Jeremiah under the Shadow of Duhm

Jeremiah under the Shadow of Duhm

A Critique of the Use of Poetic Form as a Criterion of Authenticity

Joseph M. Henderson

LONDON • NEW YORK • OXFORD • NEW DELHI • SYDNEY

T&T CLARK
Bloomsbury Publishing Plc
50 Bedford Square, London, WC1B 3DP, UK
1385 Broadway, New York, NY 10018, USA
29 Earlsfort Terrace, Dublin 2, Ireland

BLOOMSBURY, T&T CLARK and the T&T Clark logo
are trademarks of Bloomsbury Publishing Plc

First published in Great Britain 2019
Paperback edition first published 2021

Cover design: Charlotte James

A catalogue record for this book is available from the British Library.

Library of Congress Cataloging-in-Publication Data
Names: Henderson, Joseph M. (Joseph Michael), author.
Title: Jeremiah under the shadow of Duhm: a critique of poetic form as a
criterion of authenticity / by Joseph M. Henderson.
Description: London; New York: T&T Clark, [2019] |
Includes bibliographical references and index.
Identifiers: LCCN 2019021447 (print) | LCCN 2019981622 (ebook) |
ISBN 9780567676467 (hardback) | ISBN 9780567676436 (epub) |
ISBN 9780567676443 (pdf)
Subjects: LCSH: Bible. Jeremiah–Criticism, interpretation, etc. |
Jeremiah (Biblical prophet) | Duhm, Bernhard, 1847–1928. Buch Jeremia.
Classification: LCC BS1525.52 .H46 2019 (print) |
LCC BS1525.52 (ebook) | DDC 224/.2066–dc23
LC record available at https://lccn.loc.gov/2019021447
LC ebook record available at https://lccn.loc.gov/2019981622

ISBN: HB: 978-0-5676-7646-7
PB: 978-0-5677-0178-7
ePDF: 978-0-5676-7644-3
eBook: 978-0-5676-7643-6

Typeset by Newgen KnowledgeWorks Pvt. Ltd., Chennai, India

To find out more about our authors and books visit
www.bloomsbury.com and sign up for our newsletters.

To John Goldingay

For his models of faithfulness to the Scriptures, the Church, his family, and his students

Contents

Acknowledgments   viii

List of Abbreviations   ix

Introduction: The Road to Duhm   1

Part 1 The Roots of Duhm: The Historical Origins of Duhm's Model

1   Introduction to Duhm's 1901 *Das Buch Jeremia*   31

2   The Roots of Duhm's Understanding of Poetry and Prophecy   51

3   The Roots of Duhm's Biography of the Prophet   113

4   The Roots of Duhm's History of Israel's Religion   171

Part 2 The Fruits of Duhm: The Standard Form of Duhm's Model in the
Twentieth Century

5   Skinner's Biography of the Prophet   205

6   Mowinckel's Theory of the Composition of the Book   227

Part 3 Moving beyond Duhm: Discerning the Coherence in Jeremiah 2–20

7   Rhetorical Critics and Jeremiah 2–10: Scholars Look for Literary
     Coherence and Find Dramatic Portrayal   251

8   Redaction Critics and Jeremiah 11–20: Scholars Look for Theological
     Coherence and Find Dramatic Portrayal   283

9   Dramatic Portrayal and Narrative Coherence in Jeremiah 2–10
     and 11–20   319

Epilogue: Pete Diamond and the Voice of Yahweh   349

Bibliography   357
Subject and Author Index   365
Scripture Index   378

Acknowledgments

Writing this book has been a long journey. I couldn't have done it without help all along the way, so I have many people to thank. The first is Lawson Stone, whose seminars sparked my interest in both the book Jeremiah and the history of biblical scholarship and who guided me through my first extended study of Jeremiah. He was a model for me of rigorous and faithful Old Testament scholarship as were three other scholars from my small hometown of Wilmore, Kentucky: Dennis Kinlaw, Victor Hamilton, and John Oswalt. I had the privilege of working with another Old Testament scholar I admired when our paths crossed in the big city of Los Angeles. John Goldingay, who had come from England, guided my doctoral studies and my work on the first form of this book. I'm grateful for his personal encouragement and his example of testing biblical scholarship against the biblical text. Three other scholars from England encouraged my work as well. Two read my dissertation and gave me helpful criticism and encouragement: Leslie Allen, who was writing his own commentary of Jeremiah, and John Rogerson, who wrote a history of biblical scholarship that informed this work. The third was David Clines, who first accepted my book for publication. He said he liked to find works that were "deviant," which I took as a compliment. In retrospect, I'm also grateful for those who rejected earlier forms of my work because they gave me the opportunity to add "many similar words" (Jer. 36:32).

I would like to thank Biola University for supporting my doctoral work and allowing me a semester leave to revise my dissertation. I'm also grateful to my colleagues in the Torrey Honors Institute for their friendship and encouragement. Several people made this book better by reading parts of it and offering feedback: my colleagues, Fred Sanders and Rob Price; my students, Ian Heisler and Micah Hogan; and my father, Mike Henderson.

Sometimes on this journey I've felt like Frodo on his long, lonely journey to Mount Doom. Of course, he wasn't really alone. He could hardly have made it out of the Shire without many unlooked-for sources of help. He was blessed by a fellowship of friends and a faithful companion who said about his burden: "I can't carry it for you, but I can carry you." I'm thankful for the friends who have carried me. I had an international support team who stuck with me for over a decade: Nancy Crawford and Jon Stocksdale in Kenya, and Andy Bowen in Paraguay. (It was Andy who suggested I title my book "Indiana Joe and the Temple of Duhm.") I also had local support (including Andre Stephens and Gil Mellis) and family support (including my mother, Martha Henderson).

My three children—Kip, William, and Laurel—have borne part of the burden of writing a long book. They can hardly remember a time in their lives (vacations, in particular) when I wasn't working on it. My deepest appreciation is due to my wife Conchie who has been my faithful companion every step of the way.

Abbreviations

AB	The Anchor Bible
AJBI	Annual of the Japanese Biblical Institute
AThANT	Abhandlungen zur Theologie des Alten und Neuen Testaments
BZAW	Beihefte zur *Zeitschrift für die alttestamentliche Wissenschaft*
CBET	Contributions to Biblical Exegesis and Theology
CBQ	*Catholic Biblical Quarterly*
FCBS	Fortress Classics in Biblical Studies
FRLANT	Forschungen zur Religion und Literatur des Alten und Neuen Testaments
HAT	Handbuch zum Alten Testament
HSM	Harvard Semitic Monographs
IB	The Interpreter's Bible
ICC	The International Critical Commentary
JBL	*Journal of Biblical Literature*
JR	*Journal of Religion*
JSOT	*Journal for the Study of the Old Testament*
JSOT Sup	*Journal for the Study of the Old Testament*, Supplement Series
KHC	Kurzer Hand-commentar zum Alten Testament
LHB/OTS	Library of Hebrew Bible / Old Testament Studies
LXX	Septuagint
MLR	*The Modern Language Review*
MT	Masoretic Text
NAmerR	*North American Review*
NCE	Norton Critical Edition
NICOT	The New International Commentary on the Old Testament
NVBS	New Voices in Biblical Studies
OTL	The Old Testament Library
TTFL	Theological Translation Fund Library
VT	*Vetus Testamentum*
VTSup	Supplements to *Vetus Testamentum*
WBC	Word Biblical Commentary
WMANT	Wissenschaftliche Monographien zum Alten und Neuen Testament
WUNT	Wissenschaftliche Untersuchungen zum Neuen Testament
ZThK	*Zeitschrift für Theologie und Kirche*

Introduction: The Road to Duhm

Looking back over the course of my adult life, it is somewhat of a mystery to me that for most of it (about twenty-five years) I have been thinking and writing about a German commentary published in 1901: *Das Buch Jeremia* by Bernhard Duhm.[1] The obvious explanation is that it was the captivating book of Jeremiah itself that initially drew me in and set me on this path. Although this book has many alluring features, I doubt I would have chosen it as my chief scholarly interest if I had thought through what was involved. Jeremiah is a hard book in many ways, beginning with its subject matter. Its primary subject is a horrific catastrophe that brought the nation of Israel to an end, a catastrophe the book portrays as the breakdown of the marriage between Yahweh and his people. When I hear about scholars who have dedicated their careers to studying genocide or domestic violence, I have the utmost respect for them. But I can't say I envy them.

The prophet Jeremiah complains that he was seduced into his work by the delight he found in God's words (20:7, 15:16). I was first seduced by the words of Jeremiah in a seminar on the book at Asbury Theological Seminary (offered in 1993 by Lawson Stone). As a lover of great literature and as a newly minted English major, I found Jeremiah to be a work of great beauty and power. I savored its rich poetry, alive with striking imagery, and I loved its powerful evocation of the tragic story of the doomed nation, of the anguished prophet, but most of all, of the wrathful and anguished God. I resonated deeply (and still do!) with Abraham Heschel's depiction of the prophet coming to share "the pathos of the Lord."[2] In my first lectures on the book, my theme was "The weeping prophet reveals the heart of the weeping God."

When I turned from the book of Jeremiah to the scholarship about the book, I was surprised to find how seldom the very knowledgeable scholars shared my enthusiasm for the book's literary qualities. Many seemed to have a tin ear when it came to appreciating and understanding the literary composition. They often had some sense of the power of Jeremiah's poetry, particularly his personal laments. However, instead of attending to the book's tragic portrayal of the prophet, they

---

[1] Bernhard Duhm, *Das Buch Jeremia*, KHC 11 (Tübingen: J. C. B. Mohr, 1901).
[2] Abraham J. Heschel, *The Prophets: An Introduction* (New York: Harper & Row, 1962), 126.

were often more interested in exploring prophetic experience or reconstructing a historical biography using isolated passages as bits of historical evidence. The situation was much worse regarding the book's rich portrayal of its central character, Yahweh. Scholars routinely treated his poetic speeches as evidence of the psychology of the prophet, and his prose speeches (the messages he gave the prophet to deliver to his people) as evidence of the political or theological agendas of various exilic and postexilic parties.

I was also taken aback by the inability of the scholars to appreciate the coherence of the book. Admittedly, one of the features of Jeremiah that makes it a hard book is that it appears to have been composed (at least in part) by combining disparate preexisting materials. Still, the reader of the book can find ample confirmation for the initial presumption that despite the composite nature of the book, whoever was responsible for the composition (whether the prophet himself or a later editor, or editors) had some degree of intelligence and intentionality. However, most of the scholars seemed to have resigned themselves to the judgment that the book is a "hopeless hodgepodge thrown together without any discernible principle at all"[3] and to the corresponding belief that "the exploration of supposed, larger, cumulative, literary entities w[ould] not repay the labour."[4]

As I read Jeremiah, I found it full of indications of intentional ordering, and I was eager to explore the book to understand better how the parts worked together as a whole. At Asbury Seminary, I was taught a particular method of inductive study that began with identifying units of text and then describing the relationships between them.[5] The aim was to work up to an understanding of the "structure" of the whole book, which would contribute to discerning its purpose (on the principle that "form follows function"). This approach was congenial to me—in part because in my undergraduate studies in literature, I had followed a similar approach for grappling with difficult texts, especially modernist fiction (like James Joyce's *Ulysses*) and modernist poetry (like T. S. Eliot's "The Wasteland"). What might initially appear to be a random conglomeration of disparate materials or a desultory stream of consciousness in these modern works often proved on closer reading to have a high level of intentionality; they were designed to have a particular effect on the reader. I had a similar experience as I studied the text of Jeremiah.

I found some help in this work of discerning and describing the structure of the book in works on Jeremiah by William Holladay and his student Jack Lundbom, who followed a rhetorical-critical approach suggested by James Muilenburg. These scholars had a greater appreciation than most for the literary artistry of the book and higher expectation of intentional ordering. They were also working on the task of delimiting units and describing relationships between them. However, I was disappointed by their somewhat narrow understanding of rhetoric, which mainly focused on artificial rhetorical techniques (like chiasms and "catch words"), and especially by their focus

---

[3] John Bright, *Jeremiah*, 2nd ed., AB 21 (Garden City, NY: Doubleday, 1965), lvi.

[4] William McKane, *A Critical and Exegetical Commentary on Jeremiah*, ICC (Edinburgh: T&T Clark, 1986 and 1996), vol. 1, lxxiv.

[5] Robert Traina, *Methodical Bible Study* (New York: Biblical Seminary in New York, 1952).

on discovering the situations in which the book was written rather than the story it was written to tell.

In my first extended study of Jeremiah, I sought to show that a broader understanding of rhetoric (which focused on understanding the effects a text would have on an audience and the techniques used to create these) proved more fruitful for discerning the nature and structure of text.[6] In investigating the rhetorical structure of the text (treating as primary units of meaning the speeches by various speakers and with various audiences), I began to see two other important features of the text: first, that these speeches are often components of dramatic dialogues; and second, that the primary relationship between the speeches and dialogues is narrative progression. The text tells stories in the form of a succession of dramatic vignettes. Appreciating the coherence of the text depends on recognizing first its dramatic, and then its narrative, character.

This initial investigation of the book's structure was limited to a small section of the text (chs 4:5–6:30). Later in an article and a paper, I extended my argument for literary coherence to Jeremiah 2–10 and then 11–20, demonstrating the presence of dramatic presentation and narrative progression throughout these initial sections of book. I argued that Jeremiah 2–10 tells the story of Yahweh and Israel from the exodus to the exile and that Jeremiah 11–20 tells the story of Jeremiah from his initial enthusiasm for his role as a prophet of reformation to his desperation at realizing he would be a prophet of doom.[7] In another article, I made an effort to justify and clarify the presence of consistent dramatic characterization and artful dramatic dialogue as major literary features of these chapters.[8] The aim of this writing was to help readers appreciate the nature and coherence of a part of Jeremiah that scholars had often approached as an incoherent jumble of historical evidence.

I was not the only one looking for coherence in the book at this time. In Jeremiah scholarship as well as in biblical scholarship as a whole, the last decades of the twentieth century were marked by dissatisfaction with the critical approaches that had dominated the greater part of the century—the sense that they were not helping readers discern the nature and significance of the biblical books in their present form. The rhetorical-critical studies of Jeremiah (by Holladay and Lundbom) posited that the complex rhetorical patterning they found in the book showed the artistry of the primary author, Jeremiah, whose historical message provided the key to the book's meaning. Another group of Jeremiah scholars, employing a redaction-critical method,

[6] Joseph M. Henderson, *The Structure of Jeremiah 4:5–6:30* (Master's Thesis, Asbury Theological Seminary, 1998).
[7] Joseph M. Henderson, "Jeremiah 2–10 as a Unified Literary Composition: Evidence of Dramatic Portrayal and Narrative Progression," in *Uprooting and Planting: Essays on Jeremiah for Leslie Allen,* ed. John Goldingay, LHB/OTS (New York: T&T Clark, 2007), 116–52; Joseph M. Henderson, "The Drama of Jeremiah 11–20" (Unpublished, Fuller Theological Seminary, 2007). I have incorporated parts of these two papers written during my doctoral program into Part Three of the present study.
[8] Joseph M. Henderson, "Who Weeps in Jeremiah VIII 23 (IX 1)?: Identifying Dramatic Speakers in the Poetry of Jeremiah" *VT* 52 (2002): 191–206. Although this article took the form of an argument for an alternative identification of speakers in Jer. 8:18–9:3 to that offered by Mark Biddle, the primary aim was to demonstrate the kind of dramatic analysis of the text that Biddle had helped to pioneer.

argued that what coherence there was in the book was primarily due to the anonymous editors, who gave the book both its structure (by their arrangement of the preexisting material) and its theological agenda (which could be seen most plainly in the prose speeches they had added to the book).

Three redactional-critical studies of the very chapters I was working on appeared just before I began my study. All three studies, by O'Connor, Diamond, and Smith, focused on the "confessions" of Jeremiah "in context" and made significant progress in understanding the coherence of Jeremiah 11–20 (in which most of the "confessions" occur) by showing the connections between the poetic laments spoken by the prophet and the speeches (in both poetry and prose) in their immediate contexts. Each study was also able to observe some of the structural features holding together the whole unit (11–20).

Despite all of their gains in describing the coherence of these chapters, what stands out about all three studies is the odd (and oddly similar) conclusions they came to about the nature and purpose of the unit. All three concluded that the basic nature of Jeremiah 11–20 is homiletical, or didactic—that it functions as a kind of extended sermon, or lesson—and that its purpose can be described as theodicy—that it is intended to show that God's actions in bringing about the destruction of Judah and Jerusalem were just. Within this homiletical structure, they each found the "confessions" of Jeremiah to function as illustrations—historical evidence incorporated into the theodicy argument to establish the sinfulness of the people and leaders of Judah by showing their opposition to the prophet.

These conclusions would be far from obvious to most readers of the book (at least those who were not familiar with the scholarship of the twentieth century). The description of these chapters as homiletical, sermonic, and didactic is puzzling because (at least on the surface) they contain almost no material that takes the form of a sermon or lesson. Instead, they are full of verbal exchanges between Yahweh and the prophet, messages warning of (or announcing) coming disaster, complaints, tirades, prayers, rebukes, and, most notably, laments. The idea that the whole unit is intended to justify Yahweh's action does not sit well with the contents of the chapters, which include some of the most pointed criticism of divine justice in the Hebrew Bible and in which the dominant impression of Yahweh is not of an impartial judge administering the penalties for breaking the law but of an enraged lover seeking revenge for having been personally betrayed. Jeremiah's anguished laments, the most striking feature of these chapters, hardly appear to be mere appendages included to support the main points of a didactic argument. For most of the sections, they provide the heartrending conclusions—notably in the conclusion of the whole unit, Jeremiah's curse of the day of his birth (Jer. 20:14-18).

The degree of disparity between the accounts of these scholars and the impressions of an ordinary reader, together with the degree of conformity between the scholarly accounts themselves, calls for an explanation. A likely one is not hard to find. The three redaction critical studies of the passage share a set of methodological practices and priorities and a set of assumptions about the composition of Jeremiah (and the history of Israel's literature and religion) that predetermined their conclusions. The methodology followed by each of the scholars prioritizes determining the original author and historical situation of each isolated passage in the text. However, they also hold that it is the latest authors or editors, who incorporated and organized the earlier sources, who give the text its structure and significance. These attempts to identify the original authors of the passages are guided by a shared foundational assumption about the book of Jeremiah: that the division between poetic speeches and prose speeches is due to different authors writing in different periods. The poetic speeches are assumed to be authentic words of the prophet (or at any rate, the earliest source of the text), and the prose speeches are assumed to have been written by later authors. The poetic sections are considered to be records of the prophet's speech before or during the catastrophe, and the prose sections are considered to be sermons interpreting the catastrophe in terms of the legal covenant of Deuteronomy after its aftermath.

With this particular set of shared methods and assumptions, it is not surprising that the redaction critical studies would come to what are basically the same conclusions. In fact, despite their painstaking investigations of each text, it could be said that these critics would have hardly needed to read the text to come to their conclusions. If the prose speeches are considered to be the work of the editors who gave the text its present form, then the work as a whole is likely to share the homiletic character of the prose speeches understood as sermons. If these author-editors are identified in some way with the author-editors assumed to have given the books of Joshua through Kings their final form (the "Deuteronomists"), then the purpose of the unit will likely be aligned with their supposed project: to explain the catastrophe as the result of disobeying the law of Deuteronomy (or breaking the covenant of Deuteronomy). Thus, the whole unit would have the same agenda of showing that God was just in punishing the people (theodicy) by proving the people were lawbreakers. If these same editors are assumed to be the ones responsible for incorporating the poetic passages into this section (on the assumption that the poetry is authentic, or from a pre-existing source), then the explanation for their inclusion will have to be that they helped fulfill this agenda. The editors must have taken the authenticity of the poetry as making it suitable as supporting evidence, and they must have taken the suffering the poetry evinces as proof of the people's sinfulness (since they certainly wouldn't have included the poems if they thought they would impugn the justice of God).

What I saw in these redaction-critical studies of Jeremiah 11–20 was not only that adherence to a particular set of approaches and assumptions had predetermined that these scholars would reach conclusions at odds with the impressions of an ordinary reader (i.e., one who was not guided by these approaches and assumptions), but also that these approaches and assumptions had blinded them to the presence (or significance) of the features of the text that allow readers to grasp its actual nature, coherence, and purpose. The presence of dramatic exchanges throughout Jeremiah 11–20 is an indicator of the unit's dramatic nature (that it uses speeches to portray characters and situations). However, this is very hard to see when the speeches of one principal character, Jeremiah, are treated as evidence of the situations in which they were written and the speeches of the other principal character, Yahweh, are treated as sermons that express the agendas of a hypothetical historical group who do not appear in the drama. It is clear from the text that it means to portray situations before the destruction of Jerusalem (the dramatic setting of the entire unit), but this is hard to see when the warnings or announcements of the future destruction (mostly in the prose speeches) that are the main features of the unit that anchor its scenes in this period are read as sermons looking back on the destruction from a later period. Failure to discern the dramatic settings, in turn, keeps the scholars from recognizing the narrative progression of the scenes: it's hard to discern the story when the contexts of the speeches jump back and forth between the preexilic time of the prophet and the exilic time of the later authors. The possibility of following the story is further undermined by the conclusion that the genre of the whole is homiletical or didactic—since the typical structure of sermons or speeches is an atemporal arrangement of arguments and evidence. The ironic result in the case of these redactional studies is that their efforts to read the "confessions" of Jeremiah in context and discern the coherence of the entire unit (11–20) end up overlooking the primary unifying feature of the unit (narrative progression) because they fail to read the prophet's speeches in their (dramatic) contexts.

The failure to discern the nature and coherence of the text of Jeremiah because of adherence to a shared set of approaches and assumptions that I found in these redaction-critical scholars is hardly an isolated instance. In fact, the more I read scholarly works on Jeremiah, the more it became apparent to me how pervasive this particular failure, and this particular cause of the failure, is throughout Jeremiah scholarship since the beginning of the twentieth century. Whereas redaction-critical scholars had misjudged the nature and coherence of these chapters, the majority of scholars before them had missed them altogether. For most of the twentieth century, mainstream scholars of Jeremiah either failed to look for coherence in the present form of the book or denied that it existed. They did not share the redaction critics' interest in discerning the shape and purpose of the present form of the book or their distinctive theory that the shape and purpose came from the latest source; rather, the primary interest of the earlier scholars was to discover the authentic prophetic element in the book, which they identified with the earliest source. These different interests and different judgments of the value of the different sources led to radically divergent outcomes. Despite the differences between the scholars from the last decades of the twentieth century who took a greater interest in the present form of the book (of whom the redaction critics are representative) and the scholars from earlier in the century, the common element was that the outcome of their work was in large measure predetermined by a common methodological approach and the common assumption they brought to their study of Jeremiah. They shared the methodological priority of determining the authors of the various units of the text (and the historical situation in which the authors wrote them), and they shared the assumption that poetic form was the primary indication that a unit of text had been authored by the prophet.

I became convinced that this common methodological approach and assumption were the primary obstacles to discerning the nature and coherence of the text of Jeremiah. This meant that in my efforts to promote appreciation of the book, it would not be enough to draw attention to the features that point to its nature or to describe the relationships between the individual units of the text. After all, those are there for any reader to see. Instead, it would be necessary to address directly what was blinding scholars to these aspects or their significance.

Why did scholars accept this compositional theory? Looking back over Jeremiah scholarship of the twentieth century, it became apparent to me that this assumption facilitated investigation of several questions that interested scholars most about the book. For the redaction critics, it provided the key to the structure and significance of the present form of the book. Before them, however, the interest lay more in reconstructing the history behind the book. The assumed authenticity of the poetry made it available as historical evidence for reconstructing the biography of the prophet or examining the basic form of prophetic speech (which in turn could be used as evidence of the essential nature of prophetic experience. The assumption that the poetry came from a prophet and the prose from later non-prophetic authors gave the book value in understanding the tension between prophetic religion and scribal religion, or a prophetic stage and a scribal stage in the development of Israel's religion.

This is one way of answering the question of why scholars based their work on this theory, but it leaves unanswered the more important question of the basis on which these scholars come to believe this theory was true: that it was the best explanation of the phenomenon in the text, that it provided the best account of how the text was actually composed. On turning to Jeremiah scholarship based on this theory, I was surprised to find how seldom any justification was offered. Scholars would present an argument that a particular text was poetic as proof that it was written by Jeremiah (or an accurate record of his speech), or treat the fact that a particular text was not poetic (or shared some of the diction or phraseology of Deuteronomy or of the speeches in Joshua through Kings) as an indication that Jeremiah could hardly have written or said it. There was seldom an explanation of why Jeremiah couldn't speak in ("Deuteronomistic") prose, and I don't recall ever seeing an explanation of why another (later) author could not have written poetry. Although it was hard to find arguments for the theory about poetry and prose, it was easy to find its source.

Many of the scholars included a history of the scholarship of the book, and these regularly started at the same point: the 1901 commentary on the book of Jeremiah by Bernhard Duhm. It was this commentary, *Das Buch Jeremia*, which first used poetic form as the principal criterion of authenticity and attributed the prose speeches the book assigns to Jeremiah to later scribal authors who put their sermons in the prophet's mouth. In this book, Duhm not only introduced the foundational theorem of modern Jeremiah studies, but he showed how it could be used to reconstruct a biography of the prophet, recover the true body of the prophet's literary works, and distinguish his prophetic religion from the religion of the scribes. It was in this way that Duhm set the course for twentieth-century Jeremiah scholarship.

Although Jeremiah scholars writing since Duhm's book often hailed him as the pioneer of the modern approach to Jeremiah, very few of them offered an account of how he had come to his distinctive belief, or why it should be considered true. The accounts of modern scholarship often observed that it was Sigmund Mowinckel's modified form of Duhm's theory that came to provide the dominant paradigm for understanding the composition of the book. It is not hard to see that in his understanding of the three main types of material (which he labeled A, B, and C), he has preserved Duhm's fundamental distinction between authentic poetry (Type A) and later scribal prose (Type C).

It was Duhm's role in introducing what I considered the primary obstacle preventing scholars from perceiving the nature and coherence of the book that caused me to devote my attention to his commentary. My object in studying Duhm's work was not simply to redress the general lack of scholarly attention to the source of his theory about the poetry and prose, but to see if he offered a compelling reason to accept its validity. If he didn't, and a new generation of scholars was willing to reevaluate the foundational assumption of modern Jeremiah scholarship, it might allow them to come out from under the long shadow Duhm has cast over more than a century of work on Jeremiah.

The Roots of Duhm

As I became familiar with Duhm's commentary, I was struck by the fact that although the obvious difference between the material Duhm considered the authentic work of the prophet and what he considered the inauthentic scribal additions was that one was in poetry and the other in prose, he never mentions or defends poetic form as a criterion of authenticity. Perhaps this is because, stated plainly, the assertion that the prophet could only write poetry might appear silly or indefensible. Duhm's basic approach is to draw attention to what he perceives as a striking clash in the book between material of high literary, religious, and historical value and material with little to no value of any kind and then resolve the tension by positing that the prophet must be the author of what is valuable but could hardly be the author of what is worthless. Once he has sorted out what is valuable from what is worthless, the fact that the first is all in poetic form and the latter is all in prose then appears as a striking objective confirmation that he has correctly divided the authentic from the inauthentic.

When I began to investigate Duhm's standards for what he considered valuable (and thus authentically prophetic literature), I made a discovery about how Duhm divided the book. He describes the material he believes to be of high quality (his word is *allerherrlichsten*, "exceedingly glorious") in terms that I recognized from my study of English literature. In the authentic words of Jeremiah, Duhm finds that "the simple form corresponds to the poetical diction, which is never artificial, forced, or even melodramatic, but always natural, appropriate to the thought, and popular in the best sense of the word."[9] These qualities, particularly in contrast to their opposites (simple not elaborate, natural not artificial, spontaneous not forced, sincere not melodramatic, popular not elitist), are the very qualities that the Romantic poets and literary theorists of the eighteenth and nineteenth centuries used to explain the superiority of Romantic poetry over neoclassical poetry. It appeared that Duhm was extracting from the book of Jeremiah the parts that could be read and appreciated as Romantic poetry. This suspicion was further confirmed when I saw that his understanding of the nature of prophecy was almost identical to the Romantic conception of poetry as

---

[9] "*Der einfachen Form entspricht die poetische Diktion, die niemal künstlich, geziert, nicht einmal pathetisch, sondern immer natürlich, dem Gedanken angemessen, im besten Sinne volkstümlich ist, aber eben darum uns ergreift, rührt, oft erschüttert und in ihrem Reichtum an treffenden und originellen Bildern den geborenen Dichter verrät.*" Duhm, *Jeremia*, xii–xiii.

"the spontaneous overflow of powerful emotions."[10] According to Duhm, what makes Jeremiah's prophetic writing poetic is that it gives "masterful expression (*Ausdruck*)" to "the feelings, and the emotional states" of the prophet.[11] Additionally, I saw that Duhm's reconstructed biography of the prophet closely followed the biographies of Romantic poets and artists (*Künstlerromane*) that proliferated in the nineteenth century. Duhm's assumption that only the poetry of the book was the authentic work of the prophet allowed him to interpret Jeremiah's work as Romantic poetry and Jeremiah's life as the life of a Romantic poet.

The striking resemblance between Duhm's reconstructed Jeremiah and a Romantic poet raised the question of why his choice to treat only the poetic sections as authentic proved so successful in facilitating this result. I began investigating this question by examining the history of scholarship on the poetry of the prophetic books, and I made a surprising discovery: that the person who was most responsible for the modern recognition of the presence of poetry in the book of Jeremiah also helped to lay the foundations for the Romantic movement. Robert Lowth, in his *Lectures on the Sacred Poetry of the Hebrews* (1753), was attempting to demonstrate that prophetic books contained poetry and to win a hearing for this prophetic poetry as great literature. To do this, he had to challenge the regnant neoclassic conception of poetry: the poetry of the Bible could hardly measure up to the neoclassical expectations of decorum, wit, refinement and erudition, and particularly to the expectation of strict conformity to stylized poetic diction, approved tropes and figures, and classical metrical forms. He fought the neoclassical conception of poetry by portraying the qualities believed to define poetry as characteristic of a cold, aloof elite, who were out of touch with the people and the land. In contrast, he portrayed Hebrew poets as living close to the land (the whole nation was a nation of farmers), whose piety and passion found expression in a poetry characterized by simplicity, sincerity, earthy imagery and language, and the natural rhythms of passionate expression. These are the very qualities that the Romantics used to describe true poetry and that Duhm used to determine authentic prophetic speech. The portrayal of the poetic prophet in Lowth's work laid the foundation for the Romantic revolution in literature and art, because it provided a model of poetry that did not come from formal training, classical imitation, or intentional craft, but from "inspiration," understood as the passionate or ecstatic experiences of a great soul that spontaneously flow out in original artistic expressions. Lowth's understanding of inspiration lies at the root of the Romantic conception of the prophetic poet and Duhm's conception of the poetic prophet.

Uncovering this shared source in Lowth's work on biblical poetry provided some possible explanations of why Duhm's limitation of the authentic works of Jeremiah to the poetry in the book was able to produce a body of work that met his Romantic standards of good literature and facilitated his transformation of the prophet into a Romantic poet. One possibility was that Duhm had actually uncovered the truth about Jeremiah and about the book: that a kind of Romantic poet, called a prophet, had

---

[10] William Wordsworth, "Preface to *Lyrical Ballads*," in *William Wordsworth: The Major Works*, Oxford World's Classics, ed. Stephen Gill (New York: Oxford University Press, 2000), 598.

[11] Duhm, *Jeremia*, xiii.

appeared in seventh and sixth centuries BC; that for over two millennia, this poet's inspired work had lain hidden in a book underneath a pile of material attributed to him but actually composed by uninspired imitators; but that the advent of Romanticism (in the eighteenth and nineteenth centuries AD) had enabled one scholar (Lowth) to recognize the authentic Romantic poetry in the book and another scholar (Duhm) to free it from inauthentic prose and thereby to recover the true character of the prophetic poet.

Another possibility is that the standard for prophetic literature and the figure of the poetic prophet that Duhm used to distinguish between the authentic and inauthentic speech of Jeremiah and to reconstruct the biography of Jeremiah was simply a popular contemporary understanding of poetry and prophecy, and that Duhm's radical alteration of the book of Jeremiah was compelled by his need to make the prophet and his work fit this mold. Although the basic materials of this Romantic understanding were drawn (by Lowth and others) from the poetic parts of the prophetic books, the poetry had been reinterpreted and shaped to meet various needs of the eighteenth and nineteenth centuries. First, the idea of prophetic poetry as the product of (ecstatic) inspiration provided an alternative to neoclassical poetic theory and made the poetry of the prophetic books available as a model for a new kind of poetry. By extension, it provided a foundation for a theory of artistic creation grounded in personal expression rather than imitation and representation. By further extension, it provided a model for human history in which the high points were the achievements of creative geniuses who heroically broke free from conventional ideas and institutions and by fidelity to their own personal visions actually gave expression to the spirit of their nations or to the spirit of history. The idea of the poetry of the prophets as the greatest achievement of the nation of Israel (the fullest expression of its national spirit) provided a rationale for the promotion of national literatures that gave expression to the spirit of each nation. Among the German-speaking peoples, in particular, it provided a model for how national identity and unity could come through a national literature (or culture) and a reason for grounding that literature in the work of inspired bards of the Germanic people, rather than in classical models associated with the courtly culture of France. The idea that prophetic inspiration (which issued forth in poetic expression) was the true source of religion provided an alternative model to dogmatic traditional religion as well as to rationalistic "natural" religion.

All of these great cultural and historical movements of the eighteenth and nineteenth centuries drew on the idea of the creative "or expressive" individual that was rooted in Lowth's presentation of the Hebrew prophets as inspired poets. To serve as models for these movements, the prophets had to be made to conform to various roles: Romantic poet, visionary innovator, creative genius, national leader, or religious reformer. However, the extent to which the biblical prophets could be manipulated to fit these roles was always constrained by the necessity of fitting the new portrayals with their speeches and portrayals in the biblical text—the only source of knowledge about them and their work. Duhm's breakthrough was to free the portrayal of Jeremiah and his writings from these constraints with his theory that the authentic work of the prophet was limited to the poetry (thus eliminating over half of the book as evidence that had to be taken into account). That this theory allowed Duhm to bring Jeremiah into closer conformity than ever before with the roles of the inspired individuals in modern historical movements and systems of thought is hardly surprising considering these were grounded in an interpretation of the poetry in the prophetic books. The figure of the prophet as an inspired poet that Lowth had used to argue for the presence of poetry in the prophetic books Duhm was able to bring to full realization by treating only the poetic sections of the books as the work of the prophets.

Through my investigation of Duhm's commentary on Jeremiah and its roots in the history of eighteenth- and nineteenth-century thought—particularly the common roots of (German) Romanticism and (German) "higher criticism" of the Bible in the work of Lowth—I became convinced of the latter explanation of the relationship between Duhm's preconceptions and his outcome. I came to believe that Duhm had not uncovered the truth about the book's composition and the prophet's life but rather had played fast and loose with the text of the book to create a prophet of his own liking, one that conformed to the image of an inspired prophet needed to validate certain ways of understanding artistic production, historical achievement, national identity, and religious worth.

In a chapter in which I contended that Duhm's biography of the prophet was not a discovery but an invention, I concluded by noting that it was surprising a century after Duhm's commentary, a century which has seen waning support for his biographical reconstruction, that scholars were still taking as foundational the compositional theory Duhm had used to achieve his creation.[12] The doubtful validity of Duhm's results should have given scholars good reason to question the validity of the expedients he employed to attain them: the dissolution of the book into isolated pieces of historical evidence, the explanation of each piece according to its supposed historical origin, and the belief that the key to determining those origins (whether in the experience of the prophet or in the agenda of the scribal redactors) was the division between the speeches in poetry and the speeches in prose. It is the third part of Duhm's methodological legacy that is my primary concern because of my conviction that it is this assumption about the poetry and the prose that continues to present the primary obstacle to understanding the nature, coherence, and significance of the book.

I have not been alone in decrying the inability of modern Jeremiah scholarship to give a satisfying account of the book of Jeremiah or even in pointing to Duhm's commentary as the primary source of this inability. Many scholars have suggested that the failure of modern scholarship to perceive the coherence and purpose of the present form of the Jeremiah is due to the methodological approaches, priorities, and assumptions that have dominated the mainstream of biblical scholarship, and they have identified Duhm as the main person responsible for introducing these methods and aims into studies of Jeremiah. In fact, calls for Jeremiah scholarship to "move beyond Duhm" have been a feature of twenty-first-century works on the book. For example, in

---

[12] Joe Henderson, "Duhm and Skinner's Invention of Jeremiah," in *Jeremiah Invented: Constructions and Deconstructions of Jeremiah*, ed. Else K. Holt and Carolyn J. Sharp (New York: Bloomsbury T&T Clark, 2015), 15.

the preface to a 2004 collection of essays titled *Reading the Book of Jeremiah: A Search for Coherence*, Walter Brueggemann wrote, "The current discussion seeks to move beyond the historical-critical categories of Sigmund Mowinckel and Bernhard Duhm and the classic formulation of three sources, A, B, and C."[13] Brueggemann's assessment that scholars in the twenty-first century are ready to move beyond the historical categories of Duhm might suggest that they had come to reject the compositional model and undergirding theory that prevented scholars in the twentieth century from perceiving the coherence of Jeremiah. However, this suggestion is thrown into doubt by his following clarification: "In Jeremiah as in other parts of biblical scholarship, the new questions concern the inadequacy of historical readings of a positivistic kind and the prospect of synchronic readings."[14] This makes it unclear whether scholars are willing to reject or at least reexamine Duhm's compositional model or assumptions, or whether they are simply eager to move beyond these diachronic questions to synchronic questions. It becomes clear that the latter is the case further down the same page. In a list of features shared by all of the articles in the collection, Brueggemann includes that these scholars all believe that "the distinction between poetry and prose is an important one," and from their contributions, it seems "apparent at the present time that the prose material with a Deuteronomic accent is a powerful shaping force for the final form of the text."[15] The identification of the "Deuteronomic" prose with the final form, or the last additions and editing of the text, shows that, like the redaction critics considered above, these scholars take for granted that the division between poetry and prose is best explained as a division between what is early (authentic prophecy) and late (additions by Deuteronomists).

It is my belief that in order to actually "move beyond Duhm" in a way that will allow scholars to achieve their aim of identifying what makes the elements of the book cohere—or even their more modest aim of "reading the book"—it will be insufficient merely to adopt a different focus (the final form of the book) or aim (reading the book synchronically) without relinquishing Duhm's foundational assumption. However, I'm not arguing against Duhm's assumption simply because it obscures the literary coherence of the text; I'm arguing against it because it's unlikely to be true. Duhm's notion that poetic form is the primary criterion for distinguishing authentic prophetic speech is not demanded by the text; nor is it the most likely explanation of book's inclusion of speeches in both prose and poetry. Thus, attempts to move beyond Duhm and understand the true nature, structure, and purpose of the book of Jeremiah will be flawed to the extent that they are founded on the unquestioned use of Duhm's false assumption. To use Jeremiah's words, before scholarship can move on to "building and planting" a new approach to the book of Jeremiah, it must first complete the work of "plucking up, breaking down, destroying, and overthrowing" the errors of the old approach. Otherwise it will be guilty of treating too lightly the wound inflicted by Duhm.

---

[13] Walter Brueggemann, "Preface," in *Reading the Book of Jeremiah: A Search for Coherence*, ed. Martin Kessler (Winona Lake, IN: Eisenbrauns, 2004), ix.

[14] Brueggemann, "Preface," ix.

[15] Brueggemann, "Preface," ix.

The Aim of the Present Study

This book addresses the primary obstacle to perceiving the nature and unity of the book of Jeremiah by challenging the validity of the dominant compositional model founded on Bernhard Duhm's use of poetic form as a criterion for distinguishing authentic prophetic speech in the book. This book takes the form of an extended argument against continued adherence to Duhm's model. Although it includes exposition of the text of Jeremiah and advances theories about its nature, structure, and purposes, its focus is not the book of Jeremiah but the history of modern scholarship about Jeremiah: the 1901 work of Duhm, its roots in eighteenth- and nineteenth-century biblical scholarship, its embodiment in the compositional paradigm that dominated twentieth-century Jeremiah scholarship, and its continued influence in the late twentieth and early twenty-first century. The primary structure is chronological, following the course of scholarship from the eighteenth to twenty-first century. It does not follow the standard form in which the constructive argument follows the historical survey; both the argument against Duhm's assumptions and the historical survey begin in the first chapter and end in the final chapter.

The Plan of the Study

Part One argues against Duhm's compositional theory by showing the extent to which it was driven by the need to bring the book and the prophet into conformity with literary and theological systems of the nineteenth century and by arguing that the seemingly surprising congruence of the various results of his theory are best explained not by their common purchase on the historical reality behind the book but by their common source in an influential eighteenth-century account of the nature of poetry in the prophetic books.

Chapter 1 offers an overview of Duhm's 1901 commentary, *Das Buch Jeremia*, focusing on its role in establishing the compositional and biographical models that were the principal parts of the dominant paradigm for understanding the book in the twentieth century. It observes that although Duhm presents his commentary as a work of objective historical research, it is characterized by his strong judgments about the worth of each passage in the book. Moreover, these judgments of literary and theological worth constitute the primary rationale he offers for his conclusion that over half of the book is inauthentic—the claim that distinguished Duhm's work from all previous work on the book. The suspicion that these judgments are subjective (or based on the preferences of the late nineteenth century) seems to have been overcome in the minds of Duhm and those who built on his work by three other features of his work.[16] First, the division between the material he judged authentic and the material

---

[16] Another factor that helps to explain the confidence Duhm and his followers had in his judgments is that his standards for good literature and theology (which may appear to twenty-first-century readers to be merely the particular predilections and prejudices of the turn of the twentieth century) appeared to them as universal standards of what is good and true.

considered inauthentic coincides almost exactly with the division between the speeches in poetry and the speeches in prose—an objective feature of the text. Second, Duhm is able to construct a compelling biography of the prophet using only the poetry as historical evidence, and he is able to explain virtually every isolated piece of that poetic material in terms of a context in his reconstructed biography. Third, the stark contrast between Duhm's portrayal of the prophet and his message and his portrayal of the later scribal authors fits well with the reconstruction of the history of Israel's religion (and literature) that came to dominate twentieth-century studies of the Hebrew Bible. The next three chapters consider each of these three features in turn to see if they add to the credibility of Duhm's understanding of Jeremiah.

Chapter 2 shows that it is no surprise—and no confirmation of Duhm's results—that the material that he determined to be inauthentic because of its poor literary quality turns out to be identical with the prose sections of the book. This can be explained historically. Duhm's literary standards are characteristic of the widespread Romanticism of his day, and Romanticism (particularly its view of poetry) is deeply rooted in an eighteenth-century work, Robert Lowth's *Lectures on the Sacred Poetry of the Hebrews* (1751). Lowth aimed to demonstrate the presence of poetry in the prophetic books—and argue that it is great literature. This involved challenging the neoclassical conception of poetry as intentional artistry with an alternative conception of poetry as passionate expression. Lowth grounded this new conception of poetry in the identification of prophetic and poetic inspiration (understood as ecstatic experiences), and this provided foundation for Romantic expressivism. The Romantic conception Duhm uses to judge what is great literature—and thus authentically prophetic—in Jeremiah was actually designed to show that the poetic parts of the prophetic books are great literature because they are "inspired"—that is, they are prophetic.

Chapter 3 argues that it does not make Duhm's theory more believable that, using only the material he deemed authentic, he was able to construct a biography of the prophet that his contemporaries found compelling. The historical explanation is that they found it compelling because it conformed to the popular genre of biographies of creative geniuses. These built on the accounts of the development of Romantic poets and artists (*Kunstlerromane*), which were grounded in Lowth's reconception of prophets as inspired poets. In German Romanticism, the Hebrew prophets were not only the models for creative artists but for inspired geniuses of all types, especially the types that German-speaking peoples needed in order to consolidate a national literature and work for national independence and unification. This was due in large part to the work of J. G. Herder, a leading figure in German Romanticism, German nationalism, and German biblical studies. Herder's dependence on Lowth is evident in his work, *On the Spirit of Hebrew Poetry* (1783–5). It is not surprising that Duhm was able to create a prophet who resembles a Romantic poet using only the parts of the book that were used to provide the foundation for the Romantic theory of poetry.

Chapter 4 argues that it does not make Duhm's theory more believable that his compositional and biographical reconstructions cohere with the model of Israel's religious history that provided the dominant framework for Old Testament studies for much of the twentieth century. The "Grafian" reconstruction of the history of Israel's religion is best known as the historical framework of the "Documentary Hypothesis" explaining the compositional history of the Pentateuch. Its central feature is the idea of a decline from the preexilic prophetic religion of the Israel, characterized by freedom and universalism, and the postexilic religion of Judaism, characterized by legalism, ritualism, and particularism. The principle architect of this scheme was W. M. L. de Wette, a student of Herder's who drew on elements from his work including his opposition of inspired prophets and institutional religion, his historical theory of the decline from the age of inspired poetry to the age of derivative prose, and his use of literary quality as an indicator of religious value. Duhm's theories that the primary opponents of the historical Jeremiah were scribes and that the main obstacle to appreciating the authentic words of the prophet in the book of Jeremiah are the additions of later scribes conform to the Grafian theory. This is no surprise because the Grafian reconstruction is rooted in the Romantic opposition between inspired artists and uninspired traditionalists (which is rooted in Lowth's interpretation of the poetry of the prophetic books). It is also observed that Duhm was one of the earliest and most ardent advocates for the Grafian historical model in Germany and that it could be considered the main purpose of his life's work to bring the prophetic books of the Hebrew Bible into alignment with the Grafian model.

Part Two answers a possible defense of the model built on Duhm's assumption: that it was only after it had been revised and backed up by additional scholarship that the model came to be the guiding paradigm for Jeremiah scholarship for most of the twentieth century. Chapter 5 argues that the best-known presentation of the biography of Jeremiah based on Duhm's theories and methods has no more claim to objectivity than Duhm's own biographical reconstruction. John Skinner's *Prophecy and Religion: Studies in the Life of Jeremiah* (1922) presents a book-length biography of the prophet that can be considered the fullest achievement of Duhm's vision. Its more nuanced presentation of the opposition between Jeremiah and Deuteronomistic scribes offers a somewhat more plausible account of the book. However, the lengths to which Skinner went to transform Jeremiah into the mold of a Protestant liberal theologian discovering interior religion or a higher-critical Old Testament scholar coming to doubt the Mosaicity of the Law raise doubts about his objectivity. Although the popularity of Skinner's biography waned in the late twentieth century, the assumptions about the nature of the book that allowed him to produce it have become further entrenched.

Chapter 6 argues that Sigmund Mowinckel, who is responsible for the best-known presentation of Duhm's compositional model (the division of the book's materials into Types A, B, and C), is not able to place it on a firmer footing with form criticism. Mowinckel, like other form critics, insists on treating poetic speeches as messages although they rarely take that form and on treating prose speeches as sermons although they often have message form. His eventual abandonment of the theory that poetic form is the result of ecstatic experiences removes a foundational reason for denying the authenticity of the prose and for treating the poetry as historical evidence. However, Mowinckel claims that it is the "assured result" of scholarship that units of poetry must be very short and can only be understood when removed from their literary contexts and relocated in hypothetical historical contexts. Given the weakness of the textual support Mowinckel offers for his claim, it is suggested that his insistence is best explained by the fact that this view of poetry is necessary to maintain certain historical-critical methods and models like Duhm's.

Part Three argues against Duhm's theory by showing how efforts in the final decades of the twentieth century to move beyond Duhm's agenda by focusing attention on the structure and purpose of the present form of the text were stymied due to their continued adherence to Duhm's foundational assumptions. Chapter 7 shows how failure to relinquish Duhm's biographical agenda and Mowinckel's form-critical assessments hindered attempts of two rhetorical critics to perceive the coherence of Jeremiah 2–10. James Muilenberg introduced rhetorical criticism (1968) as a way to move beyond the failures of historical-critical studies to perceive the intentional artistry and coherence in biblical texts. Two of his students, Lundbom and Holladay, challenged skepticism about the authenticity of the prose and the coherence of the present text by arguing that it was intentionally ordered by a complex web of rhetorical devices (notably chiasm). Accepting the possibility of intentional artistry helped Holladay discern evidence of dramatic portrayal. However, commitment to Duhm's agenda of biographical reconstruction and acceptance of the form-critical designation of the poetry as messenger speech kept him from fully appreciating the rich variety of dramatic speakers, audiences, and situations in the text and from perceiving the true nature of its coherence.

Chapter 8 shows how three redactional critics were unable to discern the theological perspective of Jeremiah 11–20 because they failed to break free from Duhm's foundational assumption: that poetry is prior to prose. Based on this assumption, Diamond, Smith, and O'Connor incorrectly identified the perspective of the final form of the text with what they believed was the perspective of the latest redactional layer—the prose speeches read as Deuteronomistic sermons. Their assessment that the aim of the section is to justify Yahweh does not fit with its most distinctive element: laments challenging Yahweh's justice. They were not able to see that presence of dramatic presentation in the text (which Diamond was able to discern) makes the standard historical-critical approach—which begins by discerning the sources, or redactional layers—poorly suited to the passage and suggests an approach that begins by identifying the dramatic speakers and audiences.

Chapter 9 will conclude the study by showing how continued adherence to Duhm's assumptions and his historical-critical aims and methods stymied the attempts of scholars to illuminate the structure and nature of the present form of the text. They were unable to perceive how, through temporal progression of dramatic scenes, Jeremiah 2–10 tells the tragic story of Yahweh and Israel from exodus to exile because they persisted in using these chapters to reconstruct the story of Jeremiah's ministry. They were unable to perceive how Jeremiah 11–20 tells the tragic story of Jeremiah (before the exile) from hopeful Deuteronomistic reformer to despairing prophet of doom because they persisted in using these chapters as evidence of the theology of exilic Deuteronomists. These failures are due to the continued influence of the foundational assumption Duhm bequeathed to Jeremiah scholarship: that the division between poetry and prose is a division between early and late, authentic and inauthentic.

The Question of Authenticity

One misunderstanding of this book I am determined to prevent is that it is an argument for the authenticity of the prose speeches of the book. This presupposition about its aim would be understandable given that the book is intended to challenge Duhm's compositional model and that his denial of the authenticity of the prose speeches is the best-known, or at least most-debated, aspect of his model. Since so many previous books challenging Duhm's model have sought to dispel his belief that the prose is inauthentic, the title of this book, which presents Duhm's approach as a shadow over a Jeremiah scholarship to be dispelled, might raise the expectation of a similar aim. My hope is that this section would relieve this book of that expectation so that it won't be disappointed by the contents. The main argument of this book does not concern the authorship of the original component parts of Jeremiah but rather an obstacle to perceiving the nature of the present form of the book. Duhm's denial of authenticity of the prose is not the reason this argument takes issue with his compositional model; the reason is, rather, that his model embodies assumptions about these speeches in prose and poetry that have prevented scholars from discerning their actual nature and the nature of the compositions of which they are parts.

These assumptions are implicit in the question of authenticity itself—at least as it is understood by Duhm and many scholars after him (including both those who affirmed his approach and those who opposed it). Their judgment about whether a passage is authentic or not often assumes that its chief value is its ability to provide historical evidence about its author or about the historical situation in which it was produced. This assumption about the passages in the book corresponds to assumptions about the aims of interpreting them: that the goal is either to maximize their potential for historical reconstruction or to explain them as fully as possible in terms of their historical (or biographical) contexts.

Although the use of the book for historical information is a valid practice (most obviously for historians) and questions of authorship and historical context certainly play a role in interpretation, it should be recognized that the book may not have been written in a way that facilitates this use or that rewards the attempt to find answers to these questions. The nature of the book itself will determine not only its value for historical information but also how important historical questions are for interpretation. The aims and methods that are appropriate for interpreting any given text are determined not only by the interests and needs of the interpreter but also by the purposes it was designed to achieve by its author (or its authors and editors). Identification of the purposes of a text (and the roles that the components of the text play in achieving those purposes) is closely tied with identification of its nature, and it is usually the case that the most important considerations for identifying the purposes concern the form and genre of the text.[17]

---

[17] The "form" and "genre" of a text are closely related to its "nature." However, I am using them in slightly different senses. I use "nature" as the general term answering the question "What is this text?"; "form" as the answer to the question "How do the parts of the text work together to fulfil its purpose?"; and "genre" as the answer to the question, "How does the form of the text relate to texts with similar forms and purposes?"

Correctly identifying the nature of a text is critical for determining the degree to which establishing its author and historical background will be necessary or useful for interpretation. For example, fictional narratives (myths, epics, gospels, dramas, etc.) often require little knowledge of the authors or the historical situations in which they were produced for fruitful interpretation. On the other hand, for interpretation of messages (love letters, royal decrees, epistles, reports from the front, etc.), knowledge of the author, the recipient, and the historical or biographical situation are often crucial. Before a historian can determine the value of a text for historical information and before an interpreter can determine the extent to which historical background will be necessary, they must determine its nature.

It is my contention not only that Duhm bequeathed false judgments of the nature and aims of the book of Jeremiah (of the poetic and prose speeches in the book) to subsequent Jeremiah scholarship, but that these judgments encourage misguided approaches to the book, the chief of which is an unwarranted prioritization of historical concerns—including determining authenticity. Although the best-known effect of Duhm's work was to spark a debate about the nature of the prose speeches, its equally important—but largely unnoticed—effect was to further entrench a judgment about the nature of the poetic speeches that was widespread in biblical studies of his time and had been forged over a hundred and fifty years earlier. His novel theory about the prose speeches (that they are not the divine warnings, or announcements, of coming judgment they appear to be but rather post facto theological reflections on past judgment) depend an already common judgment about the nature of the poetic speeches. His primary rationale for claiming that prose speeches are inauthentic is that they are so different from the authentic poetic speeches that they could hardly be attributed to the same author. The commonly held view that the poetic speeches should be accepted as authentic prophetic speech was not merely acknowledgment that they were spoken, or written, by Jeremiah but also that they were records of particular public pronouncements of the prophet made in response to events throughout his historical career. This understanding of the nature of the poetic speeches made them admissible as historical and biographical documentary evidence and made their interpretation dependent on determining their historical and biographical context, or explaining them in terms of historical events and stages of the prophet's development. These assumptions were included in the designation "authentic."

Belief in the authenticity of the poetic speeches was accompanied by corresponding conceptions of prophecy, poetry, inspiration, revelation, religious progress, and so on. These conceptions, in turn, were foundational for revolutions in the areas of literary and artistic theory, historiography, political theory, philosophy, and theology in the eighteenth and nineteenth centuries. In biblical studies, they were closely associated with beginnings of historical criticism, and they supplied the cornerstone for the most recognizable achievement of that criticism: the Grafian reconstruction of the history of Israel's religion embodied in the Documentary Hypothesis of the composition of the Pentateuch popularized by Wellhausen—and in the source-critical theory of the composition of Jeremiah proposed by Duhm. The widespread historical influence helps to explain why this assumption about the nature of the poetry in the prophetic books was so fully entrenched by the time of Duhm.

It might have been expected that in the twentieth century—when the Hebrew prophets and prophetic literature no longer played such a prominent role in the central intellectual and cultural movements and their foundational role in the great revolutions of the previous centuries was largely unacknowledged or forgotten—the time would have been ripe for a reassessment of these assumptions about the nature of prophetic poetry. However, in the specialized field of biblical criticism, where most of the study of the Hebrew prophets took place, this view of prophetic poetry played an important role in validating the dominant historical approaches and the model of history that together formed the dominant paradigm in which much of twentieth-century scholarship took place. Even in the late twentieth and early twenty-first centuries, when support for this model had begun to crumble, the accompanying view of prophetic poetry, represented by the designation of "authenticity," has proven to have remarkable tenacity.

If "authenticity" is understood in this sense (i.e., treating texts primarily as historical evidence of their origins and understanding their interpretation primarily as explanations in terms of historical context), it can be said that this entire book is an argument against understanding and treating not only the prose but particularly the poetry as authentic. It is my contention that the natures, or intrinsic genres, of the poetic speeches and of the compositions in which they and the prose speeches play a part place significant limits on what can be known (and with what degree of confidence) about the historical context in which they were written (including the identity of the author), and that their natures also indicate that recovering their supposed historical contexts has relatively less importance than it does for texts with other natures. This contention about the limited role historical context plays in the interpretation of the text could be easily misunderstood as simply a preference for reading the text as literature rather than as history, or a preference for a "synchronic," rather than a "diachronic," approach. There have been many studies of this kind in recent decades that have attempted to "move beyond" Duhm's approach to Jeremiah because they are weary of historical approaches or see that they are no longer producing much fruit. My reasons for leaving Duhm's approach behind are different. I believe it is a misguided approach to the book based on a false assessment of its nature and the nature of its parts and that it prevents understanding of the present form of the text.

The Question of Authorship

Although the attempt to determine the authenticity of the various parts of Jeremiah has often been entangled with a host of false assumptions, unsuitable aims, and unwarranted methodological priorities, it can also be the result of simple curiosity about who wrote the book or its parts. The reader of my book who is willing to accept my assertion that answering the question of authorship (or defending an answer) is not the intended purpose of my argument may still be curious about my opinion. To save that reader the trouble of having to try to discern my opinion by searching the book for clues, reading between the lines, or speculating about my theological commitments,

I will simply state my opinion here along with a brief indication of why I think it's likely to be true.

In addressing the question of who is responsible for the prose and poetic speeches in Jeremiah 2–20, I believe the nature of these chapters calls for a different approach than that followed by Duhm and the majority of Jeremiah scholars since his time. (I argue in chs 7–9 that they comprise two coherent literary compositions: one in chs 2–10 and one in chs 11–20.) Rather than starting with the attempt to identify the authors of what these scholars consider to be the original materials found in the text and only then moving on to consider who might have brought them together, I believe it a more sound approach to start with asking who might be responsible for the unified compositions and then considering whether they may have drawn on previous materials by other authors. The primary inference about authorship, I believe, that can be drawn from the two compositions is that the high degree of literary coherence in each suggests that it is the product of a single vision[18]—and, most likely, the product of a single individual, who could be called the dramatist, or story teller. This view does not rule out the possibilities that the dramatist incorporated earlier materials (perhaps by other authors) or that later authors added materials to enhance the story. The first seems quite likely and the second quite possible.

Although these two dramatic narratives that tell the story of Israel over the course of several centuries and the story of Jeremiah over the course of a few decades could have been composed by any number of known or unknown individuals from Jeremiah's time to centuries later, I think it is most likely that Jeremiah himself is responsible for both compositions. One indication that this is the case is that although Jeremiah mainly appears in these compositions as a dramatic speaker/character, at points throughout both compositions he also appears as the narrator.[19] Although this is hardly conclusive evidence (a dramatist or compiler could be responsible for employing Jeremiah as a narrator as well as a character), it does seem that the most likely explanation of this feature of the text is that Jeremiah is not only its narrator but also its composer.

There do not seem to me to be any compelling obstacles to identifying Jeremiah as responsible for the present form of chs 2–10 and 11–20. I do not find the presence of

---

[18] Gordon McConville comes to a similar conclusion "that the book is the product of careful and sophisticated editing, substantially the work … of one mind" as the result of following a similar methodological approach: he counsels that reading the work of Jeremiah should not begin "with the small component, and work out towards the whole composition," but rather it should begin "with the whole, in whose context the disparate parts should ultimately be evaluated and understood." *Judgement and Promise: An Interpretation of the Book of Jeremiah* (Winona Lake, IN: Eisenbrauns, 1993), 22–3.

[19] A number introductions to speeches throughout both dramas appear to speak directly to the audience (in theater terms, to "break the third-wall") to tell them who is speaking: "The word of Yahweh came to me" (2:1, 13:8, 16:1, 18:5); "Yahweh said to me" (3:6, 3:11, 11:6, 11:9, 13:1, 14:11, 14:14, 15:1, 17:19), "Then I said" (4:10, 5:4, 14:13); and "Then I answered" (11:5). It is evident that it is Jeremiah who addresses the audience. However, there are a few speeches that are introduced with a third-person reference to Jeremiah: "The word that came to Jeremiah from Yahweh" (7:1, 11:1, 14:1, 18:1) and a prose story told about him (19:14, 20:1-3). It is interesting to note that three of these passages soon revert to a first-person narrator: "Then I answered" (11:5), "Yahweh said to me" (14:11), and "So I went" (18:3). This feature and the fact that the first-person introductions are much more common suggest that the five third-person references are an anomaly. One explanation would be that they are drawn from earlier material written down by another writer (perhaps the "biographer" responsible for the prose narratives about Jeremiah).

"Deuteronomistic prose" in these chapters to be a credible defeater. I argue at length (mainly in chs 3–5) that there is no good reason to deny that the prophetic persona, or the historical prophet himself, could have employed the style or held the theological perspectives of the prose speeches.[20] It also appears to me that there are no events or speeches portrayed in the dramatic narrative that he couldn't have written because they come from after his time.[21] The story of Jeremiah in chs 11–20 appears to end just after Jeremiah's public identification of Babylon as the northern foe who would conquer Judah (20:4), and this was most likely early in the reign of Jehoiakim.[22] The story of Israel in chs 2–10 appears to end at a time when Jerusalem had been invaded and conquered and her citizens exiled to Babylon (9:19, 10:20) but when the threat of another wave of Babylonian invasion was looming on the horizon (10:22). If the invasion (and conquest and exile) the text portrays is the one that took place in 597 BC (when Jehoiachin was taken into exile), then the approaching one could be the final one in 587 (when Jerusalem was destroyed and Zedekiah was taken into exile). On the other hand, if the invasion portrayed in the narrative is this final one (587), then the invasion thought to be approaching could be the one that was feared (41:18, 43:3) after the rebels assassinated Gedeliah, the governor of Judah installed by the Bablonians after the destruction of Jerusalem (40:7). In either case, both compositions could have been written during the lifetime of Jeremiah.

While the consideration of the earliest dates of composition makes it possible that Jeremiah was the dramatist responsible for these compositions, and the fact that he appears as the narrator makes it likely that he could be the dramatist as well as character in the drama, the main question is who is most likely to have wanted to portray Israel, Jeremiah, and Yahweh (and the other characters and events in the works) in this way. Chapters 11–20 appear to have been designed (among other things) to portray Jeremiah as a reluctant participant in the announcement of his nation's doom, a doom made inevitable by the people's treacherous rebellion against Yahweh, which culminated their mistreatment of his messenger Jeremiah. Chapters 2–10 appear to have been designed to portray the conquest of Jerusalem as an outpouring of the wrath of Yahweh provoked by his bride's repeated infidelities and deep-seated wickedness. The portrayal appears to be intended to urge the citizens of Jerusalem (portrayed as her children) to throw themselves on Yahweh's mercy in hopes that his steadfast love for his city would cause him relent from bringing further invasions. Although these perspectives and

---

[20] It is also worth considering that most of the prose speeches are presented as messages in which Yahweh is the first-person speaker. Thus, in terms of the drama, they represent not Jeremiah's style and perspective but Yahweh's.

[21] One obvious caveat to this general principle is that, a story about a prophet will be likely to include portrayals of him prophesying future events and these might take place after the end of the story, or even after the composition of the story. This seems likely to be the case, for example, with the prophecies of exile in Jer. 12:14, 13:17, and 13:19.

[22] The fact that Jeremiah was able to speak in the temple court (19:14), from which he was debarred in the fourth year of Jehoiakim (36:6) seems to indicate that the last events in 11–20 were before that time. However, Jeremiah's public identification of Babylon as the northern foe in 20:4, like his identification of Babylon in the fourth year of Jehoiakim (25:11, the year that Nebuchadnezzar became king [21:1] and the year of his triumph at Carchemish, 605 BC) suggests that it was close to that time. Another factor to consider is that although a major subject of 11–20 is the opposition suffered by Jeremiah because of his message, the composition includes no mention of opposition he faced from Jehoiakim or Zedekiah (including his imprisonment).

purposes of the dramatic portrayals could possibly be those of a number of individuals from Jeremiah's time onward, it appears most likely to me that Jeremiah himself is the dramatist primarily because the evident purposes of the portrayals fit best with Jeremiah's concerns when his loyalty to his nation was in question (26:11, 43:3) and when further invasions from Babylon were still a threat (21:2 or 41:18).

If Jeremiah is likely to be the dramatist of these compositions, then the main question about the source of the speeches they include is not who wrote them (since it is unlikely—though possible—that Jeremiah included sources by other authors), but whether Jeremiah wrote them when he composed the drama or at the time of the events they help to portray in the compositions. Were any of them written to address or to respond to earlier historian situations and then later incorporated into the dramatic narrative? Did they have different functions in earlier historical contexts than their present function in the literary contexts of the dramatic compositions?

For most of the poetic speeches, this question is difficult to answer because of their inherent dramatic character. They appear to have been designed to convey the identities, perspectives, emotions, and purposes of their (usually unnamed) speakers and to evoke situations in which these speakers find themselves. The dramatic character of the speeches is facilitated by the inherent dramatic poetical of poetic form. Poetry is naturally artificial: it is intentionally crafted to be different from naturally occurring speech. People don't usually speak to each other in poetry. Thus, the natural assumption of a person encountering a text in poetic form is that it is not a record of actual speech but rather an artistic representation of speech. The arguments that prophetic speech is an exception because of the poetic souls of the prophets or their ecstatic experiences seem to be special pleading.[23] While there certainly are accounts in the biblical literature of ecstatic individuals and schools of ecstatics who were called "prophets" and were associated with music and singing—and perhaps rhythmic speaking—ecstatic experiences hardly seem to be a likely explanation of the poetic form of the sophisticated compositions in Jeremiah 2–10 and 11–20. Hebrew prophets did sometimes put their messages or public prophecies into poetic form, but for most of the poetic speeches in Jeremiah 2–20 there is little indication whether they were ever publically delivered or not.

For most of the prose speeches, on the other hand, there are several features that suggest they were delivered publically at particular moments in Jeremiah's ministry. Some of the speeches are tied with specific occasions: when Jeremiah went to the potter's house (18:3), when he spoke in the temple (7:2, 19:14), when he recovered his loincloth (13:17), and when Pashur released him from the stocks (20:3). Several are presented as messages Jeremiah was to deliver to the people, which he presumably did (e.g., 7:27, 11:3, 13:12, 16:10).[24] It is worth noting that, in the prose narratives of the book, the prophet

---

[23] I argue at length against this understanding of the poetry in the prophetic books in Chapters 2, 6, and 7.

[24] Although the poetic speeches are often said to be "messenger speech," I argue (primarily in Chapter 7) that this is a false assessment of their form. Conversely, the prose speeches, which are regularly explicitly introduced in them as messages and take the form of messages, are often regarded as homiletical sermons. One indication of which speeches are correctly identified as messages is that, although the prose speeches regularly directly address (with m.s. and m.pl. pronouns) historical

is regularly pictured speaking prose, often delivering messages from Yahweh (like the prose messages in 2–20) to historical individuals and groups.[25] It is possible that these prose accounts are false, or fictional, and that the prose speeches in them as well as the prose speeches in 2–20 are not based on reports of actual speeches given by the prophet. However, the rationale most often given for this judgment is the belief that it is impossible that the historical Jeremiah could have employed the form or diction of the speeches, or could have held their perspective. The evidence most often given for this belief, in turn, is the discrepancy between them and the poetic speeches, assumed to be authentic records of how the historical Jeremiah actually spoke. That assumption seems dubious to me. Thus, one answer to the question of whether the poetic and prose speeches that function dramatically in Jeremiah 2–10 and 11–20 are likely to have been drawn from records of earlier historical speeches is that it is more likely for the prose speeches than the poetic ones.[26] In this sense, the poetic speeches are less likely to be "authentic."

The Question of Historicity

As with the question of who wrote chs 2–20, so with the question of their historical value, I believe that the nature of the chapters calls for a different approach than the one that has been followed by the majority of scholars since the time of Duhm. The basic approach as seen in Duhm's work is to start with determining the sources of isolated texts, then assess the historical value of each text (on a spectrum from authentic documentary evidence to ideologically motivated fabrications), and then work up a reconstruction of the historical background based on these assessments. My judgment that 2–10 and 11–20 are coherent dramatic narratives portraying the history of Israel and the career of Jeremiah suggests that the first questions about their historical value should be about the relationships between their portrayals of the history of Israel and the ministry of Jeremiah and the actual history of Israel and career of Jeremiah. Does the narrator expect the audience to understand events portrayed as things that actually happened? Does the narrative order follow the order of events in history? Is the purpose or perspective of the work likely to have caused distortions

---

audiences (the people or leaders of Judah and Jerusalem), the poetic speeches are addressed to a variety of audiences (such as enemy generals, a woman who represents Jerusalem, the heavens and the earth, the divine council, spiritual messengers, or Jeremiah), none of whom are the audience the designation "messenger speech" would lead a reader to expect. This reversal of the apparent nature of these speeches is necessary to maintain the practice of treating the poetic speeches, and not the prose, as authentic historical evidence.

[25] However, 2 Chron. 35:35 pictures Jeremiah lamenting for Josiah.

[26] If the prose speeches are considered to be preexisting material, it appears that the dramatist has employed them in different ways in the two compositions. In chs 2–10, the prose passages seem to have been added to a drama primarily conveyed in poetic form, a drama that could mainly tell its story without the prose speeches. Many of the prose speeches in this composition are prophecies of the future and often seemed to have been placed at the point in the story when the events they prophesy take place, rather than at the point when they were first spoken. In chs 11–20, which has considerably more prose speeches, the temporal progression of prose speeches provides the framework for the story and the poetic speeches seem mainly to have been added, or written, to develop the scenes that the prose speeches introduce.

in the portrayal? Are its depictions of individuals and events in conflict with what is known to them from other sources? Does it include depictions of things that modern interpreters or readers will judge to be impossible (or highly improbable) because of their views of reality?

Readers can ask those questions of the basic events portrayed in the two compositions. Jeremiah 2–10 presents a history of Israel that includes the following elements: that the ancestors of the nation came out of Egypt through the wilderness and into the land of Canaan (2:6-7), that they had a written law from that time that demanded sole devotion to the god Yahweh (2:8), that in land the people often worshiped other gods (2:11), that in times of distress they sought out the help of Egypt and Assyria (2:18, 36), that the people of the northern tribes were exiled to the land of the north (by Assyria) (3:8, 18), that when threatened by invasion from the north (by Babylon) the people of the southern tribes trusted in the inviolability of the Temple (7:4), but Jerusalem was destroyed and the people were taken into exile (9:19), as Jeremiah the prophet had warned (7:14-15). Jeremiah 11–20 presents a story of the Jeremiah that includes these elements: Jeremiah (apparently enthusiastically, 11:5) proclaimed that to remain in the land the people of Judah would have to obey the commands of Yahweh in accordance with the covenant Yahweh made with their ancestors when they left Egypt (11:1-5), that instead of repentance and obedience Jeremiah's message met with opposition (15:10, 18:18) including a plot against his life by men in his hometown (11:21), that he initially prayed that Yahweh would spare the people (11:14, 14:11), but later that Yahweh would judge his enemies and vindicate his message (18:23), that after some time he proclaimed that the people's stubborn disobedience made destruction unavoidable and he enacted this by smashing a pot in front of the elders and speaking to the people in the temple court (9:1-15), that in response a priest named Pashur had him beaten and put in stocks and Jeremiah announced that Babylon would take the nation of Judah into exile (20:1-6).

It appears to me that although the portrayals of history in two compositions have been shaped by strong theological convictions and agendas, there is little reason for historians (or readers, or interpreters) to doubt that they meant to portray things that actually happened. Furthermore, I find that there are no compelling reasons to doubt that these things actually did happen—and in the basic order in which they are portrayed. The portrayals do not appear to be in conflict with what is known about the period from other ancient sources (or archeology), and the events they describe are not hard to believe for modern readers who do not share the belief-system of the writers (and would not believe text's explanations of the events: e.g., that they were caused by Yahweh).

To affirm the basic historicity of the events portrayed in the accounts is not the same as saying that the portrayals are true. This is because the stories are not a bare presentations of historical events but stories of Yahweh's interaction with Jeremiah, the people of Israel, and the nations of the ancient Near East. The narratives understand the destruction of Jerusalem and Judah at the hands of the Babylonians (and the earlier destruction and exile of the northern tribes by the Assyrians) to be brought on by Yahweh's rage at the treachery (12:17-13) and infidelity of the people he chose, and his exasperation with their repeated refusals to change their ways (13:22-27). The narratives understand Jeremiah's messages as personal communications from Yahweh to his chosen people: first calling her back to into relationship with him and later announcing that because of her repeated rebuffs of his overtures that he would no longer listen to her but would hand her over to her enemies (18:17), bring death and exile to her people, and give her wealth to her Babylonian conquerors (20:4-5). These stories assume a number of foundational beliefs that readers would have to share before they could affirm the stories are true: that Yahweh is the one, true, living god (10:10); that as the creator of the heavens and earth and the king of the nations (10:7, 12), he has the power and authority to control the actions of empires; that he chose the people of Israel to be his people (10:16), delivered them from slavery in Egypt (2:6, 20), and gave them the good land of Canaan (2:7); that he bound himself in a covenant relationship with them (11:3-4) that has both the nature of a treaty that demands obedience to its stipulations to avoid consequences (11:6-11) and of marriage vows that demands fidelity (3:1); and that for centuries he spoke to them (warning them of coming judgment through prophets, 7:25) and he listened to them (relenting from judgment in response to their prayers, 15:1). Assessing the truth of these beliefs, which is necessary for understanding their present-day significance to people today, goes far beyond the work of historians and literary critics. Although I am committed to these beliefs as a Christian, it is no part of my intentions for this work to persuade others to accept them, and I have attempted in so far as I am able not to let these beliefs influence my argument.

It is not necessary to share the beliefs about Yahweh's relationship with Israel that the text assumes, or encourages, to accept the basic historicity of the events it portrays or the role of Jeremiah in its composition it implies. A reader of the book of Jeremiah who didn't believe Yahweh had chosen Israel (or that God exists, or that there could be supernatural events in history), could find good reason to believe that the events portrayed in these compositions actually happened and that the prophet portrayed by them is also responsible for the portrayal. Furthermore, it is not necessary to share these views about the historicity of stories, or about the authorship of the texts, to appreciate their literary coherence. A reader who believed that these compositions were largely fictional accounts written centuries after the events they purport to portray could still be convinced that 2–10 and 11–20 are unified dramatic works in which the various components in each work together to tell a story. Finally, it is not necessary to share this assessment of the nature and structure of these chapters to accept that Jeremiah studies of the past century have followed a misguided approach, understanding chs 2–20 based on a false assumptions about the origins of the individual passages in them. A reader who held a different understanding of the coherence of these chapters, or who believed there was very little coherence at all, could still recognize that it is dubious to assume that poetic form is an indication of authenticity and to ground interpretation on a reconstruction of the biography of the prophet or a compositional history of the book based on that assumption.

The argument of this book is intended to challenge that dubious assumption and show the unsoundness of approaches based on it in the hope that it will enable future readers and interpreters to better perceive the nature of the text and the kind of interpretive approaches it invites.

The Scope and Limitations of the Study

From the aim and plan of this study, it should be apparent that it will deviate in significant ways from what might be considered the standard form of studies of biblical texts. In order to prevent false expectations, two distinguishing characteristics and the limitations they impose on the study should be noted. First, given that the scope of the argument covers roughly three centuries of biblical scholarship, there is no claim (and no attempt) to be exhaustive. Instead, it traces the broad outlines of what it judges to be a central story in the history of scholarly study of the Hebrew Bible and of Jeremiah in particular. Furthermore, rather than argue from a broad survey of scholarship, this study primarily engages a select number of scholarly works that illustrate the story, either because they are especially influential or especially representative.

Second, the argument of the whole is intended to be negative: It is an argument *against* the standard historical-critical model of Jeremiah's composition and its foundational assumptions. Although the last three chapters do draw attention to features of the text that previous scholars have passed over, observation of these features is not primarily presented as the exegetical results of this study. Instead, the failure of recent scholars to perceive these features is presented as an argument against continued adherence to the standard model (which guided their work). The reason for this negative argument is the judgment that the primary obstacle to progress in Jeremiah scholarship is the failure to reject the erroneous system that dominated the twentieth century.

In keeping with the negative form of the argument, I primarily chose works to illustrate the adverse effects of adherence to Duhm's assumptions or methodological approach. In this way, the negative approach imposes two unwanted limitations on this work. First, many of the most illuminating scholarly works on Jeremiah are not included because they are relatively free of Duhm's influence. Second, in treatment of the works that are included, the evaluation necessarily focuses almost entirely on their most problematic aspects. I regret that the nature of the argument prevents me from fully expressing my great appreciation for these scholarly labors and my gratitude for all that I have learned from them.

One of the happiest parts of my long journey with Jeremiah has been the opportunity to meet other scholars traveling the same road. I can well remember the first time I attended a session of the Jeremiah group at the national Society of Biblical Literature meeting. It was 1998 in Orlando. On first seeing the scholars whose books I'd read, I felt like a visitor at the Walt Disney World Resort next door catching sight of their favorite Disney characters. There was Kathleen O'Connor wearing a bright scarf with panache and Robert Carroll with the gleeful grin of a gadfly; there was Mark Biddle looking every bit the professor with his tweed jacket and pipe and Louis Stulman, the Midwestern gentleman. Even the aquiline Walter Brueggemann swooped in. (His Old Testament theology published that year made him something of a rock star at the meeting.) One other character was a tall quiet man with twinkling blue eyes. This was Pete Diamond. That he was a beloved member of this community of Jeremiah scholars is evident from the dedication of a 2015 collection of essays from the group: "Dedicated to the memory of a brilliant colleague and a dear friend, A. R. Pete Diamond (1950–2011)."[27] I wrote the epilogue to this book as a tribute to his work, and I offer it here as a tribute to my fellow travelers.

---

[27] Dedication of *Jeremiah Invented: Constructions and Deconstructions of Jeremiah*, ed. Else K. Holt and Carolyn J. Sharp (New York: Bloomsbury T&T Clark, 2015), xv.

Part One

The Roots of Duhm: The Historical Origins of Duhm's Model

1

Introduction to Duhm's 1901 *Das Buch Jeremia*

Since the beginning of the last century, those intrepid souls who dare to actually read the book of Jeremiah have been warned by biblical scholars not to go out to confront this unruly giant of a book unarmed. Commentators from this modern period have been anxious to equip readers with all the gear they deem necessary for grappling with the book. In the amply stocked introductions to their commentaries, they offer readers a set of critical implements, which have remained remarkably constant throughout these years. Two elements of the critical apparatus have been almost universally urged on readers. At the minimum, readers must be provided with a genre classification system and a biography of the prophet. The classification system is offered to enable readers to recognize three types of material they will encounter: "prophetic oracles," "biographical narratives," and "prose sermons" (usually designated Types "A," "B," and "C," respectively). The biography of the prophet is given so that when readers are faced with the barrage of various speeches and incidents they will have a historical framework for sorting them out.

It might be thought that the reason these two critical implements are so widely recommended is simply that they are demanded by the nature of the book: particularly its intermingling of various literary forms and non-chronological presentation of events. However, a closer look at the specific way scholars present these two implements reveals a unanimity that cannot be wholly explained by the common issues the book requires them to address. It must also be attributed to shared scholarly aims, or a shared approach to the book. The common approach is a historical one that prioritizes distinguishing between sources and determining their reliability as evidence for historical reconstruction. This historical approach is apparent in the classification system, particularly its central feature: training readers to distinguish between the "prophetic oracles" (Type A)—considered to be authentic (i.e., reliable as historical evidence)—and the "prose sermons" (Type C), thought to have been added later and thus less reliable as evidence about the historical prophet.[1] Thus, what the classification system supplies is not merely a guide to the literary forms but a history of

---

[1] That distinguishing between Type A and Type C is the main aim of the A-B-C classification system is evident when one considers that readers can easily distinguish the Type B material (and the fact that Jeremiah is not the writer) for themselves. Type B's third-person narratives are quite distinct from the first-person speeches in A and C.

the composition of the book given to enable readers to judge what contribution each type of material makes to understanding the history behind the book.

The biography of the prophet is likewise not merely a chronological presentation of events narrated in the book; it is a scholarly reconstruction of the prophet's life based on the authentic historical evidence in the book. The focus of most of the biographies is filling in the gaps left by the historical narratives[2] (deemed to be fairly reliable) by discerning the historical situations that occasioned the various "authentic prophetic oracles." The reconstruction of the history of the book's composition (embedded in the A-B-C classification system) and the reconstructed historical biography of the prophet are the primary aims and outcomes of the historical approach to the book. They become, in turn, the recommended starting point for modern readers trying to make sense of the book: together they provide an interpretive framework within which the individual parts of Jeremiah are to be understood.

Of course, there are several varieties of the modern interpretive framework, and there are debates over individual points. The central debate about the history of composition has been over the degree to which the Type C prose speeches preserve the authentic words (or at least the authentic message) of the prophet Jeremiah. However, all sides in this debate are united in prioritizing the question of authenticity: which materials provide reliable evidence for reconstructing the historical message and ministry of the prophet (and additionally, in some scholarly studies, which materials provide evidence for determining the concerns of the later authors or editors). Likewise, debates about details of the prophet's biography also presume an approach and an aim common to all the parties involved. The familiar debating points—such as the date of Jeremiah's call, the extent of his involvement in the reform of Josiah, and the identity of the "foe from the north"[3]—share the interest of reconstructing the life of the historical Jeremiah, particularly the parts of his life the book does not directly narrate.

Taken together, the similar compositional theories and reconstructed biographies along with the underlying historical-critical aims and methods form what is a recognizable paradigm, or interpretive model, which has provided the primary guidance Jeremiah scholars have offered readers for over a hundred years. The paradigm has shown a remarkable degree of consistency and durability.[4] It is also remarkable that virtually the whole paradigm was introduced by one man in one book. Bernhard Duhm's 1901 commentary, *Das Buch Jeremia*, lays out for the first time both the three-source compositional theory and the outline of the standard modern biography of the prophet. It turns interpretation of Jeremiah to the aim of historical reconstruction based on determining which parts of the text offer reliable evidence.

---

[2]   The primary gap is in the early years of the prophet's ministry between his call in the thirteenth year of Josiah (*c.* 627 BC) and his first dated sermon in the beginning of Jehoiakim's reign (*c.* 609 BC).

[3]   See the collection of essays grouped under the section headings: "The Date of Jeremiah's Call," "Jeremiah, Deuteronomy, and the Reform of Josiah," and "The Foe from the North" in Leo G. Perdue and Brian W. Kovacs, *A Prophet to the Nations: Essays in Jeremiah Studies* (Winona Lake, IN: Eisenbrauns, 1984).

[4]   Those familiar with Jeremiah studies of the past hundred years might object that in the last few decades there has been an effort to "move beyond" the historical approach and Duhm's theory. The final chapters of this study are intended to demonstrate the degree to which the historical approach and specific elements of Duhm's theory still guide recent work.

The introductions to Jeremiah commentaries, where readers often first encounter the scholarly paradigm, sometimes include a passing reference to Duhm as the pioneer of the modern approach to the book. However, given Duhm's role in establishing the paradigm, it is surprising to discover the scant consideration most of them afford to his work—what led him to the view of the book they follow. Understanding the impetus for the modern paradigm is important for readers trying to judge whether they need to make use of the recommended historical apparatus as they read the book of Jeremiah—whether, that is, they must go out to meet the giant book clothed in Duhm's armor.

The Introduction to Duhm's 1901 *Das Buch Jeremia*

To explore the origins of the modern scholarly paradigm for interpreting Jeremiah, an obvious place to begin is an investigation of Duhm's commentary itself. Readers who have some familiarity with the paradigm will be surprised to find how fully it is enunciated in Duhm's commentary. The modern Jeremiah appears to have sprung forth from his forehead fully armed with the standard critical apparatus. Duhm lays out all the central elements in the commentary's introduction. Readers who turn to the introduction can discern the division of the book of Jeremiah into three types of material (the basis of the standard compositional model) in its outline:

I. General Overview of the Book of Jeremiah
II. The Prophetic Poems (*Gedichte*) of Jeremiah
III. The Book of Baruch
IV. The Additions (*Ergänzungen*) to the Writings of Jeremiah and Baruch
V. The Genesis (*Enstehung*) of the Book of Jeremiah
VI. Bibliography[5]

Sections II, III, and IV deal with the materials of the book as three sources, which are clearly the precursors of Types A, B, and C: The "Prophetic Poems" are what was later described as "authentic prophetic oracles"; the "Book of Baruch" is the prose narratives; and the "Additions" are mainly what came to be known as "prose sermons." Along with the standard compositional history, the second standard element of the modern paradigm is also easy to see in Duhm's introduction. The subsections of Section II, "The Prophetic Poems of Jeremiah," present the biographical reconstruction in its now familiar form:

1. Concerning the life of Jeremiah
2. The prophetic poems of Jeremiah
3. Overview of Jeremiah's poems

The first subsection presents the biography of the prophet with almost all the details that characterize the modern scholarly presentation, particularly the reconstruction

---

[5] Bernhard Duhm, *Das Buch Jeremia*, KHC 11 (Tübingen: J. C. B. Mohr, 1901), ix–xxiii.

of the events of Jeremiah's early ministry not explicitly referred to in the book: his idyllic rural childhood, his alarm at the Scythian invasions (the "foe from the north"), his initial shock at the immorality of Jerusalem, and his disillusionment with the reforms of Josiah. After giving an account of the nature of "The Prophetic Poems of Jeremiah," Duhm's third subsection, the "Overview of Jeremiah's Poems," turns to the task of assigning each speech of Jeremiah that he considers authentic to a period in his reconstructed biography. In this way he completes the historical reconstruction.

Three Characteristics of Duhm's Commentary

Although scholarly works later in the century offer more nuanced and more comprehensive presentations of the modern paradigm for understanding Jeremiah, Duhm's 1901 commentary allows readers to be present at the moment of its birth. They have the opportunity to observe the paradigm in its raw form before it was amended and refined. Even in the introduction to the commentary, they will readily perceive characteristics that distinguish the paradigm introduced by Duhm from previous ways of interpreting Jeremiah: its thoroughgoing historical character, its oppositional stance toward the present form of the book, and its strong aesthetic and theological predilections. Consideration of these three distinctives will help readers trying to assess the value of the paradigm founded on Duhm's approach.

Historical Approach

The first characteristic of Duhm's work that strikes the reader has to do with its basic character, its genre. His commentary presents itself as a historical investigation. Likewise, although the title page introduces Duhm as an "Ord[inarius] Professor der Theologie in Basel," Duhm does primarily present himself a theologian but rather a historian.[6] From the first page, Duhm appears in the role of a historical investigator, guided by the methods and aims of historical study. He comes to the book looking for reliable evidence that will enable him to reconstruct the life of the historical Jeremiah and place his writings in their original historical contexts.

The search for historical evidence is the context of Duhm's first introduction of his three-source theory. In the "General Overview of the Book of Jeremiah" that opens the introduction, Duhm postulates that the book is just one part of an extensive Jeremiah literature that is now mostly lost. Like most of this literature (which includes the "Letter of Jeremiah," "The Book of Baruch," and "Lamentations"), most of the material in the book of Jeremiah is of little historical value. The "Additions," which make up the greatest part of the book, only appear to be the speeches of Jeremiah, but in actuality they originated long after the life of the prophet (they are "with very few exceptions post exilic"), and they were written not as historical reports but in the

---

[6] The tension between Duhm's job description as a professor of theology and his actual work as a historian parallels the tension Wellhausen tried to resolve in 1882 when he resigned from theology department of his university. Henning Graf Reventlow, *History of Biblical Interpretation: Volume 4: From the Enlightenment to the Twentieth Century*, trans. Leo Perdue (Atlanta, GA: Society of Biblical Literature, 2010), 312.

spirit of "morality tales and synagogue sermons."[7] The book's value, which is greater than all the rest of the ancient Jeremiah literature, comes solely from the two other sources: "the authentic prophecy [*die echte Prophetie*] of the ancient prophet Jeremiah," and various accounts from a "biography" (*die Lebensgeschichte*) that he attributes to Jeremiah's scribe, Baruch.[8]

In his initial evaluations of the three sources, the historical nature of Duhm's project is clear from his criteria for assessing worth. His primary measure of value is "authenticity" (*Echtheit*). Authenticity is what chiefly distinguishes the first and second source (the prophecies and biography) from the third (the additions). Duhm's description of certain speeches as "authentic" is not simply an attribution of authorship; it is a judgment that those speeches are valuable, and, even more, it is an indication of the nature of their value: namely, they provide evidence of the historical, social, or biographical situation (or even the psychological state) in which they originated.

The historical nature of Duhm's work is also evident in a secondary criterion of worth. He values material that is factually accurate in its depiction of historical reality. This is what makes him judge "Baruch's biography" as "probably most important"[9] even though he clearly believes Baruch's work to be inferior to Jeremiah's in terms of its literary and theological value. For Duhm's purposes, his impression that Baruch is an artless chronicler[10] helps to secure the historical value of his writings because it takes away the possibility that any distortion has crept in due to his literary or theological aims (in contrast to the additions, in which Duhm discerns a heavy-handed theological agenda). Baruch's work is valuable for Duhm's work because as biographical material it has aims and interests that approximate his own historical aims and interests. Conversely, the additions have little value because they were not written in the "historical spirit."[11] Duhm complains that authors of the additions "write theology not history."[12] Baruch writes history, and the value of his work is not simply that it is reliable but also that it provides abundant biographical and historical facts about Jeremiah and his time.

On the basis of the historical evidence in the "authentic works of Jeremiah" and the "biography of Baruch," Duhm produces his historical reconstruction of the biography of the prophet and the corresponding designation of a biographical context for each of the prophet's authentic works. These are the primary results of Duhm's work: his aim, which, in keeping with his method, is unapologetically historical. Duhm lays out these historical achievements in his introduction, primarily in the section on Jeremiah's "Prophetic Poems" (the primary historical evidence). In the section on "Baruch's Biography," Duhm completes his biographical reconstruction by rearranging the narratives into chronological order.

---

[7] Duhm, *Jeremia*, x.
[8] Duhm, *Jeremia*, x.
[9] Duhm, *Jeremia*, x.
[10] "[Baruch] is neither a great spirit nor a brilliant writer [*kein grosser Geist und kein glänzender Schriftsteller*]; he is an upright, honest soul [*eine biedere, ehrliche Seele*], and relates his experience with an affectionate absorption in the smallest details (e.g., 36:9) and in a reliable manner." Duhm, *Jeremia*, xv.
[11] Duhm, *Jeremia*, xvii.
[12] Duhm, *Jeremia*, xviii.

To recognize that these historical reconstructions are the primary contribution of Duhm's book is to see that what Duhm's book actually provides is somewhat different than what is offered by its title, *Das Buch Jeremia Erklärt*. Although in the body of his work Duhm does provide clarification, or explanation (*Erklärung*), for each individual passage (primarily an estimation of its significance in a proposed historical context), he provides very little explanation of the book of Jeremiah as whole (its structure, purpose, message, etc.) or how the individual passages contribute to it. The book and its presentation of the prophet are clearly less important to him than the historical prophet that lies behind it.

Although it might not be unexpected that Duhm's interests would be primarily historical in the sections on the sources he deemed to contain authentic historical evidence, it is somewhat surprising to find that his relative lack of interest in the book as it stands extends even to the final sections of the Introduction: "The Additions" and "The Genesis of the Book." The main concern of the section on the additions is to demonstrate their inferiority to the other material in order to discredit them as historical evidence. The main concern of the section on the compositional history of the book is to argue that the extensive accretions and poor editing have obscured the historical evidence and original (chronological) ordering. In short, these sections present the additions and the present condition of the book as obstacles to be overcome before the work of historical reconstruction can proceed.

Antagonism toward the Book and Contempt for Its Authors

Duhm's treatment of the additions and compositional history are instances of a second notable characteristic of his commentary: his adversarial stance toward the present form of the book. His approach is characterized by disinterest in the book's structure, opposition to its portrayal of Jeremiah and his times, and contempt for the authors and editors he believed to be responsible for most of the book's materials. His disinterest in the structure of the book arises from both his general historical approach and his specific theories about the compositional history of the book. Since Duhm valued the book primarily as a repository of historical evidence, it is not hard to understand his lack of interest in how the evidence has been deposited in the book. The only kind of order that would be of much help to a historian would be chronological order, and Duhm expresses his frustration with the editors, who made his work difficult by failing to keep the historical records in the book in good order. Writing about chs 1–25, where he believes the majority of the authentic materials were stored, he observes that these materials could have been preserved in chronological order "if the editors had taken a little more interest in the real meaning of Jeremiah's works instead of allowing themselves to be led by their own fantasies … and if some of his works had not been separated for thematic reasons from what were presumably their original places."[13] In Duhm's view, the incompetence of the editors and the random nature in which the book took on its present form mean that what is now called the book of Jeremiah is not really a book at all. "The book grew up very slowly, much like the way an uncontrolled

---

[13] Duhm, *Jeremia*, xxi.

forest grows and spreads. It came into existence like a body of literature comes into existence; it wasn't made like a book is made, by orderly arrangement. There can be no question of a uniform composition."[14] Since Duhm understands the present form of the book as a "chaotic mess" or simply "a heap" (*Haufen*) of materials,[15] there is no reason for him to try to understand its structure or order; instead, his work is to consider the individual pieces of historical evidence and then fit each one into his own order: his reconstruction of the biography of the prophet and the compositional history of the book.

Duhm's low opinion of the compositional order of the present form of the book is not as low as his opinion of the largest part of the materials that make up the book. His perception of the contents of the book finds an apt parallel in Thomas Jefferson's famous comparison of the authentic words of Jesus found in the gospels to "diamonds in a dunghill."[16] Although it has been noted that Duhm believed that the "authentic literary work of Jeremiah" and "Baruch's biography" raised the book of Jeremiah over all the other extant Jeremiah literature, he also believed that these diamonds have to be carefully distinguished from the inauthentic dung that makes up the majority of book.

What particularly distinguishes Duhm's view of the book from the views of his predecessors is his estimation of the extent of this inauthentic matter. Whereas previous scholars may have raised questions about the authenticity of this or that passage, they viewed the book as generally sound. They approached the task of identifying late additions like textual critics "establishing" a text by removing isolated interpolations or like art historians restoring a painting by removing blemishes. Duhm, on the other hand, operates under the assumption that there is so little authentic material in Jeremiah that it can only be unearthed by bulldozing away a tremendous heap of rubbish. He calculates that of the roughly 1,350 verses in Jeremiah, only 280 are the authentic work of the historical prophet. Even when the roughly 220 verses written by Baruch are added, over 850 verses remain that are inauthentic additions. To use Jefferson's words, the book is less than two-fifths diamonds (550 verses) and over three-fifths dung (850 verses). Given this diamonds-to-dung ratio, it is no surprise that Duhm had little appreciation for the book of Jeremiah in its present form.

It might be asked whether "dung" is the right word to express Duhm's estimation of the materials that make up the majority of the book. His extremely low estimate of the *literary* and *theological* value of the additions will be detailed below. At this point, Duhm's estimation of the *historical* value of the additions can be considered. It has already been observed that Duhm believed the additions to be of little value in recovering the historical Jeremiah (even though they might have some value for understanding postexilic Judaism). However, it is not enough to say that Duhm found the additions to be of little use for his historical project; he viewed them as the principal agents responsible for propagating the false view of history that his work is written to correct. This is particularly true of the portrait of Jeremiah he finds in the additions. They have hidden the actual historical prophet Jeremiah with

---

[14] Duhm, *Jeremia*, xx.
[15] Duhm, *Jeremia*, xx, xxi.
[16] From a letter to John Adams (October 12, 1813).

the embodiment of an abstraction that the later Jews made themselves from the prophets in general. … He is, as far as something human remains, not primarily a prophet, but rather a Torah teacher, a scribe, like the redactors, who brings … no new revelation of God.[17]

Duhm charges the authors of the additions with transforming the Jeremiah of history—a true prophet—into Jeremiah of their own imagination, a Jeremiah in their own image—a Torah teacher and a scribe. Duhm believes that the true Jeremiah can be recovered from under the false Jeremiah of the scribes only by exposing as unhistorical the picture of the prophet created by the scribal additions that make up the majority of the book.

Duhm's low opinion of the book and its portrait of the prophet is closely related to his contempt for the authors and editors believed to be responsible for the largest part of its contents and its present order. His disdain is summed up in the word he commonly uses to refer to them: "scribes" (*Schriftgelehrte*). Duhm's designation of the authors of the additions (*Ergänzer*, "supplementers" is his most common term for them) as "scribes" is highly significant for understanding his view of the book they produced. He directly attributes the 850 verses added to the writings of Jeremiah and Baruch to "scribes," who "created their book of Jeremiah as their contribution to a kind of popular Bible (*Volksbibel*)."[18] He goes on to explain, "the scribes [believed themselves to be] entitled to explain actual or putative ideas of the old prophet and to publish these additions in Jeremiah's name, even though in actuality the style, imagery, and interests betray their origins in later synagogue sermons and morality tales about prophets."[19] Thus Duhm believes that most of the speeches in the book that "present themselves as the 'word of Yahweh' spoken by Jeremiah" were actually put in his mouth by the scribes. By this contrivance, the scribes were able to transform Jeremiah himself into a scribe. This transformation is their aim for all their people: their "highest ideal," as expressed in the New Covenant passage (31:31-34, which Duhm describes as an "outburst from the scribes"), is "that every member of the Jewish people would know the law by heart and understand that all Jews are scribes."[20]

What makes Duhm's designation of the authors of the additions as "scribes" (or "Torah teachers," *Thoralehrer*, or "people of the book," *Buchmänner*)[21] so significant is that these are the very same terms he uses to denote the enemies of his historical Jeremiah. "His most toxic opponents," writes Duhm, "are the 'wise' [cf. Jer. 18:20], the representatives of Torah, the scribes."[22] It was the "scribes," in collusion with the priests, who "cooked up schemes to bring about Jeremiah's downfall—just as the priests and scribes in the New Testament used similar tactics to bring down Jesus."[23] In Duhm's presentation, prophets and scribes are polar opposites, natural

---

[17] Duhm, *Jeremia*, xviii.
[18] Duhm, *Jeremia*, vi.
[19] Duhm, *Jeremia*, x.
[20] Duhm, *Jeremia*, 255.
[21] Duhm, *Jeremia*, 184, 211.
[22] Duhm, *Jeremia*, 158.
[23] Duhm, *Jeremia*, 157.

enemies. Whereas, prophets are inspired with fresh revelation from God, scribes have no revelation of their own and thus insist that revelation is limited to written texts. They are "text scholars" (*Schriftgelehrte*) who believe that the Torah is the "complete revelation, an eternally given law, the word of God that only requires interpretation and application."[24] As "boundary guards" (*Schwellenwächter*) for the Torah, they "fight against the ecstatic with the clear [written] Word of God."[25] However, despite their self-understanding, the scribes are not true representatives of God's law, because they are "supplementers," who have added their own uninspired teachings and traditions to the law. They are the ones of whom Jeremiah said (in 8:8), "the false pen of the scribes has made the Torah into a lie."[26] Duhm's identification of those who created the book of Jeremiah with scribes who add their own words presented as the Word of God strongly suggests that in his view the pens of these scribes also made Jeremiah's words into a lie.

Approval and Disapproval

Duhm's low opinion of the additions that make up the majority of the book of Jeremiah is one aspect of a third feature that stands out in his commentary: the strong note of approval and disapproval. Duhm's discussion of the various sources and authors and their contributions to the book is not an impartial, disinterested description. He offers his appraisal of the worth of each part of the book, and he is not simply making a pragmatic assessment of the degree to which the parts will contribute to the historical project. His critical appraisal extends to evaluation of each part's theological and aesthetic value. The three principal aspects of each type of material that Duhm evaluates can be observed in the three central subsections of his introductory section on the additions.

IV.   The Additions to the Writings of Jeremiah and Baruch

　　　…

　　4. Their Value for History
　　5. Their Theological Character
　　6. Their Literary Character[27]

In each of these three sections, Duhm draws a contrast between the low quality of the additions and the high quality of the authentic writings.

　　Duhm's low estimate of the historical value of the additions has already been noted. However, the subsection he devotes to assessing their historical value is worth considering because it helps clarify the specific nature of his disapproval. The primary failure of the redactors, in his eyes, is their inability to offer a credible

---

[24] Duhm, *Jeremia*, 189.
[25] Duhm, *Jeremia*, 235.
[26] Duhm, *Jeremia*, 82, 86.
[27] Duhm, *Jeremia*, xvi–xix.

portrait of the prophet. He castigates them for their failure to portray a prophet worthy of the reader's respect: "If they had had only half as much spirit as the author of the fourth gospel, they could have given us a prophet that we could look up to with admiration."[28] They were unable to produce such a prophet because they were uninspired Jewish scribes and Torah teachers. Their lack of inspiration explains the paltry Jeremiah they produced: "the personified vehicle of the divine messages"; the "automaton"; the "Torah teacher, [or] scribe, who, like the redactors, brings … no new revelation of God."[29] Throughout Duhm's section on the historical worth of the additions, there is a contrast between the Jeremiah the scribal redactors were able to create and the historical Jeremiah whose life Duhm presented in his section on the authentic writings. "The prophet that [the redactors] offer us, has almost nothing in common with the real Jeremiah (*dem wirklichen Jeremia*), as we know him from his literary works and Baruch's biography."[30] The redactors fail as historians because even though they had access to evidence of the real Jeremiah (in the poetic oracles, the same evidence available to Duhm), they did not have the spirit to imaginatively recreate an inspired prophet.

The contrast between the inspired prophet and the uninspired scribes also provides the foundation for Duhm's assessment of the theological value of the works of Jeremiah and additions. Duhm finds in passages that he attributes to the historical prophet the theological insights of a "delicate observer" of the religious state of his people.[31] In his youth, the budding prophet is dismayed at the local cultus of the rural neighbors, which he finds "crude, lecherous, and cruel," and on his first trip to the city, he is shocked to find the Jerusalemites "frivolous, false, complacent, and adulterous."[32] His inspired prophecies flow out of turmoil in his sensitive heart caused by the degeneracy of his people and his premonitions concerning ominous military threats. His inner despair reaches a climax when he comes to the realization that nothing can save his people, not even the Torah of the Josianic reforms, unless there is a true inner change of heart.[33] It is this theological insight that brings Jeremiah into conflict with the scribes and Torah teachers of his time, and it is also what distinguishes his authentic works from the additions of the scribes and Torah teachers who produced the book of Jeremiah.

The scribes who added to Jeremiah's writings have no understanding of Jeremiah's insistence on inner spiritual transformation. Instead, they are preachers of external conformity to written laws: "Their theology is that of legalism [*Nomismus*]; the Torah is their one and all."[34] They are not concerned with "a higher form of religion [*höhere Religionsstufe*]" of inner moral reform but only with achieving a state free of external guilt.[35] They are not burdened with the religious degeneracy of their people but simply want an end to the suffering that resulted from breaking the law.[36] Their understanding

---

[28] Duhm, *Jeremia*, xvii–xviii.
[29] Duhm, *Jeremia*, xviii.
[30] Duhm, *Jeremia*, xviii.
[31] Duhm, *Jeremia*, xi.
[32] Duhm, *Jeremia*, xi.
[33] Duhm, *Jeremia*, xi.
[34] Duhm, *Jeremia*, xviii.
[35] Duhm, *Jeremia*, xviii.
[36] Duhm, *Jeremia*, xvii.

of the exile can be reduced to this simplistic "theory of retribution [*Vergeltungslehre*]."[37] Rather than urging their hearers to examine their own hearts, they place the blame for their present problems on the "alleged idolatry" of previous generations. In comparison to their ancestors, they believe they are much more pious, and in comparison to the heathen "they are infinitely superior as Jews."[38] In sum, whereas the authentic prophecies of Jeremiah can be identified by the keen observations and heartfelt sympathy of an inspired prophet, the speeches the scribes put into his mouth betray the simplistic application of old law codes by smug legal practitioners.

Duhm's strong expressions of approval and disapproval extend to his discussion of the literary quality of the various materials. As with his evaluations of the historical and theological value, his assessment of literary value is marked by the extreme contrast he finds between what he considers authentic prophecies and what he considers later additions: he offers laudatory appreciations of the former and disparagement of the latter. In Duhm's eyes, the authentic literary works (*die Dichtungen*) of Jeremiah "betray such a keen sense of nature that one may say that if God had not selected him for the office of a prophet, he would have become the greatest lyric poet [*Idyllendichter*] of Israel."[39] In contrast, the stories that the editors created to frame the speeches they created for Jeremiah are so childish and unbelievable that "one often senses that the editors belonged to the lower strata of society." One might even suspect that they "were craftsmen [*ein Handwerk betrieben*]." In any case, they "certainly did not undergo any literary training [*schriftstellerische Schulung*]."[40] Whereas the authentic literature is characterized by the "simple candor [*schlichten Freimut*]"[41] of the prophet, the inauthentic speeches are marked by "rhetorical exaggerations."[42] The authentic speeches are expert in their use of "appropriate and original pictures" that are never "artificial [*künstlich*] or affected [*geziert*],"[43] but the inauthentic speeches repeat the same "shabby [*ärmlichen*] thoughts and phrases" again and again whether they are appropriate or not.[44] The poetry of Jeremiah gives masterful expression to the prophet's own feelings and sentiments,[45] but anything of literary worth in the editors' attempts to represent prophetic speech has been stolen from previous prophets, whom they were too simple to understand.[46] As in Duhm's evaluation of the historical and theological value of the two kinds of material, his foundational explanation of why the authentic prophecies are great literature and the additions of the editors are not is that the historical Jeremiah was an inspired poet and a prophet but the editors were only uninspired Torah teachers and scribes.[47]

---

[37] Duhm, *Jeremia*, xix.
[38] Duhm, *Jeremia*, xix.
[39] Duhm, *Jeremia*, xi.
[40] Duhm, *Jeremia*, xix.
[41] Duhm, *Jeremia*, xi.
[42] Duhm, *Jeremia*, xix.
[43] Duhm, *Jeremia*, xiii.
[44] Duhm, *Jeremia*, xviii.
[45] Duhm, *Jeremia*, xiii.
[46] Duhm, *Jeremia*, xx.
[47] Duhm, *Jeremia*, xvi.

Factors to Consider When Evaluating Duhm's Model

The Context of Duhm's Work in the History of Biblical Criticism

Three noteworthy features of Duhm's commentary have now been observed: its historical genre and aims, its oppositional stance toward the present form of the book, and its strong value judgments of the literary and theological worth of the materials. The significance of these features can now be considered. Those familiar with the history of modern biblical interpretation will have recognized these characteristic features of Duhm's approach to Jeremiah as somewhat typical of biblical scholarship of his time (or at least of one prominent stream of biblical scholarship). Biblical scholarship in the time of Duhm is characterized by the ascendency of a kind of criticism that offered itself as an objective scholarly approach to the Bible, an alternative to older theological or dogmatic interpretations. The various designations of this "modern" approach correspond to features of Duhm's approach to Jeremiah. Duhm's presentation of his work as objective research into the historical facts about the prophet is typical of biblical scholarship that understood itself as "scientific" or "historical criticism." The priority he gives to distinguishing the literary genres of the various components and identifying their authors and dates is consonant with what was called "literary criticism." Duhm's division of the book into three main sources is characteristic of what is now recognized as an era when "source criticism" was the dominant critical approach. His willingness to challenge the authenticity of material the book attributes to Jeremiah and his adversarial stance toward the present form of the book align him with historical critics trying to break free from traditional and dogmatic readings of the Bible. Thus, although Duhm's approach to Jeremiah represents a significant break from previous studies of the book, it also has a high degree of continuity with prominent streams of biblical scholarship in his day.

The nature of Duhm's Jeremiah work can also be considered in light of Jeremiah scholarship since the time of Duhm. Readers familiar with twentieth-century works on Jeremiah will see that although Duhm's basic categories have enjoyed remarkable persistence, there have been significant changes as well. In the century following Duhm, few have been willing to limit the authentic passages as drastically as he did. In addition, scholars have often been more willing to find traces of Jeremiah's original message in much of the material Duhm identified as secondary. As source criticism was augmented with form criticism and tradition criticism, there was a greater acceptance of the idea that the additions represented developments and reapplications of authentic Jeremianic material—not whole-cloth inventions as Duhm proposed. The most significant changes have come in the last few decades as scholars have virtually reversed Duhm's adversarial stance toward the additions and the final form of the book. With the rise of redaction criticism, the focus has shifted from the earliest materials to the final form of the book and the contributions of those who added to and edited the materials to produce the book. Canonical and theological (or confessional) interpretation of the book has countered Duhm's disparagement of the theological value of the additions and urged that the theological agenda of those responsible for the final form is integral to the book's enduring significance.

Throughout all these changes and reversals, however, Duhm's basic account of the composition of the book and its relationship to the historical prophet have continued to provide the dominant interpretive model.

These observations, which help to locate Duhm's approach in the history of biblical scholarship, do not directly address the question of the value of his central contribution to Jeremiah scholarship. The primary interest this study takes in Duhm's work is not that it exemplifies a certain stage of the history of criticism but that it introduced a model of Jeremiah scholarship that is still foundational for scholarship today. The reason for investigating his 1901 commentary is to help the readers of Jeremiah decide whether the model of the book Duhm introduced was necessary, or even helpful, for grappling with the book itself. Answering this question of practical utility involves answering the simple question of accuracy: Is Duhm's model correct? Does it accurately describe what the book is and how it came to be? Is his biography of the prophet true to what actually happened or not? These questions of truth and historical accuracy, which should concern anyone considering the merits of an explanatory model, are demanded by the particular nature of Duhm's work. He offers his work as the recovery of the factual history of the prophet and his authentic work that has been obscured for millennia by a blind trust in the accuracy of the book's portrayal of the prophet and his work. Readers must decide whether Duhm's account of the history is more accurate than the account given by the book.[48]

Duhm's Grounds for Preferring His Account to the Book's Account

To make this decision, readers must consider what grounds Duhm offers for the superiority of his account. When they first read his commentary, it may surprise them how little Duhm provides in the way of evidence and arguments for his bold claims that the majority of the book is a late fabrication that offers a false portrayal of the prophet. His general mode of writing is confident assertion without rationale. For example, when he first introduces the third-person narratives, he simply calls them "the biography of Jeremiah written by Baruch."[49] Later he lays out his discussion of these narratives in a section titled "Baruch's biography," which begins with his reconstruction of the life of Baruch. However, in neither place does he pause to explain why he believes Baruch is the author of these narratives.

What makes Duhm's confident assertion that Baruch is the author of the biographical prose significant is that it has no basis whatsoever in the only evidence he has about Baruch, the book of Jeremiah. The book introduces the narratives with no attribution of authorship.[50] As for Baruch, although the book does portray him as writing, it never

---

[48] Of course, Duhm would describe the choice as between an account based on the authentic elements of the book and the account given by the later scribes responsible for the inauthentic elements. However, the distinction between these elements is Duhm's, not the book's.

[49] Duhm, *Jeremia*, x.

[50] The main clues the prose narratives provide about their author are the following: the third-person references to Jeremiah, which makes it less likely that the prophet was author (the narratives only refer to Baruch in third person as well); the knowledge of Jeremiah's actions, which might (but need not) suggest an associate of the prophet; the fact that they are written, which indicates an educated person; and their prose style which has some similarities to the prose of Joshua–Kings and the prose sermons in Jeremiah.

presents him recording events—only writing "at the dictation of Jeremiah all the words Yahweh had spoken to him,"[51] words "against Judah, and Israel and all the nations … that every one may turn from his evil way" (36:4, cf. 36:18, 27, 33; 45:1).[52] If these words Baruch wrote down are included in the book, the most likely passages are the words against Judah and Israel in chs 1–20 or the words against the nations in chs 25 and 46–52. Among these, it would appear that the most likely candidates are the so-called "prose sermons" since they usually threaten destruction and often urge repentance (7:3, 11:4, 12:16, 17:24, 18:11, 26:13) and are regularly introduced (thirty-six times) as "the word of Yahweh that came to Jeremiah [or "to me"]."[53] However, these latter are attributed by Duhm to "scribes," whom he sharply distinguishes from Baruch—even though Baruch is explicitly designated a "scribe" by the book (36:32).[54] The grounds on which Duhm appears to expect his readers to accept his attribution of authors is primarily stylistic: the "rhetorical exaggeration"[55] of the prose speeches betray their authors to be uninspired scribes,[56] and the "simple style"[57] of the prose narratives show that they were written by Baruch, an "upright, simple soul."[58] Duhm's characterization of Baruch, however, has no basis in the book: its few references to Baruch suggest that Baruch was a bold and ambitious man, an outspoken yet shrewd public figure.[59] Duhm's alternative portrait of Baruch appears to be drawn wholly from the style of the prose narratives he assumes to be written by him. His confident attribution of the prose

[51] Commenting on this passage, Duhm does appear to take it as historically reliable. He writes that Baruch "wrote down Jeremiah's prophetic poems at his dictation" (*Jeremia*, xv). Thus he appears to believe that Baruch recorded (at least some of) the speeches in the book that he deems to be authentic: the speeches in poetic form. However, as has been noted, these are only roughly a quarter (280 authentic verses out of 1,130 total authentic and inauthentic verses) of speeches the book presents as spoken by Yahweh or Jeremiah. Duhm appears to be attempting to limit what Baruch wrote down to the poetic words of Jeremiah (the "prophetic *poems* [*Gedichte*]"), but there is no basis for this limitation in the text. In any case, there is no reference here or elsewhere to Baruch writing narratives.

[52] It should be noted that in the prose narrative of ch. 36, as well as in the other narrative in which Baruch appears (chs 32 and 43), Baruch is referred to in the third person, making it less likely that he was the author.

[53] Duhm takes these introductions as evidence that the prose speeches are not words of Jeremiah (or Yahweh): "Because they are put into the mouth of the prophet (or actually, into Yahweh's mouth), they are overloaded with introductory and concluding formulas, such as: 'Thus says Yahweh,' and 'speech of Yahweh,' etc." (Duhm, *Jeremia*, xvii).

[54] *Sofer*, the Hebrew word used to describe Baruch is the same word employed in 8:8 "the lying pen of the scribes"). Duhm, trying to distinguish Baruch from the scribes to whom he attributes the majority of the book, interprets 36:32 to indicate that Baruch "was a writer (*Schrieber*), i.e. probably not a scribe (*Schriftgelehrter*), but a copyist (*Abschreiber*) of writings, documents, etc., maybe even writing teacher (*Schreiblehrer*)" (Duhm, *Jeremia*, xiv–xv).

[55] Duhm, *Jeremia*, xix.

[56] Duhm, *Jeremia*, xvi–xx, 284.

[57] Duhm, *Jeremia*, 227.

[58] Duhm, *Jeremia*, iv.

[59] In 36:10 and 15, Baruch boldly reads Jeremiah's prophecies of judgment at the temple and then to the officials in the king's house. In 43:3, the people suspect that Baruch is a Babylonian collaborator who is using Jeremiah as a puppet. A popular impression that Baruch was actually the source of Jeremiah's prophecies may explain the book's repetition of the assertion that Baruch's words were dictated to him by Jeremiah (36:4, 6, 17-18, 27, 32; 45:1). In 45:4, Baruch has to be warned not to "seek great things for [him]self."

narratives to Baruch is thus not only without evidence in the book but also relies on highly circular argument.

Duhm's attribution of the narratives to Baruch is not central to his argument, but it is noteworthy because the way he distinguishes between the authentic writings of Baruch and the inauthentic writings of the later scribes is closely parallel to the way he makes his central distinction: the division between the authentic words of Jeremiah and the inauthentic words of the scribes. The primary grounds he offers for denying Jeremianic authorship to the majority of the words the book attributes to him is his contrasting descriptions of the style and theology of what he believes to be authentic and inauthentic. As was described above, Duhm's discussion of what he designates "the additions to the writings of Jeremiah and Baruch" is primarily a demonstration of their paltry portrayal of the prophet, their shabby literary style, and their narrow-minded theological perspective. Duhm rests his case for the inauthenticity of these speeches almost wholly on creating the impression that these sections are unworthy to be ascribed to the prophet he has discovered in the sections he considers to be the authentic words of Jeremiah.

Initial Evaluation and Plan for Investigation

Three Weaknesses of Duhm's Model and an Underlying Concern

The foundations Duhm offers for his conception of the book of Jeremiah appear to have several significant weaknesses. First, to accept Duhm's denial of the authenticity of most of the passages in the book, readers will have to accept his characterization of their literary style and theological perspective. For example, if readers are to be convinced that passages such as the "Temple Sermon" (7:1-15) or the "Promise of a New Covenant" (31:31-34) are inauthentic, Duhm must first convince them that these passages have poor literary style and dubious theology. Second, to accept the distinctions between the types of materials as indicative of multiple authorship, readers must be incapable of coming up with alternative explanations. If readers are able to provide plausible explanations of the differences between passages in terms of different contexts, audiences, or authorial aims (or even differences in the author at different stages of his career), Duhm's explanation will appear as simply one among several options. Third, as with Duhm's designation of Baruch as the author of the narratives, his designation of the scribes as the authors of most of Jeremiah's speeches relies on somewhat circular reasoning. Duhm's case for asserting that the additions of the scribes can be distinguished from the authentic writings rests primarily on his intuition that they are unworthy of the true character of Jeremiah, but Duhm primarily develops the "true character of Jeremiah" by considering only "the authentic writings"—the speeches of Jeremiah once the additions Duhm attributes to the scribes have been removed. Duhm's understanding of the literary style and theological perspective of the historical Jeremiah are at the same time the outcome of his division of sources and the basis (i.e., principal criterion) for his division.

These weaknesses may raise doubts for readers considering the validity of Duhm's model, but an even more basic concern arises from the noteworthy characteristics of his commentary described above. Duhm's division between authentic and inauthentic material coincides almost exactly with the division between what he likes and dislikes in literature and in theology. Of course, it is hardly surprising that in a book as large and varied as Jeremiah a reader would find passages that appeal more to his literary taste than others, or that fit better with his theological framework; however, when a reader claims that only the passages that he likes are authentic, he invites the criticism that his understanding of the book is more of a product of his own predilections than the explanation demanded by the evidence in the book. The force of this criticism is made more acute in Duhm's work because he presents it as an objective historical analysis. His privileging of some of the materials of the book would be understandable if he were simply drawing on Jeremiah for inspiration to create the portrait of a prophet in a fictional work. His selective approach could be defended if he were merely attempting to illustrate from Jeremiah what he considered to be an ideal prophet or even if he were choosing prophetic speeches he found notable for an anthology. Instead, he asks for his selections from the book to be considered as the only historically reliable evidence and for his portrayal of the prophet to be accepted as the one true Jeremiah of history.

Duhm's presentation of his work as a historical analysis opens his conclusions to the kind of suspicions one would have of a biographer of a historical figure who rejected as inauthentic anything she felt detracted from her high view of her subject. One would have good reason to question a biographer of Washington on Jefferson who questioned the authenticity of any purported historical documents that gave rise to a portrayal of the founding fathers that Americans could not "look up to with admiration." Similarly, Duhm's use of theological worth and literary worth as criteria of authenticity could be compared to a biographer of Lincoln who, because Lincoln was a Republican, used conformity to the platform of today's Republican Party as indicator of which speeches, or parts of speeches, could be considered the authentic words of the first Republican president. It might be considered dubious literary criticism if a literary critic from the modernist period thought so highly of Donne's witty, ironic erotic poems that she doubted whether it was possible for Donne to be the author of the more conventional "Elizabethan" lyrics attributed to him and dismissed out of hand the claim that Donne was the author of religious poetry and prose sermons.

The reader of Jeremiah who took up Duhm's commentary trying to evaluate the viability of the model he introduced could be forgiven for wondering how Duhm was able to convince anyone that his model was reliable. The reader might wonder how Duhm was able to persuade even himself that his portrait of the prophet was anything more than a personal fantasy. Duhm asks his readers to discount the account of Jeremiah found in the majority of the book, an account accepted almost universally by readers and interpreters for over two thousand years. He asks them to prefer his account with the explanation that whereas the authors of the book of Jeremiah (and implicitly all interpreters before him) were bound to their theological agendas, his account can be trusted because he approaches the book with the objectivity of modern literary and historical criticism. But when Duhm offers as his primary criteria for historical authenticity the literary and theological worth of the materials, it is hard to escape the impression that Duhm has merely replaced the theological perspective of the book and its previous readers with his own theological perspective and aesthetic judgment.

Three Features of Duhm's Model Scholars Found Compelling

Whatever misgivings a reader might have about the reliability of Duhm's model, it is quite clear that Duhm himself was thoroughly convinced that he had uncovered the Jeremiah of history and exposed the true history of the book's composition. Moreover, the majority of the prominent Jeremiah scholars since Duhm's work have accepted the central elements of his account as discoveries about the true compositional history of the book and the true biography of the prophet. To explain how this was possible is one of the aims of the next few chapters. As an initial step, it must be acknowledged that what might appear to readers today as the particular literary tastes and theological opinions of a scholar around the turn of the twentieth century appeared to Duhm and many of his readers as simply the self-evident principles of good theology and good literature. The objective nature of the literary and theological criteria Duhm used to evaluate the worth of Jeremiah was rarely questioned. He wrote at a time of high confidence in the objectivity of historians (and literary critics), a time when authors had less misgivings about their ability to free themselves from the limitations of their place in history. This historical situation helps to explain Duhm's self-confidence and authoritative tone; his authoritative confidence, in turn, helps to explain his appeal. At the same time, the confidence of his age in the objectivity of their methodical approach to history seems to have prevented awareness of the strength of their underlying needs. In retrospect, there appears to have been a strong need for Jeremiah to be the kind of prophet Duhm portrayed, and a need that he not be the kind of prophet the book portrays him to be.

Each of these considerations about Duhm's historical situation has something to contribute to understanding the success of his model, and some of them will be further explored in the following chapters. However, none of them can wholly explain why Duhm and so many later scholars came to believe that this model was true. These scholars (particularly Duhm himself) brought an incredible amount of learning and intellectual ability to bear on the interpretation of the book, and their work spans more than a century of scholarship including scholars with quite a variety of literary, theological, and historical perspectives and agendas. There must have been something more compelling about Duhm's model than is evident in its first appearance in the introduction to his commentary.

In fact, the grounds of Duhm's theory that subsequent scholars found most convincing are poorly represented in the Introduction to his commentary. Scholars who know anything about Duhm's contribution to Jeremiah studies will be surprised when reading the Introduction to find no direct reference to (or, even less, any justification for) what can justly be considered his most distinctive contribution: the limitation of the authentic words of Jeremiah to passages composed in a particular meter (the *qinah* lament meter). Nowhere in the Introduction does Duhm mention that he is using poetic form as his principal indicator of authenticity. The reader is left to infer it from the fact that he deals with the material he deems authentic under the heading "Jeremiah's authentic poems [*Gedichte*]" and that he only includes poetic passages in his catalogue of Jeremiah's authentic works. He never brings up metrical analysis as part of his method for discerning authenticity. In fact, in his Introduction, he only mentions meter once, in passing, as part of his description of the literary excellence of Jeremiah's works, "The meter is everywhere the same, an indication of Jeremiah's simple style: quatrains with [lines] alternating between three and two beats [*Hebungen*, i.e., accented syllables]."[60] It almost seems as if Duhm is unaware of the potential that the poetry–prose distinction has for providing an objective foundation for his compositional theory. There could hardly be a more objective criterion for distinguishing sources than simply counting accented syllables. If Duhm or later adherents to his model are accused of dividing the book according to their literary and theological tastes, they can respond that their divisions are simply the result of metrical analysis. Duhm's observation and demonstration that the division between poetry and prose in the book corresponds to differences in diction and themes and seemingly to differences in literary quality and theological perspective have proved to be the features of his theory with the most persuasive power and enduring appeal.

A second feature of Duhm's theory that scholars found compelling is better represented in the Introduction. It is the primary result of his work: the reconstructed biography of the prophet. Duhm's biography of Jeremiah is perhaps more compelling, coherent, and comprehensive than any that had appeared before. It is compelling in the sense that it tells the believable story of the rise of a great man, one that readers could "look up to with admiration." It also has a remarkable internal coherence: every part of Jeremiah's story is coordinated into one grand narrative and unified portrait of his character. What many found most convincing is the comprehensiveness of Duhm's biography in terms of its explanation of every last word that Duhm deemed authentic in a way that simultaneously adds to the reconstructed biography and makes sense of the passage being considered. This feature is adumbrated in the Introduction in the biographical overview and in the section that assigns every fragment of poetry to a stage in Jeremiah's career. However, the full explanatory power only comes out in the commentary itself, in Duhm's explanation of one poetic passage after another according to its place in his reconstructed biography. Reading Duhm's commentary is like listening to Sherlock Holmes deduce a person's whole life story by ingenious inferences made from minute observations of a multitude of seemingly insignificant features of the person's hat or cane. In his portrait of the prophet, Duhm not only weaves in every authentic word in the book, but seemingly every known detail about the historical and social background of Jeremiah's time. His bravura performance could hardly fail to impress generations of scholars.

A third feature of Duhm's model that helps to explain its enduring influence comes into the Introduction as what seems to be an offhand comment about the character of the material he deems secondary. In the section where he is describing what he considers to be the inferior literary and theological worth of the scribal additions, he brings up a more objective observation about their style and theological perspective:

---

[60] Duhm, *Jeremia*, xii.

They … speak the same language [as the authors of 2 Kings], down to the particular phrases and idioms, and share the same opinions that we find in the latest ("Deuteronomistic") components of the Former Prophets. And this is true to the extent that one is forced to conclude that the same hands have worked on the book of Jeremiah and the history books.[61]

The similarities between the speeches of Jeremiah that Duhm deems inauthentic and parts of Joshua–Kings are an observable feature of the book of Jeremiah. Although this feature alone is not enough to demonstrate the inauthenticity of the speeches, it was closely connected in Duhm's mind (and in the minds of many biblical scholars down to the present time) with a model of Israel's history, and the development of the literature in Israel's scriptures that sharply distinguished between the pre-exilic prophets and the later "Deuteronomists" (thought to have edited Joshua–Kings) and that placed the authorship of the "deuteronomistic" writings well after the time when the book portrays Jeremiah delivering speeches with "deuteronomistic" language. Given this model of Israel's literary history, it would be improbable that Jeremiah could have spoken these speeches. The historical model thus provides an external support for Duhm's model for Jeremiah such that his reconstruction of the prophet's life and work based on the exclusion of most of the speeches attributed to him in the book cannot be described as his personal fantasy.[62]

The following three chapters will examine these three aspects of Duhm's model that scholars found most compelling: the alignment of the passages he deemed authentic with poetic form, the compelling biographical reconstruction based on these poetic passages alone, and the deuteronomistic character of the passages deemed inauthentic. Each chapter will attempt to trace currents in the intellectual history of the eighteenth and nineteenth centuries that help to explain both how Duhm came to his theory and why his adherents were inclined to accept it. The aim is to help readers of Jeremiah determine whether the reconstructions of the biography of the prophet and the history of Israel's religion that Duhm's commentary supports (and the compositional model necessary to allow the book to support them) are true. This will help readers determine whether the biographical, historical, and compositional frameworks they are offered in the introductions to commentaries are necessary, or even helpful, for reading the book of Jeremiah.

---

[61] Duhm, *Jeremia*, x.
[62] Duhm appeals to this same model of Israel's history when he writes, "Like the latest editor of the former prophets, [the editors of Jeremiah] operate on belief that the centralization of the Cult at the Zion temple (as it is demanded in the Deuteronomic laws and presupposed in the Priestly laws) had been always valid and well-known law." Duhm, *Jeremia*, xvi.

2

The Roots of Duhm's Understanding
of Poetry and Prophecy

Duhm's Belief That Poetic Form Indicates Authenticity

It is an oddity worth consideration that when Duhm first laid out his new model for understanding Jeremiah, he almost completely avoided mention of its most distinctive feature: the use of poetic form as a criterion for determining authenticity. The idea that poetic form indicates authenticity is not only the most distinctive feature of Duhm's model; it is also the most enduring and widespread feature in subsequent scholarship. It is the foundational assumption of the paradigm that has dominated Jeremiah studies since the time of Duhm. The assumption is embodied in the two standard elements of the paradigm: the compositional history embodied in the classification of materials (e.g., Mowinckel's Types A, B, and C) and the reconstruction of the biography and message of the historical Jeremiah. The central functions of the classification system are to draw attention to the difference between the "prose sermons" (Type C) and "poetic oracles" (Type A) and to raise the question of the authenticity of prose in light of the assumed authenticity of the poetry. The biography is also built on Duhm's assumption: it offers, as an alternative (or at least a supplement) to the life of Jeremiah presented by the final form of the book (with its large amount of prose), a historical reconstruction obtained by discounting the reliability of the "prose sermons" as evidence and relying on passages of poetry as records of speeches Jeremiah delivered on various historical occasions. The assumption that poetic form is an indicator of authenticity allows the poetic speeches to function as historical evidence.

Duhm's belief that poetic form indicates authenticity is certainly there to be found in the introduction to his commentary. If a reader simply compares Duhm's catalog of authentic passages with those he deems inauthentic, the most obvious difference is that the former are mostly in poetic form and the latter are in prose. Yet, Duhm does not draw attention to this difference, and he provides no explicit defense for the idea that Jeremiah only wrote poetry.

Duhm is not unaware that his limitation of the authentic words of Jeremiah to the poetic parts of the book is the distinguishing feature of his theory. Although he does not bring it to the fore in his introduction, he does mention it in a one-page foreword, in which he describes his own struggle to understand the book. The foreword helps to clarify the relationship between Duhm's most distinctive contribution and the general characteristics of his approach as observed in the introduction. He writes,

> To accept the task of writing a commentary on the Book of Jeremiah, was for me a kind of gamble. I'd always feared this book more than any other Old Testament scripture. The book contains exceedingly glorious prophetic writings alongside passages of fairly low quality. With each sermon, the differences appear to me more pronounced, and the author, Jeremiah, more puzzling. Although Stade and Schwally in particular had demonstrated the inauthenticity of some smaller or larger sections, there remained many pericopes that combine apparently important content with a strangely clumsy form or that cannot be objectively brought into line with the undoubtedly genuine creations of Jeremiah. A watershed for me was the bold judgment of [Rudolf] Smend about Chapter 31, [in his 1893 *Lehrbuch Der Alttestamentlichen Religionsgeschichte*]. I long fought against it, but finally realized that Smend was right, at least for the most part. The result was that I dared to critically examine other passages to which up till then I hadn't given a second thought; their importance had assured me of their jeremianic origin. The end result, namely that *only prophetic poetry of a particular form can be attributed to Jeremiah (and no prose or even half prose)*, I have never seen before, not even a tendency toward it.[1]

In this brief foreword, as in his introduction, it is clear that the central problem the book of Jeremiah presents for Duhm is not one of mixed literary form (the intermingling of poetry and prose) but of mixed literary and theology worth (the intermingling of "glorious" and "low-quality" passages). Furthermore, his primary solution is not a literary one (one that attempts to explain differences in terms of formal or generic constraints) but a historical one (one that attempts to explain differences in terms of the authenticity or inauthenticity of the evidence). The novel feature of his book, his daring departure from previous scholarship, is his negative evaluation of the literary and theological quality of a much greater part of the book and his explanation that all of this part was not written by the prophet. The striking example in the foreword is his denial of authenticity to Jeremiah 31, "The Promise of a New Covenant," which, before Duhm, had almost universally been considered central to Jeremiah's message and indubitably authentic (Smend is the rare exception). Thus, Duhm's novel approach, as described in the foreword, has the same characteristics that were observed in the introduction: historical methodology, negative evaluation of the present form of the book, and strong judgments of literary and theological worth.

The aspect of Duhm's approach that he highlights in the foreword and does not revisit in his introduction is his belief that the authentic works of Jeremiah are limited to the passages with poetic form. In the foreword, he presents this belief not as one element of this approach (a tool for determining authenticity) but as its "end result" (*Endergebnis*). The impression he gives of his interpretive process is that he simply sorted out all the passages of the book, distinguishing the authentic ones from the inauthentic based on

---

[1] Bernhard Duhm, *Das Buch Jeremia*, KHC 11 (Tübingen: J. C. B. Mohr, 1901), vii (emphasis added).

whether the literary and theological quality of each passage is worthy of the prophet. Then, at the end of his sorting process, he made the surprising discovery that while all those passages of low worth are composed in prose, all those of high worth are in poetry, and what is more, all of the poetry has the same meter: "quatrains with [lines] alternating between three and two beats."[2] This supposedly unlooked-for outcome appears to provide a remarkable objective confirmation that he has correctly discerned two very distinct types of material with two very distinct sources.

The attempt to create this impression of his process may explain why Duhm does not introduce poetic form as a criterion of authenticity in his introduction. If he wants the alignment of authentic material with poetic form to appear as a surprising result of his method, the effect would be weakened if determining authenticity by poetic form were introduced as part of his method. He may also recognize that as a methodological assumption, the use of poetic form as a criterion to determine authenticity would be hard to defend (it would be hard to convince his readers that Jeremiah could only speak or write poetry), but as an unanticipated result, the observation that all the passages deemed authentic happen to be in poetic form provides an excellent confirmation of his critical method. Leaving it to readers to make this observation for themselves may be intended to shore up their confidence in Duhm's judgments of authenticity. Here, as elsewhere, Duhm appears to rely heavily on the persuasive power of his own confidence in the soundness of his judgments. He concludes his foreword with the bold statement: "I have complete confidence [*volle Überzeugung*] that my findings are, in the main, right."[3]

The previous chapter raised the possibility that readers of Jeremiah trying to discern how confident they could be in Duhm's theory might be troubled with doubts that Duhm's "findings" were largely shaped by what he was looking for and that his confidence in them was grounded in the way they confirmed his own presuppositions. It was noted there that Duhm's basic aims and assumptions were guided by dominant currents in biblical interpretation specific to the turn of the twentieth century. It will be shown in this chapter how Duhm's standards of literary worth (which he used to determine authenticity) are those of a particular literary school that achieved its greatest prominence during this same period. However, it was also suggested that readers' doubts about the subjectivity of Duhm's judgments of authenticity based on literary (and theological and historical) worth might be allayed by the remarkable fact that all the passages he considers authentic have poetic form, an objective feature of the text. The present chapter seeks to evaluate the support this feature should add to readers' confidence in the validity of Duhm's theory. It will do this largely by examining the historical roots of Duhm's literary presuppositions: both his understanding of the poetry in the prophetic books and his standards of literary quality.[4] The examination

---

[2] Duhm, *Jeremia*, ii.

[3] Duhm, *Jeremia*, viii.

[4] Scholarly works on Jeremiah since the time of Duhm, if they give an account of the history of scholarship, often begin with Duhm but give little or no indication of his historical situation or of the history of interpretation that led up to his work. If they give any consideration to interpretation of Jeremiah before Duhm, it is usually an account of the traditional or orthodox interpretation that Duhm broke from. In this way, they perpetuate Duhm's self-presentation as the pioneer who made the decisive break from dogmatic interpretation, the objective modern historian whose

will explore the significance of the remarkable historical fact that has received little consideration: that both of these aspects of Duhm's literary presuppositions are grounded in the work of one man in the mid-eighteenth century.

In the early twentieth century, Duhm's understanding of literary value and his assumption that the book of Jeremiah could be divided between poetry and prose were widely shared; but it would be hard to find anyone who shared his views in the early eighteenth century—until the work of Bishop Robert Lowth. Lowth not only laid the foundation for the literary movement that informed Duhm's literary judgments; he was also the first major biblical scholar to distinguish poetry from prose in Jeremiah. The fact that the identification of poetry in Jeremiah (and the other prophetic books) was used to launch a revolution in literature and the arts is highly significant for the evaluation of the nature and validity of Duhm's compositional theory—a theory that explains the difference between Jeremiah's poetry and prose in the terms of that movement. Understanding the roots of Duhm's theory can help a reader evaluate its fruits. Consideration of the effects that Duhm's explanation of poetry and prose at the end of this chapter will help the reader assess not only the validity of Duhm's theory but also its utility for reading and making sense of the book of Jeremiah.

Lowth's Use of Biblical Poetry to Transform Poetic Theory

Lowth Argues the Prophetic Books Contain Poetry

Duhm's model for interpreting Jeremiah would hardly have been possible without the work of Bishop Robert Lowth. Almost every characteristic aspect of his work on Jeremiah was anticipated by Lowth's 1753 work *De sacra poesi Hebraeorum praelectiones*. These thirty-four lectures on Hebrew poetry were delivered in Latin at Oxford over the years 1741–50 as part of Lowth's role as Oxford's praelector of poetry. Latin editions were published in England in 1753 and in Germany (in two volumes) in 1758 and 1761.[5] Most biblical scholars will recognize the name of Lowth as the scholar credited with "discovering poetry" in the Hebrew Bible and introducing the idea that the distinctive characteristic of biblical poetry is semantic parallelism. Even this slight acquaintance with Lowth makes it apparent that Duhm could hardly have begun to formulate his theory of Jeremiah's composition without Lowth's work since his theory is founded on the division of poetry and prose. However, the

---

disinterested application of historical principles allowed him to break free from personal or societal prejudices. An exception is Jack Lundbom, *Jeremiah 1–20: A New Translation with Introduction and Commentary*, AB 21A (New York: Doubleday, 1999).

[5]   The German volumes were produced by the famous German orientalist Michaelis along with his copious notes. The lectures were translated to English by George Gregory in 1787, the year of Lowth's death. The edition used for this study was published in 1815 and includes the annotations of Michaelis. Robert Lowth, *Lectures on the Sacred Poetry of the Hebrews*, trans. G. Gregory (Boston, MA: Joseph T. Buckingham, 1815).

scope of Lowth's influence on Duhm is much more extensive and has rarely been acknowledged.

The relevance of Lowth's work as a precursor of Duhm's model of Jeremiah can be focused by observing that a central aim of Lowth's lectures was to demonstrate the prevalence of poetry in the prophetic books. Before Lowth, it was widely recognized that the Bible contained poetry—or at least lyrics, compositions that were originally intended to be sung. It would be hard to deny the presence of poems or songs in the Hebrew Bible: both individual songs embedded in book (such as those attributed to Miriam, Moses, and David), and whole books of songs or poems (such as Psalms, Song of Solomon, and Lamentations). It was a distinguishing contribution of Lowth's project to extend the category of biblical poetry to include most of the material in the prophetic books. The idea that biblical prophecy is poetry, observes James Kugel, is "the single, overriding theme [of Lowth's lectures], an idea that Lowth thought was of immense importance and on which the success or failure of his whole enterprise depended."[6] For this reason, it would be more accurate to characterize Lowth's achievement not as the discovery of poetry in the Hebrew Bible, but as the discovery of poetry in the prophets.

Lowth Uses Parallelism to Overcome the Absence of Obvious Meter in the Prophets

It was in pursuit of this aim, to demonstrate that the prophetic books contain poetry, that Lowth offered his best-known contribution to biblical studies: the idea that biblical poetry is characterized by parallelism, in his words, "the poetical conformation of the sentences, which … consists chiefly in a certain equality, resemblance, or parallelism between the members of each period."[7] Lowth makes this observation in Lecture XIX, a lecture designed "to demonstrate that the compositions of the prophets are truly poetical."[8] Lowth offers the presence of parallelism in the prophets as evidence of their poetic nature.

Parallelism provided Lowth with the means to overcome one of the primary obstacles to recognizing prophetic literature as poetic—its lack of meter. The nearly universal idea that poetry should have metrical regularity presented a problem for discerning poetry in any of the biblical books, but in the case of the prophetic books, the common expectation was reinforced by the weight of long and formidable traditions. One barrier was embedded in the Hebrew text of the prophets. The Masoretic texts of the prophetic books seem to indicate that they are not to be read as poetical because they lack the special set of *tü´amîm* (accent marks) found in Psalms, Proverbs, and Job.[9] Another barrier came from the direct comments of

---

[6] James Kugel, *Poetry and Prophecy: The Beginnings of a Literary Tradition* (Ithaca, NY: Cornell University Press, 1990), 22.

[7] Lowth, *Poetry of the Hebrews*, 259.

[8] Lowth, *Poetry of the Hebrews*, 252.

[9] On the special *tü´amîm* in Psalms, Proverbs, and Job (the three poetic books called *siprê ´emet*, an acronym of the first letters of their titles) see James Kugel, *The Idea of Biblical Poetry: Parallelism and Its History* (New Haven, CT: Yale University Press, 1981), 114–15, 281.

earlier interpreters whose judgment carried great weight. In the fourth century, the Church father Jerome explicitly denied that the prophets were written in poetry. "Let no one," he wrote, "when he sees the prophets written down in verses, think that they are read metrically in Hebrew or have something in common with the Psalms or the works of Solomon."[10] In contradicting these authorities, both Jewish and Christian, Lowth was attempting to overthrow more than a thousand years of interpretive tradition.

Lowth's argument does not depend on denying the expectation that poetry should be metrical. He readily acknowledges that "it appears essential to every species of poetry, that it be confined to numbers ... for indeed wanting this ... it would scarcely deserve the name of poetry."[11] He deals with the apparent lack of meter in the prophetic texts by arguing that the meter of Hebrew poetry has been lost. By the time the Masoretes came to that point in the text of the Bible, Lowth contends, Hebrew had already become a dead language and the memory of the ancient metrical system had completely disappeared. As evidence, he points out that the special *tü'amîm* are missing not only from the prophets but also from the Song of Solomon and Lamentations, both of which most of his contemporaries would recognize as poetic.[12] Turning to Jerome, Lowth argues that if the Jews had forgotten their own system of poetry, it could hardly be any more likely that the church fathers would have known it. He points to the attempts of Jerome and other church fathers to reduce the Psalms to classical tetrameters and hexameters as an indication of their poor understanding of Hebrew poetry.[13] Whether or not one finds Lowth's theory of the lost knowledge of meter convincing—or even necessary, since readers today are much more likely to be open to the idea of poetry without meter—it cleared the way for him and for succeeding generations of scholars to look for poetry in the prophetic books.[14]

Having dealt with obstacles from Jewish and Christian traditions, Lowth continues his argument for finding poetry in the prophetic books by introducing the notion of parallelism. He asserts that parallelism is evidence of the underlying meter that has now been lost. By pointing out parallel structures and other "vestiges ... of the metrical art" in the prophetic books, Lowth hopes to persuade readers that they contain poetry.[15] His well-known division of parallelism into three categories (synonymous, antithetical, and synthetic) is designed to make this point. In his illustrations of each of the three types, Lowth carefully chooses examples both from the books then widely acknowledged to be poetic and from the prophetic books.[16] The presence of all three kinds of parallelism in both sets of books provides a bridge for extending the territory of poetry into the prophets.

---

[10] Jerome's claim, found in the preface to his commentary on Isaiah (J. P. Migne, *Patrologiae cursus completus*, series latina [Paris 1844–64] 28:771) is quoted by Kugel, *Idea of Poetry*, 152.

[11] Lowth, *Poetry of the Hebrews*, 38.

[12] Lowth, *Poetry of the Hebrews*, 241–2.

[13] Lowth, *Poetry of the Hebrews*, 243–4.

[14] Duhm was not convinced: he believed himself capable of discerning the meter in poetic sections. The majority of his followers, however, seem to be content with Lowth's looser criteria for identifying poetry.

[15] Lowth, *Poetry of the Hebrews*, 270.

[16] Lowth, *Poetry of the Hebrews*, 259.

Lowth's Discovery Embedded in the Text of Modern Translations

Lowth's attempt to win a hearing for his belief that the prophets wrote poetry is not confined to his famous lectures. His crowning achievement, a translation of Isaiah published in 1778, probably did even more than his lectures to secure acceptance of his belief.[17] In this work, Lowth introduces a way of presenting the text of the prophetic book that has become almost universal in modern translations.[18] He prints the sections he deems poetic in such a way that each unit of poetry (each parallel member) is given its own separate line. Thus, for example, Isa. 1:3, which the Authorized Version renders "3. The ox knoweth his owner, and the ass his master's crib; but Israel doth not know, my people doth not consider," appears this way in Lowth's translation:

> 3. The ox knoweth his possessor;
>   The ass the crib of his lord:
>   But Israel knoweth not me;
>   Neither doth my people consider.[19]

With this typographical innovation, Lowth overcame the problem of the poetry's lack of meter by giving the prophetic text the feature that was to replace meter as the most recognizable characteristic of poetry in subsequent centuries: lines that stop before the right edge of the page. Before Lowth, there had been poetic versions of prophetic texts. These also printed the text in poetic lines, but the lines had meter and rhyme. Lowth's innovation was to print the lines as poetry with no attempt to give them poetic meter.[20] The reader is encouraged to read the lines as poetry, noting particularly the parallelism between the lines. In Isa. 1:3, for example, the reader can see repetition of what is owned (ox, ass, Israel) at the beginning of each line and the owner (possessor, lord, me) at the end. The widespread practice of printing passages in this manner, especially printing most of the prophetic literature this way, is perhaps the best measure of the success of Lowth's argument. When readers today open their Bibles to the prophetic books, they see poetry.

Lowth's innovation soon reached the book of Jeremiah. In 1784, just three years before Lowth's death, Benjamin Blayney published a new translation of Jeremiah intended as a sequel to Lowth's *Isaiah*.[21] Following Lowth, Blayney printed the sections he identified as poetry in poetic lines. However, the book of Jeremiah had a significant

---

[17] Robert Lowth, *Isaiah: A New Translation with a Preliminary Dissertation and Notes, Critical, Philological and Explanatory*, 2 vols. (London: J. Dodsley, T. Cadell, 1778).

[18] It is also followed in modern presentations of the original Hebrew text including the Biblia Hebraica Stuttgartensia (BHS) and Jerusalem Publication Society (JPS).

[19] Lowth, *Isaiah*, vol. 1.

[20] Murray Roston points out that by abandoning the attempt to create a metrical translation, Lowth was able to provide translations that follow the Hebrew grammar and word order more closely. This ability allowed him to retain more of the parallelism in the Hebrew clauses. Murray Roston, *Prophet and Poet: The Bible and the Growth of Romanticism* (Evanston, IL: Northwestern University Press, 1965), 129, 136, 138.

[21] Benjamin Blayney, *Jeremiah and Lamentations: A New Translation with Notes Critical, Philological, and Explanatory*, 2nd ed. (Edinburgh: Oliphant & Balfour, 1810).

difference from the book of Isaiah: only about half of it could be considered poetic by Lowth's standards, and in many passages the poetry appeared to be mingled with the prose. This curious feature became obvious in Blayney's work, in which poetry and prose were clearly distinguished for the first time. However, Lowth had already recognized this characteristic of Jeremiah; he wrote, "On the whole ... I can scarcely pronounce above half the book of Jeremiah poetical."[22] With Blayney's presentation, the feature of Jeremiah Lowth had observed became obvious to any reader and called for an explanation.

Duhm Answers the Question Raised by Lowth and Blayney's Division of Poetry and Prose

It is somewhat surprising that the standard modern explanation did not appear for another hundred years. Duhm's explanation, that poetic form is an indicator of authenticity, is not confined to its exposition in his 1901 commentary. The question posed by Blayney's typographical presentation of Jeremiah is answered by Duhm's own typographical presentation. In 1903, two years after he published his commentary, Duhm published a German translation of Jeremiah with a further typographical innovation.[23] Like Blayney, Duhm distinguishes the poetry from the prose by printing it in individual lines. He indents it from the right margin and cuts if off before it reaches the left. As much as possible, he prints the poetic lines in quatrains with the second and fourth lines further indented. Then Duhm goes beyond Blayney by adding a new feature: he draws boxes around all of the passages he considers original compositions of Jeremiah. Since only passages printed as poetry are included in the boxes, Duhm's presentation of the text [needs object] makes clear to any reader his answer to the question raised by Blayney and Lowth: the division between poetry and prose is a division between the authentic words of the Jeremiah and the additions of other authors.

Although it will be readily admitted that Duhm's work answers a question raised by Lowth, it is seldom acknowledged that Duhm's answer can also be traced directly back to Lowth. This is because Lowth not only discovered poetry in the prophetic books; he also provided an influential account of the significance of his discovery. Although he did not explain the difference between poetry and prose in the prophetic books in terms of authorship, his explanation of the relationship between poetry and prophecy laid the foundation for Duhm's conclusion. Curiously, Lowth's influence on biblical scholars like Duhm did not primarily come through his comments on the prophets but rather through his novel ideas about poetry. Lowth's account of the poetry in the prophetic books involved a rethinking of the nature of poetry, and this in turn led to a revolution in literature and literary theory that in the next century led to a revolution in Biblical studies—and in works like Duhm's commentary on Jeremiah returned to its source in the explanation of poetry in the prophetic books.

---

[22] Lowth, *Poetry of the Hebrews*, 291.
[23] Bernhard Duhm, *Das Buch Jeremia* (Tübingen: J. C. B. Mohr, 1903).

Lowth Uses Biblical Poetry to Stretch the Boundaries of Poetry

Today it is not difficult to persuade readers that the book of Jeremiah has poetic sections. This is not only because, following Lowth's and Blayney's work, generations of readers have grown familiar with translations that present sections in poetic form. It is also because they have gotten used to the idea that rhyme and regular meter are not essential to poetry. For over a century, readers have grown accustomed to reading (and writing) "free verse" with its deliberate abandonment of metrical regularity. Modern readers are not only unconcerned about meter's absence; many hardly notice meter even when it is present (in Shakespeare's plays, for example). C. S. Lewis observed that many modern readers, even well-educated readers, do not know how to scan a poetic text for meter. He suggests that "the ignorance, and the deliberate abandonment, of accentual meters are correlative phenomena, and both the results of some revolution in our whole sense of rhythm."[24] This revolution in the expectations for poetic meter is only one part of a broader revolution in conceptions of the basic nature of poetry that occurred in the late eighteenth and early nineteenth centuries. An attempt to identify the origins of this revolution cannot ignore Lowth's arguments for the poetic nature of the prophetic books.

Because Lowth's work appeared before this revolution, the expectation of regular meter posed a much greater obstacle to his argument that the prophetic books contained poetry. It has already been observed how in Lowth's attempt to demonstrate that the prophetic texts had originally been composed with meter, he introduced the idea of parallelism, an idea that was to transform the understanding of ancient Hebrew poetry in the realm of biblical scholarship. However, Lowth's efforts to win a hearing for the prophets as poets had an even greater effect in the realm of European literature. In his arguments that the prophetic books contain poetry, Lowth expanded the boundaries of what could be considered poetry. This expansion was one part of what may be called a redefinition of the nature of poetry, a redefinition that laid the foundation for a revolution in poetic theory. Lowth's part in this literary revolution is better known among literary scholars than it is among biblical scholars; however, knowledge of the new literary era Lowth helped to usher in is essential for understanding the context of biblical scholarship in the following centuries.

Lowth Provides an Alternative to Neoclassical Literature and Literary Theory

In order to understand the revolutionary nature of Lowth's contribution to the history of European literature, his work must be understood against the background of the poetry and poetic theory of his day. The first part of the eighteenth century saw the final flourishing of neoclassicism in literature (as well as in art, music, and architecture), and authors and critics looked to the literature of Greece and Rome as the standard of literary taste. The period is referred to as the Augustan age in English literature not only because of King George's personal identification with Augustus Caesar but also

---

[24] C. S. Lewis, "Donne and Love Poetry in the Seventeenth Century," in *John Donne's Poetry*, ed. A. L. Clements, NCE (New York: W. W. Norton, 1966), 151.

because of the strong identification that authors of this age felt with the literature and criticism of the early Roman empire. Augustan literature abounded in imitations and translations of classical authors, and even the more original works usually took their forms from classical models. Poets of this period were primarily classically educated gentlemen, who had been trained in reading, scanning, and producing Latin verse with its complicated metrical system of long and short syllables. Their English poetry was also expected to conform to strict metrical forms and guides to poetry that laid out the various options: iambic, trochaic, dactylic, anapestic, and so on.

As was observed above, Lowth himself did not deny that meter was essential to poetry; however, the effect of his work was to undermine the use of meter to delimit the boundaries of poetry. His efforts to expand the part of the Bible considered poetic to include the prophets resulted in an expansion of the territory of poetry in general. In an age characterized by strict adherence to traditional forms, it was something of a novel feat for Oxford's praelector of poetry to give fifty-two lectures on a body of "poetry" that had no obvious metrical form. The new account of poetry Lowth offered—which relied on other features to identify poetry (most notably, but not confined to semantic parallelism)—represents a significant break from the poetic theory of the day. His lectures made it possible for poets and critics to break free from the constraints of neoclassical poetic theory.

For breaking down the poetic theory founded on the classical models, the effect of Lowth's arguments was surpassed by his translations of biblical poetry. Lowth's lectures were amply illustrated by biblical passages presented as nonmetrical poetry. Even more influential than the nonmetrical Latin poetry in his lectures was the nonmetrical English poetry in his translation of Isaiah. Lowth's work made Isaiah, Jeremiah, and the other prophetic books available as the most prominent and authoritative models of a kind of poetry that did not adhere to classically derived poetic conventions. Lowth's explanations and translations of the *Sacred Poetry of the Hebrews* opened up a hole in the dike of neoclassical poetic theory, and a new kind of poetry began to flow out.

Lowth Inspires a New Kind of Literature

Within a few years of Lowth's lectures, new forms of poetry began appearing that made heavy use of parallelism and were relatively free from metrical regularity. In 1756, the poet Christopher Smart read Lowth's lectures and published an enthusiastic review urging others to read what he found to be "one of the best performances that has been published for a century."[25] Sometime in the next three years, Smart wrote "Jubilate Agno," a poem now celebrated for its dynamism and freedom from conventional forms. The break from metrical regularity can be observed in the opening lines:

> Rejoice in God, O ye tongues; give glory to the Lord and the Lamb
> Nations and Languages, and every creature in which is the breath of Life.
> Let man and beast appear before him, and magnify his name together.

[25] In Smart's *Universal Visiter*, quoted in Roston, *Prophet and Poet*, 148.

Let Noah and his company approach the throne of Grace, and do homage to the
Ark of their Salvation.[26]

These lines and the hundreds that follow them are remarkable for being some of the
first poetry in English to be presented in lines that look like verse but show no attempt
at consistent meter. Their chief poetic feature is verbal and semantic parallelism. Their
diction and theme are clearly modeled on biblical poetry as explained and illustrated
by Lowth. It is obvious that Smart's break from neoclassical norms was enabled by
Lowth's use of biblical poetry as an alternative model.

Before Lowth's lectures and Smart's poetry, there are isolated examples to be found
of poetry that does not adhere to the rigid formal patterns dictated by neoclassical
theory. A notable example is Milton's tragedy *Samson Agonistes* (1671) with its lines of
various length and meter. Milton, like Lowth and Smart, saw himself as a rebel against
the formal constraints of his time. He offered his unrhymed poetry in *Paradise Lost* as
"an example ... the first in English, of an ancient liberty recover'd to Heroic Poem from
the troublesome and modern bondage of Riming."[27] In an argument that curiously
anticipates Lowth's, Milton defended his free use of meter in the tragedy of Samson by
arguing that the complicated system of strophe, antistrophe, and epode observed in
Greek tragedy reflected the musical settings of the original plays, music which has now
been lost. Other poets before Lowth presented their nonmetrical poetry as "Pindaric,"
justifying the form with reference to the odes of the Greek poet Pindar (fifth century
BC). In the neoclassical period, deviations from the classical norms had to be justified
by other classical models. Lowth's work provided an alternative model for poetry: the
poetry in the Bible. Lowth's recovery of ancient Hebrew poetry as a model for literature
soon became the primary inspiration and justification for poetry whose meter departed
from classical norms. Lowth had forged a powerful instrument for those struggling to
break free from the constraints of neoclassical expectations.

A later poet exploring the new poetic territory opened up by Lowth's recovery
of biblical poetry was William Blake. He explicitly rejects the necessity of metrical
regularity, the "Monotonous Cadence ... derived from the modern bondage of
Rhyming."[28] He instead takes his inspiration form the "Primeval" poetry of the Bible,
famously stating that "The Old and New Testaments are the Great Code of Art."[29] Like
Smart, Blake builds on Lowth's use of biblical poetry as an alternative model of poetry.
Additionally, Blake illustrates the influence of a central element of Lowth's work: his
inclusion of parts of the prophetic books as examples of poetry. Blake often presents
himself as prophetic bard, and he titles some of his major works prophecies (e.g.,

---

[26] Christopher Smart, "Jubilate Agno," in *Selected Poems*, ed. Karina Williamson and Marcus Walsh,
Penguin Classics (New York: Penguin Books, 1990), 47.

[27] John Milton, *Paradise Lost*, in *Complete Poems and Major Prose*, ed. Merritt Y. Hughes
(New York: Prentice Hall, 1957), 210.

[28] "To the Public" from *Jerusalem* (1820) in *Blake's Poetry and Design*, ed. Mary Lynn Johnson and John
E. Grant (New York: W. W. Norton, 2008), 209.

[29] William Blake, "[Yah] & his two Sons Satan & Adam," or "The Laocoon," (1826) in Blake, *Poetry and
Designs*, 352. Stephen Prickett argues that Blake's aphorism is a direct reference to Lowth's comments
in the preface of his translation of Isaiah. Stephen Prickett, *Words and the Word: Language, Poetics
and Biblical Interpretation* (New York: Cambridge University Press, 1986), 116–17.

America a Prophecy and *Europe a Prophecy*). The significance of poets understanding themselves as prophets will be given further attention in the next chapter, but here, Blake's presentation of his poetry as prophetic can be taken as clear evidence of the influence of Lowth. Blake's new poetry and his new poetic persona is founded on Lowth's development of a new understanding of poetry in an attempt to win a hearing for the prophets as poets.

Another remarkable instance of the new poetry that Lowth's discovery made possible is the poetry of "Ossian" or the "Fragments of Ancient Poetry collected in the Highlands of Scotland." This poetry published in 1760 by James Macpherson, who claimed his work was based on translations of ancient Celtic manuscripts, was greeted with enthusiasm in both the Great Britain and Germany, especially among those poets and critics looking for alternatives to neoclassical poetry. Whether or not there were any actual Celtic manuscripts behind the poetry—even in Macpherson's day some suspected a forgery—it is clear that the literary artistry of the work comes from Macpherson. It is also clear that Macpherson's artistry is heavily indebted to biblical poetry as explained by Lowth. The biblical parallelism is obvious in lines like these: "If on the heath she moved, her breast was whiter than the down of Cana; if on the sea-beat shore, than the foam of the rolling ocean." It is significant that although these lines are intended to be understood as a translation of "ancient poetry," they are set out like prose.[30] Because of Lowth, the poetic nature of the work is not only independent of rhyme and meter but even of presentation in poetic lines.

Another body of nonmetrical text that came to be recognized as poetry in the wake of Lowth's work was in the Authorized (or King James) Version of the English Bible. David Norton chronicles how the Authorized Version, which had previously been less used than other versions, came to prominence in the second half of the eighteenth century.[31] A key factor in its rise was the recognition of its literary qualities—in particular, the quality of its poetic books. Before Lowth's work, the text of the Psalms and other poetic books and passage in the Authorized Version could hardly be recognized as poetry. In order to appear poetic in English translations, the Hebrew poetry had to be converted into metrical, rhyming verse. Many English poets tried their hands at converting the Psalms into poetry. The sixteenth and seventeenth centuries saw an outpouring of these metrical psalms in English, from the popular metrical psalter of the Scottish Presbyterians to the refined and complex work of poets like Milton. This poetry "restored" the poetic nature of the ancient Hebrew poetry by bringing it into conformity with neoclassical expectations for form and style. In comparison, the literal nonmetrical translations of the Psalms and other

---

[30] Murray Roston illustrates the parallelism of these lines and others by printing them in poetic lines as Lowth printed the poetry in his *Isaiah*. Roston, *Prophet and Poet*, 144.

[31] See, in particular, Chapters 11 and 12 ("The critical rise of the King James Bible" and "Writers and the Bible 2: the Romantics") in David Norton's *History of the English Bible as Literature* (Cambridge: Cambridge University Press, 2000). For Lowth's role in this rise, see, especially, pp. 219–29 and 244–51, particularly the quotation from Lowth's "Short Introduction to English Grammar" (1762): "The vulgar translation of the Bible [i.e., the Authorized Version] ... is the best standard of our language." Norton, *English Bible as Literature*, 245.

poetic books or passages could hardly be considered poetry. Lowth's lectures and, even more, his translation of Isaiah opened the door for the nonmetrical translations in the Authorized Version to be considered poetry; its parallelism and other poetic features could be appreciated even though (like the poetry of "Ossian") it continued to be printed like prose.

In this way, the Authorized Version—although it was translated in the early seventeenth century—came to be celebrated as English poetry, or literature, in the late eighteenth century and thus can be considered as part of the new literature of that period that provided an alternative to earlier neoclassical literature. Although it was primarily the parts of the Bible recognized as poetry (now including parts of the prophetic books) that gave it this new literary status, the very nature of the new standards of poetry meant that much of the prose, especially the narratives, could be considered poetic as well. If meter is not considered to be essential poetry, then nonmetrical compositions could be read like poetry, or as great literature, if they shared poetry's essential qualities. The foundational exposition of those qualities is the work of Lowth on biblical poetry.

The rise in appreciation for the Authorized Version as a great work of English literature finds a parallel in the rise of Luther's translation of the Bible as a great work of German literature in the same period. This happened in the context of a revolution in German literature that, like its English counterpart, defined itself against the classical formalism of the earlier part of the eighteenth century. As will be shown more fully in the next chapter, this revolution drew inspiration from Lowth—both directly and through the example of the English authors who built on Lowth's work. The Luther Bible, translated in the sixteenth century, took its place in a body of new German literature that blossomed in the late eighteenth century and continued to grow throughout the nineteenth century.

Duhm Presents the Poetry of Jeremiah as Great Literature

Duhm's commentary on Jeremiah at the beginning of the twentieth century returns to the roots of this literature—the prophetic books of the Bible read as great poetry—and his 1903 translation of Jeremiah can be considered a contribution to this body of literature. Duhm's presentation of the poetry of Jeremiah as great literature brings to a particular culmination Lowth's aim to win a hearing for the poetry of the prophets as great literature. Lowth sought to win a place for the Hebrew prophets alongside the Greek poets in the pantheon of great writers. In Lowth's judgment, "Isaiah, Jeremiah, and Ezekiel … hold the same rank among the Hebrews as Homer, Simonides, and Æschylus among the Greeks,"[32] and Duhm's work on Jeremiah is designed to secure Jeremiah's as one of humanity's great poets. Duhm is carrying out Lowth's program of promoting the works of the prophets as literary classics. Two features of Lowth's inclusion of the prophets in the pantheon of great poets reappear in Duhm's work. First, Lowth seeks to introduce the prophets into the company of classic authors as poets. Jeremiah does not take his place alongside Greek philosophers like Plato and

---

[32] Lowth, *Poetry of the Hebrews*, 294.

Aristotle, Greek historians like Herodotus and Thucydides, or even Greek orators like Demosthenes and Isocrates. Instead, Lowth ranks Jeremiah with Greek poets, perhaps particularly with Simonides, who was known for his lyrics and laments. Duhm attempts to secure Jeremiah's literary status by denying that he could have authored the decidedly unpoetic prose the book attributes to him. Second, Lowth accomplished the inclusion of the prophets with the classical Greek poets by redefining the marks of great poetry. He did not win appreciation for Jeremiah by arguing that his poetry had the same qualities the neoclassical critics admired in Homer or Aeschylus, but by creating a new set of standards. These are the very standards Duhm employs to argue for the excellence of the poetry in Jeremiah and the worthlessness the prose. They are also the standards of the literary revolution that can be traced back to Lowth, and it is now time to give that revolution a name.

Lowth Lays the Foundation for Romanticism

The identity of the literary revolution that Lowth's work on Hebrew poetry helped to launch can be established by considering the work of William Wordsworth. Wordsworth, whose poetry and poetic theory are both heavily dependent on Lowth, is well known as a central figure in the Romantic movement. The preface to his *Lyrical Ballads* (1798) is regarded as kind of manifesto of literary Romanticism and is commonly used today as a landmark in literary history, the turn of the nineteenth century that saw the full flowering of English Romanticism. Wordsworth and his contemporaries—including Coleridge, Shelley, Keats, and Byron—are considered the primary representatives of English Romanticism, and poets that anticipated their work—including Smart, MacPherson, Blake, and often Lowth himself—are often designated "pre-Romantics." However, particularly in the case of Lowth, this designation should not be interpreted in a way that underestimates his contribution to the movement. Lowth was not merely "ahead of his time" in anticipating the poetic tastes of a later literary age. He forged the poetic forms, the artistic values, the theory of inspiration, and the figure of the artist that the Romantics took up in their literary revolution. His role can be seen by observing, as will be done below, how Wordsworth's preface is dependent on Lowth's lectures. The new understanding of poetry Lowth worked out to win a hearing for biblical poetry is the same understanding Wordsworth proclaimed as the herald of Romanticism.

Wordsworth's Romantic poetry can be added to the list of poetry made possible by Lowth's recovery of biblical poetry. The influence of biblical poetry as understood by Lowth is clear in the poems in Wordsworth's *Lyrical Ballads*. A typical ballad in this collection, "The Thorn," includes as a kind of refrain the cries of a mother of a dead child: "O misery! o misery! / O woe is me! o misery!" The lines are more notable for their parallelism than their strict meter or rhyme. In the 1800 edition, Wordsworth felt it necessary to defend this kind of poetry and added a "Note to The Thorn," in which he argues that "repetition and tautology are frequently beauties of the highest kind." He defends this claim by pointing to the parallelism in biblical poetry. He writes, "The truth of these remarks might be shewn by innumerable passages from the Bible," and gives as an example parallel lines from the Song of Deborah (Judges 5:12, 27, 28a), a song that Lowth employs throughout his lectures as an illustration of Hebrew poetry.[33] Wordsworth's use of biblical poetry as a model for his poetry and a justification for his departures from accepted norms shows how biblical poetry was foundational for the Romantic revolution, a foundation laid by Lowth.

Lowth Makes Biblical Poetry an Alternative Ancient Model

The importance of Biblical poetry as understood by Lowth for the Romantic movement can be better understood by considering the importance of classical poetry for Augustan literature. The artists, poets, and theorists of Romanticism understood their artistic movement as a revolt against neoclassical art, literature, and theory. They were striving to break free from the constraints of rigid formalism and slavish imitation of classical models. Their work can be considered an outburst of undercurrents of discontent with the dominant artistic model in the eighteenth century. It is true that before Lowth's work, there was a growing interest in alternatives to classical literature: the beginnings of primitivism and orientalism. Readers were seeking out literature that was more simple, free, sincere, and passionate. However, it was difficult for anyone in that era to envision a radical break from the dominant system supported by the classical tradition. How could one set an individual poetic taste against the objective greatness of Virgil or Homer? By what authority could a modern literary theorist oppose the received wisdom of Aristotle or Cicero?

It was in answer to questions like these that critics of neoclassicism found biblical poetry as expounded by Lowth to be such a powerful tool. If neoclassical theory could claim to be founded on ancient Greek and Roman literature, its critics could counter with Lowth's literary theory founded on the even more ancient Hebrew literature. To the literary tradition embodied in the classical canon, Lowth's work offered a counter-tradition that enjoyed an unparalleled claim to canonical status.

Lowth Uses Biblical Poetry to Attack Neoclassical Culture

Lowth's role in the Romantic revolution was not accidental. It was not as if in his efforts to win a hearing for some ancient poetry he enjoyed, he happened to turn up poetic principles that later writers seized on to launch a revolt against the dominant school of poetic theory. Lowth himself was intentionally using biblical poetry to challenge the dominant theory. His direct attack on neoclassical poetic theory and the culture it represented can be seen in his criticism of the kind of poetic diction expected in Augustan poetry. In a lecture defending the poetry of the Bible from the charge that its language and imagery are too commonplace, Lowth lashes out at critics who might find the Hebrew poets uncivilized: the critics are right to "boast of their superior civilization … if luxury, levity, and pride, be the criterions of it."[34] In this critique, Lowth has clearly gone beyond merely defending Hebrew poetry

---

[33] William Wordsworth, "Preface to *Lyrical Ballads*," in *William Wordsworth: The Major Works*, Oxford World's Classics, ed. Stephen Gill (New York: Oxford University Press, 2000), 595.
[34] Lowth, *Poetry of the Hebrews*, 91.

to attacking the social structures of his day. His subsequent description of the character of the Hebrew nation that produced the poetry in the Bible functions as a backhanded critique of the "civilized" nations of his day. The ancient Hebrews, he writes, because they were "the offspring of the same ancient stock, boasted an equality of lineage and rank [with] no empty titles, no ensigns of false glory." Many of their kings and prophets, he continues, were called "from the plough and from the stalls," but "not even the greatest among them esteemed it mean and disgraceful to be employed in the lowest offices of rural labor."[35] These descriptions of Hebrew society go beyond a defense of the common language of Hebrew poetry; Lowth is exploiting the contrast with the refined poetic diction of his day to portray the privileged classes that produced and consumed the poetry as illiberal, undemocratic, and elitist. When Lowth defends Hebrew poetry as consonant with the Hebrew's "simple and uncultivated (or rather uncorrupted) state of life,"[36] he implies that the elaborate decorative language of the poetry of his day is not evidence of refinement but of corruption.

Lowth's preference for the simple, uncultivated life over the refinements of advanced civilization and the corresponding taste for a simple, uncultivated poetry turn neoclassical aesthetic values on their head. Poetry in the Augustan Age was the apotheosis of the refined tastes of the classically educated upper class. The educated elite looked to the classics not only for poetic form, but for the civilized manners and taste that could elevate their artistry above the common speech. Poetry became an opportunity to display wit and artistry, refinement and erudition along with a stylized, formal poetic diction that was considered essential to poetry.

The sense that verse could hardly be considered poetry without the requisite poetic diction can be illustrated by considering the poetic paraphrases of the seventeenth and eighteenth centuries. These "translations" of the parts of the Bible considered to be poetic not only supplied rhyme and meter to the Hebrew original but also suitably poetic language and imagery. Murray Roston observes, "The neo-classicist felt compelled to clothe the Bible in the garb of Augustan diction in order to make poetry of it."[37] Roston provides an excellent example of the neoclassical cloaking of biblical poetry. In the Authorized Version, Job 41:1-2 reads, "Canst thou draw out leviathan with an hook? or his tongue with a cord which thou lettest down? Canst thou put an hook into his nose? or bore his jaw through with a thorn?" But in a poetic paraphrase, Edward Young (1683–1765) renders the passage:

> Go to the Nile, and, from its fruitful side,
> Cast forth thy line into the swelling tide:
> With slender hair leviathan command
> And stretch his vastness on the loaded strand.

> (Young, *Poetical Works*, 1834)

---

[35] Lowth, *Poetry of the Hebrews*, 91.
[36] Lowth, *Poetry of the Hebrews*, 91.
[37] Roston, *Prophet and Poet*, 38.

Roston notes,

> The "unpoetic" words *hook, jaw*, and *thorn* are replaced with delicate paraphrases such as *commanding* the leviathan *with slender hair* from the *swelling tide*. ... The total effect is that the sharp picture of man's puny efforts to subdue the monster is blurred to become the conventional eighteenth-century landscape painting of the angler calmly fishing by the stream, acknowledging that the leviathan is a trifle too heavy for his fishing-rod.[38]

Lowth's writing on poetic style was an attack on this kind of dainty and genteel diction. By his defense of the common language in biblical poetry in his lectures and, even more, in his translation of Isaiah into common English, Lowth set a new standard for the kind of language that could be considered poetic. The difference can be seen by comparing the opening of Lowth's Isaiah with a contemporary poetic paraphrase. In William Langhorne's poetic paraphrase, Isa. 1:2 is rendered:

Jehovah speaks—let all creation hear!
Thou Earth attend! Ye rolling Heavens give Ear!
Reared by my care and fostered by my Hand
My rebel sons against their Father stand.[39]

To the Hebrew text, Langhorne has added Latinate words ("creation"), adjectival epithets ("*rolling* Heavens," "*rebel* sons"), and he has replaced single words of the Hebrew with poetic phrases ("reared by my care," "fostered by my Hand," "stand against"). Neoclassical propriety is most evident in his replacement of the direct first-person "rebelled against me" with a detached, third-person circumlocution "against their Father stand." Lowth's translation hews much closer to the Hebrew original:

Hear, O ye heavens; and give ear, O earth!
For it is Jehovah that speaketh.
I have nourished children and brought them up;
And even they have revolted against me.[40]

Lowth has hardly added a word to the Hebrew text. There is no attempt to refine the language to make it more poetic. The only indicators of the poetic nature of the text are presentation of the lines in a way that emphasizes their parallelism. Lowth relies for poetic effect on the text's presentation of Jehovah's simple, direct speech.

Lowth's defense of common language with imagery drawn from the daily life of rural people is not simply aimed at winning appreciation for biblical poetry. Lowth

---

[38] Roston, *Prophet and Poet*, 38–9.
[39] William Langhorne, *A Poetical Paraphrase on Part of the Book of Isaiah* (London: for R. Griffiths, 1761), quoted in Roston, *Prophet and Poet*, 136.
[40] Lowth, *Isaiah*, vol. 1, 1.

wields biblical poetry in an attack on the poetry of his age: its pride and extravagance, its lack of seriousness and sincerity, and its failure to give voice to anyone but the rich and powerful in the city and the court. Lowth is a deliberate and active participant in the revolt against the culture of neoclassicism, a revolt that would later be identified as Romanticism. Other writers in Lowth's time gave voice to a longing for a simpler, more natural life, one free from the corrupting influence of civilization. The best-known example is Rousseau, who countered the pride eighteenth-century Europeans took in the superiority of their civilization, with an account of human history in which the civilized state is a degeneration from the happy primitive, or "savage," state of humanity.[41] Just three years before the publication of Lowth's lectures, Rousseau published his first major philosophical work, an essay in which he argued that arts and letters merely "spread garlands of flowers over the iron chains" that constrain humanity's original freedom "and make them love their slavery by turning them into what are called civilized people."[42] Lowth's work takes part in this indictment of the current culture. His particular contribution was to make the Bible, particularly the Hebrew prophets, a tool for questioning the assumed virtues of classical and neoclassical civilization.

Lowth's attack on the culture of neoclassicism and the particular means (criticism of artificial poetic diction) show him in the vanguard of the Romantic revolution. Like Lowth, the Romantic authors censure the poetry of the Augustan age as a product of a corrupt upper class; in Wordsworth's description,

> A light, a cruel, and vain world, cut off
> From the natural inlets of just sentiment,
> From lowly sympathy, and chastening truth.[43]

Like Lowth, the Romantics celebrate the simple life of rural people who live close to nature. They countered the taste for the refined, learned, witty, and sophisticated with the virtues of the natural, simple, sincere, and common. The change in setting from city to countryside, and in characters from courtly gentlemen to yeoman farmers, was accompanied by a change in language. Wordsworth states that the aim of his *Lyrical Ballads* is "to chuse incidents and situations from common life, and to relate or describe them throughout in a selection of language really used by men."[44] Poets like Wordsworth could look to the folk ballad and other forms of popular literature for models for their new poetry, but because of the work of Lowth, the most authoritative example would be the poetry of the "husbandmen and shepherds" found in the Hebrew Bible.[45]

---

[41] The primitive is not the original natural state of humanity, in Rousseau's scheme, but a happy medium between the independent, animal-like natural state and the civilized state.

[42] Jean-Jacques Rousseau, *Discourse on the Sciences and Arts*, trans. Judith R. Bush, eds. Roger D. Masters and Christopher Kelley, vol. 2 of *The Collected Writings of Rousseau*, (Hanover, NH: University Press of New England, 1992), 5.

[43] Wordsworth, *The Prelude*, Book 9, "Residence in France," lines 348–50.

[44] Wordsworth, "Preface to *Lyrical Ballads*," 596–7.

[45] Lowth, *Poetry of the Hebrews*, 91.

Duhm's Primary Criteria Derived from Romantic Aesthetics

The revolutionary Romantic aesthetic that champions the simple, natural language of common people—in contrast to the artificial and imitative poetic diction of neoclassicism—is the informing principle of Duhm's approach to Jeremiah. It explains the central division he found in the book between the passages of "glorious" quality and the passages of "fairly low quality." What makes passages "glorious" in Duhm's eyes is their conformity to Romantic literary values. His description of what makes the authentic poetry of Jeremiah recognizably glorious is virtually identical to Wordsworth's description of his poetry. In Jeremiah's poetry, writes Duhm, "The simple form corresponds to the poetical diction, which is never artificial, forced, or even melodramatic, but always natural, appropriate to the thought, and popular in the best sense of the word."[46] The characteristics Duhm uses to distinguish the passages he finds glorious and those of low quality in Jeremiah are the very characteristics Romantic authors use to demonstrate the superiority of their poetry over neoclassical poetry: simple rather than elaborate, natural rather than artificial, spontaneous rather than forced, sincere rather than melodramatic, and popular rather than elitist. As in Romantic thought, Duhm explains the difference between the splendid and the shoddy styles of the passages in terms of the different cultures of the authors. The simple form and common diction of the authentic passages, Duhm explains, reveal the prophet's idyllic rural upbringing in Anathoth. By way of contrast, the clumsy form and "rhetorical exaggerations"[47] that characterize the additions reveal that the priests, scribes, and Torah teachers responsible for them come from the decadent culture of the city and the academy. This is Duhm's theory of the book in brief: only those passages of the book that can be read as having the characteristics valued in Romantic authors can be accepted as the authentic work of the prophet; the remaining passages should be read as having the characteristics the Romantic authors saw in their eighteenth-century neoclassical predecessors. The result is the isolation of a body of writing worthy of a Romantic author. The project of abstracting Romantic literature from an ancient book might seem odd. However, it should be easier to understand when it is recalled the Romantic aesthetic is grounded in a work about poetry in the prophetic books. Lowth's lectures made the poetry in the prophetic books not only the primary example for Romantic literature but also its justification and its grounds for criticizing the neoclassical literature of the day. Lowth had used the poetry in the prophetic books to critique the poetry and culture of his day; now Duhm returns the favor by using the Romantic literary theory that issued from Lowth's work to critique the literature and culture of the authors of the prophetic books.

---

[46] "Der einfachen Form entspricht die poetische Diktion, die niemal künstlich, geziert, nicht einmal pathetisch, sondern immer natürlich, dem Gedanken angemessen, im besten Sinne volkstümlich ist, aber eben darum uns ergreift, rührt, oft erschüttert und in ihrem Reichtum an treffenden und originellen Bildern den geborenen Dichter verrät." Duhm, *Jeremia*, xii–xiii.
[47] Duhm, *Jeremia*, xi, xix.

Lowth Uses Biblical Poetry to Redefine the Purpose and Nature of Poetry

Lowth's criticism of neoclassical poetic theory goes beyond a critique of its artificial forms and language and the genteel culture that produced it; he used the poetry he found in the Bible to effect a transformation of the perceived purpose of poetry, a transformation that would be fully embraced by the Romantic movement. Lowth's transitional role in this transformation helps to explain the appearance of conventional statements alongside his more novel contributions. His adherence to conventional poetic theory seems to come in his more unreflective, initial considerations. For example, Lowth's inaugural lecture on poetry begins by rehearsing the conventional aims of poetry: "Poetry is commonly understood to have two objects in view, namely advantage and pleasure, or rather both."[48] This dual function of poetry echoes the neoclassical commonplace that poetry's function is "to teach and to delight," a phrase from Philip Sidney's *Apology for Poetry* (1595) that has its roots in the poetic theory of Horace, who wrote during the reign of Augustus Caesar. The conventionality of Lowth's definition may be ascribed to the strength of the conventional view, to the delayed appearance of Lowth's mature view, or to the brevity of the time he had to prepare his first lecture after being made Oxford's professor of poetry.[49]

In the conventional neoclassical view, poetry's ultimate aim was its pedagogical or moral purpose, and the secondary aim of delight, or pleasure, served this end by making the teaching appealing, or at least palatable. Poetry achieved its pedagogical aim primarily by representation of worthy subjects. However, even though poetry was considered to be fundamentally a mimetic art, its distinguishing features came for the particular things poets added to make their portrayals pleasing: meter, rhyme, poetic diction, and figurative language. The way in which Lowth's theory challenged the necessity of meter, rhyme, and formal poetic diction has already been shown. In the case of figurative language, Lowth believed it to be essential to poetry, but he gave new account of its contribution that realigned the basic aims of poetry.

Figurative Language Gives Expression

As in his discussions of meter and poetic diction, Lowth's initial concern in his discussion of figurative language is to challenge the aspects of the conventional theory that kept Hebrew poetry from being appreciated as great poetry. The figurative language of biblical poetry did not measure up to the expectations of classically trained Augustan poets and critics. Poetry was expected to please or delight by the elegance and grace of the figures of speech that adorned it. For such embellishments, poets could turn to rhetorical guides that provided catalogs of approved tropes and figures as well as guidelines for selecting which ones would be most fitting. The Hebrew prophets and psalmists, of course, did not have access to these rhetorical guides. Thus, although their poetry often employs figurative language, their work could not achieve highest levels of classical decorum. Lowth expects his readers to recognize how unsuitable

---

[48] Lowth, *Poetry of the Hebrews*, 6.

[49] Lowth begins his first lecture with the apology: "Our present meeting [is] on some accounts rather earlier than I could have wished." Lowth, *Poetry of the Hebrews*, 9.

these classical guidelines are for appreciation of the more ancient *Poetry of the Hebrews*. Thus he begins his discussion on figurative language in biblical poetry with the recommendation that the "almost innumerable forms of the Greek rhetoricians"[50] be set aside.

In place of the classical tropes and figures, Lowth asks readers to consider the Hebrew concept of the *mashal*, or parable, as a comprehensive term for poetic figures.[51] Although he observes that many of the classical techniques fall under the scope of the *mashal*, he finds them employed in the Hebrew poets for a different reason: "It is the peculiar design of the figurative style ... to exhibit objects in a clearer or more striking, in a sublimer or more forcible manner."[52] With this statement Lowth reorients the purpose not only of figurative language in Hebrew poetry but of poetic technique as a whole. Figurative language is not primarily for pleasant and decorous embellishment; it is for conveying the message of the poet with clarity, sublimity, and force. The purpose not merely of figurative language, but of poetic technique in general is not to decorate what could have been communicated in prose; it is to give the poet's expressions power.

In the succeeding generations, particularly in Romantic literary theory, Lowth's account of figurative language in Hebrew poetry became the standard account of figurative language in all good poetry. Wordsworth, building on Lowth, rejects the neoclassical understanding of figurative language. He argues that adding "transitory and accidental ornaments" to a poem is evidence either of the poet's attempt to "excite admiration of himself by arts" or of "the assumed meanness of his subject." In true poetry, Wordsworth argues, figurative language is a natural accompaniment of the poet's passions expressed in the poem: "it will naturally ... lead him to the passions the language of which ... must necessarily be dignified and variegated, and alive with metaphors and figures."[53]

Romantic Expressivism

Wordsworth's explanation of figurative language in terms of the passion of the poet is an instance of what is perhaps the most recognizable characteristic of Romanticism: the idea that art is primarily the result of an artist's passions. Prior to the rise of Romanticism, art was understood, for the most part, to be the result of artistry: that is, an artist's intentional use of labor and skill to produce a work of art. In the older understanding of artistic creation, passion did not play the role that it did in the Romantic conception of artistic creation. The artist might design a work to move the passions of audience; the artist might depict passion (perhaps even his or her own); but the passions of the artist would be incidental to the creation and the appreciation of the work. In neoclassical poetic theory, the poet was primarily thought of as a

---

[50] Lowth, *Poetry of the Hebrews*, 67. James Kugel provides a helpful overview of what he calls the "tropes-and-figures approach" to biblical literature (Kugel, *Idea of Poetry*, 161–7, 226–33) and the rejection of this approach by Lowth, *Poetry of the Hebrews*, 275–6.

[51] See Ian Balfour's enlightening discussion of Lowth's use of the concept of *mashal*. Ian Balfour, *The Rhetoric of Romantic Prophecy* (Stanford, CA: Stanford University Press, 2002), 62–9.

[52] Lowth, *Poetry of the Hebrews*, 71.

[53] Wordsworth, "Preface to *Lyrical Ballads*," 607, 603.

craftsperson who shaped the chosen subject matter into poetic form and adorned it with poetic graces.

The emphasis placed on the passions of the artist distinguishes Romanticism not only from neoclassical poetic theory but also from Enlightenment thought with its emphasis on reason. The most familiar designation of the eighteenth century in European culture is the "Age of Reason," and the rise of Romanticism can be understood, by way of contrast, as the gradual dawn of an "Age of Passion," or an "Age of Sentiment." Of course, these two ages overlapped, and elements of both can be found in many individual authors from this time, particularly those who draw a strong distinction between the realms of reason and passion (or "the head" and "the heart") each having its natural claims. However, if the two ages grew up side by side, Romanticism is clearly the younger of the two and understood itself as supplying what was lacking in an era whose emphasis on reason and common sense it found dull, sterile, and dry.

In his Enlightenment context, Lowth clearly believed that by championing Hebrew poetry he was striking a blow for the passions in poetry. He distinguishes sharply between reason and the passions and defines poetry as the latter:

> The language of reason is cool, temperate, rather humble than elevated, well arranged and perspicuous, with an evident care and anxiety lest anything should escape which might appear perplexed or obscure. The language of the passions is totally different: the conceptions burst out in a turbid stream, expressive in a manner of the internal conflict; the more vehement break out in hasty confusion; they catch (without search or study) whatever is impetuous, vivid, or energetic. In a word, reason speaks literally, the passions poetically.[54]

Poetry, for Lowth, is an expression of the turbulent soul of the poet, an outburst of the poet's passions. Lowth's account of poetry became the standard Romantic explanation and remains a widespread conception today. In Lowth's day, it was certainly not the dominant account. Lowth's lectures stand near the source of this new stream of poetic theory, though in his account it issues from an ancient spring: the *Poetry of the Hebrews*. "Hebrew poetry," he writes, "instead of disguising the secret feelings of the author, ... lays them quite open to public view; and the veil being as it were suddenly removed, all the affections and passions of the soul, its sudden impulses, its hasty sallies and irregularities, are conspicuously displayed."[55]

When Lowth used Hebrew poetry to argue that poetry is an unveiling and display of the secret feelings of the author, "expressive ... of the internal conflict," he was laying the foundation for what Isaiah Berlin called "expressionism."[56] In contrast to "the normal eighteenth-century view," in which the "value of a work of art consisted in the [intrinsic] properties it had" and "had nothing to do with who made it," expressionism taught that "when we appreciate a work of art, we are put into some

---

[54] Lowth, *Poetry of the Hebrews*, 190.
[55] Lowth, *Poetry of the Hebrews*, 192.
[56] Isaiah Berlin, *The Roots of Romanticism*, 2nd ed. (Princeton, NJ: Princeton University Press, 2013), 67.

kind of contact with the man who made it, and it speaks to us."[57] The expressionistic account of artistic creation has a strong claim to being the primary constitutive belief of Romantic poetics, its fundamental difference from previous poetic theories. With Romanticism comes a great shift in poetic theory from an emphasis on the work of art itself—and its relationship to its subject—to an emphasis on the artist and the psychological and biographical origins of artistic creation. The shift from objective mimesis to subjective expression is identified by M. H. Abrams as central to the transition to Romanticism. In his depiction, it is a transition from the poetics of the mirror (which merely reflects objects) to the poetics of the lamp (which illuminates objects from its interior light).[58]

Lowth's Sublime: Transition to Expressionism

Perhaps the best-known statement of Romantic expressionism is Wordsworth's definition of poetry as "the spontaneous overflow of powerful emotions."[59] It deserves to be better known that, over fifty years earlier, Lowth had written of Hebrew poetry that it "lays ... open the all the affections and passions of [the author's] soul" with language that "burst[s] out in a turbid stream, expressive ... of the internal conflict." In Lowth's work, the transition to an expressionist poetics is taking place. The transition can be observed in his treatment of the sublime, a concept that came to be central to Romantic poetics. Lowth's definition of the sublime stands astride the watershed between a poetics of mimesis and a poetics of expression:

> The word [sublime] I wish in this place to be understood in its most extensive sense: I speak not merely of that sublimity which exhibits great objects with a magnificent display of imagery and diction; but that force of composition, whatever it be, which strikes and overpowers the mind, which excites the passions, and which expresses ideas at once with perspicuity and elevation; not solicitous whether the language be plain or ornamented, refined or familiar: in this use of the word I copy Longinus.[60]

---

[57] Berlin, *Roots of Romanticism*, 68, 69. Berlin introduces expressionism to explain the thought of Herder and says that Herder learned it from Hamann. He does not mention the profound effect that Lowth's work on Biblical poetry had on both Hamann and Herder. This influence will be discussed in the following chapter.

[58] M. H. Abrams, *The Mirror and the Lamp: Romantic Theory and the Critical Tradition* (New York: W. W. Norton, 1958), 58–60. Abrams bases his terms "mirror" and "lamp" on the writings of the English Platonists, William Hazlitt, Wordsworth, and Coleridge who all depict the human mind as projecting (not merely reflecting) light. Abrams, *Mirror and the Lamp*, 52, 54, 58–60.

[59] From the 1802 "Preface to *Lyrical Ballads*." Wordsworth, "Preface to *Lyrical Ballads*," 598. Stephen Prickett notes that Wordsworth's poetic formulation was directly dependent on the works of Lowth and Hugh Blair. Prickett, *Words and the Word*, 43. Hugh Blair himself was drawing directly from Lowth. One piece of clear evidence is the lecture on Hebrew poetry (XLI) in Blair's influential *Lectures on Rhetoric and Belles Lettres* (1783), which is basically a summary of Lowth's lectures. For more on Lowth's influence on Blair and Wordsworth, see Anna Cullhed, "Original Poetry: Robert Lowth and Eighteenth Century Poetics," in *Sacred Conjectures: The Context and Legacy of Robert Lowth and Jean Astruc*, ed. John Jarick, LHB/OTS (New York: T&T Clark, 2007), 44.

[60] Lowth, *Poetry of the Hebrews*, 189.

In its context, this definition can be seen as one more instance of Lowth challenging the limitations of conventional theory as unable to account for biblical poetry. In this case, the conventional understanding of the sublime (in the first phrase of Lowth's definition) is a veritable summary of the mimetic and decorative poetic theory of neoclassicism: the sublime "exhibits [or imitates] great objects" and dignifies them "with a magnificent display of imagery and diction." The new understanding Lowth introduces (in the second phrase of his definition) fully anticipates the expressive poetic theory of Romanticism. The sublimity of a work does not depend on the artist's conscious choice of a grand subject or skill with "refined" poetic diction or "ornament[al]" figures of speech. Its sublimity comes from the mysterious force that "overpowers the mind, … excites the passions, and expresses the ideas [of the artist]." In fact, sublimity no longer primarily refers to an aesthetic quality in the work but to a force of composition in the artist.

It might be thought that Lowth derived his novel expressionist theory from classical sources, and in fact, as support for his definition of the sublime, he employs the authority of Longinus. The first-century treatise "On the Sublime" (popularly attributed to Longinus) was indeed an important source for authors like Lowth who were seeking alternatives to neoclassical poetic theory. At one point, the author of the treatise takes issue with an earlier writer on the sublime who denied that passion could be a source of elevated poetry: "I would affirm with confidence that there is no tone so lofty as that of genuine passion, in its right place, when it bursts out in a wild gust of mad enthusiasm."[61] The eighteenth-century exponents of an expressionistic poetic theory seized on lines like this. However, as a whole, the work is much more conventional. Its outline is based on the enumeration of five sources of elevated style: "the power of forming great conceptions"; "vehement and inspired passion"; "formation of figures"; "noble diction"; and "elevated composition" (which includes elegant and rhythmic arrangement of words).[62] Of these, the last three (which the author categorizes as "art") are the common classical—and neoclassical—rhetorical graces that the poet or speaker adds to a work, and discussion of them makes up the bulk of the treatise. The first two (which the author categorizes as "nature") are the ones that Lowth (and others who helped to launch the Romantic revolt) found useful. However, the author leaves discussion of the passions for another treatise, which has never been discovered. The mere existence of a classical author who acknowledged the possibility that sublimity could be a natural result of the great conceptions and passions of the poet was enough to make the treatise a threat to the traditional certainties of Augustan poetic theory, what William Wimsatt called "the Trojan horse in the camp of neo-classicism."[63]

---

[61] Longinus, "On the Sublime," trans. W. Rhys Roberts, in *Criticism the Major Works*, ed. Walter Jackson Bate (San Diego, CA: Harcourt Brace, Jovanovich, 1952), 66.

[62] Longinus, "On the Sublime," 65–6.

[63] William K. Wimsatt Jr. and Cleanth Brooks, *Literary Criticism: A Short History* (New York: Random House, 1957), 285.

In fact, Lowth's transformation of the concept of the sublime owes little to theories of Longinus.[64] His primary source of authority is the models in Hebrew poetry. The definition of sublimity that he attributes to Longinus is intended to clarify a quality that he finds characteristic of Hebrew poetry. He introduces it to support his claim (in the previous sentence) that "the Hebrew poetry expresses in its very name and title [*mashal*], the particular quality [sublimity] in which it so greatly exceeds the poetry of all other nations."[65] In four lectures on the sublime, Lowth provides numerous examples from Hebrew poetry to illustrate its sublimity. Once again, it is his efforts to defend the poetic worth of biblical poetry entail a transformation of poetic theory. His new understanding of sublimity is apparent in the titles of four of his lectures on Hebrew poetry: "XIV: Of the Sublime in General," "XV: Of Sublimity of Expressions," "XVI: Of Sublimity of Sentiment," and "XVII: Of the Sublime of Passion."[66] These four lectures are intended to illustrate a feature of Hebrew poetry and they are full of examples from the poetic parts of the Bible. But the sublimity Lowth sees in this poetry is clearly the new sublime—one that expresses the soul of the artist, particularly the passions, or sentiments—and Lowth's work made biblical poetry the prime justification and example of a sublimity that was not due to formal graces, elevated diction, or use of classical figures of speech, but due to the intensity of the poet's passions. In short, Lowth made the Bible the prime example of sublimity for Romantic poetry and poetic theory.

This contribution of Lowth's can be seen in Wordsworth's comments on the sublimity of Milton (whose *Paradise Lost* he judged to be more sublime than all the classical epics): "The grand storehouses of enthusiastic ... language ... are the prophetic and lyrical parts of the Holy Scriptures, and the works of Milton. ... Our great epic poet ... however imbued the surface might be with classical literature ... was a Hebrew in soul; and all things tended in him toward the sublime."[67] Coleridge agreed on the ultimate source of the sublime. "Could you ever discover anything sublime ... in the classical Greek literature? Sublimity is Hebrew by birth."[68] These comments make it clear that the Romantic understanding of the sublime, one that embodies their vision of great art as the expression of the great passions of the artist, was grounded in biblical poetry as read by Lowth.

---

[64] One feature, often overlooked, that made Longinus's work especially effective as an agent for spreading a new vision of poetry in the eighteenth century is its use of the Bible as an example of the sublime. With its quotation of Genesis 1:1 "Let there be light, and there was light," Longinus is one of the first pagan literary critics to use Hebrew scripture to illustrate a literary quality. This distinction of Longinus's treatise was greatly enhanced in the version, which most eighteenth-century English readers would have encountered. Murray Roston observes that in the English translation "On the Sublime" by William Smith, the translation Roston argues was most influential in the eighteenth century, the annotations cite the Old Testament more frequently than any other source as the noblest illustration of the sublime. Roston, *Prophet and Poet*, 123. Smith's translation was first published in 1739, two years before Lowth's first lecture.

[65] Lowth, *Poetry of the Hebrews*, 189.

[66] Lowth, *Poetry of the Hebrews*, xv–xvi.

[67] Wordsworth, "1815 Preface to *Lyrical Ballads*," in *William Wordsworth: The Major Works*, Oxford World's Classics, ed. Stephen Gill (New York: Oxford University Press, 2000), 634.

[68] Samuel Taylor Coleridge, *Table Talk and Omniana*, ed. T. Ashe (London, 1884), 174, quoted in Roston, *Prophet and Poet*, 125.

Duhm Makes the Poetry in Jeremiah an Expression of the Prophet's Passions

The Romantic conception of great poetry as the expression of the great passions of the artist lies at the foundation of Duhm's approach to Jeremiah. This is evident in his description of Jeremiah's poetry. It has already been noted how Duhm's description of its distinctive form and diction corresponds exactly to the qualities of poetry the Romantic poets felt distinguished their poetry from neoclassical poetry: "The simple form corresponds to the poetical diction, which is never artificial, forced, or even melodramatic, but always natural, appropriate to the thought, and popular in the best sense of the word." Duhm goes on to say that the fact that Jeremiah's poetry uses simple form and common diction does not prevent it from communicating his feelings; instead, "for that very reason, it touches, moves, and often shakes us, and in its richness of fitting and original images, it betrays the born poet."[69] For Duhm, like earlier Romantics, the ultimate test of the worth of the poetry is its power to move the emotions of the readers by what Wordsworth called the "spontaneous overflow of [the poet's] powerful emotions."[70] The poetry moves and shakes the reader because the poet was moved and shaken. Its imagery is fitting because it is a natural product of the poet's original experience, a passionate experience that, as Wordsworth says, "will naturally … lead him to" the language of passion, which "must necessarily be … alive with metaphors and figures."[71] The poetic features are not evidence of the poet's skill and familiarity with previous poetry but of poetic experience that is the result of a poetic temperament—evidence, in short, of a "born poet."

That Jeremiah is "a born poet"—more of a poet than all of the prophets who preceded him—is evident to Duhm from the distinctive nature of his poetry:

> The primary distinction of Jeremiah's poetry is that more than any the prophetic poetry of the previous centuries it gives voice to the individual self (*das eigene Ich*), the feelings (*die Gefühle*), and the emotional states (*die Stimmung*) of the prophets, and these are often given masterful expression (*Ausdruck*). Amos and Isaiah are the orators (*die Redner*); Jeremiah is the poet (*die Lyriker*).[72]

This characterization of Jeremiah's poetry reveals that for Duhm the essential element of poetry is not poetic form. Isaiah and Amos employed poetic form, but only Jeremiah is the true poet. What makes Jeremiah's poetry truly poetic is its expression of his passions, his interior experiences, and his individuality. This is Romantic "expressionism" in a nutshell: artistic worth can be measured by the degree to which it gives expression to individual temperament and passions of an artist.

Conformity to this understanding of literary worth supplies Duhm's primary criterion for dividing the speeches the book of Jeremiah attributes to the prophet between authentic and inauthentic material. While the authentic passages use fitting and original images to express the passions of a born poet, the inauthentic material can

---

[69] Duhm, *Jeremia*, xii–xiii.
[70] Wordsworth, "Preface to *Lyrical Ballads*," 598.
[71] Wordsworth, "Preface to *Lyrical Ballads*," 607, 603.
[72] Duhm, *Jeremia*, xiii.

only "repeat over and over the same shabby phrases, fitting or not,"[73] and this is because they have no original experiences themselves but can only pass on thoughts not based on experience but on tradition the authors hardly understand.[74] Duhm's contrast between the shabby and the sublime was clearly drawn from Romantic aesthetics, but this in turn was drawn from Lowth's work on the prophets.

Lowth Makes Prophetic Inspiration the Measure of Poetry

Wordsworth's assertion that sublimity was to be found not only in the "lyrical" but also in the "prophetic" parts of the Bible is a clear indication of his dependence on Lowth. As has been shown, a primary aim of Lowth's lectures was to expand range of biblical poetry beyond the parts commonly accepted as "lyrical" (Psalms, Song of Songs, and Lamentations) to include the parts of the prophetic books. Now that Lowth's role as a critic of neoclassical poetic theory has been shown, a further significance of his expansion of poetry to include the prophets begins to appear. Lowth was not merely making a greater part of the Hebrew Scriptures available for appreciation (or even imitation) as poetry. The poetry he found in the prophetic books was his prime example of what he considered to be the truest form of poetry, poetry that had the qualities the conventional poetry of his day lacked.

> This species of poetry [i.e., prophetic poetry] … possesses all that genuine enthusiasm, which is the natural attendant on inspiration; it excels in the brightness of imagination and in clearness and energy of diction, and consequently rises to an uncommon pitch of sublimity: hence also it often is very happy in the expression and delineation of the passions.[75]

Lowth's description of prophetic poetry is remarkable for the degree to which it anticipates the central themes of Romantic literary theory. In this brief description, Lowth employs the essential vocabulary that would come to express what the Romantics valued in poetry: "enthusiasm," "inspiration," "imagination," "sublimity," "expression," and "passion." The qualities of poetry Lowth found lacking in the poetry of his day are the very qualities he believed he had found in the prophetic books of the Bible. For Lowth, the prophetic books contained the desired alternative to neoclassical poetry, and through his work they became the prototype for Romantic poetry.

"Inspiration"

In Lowth's description of prophetic poetry, one quality stands apart as the source of all the others. "Inspiration" is the master concept that allowed Lowth to use the poetry he found in the prophetic books to transform poetic theory. In his description of prophetic poetry, "inspiration" is the primary quality, and the others are the "natural

---

[73] Duhm, *Jeremia*, xviii.
[74] Duhm, *Jeremia*, xx.
[75] Lowth, *Poetry of the Hebrews*, 279.

attendant[s]." Lowth's critique of the poetry of his day is not simply that it lacked certain poetic qualities, but that this lack showed that it did not flow from the true source of poetry: inspiration. He found contemporary poetry, with all its artificial constructions and labored imitations, uninspired. As with the case of "sublimity," "inspiration" was not a novel concept in the poetic theory of Lowth's day, but he helped to elevate its importance and, more importantly, to effect a transformation of its meaning that distinguished it from previous use and paved the way for its use by Romantic authors.

Lowth forged the new significance of "inspiration" in reference to prophetic poetry. The new significance, and its roots in the prophetic poetry, can be seen in a statement Lowth makes about the effects of inspiration: "To decorate the worship of the Most High with all the charms and graces of harmony; to give force and energy to the devout affections was the sublime employment of the sacred Muse."[76] The "Muse" is, of course, the traditional, or classical, source of poetic inspiration, and Lowth's term "sacred Muse" allows him to attribute the inspiration of the *Sacred Poetry of the Hebrews* to the muse as well. Although his description of what the muse contributes to poetry begins with the traditional effects of inspiration, it moves on to Lowth's new understanding of its effects. The first phrase is a neat summary of the (neo)classical understanding of inspiration. The muse enables the poet, who has chosen a fitting theme ("the worship of the Most High"), to "decorate" the theme with "all the charms and graces of harmony." The effects of inspiration can be seen in the rhyme and meter, the tropes and figures that raise the poet's presentation (*mimesis*) of the exalted subject to the appropriate level of poetry. In the second phrase, Lowth breaks though to a new understanding. The work of the muse is no longer confined to adding decorative graces; it is a power that works on the source of the poetry in the heart of the poet. Inspiration empowers and energizes the poet's affections, or passions, to such a degree that their expression will be sublime, or inspiring. Once again, in this brief description Lowth makes the transition from neoclassical to Romantic poetics.

A closer look at the two phrases in Lowth's description of inspiration reveals the source of the transition. In the first phrase with its traditional neoclassical notion of poetry, Lowth seems to have in mind the odes and lyrics found in the Psalms ("the worship of the Most High"), but in the second phrase with its new proto-Romantic notions, Lowth has in mind prophetic poetry. It is primarily in prophetic poetry that Lowth finds the sublime expression of ardent passion. Thus, once again it can be seen that Lowth's expansion of the realm of poetry to include the prophets provided the grounds on which he, and those who followed him, built their new paradigm for poetry.

The term "sacred Muse" represents the transformation of the meaning of "inspiration" that is at the heart of Lowth's redefinition of poetry. He took two relatively distinct ideas of inspiration that were widely accepted—the classical idea of the inspiration of poets by the muse and the biblical idea of the inspiration of prophets by God—and fused them into a single concept. The "sacred Muse" is at once the classical Muse that inspires secular poetry and the Holy Spirit who inspired the Scriptures.

[76] Lowth, *Poetry of the Hebrews*, 253.

History of Inspiration: *Saul a Nabi'*

As in the case with Lowth's redefinition of "sublimity," the initial purpose of his redefinition of "inspiration" is to win a hearing for the prophetic books as poetry. The relationship between his new understanding of inspiration and his new understanding of prophetic literature can be seen in a passage in which Lowth offers a historical, or etymological, argument for understanding prophets as poets. Lowth attempts to demonstrate that the Hebrew word for prophet (*nābi'*) was used with "an ambiguous sense and that it equally denoted a prophet, a poet, or a musician, under the influence of divine inspiration."[77] He cites the examples of Saul who "prophesied" (*nābā'*) when he met with the companies of "prophets" playing instruments, and the Levitical singers appointed by David who "prophesied" on their instruments, and he finds it particularly significant that on one occasion Elisha would not begin prophesying until a minstrel was brought and began to play his harp.[78] "From all these testimonies," he concludes, "it is sufficiently evident, that the prophetic office had a most strict connection with the poetic art. They had one common name, one common origin, one common author, the Holy Spirit."[79] Here is Lowth's fusion of prophetic and poetic inspiration in a nutshell.

The historical argument Lowth provides for his bold claim is not very strong. The handful of passages he provides do not make it "sufficiently evident" that prophets and musicians shared a common name. These passages merely show that people called "prophets" could play music and that musicians could do something called "prophesying." His evidence that poetry and prophecy have as their common origin the Holy Spirit is even less adequate. Only one of his example mentions a spirit as a source of prophecy or poetry. In the story of Saul and prophets, the "prophesying" that Saul does when the spirit comes on him seems to be some kind of ecstatic behavior. In a related story, "prophesying" involves Saul taking off his clothes and lying naked for a whole day (1 Sam. 19:24). It would take much more evidence than Lowth provides at this point to demonstrate that the "inspiration" that resulted in Saul's ecstatic behavior in the eleventh century is of the same kind as the "inspiration" that resulted in the literary production of the prophetic books beginning in the eighth century.[80] However, it is just this transformation of his audience's understanding of how the prophetic books were inspired that Lowth is attempting to achieve with the examples.

What makes Lowth's audience likely to accept his view is not so much the historical evidence he provides but the assumptions the audience brings to his work. Lowth can count on most of his audience already believing that both what he calls the "sacred hymns" in the Psalms and the "oracles of God" in the prophetic books were inspired by the Holy Spirit. It is a tenet of Christian doctrine that the whole of the canonical Scriptures are "God-breathed."[81] Lowth trades on this theological affirmation of

---

[77] Lowth, *Poetry of the Hebrews*, 246.
[78] 1 Sam. 10:5-10, 19:20-24; 2 Chron. 25:1-3; 2 Kgs 3:15. Lowth, *Poetry of the Hebrews*, 245–8.
[79] Lowth, *Poetry of the Hebrews*, 248.
[80] The authors of the prophetic books rarely attribute their prophetic words to the work of the Spirit. The only passages that make this connection are Ezek. 3:23, 11:5; Isa. 59:21, 61:1; Joel 2:28; and Zech. 12:1.
[81] 2 Tim. 3:16. Orthodox Christians of all times would readily admit that the ultimate source of both the Psalms and the prophetic books is God through the agency of his Spirit. However, Lowth's concern

common inspiration to make his case for the literary theory that the poetry and prophesy are closely related because they both originate in an experience analogous, if not identical, to the ecstatic behavior of Saul. He is bringing together poetry and prophecy by portraying them both as the result of "inspiration" thought of as a force that seizes a person and stirs up the passions such that they flow out in music and rhythmic poetry.

"Enthusiasm"

Lowth's emphasis on "inspiration" as the cause of prophecy is paralleled by his emphasis on "enthusiasm" as the source of poetry. As with prophecy, he seeks to (re-) define poetry with reference to its earliest form:

> The origin and first use of poetical language are undoubtedly to be traced into the vehement affections of the mind. For what is meant by that singular frenzy of poets which the Greeks, ascribing to divine inspiration, distinguished by the appellation of "enthusiasm," but a style and expression directly prompted by nature itself and exhibiting the true and express image of a mind violently agitated? when, as it were, the secret avenues, the interior recesses of the soul are thrown open, when the inmost conceptions are displayed, rushing together in one turbid stream, without order or connection.[82]

The idea that poetry is the result of "enthusiasm," a venerable theory, had been eclipsed in Lowth's time by the idea that poetry was the result of intentional artistry. Lowth helped to resuscitate the enthusiasm explanation in his attempt to show that poetry and prophecy have a common origin. Like attributing prophecy to ecstatic inspiration, attributing poetry to enthusiasm makes poetry simultaneously the result of a natural, psychological experience and of divine agency (*en-theos* in Greek, referring to possession by a god). By explaining prophetic inspiration in terms of the experience of early ecstatics and privileging enthusiasm over artistry as an explanation for poetry, Lowth is able to make inspiration and enthusiasm virtually synonymous and thus to unite poetry and prophecy as the common results of a common experience.

Although Lowth's ostensible aim in fusing poetry and prophecy as the result of a common experience is to strengthen his case that the prophetic books in the Bible contain poetry, his larger achievement was to transform how people in his age understood poetry. If poetry in its essence is the result of a passionate experience in the soul of a poet, one that the ancients could only explain as an encounter with divinity, then the mere presence of rhyme, and meter, or figures of speech would hardly be adequate to qualify a composition as poetic. To be truly poetic, a composition must betray evidence of this experience: passion, sublimity, spontaneity, energy, sincerity,

---

is not the theological question of the God-givenness of all Scripture, but the literary question of the genre of the prophetic literature: whether it originated from the same kind of (poetic) inspiration from which the Psalms and other poetic works originated.

82 Lowth, *Poetry of the Hebrews*, 52.

originality, and so on. It must speak the "language of the passions" because it is an expression of the passions of the artist. If it lacks these qualities, and can only speak the "language of reason," it is not only bad poetry; it can hardly be considered poetry at all. This is the critique of neoclassical poetry that Lowth's reconception of the source of poetry allows. Its formal elegance can be discredited as artificial, imitative, labored, "the effect of study and diligence, not of imagination and enthusiasm."[83] The dichotomy Lowth draws between imitation and imagination, diligence and spontaneity, stimulation of stock responses and sincere expression of individual experience became the foundation of the Romantic movement's self-understanding. Because the cornerstone of this foundation was Lowth's work on the prophets, the Romantic authors would explain what made their poetry better than previous poetry in terms of inspiration. Their poetry was inspired, or simply "prophetic." It is due to Lowth's work on the poetry of the prophets that Schlegel, a leading figure in German Romanticism, could write, "No one is a poet except the prophet." Stephen Prickett writes that Lowth's lectures "did more than any other single work to make the biblical tradition, rather than the neo-classical one, the central poetic tradition for the Romantics."[84] It would be more accurate to say that the lectures made "the *prophetic* tradition rather than the *classical* one" the central tradition of the Romantics. They looked to the poetry in the prophetic books as evidence that true poetry must be the result of an overwhelming interior experience.

Duhm Discerns Inspiration by Literary Means

The Romantic contrast between inspired and uninspired writing supplies the foundation for Duhm's approach to the book of Jeremiah. Like other Romantic authors, Duhm accounts for the difference between good and bad literature by positing a division between two types of writers: inspired and uninspired. "In every age," Duhm writes, there is a "deep opposition between inspiration and study, between the living force that impels creative spirits forward and the endeavors of epigones and imitating amateurs that rest on the accomplishments of an earlier time."[85] Duhm's statement is a clear expression of Romantic poetics. It is interesting to note that his synonym for "inspiration"—"the living force (*Drang*)" behind creative spirits—is one frequently employed in German Romanticism, which had its first blossoming in what was referred to as the *Sturm and Drang* movement. Duhm's is also clearly dependent on Lowth's work. He uses "inspiration" in just the same way. Its opposites are the "study" and "imitation" characteristic of neoclassical literature, and its ally is the "creativity" that would characterize the Romantic literature that looked to Lowth. Most significantly, Duhm, like Lowth, understands "inspiration" as both the defining characteristic of true literature and the defining characteristic of prophecy. Duhm's explanation of the divide between inspired and uninspired writers comes in a passage in which he is distinguishing prophets on the one hand and scribes and Torah teachers on the other.

---

[83] Lowth, *Poetry of the Hebrews*, 244.
[84] Prickett, *Words and the Word*, 105.
[85] Duhm, *Jeremia*, 90.

The difference is between those who look back to previous tradition and those who create something new: those whose achievements come through "study" (either reading and imitating previous writers or acquiring news skills through practice) and those whose creations flow from them naturally. This is how Duhm accounts for the difference between the high-quality literature of the prophet and the low-quality literature of the Torah teachers and Scribes. It is the same way that people in the age of Romanticism explained what differentiated their original works of imagination from the derivative works of those who simply imitated the classics.

The basic difference is "inspiration." Some writers are inspired, but others, lacking inspiration, can only rely on the inspiration of previous writers. Duhm believes he can distinguish between the authentic writings of the prophet and the inauthentic additions of the scribes because prophetic writings display the marks of inspiration and scribal writings betray their lack of inspiration. Of course, the idea that prophets are inspired has a long history. What is noteworthy about Duhm's understanding of prophetic inspiration is that it is almost identical to the way Romantic poetics learned to understand inspiration from Lowth. Duhm's "living force [*Drang*] that impels creative spirits forward" is the same inspiration that characterizes the "*Sturm und Drang*"[86] movement that was the first blossoming of German Romanticism. It is also the same inspiration Lowth describes as "force of composition, whatever it be, which strikes and overpowers the mind, which excites the passions."[87]

Lowth Makes Biblical Poetry Useful in the Wake of the Enlightenment

Prophecy as Poetry and Enlightenment Skepticism

Lowth's fusion of prophetic and poetic inspiration played an important role in the thought of his century and the following centuries. Up to this point, consideration of the significance of Lowth's work has been mainly confined to effects on the realm of literature and the arts. It has been shown how his recovery of prophetic poetry laid the foundation not only for a new kind of poetry but for a new conception of the role of the artist. This contribution to the literary field appears to have been part of Lowth's aim in these lectures delivered in his role as Oxford's praelector of poetry. However, Lowth's reconception of prophecy as inspired poetry soon had effects that went far beyond his original intent. The revolution Lowth started in the realms of biblical studies and literature soon reached the realms of religion, science, philosophy, and history as part of a great shift in the understanding of how the natural relates to the supernatural.

Understanding the significance of Lowth's work for the momentous changes that were taking place in his age begins by considering his cultural context. The early eighteenth century was not only the age of Augustan neoclassicism, it was also the age of Enlightenment. It was the Age of Reason and the Age of Science and Empiricism.

---

[86] Although this title has conventionally been translated "Storm and Stress," "*Drang*" is better translated with a word like "compulsion," "drive," "urge," or "force."

[87] Lowth, *Poetry of the Hebrews*, 189. This is actually Lowth's definition of "sublimity," but "inspiration" and "sublimity" (particularly as a force of composition in the poet) are closely allied as can be seen in his reference to inspiration as "the sublime employment of the sacred Muse," 253.

The rising confidence in human reason and common sense undermined reliance on religious authority and tradition. At the same time, the ability of scientists like Galileo and Newton to explain the entire natural world in terms of simple, universal and unalterable laws of nature led to skepticism about claims of miraculous or supernatural events that would suspend these laws. These factors and others contributed to an erosion of the traditional understanding of the prophetic books. Scientific doubts about the supernatural made it harder to believe that prophets could foretell future events, and the Enlightenment preference for universally held truth made it harder to believe that the architect of the universe had primarily made himself known through the prophets of one particular nation in the ancient Near East. In this context, Lowth's attempts to win an appreciation for the prophetic books as poetry provided an alternative way of understanding their value. The decline of their authority as divine revelation was accompanied by a rise in their value as sublime literature.

Some enlightenment thinkers found in Lowth's presentation of the prophets as poets a plausible account of the prophetic literature that fit with their rationalistic presuppositions by avoiding any reliance on supernatural explanations. If prophetic inspiration was no different in kind than the inspiration claimed by poets, then the phenomenon of prophecy could be reconciled with the world that always operated according to the laws of Newtonian science. A striking example of this use of Lowth's arguments appears in Thomas Paine's deistic pamphlets, published together as *The Age of Reason* in 1794. In a passage arguing against the supernatural origins of the Bible, Paine writes,

> The word *prophet*, to which later times have affixed a new idea, was the Bible word for poet, and the word *prophesying* meant the art of making poetry. It also meant the art of playing poetry to a tune upon any instrument of music …
>
> We are told of Saul being among the prophets, and also that he prophesied; but we are not told what they prophesied, nor what he prophesied. The case is, there was nothing to tell; for these prophets were a company of musicians and poets, and Saul joined in the concert, and this was called prophesying …
>
> The manner in which [the word *prophesy*] is here used strips it of all religious meaning, and shews that a man might then be a prophet, or he might *prophesy*, as he may now be a poet or a musician, without any regard to the morality or the immorality of his character.[88]

Paine does away with the traditional ideas of prophecy as speaking for God or foretelling future events using Lowth's argument that in ancient Israel there was no distinction between a prophet and poet. One indication that this passage is dependent on Lowth (whether directly or indirectly) is his use of the very same examples Lowth used to demonstrate the poetic roots of prophecy. However, whereas Lowth was simply arguing that the prophets could be thought of as poets, Paine takes the idea further and argues that the prophets were strictly poets and no more—with the result that prophecy is "strip[ped] … of all religious meaning."

---

[88] Paine, *The Age of Reason*, Part I, Chapter IV.

Prophetic Poetry as an Antidote to Arid Rationalism

Although Paine's use of Lowth's arguments demonstrates the potential they have for founding a totally secular understanding of prophecy, his work is representative of the effects of Lowth's work only as radical extreme of a general secularizing tendency. Lowth himself, an Anglican bishop, seems to have entertained little doubt about the supernatural aspects of prophecy. He continues to accept that foretelling of future events is the primary definition of prophecy. The difference between Lowth and secularizers like Paine is evident in the very title of his book: *On the Sacred Poetry of the Hebrews*. For Lowth and many after him, prophecy could be simultaneously the result of poetic inspiration and divine revelation.

The religious controversy stirred up by writers like Paine made the skeptical use of Lowth's fusion of poetry and prophecy its most obvious outcome. However, as has been shown in the field of literature, the primary effect of Lowth's work was not to drag Hebrew prophecy down to the level of secular poetry but to raise contemporary poets up to the level of biblical prophets. The possibility that the prophets, considered as inspired poets, could provide a model for contemporary artists was seized on by Romantic poets, but it also offered a way to fill a spiritual void left by the Enlightenment. In the eighteenth century, the ascendency of science and empiricism (and the waning authority of dogma and tradition) resulted in a view of reality in which everything could be explained by rational scientific laws. With this view, the universe could seem to be reduced to a giant machine, one in which humans were merely cogs and God was at most the original designer who had stepped away once he had set the machine in motion. Many people of this age experienced this new universe as flattened and stripped of significance. They yearned for the transcendence and meaning that traditional religion had offered, but they found themselves unable to return to a system they believed reason and science had shown to be naïve and superstitious. They needed an alternative to traditional religion that could withstand the critique of science. Many found that this need could be met by some form of the expressivist theory of artistic creation foundational to Romantic literary theory, a theory that drew heavily on Lowth's recovery of biblical prophecy as poetry and his fusion of prophetic and poetic inspiration.

William Blake provides an early example of the way the expressivist theory of artistic creation could provide a viable alternative to the loss of religious transcendence in the Enlightenment age. A portion of his 1788 work, "There Is No Natural Religion," lays out the problem and solution in a series of aphorisms.

> The Desires and Perceptions of Man, untaught by anything but Organs of Sense, must be limited to Objects of Sense.
>
> If it were not for the Poetic or Prophetic Character, the Philosophic and Experimental would soon be at the Ratio of all things; and stand still, unable to do other than repeat the same dull round over again. ... The same dull round, even of a Universe, would soon become a Mill with complicated wheels.[89]

---

[89] Blake, "There Is No Natural Religion" (1788) in Blake, *Poetry and Designs*, 6–7.

The dull mechanical universe, explains Blake, is the result of relying solely on the empirical ("experimental") data of the senses and rational ("Philosophic") analyses. But there is another source of knowledge, "the Prophetic or Poetic." Blake's approach concedes that empirical scientific approach can offer a comprehensive explanation of the whole universe; the problem with the explanation is not that it is false, but that it is dull. The alternative he proposes posits that there is another way that humans relate to the natural world: not through the senses and reason but through the creative powers that find expression in poetry and art. The empirical scientist passively observes nature, but the inspired prophet/poet invests nature with significance, beauty, and sublimity. The apposition of poet and prophet in Blake's aphorism was made possible by Lowth; but whereas Lowth (and Romantic literary critics) primarily used the prophetic poet as a counter to the neoclassical poet, here it is set in opposition to the rationalistic philosopher and the empirical scientist.

Blake is typical of many Romantic artists who followed him in offering poetic expression as a necessary complement to Enlightenment rationalism and empiricism. The expressivist poetics of the "lamp" that characterized Romanticism could be considered as an answer to the mimetic poetics of the "mirror" of neoclassicism. But this feature of Romanticism could function as counter to Enlightenment thought as well: it urged that human mind could do more than coldly reflect nature; it could shine light and warmth on its surroundings. This way of criticizing Enlightenment rationalism and empiricism by emphasizing the active powers of the mind was not limited to Romantic poets but widespread among the late eighteenth- and early nineteenth-century thinkers. A key figure in the move beyond empiricism was Kant, who offered a philosophical account of the limitations of the world that could be known by the senses (the "phenomenal" world) and the powers of the human mind to create rational order and moral and aesthetic value. However, his philosophic work is just one part of a much larger movement to counter (or complement) the Enlightenment emphasis on external and objective knowledge with an appeal to the significance that could only come from an internal subjective source. The passage from Blake shows how what was felt to be lacking in the intellectual systems of the scientist or philosopher could be supplied by the character of the prophet or poet.[90] The poetic prophet, or the prophetic poet, that Blake believes reanimates the dull Enlightenment universe is drawn from the prophetic books of the Bible presented as poetry by Lowth.

Lowth's poetic prophet provided Blake's age with a model for what M. H. Abrams (borrowing a phrase from Carlyle) terms "natural supernaturalism." Lowth's account of the poetry of the prophets allowed for a poetry that was "supernatural" in the sense that it could invest the world with the wonder and transcendent significance that were

---

[90] "Since about 1800, there has been a tendency to heroize the artist" in other words, "the artist becomes in some way the paradigm case of the human being" and this rise of the artist has been accompanied by a new understanding of art: "No longer defined mainly by imitation, by *mimēsis* of reality, art is understood now more in terms of creation." (Charles Taylor, *The Ethics of Authenticity*, [Cambridge, MA: Harvard University Press, 1991], 62). Taylor refers to this as the rise of "expressivism" (*Authenticity*, 61) and although he does not indicate its roots in Lowth's work on the biblical prophet, he does single out Herder as one of the main author responsible for this rise. The next chapter will discuss the central place of Herder in transmitting Lowth's ideas to (German) Romanticism, historicism, and higher critical approaches to the Bible.

formally found in supernatural religion. This is the significance of the transformation of the "sublime" in Lowth's work: it kept alive the possibility of experiences that transcend the world of material causation, the experiences of the sublime. The experience of nature charged with beauty and meaning was not limited to poets but lay behind all true artistic expression. Even more broadly, the ability of humans to experience beauty and meaning in the world could be attributed to powers of the creative mind or human imagination analogous to prophetic inspiration.

At the same time, Lowth's account of the poetry in the prophetic books allowed an explanation of prophecy that could be understood as "natural" in the sense that it did not require an explanation that involved a suspension of the laws of nature as understood by the science of the day. This is the significance of Lowth's reinterpretation of "inspiration" as it relates to the prophets. It provided an explanation of prophecy (and by extension, all religious experience and all the religious literature that flowed from it) that could be understood in a way analogous to the "muse's" inspiration of poets from the classical period or even from the present. More broadly, prophetic inspiration could be understood in the terms of natural and universal human psychology, the experience of powerful passions. Lowth's "natural" explanation of prophetic inspiration protected the prophetic books from the attacks of Enlightenment skepticism and made them valuable not only as sublime poetry but also as the very models of the way that the spirit of human artists can reinvest the natural world with beauty and significance.

Duhm's Hero of the Imagination

It has already been shown that Duhm not only understood Jeremiah as an inspired Romantic poet but that he found him the most fitting representative of the prophetic poet among all the Hebrew prophets. Duhm's Jeremiah is the "born poet" whose poetry is primarily distinguished by its "masterful expression" of the feelings of "the individual self." He is the "creative spirit" whose work represents the "inspiration" that is always opposed by the uninspired who are forced to rely on "study." Although Duhm's contrast between "inspiration" and "study" is more closely parallel to the contrast between the creativity of Romanticism and the imitation of Classicism than to the contrast between artistic expression and scientific empiricism, his appreciation of the prophet is primarily for his expression of his own subjectivity. Duhm writes, "We must be thankful that Jeremiah allows us to look so deeply into his inner life—as no other Old Testament writer. He is the most subjective of all the prophets."[91]

To achieve this presentation of the prophet as the self-expressive poet, Duhm must overturn the traditional understanding of the prophet as the messenger of God. However, Duhm recognizes that the tradition he is opposing is not simply a misinterpretation of the book that arose sometime in the two and half millennia since the book was composed; it is a view of the prophet that appears in over half of the book. This is what makes his compositional theory necessary. He must deny the authenticity of the prose speeches Jeremiah speaks in the book not only to bring Jeremiah into conformity with the view (held by Paine, for instance) that a prophet is a poet and

---

[91] Duhm, *Jeremia*, 168.

no more, but because it is difficult to read them as self-expression. Most of them take the form of first-person speeches of Yahweh delivered by Jeremiah in the role of a messenger. Duhm finds the book's presentation of Jeremiah as a divine messenger repugnant. He derides it saying that the picture of Jeremiah as "an automaton, a personified vehicle of divine messages" is one that the "Jews made for themselves."[92] It is only by means of his compositional theory that the prose speeches are inauthentic that Duhm believes he can finally "understand Jeremiah as a man, a writer, and a prophet,"[93] in other words, as a self-expressive poet.

Duhm's way of using the book of Jeremiah as evidence that the historical prophet fits the model of the poetic prophet from the eighteenth and nineteenth centuries might raise the question of why he stopped where he did in his compositional theory. After all, it is not only the prose speeches that take the form of first-person speeches of Yahweh; this is true of the majority of the poetic speeches as well. It would seem more consistent to limit the authentic speeches of Jeremiah exclusively to those passages in which the prophet is the first-person speaker (e.g., the "confessions" in chs 11–20). The basic reason that Duhm includes the poetic speeches of Yahweh as authentic works of the prophet is that, following Lowth, he believed that poetry is inherently prophetic, and he was able to find ways to read Yahweh's poetic speeches as instances of the prophet's inspired self-expression. Thus, for example, Yahweh's warnings to his people of the severity of the coming judgment are celebrated by Duhm for their sublimity and treated as marks of Jeremiah's growth as poet. Yahweh's speeches raging at his people's unfaithfulness are taken as evidence of the moral sensitivity of Jeremiah. Yahweh's speeches comforting his people with promises of future deliverance are treated as indications that Jeremiah was filled with hopeful idealism at some point in his youth. Duhm's translation of Yahweh's messages into aspects of the prophet's literary sensibility and psychology is not original with him but represents a way of interpreting the poetry in the prophetic books that stretches back to Lowth. The poetry is understood as the sublime expression of the passionate interior experiences of the prophet—whether he speaks as himself (or about himself) or not. The effort to secure for Jeremiah a body of literary work worthy of a Romantic poet requires not only the denial of the authenticity of the prose but also a novel way of reading the poetry.

The Effects of Lowth for Reading Biblical Poetry

This review of the origins of Duhm's literary sensibility allows a fresh evaluation of his approach to the book of Jeremiah. Although it is his denial of the authenticity of the prose that has attracted the most attention, it can now be seen that the foundation of his approach is a particular way of understanding the poetry—a Romantic poetics that has its roots in Lowth's work on Hebrew poetry. Having considered the roots of Duhm's work, the remainder of this chapter will consider its fruits for reading the book of Jeremiah. The evaluation can begin by considering the effects of Duhm's work

---

[92] Duhm, *Jeremia*, xviii.
[93] Duhm, *Jeremia*, vii.

for reading the poetry, move on to considering its effects for reading the prose, and conclude by briefly considering the effects for reading the book as a whole.

As regards the effects of Duhm's approach to the poetry, it has been shown here that his understanding of the poetry is almost indistinguishable from the understanding Lowth forged over a century earlier. Thus the effects of Duhm's understanding of the poetry of Jeremiah can be evaluated by evaluating the effects of Lowth's understanding of prophetic poetry in general.

Prophetic Poetry Becomes Literature

The first aspect of Lowth's understanding of prophetic poetry to be considered is the foundational one: the primary achievement of Lowth's work was to move the poetic parts of the prophetic books into the realm of literature and establish them there as the model of literary greatness. Before considering the effects this had for interpreting the biblical prophets, it is worth pausing to consider the effects on the realm of literature (and the broader realms of art and culture). The effects are inestimable. Lowth's idea that art should be an authentic expression of the experiences of the artist permeates modern thinking in many realms. Its effects on literature can hardly be limited to the work of Romantic poets and artists. The idea that art should be original and creative—an expression of the individual vision of the artist—is foundational for much of the art from Lowth's time until today: from paintings to novels to popular music; from Beethoven to the Beatles. Lowth's work is a mainspring of the modern expectation that artistic expression should be sincere, heartfelt, and rooted in the experiences of the artist. That Lowth drew this vision of artistic expression from the prophetic literature and set up the prophets as its primary models has created the (largely salutary) expectation that artists, like prophets, should be speaking the uncomfortable truth, confronting the powerful, exploring the realm of the spirit, and advancing the cause of social justice.

When evaluating the effects on interpretation of the biblical prophets that followed from considering them as literature, it must first be recognized that this move was accompanied by remarkable gains. Lowth's work on biblical poetry was central to a revolution in biblical studies that brought greater understanding and knowledge of the biblical text than had been seen in centuries. The basic idea that, whatever their ultimate source, these books are written by humans for humans in human language has allowed readers and interpreters to use the tools used for understanding other kinds of literature and human speech to understand the prophets. They can examine them for figurative speech, hyperbole, rhetorical ploys, and so on. They also recognize that these books are historically situated. The aims and ideas of the books arose from the events of the time when they were composed and were intended to communicate to people of their day.

Despite these undeniable gains, readers may still find some of the implications considering prophetic books as literature problematic. Some readers may have concerns about this characterization of the prophetic books because of religious beliefs. These are not new concerns. The resistance to the including parts of the Bible among the classics of literature is (at least in part) what led some early Jewish and Christian writers (like Jerome, as seen above) to reject the idea that the prophetic books are poetic.[94] They objected to ranking Isaiah, Jeremiah, and Ezekiel with Homer, Simonides, and Æschylus, as Lowth did.[95] Whether this was because their high regard for classical authors made them anxious about the ability of the biblical authors to measure up by literary standards or whether their low regard for "pagan" authors made them anxious that the biblical authors would be degraded by the association, they wanted to preserve a distinction between biblical literature and secular literature. They resisted the desacralization, or secularization of the books of Scripture.

The nature of the religious concerns raised by Lowth's new vision of the prophetic writings becomes clearer when it is recognized that it is based on a religious claim. Lowth was not content simply to point out similarities between secular poetry and the poetry of the prophets (parallelism, figures of speech, etc.); he grounded his attempt to win appreciation for prophetic poetry in a claim about the origin—and thus the nature—of prophecy. As has been seen, Lowth's foundational argument for the poetic nature of the prophetic literature was a novel theory of its inspiration. He argued that prophecy could be identified with poetry because they share "one common name, one common origin, one common author, the Holy Spirit."[96] Lowth's statement is not simply a theory of the source of poetry; it is at the same time an explanation of prophetic inspiration. He is making the claim about the inspiration of the prophetic books in the scriptures. The claim on which Lowth rests his explanation of prophetic poetry is not merely about the inspiration of Scripture; it is about the Holy Spirit—that is, about God.[97] Lowth is arguing that poetry and prophecy are both rooted in ecstatic experience, which is ultimately caused by God.

Not only is Lowth's understanding of prophetic poetry grounded in what is essentially a religious claim, this claim has significant religious implications. Although Lowth may have focused on the literary implications of his claim, the religious implications were not lost on his readers, readers like Blake and Paine. On the one hand, this identification suggests that the authority of the biblical prophets was not unique but one that they held in common with poets, or inspired individuals (whether creative artists, intellectual geniuses, or visionary leaders), from every time, place, culture, or religion. On the other hand, it suggested that the authority or worth of the various parts of the Bible could be measured by the characteristics used to evaluate the "inspiration" of secular poetry: intensity of passions, fittingness of speech and imagery, originality of thought, power of persuasion, imagination.

---

[94] Kugel writes, "Certain elements of the Early Church maintained a hostile attitude toward 'pagan' … literature, and were consequently reluctant to speak of Moses and David as 'Poets'" (Kugel, *Idea of Poetry*, 142). Others of the church fathers (e.g., Athenagoras and Origen) had a greater appreciation of the classical literature, and this produces a "clash … with the exclusive nature of Divine inspiration as presented in the Bible and Christian Doctrine. For Origen, especially, it was a difficult problem" (Kugel, *Idea of Poetry*, 146).

[95] Lowth, *Poetry of the Hebrews*, 294.

[96] Lowth, *Poetry of the Hebrews*, 248.

[97] The term "Holy Spirit" is only used three times in the Hebrew Bible (Ps. 51:11, Isa. 63:10-11)—not in the passages Lowth employs to make his argument about prophetic inspiration and, in fact, never in reference to poetry or prophecy. It is primarily a Christian term (occurring over ninety times in the New Testament). In Christian theology, the term refers to the third person of the Trinity, who is God.

Lowth's understanding of prophetic inspiration stands in tension with traditional Christian and Jewish belief. In the traditional view, prophecy is essentially the communication of a personal God to humans through the agency of a human chosen by God for that task; thus, it cannot be defined as the exalted expressions of an extraordinary human under the influence of powerful emotions. The traditional description of the prophets and prophetic books as "inspired," or "God-breathed,"[98] has this same basic meaning: it designates the divine origin of their words—they came from God; thus inspiration cannot primarily refer to a particular kind of human experience or to the literary quality of the resulting words. Lowth's redefinition of inspiration in terms of the ecstatic experience and the resulting literature can be taken in two main ways either of which is out of keeping with traditional Christian doctrine: either it invests all literary works that display the marks of inspiration with a degree of divine authority or, as Paine concluded, it "strips [the prophetic literature in the Bible] of all religious meaning." For this reason, to evaluate Lowth's understanding of prophetic poetry—or theories founded on Lowth's understanding, like Duhm's—necessarily involves consideration of religious questions.

Although the way Lowth attempted to win recognition for poetry of the prophetic books as great literature raises questions that go far beyond the realm of literary theory, their approach raises literary questions as well. The basic question is to what extent prophetic poetry belongs in the category of classic literature. It can be asked how similar it is to other texts in that category in nature, content, aims, and appropriate use. To read any text well, the reader must form a good idea of what the text is and what it is intended to do. Much of what was considered classic literature before Lowth is characterized by the aim to entertain or delight (*delectare*). It could be asked of the poetry in the prophetic books, whether it shares that aim. The book of Ezekiel describes hearers who fundamentally misunderstood the purpose of the prophet's poetry because they went to hear the prophet like those who go to hear one who "sings lovely songs with a beautiful voice and plays an instrument well" (33:32). It seems unlikely that the poetry in the book of Jeremiah aims to entertain when it is self-described as a "fire" that burns and a "hammer that breaks into pieces" (23:29). Of course, as has been shown, Lowth recognized that the inclusion of the prophets as great literature would alter the conceptions of literary greatness and make room for a new kind of literature. He ushered the prophetic books into the category of literature as a specific kind of literature that came to be identified as Romantic. That recognition only focuses the question: it is not simply a question of whether the prophetic books belong in the broad category of literature, but whether they should be read as Romantic literature.

Prophetic Poetry Becomes Romantic Poetry

What it means for prophetic poetry to be read as Romantic literature can be investigated by considering the circumstances of the modern "discovery" of poetry in the prophetic books by Lowth. Although the reality of what Lowth discovered (or

---

[98] Cf. 2 Pet. 1:21 and 2 Tim. 3:16.

recovered) can be wholly affirmed (poetic form is an objective feature of the text), it must be recognized that the significance given to any discovery is determined to a large extent by the situation of the discovery, or more particularly, the identity of the discoverers and what they were looking for. The significance of the discovery in 1945 of a means to unleash immense power from an atom was shaped by the fact that the discoverers were working for the American military in the midst of a great world war. The significance of the European "discovery" of the Americas beginning in the fifteenth century was shaped by the fact that the explorers and their patrons were looking for a trade route to the Indies. This explains, among other things, how the native population of the Americas came to be called "Indians." In the case of the discovery of poetry in the prophetic books, it is highly significant that the discoverer was looking for an alternative to neoclassical formalism in literature and literary theory and became one of the founders of the Romantic revolution. What Lowth was believed to have discovered in the prophetic books was not just poetry, it was what came to be known as Romantic poetry.

The legacy of Lowth is that the poetry in the prophetic books has continued to be read as Romantic poetry. Understanding prophetic poetry as Romantic poetry has shaped the preconceptions of readers and interpreters coming to the prophetic books. They expect the poetry to be original, free, spontaneous, sincere, sublime, and passionate. This understanding has also provided a standard account of the composition of the prophetic poetry. The poetry was composed under the influence of inspiration, and inspiration is understood to be an overwhelming, passionate, interior experience that overflows into poetic expression. These experiences came in response to events in the life of the prophet, the natural responses of a finely tuned poetic sensibility. This explanation, in turn, determined why the poetry was to be valued and how it was to be used. It was valued as an expression of the experience of the prophet. It allowed access to his interior experiences, and could allow the sympathetic reader to have a similar experience. The reader was to trace the flow of the poetry from the written poem back to its source in the interior life of the poet.

The Romantic understanding of poetry provides a plausible and often compelling account of much of the poetry in the prophetic books. This is hardly surprising since, as has been demonstrated, mainly due to Lowth's work, the poetry in the prophetic books was both a foundation and an inspiration for Romantic poetry. The poetry of the prophetic books will obviously have more in common with Romantic poetry, which looks to them as models, than neoclassical poetry, which looks to Greek and Roman poetry as models. However, the similarities are only partial mainly because Romantic poetry, which grew to prominence in the eighteenth and nineteenth centuries AD (not the ninth and eight centuries BC), was also heavily shaped by forces and ideas from that period. In particular, as has been shown, it was heavily influenced by the need for an alternative, first, to neoclassical formalism and, later, to enlightenment rationalism and empiricism. Among many other shaping influences, a prominent one is the particular aims and concerns of the individual Romantic poets. The danger is that because of these contemporary aims and concerns, contemporary needs and preconceptions would exert undue influence on interpreters trying to discern the nature of the ancient prophetic poetry.

Other Possible Explanations of Prophetic Poetry Prevented

A particularly problematic effect of considering the poetry in the prophetic books as Romantic poetry is that it comes with a particular theory of the origin and nature of poetry that keeps readers and interpreters from considering alternative accounts of the presence of poetic features. One can consider the possibility of an alternative understanding of prophetic poetry by imagining a different account of a person discovering poetry. The person is taking a walk when she discovers a piece of paper (or perhaps, a piece of an ancient scroll) with writing on it. On examination, she determines that the writing is poetry. Her determination is likely to be based on finding instances of formal patterning (significant repetitions like semantic or verbal parallelism, rhyme, alliteration, elements of similar length, and rhythm), as well as other features such as unusually high incidence of nontypical diction and syntax or figurative language. Having determined she has found poetry, the discoverer makes a few basic inferences. First, she deems it likely that the reason the writing has the features that led her to determine it was poetry is that the writer intended to have those features. The writer intentionally shaped the writing (or the speech that the writing records) to have features that distinguish it from what could be called naturally occurring speech: for example, the speech in everyday conversations. Second, she assumes the writer gave it these features in conformity with conventions of the kind of speech or writing that is set off from naturally occurring speech by these conventions. These conventions not only serve to distinguish this kind of writing but are also designed to have certain effects on readers: for example, to make the writing aesthetically pleasing, or memorable, or emotionally moving. Third, she assumes the speech in the writing is not related to naturally occurring speech as a record but as a representation. Similarities between the writing and naturally occurring speech (e.g., the use of first- and second-person pronouns) are due to the writer's intention to create speech that resembles, or portrays, natural speech.

The assumptions of this nameless discoverer of poetry could be said to be "common"—with either the meaning "universal" or "commonsensical." The idea that poetry is the result of intentional craft is reflected in the etymology of "poet" and "poem," which ultimately derive from the Greek ποιητής (a maker) and πόημα (something made). The idea that poetic language has its own distinctive conventions is borne out by the existence of large bodies of similar speeches in most languages that have features common to each other but not to naturally occurring speech. The idea that poetic speech imitates or represents naturally occurring speech is reflected in the often-recurring judgment that poetry is a mimetic art, like sculpture or painting.[99] It is also the reason that (until the last few centuries) poetic form was considered to be the natural form for dramatic and fictional narrative works.

The peculiarity of Lowth's understanding of the poetry in the prophetic books can now be more fully grasped: the person who discovered this particular poetry did not make any of the inferences one would commonly make on having discovered poetry. Lowth did not acknowledge that the poetic features of the poetry in the prophets were

---

[99]   Aristotle, *Rhetoric*, 1355b26-35; *Poetics*, 1448b3-24.

the result of intentional poetic craft. Instead, he developed the theory that they were the involuntary products of powerful emotional experiences. The "style and expression" of poetry is "directly prompted by nature itself." They exhibit "the true and express image of a mind violently agitated."[100] Lowth did not understand features like rhythm, repetition, figurative language, and altered syntax as conventions of a particular type of speech that authors of the prophetic books intentionally adopted. In place of the idea that authors were attempting to write in conformity with the conventions of certain modes of speech (i.e., that poetry comes from someone attempting to produce poetry), Lowth offers an alternative explanation: that these features were compelled by the power of the experience. The prophets under the influence of violent passions naturally spoke "the language of passion"; "the passions [speak] poetically"; "they catch (without search or study) whatever is impetuous, vivid, or energetic."[101] The common linguistic features of the Hebrew poetry are not due to common conventions but common experiences. Finally, Lowth does not understand the poetry of the prophets to be fictive speech (speech crafted to dramatically portray naturally occurring speech). Instead, he depicts the poetry of the prophets as naturally occurring effusions that give direct expression to the emotions of the author. "Hebrew poetry," he writes, "instead of disguising the secret feelings of the author ... lays them quite open to public view."[102] In short, Lowth understands the poetry he finds in the prophets not as artistically crafted speech but naturally occurring speech.

His novel theory of inspiration and his theory that the writing prophets derive from musical ecstatics are the foundation of this understanding. These were shown to be possible but not necessary or even likely.

The study of Lowth's work on Hebrew poetry has indicated the main motivations for Lowth's peculiar theory of poetic composition. The basic reason is that he was offering an alternative to neoclassic poetry and poetic theory, which placed a strong emphasis on poetic craft and adherence to poetic convention. In his narrow task of winning a hearing for biblical poetry, Lowth had to create alternative standards and expectations for poetry because it seemed apparent that biblical poetry could not measure up to the standards of neoclassical artistry and it obviously did not meet the expectations formed by classical conventions (of meter, rhyme, figures of speech, etc.). In his larger task of providing an alternative to contemporary poetry of his day, Lowth called for a new kind of poetry that was spontaneous rather than intentionally produced, natural rather than artificial, original rather than conventional, and sincere rather than calculated.

The upshot of Lowth's work and its blossoming in the Romantic revolution is that now there are two main understandings of poetry. C. S. Lewis illustrates the transition by citing the definition of "poet" in Samuel Johnson's dictionary (published in 1755, the same decade as Lowth's lectures on Hebrew poetry) and a modern dictionary. In Johnson's dictionary, "poet" is simply defined as "an inventor; an author of fiction; a writer of poems; one who writes in measure." Lewis comments that before this time "fiction and metre were the chief *differentiae* of the 'poet'." Turning to a

---

[100] Lowth, *Poetry of the Hebrews*, 52.
[101] Lowth, *Poetry of the Hebrews*, 190.
[102] Lowth, *Poetry of the Hebrews*, 192.

mid-twentieth-century dictionary, Lewis observes its definition of "poet" begins with a definition like Johnson's but feels obliged to add as a second definition the following: "a writer in verse (or sometimes elevated prose) distinguished by imaginative power, insight, sensibility, and faculty of expression."[103] In the second dictionary, the older understanding of a poet and the one introduced by Lowth and the Romantics stand side by side. Poetry can either be thought of as a result of an author's intention to create fictive speech distinguished from naturally occurring speech by giving the work meter (or other formal features of poetry) or a naturally occurring expression of the inner experience of a person with poetic insight and sensibility.

Although the result of Lowth's work for poetry in general has been to give writers and readers of poetry another option for understanding poetry, the result for biblical poetry has been to limit interpretation to his novel understanding. Because biblical poetry (and prophetic poetry in particular) was the material out of which the Romantic understanding was created and it continued to serve as a primary model for Romantic poetry, the older, more universal explanations of why people compose poetry have seldom been considered in relation to the poetry in the prophetic books. This is especially true within the realm of biblical studies. As will be shown in the following chapters, the Romantic theory that poetry is the natural result of inspiration in the soul of a person of powerful insight and refined sensibility was foundational for much of the interpretive framework built in the nineteenth century. In the twentieth century, the relative isolation of biblical studies from the broader realm of literary studies (until its last decades) had the result that the Romantic understanding of the nature of poetry remained entrenched even when it faced significant challenges in literary scholarship.

Evaluation of Duhm's Understanding of Poetry and Prose in Jeremiah

Duhm's Understanding of the Poetry in Jeremiah

With this evaluation of Lowth's approach to prophetic poetry in general in mind, the reader of Jeremiah is now in a better position to evaluate Duhm's approach to the poetry in the book of Jeremiah. The historical survey above has shown how fully Duhm's work on Jeremiah's poetry is an extension, or a kind of culmination of Lowth's work. Now Duhm's work can be evaluated by considering the way he develops the three aspects of Lowth's work on poetry just discussed: Duhm's treatment of Jeremiah's poetry as great literature, his adherence to Romantic poetics, and his neglect of other ways of understanding poetry.

In regard to Lowth's efforts to move prophetic poetry into the realm of literature, Duhm's work on Jeremiah represents a kind of absolute limit to this campaign. Duhm's efforts to win recognition for Jeremiah as one of the "heroes of world literature" (*Heroen der Weltliteratur*)[104] primarily take the form of isolating a set of texts from

---

[103] C. S. Lewis, *Studies in Words*, 2nd ed. (New York: Cambridge University Press, 1967), 95.
[104] Duhm, *Jeremia*, 47.

the book that can be read as great literature. His denial of the authenticity to any text that does not measure up to his standards of literary worth allows him to preserve this body of literature from the taint of poor-quality work. Although Duhm does allow for variance in the quality of the work he finds authentic, he excuses the work of lesser quality or originality as the work of Jeremiah's youth or work hindered by his tragic career.[105] In fact, as the next chapter will show, Duhm creates an entire biography for Jeremiah that takes the form of the literary education of a poet. In short, Duhm's efforts to bring Jeremiah's literary output into conformity with Lowth's vision involve rejecting over half of the book of Jeremiah as spurious and creating a biography largely unknown to the book. This kind of radical reconfiguration of a work to make it fit a preconceived mold will appear a dubious interpretive approach to many readers. The roots of Duhm's approach in the work of Lowth does offer one consideration that could mitigate this critique. In Duhm's defense, it can be noted that the literary ideal he is trying to make the text fit is not extrinsic to the text. It was actually derived from Lowth's interpretation of the poetry in the prophetic books including Jeremiah. Even so, Duhm's work on Jeremiah can at best be characterized as an attempt to bring the entire book into conformity with a vision of literary excellence drawn from a particular interpretation of one part of the book. This attempt is not to be necessary to win recognition of the existence of poetry in the book or of the literary excellence of the poetry. What makes it necessary is a particular view of the relationship between prophecy and poetry.

The relationship between poetry and prophecy that provides the foundation of Duhm's approach can be identified as Lowth's fusion of poetic and prophetic inspiration. However, whereas Lowth used this theory to argue for the presence of poetry in the writings of Jeremiah, Duhm uses it to deny the prophetic authenticity of anything not in poetic form. Since there is nothing in the book that relates poetry and prophecy or that pictures poetry or prophecy as the result of inspiration (i.e., from the spirit), the reader's judgment of the validity of Duhm's method will be largely determined by whether she accepts or rejects Duhm's radical version of Lowth's belief on other grounds.

As was observed in relation to Lowth, this question of the nature of prophetic inspiration has a religious dimension both because Lowth's theory concerns the relationship between God and humans and because his theory is in tension with traditional Christian and Jewish belief.

Lowth, an Anglican bishop, may have been unaware of the tension between his theory of inspiration and the traditional understanding of prophetic inspiration, but Duhm actively opposes the traditional belief. It is the picture of prophecy he believes to be responsible for the portrayal of Jeremiah in prose additions, a portrait of the prophet he derides as "an automaton, a personified vehicle of divine messages" that the "Jews made for themselves."[106] The traditional view of Jews and Christians is considered by its adherents to be grounded in their scriptures, including the book of Jeremiah (as a whole). Duhm also believes his view to be grounded in the biblical books, but only the parts he believes to be authentic,

---

[105] Duhm, *Jeremia*, 47.
[106] Duhm, *Jeremia*, xviii.

or inspired. His compositional model of Jeremiah can be understood as part of a radical reshaping of Jewish and Christian scripture to create a new scripture that fits with his alternative religious beliefs:[107] a new way of understanding the way the divine relates to the human.[108]

Recognition of the religious nature of Duhm's explanation will help the reader of Jeremiah determine what is entailed in evaluating the truth of Duhm's theory. The reader is being asked to judge between the competing claims of (at least) two religious viewpoints, or, to put it another way, two views of the relationship between God and humanity. The nature of the disagreement between Duhm and his opponents means that at a fundamental level the question to be answered is, To what extent is prophetic inspiration to be identified with poetic inspiration? Or, more basically, Are the poetic parts of the Hebrew prophets inspired in such a way that they should be ranked among the great achievements of the human spirit? Or, Is the Spirit of Yahweh the same as the muse of poetry?

The questions raised by Duhm's interpretation of the poetry of Jeremiah according to Lowth's theory of inspiration are not only theological but also literary. One reason for this is that Lowth's theory is closely related to one particular school of literary interpretation: Romanticism, with its understanding of art as the expression of emotion. Duhm's approach to Jeremiah's poetry has been identified as Romantic, and now the effects of his Romantic perspective can be considered and evaluated. The basic effect is that Duhm primarily values the poetry for what it reveals about the interior experiences of the prophet. He understands these experiences as emotional reactions of the poetic soul of the prophet to various events in his life. Thus, the most important elements of interpreting each poetic passage are determining its biographical setting and explaining what it was about circumstances and the soul of Jeremiah that caused him to have the particular reaction expressed in the poetry. This understanding of interpretation in turn makes historical or biographical reconstruction essential to interpreting Jeremiah. This is why Duhm's commentary includes in its introduction a recreation of the life of Jeremiah with every poetic passage (all the material in the book he considers authentic) assigned to a specific time in the biography. One result of this biographical or historical approach based on the Romantic interpretation of the poetry is that it prevents Duhm from considering whether the elements in the poetry he treats as accidental evidence that betray the situations that sparked the composition could be intentional elements that the poet chose to portray a situation.

Duhm's inability to consider alternatives to his biographical method is just one example of the way his Romantic poetics prevent him from considering other possible

---

[107] As with Duhm's aesthetic theory, his theological perspective is not primarily his unique personal system but rather is mostly in keeping with what can be described as (German) Protestant Liberalism, which was prevalent among intellectuals in his day. This will be discussed more fully in Chapter 4.

[108] In his reconstruction of Scripture, Duhm bears comparison to Marcion (*c.* AD 86–160), who likewise created his own alternative scriptures by paring away writings accepted as authoritative by the mainstream of Christian tradition that he found out of keeping with his alternative version of Christian belief. An interesting point of comparison is that what both found objectionable in the traditionally accepted scriptures were the Jewish elements, particularly those that enjoined obedience to the revealed law and portrayed God as punishing disobedience.

significances of the poetic form. The Romantic explanation of poetic form derived from Lowth (that it is a function of the intensity of the author's emotional experience) kept Duhm and interpreters who followed him from considering the possibility that the poetic form is due to an author's intention to write poetry. The conception of Jeremiah's poetry as the sublime effusions of the prophet under the influence of his powerful emotions stands in the way of considering whether the author of the poetry was expressing his own emotions or portraying expressions of emotion (whether Jeremiah's emotions or those of one of the other speakers like Yahweh or Lady Jerusalem). It causes Duhm and those who follow him to ignore the possibility that the poetic form is intended to be an indicator that the speech is not naturally occurring but artistically crafted to represent speech. This keeps them from considering what could be intentional characterization of the speakers. It keeps them from considering whether the successive speeches were created to evoke dialogues, or dramatic scenes, or changes of emotion or character development over time. The idea that there may be temporal progression in the speeches, that they could work together to present a story, is not considered because the speeches are read as a collection of records of speeches that poured out of the prophet on various historical occasions.

The Romantic idea of poetry as spontaneous effusions helps explain why Duhm treats Jeremiah's poetry as individual short units. He regards the poetry as hundreds of individual short poems mostly one to three verses long. This keeps him and the interpreters who follow his approach from looking for the kind of artistic formal patterning characteristic of poetry. It also keeps them from considering the possibility that the extended sections of the poetry were crafted in such a way that all the parts work together to create an effect. The idea that the poetry was crafted to have an effect (or evoke a response) from the audience is also kept off limits because it does not fit the expectation that the poetry should be artlessly sincere. These are all effects of the tight connection between the poetry of the prophets and Romantic literary theory. It was reinforced and made the standard approach to Jeremiah's poetry by Duhm's work. Although it has continued to dominate scholarly approaches to the book, alternative approaches began to appear in the last decades of the twentieth century. There has been a greater openness to considering alternative accounts of the poetry. Particularly in those scholars approaching the book of Jeremiah from the standpoint of "rhetorical criticism," there was a fresh willingness to reexamine the significance of the poetic form. The work of these scholars—both the promising fruits of their work and the limited degree that they were willing to break from Lowth's understanding of prophetic poetry—will be explored in the final chapters of this work.

Duhm's Understanding of the Prose of Jeremiah

Evaluation from the History of Criticism

Duhm Completes a Trajectory That Begins with Lowth

Duhm's Romantic understanding of the poetry in Jeremiah, which provides the foundation of his 1903 commentary, was not particularly novel at the beginning of the twentieth century and could be found in many interpretations of Jeremiah between Lowth's work and his own. In the eighteenth century, when Lowth first enunciated his views of poetry and prophecy, it represented a major break from contemporary thought. However, his ideas had great influence in his own century and were widespread in Europe in the nineteenth century. This was particularly true in the realm of literature and literary theory, so much so that Romanticism can be called the dominant school of literary thought in Europe for most of the century. In the realm of biblical studies, Lowth's understanding of prophetic inspiration was especially influential among German biblical scholars. Aspects of the influence of Lowth's theory in the historical development of biblical scholarship in Germany will be considered in the next chapter. Here it is sufficient to note that at the turn of the twentieth century, Duhm's understanding of the qualities of good literature and (to some extent) the characteristics of true prophecy were widely accepted.

Although Lowth's theory of prophetic poetry is foundational for Duhm's commentary on Jeremiah, what made his work novel—the aspect of his work that distinguished it from all previous interpretation of the book—was his theory about the prose. No one had argued for Duhm's audacious theory that among the speeches the book attributes to the prophet, all of those written in prose (roughly two-thirds of the speeches) were not authentic but were composed by later editors who employed the prophetic persona to speak their ideas. In his foreword, Duhm draws attention to the novelty of his theory: "I have never seen it before, not even a tendency toward it."[109]

Although it is quite likely that no one had proposed limiting the authentic words of Jeremiah to the poetry in the book before Duhm, it is not true that there had been no tendency toward his theory. In fact, the use of literary quality to judge whether or not passages were written by a prophet stretches back to the work of Lowth. The idea that poetry is more authentically prophetic than prose is a natural conclusion of his fusion of poetry and prophecy. Lowth had achieved his aim by transforming not only the idea of poetry but also the ideas of inspiration and prophecy. Inspiration according to Lowth could be ascertained by literary qualities. Truly inspired writing would naturally be sincere, passionate, and sublime and, as a result, would move the emotions of the reader. Inspired writing will be inspiring. The corollary is that if writing lacks these qualities and fails to move the reader, then it cannot be inspired. If the prose of Jeremiah fails to inspire the readers or lacks the qualities of Romantic poetry, it can be judged to be uninspired, and the question is raised whether an inspired prophet like Jeremiah could have written it.

Even more than Lowth's reformulation of the nature of poetry, his reformulation of the nature of prophecy leads to Duhm's conclusion about the prose. Lowth makes prophets and poets virtually identical: they have "one common name, one common origin, one common author, the Holy Spirit."[110] The identity of poet and prophet is the point not only of his theory of inspiration (that the Holy Spirit and the poetic muse are one and the same) but of his historical account of the origin of prophecy (that prophets were originally musical ecstatics). If prophets are fundamentally poets,

---

[109] Duhm, *Jeremia*, vii.
[110] Lowth, *Poetry of the Hebrews*, 248.

then it is hardly an unexpected conclusion that the authentic prophecy in the book of Jeremiah is limited to the poetic sections and excludes the prose.

Lowth's recharacterization of prophetic speech led to a dramatic, if predictable, outcome: prophecy was no longer judged by whether or not it was in a prophetic book (or attributed to a prophet in the scriptural text) but by whether it conformed to the true characteristics—or to the spirit—of prophecy. The use of Lowth's redefinition of prophecy to distinguish whether a passage in a prophetic book is truly prophetic—and thus authentic—is the distinguishing mark of Duhm's work on Jeremiah, but it first appeared in Lowth's own work more than a century earlier. In a passage on alphabetic acrostics, Lowth exclaims, "It would be unnatural and absurd to look for instances of that kind in the prophetic poetry ... since such an artificial arrangement would be utterly repugnant to the nature of prophecy; it is plainly the effect of study and diligence, not of imagination and enthusiasm; a contrivance to assist the memory, not to affect the passions."[111] If poetry is artificial, contrived, studied, and labored and does not move the emotions of the reader, it cannot be prophetic because prophetic poetry by nature is enthusiastic, imaginative, passionate, and moving. One hundred and fifty years before Duhm, Lowth used his idea of the nature of prophecy to deny the authenticity of a passage that might otherwise have been attributed to a prophet.

A similar instance occurs in the notes provided by Michaelis to the first German edition of Lowth's lectures (published less than ten years after their original publication).[112] Commenting on Psalm 137,[113] Michaelis writes that "nothing could be more absurd" than to attribute one of the "most sublime" psalms to Ezra "than whose style nothing can be meaner or more ungraceful." He is inclined to attribute it instead to Jeremiah because he can so plainly discern in it "the taste and spirit of the bard."[114] For Michaelis, as for Lowth, Jeremiah is primarily "the bard, who sung so sweetly ... of the miseries of his nation."[115] Here Michaelis directly anticipated Duhm's approach to Jeremiah: the authentic writing of Jeremiah can be distinguished by its taste, spirit, sweetness, and sublimity.

It was observed above how Lowth's arguments for the poetic nature of the prophetic writing were used by Thomas Paine to reduce biblical prophecy to nothing more than poetry. Paine concluded his comments on the prophets saying, "The writings of the Jewish poets deserve a better fate than that of being bound up, as they now are, with the trash that accompanies them, under the abused name of the Word of God."[116] Lowth's re-presentation of the prophets as (Romantic) poets enables a new approach

---

[111] Lowth, *Poetry of the Hebrews*, 244.
[112] Michaelis published the lectures with his notes in two volumes that came out in 1758 and 1761. Brian Hepworth, *Robert Lowth*, Twayne's English Authors 224 (Boston, MA: G. K. Hall, 1978), 39.
[113] Although the text of Michaelis's note refers to Psalm 139, it appears likely that he means Psalm 137, since that psalm, "By the Rivers of Babylon," clearly "[sings] sweetly ... of the miseries of [the bard's] nation."
[114] Michaelis in Lowth, *Poetry of the Hebrews*, 276, n. 2.
[115] Michaelis in Lowth, *Poetry of the Hebrews*, 276, n. 2. These are the words of Michaelis. However, when Lowth wrote that "Isaiah, Jeremiah, and Ezekiel ... may be said to hold the same rank among the Hebrews as Homer, Simonides, and Æschylus among the Greeks," the parallel structure suggests that Lowth associated Jeremiah with Simonides, the Greek poet noted for the pathos he evoked in poems like his lament for soldiers who died at Thermopylae. Lowth, *Poetry of the Hebrews*, 294.
[116] Paine, *The Age of Reason*, Part I, Chapter IV.

to determining which parts of the prophetic literature are truly prophetic: the primary criterion is not whether the words are God's words (Jer. 23:22) but whether considered as poetry they are sublime or trash. Paine's understanding of the prophetic books, which is clearly derived from Lowth's understanding of prophecy and poetry, is the one that informs Duhm's work on Jeremiah. Paine not only enunciates Duhm's point of view, he anticipates Duhm's agenda: to recover the sublime poetry of the prophet from the trash that accompanies it.

Although it would be another hundred years after Paine before Duhm carried out his program in regard to the book of Jeremiah, throughout the nineteenth century there were influential scholars whose work was characterized by an attempt to distinguish authentic prophetic literature in the Bible from later (and earlier) literature of lesser value. As was shown to be the case with Duhm's characterizations of the material he believed to be in authentic additions to Jeremiah's poetry, the aspects that made the lesser parts of the Hebrew Scriptures unworthy in the eyes of these scholars were not confined to their failures to measure up to Romantic taste in literature. Like Duhm, these scholar predecessors also devalued the scripture they saw as non-prophetic because they found themselves at odds with its presentation of Israel's history, portrayals of prophets, and theological perspectives. Although their scholarly work is distinguished by the historical models and theological systems they offered as alternatives to the history and theology in the Bible, like Duhm they presented themselves as literary critics. They believed they could discern the prophetic nature, or inspiration, of a text based on literary characteristics.

In retrospect, Duhm's commentary on Jeremiah can be seen the moment when the book of Jeremiah was brought into full alignment with this nineteenth-century effort. However, the fact that this stream of scholarship has its source Lowth's presentation of the prophets as inspired poets is an indication that in his use of literary quality and poetic form to isolate authentic prophetic literature, Duhm's novel work is not simply an extension of nineteenth-century biblical scholarship but the expected conclusion of the eighteenth-century literary work of Lowth. Lowth, it was observed, was not attempting to show that the prophetic books were great literature, but rather that they contained great literature: namely, the poetic parts. Duhm brings Lowth's work to a kind of culmination by isolating the poetry of Jeremiah as a body of great literature and dissociating it from the poor-quality (prose) literature that could hardly be the work of an inspired literary artist.

Given the widespread influence of Lowth's association of prophetic inspiration with the poetic nature of the prophetic books, one might wonder why it took over a hundred and fifty years for a scholar to work out the implications of Lowth's theory and extend the work Lowth and Michaelis had begun of distinguishing the authentic work of Jeremiah on literary grounds. The basic reason is that it stands in opposition to the traditional view of the authorship of Jeremiah, or to be more precise, the book's own presentation of its speakers.

Duhm's denial of Jeremianic authorship to the prose speeches directly contradicts the presentation of the book, which regularly attributes them to the prophet (or to Yahweh, who put them into the prophet's mouth). The prose speeches, which the book attributes to Jeremiah (as opposed to the prose narratives about Jeremiah, which are mostly anonymous), amount to somewhere between 725 and 850 verses of the roughly 1,350 verses in the book (as compared to the 280 to 400 verses of poetry). On Duhm's theory, all of the prose speeches are inauthentic. Furthermore, as has been observed, Duhm's description of the prose speeches as inauthentic is not merely a judgment about authorship. It is intended to indicate the worthlessness of the prose for literary appreciation, for historical and biographical reconstruction, and for theological instruction. This means that Duhm's expedient for bringing the book into conformity with the vision inspired by Lowth came at the cost of dismissing and devaluing of over half of its contents.

Evaluation from Literary, Historical, and Religious Perspectives

Duhm himself recognizes the audacity of his way of dealing with the book. He describes in the foreword to his commentary how, for many years, he had hardly dared to question the Jeremianic origins of many of the passages he finally came to view as inauthentic. He goes on to predict that his conclusions will meet with the "usual cries of indignation and wonderful teachings *ex cathedra*." Duhm's prediction implies that opposition to this theory would come mainly from religious readers. However, those who come to the book for literary or historical reasons might also find Duhm's treatment of the prose speeches problematic, and the concerns of these readers can be considered first.

Readers who attempt to understand the book of Jeremiah as literature are in for a strange literary experience if they follow Duhm's approach. His suggested way of reading the text as a chaotic mixture of authentic and inauthentic texts is hardly one that would occur to readers if they approached the text without the guidance of Duhm or a later scholar who followed his approach. One indication that this is an unnatural way to read the book is that there is no evidence that it occurred to any of the readers of Jeremiah for over two millennia before the modern period. Duhm's own translation of Jeremiah shows what is necessary to produce this reading. It is not enough to distinguish how poetry and prose are printed; there must be another feature to distinguish the authentic from the inauthentic material: in Duhm's translation, the boxes that fence off the authentic material. Besides this, there must be an extensive introduction that explains the differences in style in terms of authenticity and inauthenticity. The introduction must also include a biography of the prophet because when the prose Duhm deems inauthentic is removed from the book, the connection of the poetry with the life of Jeremiah disappears.

To follow Duhm's approach, the reader must also adopt the tastes of nineteenth-century Romanticism. In the case of the prose, it is not enough to evaluate it according to the literary values of a Romantic critic; the reader must keep in mind that the prose was written by uninspired traditionalists and interpret its significance, or judge its value, in that light. Only in this way can passages formerly thought to have high literary worth (e.g., the "temple sermon" in ch. 7, the letter to exiles in ch. 29, and the promise of a new covenant in ch. 31)[117] be understood to be of poor quality. These measures may allow the reader the ability to appreciate the poetry as Romantic lyrics, but the question may arise if this gain has been too dearly bought.

---

[117] Duhm denies the authenticity of each of these passages the book attributes to Jeremiah. Duhm, *Jeremia*, 74, 228, 254.

Historians studying Jeremiah and his period, or those investigating prophecy or Israel's religion, might likewise have cause for resisting Duhm's severe limitation of the material deemed admissible as historical evidence. The denial of authenticity to such a large portion of the book on the basis of literary style not only takes away a great deal of the evidence for the life and thought of the prophet (since the book is almost the sole source of evidence); it also raises questions about whether any part of the book offers sufficient assurance of authenticity. As has just been noted, if the prose that Duhm believes is inauthentic is dismissed, there remains no indication that the poetry is related to Jeremiah except that it has been included in a book with stories about Jeremiah. Duhm might seek to bolster the case for the authenticity of the poetry by arguing that its literary greatness is evidence that it came from an inspired poet. However, this evidence from literary form is unlikely to provide the same assurance to historians today as it gave to Duhm and his initial followers.

Duhm's prediction that his book would meet opposition from religious readers proved true in the following century, and for good reason. Jewish and Christian believers who read Jeremiah as a part of their Scriptures would certainly find Duhm's theory at odds with their beliefs on several counts. These believers (whether laypeople, religious leaders, or scholars) would find his denial that Jeremiah spoke the prose speeches attributed to him in the book contradictory to their belief in the truth of the book. Duhm's theory denies the veracity of the book's repeated designations of the prose passages as the speech of Jeremiah. This involves Duhm in arguing that over half of the book is uninspired and misleading. Since this material mainly consists of passages the book presents as messages that Yahweh spoke through the mouth of the prophet, Duhm's claim that they were put into the prophets mouth by uninspired human writers is tantamount in the eyes of the believing readers to a claim that they are false prophecies.

Opposition to Duhm's theory has primarily focused on his denial of the authenticity of the prose, and it may well be that many opposed it because of the challenge it presents to religious belief in the truth of the book's self-presentation. However, Duhm's theory presents a deeper challenge to religious readers who accept the book as part of their scriptures. As was noted in the discussion of Lowth and Duhm's understanding of the poetry, at the foundation of Duhm's theory is a revised understanding of the nature of inspiration. Their belief that the inspiration of prophets can be identified with the inspiration of poets is a religious claim. Thus, Duhm's work on Jeremiah does not merely question the veracity of the book and the traditional ascription of authorship; his reconstruction of the book is in the service of an alternative to the book's portrayals of prophecy and thus how God speaks to humans. He also offers an alternative to the book's understanding of God's character, how he relates to Israel, and what pleases or angers him. In essence, Duhm's theory of Jeremiah is in support of a religious system that stands as an alternative to traditional Judaism or Christianity or to the religious view of the book of Jeremiah.

These observations about the opposition between Duhm's theory and Christian or Jewish belief should help the reader of Jeremiah see what is at stake in accepting or rejecting Duhm's theory. The reader is being asked to choose between two vying religious systems. The reader may find ways to adopt elements of Duhm's theory without denying the truth of orthodox Christian or Jewish belief or the veracity of the book believed to be inspired scripture, but it should be clear that Duhm's theory is an attack on both from an alternate religious view.

Evaluation of Duhm on His Own Terms

Ultimately, the judgment the reader of Jeremiah has to make about Duhm's theory is whether or not it is true: whether or not Duhm's account of the life of the prophet and the composition of the book accurately describes what really happened. The evaluation of the truth of Duhm's theory should not be determined by the literary critic's desire for a coherent book, the historian's desire for a large amount of evidence, or the religious believer's desire to safeguard traditional beliefs. At the same time, it must be recognized that determining whether or not something is likely to be true will involve considering how well it fits with what readers already believe to be true. The literary critic will have ideas of how books usually come to be composed, the historian will have ideas about what kind of things could possibly happen or what explanations are likely, and the religious believer will have ideas about these as well—ideas that take into account the possibility of divine involvement. The last two chapters have shown that Duhm's theory was strongly driven by the literary, historical, and religious ideas he brought to his interpretation of the book.

This is not how Duhm understands his theory—or how he presents himself in his commentary. In his presentation, consideration of underlying religious commitments is only relevant to understanding opposition to his view. It is only his opponents who are guided by religion. Their "cries of indignation" and "wondrous pronouncements ex cathedra" provoked by Duhm's discovery about Jeremiah are the angry reactions of hide-bound dogmatists whose religious certainties are threatened or the attempts of religious authorities to stifle dissent. Emotional outbursts and demands for ideological conformity are all they can oppose to the "findings" and "results" of his own "critical investigation." The contrast Duhm draws between the religious views of his opponents and his nonreligious view is an instance of a foundational characteristic of his approach that was observed in the investigation of his introduction: his presentation (and his understanding) of his work as a historical investigation. His adherence to the methods and aims of historical research are intended to provide an objectivity that allows his work to break free from the unquestioned assumptions of religious dogma and tradition. In his presentation, his theory is superior because it is untainted by religious presuppositions.

Although Duhm might acknowledge that his explanation of the book Jeremiah has religious implications, he implicitly asks the reader to believe that his understanding of the work is the result of a purely objective, or scientific, investigation of the evidence. Thus he asks for his work to be evaluated by the same standards used to evaluate other historical works. The reader seeking to evaluate Duhm's work on its own terms can ask whether his method ensures such a clear, objective result that the religious perspective of the investigator or the religious implications of his results are irrelevant to assessing the work's validity. First, the reader can assess whether Duhm's handling his evidence allows him to characterize his observations as "findings" rather than his interpretations. Second, the reader can judge whether Duhm's adherence to a historical method gives his conclusions the nature of "results"—that is, the necessary, or obvious, outcome of a straightforward process. Third, the reader can judge whether Duhm's arguments for his judgments of authenticity are so compelling that his claim that only the poetry is authentic can properly be called a "conclusion."

Duhm's Evidence

In regard to Duhm's treatment of his evidence, the aspects that can be evaluated at this point are his division of the text between passages of "exceedingly glorious" quality and "passages of fairly low quality"[118] and between poetry and prose. A reader might initially be inclined to question Duhm's aesthetic judgment of what is high- and low-quality literature as likely to be quite subjective; however, it has been shown here that his understanding of literary quality, which is basically that of nineteenth-century Romanticism, was actually quite established and widely shared in his time. However, it must be admitted that the literary qualities admired by Romantic critics allow quite a bit more room for individual judgment than those of other schools of literary criticism. Their basic criterion for judging quality is inspiration, conceived of in terms of an emotional experience: how clearly it flows from the deeply moved heart of a poet and how deeply it moves the hearts of the readers. Judgments about both the poet's and the readers' emotions could differ widely between interpreters; what one reader finds "moving" might fail to "move" another. The specific qualities that distinguish good literature for Duhm and other interpreters also allow ample room for judgments that are open to dispute. There is more room for argument about whether a passage has a high degree of simplicity, naturalness, sincerity, or spontaneity than there could be about whether a passage displays, for example, a high degree of metrical complexity, rhetorical ingenuity, erudition, or verisimilitude. A case in point would be the biblical example used by Longinus to illustrate sublimity: Gen. 1:3. Whereas one reader could find the words "Let there be light, and there was light" simple and transcendent, another could find them simplistic and naïve. The pliability of the qualities Duhm values opens his judgments of the worth of passages to the criticism that they have been influenced by his preconceptions about the various authors who wrote them. It would not be difficult for him to find poetic simplicity rather than prosaic simplemindedness in a passage he had already determined to be the work of a "born poet" on other grounds—including such qualities as parallelism or metrical regularity.

Duhm would appear to be on firmer ground in his determination of which passages are poetic since poetic form (in particular, parallelism and meter) is a more objective criterion than literary quality. However, examination of Duhm's actual practices shows a considerable degree of flexibility in his use of these indications of poetry. In the case of parallelism, although a relatively clear-cut judgment can be made that many passages display synonymous (or even antithetical) parallelism, many of the passages Duhm judges to be poetry fall into the less clear-cut category of "synthetic parallelism," in which the second phrase merely completes the second in one of many ways. Regarding

---

[118] Duhm, *Jeremia*, vii.

meter, not only does Duhm's method of counting accented syllables allow for quite a bit of flexibility (e.g., a long sentence can be broken up into several poetic lines each having the desired number of accented syllables), but Duhm also allows himself quite a bit of license in emending passages to fit the meter. Throughout his comments on individual passages, he recommends deleting words on metrical grounds so many times the phrase *"durch das Metrum ausgestossen"* becomes a kind of refrain.[119] This practice allows Duhm to find metrical form in many passages that he finds to be poetic, or of high literary quality, on other grounds.

Duhm's ability to bend the boundaries between high- and low-quality literature and between poetry and prose in Jeremiah makes them amenable to be being adjusted to align with each other. Still it has already been observed that most of his judgments are convincing and the fit between the two categories is clear enough to conclude that Duhm has actually "found" an objective feature of the text. The reader must remember that what he found—the evidence of poetry—had already been found and that what he claims to have found—evidence of inauthenticity—is only an interpretation of his actual findings that requires some additional form of support. Thus, although Duhm's categorizations of his evidence in terms of poetic form and literary quality are mostly unobjectionable, the reader should be aware of the degree to which Duhm is able to manipulate the boundaries of these categories not only to allow them to align with each other but also to allow them to correspond with his judgments on whether passages display or lack prophetic authenticity and theological truth.

Duhm's Method

A second way that Duhm hopes to distinguish his theory from views guided by religious beliefs is his adherence to a clear, straightforward method. In his foreword he describes his direct inductive procedure. Once he had been convinced by other scholars of the inauthenticity of some "important" passages in Jeremiah, he worked back through the whole book, "critically examining" each passage for authenticity based on its literary quality and consistency with the contents of the "undoubtedly genuine creations of Jeremiah."[120] The "end result" of this process was a significantly limited set of authentic passages that consisted entirely of a "prophetic poetry of a particular form."[121] Examination of the criteria Duhm uses for evaluating the authenticity of passages shows that Duhm's method is less straightforward and inductive than it might appear at first. His use of literary quality (e.g., doubting the authenticity of

---

[119] This phrase could be called Duhm's version of the "dl m cs" (*delendum metri causa*) in the apparatus of some books of the BHS, although characteristically, there is nothing in Duhm's judgments that corresponds to the *"frt"* or *"prb"* ("fortasse": perhaps; or "probabiliter": probably) that usually precede these recommendations. The phrase occurs in Duhm's comments on Jer. 2:3 (p. 17), 2:17 (18), 2:20 (24), 3:1 (33), 3:20 (42), 4:1 (45), 5:6 (58), 8:13 (90), 15:9 (133), 22:22 (178), 30:20 (242). Other verses with elements that Duhm wants to *"streichen aus metrischen Gründen"* include Jer. 2:27 (p. 28), 2:35 (32), 4:14 (51), 6:3 (65), 6:4 (66), 7:28 (84), 8:4 (86), 9:2 (93), 12:9 (116), 22:13 (174), 22:21 (178), 23:9 (182), 31:7 (245), 31:8 (246), 31:11 (247), 50:24 (364).

[120] Duhm, *Jeremia*, vii.

[121] Duhm, *Jeremia*, vii.

those passages with "strangely clumsy form")[122] to determine authenticity appears to predetermine his conclusion that the authenticity can be determined by literary form. This becomes even more apparent when it is recognized that his standards for literary quality are drawn from a system (Romantic literary theory) initially designed to show the literary quality of the parts of prophetic books with poetic form. His other criterion for determining authenticity, consistency with the passages in the book that are "undoubtedly genuine," faces the same criticism. He begins the process of distinguishing authentic from inauthentic passages with a set of passages he has already determined to be undoubtedly authentic—seemingly on the basis of their literary quality. Before he begins methodical investigation, he has already concluded that the speeches the book ascribes to Jeremiah can be divided between "exceedingly glorious prophetic writings" and "passages of fairly low quality."[123] This description of the two types betrays his presupposition that the authenticity of a passage (whether or not it is "prophetic") can be determined by its literary quality (whether "exceedingly glorious" or "fairly low"). Once again his conclusion is largely determined by his assumptions about the relationship between prophecy and literary quality—or more basically, the identity of prophetic and poetic inspiration.

Duhm's description of his belief that the authentic passages are limited to those in poetic form as the "end results" of his work suggests that it was only when he finished his work that he observed that the authentic passages were all in the same poetic form. In this way, he avoids the impression of circularity: that his conclusion influenced his process. The desire to maintain this impression is the likely reason that poetic form is not mentioned as a criterion of authenticity in the introduction to his commentary. However, it is quite improbable that Duhm did not make use of poetic form when he was determining authenticity given the close association in his mind of poetry with literary excellence and prophecy. His practice of altering passages he believes to be authentic to give them poetic form is an indication that throughout his investigation he was operating with poetic form as a criterion of authenticity. If the association of poetic form and authenticity is a feature of both Duhm's method and his conclusion, it is one more reason to question the impression he labors to maintain that his theory is the inevitable outcome of applying a scientifically rigorous literary-historical method to the text of Jeremiah.

For a reader today, discovering the presence of circularity in Duhm's method is not an automatic reason for rejecting the potential validity of his conclusion. The circularity inherent in any process of discovery is a reality more widely acknowledged now than in Duhm's time. Even in the hard sciences there is a readily acknowledged cycle of forming a hypothesis from the initial survey of the evidence and then repeatedly revising the hypothesis after testing it against the evidence. In the more relevant field of literary interpretation, theorists, interpreters, and readers are even more ready to admit the circularity involved in understanding a text. Duhm's process of discovery can easily be recognized as an instance of the familiar hermeneutical circle, in which an initial impression of the whole influences interpretation of the various parts and interpretation of the parts in turn influences the impression of the whole. The circle

[122] Duhm, *Jeremia*, vii.
[123] Duhm, *Jeremia*, vii.

can be a "virtuous cycle" if the preconceptions yield insight into the text and if they are refined by repeated interactions with the text.

The concern then is not whether the method is circular or whether the interpreter comes to the text with preconceptions; it is whether the preconceptions are held so tightly that they cannot be shaped by the text and whether the cycle is a "vicious" one that simply uses the text to reinforce the interpreter's prejudgments. An interpretive process can be evaluated in terms of the degree to which the interpreter is willing to let interaction with the text reshape the pre-conceptions and re-align the purposes she brings to the text—or to put it negatively, the degree to which she has allowed her preconceptions and agenda to distort the text, perhaps by ignoring or misconstruing individual passages or by misjudging its overall nature and aims. In the case of Duhm's treatment of the division between poetry and prose, the degree to which his conclusions are already present in his preconceptions and critical judgments, his highly selective use of the evidence (he discounts over half of it), and his willingness to bend the evidence to fit his model, suggest a hermeneutical method in which the materials of the book were reshaped and reorganized to fit models (including the Romantic conception of inspired prophecy) that Duhm brought to the book rather than found in it.

Duhm's Arguments

A third way Duhm seeks to provide his theory with the unquestionable objectivity of historical research is to present it as the "conclusion" of compelling arguments. With clear evidence, valid premises, and watertight reasoning, a reader could be "forced to the conclusion"[124] that Duhm's theory was correct. If his theory is the necessary result of a logically sound argument, there would be no need for the reader to consider Duhm's religious views and aims (whether they are true or shared by the reader) to evaluate its validity. Duhm's presentation of his theory as the "conclusion" or "end result" of his historical investigation invites the reader to accept it as the only rational explanation of the evidence. However, Duhm's commentary does not provide this kind of rational persuasion. It is a curious feature of Duhm's writing how seldom he provides justification for his judgments in the form of explicit arguments. On one topic after another his modus operandi is simply to pronounce his impressions and rely on their inherent plausibility, explanatory power, and fit with the text to persuade the readers of their validity. In the specific case of his central thesis that the authentic words of Jeremiah are limited to the poetic passages, instead of offering arguments Duhm appears to rely on the readers' acquiescence to his individual judgments of each nonpoetic passage that it is not worthy of being attributed to the prophet. Duhm seeks

---

[124] "Zu dem Schluss gedrängt." Duhm, *Jeremia*, x. In this passage, Duhm argues that one is "forced to the conclusion" that the prose additions to Jeremiah and the late Deuteronomistic portions of the former prophets come from the same hands by the similar subjects, ideas, and diction. This is a fascinating feature of the prose in Jeremiah, and Duhm's explanation is a plausible one. However, there are many other plausible explanations (e.g., the author(s) of one were dependent on the other(s), the authors of the two had similar training, etc.), and for one "to be forced" to Duhm's "conclusion" would take arguments that his explanation is the best one.

to persuade by the strength of his own confidence in the rightness of his judgments. He concludes his foreword by assuring his readers that criticisms of his theory will come to nothing because his theory is right. The "cries of indignation" from his critics and their "pronouncements ex cathedra" can be ignored: they "won't do any good, but at least they won't do any harm." Duhm's reason: "I have complete confidence that my findings are, in the main, right."[125]

The nature of the contrast Duhm draws here between himself and his detractors suggests the true ground of his certainty that his reading of Jeremiah is superior to that of his opponents. The contrast is not merely between the unexamined religious beliefs of his opponents and the objective results of his historical investigation. It is between their submissive acquiescence to conventional opinions on the external grounds of tradition and authority and his daring assertion of his internal individual convictions. Duhm not only sees himself in the role of scientist or historian correcting unfounded religious dogma with evidence and arguments; he sees himself in the role of a prophet, reformer, or Romantic artist challenging the entrenched falsehoods of tradition and corrupt authority on the basis of the intensity of his own inner assurance. His ability to judge the worth of the various parts of Jeremiah comes from his own penetrating powers of discernment. The reason he can recognize what is exceedingly glorious and thus prophetic in Jeremiah is that it corresponds to something glorious and prophetic in himself. Duhm's reliance on his own refined intuitions can be recognized as an instance of Romantic hermeneutics, in which understanding a text is conceived of communion between the spirit of the reader and the spirit of author such that the reader re-experiences the original experience of the author. In Duhm's case, it appears to spring from his personal character. Rudolf Smend notes that it was well known that Duhm had a feeling for "mysterious, abnormal, irrational phenomena" and quotes a colleague as saying that Duhm knew "the occult side of the inner life from experience."[126] Alfred Bertholet, Duhm's student, says of him, "He had a strong divinatory strain, to which he willingly surrendered … taking from it the right to an extensive use of hypothesis."[127] It is this extensive use of "hypothesis," or authoritatively stated opinion, in his Jeremiah commentary that gives the impression that Duhm expects his theory to be accepted on the basis of his own inspired insight. Duhm asks for his discernment of the authentically prophetic to be recognized as in some sense prophetic itself.[128]

Readers of Jeremiah trying to evaluate Duhm's judgments about authenticity will have to ask themselves to what extent they trust Duhm's powers of divination: whether the utterances of his spirit find an echo in their own spirits. This is not as mysterious

---

[125] Duhm, *Jeremia*, vii–viii.

[126] Rudolph Smend, *From Astruc to Zimmerli: Old Testament in Scholarship in Three Centuries*, trans. Margaret Kohl (Mohr Siebeck: Tübingen, 2007), 106–7. The quotation is from Duhm's colleague at Basel, Johannes Wendland (Schweizerisches Protestantenblatt, 1927, 337). Smend notes that there were many stories about this aspect of Duhm's character including that he regularly spoke with his dead wife, 107.

[127] Alfred Bertholet, *Deutsches biographisches* Jahrbuch 10 (1928), 46, quoted in Smend, *Astruc to Zimmerli*, 107.

[128] Welhausen is said to have remarked about Duhm: "In order to be a prophet it is not enough to be a prophet oneself." Cited in Smend, *Astruc to Zimmerli*, 107.

or uncommon as it might sound. Readers will be more easily persuaded by Duhm if the parts of the book that he finds glorious strike them as glorious as well. Agreement about what is excellent in literature or praiseworthy in theology is a powerful factor in whether readers find Duhm's judgments (or Lowth's) believable. It has almost surely played a much larger role in determining which scholars up to the present time have embraced or resisted Duhm's approach than the scholars themselves would be willing to admit. The inexplicable sense of the soundness of Duhm's judgments cannot be dismissed out of hand as mere subjectivism or personal taste. People often have the experience of something having the ring of truth, or being objectively beautiful, without their being able to explain why. However, this innate sense of what is true, or good, or beautiful can also be questioned—especially in regard to its source.

The present chapter has given numerous reasons for asking whether what Duhm and his adherents found to be glorious or pedestrian in the book of Jeremiah is better attributed to an inner faculty for aesthetic judgment or to the historical conditioning of an aesthetic movement dominant in their time. It is worth recalling that before Lowth, there was little taste for the kind of poetry found in the prophets (it had to be made poetic before it could be appreciated) and that this acquired taste only spread gradually throughout the next century. These are reasons to question the timeless universality of Duhm's aesthetic judgments. However, his literary (or theological judgments) are not the main reasons to question Duhm's work on Jeremiah; it is his theory of the book's composition based on these judgments. A reader may share Duhm's (and Lowth's) appreciation for the excellence of the poetry in the book without accepting his theory that it is impossible that the prose (or the passages he finds to have less literary or theological excellence) could be the work of an inspired prophet. While Duhm's inner spiritual and aesthetic sensitivity may provide passable support for his "complete confidence" that his aesthetic judgments are "right," the question remains whether he is justified in extending that confidence to his judgments about authorship and composition. Duhm's own confidence in this extension seems to rest less on logical arguments than on his intuitions about how a prophet should talk, and these intuitions in turn were largely shaped by currents of eighteenth- and nineteenth-century thought.

Evaluation of the Confirmation Given by Poetic Form

At this point, the reader of Jeremiah trying to evaluate Duhm's theory is in a position similar to where she was at the close of the previous chapter. An initial survey of Duhm's theory as laid out in the introduction to his commentary left the reader with the question of how Duhm could escape the criticism that he had simply reconstructed the book to fit his preferences in literature and theology. The overview of the roots of Duhm's literary taste in nineteenth-century Romanticism and ultimately in Lowth's work on prophetic poetry has clarified this question. It has shown that Duhm's literary preferences were by no means his own personal preferences but rather the values of a major school of literary theory that was already over a century old by the time he wrote his commentary. Thus, the question can now be better formulated as follows: How can Duhm escape the criticism that his theory appears to be designed to bring the book into conformity with Romantic literary values? As an initial response to this question, it was noted that Duhm and his adherents could counter this criticism by pointing out that the material they deemed authentic is delimited not only by Duhm's judgments of literary quality but also by an objective quality of the text itself: poetic form. That the parts of the book Duhm judged to be Jeremiah's authentic words on the basis of their literary (or theological or historical) value turn out to be the very same as the parts of the book that display poetic form appears to confirm the objective nature of Duhm's judgments.

The investigation in this chapter of the origins of the modern study of poetry in the prophetic books provides a simpler explanation for this fit. The reason the passages Duhm found to be great literature are the same as those with poetic form is that Duhm's understanding of what makes literature great derives from a literary theory designed to show that the poetic passages in the prophetic books are great literature. Duhm's literary values have been shown to be those of Romanticism, and Romanticism has been shown to have deep roots in Lowth's effort to challenge the literary values of neoclassicism by promoting the poetic sections of the biblical prophets as new models of great literature. It is hardly surprising then that the passages in Jeremiah that appeal to the Romantic taste in literature are the poetic passages because the Romantic movement is grounded in the use of poetic passages in the prophetic books to set up and justify new standards of literary taste. The reason the glove fits the hand is that the hand was the model for the glove.

This explanation of Duhm's judgments largely dispels the impression that the fit between the passages Duhm believed authentic because of their literary quality and the passages with poetic form provides additional support or credibility to his compositional theory. However, it does not undermine the fact that Duhm was dealing with an objective feature of the text of Jeremiah: that a large number of passages in the book are related to each other by sharing not only poetic form but several other similarities. In light of the review of Lowth's work, the nature of this feature can now be more precisely expressed by saying that parts of text that display semantic parallelism also have a high incidence features such as figurative language and elliptical and nonstandard sentence structure. In light of the overview of the reception of Lowth's work, it can be added that these passages are amenable to being read as having the features valued by poets and literary critics of the Romantic age (such as simple but powerful diction) conforming to their understanding of the poetic composition (as expressions of passionate emotions). In regard to Duhm's work on Jeremiah, it should be clear that the discovery of this feature of the text was not his but Lowth's over a hundred years earlier. Duhm's contribution to Jeremiah studies was not the unearthing of a new feature of the text but a new explanation of its significance.

As has been noted, Duhm's commentary and his 1903 translation of Jeremiah provide an answer to the question raised by Benjamin Blayney's 1784 translation of Jeremiah, which typographically distinguished between poetry and prose.[129] For over a hundred years, this distinction had been staring readers in the face, leaving them with the question of what it signified. Duhm's answer was clear and simple: the poetry was

---

[129] The question was raised earlier, but less obviously, by Lowth's observation that less than half of Jeremiah is composed of poetry (*Poetry of the Hebrews*, 291).

written by Jeremiah and the prose was not. To be more precise, poetic form is one of several indicators of inspiration and thus passages that have these indicators can be ascribed to the inspired prophet, but passages that lack them should be ascribed to authors who lacked inspiration. The initial appeal of Duhm's answer can be attributed both to the degree to which readers of Jeremiah in his day shared his assumptions about poetry, prophecy, and inspiration, as well as to its elegant simplicity. For many readers, the benefits of Duhm's answer (primarily the foundation it supplied for their literary, historical, and theological systems) outweighed its costs (primarily its atomization of the text and its denial of the truth and value of such a large part of the book's content).[130] However, acceptance of his answer by scholars can also be explained by the lack of a compelling alternative. This situation still largely obtains over a hundred years after the publication of Duhm's commentary. Although readers today may have an increased awareness of the costs of adopting Duhm's theory and have less reason to share the assumptions that made it plausible, until they are presented with a more compelling answer to the question raised by the discovery of poetry alongside the prose in Jeremiah, Duhm's answer will remain the standard.

Duhm's Understanding of the Book of Jeremiah

Although throughout the twentieth century there was a vocal minority of scholars who resisted Duhm's approach primarily because of his denial of the authenticity of the prose, in the late twentieth century a growing number of scholars began to express dissatisfaction with Duhm's approach primarily because of its effects on reading the book as a whole. This was part of a larger movement in biblical studies to move beyond the historical-critical methods like Duhm's source criticism that had led to the fragmentation of the biblical books. Methods such as redaction criticism, rhetorical criticism, and canonical criticism were employed in an attempt to take account of whole books in their present form. Scholars who turned to these methods in their investigation of Jeremiah sought to counter neglect of the literary form, rhetorical agenda, and theological significance of the whole book. This neglect was an effect of Duhm's approach, which began by dividing the book into authentic and inauthentic

---

[130] The opposite question is why Duhm's radical extension of Lowth's theory into the book of Jeremiah came when it did, at the turn of the twentieth century. Of course, the examination of why Duhm wrote what he did when he did would require a reconstruction of his biography and the development of his thought (not unlike Duhm's reconstruction of Jeremiah's biography and thought, though with much more evidence available). However, the question of why his theory of Jeremiah's composition won acceptance and grew to be the dominant model of Jeremiah studies in the first part of the twentieth century can be more readily answered in general historical terms. There are three salient factors. First, the need for a corpus of Jeremiah's work different from that attributed to him by the book was relatively strong. Some of the reasons for this will be discussed in the following chapters. Second, resistance to questioning the traditional ascription of authorship to books (or in the case of Jeremiah, self-designation of authorship) was relatively weak. The increasing readiness of eighteenth- and nineteenth-century scholars to question the authorship of biblical books (notably the Mosaic authorship of the Pentateuch) is a well-known part of the history of biblical scholarship. This history will be briefly rehearsed in the fourth chapter primarily to show Duhm's place in it. Third, the inherent strength of Duhm's particular theory, its ability to provide plausible answers to long-standing questions about the book of Jeremiah.

sources. The attempts of these scholars to "move beyond Duhm" and come to terms with the book as whole will be addressed in the final chapters of this study. These chapters will assess attempts to understand the literary form of the whole book and the book's portrayal of the prophet.

This chapter can conclude by noting that Duhm had little interest in the attempt to understand the literary form of the book or its portrayal of the prophet. These are what his commentary on Jeremiah was written to dispel. In his foreword, quoted at the beginning of this chapter, Duhm sets up as his fundamental problem the literary form of the present form of the book: that in it "exceedingly glorious prophetic writings" were embedded in "passages of fairly low quality." This chapter has shown how this problem for reading the book arose from Lowth's identification of prophecy with glorious, or sublime, literature and how Duhm's solution to the problem (to deny that the low-quality, or nonpoetic, passages could have come from the prophet) also has its roots in Lowth's understanding of prophecy and poetry. Duhm's solution, the dissolution of the book into authentic and inauthentic sources, was one he and his followers eagerly embraced. They were not interested in reading the book of Jeremiah as literature, but in extracting the parts they could read as great literature from the rest of the book. Duhm concludes his foreword saying that his theory that the prophet is only responsible for the poetry of the book meant "freedom from a nightmare."[131] The present form of the book was a nightmare for Duhm. What he found nightmarish about it can be gathered from what he says next. If his theory freed him from a nightmare, what he found when he awoke was that he could "now understand Jeremiah as a man, a writer, and a prophet, as far as anyone can claim to say that of so great a man."[132] For Duhm, the portrait of the prophet Jeremiah presented by the present form of the book is a nightmare to be dispelled. His alternative is the subject of the next chapter.

---

[131] The colorful German word "*Albdruck*," translated here as "nightmare," derives from the idea that a nightmare is caused by an incubus ("*ein Alb*") that bears down on top of a sleeper in bed. So the phrase "*die Befrieung von einem Albdruck*" also suggests freedom from an oppressive weight. Edmund Wilson notes that this image was a frequent one in the writings of Karl Marx. "There is a German expression '*lasten wie ein Alp*,' which means something like 'to weigh like an incubus,' to which Marx is very much addicted. We find it on the first page of *The Eighteenth Brumaire*, where he says that 'the tradition of all the dead generations weighs like an incubus on the brains of the living.'... It is always the same oppression whether Marx has objectified it and generalized it as the oppression of the living by the dead or felt it personally as his own oppression." Edmund Wilson, *To the Finland Station: A Study in the Writing and Acting of History* (New York: New York Review of Books, 2003), 310. Duhm uses the expression in a very similar way to Marx.

[132] Duhm, *Jeremia*, vii.

3

The Roots of Duhm's Biography of the Prophet

The Reason for Duhm's Biographical Reconstruction

Although Duhm's primary and most enduring contribution to Jeremiah studies was his compositional theory, in his own assessment his primary achievement was his reconstruction of the biography of the prophet. As has been observed, Duhm goes about his work as a historian gathering authentic evidence and piecing it together to recover what really happened, and his central recovery is the biography of the historical prophet. He presents the reconstructed biography in the introduction to his 1901 commentary in the section on "Jeremiah's Prophetic Poetry."[1] The section begins by laying out his new account of the prophet's life and concludes by placing "approximately sixty authentic poems" into various periods of the prophet's life: first, his early years in rural Anathoth, then his ministry in Jerusalem during the reigns of Josiah, Jehoahaz, Jehoiakim, and Zedekiah.[2] The way Duhm presents his material makes it clear that the biographical reconstruction is the aim of his source-critical theory. The purpose served by identifying which sources are authentic and inauthentic is to allow a historical reconstruction based only on authentic materials.

As was previously noted, the influence of Duhm's compositional model and biographical reconstruction is manifest in the regularity with which Jeremiah commentaries ever since Duhm's work include sections on these two topics in their introductions. The initial question that faces a reader of Jeremiah who turns to these commentaries is, "Are these elements necessary or helpful for reading the book?" To answer this question in regard to Duhm's biography of the prophet, the reader can start by asking the question of why Duhm himself found it necessary to offer a reconstruction of the prophet's biography (but surprisingly this question is almost never asked).

The Book Does Not Require a Reconstructed Biography

Initially it might seem that the reader needs a biography of the prophet simply due to the nature of the book, that the book of Jeremiah itself invites a biographical

[1] Bernhard Duhm, *Das Buch Jeremia*, KHC 11 (Tübingen: J. C. B. Mohr, 1901), xi–xii.
[2] Duhm, *Jeremia*, xii–xiv.

reconstruction like Duhm's. The book contains more information about the life of the prophet than any of the other writing, or latter, prophets. This might call for gathering the information into a coherent whole. Like the other prophetic books, Jeremiah begins by explicitly relating the ministry and the words of the prophet to reigns of various kings.[3] This is followed up by introductory words throughout the book that situate the speeches or actions of Jeremiah in specific years in the reigns of the kings.[4] The fact that these events that are explicitly tied to certain years are not in chronological order[5] seems to invite the reader to mentally arrange these events in a chronological order different than the literary order in the book.

Although these features of the books do make a certain degree of familiarity with the historical background of the book helpful for readers, they cannot have been the primary reason Duhm felt it necessary to provide his historical reconstruction of Jeremiah's life. First, whereas the book is interested in tying the events to the history of Judah as represented by her kings, Duhm is mainly interested in locating them in periods of the life of the prophet. For the purposes of the book, the relevant historical background that provides the chronological framework would be something like 2 Kings 22–25, which presents the main events in the reigns of Josiah and his sons up through the destruction of Jerusalem and the exile. What Duhm provides instead is a chronological development of Jeremiah's ministry and message, something that the dated passages in Jeremiah appear to have little interest in. Second, whereas the explicitly dated passages in the book are almost all prose (either narratives or speeches), the passages that Duhm labors to place into historical context are almost entirely poetic. As has been noted, the heart of his project was to place around sixty isolated poetic passages into a biographical framework, and these historical contexts of these poetic passages are not given by the book.[6] Third, Duhm's primary biographical reconstruction is of a period of the prophet's life for which the book does not offer any explicit (dated) references. There are no events that the book explicitly assigns to specific periods between the beginning of the prophet's ministry (the thirteenth year of Josiah, *c.* 626, Jer. 1:2) and a message he delivered in the temple court (in the beginning of the reign of Jehoiakim, *c.* 609, Jer. 26:1).[7] This is the period to which Duhm assigns the majority of the poems (at least thirty-three of the approximately sixty),[8] and it is the central part of his biographical reconstruction. Duhm's story of the early years of Jeremiah's ministry (his opposition to the local cult in rural Anathoth, his foreboding on hearing of the Scythian invasions, his moral shock on first coming to the big city of Jerusalem, and his opposition to the (Deuteronomistic) reformers in Josiah's time) is a story that the book takes no interest in—if it knows it at all. If Duhm's biography is the

---

[3] Jer. 1:1-3, cf. Isa. 1:1, Ezek. 1:1-2, Hos. 1:1, Amos 1:1, Mic. 1:1, Zeph. 1:1, Hag. 1:1, Zech. 1:1.

[4] Jer. 21:1, 24:1, 25:1, 26:1, 27:1, 28:1, 29:1-2, 32:1, 34:1, 35:1, 36:1, 40:1, 44:1.

[5] Events from the reign of Zedekiah (21:1, 24:1, 27:1, 29:1, 32:1, 34:1) alternate with events from the reign of Jehoiakim who preceded him (25:1, 26:1, 35:1, 36:1).

[6] One exception is 38:22b, four lines of poetry embedded in a message to Zedekiah.

[7] One exception would be 3:6-10, which begins, "Yahweh said to me in the days of Josiah." However, since this passage is in prose, Duhm takes it as inauthentic (dependent on Ezekiel) and suggests that it was assigned to the time of Josiah on the editors' supposition that what comes early in the book must come early in the ministry of Jeremiah. Duhm, *Jeremia*, 36.

[8] Duhm, *Jeremia*, xiii–xiv.

actual historical story that stands behind the poetry of the book, the authors or editors have obscured it. Thus the only sense in which Duhm's reconstruction can be said to be made necessary by the book is that it fills a gap Duhm perceived in the book.

Modern Concerns Call for a Reconstructed Biography

One indication that the book does not invite the biographical reconstructions offered by Duhm and subsequent commentators is that before the modern period commentators on the book did not find it necessary to recreate the biography. This suggests that what made it necessary has less to do with the book than with factors in the modern period. Two aspects of modernity appear especially relevant to explaining the need to reconstruct Jeremiah's life. The first is the rise of historical consciousness, the idea that history is the universal framework into which everything fits, that understanding things is primarily a matter of discovering their places in this framework. In much modern interpretation, everything must be explained according to its historical causes, its origins, in this vast causal network. Historical explanations are expected both to follow universal historical principles and to be grounded in the unique elements of the specific historic context. Although this kind of historical understanding rose to prominence in nineteenth-century biblical interpretation, its roots can be traced to the eighteenth century. An early instance is the way Lowth explained Hebrew poetry both in terms of a universal theory of literary production (poetry as the result of inspiration) and in terms of its specific historical context (the peculiarities of ancient Hebrew culture). The general rise of historical consciousness is the backdrop for the specific rise of "historical criticism" in Biblical studies. The works of Duhm and his followers are instances of historical criticism, and the historical nature of their work helps to explain the need they felt to include both a reconstruction of the historical (and biographical) background of the book and a theory of its composition.

The second and related aspect of modern interpretation is the rise of a hermeneutical theory that held that all literature can be interpreted by accounting for the experience of the author (both the thoughts and feelings and the situation that produced them) when the literature was written. This hermeneutical approach, most associated with Schleiermacher, is closely related to more the general rise of historical consciousness and was widespread in nineteenth- and twentieth-century historical criticism. It is sometimes referred to as Romantic hermeneutics because it is the counterpart of the expressive theory of artistic creation that lies at the core of Romanticism.[9] This expressive theory has been shown to have deep roots in Robert Lowth's championing of the poetry in the prophetic books as the model for good poetry. To interpret poetry of Jeremiah according to this Romantic hermeneutic, it is essential to determine what the prophet's thoughts and feelings were when he wrote it. For each piece of poetry, interpretation means explaining it as the effect a particular historical event had on the particular psychology of the prophet at this particular moment in his development. Thus determining when a poem was composed is necessary not only for identifying the external events that provoked it but also for discerning the stage in the development of

---

[9]   Anthony Thiselton, *New Horizons in Hermeneutics* (Grand Rapids, MI: Zondervan, 1992), 204–33.

the prophet's interior life that caused him to experience the events the way he did. For these tasks, recreating the prophet's biography becomes essential.

Duhm's Biography Intended to Replace the Book's Biography

Although these features of modernity help to explain why Duhm (and readers and interpreters from his time to the present) has been interested in the historical background of the book and the biography of the assumed author, there is a more fundamental reason why Duhm felt his biographical reconstruction necessary. In Duhm's eyes, the portrait of the prophet offered by the book is not merely incomplete or in need of historical arrangement and grounding; it is false and unworthy of the historical prophet. As was seen in the overview of Duhm's introduction, he believes that the majority of the book was added long after the time of Jeremiah, and that thus that the book's portrait of the prophet is mainly a fabrication of the later editors. He describes their creation as "the embodiment of an abstraction that the later Jews made themselves from the prophets in general. ... He is, as far as something human remains, not primarily a prophet, but rather a Torah teacher, a scribe, like the redactors, who brings ... no new revelation of God."[10] From this description it can be seen that Duhm finds fault with the book's portrait of the prophet for two broad reasons. First, the book's prophet is not historically described: "Space and time do not exist for [the prophet. He] float[s] high above all concrete reality, as does the theology for which he must be the mouthpiece."[11] Second, its prophet is not worthy of the name prophet but is only a Torah teacher, a scribe, created in the image of those who added to the book.

Duhm's biography of the prophet is offered as an alternative to the portrait of the prophet given by the editors. It remedies the two main problems Duhm found in the book's portrayal. First, it is fully historical: Jeremiah's life is coordinated with known events in world history, and each of his sayings is rooted in a concrete historical context. Second, it presents a prophet that readers can "look up to with admiration."[12] His Jeremiah is no uninspired scribe, mindlessly repeating the words of others; he is an inspired and inspiring prophet who broke through to a new level of authentic spiritual vision. Duhm believes his historical biography of the great prophet is necessary to replace the deceptive and contemptible portrait of the prophet offered by the book.

As Duhm presents it in his foreword, his new portrait of the prophet was the primary outcome of his method. More than that, it provides the justification for his primary methodological innovation:

> The end result, namely that only prophetic poetry of a particular form can be attributed to Jeremiah (and no prose or even half prose), I have never seen before, not even a tendency toward it. But for me, it means freedom from a nightmare: I

---

[10] Duhm, *Jeremia*, xviii.
[11] Duhm, *Jeremia*, 36.
[12] Duhm, *Jeremia*, xviii.

can now understand Jeremiah as a man, a writer, and a prophet, as far as anyone can claim to say that of so great a man.[13]

Duhm had described how the initial consternation of trying to understand a book with contents of such mixed literary and theological quality had begun to be eased by his increasing willingness to admit that parts of the book were inauthentic. Finally, he came to his radical solution: that the authentic passages were limited to the poetry. Although he realized that this would be highly controversial, he had complete confidence in his new theory, and the reason was that it provided the solution to the problem the book presented him. It gave him freedom from a nightmare, or release from heavy burden. The freedom did not come primarily from the ability his theory about the poetry gave him to disentangle the good literature from the bad, but from the new portrait of the prophet he was able to paint when he drew exclusively from the (authentic) poetic materials. The nightmare was not only the inferior material in the book, but its problematic portrait of the prophet. Duhm explained what made his new portrait superior to the one found in the book: Jeremiah could now be understood as a real historical human being rather than a theological abstraction, as an inspired author (or poet) rather than an uninspired editor, as a prophet with divine revelation rather than a mere mouthpiece for the Law or a theological system. In sum, Duhm's compositional theory allowed him to offer modern readers a Jeremiah they could accept as a believable historical figure as well as look up to with the admiration due a great man.

If Duhm's confidence in the validity of his theory rests on his sense that the resulting portrait of the prophet is highly compelling, the reader of Jeremiah trying to determine whether she needs the help of Duhm's theory will want to judge for herself how compelling she finds Duhm's portrait—and how problematic or distasteful she finds the portrait offered by the book. If Duhm's compositional theory (that only the poetic passages are authentic) is necessary for his biographical reconstruction, and his biography is necessary for replacing the book's portrayal of the prophet, the necessity for his theory heavily depends on the merits of his novel portrayal. A starting place for this investigation is to try to determine what made it so compelling for Duhm and, for the other scholars who accepted his theory, so compelling that Duhm's theory became the dominant paradigm for twentieth-century Jeremiah scholarship.

Duhm Attempts to Make Jeremiah's Biography Believable

As was noted, Duhm found the new portrait of the prophet compelling in two main ways: his Jeremiah is both believable (*glaubwürdig*) and praiseworthy (*würdig*). For Duhm and those who followed him, "believable" is roughly synonymous with "historical." Thus, a speech from Jeremiah is more believable if it can be linked with a historical event known from another source. An example from Duhm's biographical reconstruction would be his explanation of Jeremiah's speeches warning of destruction from a "foe from the north" as expressing the prophet's sense of foreboding at hearing about the Scythian invasions that happened around 625 BC (an event not mentioned

---

[13] Duhm, *Jeremia*, vii.

in the Bible but recorded by the Greek historian Herodotus). "Historical" can also be opposed to "mythical" or "legendary." Part of what makes legends and myths hard to believe is that they contain elements that cannot be easily explained according to the universal laws of causation. Believable historical accounts are ones that can be explained in the same terms as commonly occurring events in the present. Consideration of believability helps to explain why Duhm is willing to incorporate most of the prose narratives (which he attributes to Baruch) into his biography[14] but not the prose speeches or short prophetic narratives[15] (which he attributes to the later scribes). The reason is that whereas the former—unlike the accounts of prophets like Samuel, Elijah, Elisha, or Jonah[16]—do not describe anything outside of common experience (or that cannot be explained by universal laws), the latter do.

The narratives and speeches that Duhm deems to be inauthentic do not include obvious miracles or supernatural occurrences. However, they do contain two elements of prophecy that Duhm and other modern interpreters have found problematic in terms of historical believability: the implication that the prophet received verbal communication from God and the idea that the prophet could predict the future. For some interpreters, these aspects of prophecy appear to be too great a departure from the normal way things occur in history. This presents an interpretive problem since these aspects are central to, almost definitive of, the understanding of prophecy in the book of Jeremiah (e.g., 1:9, 12; 23:22; 28:9, 16-17) and throughout the Hebrew scriptures (e.g., Deut. 18:18-22). If modern interpreters cannot accept that these were aspects of actual, historical prophecy, they have recourse to the theory that they have been projected back onto the prophets by later authors who were either unfamiliar with actual prophecy or had an agenda that required making it appear as if the prophets spoke God's words and predicted the future.

The degree to which Duhm and other modern interpreters felt the need for an alternative to supernatural aspects of the prophecy varied. Duhm's stance in his commentary is inconsistent. On the one hand, he denies the book's claim that Jeremiah ever predicted that the exile would be seventy years long (Jer. 25:12, 29:10).[17] On the other hand, he accepts that Jeremiah correctly predicted the immanent death of Hananiah (Jer. 28:15-17) and warns against making an absolute law that something cannot happen without fully examining the reality.[18] Still, the overall effect of his approach is to discredit as inauthentic the parts of the book that might seem historically implausible because they present Jeremiah delivering messages from Yahweh and making explicit predictions about the future.

---

[14] The main exceptions are the speeches of Jeremiah in Baruch's accounts which Duhm finds too long to be believable. Duhm, *Jeremia*, v–xvi.

[15] "*Handlungen*," e.g., enacted signs as in ch. 13. Duhm, *Jeremia*, xvii.

[16] Duhm calls these "inspirational tales about the prophets" (*erbaulicher Prophetenlegenden*). Duhm, *Jeremia*, xvii.

[17] Although the prediction occurs in a letter that Duhm takes to be authentic (Jer. 29:1-14), he regards the prophecy of a seventy-year exile as an interpolation of part of a later apocalyptic system. Duhm, *Jeremia*, 230.

[18] It appears in this case that part of his reason for crediting the story is that the rest of the story (Jer. 28:1-14) has the ring of an authentic historical account by Baruch. Duhm, *Jeremia*, 227.

The poetic speeches that Duhm does attribute to Jeremiah might seem to present similar problems in terms of historical plausibility: after all, they are mainly the first-person speech of Yahweh and often deal with what is coming in the future. However, Duhm is able to present these as poetic conventions, ones that the young Jeremiah learned from the poetry of Hosea.[19] That Jeremiah speaks in the voice of Yahweh is an indication of his confidence in his message, and his visions of the future are provoked by current events (e.g., his vision of the northern invaders is based on the fears raised by the Scythian invasions). Duhm rejects as a later priestly view of prophecy (a view reflected in Ezekiel) the picture of the words of Yahweh being placed in the mouth of the prophet (1:9), but he is willing to concede that this could serve as a picture for the inspiration that stands behind Jeremiah's poetry.[20] In these ways, Duhm is able to craft a portrait of the prophet that is more compelling to him and his modern contemporaries than the portrait offered by the book.

Duhm Attempts to Make Jeremiah Praiseworthy

It is important to observe that the elimination of what modern readers might deem crude supernaturalism is only part of what made Duhm's new portrait of the prophet more compelling. Its primary attraction is that his portrait allowed the prophet to be understood "as a man, an author, and a prophet." By "a man," Duhm appears to mean a believable historical figure. However, he did not think Jeremiah was simply an ordinary person; he stands in reverential awe of "such a great man," and it is Jeremiah's figure as a prophet and an author by which Duhm measured his greatness. Duhm believed that his work had restored Jeremiah to his lofty status as not only one of the great men of Israel but of the world, a "hero of world literature"[21] and the "first true martyr of religion."[22] Duhm's Jeremiah was truly one whom readers could look up to with admiration, and that is what made him so compelling.

Although Duhm achieved his portrait of the great man by stripping away what he felt was inauthentic and restored the poet's literary reputation by exposing over half the speeches attributed to him by the book as spurious, this was only the first step. Using only the authentic historical and literary evidence he isolated, Duhm was able to piece together a biography that had not been known for over two thousand years. Duhm understood his biographical achievement to be a work of discovery—or recovery—unearthing the historical Jeremiah from under layers of inauthentic tradition. However, although Duhm's biography of Jeremiah is certainly unlike any previous portraits of the prophet, it bears a striking resemblance to a new type of biography that had grown to prominence in the nineteenth century: in particular, the biography of the "man of Genius," rooted in the biography of the Romantic poet or artist. Like other aspects of Duhm's Jeremiah, his biography of the prophet has its roots in the work of Robert Lowth.

---

[19] Duhm, *Jeremia*, 16.
[20] Duhm, *Jeremia*, 4.
[21] Duhm, *Jeremia*, 47.
[22] "Unlike some Christian martyrs of the first centuries he was not enticed by other-worldly reward; he was a martyr, but not a fanatic, and thus his bravery was doubly great and truly moral." Duhm, *Jeremia*, 14.

Duhm's Romantic Biography of Jeremiah

Lowth and the Biographies of Prophetic Poets

It was observed in the previous chapter that Robert Lowth's *Lectures on the Sacred Poetry of the Hebrews* (1753) not only argued that there was poetic material in the prophetic books, but also established this poetry as the model for a new type of poetry, an alternative to the poetry shaped by the neoclassical formalism of the early eighteenth century. Because this new poetry and poetic theory that justified it came to be known as Romantic, Lowth's rehabilitation of the poetry in the prophetic literature can be identified as one of the main sources of Romanticism. As was observed, a key feature of Romanticism was its expressive theory of artistic creation. In contrast to the neoclassical idea of art as the intentional product of the artistic efforts of a skilled artisan, the Romantics understood art to be the spontaneous overflow of the interior experience of an artistic soul. The value of the art lay in the access it provided to the sublime experiences and elevated mind of the artist. This understanding of artistic creation grounded in Lowth's theory of poetic and prophetic inspiration turned attention in literary studies from poetry to poets, and in biblical studies from prophetic literature to prophets.

Because of Romanticism's deep roots in Lowth's work on Biblical poetry, not only did the prophetic books become models for Romantic poetry, but the prophets themselves became models for Romantic poets. In the previous chapter, the influence of the poetry in the prophetic book as understood by Lowth was observed in the poetry of three poets of the late eighteenth century: William Blake, William Cowper, and Christopher Smart. In this examination of Duhm's biography of Jeremiah, it can be further observed how the personal lives of each of these "pre-Romantic" poets conformed to the model of the prophetic poet that Lowth had developed from his interpretation of the biblical prophets. They understood themselves and were understood by their contemporaries as prophets in the tradition of Amos, Hosea, Isaiah, and Jeremiah. In varying degrees the pre-Romantic poets fostered this identification. Blake, for example, famously pictures himself dining with the prophets Isaiah and Ezekiel discussing poetic genius[23] and begins one of his earliest works identifying his authorial persona as "a voice crying in the wilderness."[24] For each of them, as Murray Roston points out, Lowth's recovery of biblical prophets as poets was an important influence.[25] Although they had quite distinct personalities—Blake, the fiery visionary; Cowper, the melancholy hymn writer; and Smart, the religious madman—each of them was characterized by personal visions, extreme emotions bordering on pathology, and a sense of prophetic vocation. They became contemporary embodiments of the amalgamation of prophet and poet that Lowth had found in (or created from) the biblical prophets.

---

[23] William Blake, "The Marriage of Heaven and Hell," in *Blake's Poetry and Designs*, 2nd ed., NCE (New York: W. W. Norton, 2008), 352–74.

[24] "All Religions Are One" in *Blake's Poetry and Designs*, 5.

[25] Murray Roston, *Prophet and Poet: The Bible and the Growth of Romanticism* (Evanston, IL: Northwestern University Press, 1965), 165 (Blake), 104 (Cowper), 148 (Smart).

In the next century, the great poets of the Romantic age such as Wordsworth, Coleridge, and Shelley each attempted to take up the mantle of the poetic prophet, or to fill the role of the "prophetic bard." The figure of the bard, which Blake had a large part in developing, combined Hebrew prophet with national poet. A foundational example of a poetic bard for Blake and other Romantics was Milton, a great English poet whose poetry they found to be infused with the enthusiasm, moral vision, and sublimity of the biblical prophets. In Wordsworth's estimation, Milton was "a Hebrew in soul; and all things tended in him toward the sublime."[26] Milton, like the biblical prophets, denounced the evils of his day but also gave a vision of how humanity could be restored and paradise regained by interior renewal. The inspired vision proclaimed by the bard, or poet-prophet, offered an alternative in the nineteenth century to the failed promises of rationalism, science, and political revolution in the eighteenth century. A signal event for many of the Romantics was the failure of the French Revolution, which many had initially hoped would usher in a new age of freedom. The disappointment of this dream had left many of the leading European intellectuals and artists cynical about the possibility of human progress. The central Romantics authors saw themselves as called to confront this despair, in Wordsworth's self-description, "singled out as might seem for Holy services."[27] Though the rest of the people of "this Age fall back to old idolatry," says Wordsworth to Coleridge, we will address them as

> Joint labourers in the work
> (Should Providence such grace us vouchsafe)
> Of their redemption, surely yet to come.
> Prophets of Nature, we to them will speak
> A lasting inspiration.[28]

In this way, Wordsworth and the other Romantics hoped to serve as inspired prophets in the crisis of their age as the Hebrew prophets had in theirs. They would offer a prophetic vision of the future restoration of humanity, a restoration that would come from the renewal of authentic vision and creative powers reawakened by their prophetic poetry.

Wordsworth makes it explicit that he sees his work as a poet as equivalent to the work of a Biblical prophet in a passage where he describes his response to the reports of the Reign of Terror that followed the French Revolution:

> But as the ancient Prophets, were enflamed
>   … when they denounced,
> On towns and cities, wallowing in the abyss
> Of their offences, punishment to come;…
> …
> So, did some portion of that spirit fall
> On me, to uphold me through those evil times,
> And in their rage and dog-day heat I found …
> …

---

[26] Wordsworth, "1815 Preface to *Lyrical Ballads*," in *Major Works*, 634.
[27] Wordsworth, *Prelude* I: 62–3, in *Major Works*, 376.
[28] Wordsworth, *Prelude* XIII: 432, 439–43, in *Major Works*, 589.

Motions raised up in me, nevertheless,
Which had relationship to highest things.[29]

In this passage, Wordsworth explicitly identifies himself with the Biblical prophets: he shares the same spirit and is a successor to their prophetic ministries as Elisha was to Elijah (like Elisha, he received "a portion of [the prophetic] spirit").

The Romantic Reconstruction of Biblical Prophets

At the same time as the Romantic poets' self-identity was being shaped by the model of the biblical prophets, they were also shaping the model to make it accommodate their own experience. Wordsworth's later revision of this same passage begins,

But as the ancient Prophets, borne aloft
In vision, yet constrained by natural laws
With them to take a troubled human heart. ...[30]

The inspiration and visions of the Biblical prophets are now "constrained by natural laws": they must conform to what enlightened people of the nineteenth century know to be true. They know that prophetic experience must be explained not only in terms of a divine "vision" but also in terms of a "human heart." This "natural supernaturalism" in explaining prophetic experience has been shown to have deep roots in Lowth's novel theory of prophetic inspiration, which fuses the supernatural inspiration of prophecy and the natural inspiration of poets. This kind of fusion is highly developed in Wordsworth's work. The passage in which Wordsworth describes how he assumes prophetic stature comes in the tenth book of *The Prelude*, his epic description of the education of his own poetic and prophetic heart. From the "gentle breeze" in the opening line of the epic, an actual breeze, which substitutes for the inspiration of the muse, Nature plays the role of the divine spirit in shaping the Wordsworth for his role as a poet and a prophet. It is the story of how "Nature ... frame[s] / A favored being, from his earliest dawn."[31] Nature carefully molds him by drawing out the inherent powers of his creative mind through powerful experiences of the natural world. The end product is Wordsworth the poet: "a man ... endued with more lively sensibility, more enthusiasm and tenderness ... a more comprehensive soul."[32] Wordsworth the poet is Wordsworth the prophet. His sensitive poetic soul is what makes him prophet: it causes his indignation at

---

[29] Wordsworth, *The Prelude* (1805), X: 401,403–5, 409–11, 417–18 in *Major Works*, 452–3. It is interesting to note that in the revised edition (1850), Wordsworth, who had grown more conservative in later life, added before the lines "So did a portion of that spirit fall / On me," a line trying to soften the presumption of comparing himself to the biblical prophets: "So with devout humility be it said." *The Prelude* (1850), X: 447 in *The Prelude 1799, 1805, 1850* (A Norton Critical Edition), ed. Jonathan Wordsworth, M. H. Abrams, and Stephen Gill (New York: W. W. Norton, 1979), 381.

[30] Wordsworth, *The Prelude* (1850), X: 437–9 in *The Prelude* (Norton), 381.

[31] Wordsworth, *Prelude* (1805), I: 363–4 in *Major Works*, 384.

[32] Wordsworth, "Preface to *Lyrical Ballads*," 603.

the evils of his age, allows him to transcend historical crises, and gives him the hopeful vision of a glorious future of human potential. The new understanding of a prophet developed by Wordsworth and other Romantic writers adapts Lowth's understanding of the biblical prophets to meet the needs of the late eighteenth and early nineteenth centuries.

Duhm's Biography of a Romantic Poet

In the previous chapter, it was noted how closely Duhm's understanding of what makes excellent literature (the criteria by which he was able to discern the authentic speeches of Jeremiah) conforms to what Romantic critics valued in literature. Now it can be observed how closely his portrait of the Jeremiah conforms to the character of the Romantic poet-prophet. One simple way to demonstrate the likeness is to observe the subheadings of the "Jeremiah" entry in the index at the back of Duhm's commentary; they include "Sensibility" (*Feinfuehligkeit*), "Honesty," "Empathy" (*Mitlied*), and "Idyllic personality."[33] In the text of his commentary, Duhm describes the prophet as "by nature a tender, shy creature, a gentle personality." He continues, "His poetry seems to indicate that he was a man created for an idyllic peaceful life, a childlike soul, who longed for the innocent pleasures of life."[34] These characteristics of the historical Jeremiah that Duhm discerns from his poetry are virtually identical to the characteristics of Wordsworth's poet. In fact, Duhm sees Jeremiah as more like the Wordsworthian poet than any of the other prophets: "He looked more deeply into his own interior life than any other Old Testament writer. He is the most subjective of all the prophets";[35] "Amos and Isaiah are the preachers [*die Redner*], Jeremiah is the poet [*der Lyriker*]."[36] Commenting on the sensitivity of Jeremiah's perception, Duhm writes, "If God had not selected him for the office of a prophet, he would have become the greatest lyric poet [*Idyllendichter*] of Israel."[37]

Although it is interesting to note how much Duhm's portrait of Jeremiah's character conforms to the character of a Romantic poet, what is even more striking is the conformity of his reconstructed biography of the prophet to the biographies and autobiographies of the poets in the Romantic era. In the late eighteenth century, an intense interest grew in the biographies of poets and artists. A well-known work from this period is Samuel Johnson's *Lives of the Poets* (1781).[38] The life of the artist, or *Künstlerroman*, is a genre that sprung up during this time and there are hundreds

---

[33] Duhm, *Jeremia*, 386.
[34] Duhm, *Jeremia*, 14.
[35] Duhm, *Jeremia*, 168.
[36] Duhm, *Jeremia*, xiii.
[37] Duhm, *Jeremia*, xi.
[38] Samuel Johnson's work is usually considered to be representative of Neo-Classicism rather than Romanticism. However, like many in his age, Johnson can be considered a transitional figure, and the interest of contemporary readers in his lives of the poets can be seen as a characteristic of the growth of Romanticism. One might be able to observe the shift in focus from poetry to poet in the difference between the original title Johnson gave for his work, *Prefaces, Biographical and Critical to the Works of the English Poets* (1779), and the title his publishers gave to a later edition of the work, *The Lives of the Poets* (1781).

of representative works from that period down to the present. The rise in biographical interest corresponds to the rise of the Romantic understanding of art as the expression of the personal experiences of the artist. The personality, psychology, and spiritual life of the artist became not only the essential context for understanding the art but often the true subject matter of the art as well. The particular interest was in the development of the artist's personality: the mix of natural talent, early environment, and significant experience that gave shape to the unique temperament expressed in the art. These are the very elements that Duhm found the portrait of the prophet in the book of Jeremiah to lack—and that he supplied in his alternative biography.

The correspondence between Duhm's biography of Jeremiah and the autobiography of Wordsworth in his *Prelude* are remarkable. *The Prelude*, subtitled *The Growth of a Poet's Mind,* is perhaps the best-known and most representative work in the genre of *Künstlerromane*. Wordsworth's epic-length poem traces the gradual development of his artistic temperament, which climaxes, as has been seen, with his assumption of the role of prophet-poet for his age. Duhm's recreation of Jeremiah's biography, particularly (as has been noted) the early years of his ministry passed over by the book, follows Wordsworth's account of his development as poet almost point by point. Wordsworth's poetic education begins with his childhood in the idyllic, rural Lake District where Nature stocks his mind with beautiful images (Books I and II of *The Prelude*). Duhm finds in Jeremiah's poetry evidence of a superior knowledge of country life that is due to his upbringing in rural Anathoth.[39] Wordsworth comes to Cambridge where he (like Milton before him) is disappointed by the frivolity of the future leaders of his country, particularly the ecclesiastical leaders (Books III and IV). Duhm's Jeremiah is likewise put out when he comes into contact with the urban prophets and priests.[40] In the section on his formal education, Wordsworth gives a full account of the literature he read that shaped him (Book V). Duhm is at pains to trace the effects of earlier authors from Jeremiah's library (particularly Hosea) on the young author. A defining moment in Wordsworth's life comes when he goes to live in London for the first time and is shocked by its moral depravity (Book VII). Duhm also reads passages denouncing Israel's sin as evidence of Jeremiah's shock at the depravity of the people in Judah's capital, when he first comes from rural Anathoth to the big city of Jerusalem.[41] Wordsworth is initially filled with great hope at the prospects for political change emanating from the French Revolution, but he is later disappointed and realizes that it was merely a superficial change, which could not fully address the deep wounds resulting from centuries of injustice (Books IX and X). Duhm likewise claims that Jeremiah found himself in opposition to the advocates of the Deuteronomistic reforms during the reign of Josiah. In Duhm's retelling, these reformers were only interested in conformity to and external law, but Jeremiah knew that real reform had to be from the heart.[42]

---

[39] "The fact that he spent his youth in the country side comes out clearly from his poetry, which betrays such a distinct a feeling for nature [*Natursinn*]." Duhm, *Jeremia*, xi. Duhm takes the picture of wild asses in heat (Jer. 2:24) as evidence that "Jeremiah was obviously much more familiar with rural life than the rabbis with their scholarship." Duhm, *Jeremia*, 27.

[40] The priests and prophets in the city "have an interest in the present arrangement and thus have no desire to improve it." Duhm, *Jeremia*, 69–70.

[41] He finds the urban population "frivolous, hypocritical, blasé, and adulterous." Duhm, *Jeremia*, xi.

[42] Duhm, *Jeremia*, xi.

In the final account, Wordsworth places his hope for humanity in its realization of their personal spiritual powers, a realization that will parallel and be awakened by his account of his own growth as a visionary poet and prophet (Books XI–XIII). Duhm likewise finds Jeremiah's ultimate value as a model of fidelity to one's personal, interior vision.

Opposition in the Biographies of Romantic Poets

The one significant way in which Duhm's life of Jeremiah departs from Wordsworth's is that his life of the prophet is a tragic life of opposition, suffering, and finally martyrdom. Although the opposition and suffering Jeremiah endured is certainly not Duhm's invention (it appears in both the narratives and poetry of the book),[43] Duhm heightens this aspect of Jeremiah's life,[44] makes it central to his significance, and even adds elements that are not mentioned in the book: particularly, the opposition between Jeremiah and the Josianic reformers. Duhm even goes so far as to assert that Jeremiah was martyred because of the reformers, becoming "the first martyr of religion."[45] The suggestion that Jeremiah was martyred cannot be found in the book but only in later tradition (and in that tradition Jeremiah dies at the hands of idolaters, not advocates of the Law). That Duhm would include this element from tradition, when he presents his project as recovering the historical prophet by relying only on authentic evidence not later tradition, shows the importance to Duhm of suffering and opposition in his portrait of Jeremiah.

The persecution and suffering of Duhm's Jeremiah is not matched by Wordsworth's life. Wordsworth spent most of his adult life in peaceful seclusion at Dove Cottage in the idyllic Lake District and in his final years was honored as the poet laureate of England. However, in this aspect, it is Wordsworth's life rather than the life of Duhm's Jeremiah that departs from the model of the Romantic poet. The paradigmatic Romantic poet is the *poète maudit*, the accursed poet.[46] The poet is cursed, first, with a sensitive poetic soul, one that is closely allied with madness (as in the case of Christopher Smart who was at one time confined to Bedlam, the famous "lunatic asylum" in London). The poet's sensitivity makes him experience much more acutely the losses and cares of life: whether unrequited love, the death of a loved one, news of war, or religious doubts. The poet is also cursed with fears and sorrows, or (in terms of modern psychology) anxiety and depression (as in the case of Cowper, who attempted suicide several times). The poet is also cursed with his vision that sets him at odds with his society or his age: either they cannot understand him, or they take offense at his unmasking of their spiritual emptiness. The poet becomes a lonely outcast, whose life and death can

---

[43] See Jer. 1:19; 11:18-23; 15:10-18; 18:18-23, 20, 26, 28, 32, 36-38, 43-44.

[44] Jeremiah's "character is more tragic than any of the followers of God in the Old Testament." Duhm, *Jeremia*, 5-6.

[45] Duhm, *Jeremia*, 14. "It was because of [the Deuteronomic theologians] that Jeremiah had to die a martyr." Duhm, *Jeremia*, 90.

[46] Although the term *poète maudit* first came into common use after the publication in 1883 of *Les Poètes maudits*, (Paul Verlaine's study of several symbolist poets), the figure of the suffering artist had been developing for over a century. Perhaps the best-known early example comes from Goethe's loosely autobiographical novel *The Sorrows of Young Werther* (1776).

only be a tragedy. This picture of the suffering poet certainly draws on the figures of the Hebrew prophets (especially as interpreted by Lowth and his followers).[47] Thus, in some ways, Duhm's tragic life of Jeremiah as a suffering poet simply returns the genre to its roots. However, it is also the case that the Romantic portrait of the artist cannot be explained solely in terms of the biblical prophets, and thus the fact that Duhm's portrayal of Jeremiah fits it so completely cannot be explained solely by its similarities with the book's portrayal of Jeremiah.

It has been observed that the confidence Duhm and his followers had in his theory of the book derived in large part from the resulting portrait of the prophet, one that allowed them to understand Jeremiah as "a man, a (great) author and a prophet." Now this observation can be made more specific by saying that they found Duhm's portrait of the prophet compelling because it allowed them to understand Jeremiah as a Romantic poet. In their minds what makes a man a great author and especially what makes him a prophet were closely akin to what makes a man a Romantic poet. This is obviously related to the way in which Duhm and his followers understood the literary greatness of what they believed to be the authentic works of Jeremiah in terms of their likeness to Romantic poetry (their sublimity, originality, simplicity, spontaneity, sincerity, etc.). The simple explanation is that Duhm's understanding of great literature and great writers is basically Romantic. This is not surprising given the pervasive influence of Romanticism in the late nineteenth and early twentieth century when Duhm wrote.

The Lowthian Roots of German Romanticism

Up to this point, the influence of Romanticism on the work of Duhm has primarily been illustrated with examples from Romantic authors in England. This was in part because the aim has been to show the importance of eighteenth-century English authors (particularly Lowth) as sources of Romanticism and in part because, among the authors of the Romantic period, the English authors will be more familiar to most English readers today than the German authors. However, since this is an investigation of the influences that shaped a German author, Duhm, it will be important to give an account of Romanticism in Germany.

First, it should be remembered that the Romantic movement was as strong, if not stronger, in Germany as in England. The importance in English literature of authors like Wordsworth, Coleridge, Byron, Keats, and Shelley is matched by the importance in German literature of authors such as Goethe, Schlegel, the Schelling brothers, Novalis, and Hölderlin. The list of German Romantics grows longer if one includes philosophers and theologians like Schiller, Fichte, and Schleiermacher, and even longer if one includes artists like Friedrich and composers like Beethoven, Brahms, Schubert, and Wagner. These artists and authors are not merely representatives of German Romanticism but are also some of the central figures in German culture and literature

---

[47]   Yvonne Sherwood, *Biblical Blaspheming: Trials of the Sacred for a Secular Age* (New York: Cambridge University Press, 2012), 133.

as a whole. This is no coincidence because the rise of Romanticism in Germany went hand in hand with the rise of self-consciously German arts and letters.

Romanticism and German National Identity

The close association between beginnings of a self-consciously German literature and Romanticism has much to do with the history of the late eighteenth and early nineteenth centuries in Germany. During this period there was a resurgence of German national identity. It was not until the end of the nineteenth century (1871) that a unified German nation emerged, and in the eighteenth century, people in the hundreds of little German-speaking states of Northern Europe thought of themselves primarily as Bavarians, Hessians, Saxons, or Hanoverians rather than as Germans. The rise of German national identity that preceded unification as a nation-state was made possible by the efforts to recognize and cultivate a common German culture, which included music and the arts, as well as literature. The fragmented political state was not the only obstacle to recognition of German cultural identity. For over two hundred years, German culture had been overshadowed by the culture of France. In comparison to the glories of the court of Versailles, the little courts of the German princes seemed shabby. The French view of these courts can be seen on the opening page of Voltaire's *Candide* (1759), which introduces a certain German baron, who "was one of the most powerful lords of Westphalia, for his castle had not only a gate, but even windows."[48] As for the German rulers themselves, one historian notes, "German princes and princelings spent fortunes on building palaces to which they gave French names, imposed on their courts absurdly detailed etiquette, [and] entertained themselves with French plays of imitations."[49] Imitation was also common for German-speaking artists, composers, and authors, who often wrote their greatest works in Latin or French. By the end of the eighteenth century, many Germans had a growing desire to throw off the influence of French culture and take their stand as representatives of an authentically German national culture.

If German culture was to be more than an inferior imitation of French culture, it would have to provide a compelling alternative. French culture prided itself in being cosmopolitan, urbane, and sophisticated. France could boast of the University of Paris, and in the seventeenth century the glittering court of the Sun King at Versailles. Its symmetrical palaces and gardens, classical dramas and operas, and elaborate rules of etiquette set the standards for European culture of its era. In the eighteenth century, France was at the center of the Enlightenment with it salons, encyclopedists, and philosophes. In the early nineteenth century, when Napoleon was spreading the rationalist ideals of the Revolution across the continent, the imperial French government officially sponsored a revival of classical art forms.[50] What did Germany have that could compare to the glories of France? The answer that united

---

[48] Voltaire, *Candide, or Optimism*, trans. Henry Morley (New York: Barnes & Noble Books, 2003), 11.
[49] Jacques Barzun, *From Dawn to Decadence: 500 Years of Western Cultural Life: 1500 to the Present* (New York: HarperCollins, 2000), 391.
[50] Paul Johnson, *The Birth of the Modern: World Society 1815–1830* (New York: HarperCollins, 1991), 71.

many diverse German authors in the late eighteenth century could be summed up in one word: spirit (*Geist*). German authors believed that the German people had a depth and interiority in comparison with which all the sparkling glories of French culture could be shown to be shallow and superficial. The spiritual depth of Germany could be traced to religious pietism or to the simple life of the people (*Volk*) living close to the land. In German villages and around the hearths of German homes was a way of life untouched by the stiff, artificial manners of the French cities and courts. There was a wild beauty in the untouched German countryside that transcended the beauty of symmetrical classical gardens. The decorum and orderliness that were the pride of French culture could be seen as stifling conformity, and Germans could take pride in their freedom of expression and sincerity. In comparison to the warmth of German piety, the Enlightenment rationalism could be shown up as cold and formal. Thus, renewed appreciation of German culture was accompanied by a shift in values. The authors of the German resurgence celebrated inspiration, individuality, freedom, originality, naturalness, passion, direct expression, simplicity.

These values are, of course, the values of the literary and artistic revolution known in Germany as well as in England as Romanticism. German Romantics, like those in England, found in the idea that true art flows spontaneously from inspiration, passion, and imagination an alternative to the strictures of neoclassical literary theory and the arid rationalism of Enlightenment philosophy. However, for the Germans, more than for the English, neoclassicism and the Enlightenment rationalism were associated with France. In contrast to the rationality, order, and decorum of the French elites, German Romantic authors celebrated the passions and piety of common people and the freedom that comes from individual vision. This is especially true of the German thinkers associated with the *Sturm und Drang* movement, often considered a precursor to the full flowering of Romanticism in Germany. The "Storm and Stress" movement (as it is often translated into English) celebrated the passionate and even the irrational. Although some of the central writers in the movement drew inspiration from French sentimentalists (particularly Rousseau), their primary influences were pre-Romantic English writers. Many of them learned English; read English novels, plays, and essays; and some even travelled to England.[51] English literature provided alternative models to the literature of France and neoclassicism. The *Sturm und Drang* authors were particularly drawn to Shakespeare who was perceived as a great literary genius, one whose dramas achieved greatness by their expression of the soul of the author and the spirit of the people, not by rigid adherence to the strict rules of dramatic presentation (e.g., the "unities" of action, time, and location) prescribed by French neoclassicists. This view of Shakespeare as a national "bard" who gave voice to the spirit of his people was encouraged by works by English literary critics: notably, Joseph Warton and Edward Young.[52] The work of the English critics Thomas Blackwell and Robert Wood gave a similar presentation of Homer as the bard of Hellenistic

---

[51] Barzun, *Dawn to Decadence*, 409.

[52] Joseph Warton, *An Essay on the Genius and Writings of Pope* (London: For M. Cooper at the Globe in Paternoster Row, 1756); Edward Young, *Conjectures on Original Composition* (London: For A. Millar in the Strand; and R. and J. Dodsley in Pall-Mall, 1759).

Greece,[53] and it was according to the same model that Hugh Blair presented "Ossian" as the ancient bard of the Scottish people.[54] For German authors in the late eighteenth century, this Romantic idea of great poets giving voice to the spirits of their nations encouraged them to look for such inspired German-speaking artists and authors, the sources of German national culture.

The German Romantic authors not only looked to the great inspired authors of England, Greece, and Scotland for models of national literature. They also looked to the inspired poets of the ancient Israel found in the Bible. The idea that the Bible could be used as an earlier and greater authority to overthrow centuries of accumulated tradition found a natural home in Germany, the home of the Protestant Reformation. However, it was primarily from an English author that the German Romantics drew the idea of the Bible as a model for the literature of a simple people distinguished by the greatness of their national spirit. It was the same author who made the Hebrew poets and prophets available as models for inspired artists who made the Hebrew prophets available as leaders who unified their country by laying a foundation of vernacular literature. German authors found both of these ideas in one English work: the *Lectures on the Sacred Poetry of the Hebrews* by Robert Lowth.

Lowth's Lectures Come to Germany: Michaelis and Hamann

The story of how lectures an English Bishop gave in Oxford made their way across the North Sea and affected German authors, artists, and scholars (eventually including Duhm) can begin in 1741 with the visit to England of Johann David Michaelis, the prominent Orientalist, philologist, and theologian of Göttingen University. He was present at Oxford to hear at least one of Lowth's lectures.[55] Michaelis published an edition of the lectures in Göttingen in 1758 (only a few years after they were published in Oxford in 1753).[56] As in England, they were published in Latin, but the German edition included extensive annotations from Michaelis. In this annotated edition of Michaelis, Lowth's work was widely known in Germany and may be said to have had a greater influence there than in England. "So far as England was concerned," writes T. K. Cheyne, "Lowth was a *vox clamantis in deserto*."[57] In Germany, writes Michaelis, "we admire him and follow him like some Oriental Orpheus."[58]

---

53 Thomas Blackwell, *An Inquiry into the Life and Writings of Homer* (London: For E. Dilly, at the Rose and Crown in the Poultry, near the Mansion-House, 1735); Robert Wood, *Essay on the Original Genius and Writings of Homer* (London: For T. Payne at the Mews Gate and P. Elmsly in the Strand, 1775).

54 Hugh Blair, *A Critical Dissertation on the Poems of Ossian* (London: For T. Becket and P. A. De Hondt, at Tully's Head in the Strand, 1763).

55 Michael Legaspi, *The Death of Scripture and the Rise of Biblical Studies* (New York: Oxford, 2010), 107, 116. Legaspi's study focuses on the work of Michaelis and includes an extended discussion of what he found in Lowth's work and how he shaped it. Legaspi, *Death of Scripture*, 115–28.

56 Michaelis published Lowth's *Lectures* in two volumes the first in 1758 and second in 1761.

57 Thomas Kelly Cheyne, *Founders of Old Testament Criticism: Biographical, Descriptive, and Critical Studies* (London: Methuen, 1893), 4.

58 Quoted in Hepworth, *Robert Lowth*, Twayne's English Authors 224 (Boston: G. K. Hall, 1978), 39. Lowth was made a fellow of the Royal Society of Göttingen in 1765.

The work of Lowth was especially important for Johann Georg Hamann (1730–1788), the German author to whom the many of writers in the *Sturm und Drang* period looked for spiritual inspiration. Hamann preached a mystical philosophy of heartfelt passion and assailed the arrogance and aridity of rationalism. He found Lowth's discovery of poetry in the Hebrew prophets of immense significance. The nature of his appreciation for Lowth's work can be seen in his criticism of Michaelis. In Hamann's estimation, Michaelis was a rationalist who lacked the spiritual sensitivity to appreciate the spiritual value of Lowth's discovery that the Hebrew prophets were inspired poets. This is the burden of his cryptic essay *Aesthetics in a Nutshell*, a "nutshell" that, in the words of Isaiah Berlin, he "hurled at Michaelis' head."[59] It grieved Hamann to see Lowth's discovery in the hands of a mere historian and grammarian who could not understand the spirit of the great poetic prophets. In the essay, Hamann refers ironically to Michaelis as a "Master of Israel," an allusion to Nicodemus, who could not understand what Jesus said about the Spirit, which is like the wind that "bloweth where it listeth" (Jn 3:8-10).[60] Hamann and the writers of the *Sturm und Drang* movement hoped that the literary spirit that Lowth believed inspired the Hebrew prophets could also breathe new life into German literature. Isaiah Berlin describes Hamann as the individual "who struck the most violent blow against the Enlightenment and began the whole Romantic process,"[61] and it is significant that a primary resource for him in attacking French rationalism and classicism and inspiring German Romanticism is Lowth's establishment of the Hebrew scriptures as a model of inspired literature.

Herders's Lowthian Romanticism

If Hamann was the initial author to use Lowth's literary Bible to spark the Romantic revolution in Germany, the author who did the most to fan the flames was his student, Johann Gottfried Herder (1744–1803). Herder was a central figure not only of the *Sturm und Drang* movement but also in German Romanticism, and German literature as whole. He was a personal friend and mentor to many of the great authors of his day including Goethe. That Herder drew directly on Lowth's *Lectures* is clear in the title of one of his own works, *On the Spirit of Hebrew Poetry* (1783–5). Knowing that his title was reminiscent of Lowth's *Lectures*, Herder opens his work assuring his readers that his work is not merely "a translation or an imitation of ... the beautiful and justly celebrated work of Bp. Lowth."[62] Although Herder certainly goes beyond Lowth's work (or, in his conception, deeper into the spirit of poetry), he takes Lowth's view of the Hebrew Bible as a starting point and thus serves to extend its influence in Germany. The foundational idea that Herder takes from Lowth is that the Hebrew Bible, particularly

---

[59] Isaiah Berlin, *Three Critics of the Enlightenment: Vico, Hamann, Herder* (Princeton: Princeton University Press, 2000), 334.

[60] J. G. Hamann, "Aesthetica in Nuce: A Rhapsody in Cabbalistic Prose (1762)," in *Classic and Romantic German Aesthetics*, ed. J. M. Bernstein (New York: Cambridge University Press, 2003), 7, 9. Hamann also refers to Michaelis as "the Archangel," a play on his name, which, as Gwen Dickson suggests, is probably intended to imply that he is the (very imperfect) mediator of Lowth's work. Gwen Griffith Dickson, *Johann Georg Hamann's Relational Metacriticism* (Berlin: de Gruyter, 1995), 86.

[61] Berlin, *Roots of Romanticism*, 47.

[62] Herder, *Hebrew Poetry*, 1:51.

the parts that can be read as poetic literature, provides a viable alternative to classical and neoclassical literature, a literature that expresses both the individual spirits of great authors and the collective spirit of a nation.

Herder's aesthetic approach to the Hebrew Bible is obvious throughout his work on Hebrew poetry, which, like Lowth's *Lectures*, reads as an extended apology for the literary merit of the Hebrew texts. The first volume of Herder's work on Hebrew poetry takes the form of an extended dialogue that begins when Alciphron, a young lover of poetry, asks Euthyphron why he continues to study the "poor and barbarous language" of the Hebrews.[63] Euthyphron responds by challenging Alciphron to a discussion of Hebrew literature, and proposes that, in order to ensure that they are not swayed by the consideration of the religious value of the texts, they speak of the literature "only as an instrument of ancient poetry."[64] Although Herder, a devout Lutheran pastor and preacher, believed in the divine origin of the Bible as well as its revelatory nature and basic historicity, his choice to investigate the texts as human literary products is a further development of the nonreligious appreciation of the texts pioneered by Lowth. Herder writes, "In human fashion must one read the Bible: for it was written by men for men."[65] One indication that Herder's work goes farther in this direction than Lowth's is that whereas Lowth's title refers to the *Sacred Poetry of the Hebrews*, Herder's simply refers to "Hebrew Poetry."

As was the case with Lowth, Herder's defense of the literary worth of the Hebrew Bible involved articulating a new conception of literary values. As these new values are the very ones that Romantic authors used to challenge neoclassical values, Herder's work on Hebrew poetry, like Lowth's, can be seen as a contribution to the Romantic revolution. When Alciphron complains that the literature of the Bible is too simple and never moves beyond unrefined sketches, Euthyphron gives an answer that is a direct attack on neoclassical formalism: the literary works of the Bible, he says, "are not loaded with delicate and overwrought refinement, but vigorous, entire, instinct with life and spirit."[66] He goes on to root these literary virtues in the Hebrew language: "Their verbs ... are all action and emotion. The nouns ... are still active agents, and exhibit a continual personification. Their pronouns ... always possess the language of passion .... From all these peculiarities the language seems to me, I confess, more poetical, than any other language on earth."[67] Whereas refined and carefully wrought language was taken to be essential to poetry in classical theory, Herder's conception of the language of poetry is clearly Romantic with its preference for vigor, emotion, activity, passion, and spirit.

---

[63] Herder, *Hebrew Poetry*, 1:25. In Plato's *Euthyphro*, Euthyphro is a mystic who realizes that his divine messages will seem like madness to men of reason. Plato, "Euthyphro," in *Plato: Complete Works*, ed. John M. Cooper (Indianapolis, IN: Hackett, 1997), 1–16. Herder's teacher Hamann uses Euthyphro to refer to Francis Bacon, who he believes understood the need to complement scientific rationalism with a recognition of the divine or magical in nature. Dickson, *Hamann's Metacriticism*, 79, 87.

[64] Herder, *Hebrew Poetry*, 1:27.

[65] *Briefe, das Studium der Theologie betreffend* (vol. 10, letter no. 2). Quoted in Hans Frei, *The Eclipse of Biblical Narrative: A Study in Eighteenth and Nineteenth Century Hermeneutics* (New Haven, CT: Yale University Press, 1974), 184.

[66] Herder, *Hebrew Poetry*, 1:32.

[67] Herder, *Hebrew Poetry*, 1:32-33.

Herder's defense of Hebrew poetry can also be seen as Romantic in the way it offers an alternative to the tastes of rationalist critics. When Alciphron complains that parallelism is mere tautology and offers little to the understanding, Euthyphron counters with a Lowthian account of parallelism well suited to Romantic sensibilities:

> Poetry is not addressed to the understanding alone but primarily and chiefly to the feelings. And are these not friendly to parallelism? So soon as the heart gives way to its emotions, wave follows upon wave, and that is parallelism. ... The pulsation of nature, this breathing of emotion, appears in all the language of passion, and would you not have that in poetry, which is most peculiarly the offspring of the emotions?[68]

In poetry, heart speaks to heart in the language of passion. This conception of poetry is both clearly Romantic and clearly drawn from Lowth's presentation of parallelism and poetry.

Herder also builds on the foundational contribution Lowth's study of Hebrew poetry made to Romanticism: the expressive account of poetic creation, the idea that poetry is not the result of an intentional attempt to skillfully represent a chosen subject (mimesis) but instead comes from the spontaneous overflow from the heart of an artist moved by passion (self-expression). Herder writes,

> Instead of placing [poetic art's] essence in the imitation of nature, ... we ... place it in the imitation of that Divine agency, which creates, and gives form and determinateness to the objects of its creation .... [T]he more unsophisticated and full the impulse of feeling, which impels us to impress everything with [our] humanity, ... the more beautiful, the more perfect, and ... the more powerful will be our poetic art.[69]

It is this Romantic conception of poetry, drawn from Lowth, that allows Herder to conclude that the Hebrew poets were the greatest because, "in this feeling of natural beauty and sublimity the ... nations of the greatest simplicity have in their natural imagery and expressions of natural feeling, the most elevated and touching poetry."[70]

Herder, German Literature, and Romantic Nationalism

In Lowth's idea that Hebrew poetry is the simple expression of the Hebrew nation, Herder found a powerful justification for his endeavor: promoting German literature as the expression of the German national spirit. It is a small step from Euthyphron's defense of the "poor and barbarous" Hebrew language to Herder's defense of the German language and German literature, which might appear "poor and barbarous" in the eyes of neoclassical or Francophile critics. Like Lowth, Herder's aim went

---

[68] Herder, *Hebrew Poetry*, 1:41.
[69] Herder, *Hebrew Poetry*, II:7–8.
[70] Herder, *Hebrew Poetry*, II:8.

beyond winning a hearing for the Bible as ancient literature to laying the foundation for a new kind of contemporary literature, one that came to be recognized as Romantic literature; but Herder had the further aim of promoting national literature, specifically German literature. In the passage where Herder asserts that simple nations often produce the most elevated poetry, he continues with the further assertion that "the poetical images and feelings of one people, and of one age, can never be judged, censured, and rejected according to the standard of another people, and another age."[71] Although Herder is still ostensibly writing about Hebrew poetry, he might also have said that the literature of the Germans cannot be judged by the neoclassical standards of the French, or that the literature of the eighteenth century in the German states cannot be rejected in favor of the classical age in Greece and Rome. His rationale for this assertion is that one people will produce a different literature than another people based on their age and place—whether in contemporary Germany or ancient Israel.

To appreciate the poetry of ancient Israel, Herder—following Lowth—believed it was necessary to understand it as the work of an ancient "Oriental" people. His work encourages his readers to "become with shepherds a shepherd, with the people of the sod a man of the land, with the ancients of the Orient an Easterner."[72] As in Lowth, this exercise in historical imagination is, in part, a necessary element of the argument for the excellence of a literature that conforms so little to the tastes of the day that it is often not recognized as literature. However, by Herder's time there was a growing taste for "Oriental" and ancient literature, due in no small part to the influence of Lowth—and of Michaelis, often descried as the foremost "Orientalist" of his day. In Herder, the "Oriental" poetry of the Hebrews takes its place alongside the ancient works of Homer and "Ossian," as poetry that can only be understood in reference to the ancient and alien cultures that produced them.[73] Herder attempts to surpass Lowth in his attempt to clear away the difficulties that prevent the modern reader from fully entering into ancient Hebrew culture and literature. The title of his work suggests that it will not merely help his readers appreciate the outward forms of Hebrew literature but enable them to enter into its "Spirit."[74] The idea of a Spirit, or *Geist*, that stands

---

[71] Herder, *Hebrew Poetry*, II:8.

[72] Herder, *Briefe* (vol. 10, letter no. 14). Quoted in Frei, *Eclipse of Biblical Narrative*, 185.

[73] "Ossian," to whom Herder often refers in his work, was thought to be an ancient Scottish poet (*Fragments of Ancient Poetry, Collected from the Scottish Highlands and Translated from the Galic or Erse Language by James Macpherson*, 1760). Although the poems were a fraud, they had a great effect on early Romantic poets and scholars including Herder. It appears that Herder shared his enthusiasm for Ossian with Goethe during their first encounter in Strasbourg (1770) when Herder encouraged Goethe to give free rein to his feelings in his writing. In its parallelism and attempts at sublimity, the poems of Ossian owe much to Hebrew poetry as promoted by Lowth.

Thomas Blackwell's *Enquiry into the Life and Wrings of Homer* (1735; German translation, 1766) helped to recast Homer's poetry as bound to the national and linguistic context of ancient Greece. Stephen Prickett, *Words and the Word: Language, Poetics and Biblical Interpretation* (New York: Cambridge University Press, 1986), 50.

[74] Hans Frei detects an ambivalence in Herder's attitude toward Lowth, and attributes it to Herder's perception that Lowth had not fully freed himself from the poetic categories of the early eighteenth century and had not fully entered into the "spirit" of Hebrew poetry. Frei, *Eclipse of Biblical Narrative*, 184. Perhaps, as appears to be the case with Hamann, Herder has a greater dissatisfaction with Lowth's reception by authors like Michaelis than with Lowth himself.

behind literature became a powerful impetus for the appreciation of German literature. That German literature was a product of the German Spirit could have two important significances. It could simply mean that like the literature of other countries, German literature was a product of the unique national character—the spirit—of the German people. However, it could also mean that in comparison to the literatures other peoples who might pride themselves in the outward forms of their culture, German literature was greater because the German people were characterized by their depth in matters of the Spirit.

In Herder's work, the word "people" (*Volk*) plays similar role in his promotion of Hebrew and German literature. Like *Geist, Volk* has two overlapping significances that are important for Herder's argument. On the one hand, Herder uses *Volk* to refer to a group of people organically united by a common language and culture, a powerful idea that Herder contributed to German nationalism (and Romantic nationalism throughout Europe). On the other hand, *Volk* can also refer to the common people as opposed to the aristocratic elites, a powerful idea that Herder and other Romantics used to turn the system of classical values on its head. The idea that every *Volk* has its own literature serves to undermine the idea that there is a universal standard of literary excellence (such as the neoclassical values of France). However, the celebration of simple, natural, free literature of the common *Volk* over the artificial, constrained, elitist, literature of the urban and courtly elites sets up a new standard that allows the judgment that German literature is better. The superiority of German literature can be explained by considering it a product of the superior German "*Volkgeist*"—a word coined by Herder.

It has already been observed that the rise of a self-consciously German literature in the late eighteenth century was closely tied with a Romantic understanding of literature, one in which literature was thought of as the expression of the spirit of an individual or a culture. Now it can be added that Herder was arguably the most important proponent of German Romanticism, and that the Romantic aspects of his thinking were primarily drawn (whether directly and or indirectly) from Lowth's work on Hebrew Poetry. Lowth's conception of Hebrew poetry as the expression of the spirit of the Hebrew people is central to one of Herder's most influential ideas: what has been termed Romantic nationalism, the idea that nations should be founded on the common culture and language of the people. Herder was one of the primary architects of this cultural and political view, which not only intensified the desire of the German-speaking people to throw off French (and Austrian) imperial rule and unite as a German nation but also coupled the goals of independence and unification to the recovery and development of a common German culture, in particular, an authentically German literature. Herder's idea that a great national literature was rooted in the expression of the *Volkgeist* inspired his generation to collect and consolidate German stories, legends, and songs. This is the root of what came to be called "folklore." Herder himself made a famous collection of German songs, and it was largely due to his influence that the Grimm brothers began collecting German folk tales. Later generations were intent on discovering the national epic that would be for Germany what Homer's epics were for the Greeks or "Ossian's" for Scottish people. However, Herder's dominant role in German Romanticism meant that in the quest for authentic German literature the foundational model would be the Bible, and, particularly, the Hebrew poetry of the prophets as understood by Lowth.

Lowth's Influences on Duhm's Biography of Jeremiah

This brief survey of the pervasive influence of Lowth's work in German culture and literature helps to explain the Lowthian elements in Duhm in terms of his German context. It fills in some of the historical background needed to make sense of the observation in the previous chapter that Duhm's approach to Jeremiah is founded in a literary sensibility that could broadly be described as Romantic and more specifically as grounded in Lowth's understanding of poetry. It was noted that the Lowthian influence is particularly obvious in Duhm's idea of what distinguishes great literature from inferior literature (originality, authenticity, sincerity, passion, simplicity, sublimity) and his idea of the source of great literature (inspiration, understood as passionate experiences of sensitive poetic souls called forth by particular historical or biographical incidents). Now it can be seen that these are common elements of German Romanticism, which was widespread in the nineteenth century and rooted in the work of Herder (and ultimately Lowth) in the eighteenth century. The Lowthian influence on German literature, particularly as mediated by Herder, also helps to explain the observation made in this chapter of the close similarity of Duhm's reconstruction of the biography of Jeremiah and the lives of Romantic poets.

The Lowthian Roots of German Biblical Criticism

To explain the Lowthian influence on Duhm's understanding of the historical prophets behind the books that bear their names, it is necessary to go beyond looking at Lowth's influence in German culture and literature in general and consider his influence on German biblical scholarship in particular. It has been estimated that Lowth's impact on German literature was even greater than his impact on British literature; however, his impact on German biblical scholarship in comparison to British biblical scholarship is even more pronounced. This is particularly true of German studies of the Old Testament. In the estimation of John Rogerson, Lowth's *Lectures on the Sacred Poetry of the Hebrews* is "a British work whose influence upon the German Old Testament scholarship of its day had probably never been equaled."[75] As in the case of Lowth's general influence on German culture, the story of his influence on German biblical scholarship begins with the widespread popularity of the German edition of the *Lectures* published by Michaelis, who was one of the foremost biblical scholars of the eighteenth century. However, as was also the case in the broader story, it was primarily through the work of Herder that Lowth's influence had its most significant and characteristic influence. The foundational contribution of Lowth and Herder to German Biblical studies was the idea that the Old Testament contained great literature: that it should be classed among the great works of literature and could be appreciated in the same

---

[75] John Rogerson, *Old Testament Criticism in the Nineteenth Century: England and Germany* (London: SPCK, 1984), 23.

way. As Robert Thompson wrote, "Herder's aestheticism was in the air when [biblical] criticism began."[76]

Thompson's reference to the beginning of biblical criticism is a reminder that the late eighteenth century was not only the formative period for German literature but also for modern biblical criticism, which can be said to have primarily originated in Germany. Herder, disseminating the influence of Lowth, was at the center of it. A foundational tenet of the "higher," or "historical," "criticism"[77] that began its rise to prominence in Germany at this time was the belief that the biblical books should be studied like other ancient literature, with particular attention to their original historical contexts and the purposes of their authors.[78] This belief, as has been seen, was promoted by Herder, and Lowth before him. It was application of this belief to the interpretation of the Pentateuch in his *Introduction to the Old Testament* (1783–5) that gained Johann Gottfried Eichhorn the title "the father of higher criticism"; however, the degree to which Eichhorn's approach is derived from Lowth's might suggest that, in regard to historical criticism of the Bible, Lowth should be considered "the grandfather." As in German biblical studies as a whole, Lowth's influence on Eichhorn was primarily mediated through Herder. Eichhorn first met Herder in 1780, and afterward they remained close associates and correspondents.[79] It was during the early years of their friendship that Eichhorn published his *Introduction*—a year after the publication of Herder's *Spirit of Hebrew Poetry* (1782–3). Eichhorn's awareness of his debt to his friend is remarked by Cheyne: who writes, "Eichhorn is never weary of confessing that he lives upon Herder's ideas."[80] Many of the ideas that Eichhorn drew from Herder, Herder had drawn from Lowth. Lowth's influence on Eichhorn was not only through Herder, but also through Eichhorn's teachers Michaelis (whom he succeeded at Göttingen) and C. G. Heyne, and surely through his own reading of Lowth's *Lectures*. Eichhorn wrote of Lowth: "Let no one forget that we have become what we are, in part at least, by his aid."[81]

Lowth's contribution to the rise of the historical criticism of Eichhorn and other German biblical scholars was not only the general encouragement to a literary and historical approach to the Hebrew Scriptures, but a particular conception of the

---

[76] R. J. Thompson, *Moses and the Law in a Century of Criticism since Graf*, VTSup 19 (Leiden: Brill, 1970), 45.

[77] "Higher Criticism" is the counterpart of "lower criticism," which refers primarily to textual criticism. Higher criticism of the text (which had been established by textual criticism) primarily dealt with understanding the composition of books in terms of the authorship and dates of the various sources that lie behind the present text. The concern with discerning sources explains why "source criticism" is another roughly synonymous term.

[78] The idea that the biblical books should be studied like non-biblical literature is the reason that this kind of study could be called "literary criticism" of the Bible. The fact that the central concerns of biblical and non-biblical studies of literature at this time had to do with sources, author, and dating explains why the terms "literary criticism," "source criticism," "historical criticism," and "higher criticism" are roughly synonymous as descriptions of the biblical studies of this time (from the late eighteenth to the early twentieth centuries).

[79] Eichhorn was professor of Oriental languages at Jena when Herder was appointed court preacher at nearby Weimar. Cheyne, *Founders of OT Criticism*, 16.

[80] Cheyne, *Founders of OT Criticism*, 17.

[81] Quoted by Calvin E. Stow, review of *Lectures on the Sacred Poetry of the Hebrews*, by Robert Lowth, trans. G. Gregory (1839), NAmerR 31 (1830): 366. Eichhorn was a student of Michaelis and succeeded him at Göttingen.

prophetic writings as the greatest works of Hebrew literature and the prophets behind them as the greatest authors of Israel's literary history. As was seen in the previous chapter, Lowth's primary aim in his lectures was to win appreciation for the prophetic books as inspired poetry. Herder's work builds on Lowth's promotion of prophetic poetry by exalting the poetic prophets as historical giants who brought Israel to national glory. Herder's famous statement "A poet is the creator of the nation around him" draws on Lowth's particular way of fusing the identities of prophet and poet and adapts it to serve his vision of authors and artists raising up a great nation. Whereas Lowth's work put forward Hebrew poetry as a compelling alternative to neoclassical literature, Herder's work put forward the Hebrew prophets as models for the historical figures who could bring Germany to greatness. In this way, Lowth laid the foundation for Duhm's understanding of the poetry in the book of Jeremiah and Herder laid the foundation for Duhm's understanding of the historical prophet behind the book.

Herder's Reconception of Prophets as National Leaders and Geniuses of Humanity

The reconception of the role of prophets in Herder's work involved replacing traditional ideas of the prophecy's aims and nature. In both his departure from the traditional view as well as his creation of a new view, Herder built on the foundation laid by Lowth. While Lowth made it possible to conceive of the prophets as poets, his insight was mainly limited to the genre of their writing. He argued that poetic form was compatible with the nature and ends of prophecy, the nature and ends *traditionally associated with* prophecy. For Lowth the two ends of prophecy are (1) "to inform and amend those generations that precede the events predicted" and (2) to offer a "demonstration and attestation … of the divine veracity" to those who live after the prediction is accomplished.[82] These two purposes of prophecy make clear Lowth's traditional understanding of the basic nature of prophecy: prophecy is prediction. Herder goes farther than Lowth in breaking with tradition: he denies that prediction was an essential part of prophecy. He observes that with Moses, his great model of a prophet, "prediction, that is the foretelling of events, was as little thought of as with Abraham" (i.e., the first notable example of a prophet).[83] Instead, argues Herder, the essential nature of a prophet is "a man, through whom God spake, and by whose instrumentality he accomplished his purposes."[84] Herder's definition might appear to fit with a traditional view of a prophet—until one examines what Herder believed to be God's purposes in raising up prophets. In Herder's view, the primary ends for which God employed prophets were not to warn people of impending doom nor to induce belief in himself through miraculous predictions but rather to raise up a nation and

---

[82] Lowth, *Poetry of the Hebrews*, 277.
[83] Herder, *Hebrew Poetry*, 2:57. Herder does not deny that the prophetic message has to do with futurity. Ian Balfour notes that for Herder, "prophecy offers a vista into the future (*'eine Aussicht in die Zukunft'*), but precise prediction of any particular event is entirely contrary to the prophetic spirit." Ian Balfour, *The Rhetoric of Romantic Prophecy*, (Stanford, CA: Stanford University Press, 2002), 112.
[84] Herder, *Hebrew Poetry*, 2:57.

bring enlightenment to the human race. The prophets in Herder's presentation become leaders of their nations and benefactors of the human race.[85]

Herder's understanding of prophets as not only religious poets but also national leaders is most evident in his treatment of Moses, whom he considers the prime model of a prophet. That Moses fit the Lowthian model of an inspired poet was evident to Herder from the poetic compositions of Moses: his song at the Red Sea (Exodus 15), "the lofty Psalm attributed to him" (Psalm 90), and his "last poetical effusion" (Deuteronomy 32). These poems are not merely samples of the creativity or lofty sentiments that marked Moses as a poet; they are part of his efforts to establish the national literature of Israel: the first is the model of all the "psalms of praise, of triumph, and of deliverance" of Israel; the second, "the beautiful model of didactic poems" of Israel; and the third, the pattern of Israel's prophets. However, these poems do not simply establish the literary reputation of Moses; for Herder they are simultaneously evidence of his genius for nation building. The poetry of Moses (along with his efforts to teach his people to write) lays the foundation "for making a barbarian people … into a literary people."[86] Along with literary work of Moses in forging a national literature as a poet, Moses also established the civic and religious order of the nation through his work as a lawgiver. Since both his poetic and legislative achievements are instances of Moses carrying out God's purposes for his nation and for humanity, Herder considers them both to be prophetic actions:

> Has the Divine Being a nobler work among men than their cultivation? And was not he [Moses] who undertook to advance this in those early times, amid obstacles apparently boundless, and with no human support, whether he did it as a teacher, or as an actor on the stage of life, was he not truly a man of God, a genius of humanity? Let one but look at those nations, which have remained behind or sunk into a savage state; observe to what a condition of horrible depravity human nature sinks, when it is not forced upward by a living power and aroused from its gloomy lethargy, and he will then be able to appreciate the services of those early guardians of our race, who diffused the enlightening influence of their spirits over succeeding ages, embraced nations within the compass of their affections, and, even against their will, raised them from degradation with a giant power. Such men the Divine Being has scattered sparingly in the world.[87]

In this passage, Herder provides a new category for classifying prophets. By identifying prophets with poets, Lowth made it possible to understand them by analogy with Homer and Aeschylus. By identifying prophets with "genius[es] of humanity," Herder further expands the idea of prophets, allowing a comparison with the "enlightening influences" of all kinds of geniuses who contribute to the education of the human race. Prophets belong to the class of geniuses that includes not only artists but also creators

---

[85] Ian Balfour observes that Herder can "characterize prophecy in general as 'political art' ('*politische Kunst*')." Balfour, *Rhetoric of Romantic Prophecy*, 111.

[86] Herder, *Hebrew Poetry*, 1:277.

[87] Herder, *Hebrew Poetry*, 2:57.

and founders in many different fields.[88] In a poem celebrating the contributions of the prophets, Herder salutes Moses, Elijah, Isaiah, and Jeremiah, but along with them, "The Druids, Orpheus and Pythagoras" as well as "Plato, and whoe'er by wholesome laws has proved his people's father and their guide."[89] Prophets are those who have made creative contributions to their nations and to humanity not only in poetry (like Orpheus) but also in religion, science, philosophy, and civic order.

Needs Met by Herder's New Understanding of Prophets

Some of Herder's modifications of Lowth's position helped to make biblical prophecy more credible to the "cultured despisers" of religion in his Enlightenment audience. For those wary of "crude supernaturalism," Herder removes a major obstacle to appreciation of the prophets by his denial that prediction is essential to prophecy. However, Herder himself is not a religious skeptic; he is eager to maintain the belief that prophecy has a divine origin. In his portrayal of the prophets as the instruments of God's purposes for humanity in history, he maintains a delicate balance between the traditional theological view that it is God alone who can save the human race or enlighten them through revelation and the newer humanistic view that human progress comes through exceptional humans who educate humanity by their enlightened spirits. For example, in his comments on Moses as prophet, it remains somewhat unclear whether the "living" or "giant power" that raises humanity out of degradation is the power of God or the power of enlightened spirits and geniuses of humanity. As in Lowth's effort to win appreciation for Hebrew poetry as literature, so also in Herder's attempt to cast prophets as geniuses of humanity, a secularizing or humanizing trend is evident. Although Herder himself may have always kept one foot in traditional belief, the new position he worked out is a step along the path to the idea that prophecy is simply another name for the work of the great spirits of history who make lasting contributions to the development of the human race. Herder's view of prophecy moves closer to Lessing's perspective, which reduces revelation to what humanity learns through history: "That which Education is to the individual, Revelation is to the Race."[90] However, Herder himself attempts to resist this reduction of revelation by his assertions of the divine guidance of the prophets. According to Hans Frei, Herder understands biblical revelation as "the fullest expression of the one human spirit under the guidance of divine providence."[91]

Herder's new conception of prophets not only helped him to win over skeptics to an appreciation for biblical prophecy; it also made the prophetic writings and the

---

[88] Gadamer traces the rise to dominance of the concept of genius. From its limited place in the aesthetic theory of Kant, "in the nineteenth century the concept of genius rose to the status of a universal concept of value and—together with the concept of the creative—achieved a true apotheosis." Hans Georg Gadamer, *Truth and Method*, trans. Joel Weinsheimer and Donald Marshal, 2nd ed. (New York: Continuum, 2000), 59.

[89] Herder, *Hebrew Poetry*, 2:55.

[90] Gotthold Ephraim Lessing, *The Education of the Human Race*, trans. F. W. Robertson, 3rd ed. (London: Henry S. King [1777–80] 1872), 1.

[91] Frei, *Eclipse of Biblical Narrative*, 185.

prophets available as resources to meet contemporary needs. Herder's prophets could serve as models for his German contemporaries. As in Lowth's time, understanding the prophets as poets provided a liberating alternative for contemporary poets who felt stifled by the strictures of neoclassical literary theory; so in Herder's time, understanding the prophets as national founders and guides provided Germans with a vision of the kind of leaders who could—like Moses had done for the Israelites—unite the disparate German-speaking peoples, liberate them from their imperial rulers, and lay the foundations for national greatness. The fusion of national leader and inspired poet in Herder's portrayal of the prophets contributed to the idea that the national unity and greatness Germans hoped for could be founded on a revival of German literature.

Herder's idea that the prophets served their nation (and humanity as a whole) not only in the political but in the literary realm, applies with greater force to the prophets responsible for the prophetic books than to the prophets like Moses whose stories are told in the historical books. Moses, Samuel, and even Nathan can be credited with contributing to the rise of the nation of Israel; but the times of the writing prophets are mostly the eras of the nation's decline. Herder observes, "Isaiah and other Prophets could speak like Moses ... but where is the work which they accomplished? the political edifice, which they left behind them?"[92] What these latter prophets left behind them was literature, and this literature was not so much the foundation of the Hebrew nation, but its fruit: the expression of its national spirit and its particular contribution to the education of humankind.

Although Herder may have judged the contributions made to national greatness made by the writing prophets as inferior to the contribution of the nation-building prophets like Moses, his very inclusion of these later prophets in the category of national heroes and educators of humanity moves the understanding of their significance some way down a path opened up by Lowth. They become the prime examples of how creative artists and especially poets contribute to the progress of humanity. Other Romantic poets were exploring this same path. Wordsworth's *Prelude*, for example, not only tells the story of how he became a poet but how he came to understand that poets could make great contributions to humankind, contributions that even surpassed those of political leaders. Wordsworth lived in revolutionary times when there were great hopes that humanity would soon break through to a new golden age. Like many of his contemporaries, he had high hopes that the French Revolution would not only give birth to a new nation, but usher in a new world order. When the Revolution descended into the Reign of Terror, his hopes were dashed and only recovered by the discovery of his literary powers. He came to believe that human progress would come through breakthrough to a new level of human consciousness, one that could be sparked by his own sublime experiences as expressed in his poetry. Wordsworth's story, in which his hope in political revolution was replaced by hopes of a revolution in consciousness, is only one of many among the leading figures in English and German Romanticism. M. H. Abrams traces parallel journeys in the lives of Southey, Coleridge, Shelley,

---

[92] Herder, *Hebrew Poetry*, 1:306-7.

Hölderin, Novalis, and Carlyle. For each of them, the failure of the French Revolution was the catalyst for a process in which "faith in an apocalypse by [political] revolution … gave way to faith in an apocalypse by imagination or cognition."[93]

Many of these Romantic authors, particularly in England, looked to the example of Milton, who, disillusioned by the outcome of the Puritan Revolution, wrote his poetic masterpieces that refocused hope from the lost political paradise to the possibility of recovering "a paradise within … happier far."[94] However, particularly in Germany and in part due to the work of Herder, it was neither Milton nor Shakespeare nor their German counterparts who provided the foundational examples of the great souls who rise above the circumstances of their day to a proclaim a vision of liberation that comes from within and thus play a role in lifting not only their nations but of all humanity; these models were provided by the writing prophets of the Hebrew Bible. The great souls of all nations could be understood to be inspired in a way similar to the inspiration of the biblical prophets. Just as Lowth's work had enabled a new understanding of poetic inspiration by grounding it in prophetic inspiration, Herder's work allowed a new understanding of the inspiration of the agents of human progress by grounding it in the inspiration of the prophets.

As the Romantic use of the poetry in the prophetic books as model for contemporary poetry made it necessary for prophetic poetry to be read in a particular way (as the spontaneous effusions of sensitive souls overwhelmed by passionate emotions), so the historical use of the prophets behind the prophetic books as models for the geniuses who elevate their nations and humanity made it necessary that the lives of the prophets include particular components. The basic features of the model have been observed in the life of Wordsworth. If the prophet is to be an example of giving expression to the spirit of his land and people, then evidence must be found in his work of the shaping influence of a rural upbringing among the common folk of the nation. If the prophet is to be an example of an individual whom history has used to educate the human race, then there must be a psychologically compelling account of how he came to develop the perceptive powers that allowed him to see what no one had seen before. If the prophet is to serve as an example of those geniuses whose forward-looking visions put them at odds with those enmeshed in the current dogmas or established customs, the prophet's life must feature opposition from those who find his novel ideas threatening. Whether the prophet is a triumphant reformer who wins over his contemporaries to his new vision or a tragic hero—or martyr—who is overcome by his opponents makes little difference. What matters is the sincerity of the prophet's belief in the truth he has discovered and fidelity to his vision in the face of opposition from the unenlightened.

Although Herder provided the general pattern for the new understanding of the prophets as enlightened educators of humanity, it was left to the biblical scholars who followed him to work out the details for each of the individual prophets behind the prophetic books of the Bible. This biographical project was one of the main tasks

---

[93] M. H. Abrams, *Natural Supernaturalism: Tradition and Revolution in Romantic Literature* (New York: W. W. Norton, 1971), 334.

[94] John Milton, *Paradise Lost*, in *Complete Poems and Major Prose*, ed. Merritt Y. Hughes (New Jersey: Prentice Hall, 1957), XII, 587.

of nineteenth-century biblical scholarship, particularly in Germany, and it can be said to have reached a culmination in Duhm's 1901 study of Jeremiah in which he claimed that his method finally made it possible to understand Jeremiah as a "great man" and in particular "a man, a writer, and a prophet."[95] What Duhm meant by these terms can now be better seen in light of Herder: a believable historical figure, whose primary contribution to his nation and to humanity came through his sublime literary works, and who could be recognized as a prophet by his conviction of the truth of his individual vision, which allowed him to persevere in the face of opposition.

Ewald's Prophets: Men of Vision and Conflict

Of all of the nineteenth-century biblical scholars who contributed to the transformation of the prophets along the lines of Herder's vision, perhaps the most influential was Heinrich Ewald (1803–1875), Duhm's (and Wellhausen's) professor. A line of scholarly tradition connecting Duhm with Lowth runs back through Ewald. As Duhm had been taught at Göttingen by Ewald, Ewald, in turn, had been taught at Göttingen by Eichhorn, who, as it has been seen, was heavily influenced by Herder and Lowth. Cheyne notes that portraits of Eichhorn and Herder hung on the walls of Ewald's study, "as if to remind him of the aim and spirit of their common enterprise."[96] Ewald's work on the prophets is the clearest precedent to Duhm's work on the prophets. And he builds on the work that Herder built on the foundation laid by Lowth.

The Lowthian foundation of Ewald's work is that he understands the prophets as inspired poets and their writings as Israel's greatest literature. The aesthetic approach to the Hebrew Bible that Ewald drew from Lowth and Herder is evident in the intentional progression of his publications on the Old Testament: first, his volumes on poetry, then his volumes on prophecy, and finally his history of Israel.[97] Cheyne explains that Ewald thought it safest to begin with the poets, who he hoped would give him "a vantage-point for comprehending ... the far loftier speech of the prophets."[98]

Ewald's understanding of the prophetic vocation builds on Herder's portrayal of the prophets as the agents of God's providential cultivation of humanity. In his introduction to the phenomenon of prophecy, he offers a portrait of a prophet's calling:

If ... the heart of an individual, ... consents to be aroused by the divine thought ... to a corresponding purpose and activity, in that man a new life will be established ... in fellowship with God and all truth ... and the consequent action ... will take part in the divine operation itself, producing thus eternal and blessed fruit and reward. ...

[95] Duhm, *Jeremia*, vii.
[96] Cheyne, *Founders of OT Criticism*, 71.
[97] Five volumes of *Die poetischen Bücher des Alten Bundes* beginning with Song of Solomon (1826, 1835, 1836, 1837, 1839). Two volumes of *Die Propheten des Alten Bundes* (1840–1). Five volumes of *Geschichte des Volkes Israel* (1843–59).
[98] Cheyne, *Founders of OT Criticism*, 87.

> The sign and proof of the actual formation ... of a fellowship of this kind ... must be supplied ... by a clear and lucid view of his age and its condition, by wisdom and perfect calmness in the face of the clouds and complication of the present, by firm energetic action in overcoming the hindrances in the way of what is good, and by the subsequent certain victory.[99]

Ewald's prophet is a lonely reformer, the only person who can see clearly what is happening in his time. The prophet takes his stand against his age, confident in his own enlightenment and in his eventual vindication: "Whoever feels within himself a light, by which he divides the dark clouds of his time, will not deceive himself ... [and] will sooner or later be recognized by others."[100]

The prophet described by Ewald as a man of unshakeable conviction is not only the one he found in the biblical prophets, but the one he embodied for his contemporaries. He was dismissed twice from the faculty of Göttingen for political insubordination and was finally forbidden to lecture.[101] In his time in the German parliament, he was charged three times with insulting the king.[102] His confidence that his scholarly positions were correct and that others were in error led to Ewald's life-long antagonism toward Gesenius and the insults he directed at several other leading scholars in his books.[103] Zimmerli recounts that on his portrait of his teacher, Wellhausen had written, "His hand against every man, and every man against him" (Gen. 16:12).[104] As the Romantic poets from Blake to Wordsworth had both been shaped by and helped to give shape to Lowth's picture of the prophet as an inspired poet, Heinrich Ewald was shaped by and helped to give shape to Herder's picture of the prophet as an enlightened voice of truth at odds with his age.

The idea that prophets, as conduits of human enlightenment and progress, would necessarily come into conflict with unenlightened resistance to change was a dominant characteristic of the new understanding of prophecy developed by Lowth and Herder and their followers. Obviously, they were not the first to notice that Jeremiah and many of the other prophets encountered opposition. What they added was a particular characterization of the nature of the conflict between the prophets and their opponents. They recast the conflict as an ancient precursor to the conflicts they found themselves in. The leaders of the Romantic movement understood themselves in comparison to neoclassical formalists and Enlightenment rationalists. Thus, they understood

---

[99] Heinrich Ewald, *Commentary on the Prophets of the Old Testament*, trans. J. Frederick Smith, TTFL 9 (London: Williams & Norgate, 1875), 1:72, 1:4-5.

[100] Ewald, *Prophets of the Old Testament*, 1:5.

[101] First as part of the Göttingen Seven who protested against the Hanoverian King Augustus Ernest (1837); second, for refusing to take an oath of loyalty to the new Prussian King (1867). Cheyne, *Founders of OT Criticism*, 92–3, 114.

[102] Walther Zimmerli, *The Law and the Prophets: A Study of the Meaning of the Old Testament*, James Sprunt lectures 1963 (Oxford: Blackwell, 1965), 20.

[103] His harsh words for de Wette, Baur, Delitzsch, Hengstenberg, and Pusey were well known. Cheyne, *Founders of OT Criticism*, 61, 82, 91, 94. In a footnote to his work on Prophets, Ewald refers to "the English works of Pusey upon the Prophets, which must in our day have their origin in the desire to annihilate all Biblical science." Ewald, *Prophets of the Old Testament*, 1:105.

[104] Zimmerli also cites Wellhausen's words on Ewald's death: "He died on May 4th, 1875, in conflict with the world, but at peace with God." Zimmerli, *Law and Prophets*, 20.

Hebrew prophecy as representing artistic freedom as opposed to following traditional constraints, originality as opposed to imitation of classical models, spontaneity as opposed to artificiality, and expression of passion as opposed to dry rationality. In the nineteenth century, biblical scholars following Herder who understood the prophets as agents of human progress, portrayed as geniuses of innovation as opposed to traditional thinkers, as reformers as opposed to those invested in the status quo, as progressives as opposed to reactionaries.

This is the model of prophetic conflict by which Duhm, following Ewald and Herder before him, understood Jeremiah and his opponents. It was also the one by which Duhm understood himself and his opponents. In the foreword to his Jeremiah commentary, Duhm predicted that his conclusion that only the poetry of the book was authentic would be met with "various cries of indignation and the most wondrous censures ex cathedra." He also predicted his eventual vindication: "They won't do any good, but at least they won't do any harm. I have complete confidence that my findings are, in the main, right."[105] In this way of understanding, opposition from the powerful representatives of the established order validates the status of a prophetic individual as one of the great men of history. The opposition Jeremiah faced provided the primary evidence to Duhm of his greatness: "In the struggle with kings and priests, with prophets and scribes, Jeremiah acquired the right to be placed beside the greatest men not only of his people, but of the world's history."[106] The opposition Duhm believed his commentary on Jeremiah would provoke provided validation for the truth of its claims.

New Conception of the Opposition between Prophets and Priests and Scribes

Duhm's understanding of Jeremiah as one of the great men in the history of Israel and in the history of the world involves understanding the prophet's opponents as those who tried to silence the voice of enlightenment and stand in the way of progress because of their investment in preserving the present system. If prophets represent progress, their opponents must represent reactionary opposition to progress, and Duhm understands these opponents of prophets to be primarily priests and scribes. This way of understanding the opposition between the enlightened prophets on the one hand and backward priests and scribes on the other is hardly unique to Duhm's work. It might be identified as the cornerstone of nineteenth-century historical criticism—and like much else it has roots in Lowth's work, particularly as interpreted by Herder.

Herder's Lowthian work *The Spirit of Hebrew Poetry* not only puts forward the idea of the prophets as the creative geniuses responsible for progress in human history; it also presents priests as those responsible for opposition to progress, or "the progress of corruption." This conception of priests can be seen in a passage in which Herder presents the relationship between prophets and priests in terms of the relationship between Moses the prophet and Aaron the priest.

---

[105] Duhm, *Jeremia*, vii.
[106] Duhm, *Jeremia*, 47.

> How great is the difference, if we compare them together, between the two brothers, Moses and Aaron. The latter is the body, the former the soul, "He shall be thy mouth, and thou shalt be to him in the place of God!" So it remained always in the relations between priests and prophets. How few priests ... ever opposed themselves to the progress of corruption? Under the judges and kings did not corruption indeed always begin with them?[107]

In this passage, Herder adds to the Lowthian association of prophets with the soul or spirit, the complementary association of priests with the body. What the prophets perceived spiritually, the priests turn into carnal institutions. The prophets speak from the heart, but the priests can only mouth the prophets' words. The prophets do original work, but work of the priests is at best only derivative or parasitic on the work of the prophets. More often, the work of the priests undermines the work of the prophets. The priests relate to the prophetic agents of progress as the agents of stagnation or corruption.

Herder is certainly not the first to exalt the prophets by using the priests as foil. The superiority of prophet over priest formed part of the self-understanding of Protestants (particularly in Germany) who understood Catholic Christianity to be inferior because it is priestly religion. Similarly, Enlightenment thinkers often opposed much of traditional Christian practice and liturgy as unenlightened "priestcraft." This Enlightenment view comes close to Herder's view of the prophets as agents of human progress opposed by the priests. What distinguishes Herder's Romantic vision is that what makes the prophets superior to the priests is not so much their enlightened rationality but their creative imaginative power, and their heartfelt sincerity and conviction. The inspired prophets, who speak from the heart, are concerned with the hearts of the people, but the uninspired priests who follow traditions are only concerned with outward forms of sacred objects and rituals.

In Herder's own work, the polarization of prophet and priest was curtailed by his relatively conservative view of the historicity of the texts. If Moses, the greatest of the prophets is responsible for instituting the priesthood (as depicted in Leviticus or Numbers), then priesthood cannot be inherently bad but only potentially corruptible. It was only later, in the nineteenth century, that scholars like Duhm felt more freedom to question the historicity of the biblical accounts, that the reconstruction of the supposed actual history behind the text could be brought in to close conformity with Herder's model of prophets as the inspired agents of progress and priests as uninspired agents of corruption. Nevertheless, it was Herder's idea that set the pattern that was to prove determinative for historical critics like Duhm.

Herder's Lowthian understanding of prophecy not only provided the foundation for the new understanding of the relationship of prophets and priests but also of prophets and scribes (and "teachers of the Law"). Ranged alongside the priests in opposition to the prophetic geniuses of Herder's system are those who impede progress by clinging to the system of laws that Moses had only instituted as a "temporary ... yoke, ... a

---

[107] Herder, *Hebrew Poetry*, 1:279.

necessary step, in the process of political development."[108] He imagines how Moses would have responded if he had seen how his laws came to be used:

> What, then, would have been the conduct of that godlike man [Moses], had he appeared in those times, when his commands were made a snare to catch the souls of men, and hold them in a state of perpetual childhood? in times, when his system of laws, once living in all its members, had become a lifeless mass, when the least of his precepts had been converted into a golden calf, round which men danced and revelled in the extravagance of a hypocritical idolatry? With thousandfold reasons might he have ground it to powder, and given it, as a cup of abomination, to his sacrilegious and idolatrous people.[109]

In these people who idolize the law can be seen the outlines of Duhm's scribes and teachers of the law. Herder himself does not further specify who these legal rigorists are. If he were merely referring to those whom Jesus or Paul spoke against as corrupting parts of Jewish faith, this would hardly be a novel view. It is also an open question whether he would level this strong of an accusation against any of the authors of the text of the Hebrew Bible. Herder's high view of the biblical texts puts him at some distance from later scholars like Wellhausen or Duhm who believed that the largest part of the Hebrew Scriptures was the work of these uninspired legalists. However, here again, it can be seen that Herder has presented the contrast between prophet and legal enforcer in a way that would be determinative for later scholarship. Moses and the other prophets are agents of religious and political progress, which emerges from their original and creative genius; the legalists, who lack the creative genius to envision further progress or even to understand the spirit of the geniuses, oppose the prophets of their day—often claiming the authority of a work of a prophet from an earlier age. This is the basic outline of the opposition Duhm believed to be the defining feature of the life of Jeremiah.

The Central Feature of Duhm's Biography: The Prophet's Opposition to the Law

The central feature of Duhm's reconstructed biography of Jeremiah is the struggle between the prophet and his opponents. The idea that Jeremiah faced significant opposition will hardly surprise readers of the book. Jeremiah's message of condemnation and doom was not calculated to win friends, and the book contains many accounts of the efforts from kings, prophets, and priests to silence him, as well as Jeremiah's own complaints about the severity of the opposition he faced. In his own words, he was "a man of strife and contention to the whole land" (15:10). What is surprising about Duhm's account is his identification of the primary source of opposition to Jeremiah. It is one that readers of the book might never have guessed.

[108] Herder, *Hebrew Poetry*, 1:271.
[109] Herder, *Hebrew Poetry*, 1:272.

In Duhm's account, Jeremiah himself was surprised by his principal enemy. In his early ministry he had opposed the backward local cult of his rural hometown and then the corrupt urban society he found when he first came to Jerusalem. It was during his time in the capital that he encountered his greatest enemy:

> There arose opposition, for which he was probably unprepared: the one-sided adherents to the reform carried out on the basis of the Deuteronomy found in the kingdom of Judah in 621. Many "priests and prophets" and the "scribes" (now mentioned for the first time) believed that the time of salvation had come. Jeremiah, however, did not believe that the new Torah, which had been "made a lie" by the scribes, was all that wisdom required (8:8-9); instead he believed that without moral repentance the people would perish.[110]

Jeremiah's opponents, according to Duhm, were those associated with the reforms carried out under King Josiah on the basis of the "Book of the Law" found in the temple in the eighteenth year of his reign (as described in 2 Kings 22–23). The Book of the Law, Duhm identifies as Deuteronomy (or some version of it), but he does not consider it to be the ancient Law of Moses but rather a "new Torah" that was recently produced not simply recently discovered. Those who produced and promoted Deuteronomy Duhm calls "Deuteronomists" (*Deuternomisten* or *Deuteronomiker*)[111] and although this group included priests and prophets, its central members were "scribes" (*Schriftgelehrten*) or "bookmen" (*Buchmänner*).[112] It was these "zealous adherents to the Torah" who, in Duhm's account, were Jeremiah's greatest opponents; the ones who called for the prophet's death.[113]

Evidence from the Book as a Whole

Duhm's identification of Jeremiah's opponents might surprise readers for several reasons. First, there is no explicit mention of Josiah's reform in the book. Second, Jeremiah seems to have had a positive view of Josiah (22:15-16). Third, regarding "scribes" and "bookmen," the only scribe who plays a prominent role in the book is Jeremiah's colleague Baruch (36:26, 32),[114] and the only men who have anything to do

---

[110] Duhm, *Jeremia*, xi.

[111] Duhm uses both terms to refer both to the advocates of Josiah's reform in time of the prophet Jeremiah and to the later editors responsible for the final form and the majority of the content of the book of Jeremiah. He uses Deuteronomisten to refer to the reformers (Duhm, *Jeremia*, xiv, 47, 157) and to the editors (13, 76, 83, 84, 88, 175). He uses Dueteronomiker to refer to the reformers (82) and to the editors (Duhm, *Jeremia*, 220, 270).

[112] Duhm uses these terms interchangeably. His note in this passage, that the scribes (*Schriftgelehrten*) are first mentioned in the book of Jeremiah (or perhaps at this point in Jeremiah's life), refers to Jer. 8:8; however, in his translation of that passage, he renders *sopherim* as *Buchmänner* (Duhm, *Jeremia*, 88).

[113] Duhm, *Jeremia*, 211.

[114] There are also a few secretaries named among the officials in the court of Jehoiakim (Shapan 36:10, and Elisham 36:12, 20, 21) and of Zedekiah (Jonathan 37:15, 20, and a "secretary to the commander of the army," 52:25). None of these seems to have had anything to do with word of Yahweh or offered any opposition to Jeremiah.

with a book or scroll are Baruch (36:2, 32; 45:1) and Jeremiah (25:13, 30:2, 51:60). Of course, the books they produced are not the "Book of the Law," and that is the book in question. The question is whether Jeremiah opposed—and was opposed by—those who urged adherence to Torah that was the basis of the reforms of Josiah's time.

Another way of asking the question is to ask whether Jeremiah's opponents were "Deuteronomists." Of course, the term "Deuteronomist" does not occur in the book of Jerusalem since "Deuteronomy" as name of the fifth book of the Torah came only in the fourth century BC and "Deuteronomist" as a name for advocates of the book's perspective came only in the nineteenth century AD. However, if a Deuteronomist is understood to mean someone who urges adherence to the laws in Deuteronomy (or who understands Israel's history in terms of obedience or disobedience to those laws), it can be asked who in the book urges adherence to "the law" (or to "the covenant," since Deuteronomy presents its laws as part of a covenant; see Deut. 29:1, 9, 12).

A cursory survey of the references to "covenant," "law," and "commandments" in the book shows that they are almost exclusively associated with one person. It is Jeremiah who understands the relationship of God and Israel as a covenant that requires obeying the law or commandments (11:1-10, 22:8-9, 31:31-34, 34:13-14). It is also Jeremiah who urges obedience to the law (17:19-27, 26:4-6) or, more often, warns that judgment (particularly exile) is coming because of disobedience (6:19-21; 9:12-16; 16:10-11; 32:23; 44:10-11, 23). The idea that disobeying the commandments or breaking the covenant will bring God's judgment (with the ultimate judgment being exile from the land, Deut. 28:64-68) is, of course, central to the message of Deuteronomy (especially Deuteronomy 28–30). The particular combination of sins Jeremiah repeatedly inveighs against (social injustices as well as syncretism and idolatry) are also the central concerns of the book of Deuteronomy (and in the case of syncretism and idolatry, also central concerns of the Josianic reform as described in 2 Kings 23). Furthermore, it is not the case that the message of Jeremiah is distinguished from Deuteronomy because the book is interested in only superficial obedience to the law but the prophet understands that obedience is insufficient without moral repentance. It is worth noting that one of Jeremiah's key terms for moral repentance, "circumcision of the heart," (Jer. 4:4, 9:26) plays a prominent role in Deuteronomy as well (Deut 10:16, 30:6).[115]

Turning to the book's portrayal of Jeremiah's opponents, it is striking that there is no indication that any of them ever advocate adherence to the laws of Deuteronomy or obey them themselves. Instead, they are described as adulterous (23:14, 29:14), greedy (6:13, 23:10), and idolatrous (2:26, 8:2), and Jeremiah's chief complaint against them is that they "strengthen the hand of evildoers" (23:14) by their own bad example and by minimizing the extent of the people's sinfulness and denying that it will result in judgment. They counter Jeremiah's warnings that the sinful people will face exile with assurances that the people will not face the consequences of their sin (particularly, the exile threated by Deuteronomy) and will continue to

---

[115] Notice also that another of Jeremiah's key phrases for moral repentance—to "turn (*shub*) to God with all one's heart (*kol-leb*)" (Jer. 3:10, 24:7, cf. 29:13—also has its parallel in Deuteronomy (30:10).

enjoy peace and prosperity. It is hard to imagine how they could use the book of Deuteronomy to support their message or opposition to Jeremiah.

In light of the book's portrayal of Jeremiah and his opponents, readers might wonder how it is possible for Duhm to characterize Jeremiah's opponents as Deuteronomists. The initial consideration, of course, is that he believes the book's portrayal to be false. In Duhm's account, the present form of the work is for the most part the work of editors who freely added their own compositions (mostly speeches they put in the mouth of Jeremiah) to promote their own religious perspective and agenda, which he identifies as Deuteronomistic. Remarkably, in Duhm's system, the perspective of these editors is primarily the same as that of Jeremiah's opponents.[116] The editors are scribes and Deuteronomists themselves, and they have sought to remake Jeremiah after their own image and make him a vehicle for their message. This theory is the reason why, for Duhm, the principal indication that a particular text in the book is not authentic but has been added to the original historical words of Jeremiah is that it has the perspective, or employs the characteristic diction, of the Deuteronomists. Thus almost all of the passages referenced above in which Jeremiah shares the concerns or employs the language of Deuteronomy are judged by Duhm to be inauthentic; they were placed in his mouth by the Deuteronomistic scribes who produced the book.

Evidence from the "Book of Baruch"

Of course, Duhm has other criteria for judging the authenticity of passages in the book, the chief of which is literary style. Passages that do not rise to the literary excellence of the poetic passages Duhm considers authentic are identified as the work of lesser literary talents—scribes. A large number of the passages Duhm judges inauthentic on the basis of their Deuteronomistic perspective or terminology are also written in prose. Among the prose passages Duhm deems inauthentic are all those in which Jeremiah refers to a legal covenant (11:1-13, 22:8-9, 31:31-34)[117] and most of those in which Jeremiah refers to obedience to the law (9:13, 16:11, 17:22, 32:23, 44:10, 23).[118] Denying the authenticity of these passages may weaken the association between Jeremiah and the Deuteronomists. However, it does nothing to show that Jeremiah opposed the Deuteronomists or the Deuteronomists opposed him. For Duhm to support those claims, he would have to produce alternative textual evidence, evidence from the parts of the book he deems authentic or historically credible.

As has been noted, Duhm does not believe that all of the prose of the book lacks historical credibility. In particular, he believes the prose narratives to be (for the most part) historically accurate firsthand accounts written by Baruch. These could possibly provide evidence of the true nature of the conflict that could be contrasted with picture that arises from the prose speeches attributed to Jeremiah. One of these prose narratives is particularly relevant to the question of whether Jeremiah or his opponents shared

---

[116] This raises a difficult question for Duhm's compositional theory: Why would the Deuteronomistic editors have included in their book evidence that Jeremiah opposed the Deuteronomists in his lifetime?

[117] Duhm, *Jeremia*, 106–8, 123, 252, 255.

[118] Duhm, *Jeremia*, 94–5, 138, 149, 266, 327–8.

the perspective of Deuteronomy. Jer. 34:8-22 offers an account of Jeremiah facing off against the king, officials, priests, and people of Judah. The situation is that when a Babylonian siege of Jerusalem is unexpectedly lifted, King Zedekiah and the people go back on a covenant they had made to free their Hebrew slaves. When Jeremiah delivers God's word to them, he calls them to account not only for having broken this recent covenant but also for breaking the covenant God made with their "fathers when he brought them out of the land Egypt" (34:13). The identity of that covenant made at the time of the exodus is suggested when Jeremiah cites as part of the covenant a law about Hebrew slaves from Deuteronomy (Deut. 15:12, Jer. 34:14). That it is the covenant in Deuteronomy that Jeremiah is referring to is made more clear when the judgment Jeremiah says will come as the result of breaking the law and the covenant has elements that directly parallel parts of the covenant curses in Deuteronomy 29: Yahweh will make them "a horror to all the kingdoms of the earth" (Jer. 34:17, Deut. 28:25) and "their dead bodies shall be food for the birds of the air and the beasts of the earth" (Jer. 34:20, Deut. 28:26). All of these details suggest that Jeremiah understands the situation in terms of the covenant found in the book of Deuteronomy. He opposes the political and religious leaders with the authority of Deuteronomy, and it is more than likely that it was this Deuteronomistic message that aroused the enmity of those who later in the same year had Jeremiah arrested and thrown into a cistern (Jeremiah 37–38). Thus, this prose narrative appears to offer evidence for the nature of conflict between Jeremiah and his opponents that is closely aligned with the nature of the conflict as it appears in the speeches of Jeremiah: it is the prophet and not his opponents who can best be characterized as Deuteronomistic.

This narrative appears to offer evidence that directly contradicts Duhm's view of the conflict. However, Duhm has a way of dealing with the discrepancy without denying the reliability of Baruch's accounts. Concerning Jeremiah 34, Duhm maintains that although the incident itself may have a kernel of historical truth from Baruch, the speech attributed to Jeremiah is a complete fabrication of the scribal editors. They "use the prophet like a puppet and use hints from Baruch to write about pressing matters from their own day or about their theology."[119] In actuality, Duhm speculates, Jeremiah may not have been involved in the incident regarding the broken covenant with the slaves at all. If he had been, says Duhm, he would have been primarily concerned about the selfishness of the wealthy landowners and their lack of sympathy for their poor country men rather than with the violation of a cultic covenant that the fabricated speech condemns.[120] Because of Duhm's certainty that the Deuteronomistic perspective would have been alien to the historical prophet, he believes he can confidently judge the speech in the passage to be inauthentic even though it is embedded in prose narrative he accepts as the authentic work of Baruch. In this way, Duhm is able to keep the prophet free from the taint of Deuteronomistic legalism and ascribe it instead to the later scribes who put their words in the mouth of the prophet.

Another prose narrative is highly relevant as evidence of the nature of the conflict between Jeremiah and his opponents. Jeremiah 26 offers an account of how the conflict

---

[119] Duhm, *Jeremia*, 279.
[120] Duhm, *Jeremia*, 280.

came to its most critical point: when Jeremiah's opponents were almost able to get the prophet killed. According to this account, early in the reign of Jehoiakim, a group of the priests, prophets and common people in Jerusalem sought the death sentence against Jeremiah on the basis of a speech he gave in the temple court. The severity of the threat to the prophet's life is underscored in the text by the inclusion of an account of how the prophet Uriah was actually hunted down and put to death by Jehoiakim for speaking a similar message. The message that incited Jeremiah's opponents to call for his death was as follows:

> Thus says Yahweh: If you will not listen to me, to walk in my law that I have set before you, and to listen to the words of my servants the prophets whom I send to your urgently, though you have not listened, then I will make this house like Shiloh, and I will make this city a curse for all the nations of the earth. (Jer. 26:4-6)

What primarily incited Jeremiah's hearers to call for his death was the message that Yahweh might destroy the temple and Jerusalem. The charge they brought against him was that "he prophesied against this city" (26:11) "in the name of Yahweh, saying, 'This house shall be as Shiloh, and this city shall be desolate without inhabitant'" (26:9).

To understand the nature of the conflict, especially as it relates to the Law, it is helpful to note two key elements of Jeremiah's message that the opponents left out of their charge: first, what Jeremiah had said would cause Yahweh to destroy the temple and city, and second, the possibility that Yahweh might relent. According to Jeremiah, if Yahweh brought destruction, it would be because the people did not "walk in the Law" he set before them or listen to the prophets he sent to them. That the threatened destruction is conditional is indicated by the "If" at the beginning of Jeremiah's initial message, and reinforced by his response to the charge brought against him: "Mend your ways and your deeds and obey the voice of Yahweh, your God, and Yahweh will relent of the disaster he has pronounces against you" (26:13). In Jeremiah's message, whether the city and temple are destroyed or not depends on whether or not the people obey the voice of Yahweh as expressed in the Law. Since Jeremiah appears to believe that disobedience to the Law is what brought the destruction of Shiloh, it is likely that he thinks of the Law as having been given by Yahweh in the time of Moses (before Yahweh's "house" was at Shiloh, cf. Josh. 18:1 and 1 Sam. 1:24) before the long succession of prophets sent by Yahweh to call for obedience. When Jeremiah refers to Yahweh "set[ting] the Law before" the people (26:4), it is not clear whether he is referring to when the Law was originally given to Moses or to when it was rediscovered and publicly read to the people in the time of Josiah (a little over ten years before Jeremiah's speech in the temple).[121] However, several elements from Jeremiah's speech suggest that it is the Law as found in Deuteronomy that Jeremiah particularly has in mind. First, the strongly conditional nature of the judgment his message threatens corresponds to the conditional nature of curses threated by Deuteronomy: "If you will not obey the voice of Yahweh your God … then all these curses will come upon you"

---

[121] Assuming that the book of the Law was found in about 622 BC and Jehoiakim came to power in about 609 BC.

(Deut. 28:15). The parallel to Deuteronomy in the condition given by Jeremiah "obey the voice of Yahweh, your God," (26:13) is matched by a parallel in the consequence: he warns that Yahweh will "make this city a curse among all the nations of the earth" (Jer. 26:6), which is very similar to the warning in Deuteronomy, "you shall become ... a proverb and a byword among all the nations" (Deut. 28:37). What distinguishes Jeremiah's message from the charges of his opponents is that he makes the threatened judgment conditional on whether or not they obey the law a given by Moses. The message that caused his enemies to call for his death was a Deuteronomistic message.[122]

Duhm can hardly deny the Deuteronomistic character of Jeremiah's message in this central account of the conflict between Jeremiah and his opponents. However, he is also committed to the basic historicity of the narrative accounts (without them it would be very hard to begin to reconstruct a biography). His method of dealing with the evidence in the narrative that contradicts his view of the conflict is the same as that observed in the narrative in ch. 34: he denies as inauthentic only those parts of the passage that cannot fit his view. Thus, he judges the first part of the account (26:1-3) to be an authentic record of Baruch about Jeremiah going to the temple and delivering a message that the people must repent or face destruction. However, he cannot accept the rest of Jeremiah's message:

> Concerning the continuation of Jeremiah's message in verses 4-6, Baruch could not have written a single word .... Jeremiah cannot have made the salvation of the people dependent on the observance of the "Torah," (as is the case in v. 4), at least not so unconditionally, since according to him (8:8f.), the Torah had been made a lie by the scribes. Baruch as well must have known that those who had gathered [at the Temple], especially the priests and prophets, were precisely the most zealous followers of the Torah.[123]

Thus Duhm concludes, "The editor has interfered."

As was the case in his treatment of ch. 34, Duhm's primary criterion for determining authenticity of the textual evidence is not its form (poetry or prose) or genre (sermon or narrative): he accepts the sermonic prose in 26:3 as authentic but not the sermonic prose in 26:4. The reason he judges that 26:4-5 is inauthentic is that it is out of keeping with what he is confident a great prophet like Jeremiah would have believed. Likewise it is impossible for Duhm to believe that Jeremiah's opponents could have been incited to call for his death by a message that encouraged obedience of the Torah because Duhm knows that it was actually his opponents who were Torah zealots. The question becomes how it is that Duhm knows these things about Jeremiah and his opponents— what is the evidence?

---

[122] It is probably not a coincidence that in this instance Jeremiah was saved from death by "the hand of Ahikam son of Shaphan" (26:24). Shaphan was the scribe who read the Book of the Law to Josiah when it was found, and Josiah sent him and Ahikam to Huldah, the prophetess, to ask what to do about the wrath of Yahweh because their fathers had not obeyed the words of the book (2 Kgs 22:8-14).

[123] Duhm, *Jeremia*, 211.

Duhm's theory that later authors have falsified the text by making Jeremiah speak words they composed themselves is at least possible. However, for it to be accepted as probable, Duhm would have to produce evidence that Jeremiah did not believe that judgment could be averted by obedience to the Law as well as evidence that his opponents advocated obedience to the Law. He needs evidence that his view of the conflict is the true historical one and that the book's portrayal is false. The challenge for him is that the only available evidence for examining this question is in the book of Jeremiah.[124] This is the problem Duhm's compositional theory is meant to overcome. He believes he can isolate the authentic words of Jeremiah that allow him to reconstruct the true history that can show the falsity of the account of the book in its present form. The question then becomes whether he can find any textual evidence for his view of the conflict and whether the case for reliability of that evidence is strong enough to show all of the other evidence considered above to be inauthentic.

Evidence from the "Authentic Poetry": Jer. 8:8-9

Although there does not appear to be any evidence that would support Duhm's view of the conflict in the prose of the book (including in the prose narratives that Duhm largely accepts as reliable), he believes there is evidence in the poetry of the book, which he accepts as mostly the authentic words of Jeremiah. There is one poetic passage (two verses) that Duhm makes central to his argument. It is the passage Duhm cites as the proof (quoted above) that Jeremiah could not have urged Torah obedience in his temple sermon: "According to [Jeremiah] (8:8f), the Torah had been made a lie by the scribes." Duhm identifies Jer. 8:8-9 as "one of the most important in the book."[125] Perhaps he should have called it the most important since it may be the only passage that could be read as evidence supporting his belief about the nature of the conflict between Jeremiah's perspective and the perspective of his opponents.

Jer. 8:8-9 reads (in a standard English translation):

> How can you say, "We are wise,
>   and the Law of Yahweh is with us"?
> When, in fact, the false pen of the scribes
>   has made it into a lie.
> The wise shall be put to shame;
>   They shall be dismayed and taken;
> behold, they have rejected the word of Yahweh,
>   what wisdom is in them?[126]

---

[124] Of course, there is also textual evidence for the time of Jeremiah in the books of Kings and Chronicles. They have accounts that involve key elements of the conflict: priests, prophets, the law, the temple, the king, the people and the Babylonian invaders. What they do not indicate is how these elements relate to Jeremiah and those who opposed him.

[125] Duhm, *Jeremia*, 88.

[126] The New Revised Standard Version is used for quotations from the Bible in English. The "The LORD" had been changed to "Yahweh" without note. *The HarperCollins Study Bible: New*

In Duhm's understanding of the passage, "the Law of Yahweh" refers to Deuteronomy, or the form of Deuteronomy that was found in the temple during the reign of Josiah. Duhm takes this passage as evidence that Jeremiah (like Duhm himself) recognizes that the idea that this Law came from Yahweh during the time of Moses is a fiction and that, in actuality, the book is the product of scribes who have reduced living religious tradition of Israel to a code of written laws. When Jeremiah said that "the false pen of the scribes has made [the Law] into a lie," he meant that Deuteronomy was primarily written by scribes. Deuteronomy is a lie in two senses: it is falsely attributed to Moses [and Yahweh] and it advocates false, "scribal," religion. The "scribes," (whom Duhm identifies with "the wise") are "Deuteronomists," agents of the religious program carried out during the time of Josiah ("the reform") on the basis of the Deuteronomy, the written law they had produced. Thus, in Duhm's interpretation, Jer. 8:8-9 is evidence both of Jeremiah's view of the Law (it is false) and of the true identity of Jeremiah's opponents (they are the advocates of the reform of Josiah, understood as legalistic zealots). Whether the passage supports either of these conclusions can now be examined.

Jeremiah's View of the Law

Duhm's claim that Jer. 8:8-9 shows that Jeremiah believed that the Law (i.e., Deuteronomy) is false (or more precisely, had been falsified) faces several challenges. The first has to do with translation. Duhm's interpretation is based on his translation, which like the English one presented above, depends on revocalizing the Hebrew text to supply a direct object "it" in the phrase "the false pen of the scribes made it [i.e., the Law] into a lie." It is not clear in the Hebrew text what the direct object of "made" is (or, for that matter, what its subject is), and none of the versions understand "the Law" to be the object.[127] A possible translation of the text as it stands would be "The false pen of the scribes has worked falsehood" (as in the Vulgate) or even "He [i.e., Yahweh]," or "it [i.e., the Law of Yahweh] has made the lying pen of the scribes false." Perhaps it could mean that the people's claim, "We are wise and have the Law of Yahweh with us" is shown to be a false by the falsehoods [the people have had] their scribes write. It could even be translated: "The false pen has falsified the [work of the] scribes."[128] In any case, the extreme difficulty of determining what the second clause means (at least without help from the literary context) makes the passage a shaky foundation for Duhm's historical reconstruction. One might judge to be precarious the stability of a theory that argues that every passage in the book which appears to give Jeremiah's

---

Revised Standard Version, Including the Apocryphal/deuterocanonical Books (San Francisco, CA: HarperSanFrancisco, 2006).

[127] Neither the Septuagint, the Syriac, the Vulgate, nor the Targum understand "it" (with "The Law" as its antecedent) to be the direct object of "made." William Holladay, *Jeremiah 1: A Commentary on the Book of the Prophet Jeremiah, Chapters 1-25*, Hermeneia (Philadelphia, PA: Fortress, 1986), 281.

[128] If that translation were interpreted to mean that the good work of the scribes in copying or promulgating the law had been falsified by the bad writing of others, the meaning would be in keeping with the neutral or positive view of scribes throughout the rest of the book.

view of the Law must be inauthentic because it contradicts one interpretation of one translation of one passage when the text is altered.

Even if it is granted that Duhm is correct in translating and interpreting the passage to mean that scribes have falsified the Law, it is not clear in what way the scribes did this. Duhm assumes Jeremiah believes that the text of the Law itself is false because of the modifications and additions of the scribes (or perhaps simply because the scribes reduced the living law to a written document). If this is the case, then the passage does stand in considerable tension with all of the other passages in which Jeremiah appears to have a positive view of the Law or to give a message closely aligned to the message of the Law. However, this is not the only way the scribes could have falsified the Law. They could have offered interpretations of the Law (perhaps in written commentaries, sermons, or midrashim) that distort its message. They could have lived lives that did not back up the (possibly true) things they had written. If either of these is what the passage refers to, then there would be no reason to infer from it that Jeremiah found the Law itself to be false. These interpretations would have the advantage of being compatible with almost every other passage in the book that appears to show Jeremiah's view of the Law.

The difficulty with view of the Law Duhm finds in the passage is not simply that it stands in tension with other passages in the book, it is that there is almost no other evidence for it in the book. Duhm's theory that the form of the book presents a false portrait of Jeremiah and his view of the Law might be possible, but for readers to accept it as plausible, he would have to produce evidence with a more compelling claim to accurately represent Jeremiah's true perspective. Duhm is able to make his claim about Jeremiah's view somewhat plausible by discrediting all the passages that provide evidence that Jeremiah's view was the opposite of what he believes it to be, but he is left with only 8:8-9 as evidence supporting his belief.

There are a few passages in the book that could possibly be interpreted in a way that would allow them to be used as evidence for the view of the Law Duhm finds in 8:8-9. Two passages (2:8, 18:18) cast people associated with the Law in a negative light. In a poetic speech depicting Yahweh's judgment on the failure of Israel's leaders in previous generations, Jeremiah includes among the leaders "those who handle the Law" (2:8). However, his criticism of the leaders is not that they handle the Law but that they do not know Yahweh: "Those who handle the law do not know me" (2:8).[129]

---

[129] A similar situation may lie behind the speech in 18:18. Jeremiah's opponents plot against him, saying,

> The law shall not perish from the priest,
> Nor counsel from the wise,
> Nor the word from the prophet.

It is not clear whether Torah in this verse should be translated "Law" or "instruction." If it is the former, then it appears that some of Jeremiah's (priestly) opponents thought that their possession of the Law was enough to vindicate them and their message and to attack Jeremiah and his message. The inclusion of "the wise" in this passage makes it similar to 8:8. It seems that some of Jeremiah's opponents may have prided themselves in having the Law and perceived that Jeremiah's opposition to their message (probably a message of welfare in contrast to his message of doom) implied that

The implication is that dealing with the Law should have led to knowing Yahweh, who gave the Law. This also appears to be the implication of Jeremiah's prophecy that in the future when the Law is written on the people's hearts they will all know Yahweh (31:33-34). Duhm might have been able to use 31:33-34 as evidence that Jeremiah believed the written law to be flawed if he interpreted the passage to mean that the problem with the former covenant was the falsity of its Law. However, Duhm is unable to explain away the positive view of the Law in the passage; thus he concludes that it must be inauthentic.[130]

The meaning of these (poetic) passages about the Law suggests a similar meaning for 8:8-9: Jeremiah is denouncing the combination of having the Law of Yahweh but failing to know Yahweh who gave the Law. One indication that this is the sense of 8:8-9 comes from its literary context. In the passage that immediately precedes it, Jeremiah gives Yahweh's complaint: "My people do not know the justice (*mishpat*) of Yahweh" (8:7).[131] To know that Yahweh practices justice is to know Yahweh: "Let him who boasts boast in this that he knows and understands me, that I am Yahweh who practices steadfast love, justice, and righteousness in the earth" (Jer. 9:24).[132] The problem with the people who claim to be wise and have the Law in 8:8 is that they do not know Yahweh and his ways, not that they have the Law. The Law is not false; it is the claim that is false, and the people who made it—whether that is the people in general ("my people" 8:7 or "this people" 8:5), "the wise" (8:9), the "scribes" (8:8), or whoever has a "false pen" (8:8). Thus, when read in its literary context, the meaning of 8:8-9 fits with the conclusion about Jeremiah's view of the Law that seems apparent from every other passage in the book that can be used as evidence: Jeremiah does not find the Law false; he finds the people false because their words and actions show that they do not know Yahweh whose character is revealed in the Law. If this is how the passage is best interpreted, it would mean that there is no evidence in the book of Jeremiah (either in the prose or the poetry) for the view of the Law that Duhm believes Jeremiah to have held.

The Nature of the Conflict between Jeremiah and His Opponents

In Duhm's system, 8:8-9 is not only foundational for his belief that Jeremiah believed the Law to be false; it is also foundational for his understanding of the nature of the

---

he denied their claim to have the support of the Law. If so, then the conflict was not about the truth or falsity of the Law but about whose message was in accord with the Law. Both sides assumed the truth of the Law. The opposition to Jeremiah (the passage begins, "Come, let us make plots against Jeremiah") has arisen not because he had criticized the Law but because he had exposed the "wise" as foolish, the prophets as false, and the priests as lacking the support of the Law. In short, the opponent's speech can plausibly be read as a response to a speech of Jeremiah's like that of 8:8-9 interpreted to mean that, as good as the Law may be, merely possessing it does not make one wise. Duhm judges 18:18 to be inauthentic (Duhm, *Jeremia*, 157).

[130] Duhm, *Jeremia*, 254-5.

[131] Duhm believes that this phrase does not belong to the original but to a "later hand" and that it was probably borrowed from 5:4-5 (Duhm, *Jeremia*, 87).

[132] The idea that the Law should lead to knowledge of Yahweh and his character is consonant with the message of Deuteronomy: "Know therefore that Yahweh, your God, is God, the faithful God who keeps covenant and steadfast love" (7:9). "He executes justice for the fatherless and the widow" (10:18).

conflict between Jeremiah and his opponents. He understands the passage to reveal a conflict between the "law of Yahweh" (8:8) and the "word of Yahweh" (8:9). The "Law of Yahweh" is the product of the scribes, and the "word of Yahweh" comes from the prophets. The "scribes" and "wise men" in the passage Duhm describes as "scholars of the law who are so deluded by their Torah wisdom that they scorn the real Word of Yahweh, the word of the prophets."[133] As has been said, Duhm identified the "Law" with Deuteronomy and its proponents with the Deuteronomists who carried out the reform in the time of Josiah. However, Duhm discerned that the reform had a target that would be a surprise to a reader of the account of the reform in the book of 2 Kings. He believed that the reform was carried out in opposition to the prophets of Israel like Jeremiah. Opposition to the prophets was not only the motivation of the Deuteronomistic reformers but also of the scribal authors who originally produced the book of Deuteronomy. The written law was a ploy to wrest religious authority away from the prophets who claimed to speak for God. The prophetic word "the predictions of the ever-irrational inspiration" was a threat to the power of the scribes; it was "troublesome and hated" and thus they sought to silence it. They answered the prophetic word with the written law, which gave them control because it was "something they could master intellectually, something rational which could be understood and disputed about."[134] The written law and the reform carried out on the basis of the law shifted religious authority to the scribes: it was "something new which from this time would overshadow the authority of a prophet."[135] This understanding of Deuteronomy and the Deuteronomistic reform, means that in Duhm's system the essence of the reform in the time of Josiah and Jeremiah was a conflict between the scribes (and the priests) and the prophets.

It would be hard to guess that this is the nature of the conflict from the primary account of the reform in 2 Kings 22–23. In that account, the targets of the reform appear to be the syncretistic priests in Jerusalem and at the high places throughout Judah and Samaria (23:4-5, 20). There is no hint of opposition between scribe and prophet, or between written Book of the Law and the oral Word of Yahweh. When the Book of the Law is found, the scribes take it to the prophet, Huldah, and the reform goes forward on the basis of her prophetic word affirming "all the words that you have read in this book" (22:16). Duhm's account of the reform as a struggle between scribe and prophet cannot be told on the basis of anything in the text of 2 Kings.

Duhm's story of the reform and its opponents relies instead on his reconstruction of the biography of Jeremiah from the evidence he finds in the book of Jeremiah. According to Duhm's biography, Jeremiah, the greatest prophet of this time of conflict, recognized the threat that the Law and the scribes represented to true prophetic religion. He spent his lifetime trying to oppose the rise of the scribes and their written Law; but they silenced him and eventually he was martyred because of them.[136] Thus the tragedy

---

[133] Duhm, *Jeremia*, 90.
[134] Duhm, *Jeremia*, 90.
[135] Duhm, *Jeremia*, 88.
[136] Regarding the "Deuteronomistic theologians," Duhm writes, "it was because of them that Jeremiah had to die a martyr" ("ihretwillen musste Jer. zum Märtyrer werden." Duhm, *Jeremia*, 90). Duhm does not say on what evidence he bases this claim. Readers of the book will remember that, in its

of Jeremiah's life was that he was unable to prevent the ascendency of the scribes. The scribes were able to triumph over the prophetic word with the fiction that Moses the greatest prophet was the author of their newly written law. They were able to triumph over Jeremiah and other living prophets by persecuting and killing them. In their final triumph, they were able to triumph over Jeremiah's prophetic words and literary legacy by hijacking it and incorporating it into a work designed to cement their own authority by blaming the fall of Jerusalem and the exile to Babylon on disobedience to their new law. The present book of Jeremiah is a monument to the victory of the scribes and read uncritically (as it had been until the work of Duhm) it continues to further the agenda of Jeremiah's Deuteronomistic opponents: encouraging obedience to the Law by showing the disastrous effects of disobedience. By exposing the inauthenticity of the Deuteronomistic parts of the book, Duhm is able to overturn the scribes' victory over the prophet. He is able to recover the thought of the actual Jeremiah who knew that it was not disobedience to the law but zealous adherence to it that brought this catastrophe. It was the scribes and their book, not the prophets and their word, which were responsible for the fall of Israel. The scribes attempted to cover up the conflict between themselves and the prophet by presenting Jeremiah as an advocate of their Law (as they made the prophets Moses and Huldah advocates of their law). However, they made the mistake of leaving enough evidence of the historical Jeremiah and his message in the book of Jeremiah to allow Duhm to recover the antagonism between them and the prophet.

The challenge for supporting Duhm's view of the conflict between Jeremiah and his opponents is similar to the challenge for supporting his view of Jeremiah's opinion of the Law: finding any evidence for it in a book replete with evidence of the opposite view. The evidence in the book for the nature of the conflict in Jeremiah's life can be examined to see if any of it can support Duhm's view. The first kind of textual evidence includes explicit references to Jeremiah's opponents. Duhm's belief that the conflict is between the prophets (with the spoken word) and priests and scribes (who rely on a written word), does not fit well with the instances throughout the book in which Jeremiah's opponents include both priests and prophets (but never scribes, except possibly in 8:8). In 18:18, for example, those who make plots against Jeremiah include both the priests with their "law" (or "instruction") and the prophets with their "word." In ch. 26 (discussed above) in which Jeremiah's opponents call for his death, the instigators are identified four times as "the priests and the prophets" (26:7, 8, 11, 16); Jeremiah's deliverance, on the other hand, comes from Ahikam, son of Shaphan, a scribe associated with the finding of the Book of the Law in 2 Kings. In what is perhaps the best-known story of confrontation in the book (Jeremiah 28), Jeremiah's opponent is not a priest or a scribe but a prophet, Hananiah, and he opposes Jeremiah not on the authority of the written Law but on the authority of his own prophetic utterance. Jeremiah responds to him with a standard for judging prophets that he appears to have drawn from the written Law (Jer. 28:9, cf. Deut. 18:22). There is also the account of

account, Jeremiah is last seen in Egypt where his last recorded speech condemns the people of Judah who took him there for their worship of Egyptian gods and the Queen of Heaven (Jeremiah 44). Thus to the last, in the book's telling, Jeremiah opposes those who follow other gods, not those who insist that no other God should be worshipped but Yahweh (perhaps the most distinctive element of Deuteronomy and of the "Deuteronomistic" reforms described in 2 Kings).

Jeremiah's opposition to the prophet Shemiah, a conflict between two prophets carried out in written letters (Jer. 29:24-32, cf. Jeremiah's prophecy against the prophets Ahab and Zedekiah in his letter to the exiles, 29:20-23). In sum, none of the direct depictions of conflict in the book provide evidence of the conflict posited by Duhm, but rather conflicts that stand in tension with Duhm's account.

Besides all of these direct depictions of prophets as Jeremiah's opponents, there are many more passages in the book in which Jeremiah denounces prophets along with priests. For example, in Jer. 2:8, it is not only the priests and "those who handle the law" who come in for criticism but also "the prophets [who] prophesied by Baal and went after things that do not profit." Other passages—in both prose and poetry—in which Jeremiah censures prophets along with priests include 4:9, 8:1, 13:13, 32:32 (in prose) and 2:8, 2:26, 5:31, 6:16, 8:10, 14:18, 23:11 (in poetry). These passages assert that it is prophet and priest working together who have brought Yahweh's wrath on the nation, or who have misled the people and given them false security. Furthermore, several passages suggest that it is prophets and their words that are at the root of the problem: for example, "the prophets prophesy falsely, and the priests rule at their direction" (5:31). Examples of prophets propping up the priests in their misrule include the prophet Shemaiah who sent a letter from Babylon to support the priesthood of Zephaniah and encourage him to rebuke Jeremiah (29:24-28) and the prophet Hananiah who prophesied that the vessels the priests used in the temple would be returned from Babylon in only two years (28:3). Jeremiah warns the priests about the prophecies spoken by the prophets: "Then I spoke to the priests … saying, 'Thus says Yahweh: Do not listen to the prophets … for it is a lie they are prophesying to you'" (27:16). In contrast to this, there are no passages that portray the priests being in league with scribes or being misled or given false hope by the law.[137]

According to his usual practice, Duhm deals with most of this evidence that contradicts his view of the conflict by denying its authenticity. He claims that all of the passages presented as the prose speech of Jeremiah have been put in his mouth by later authors, scribes. He also denies the authenticity of most of the poetic passages that show Jeremiah's belief that the prophets were in league with the priests or encouraging their opposition to Jeremiah. To avoid what would appear to be a departure from his assumption that the poetry is authentic, Duhm denies that some of these passages have poetic form and says of others of them that the quality of poetry is not up to the standards of Jeremiah's authentic poetry.

This evidence that Jeremiah saw his opposition as including prophets (along with priests) presents a significant difficulty for Duhm's attempt to read 8:8-9 as presenting a conflict between the scribes and priests who represent the Law and the prophets who represent the word of Yahweh. This difficulty is intensified when the passage is read in its literary context. The very next verse is one of those (poetic) passages in which

---

[137] Among the beliefs that Jeremiah had to confront in his opponents were the inviolability of the temple and city of Jerusalem and the promise of peace and well-being (shalom). It is worth noting that none of these beliefs have any basis in Deuteronomy. The blessings it holds out (which are conditioned on obeying the law) do not include peace (shalom) or the protection of any particular place but only blessings for the people and land in general. A more likely source of confidence in God's protection of the temple would be the promises to David, who established Jerusalem and charged Solomon to build the temple. These promises were not grounded in the Law (or contingent on keeping the Law) but were given as a Word of Yahweh through the prophet Nathan (2 Sam. 7).

the prophets are included as part of the problem: "Everyone is greedy for unjust gain; from priest to prophet everyone deals falsely" (8:10). The passage goes on to explain the central issue in dispute: "They [both priest and prophet] have healed the wounds of my people lightly, saying 'Peace, peace,' when there is no peace" (8:11).[138] The conflict in this passage, as in many others, is not between prophets on one side and priests and scribes on the other. It is between Jeremiah (a prophet from a family of priests, Jer. 1:1) who declares judgment is coming because of the depth of the people's sin (a message fully in keeping with the Law as presented in Deuteronomy), and all those—prophets, priests, scribes, kings, officials—who offer assurances of peace because they deny the depth of the people's sins (a message with no basis in Deuteronomy).

Duhm's attempt to read 8:8-9 as revealing the true nature of the conflict between Jeremiah and his opponents as one between the prophetic word and the scribal law is not only at odds with the evidence that the prophets collaborated against Jeremiah with the priests and those who handle the law. His interpretation is also at odds with evidence throughout the book that Jeremiah saw the prophetic word he brought from Yahweh as in keeping with the Law of Yahweh. In 9:13, Jeremiah gives as Yahweh's reason for the exile that the people have "forsaken the Law I set before them and have not obeyed my voice." If the "voice" of Yahweh in this passage is taken to be his word through the prophets, then the passage presents the (true) prophetic word of Yahweh as closely associated with Yahweh's Law. Duhm denies this passage as evidence of Jeremiah's view.[139]

Part of the rationale Duhm offers for rejecting the authenticity of 9:13 is its prose form. However, there is poetic passage that presents an even more significant challenge to the dichotomy Duhm sees in 8:8-9 between Law and Word. This passage not only shares poetic form with 8:8-9; it is more closely related to it in content than any other passage in the book. Jer. 6:16-19 begins by recounting how the people refused to walk in "the ancient paths" or to "pay attention to the sound of the trumpet" and the "watchmen." The identity of the ancient paths and of the watchmen with their trumpets is made clear in the conclusion of the passage, which parallels the introduction:

> They have not paid attention to my words
> And as for my Law, they have rejected it.
> (6:19)

In Jeremiah's view, the ancient Law and the Words of the prophetic watchmen both come from Yahweh; they are two ways in which Yahweh intended to warn his people. This is strong evidence that Jeremiah saw the prophetic word of Yahweh that he (as one of Yahweh's watchmen) delivered to the people was aligned with the ancient Law of Yahweh.[140]

---

[138] Duhm does not believe that 8:10-11 belongs after 8:8-9. Duhm writes, that the "threats and the condemnation of the opponents" in 8:10-11 are inappropriate in a discussion of whether the prophetic Word of Yahweh or the wisdom of the Torah should be privileged (Duhm, *Jeremia*, 90). In other words 8:10-11, in which Jeremiah condemns prophets and not scribes, does not belong here because it does not fit with the conflict between prophet and scribe Duhm finds in 8:8-9.

[139] Duhm, *Jeremia*, 94.

[140] The parallel between the "Law" and the "ancient paths" in this passage is evidence that undermines Duhm's claim that Jeremiah knew that the Law was a recent product of the scribes.

The passage presents a strong challenge to Duhm's attempt to read 8:8-9 as presenting Jeremiah's view that the Law of Yahweh and the Word of Yahweh are opposed to each other—especially since the combination of Yahweh's Law and Yahweh's Word(s) make 6:16-19 the closest parallel to 8:8-9 in the book.[141] In light of the close association in 6:16-19 between the Law of Yahweh and the Words of Yahweh, it appears natural to understand that in 8:8-9 Jeremiah presents the Law of Yahweh (8:8) and the word of Yahweh (8:9) as two ways of knowing the way (*mishpat*) of Yahweh (8:7) or the warning of Yahweh (8:9a, 10a), and that he is rebuking the priests and prophets (8:10b) along with the scribes and the wise (8:8) for dealing falsely with one and rejecting the other.[142]

Duhm is only able to resist this reading of 8:8-9 by positing that all of the other evidence in the book on this question is inauthentic—including the closely parallel poetic passage 6:16-19. About verses 6:18 and 19, he writes, "They can hardly be from Jeremiah."[143] His sole reason for rejecting their authenticity is their view of the Torah:

> One need only say that the explanation of the fall as the result of contempt of the Torah and the disobedience to the divine Word has nothing to do with Jeremiah's opinions. Even if Jeremiah had composed this poem long afterwards, long after the introduction of the Torah, he would hardly have identified as the cause of judgment contempt for the Torah, but rather blind confidence in the Torah.[144]

Duhm argues that these verses cannot come from Jeremiah because they are out of keeping with Jeremiah's view of the Torah and the reason he thinks Yahweh's judgment is coming. The question is how Duhm knows Jeremiah's opinions. As should now be clear, the only textual evidence that Jeremiah holds the opinion of the Law Duhm believes he held is 8:8-9, and to find this opinion in that passage, it is necessary to alter the text and read the passage out of context and in opposition to dozens of passages in poetry and prose that give clearer evidence of Jeremiah's opinions. This situation suggests that Duhm's beliefs about Jeremiah's view of the Law and about the nature of the conflict between him and his opponents are not based on the textual evidence in the book of Jeremiah, rather they have been read into Jer. 8:8-9 and then maintained by denying the authenticity of most of the rest of the evidence in the book.

---

[141] Jer. 26:4-6 (the authenticity of which is being investigated) also contains the combination of Yahweh's law and Yahweh's word: "Thus says Yahweh: If you will not listen to me, to walk in my law that I have set before you, and to listen to the words of my servants the prophets whom I send to you urgently" (26:4b-5a). However, it is easier for Duhm to dismiss this passage as inauthentic since, even though it is a narrative, it is in prose form and uses Deuteronomistic phraseology.

[142] Jer. 8:7, the verse before 8:8-9, like the verses after it (8:10-12) stands in tension with the Duhm's interpretation of 8:8-9. As with 8:8-9, Duhm denies the authenticity of the last phrase of 8:7 (Duhm, *Jeremia*, 87) even though it (like 8:10-12) has poetic form. For Duhm to achieve his interpretation of 8:8-9, he must read the passage isolated from its (present) literary context.

[143] Duhm, *Jeremia*, 71.

[144] Duhm, *Jeremia*, 71.

Evaluation of Duhm's Biography

The almost complete lack of textual evidence for what Duhm presents as the defining conflict in the life of Jeremiah throws into doubt what he puts forward as the primary merit of his reconstructed biography: that it had a better claim to represent what actually happened in history than previous accounts because of its objective treatment of the evidence. The lack of evidence also raises intriguing questions about Duhm's work: given that there is little in the book to suggest the main feature his account (and nothing in the accounts of this period in Kings and Chronicles), where did Duhm get this idea in the first place and what made it believable to him; furthermore, what made it believable to so many Bible scholars in the following century?

The Source of Duhm's Biography

A plausible, if partial, answer to these questions is provided by the account in the first part of this chapter of how nineteenth-century German biblical scholarship was rooted in German Romanticism. Although Duhm's biography of the Jeremiah would be unfamiliar to readers who knew about the prophet from reading the book, the story he tells would be well known to those who knew the biographies of leading artists and intellectuals in the nineteenth century, biographies which follow the pattern of the lives of Romantic poets. It was shown, for example, how closely Duhm's biography of Jeremiah follows the autobiography of Wordsworth, and it will be observed that a similar story can be found in hundreds, if not thousands, of biographies, autobiographies, and novels in the century before Duhm's commentary.[145] These stories of the educations and careers of artists, intellectuals, and political or cultural leaders have familiar elements: pious youth, disillusionment with traditional beliefs and practices, personal breakthrough to a higher truth or way of life, and then perseverance in the face of opposition from the guardians of the traditions or the status quo. This is the story that provides the framework for Duhm's biography of Jeremiah. In Duhm's work, Jeremiah is transformed into the inspired artist or visionary leader, one of the geniuses of humanity raised up by the spirit of the nation or the spirit of history for the enlightenment of the human race.

This nineteenth-century biographical model helps to explain the origins of the parts of Duhm's biography of Jeremiah that are the most surprising because they have the least grounding in the book of Jeremiah. First and foremost it helps to explain Duhm's understanding of the principal conflict in Jeremiah's life: one between the prophet with his personal understanding of God and scribes and priests whose beliefs and social agenda were shaped by adherence to the Book of the Law. In the biographical model rooted in Romanticism, the personal vision of the inspired individual brings him into conflict with the uninspired traditionalists who cling to outdated forms because they have no inspiration of their own. The opposition between inspiration and tradition, between originality and imitation, between artistic or intellectual

---

[145] See page 216n43.

freedom and dogmatic conformity is foundational to the Romantic understanding. In Lowth and the Romantic poets and theorists who followed him, the opposition was between those whose poetry gave free expression to their sublime emotions and those who believed poetry should be written and evaluated according to the strictures of neoclassical formalism. In Herder and later German nationalists, the opposition was between those who give expression to the spirit of the (German) people and those who reject their expressions as not conforming to what they considered universal or rational standards (but which are actually French). In Herder and German historians of the nineteenth century, the opposition is between the men of genius whom the spirit of history has appointed for the elevation of the human race and the reactionary conservatives who stand in their way clinging to outdated forms and institutions. For Duhm, the opposition is between Bible scholars like himself and the reactionary conservatives who oppose his recovery of the true prophet with their "outrage and censures ex cathedra."[146] Duhm brings the life of Jeremiah into conformity with what he believes to be the defining characteristic of historical progress: "the deep opposition between inspiration and scholarship, between the living force that impels creative spirits forward and the endeavor of the epigones and imitating amateurs, who rest upon the achievements of an earlier period."[147] Duhm's view of his history is grounded in what for him is a basic article of faith: "The lawgiver is the antithesis of the prophet."[148] Duhm's confidence in this belief provides a more compelling explanation for the opposition he finds between the Deuteronomists and Jeremiah than any textual or historical evidence.

A second novel element of Duhm's biography of Jeremiah—his confidence that the prophet considered the Book of the Law to be false—can also be explained as derived from this antithesis between prophet and lawgiver. As an inspired poet, and a "born psychologist,"[149] Jeremiah would surely have understood that true religion is a matter of the heart and cannot be reduced to adherence to a fixed set of rules—especially rules that mainly concern avoiding external taboos and avoiding the consequences of violating them by means of cultic remedies. An inspired prophet could no more be bound by outdated cultic laws than a Romantic poet could be bound by neoclassical rules of composition. The firmness of Duhm's belief in the opposition between inspiration and following rules helps to explain how he could come up with the idea that Jeremiah opposed the Law—and how he could maintain his idea in the face of all the evidence in the book that Jeremiah urged obedience to the Law.[150] Duhm's judgment that all the textual evidence that Jeremiah was an advocate of the Law is inauthentic is supported by his foundational belief that true prophets cannot tolerate Law. It is uninspired scribes who have an interest in obedience

---

[146] Duhm, *Jeremia*, vii.
[147] Duhm, *Jeremia*, 90.
[148] Bernhard Duhm, *Israels Propheten* (Tübingen: J. C. B. Mohr, 1916), 319. Cited in Walther Zimmerli, *Law and Prophets*, 28.
[149] Duhm, *Jeremia*, 47.
[150] It may also explain how Duhm could maintain his characterization of the Book of the Law as concerned only with externals when Deuteronomy actually shows a strong and pervasive concern with the state of the heart (Deut. 4:9, 29; 5:29; 6:5-6; 8:2; 10:12, 16; 11:13, 18; 13:3; 15:7, 10; 26:16; 28:47; 29:19; 30:2, 6, 10).

to the Law, so they must be the actual source of the all the speeches urging obedience that the book attributes to Jeremiah. It is not always clear in Duhm's commentary whether he believes the scribes knowingly falsified Jeremiah's message by making him espouse a position he had opposed in life or whether they falsely assumed they were giving Jeremiah speeches he would have agreed with. In any case, Duhm believed that the scribal authors responsible for the majority of the book of Jeremiah were unconcerned with historical fact and only concerned with their own ideological position. They are poor historians both because they cannot understand the authentic evidence (they lack they capability "to read … the best sources,") and because they do not care what really happened (they "follow their own fantasies.… They have no interest in historical reality. They write theology not history.").[151] In light of Duhm's disbelief in the historical value of the book in its present form, the question Duhm's biography raises of whether Jeremiah advocated obedience to the Law and was opposed by scribes can be recast as a question of whether Duhm and his followers or those responsible for the book are better historians: Which have correctly discerned Jeremiah's actual belief about the Law and which have falsified his belief to bring it into conformity with their own beliefs about the Law? Which are writing history and which are following their own fantasies?

A third feature of Duhm's biography of the prophet which would hardly be apparent from merely reading the text can also be explained by the influence of the Romantic biographical model. It was observed how Duhm rearranges bits of poetry of the book to reconstruct a story of Jeremiah's early life which takes the form of his education as poet: the shaping of his poetic soul by his rural surroundings, early spiritual stirrings, and reading of earlier poets. These elements will all be familiar to the readers of biographies of artist and poets (the genre of *Kunstlerroman*) with Wordsworth's autobiographical poem as a notable example. The stories offer believable accounts of how the artists (and more broadly, visionary thinkers and revolutionary leaders) came to possess their extraordinary powers. Providing Jeremiah with an early life like this would make it easier for Duhm's modern audience to accept the biography of a prophet that might otherwise arouse their rationalistic skepticism. However it was suggested that the primary appeal of a historical biography like Duhm's biography of Jeremiah was not that it stripped the biblical account of its supernatural elements so that it could be fit in into a modern rationalistic account of reality, but that it made credible a kind of "natural supernaturalism" that could fill the modern need for transcendence and enduring significance in a world "disenchanted" by of the enlightenment rationalism or scientific materialism. Duhm's biography offers a believable account of how a historical person came to achieve "a tragic grandeur" that lifted him above the "passions of the ordinary mortals, the ignorance in which the eternally blind live even in the day."[152] The progression of Jeremiah's life shows how one human came to "solve the riddle of existence, at least for himself."[153] With his biography of Jeremiah, Duhm offers his modern readers what religion offered pre-modern readers in its hagiographies of saints and martyrs but without recourse to naïve supernaturalism.

---

[151] Duhm, *Jeremia*, xviii.
[152] Duhm, *Jeremia*, 5.
[153] Duhm, *Jeremia*, 5.

Duhm's creation of a *bildungsroman* about the early life of the poet/prophet may serve another function in his biographical reconstruction. The lack of textual evidence for Duhm's depiction of the mature prophet (his negative view of the Law and the opposition he faced from Deuteronomistic scribes)) raised the question of how Duhm or his readers could have any assurance this central part of his biographical reconstruction. The story that Duhm develops of the growth of the young Jeremiah as a poet and keen observer of his society provide a possible answer. If Jeremiah could be shown to have a life education like that of a Romantic poet or of a liberal reformer of the nineteenth century, then he could be assumed to have come to hold the views of those great individuals. He would share their views of traditional beliefs and institutions because, according to their biographies, their views were the conclusions to which the course of their lives had naturally led. The particular shape of the education Duhm proposes for Jeremiah also helps made credible his views as an adult. Duhm's depiction of Jeremiah receiving an education from the natural rural environment and earlier poets (Amos and Hosea) makes it more believable that he came to oppose the law and priests than if one simply considered what kind of education the son of a priest would have received. The relationship between Jeremiah's education and his adult views in Duhm's biography is not one of logical necessity. When stated as an argument (Jeremiah must have opposed the Law because he had the early life of a rural poet), it appears somewhat circular: it seems likely that some of Duhm's confidence that the fragments of authentic poetry fit into the framework of a modern *bildungsroman* derives from his confidence that the mature Jeremiah held forward-looking views of enlightened modern people and was opposed by the same kind of backward people who oppose them. All the same, it seems likely that these two aspects of Duhm's reconstructed biography (the prophet's development as an artist and the opposition to scribes and the Law) lent support to each other in the mind of Duhm and his followers.

It has been observed that for each of the three distinctive features of Duhm's biography of Jeremiah (his conflict with scribes, his negative view of the Law, and his gradual development into a poet), what made them credible to Duhm and his followers was not as much evidence from the text as it was conformity to a familiar contemporary narrative. They found the biography compelling because it fit with their preconceptions about the life of a prophetic individual. This narrative of the life of a visionary person was rooted in the portrait of an inspired poet forged in large part by Lowth's work on the poetry of the prophets. Equipped with a means for discounting the historical value of the majority of the text, Duhm was able to bring the life of Jeremiah into closer conformity to Lowth's vision of the inspired poet (and Herder's genius of humanity) than perhaps anyone had ever brought the life of a biblical prophet.[154]

---

[154] The most notable achievements in this project before Duhm would be the hundreds of nineteenth-century lives of Jesus—including the well-known *Das Leben Jesu* (1835) by David Strauss and *Vie de Jésus* (1863) by Ernest Renan. Although there is great variety in these various reconstructed biographies of Jesus, they all offer alternatives to the life of Jesus as presented in the biblical texts that their authors thought would be more compelling for modern audiences. They are perhaps best known for denying or downplaying the supernatural elements in the gospel accounts, but the way

The Aim of Duhm's Biography

Duhm's biography not only made Jeremiah's life understandable; it also made the story of the prophet useful. As Lowth's work had made prophetic poetry available as a new model for great poetry, Duhm's work made the life of Jeremiah available as a model for human greatness. Jeremiah could now be looked to as prime example of the geniuses of history who raised their nations and the human race by giving voice to their individual visions and remaining true to them in the face of opposition from those who were threatened by their visions. As Lowth's defense of Hebrew poetry helped to create new standards for what make great poetry or great art, Duhm's revision of Jeremiah's life and message (building on the work of Bible scholars like Herder and Ewald) helped to create a new standard for what makes a great person. The standard was no longer conformity to a fixed set of rules (whether adherence to traditional morality or obedience to the commands of God) but rather bold expression of—and fidelity to—the personal vision that person's life experiences called forth from their inner self. The validity of the message and the greatness of the individual could be measured by the opposition they faced from the representatives of the status quo.

The power of Duhm's model was that it grounded this new portrait of human greatness in a new account of a book of the Bible, the prime source of authority for many of the previous understandings of what it means to be a good person. Traditional interpretation of the significance of the book of Jeremiah had understood the prophet's message to be a warning about the consequences of disobeying God's laws, showing the danger of being guided by the human heart (which is "desperately wicked," Jer. 17:9) or by human dreams (which could be "lying dreams," Jer. 23:32). Duhm's work on Jeremiah is designed not only to show this message is falsely attributed to prophet, but that it was added to the book by the very same type of people who opposed Jeremiah in his lifetime and were responsible for his martyrdom. Through their additions to the book scribes not only made the prophet speak their messages but also transformed him into a "preacher of the 'Word of God'" like themselves, one who had no inspired word to speak but could only urge obedience to a written law. Duhm's work on Jeremiah is designed to expose the scribal preachers: those who opposed Jeremiah in his lifetime, those who added to his authentic works, and those "preachers of the 'Word of God'" who perpetuate their work in the present.[155] The modern equivalents of the Jeremiah's scribal enemies Duhm calls "Bible-believers," those who think that "with the Old or New Testament, the revelation of God is complete and closed."[156] These modern Jewish and Christian believers, like their ancient scribal counterparts, do not think of themselves as enemies of the ancient prophets, but they oppose all

---

they shape the life of Jesus to fit the mold of the kind of person nineteenth century culture could admire deserves to be better known. Like Duhm's biography of Jeremiah, many of them appear to be adapting the textual evidence to fit a modern biographical framework, excluding parts of the text that cannot fit in the framework and adding elements to fill in the gaps. There is definitely a strong continuity between these works and Duhm's work on Jeremiah which could be profitably researched.

[155] Duhm notes that the "pious scribes," of Jeremiah's time were called "preachers of the 'Word of God' in the same sense in which this concept is used among us. Duhm, *Jeremia*, 189.

[156] Duhm, *Jeremia*, 189.

actual prophets of their time, because they consider "the eternal law to be given, the word of God only in need of interpretation and application." As a "historian of religion" (*Religionshistoriker*), Duhm knows that all history tells the story of the struggle between these uninspired scribes and the inspired prophets: "All systematists love the classics of their choice and hate the new prophets, as the scribes saw in the prophet of Nazareth a troublemaker, and Jeremiah … found himself confronted with the wisdom of the scribes (8:8-9)."[157] Duhm's book is designed to counter the work of the anti-prophetic scribes: first, by revealing that they were the true enemies of Jeremiah (on the basis of Jer. 8:8-9) and second, by revealing how they had made not only the book of the Law (Jer. 8:8-9) but also the book of Jeremiah into a lie. In this way Duhm exposes the scribal "Bible-believers" of his own day who consider themselves to be aligned with the prophet Jeremiah when actually their acceptance of the truth and authority of the book of Jeremiah perpetuates the work of the scribes who opposed the prophet and were responsible for his death.

Final Evaluation

Whatever the theological merits of the alternative religious system Duhm's work supports (the new vision of inspiration, scripture, law, human nature, history, etc.), consideration of what made his new biography of Jeremiah compelling to him and his contemporaries has raised questions about its claims to be the necessary conclusion of a objective historical investigation of the text—and thus to be a recovery of the actual life and views of the historical Jeremiah. The likelihood that his biography is not objective but heavily shaped by his preconceptions and aims is shown not only by the conformity of his results to those preconceptions and aims but also by the paucity of textual evidence supporting his results and by the tendentious nature of the methods he used to get those results—manipulating evidence to fit his preconceptions and discrediting as inauthentic the evidence that he cannot make fit. These features of Duhm's use of the text make it reasonable to maintain that his conclusions about Jeremiah and his message are not founded on valid exegesis, but rather, eisegesis, reading his own preconceptions or wishes into the text.

This examination and evaluation of Duhm's biography of the prophet should help the reader of the book of Jeremiah determine whether such a biography is a necessary, or at least helpful, aid for understanding the book. The questions raised about the truth of Duhm's biography and the validity of his historical method suggest that not only is the biography unnecessary, it could actually be unhelpful because it is misleading. Although Duhm's biography of Jeremiah may not be helpful for understanding the historical prophet or his historical context, it may still have historical interest for understanding Duhm and his historical context. The fact that Duhm and many twentieth-century scholars found his biographical reconstruction compelling (more compelling that the book's portrait) has much to teach historians today about that period. It is not only evidence of the dominance of the task of historical reconstruction

---

[157] Duhm, *Jeremia*, 189–90.

but, even more, the interests that guided that task: for instance, the quest to find individuals who could serve as models of the kind of people who contribute to the rise of their nations or the progress of humanity.

The commentaries consulted by readers of the book of Jeremiah today may have less interest (or confidence) in the project of recovering the prophet behind the book by treating the text as historical evidence. They may feel less of a need to have a prophet they can "look up to with admiration," a model for human greatness. However, understanding Duhm's biography of the prophet still has relevance to modern readers because although the biography itself may no longer have many advocates, the compositional approach Duhm used to achieve his biography continues to be influential. Many (perhaps most) of the scholarly guides readers will encounter in commentaries and articles on the book of Jeremiah follow Duhm's compositional approach in at least two ways: they make the determination of source a methodological priority and they treat the distinction between poetry and prose as the prime factor in this determination (treating poetic passages as more likely to be authentic or early, and prose as passages as more likely to be inauthentic or late). This chapter has shown how deeply intertwined these elements of Duhm's compositional approach is with the distinctive features of his biographical reconstruction. Duhm's basic assumption that poetry is an indication of authenticity and prose an indication of inauthenticity is necessary to achieve his biographical reconstruction. The prose speeches of Jeremiah must be considered inauthentic evidence if the primary features of Duhm's biography are to be believed. It would be very hard to convince anyone that Jeremiah had a low view of the Law and faced opposition from its advocates if Jeremiah's speeches in prose are considered indicative of his views. The poetic sections must be understood as records of Jeremiah's poetic effusions in response to various events in his life if they are to be used as the raw material for creating a story of his development as poet. Duhm's biography in turn supports his compositional model. Creating a life story for Jeremiah in the form of biography of a Romantic poet makes plausible what would otherwise seem improbable about Duhm's compositional claims: that Jeremiah's only authentic compositions are in poetic form and that "Deuteronomistic" features (that show the influence of, or sympathy for, the Law) are indicators of inauthenticity. Both Duhm's compositional model and his biographical reconstruction have been shown to be rooted in Romantic conceptions of poetry and the lives of poets. Both have the same basic aim in Duhm's work: to disassociate the inspired prophet and his poetic works from uninspired lawgivers and their uninspiring compositions. This close association of Duhm's biographical and compositional reconstructions should raise a question for modern interpreters: If Duhm's biography has been largely abandoned as unlikely to be true, why are scholars still following the compositional approach and adhering to the compositional assumptions that facilitated the biography?

If Duhm's reconstructed biography of the prophet appears now to be a weaker element of his work on Jeremiah, this was not true for Duhm and his contemporaries. They accepted Duhm's radical compositional theory (his denial of the authenticity of the majority of the book) in large part because they found the resulting biography so compelling. This chapter has suggested that they found the biography compelling because it fit with their preconceptions about the lives of inspired poets and thinkers and leaders. They also found it compelling because it fit with a new model of Israel's religious history that was the primary achievement of biblical scholarship in the nineteenth century and its most influential contribution to biblical scholarship for most of the twentieth century. Although this model is best known as a theory of the composition of the Pentateuch, its underlying framework was a religious history in which Israel's religion declined into the age of law from its high point, the age of the prophets. Duhm's reconstructed life of Jeremiah provides the most detailed account of the watershed moment in this history when the last great prophet was overcome by the representatives of Law. His reconstruction of the compositional history of the book tells the same story: the living words of the prophet are overcome by the dead letters of the scribes. The close fit of Duhm's reconstructions of the prophet's biography and the book's composition with contemporary biblical scholarship's reconstruction of the history of Israel's religion helped make his work on Jeremiah compelling to both Duhm himself and his contemporaries. The next chapter will examine whether this correspondence should also recommend Duhm's work to readers of Jeremiah today.

4

The Roots of Duhm's History of Israel's Religion

As was observed in the overview of the Introduction to Duhm's commentary on Jeremiah, Duhm presents himself as historian and his work as a contribution to the recovery of the historical prophet and his place in the history of Israel. This feature of Duhm's work invites the reader of Jeremiah to evaluate his work based on the soundness of his historical conclusions. The previous chapter considered whether the biography of Jeremiah that resulted from his work had a greater claim to historical truth than more traditional accounts of the prophet's life based on taking the (whole) book's account of what the prophet did and said as what actually happened. However, the reconstructed biography of the prophet is not the only contribution Duhm's study of Jeremiah made to historical studies. His theory of the composition of the book was designed to offer a better understanding not only of Jeremiah and his period but also of Israel's national and religious history. Duhm's commentary as well his other works on the biblical prophets contributed to a sweeping reconstruction of Israel's history that was the defining work of biblical scholarship during the time Duhm was publishing (1875–1916). This particular reconstruction of Israel's history rose to prominence in the late nineteenth century and took its place as the dominant paradigm of guiding biblical scholarship in early twentieth century. Confidence in its validity was a major factor in the acceptance of the validity of Duhm's work on Jeremiah. This means that evaluating the validity of Duhm's work is hardly possible without evaluating the validity of the historical reconstruction.

The Place of the Prophets in the Grafian History of Israel's Religion

The common way to refer to this reconstruction of Israel's history is the Grafian hypothesis. The alternative name, the Documentary Hypothesis, indicates that it is ostensibly a theory about the composition of the Bible, in particular the Pentateuch. Like Duhm's theory of the composition of Jeremiah, its primary approach involves noting differences between various passages in the text and explaining the differences as indications of multiple authors or editors. Its concern with identifying the authors or historical periods from which these sources came earns it the name "source criticism."

However, the connection between the Grafian theory of the composition of the Pentateuch and Duhm's theory of the composition of Jeremiah is not simply a common method; it is a common historical product to which they contributed: a reconstruction of the history of Israel's literature and religion based on assumptions they shared.

The distinguishing claim of the Grafian hypothesis, as presented by Julius Wellhausen, its best known champion, is that the Priestly materials (the priestly laws in Exodus–Leviticus and the corresponding narratives beginning in Genesis 1) do not comprise the earliest source of the Pentateuch (its foundational text [*Grundschrift*], to which the other parts were added as supplements, but rather, the last major source, the unifying framework imposed on the earlier material. In shorthand, the thesis is represented by the chronological order of sources "JEDP" (representing the Jahwist, the Elohist, the Deuteronomistic, and Priestly sources, respectively), in which the Priestly source "P" comes last. JEDP was embraced in place of the earlier proposed order of the sources: "PJED."

The late dating of the Priestly material is not simply based on judgments about the Pentateuch, but about the historicity of materials throughout the Hebrew Bible and an alternative historical scheme than the one presented by the texts themselves. First, the reliability of the Chronicler's history is called into question, thus cancelling its presentation of the early implementation of the priestly cult. Then, the narratives of Judges–Kings are used to show the lack of knowledge of the legal material from the Pentateuch ("Priestly" and "Deuteronomic") before the reforms of Hezekiah and Josiah. This ignorance is taken to indicate that the Law had not been written at this time and thus could not possibly have been handed down from Moses. The main body of Deuteronomy is dated to the period of Josiah's reforms, and the Priestly law of Leviticus and Numbers is assigned a postexilic date, often related to the reforms of Ezra.[1]

The resulting picture of the development of Israel's religious history, as best known from Wellhausen's *Prolegomena* (1883), is a three-stage progression from a primitive, localized, polytheistic cult in the time of the judges and early monarchy (represented in the Jahwistic and Elohistic narratives) to a centralized monotheistic religion in the late monarchy (represented in the deuteronomistic materials) to a Torah-centered temple worship in the postexilic period (represented in the priestly materials).[2]

The significance of this new understanding of the Israel's religious history for work in the prophetic literature can be indicated by the summary of this theory in Wellhausen's sentence, "The prophets preceded the law."[3] This reversal of the traditional understanding of the relationship between the law and the prophets involves a comprehensive rethinking of the role of the prophets. In the traditional

---

[1] J. W. Rogerson, *Old Testament Criticism in the Nineteenth Century: England and Germany*, 1st Fortress Press ed. (Philadelphia, PA: Fortress, 1985), 265.

[2] Julius Wellhausen, *Prolegomena to the History of Ancient Israel: With a Reprint of the Article "Israel" from the Encyclopedia Britannica* (New York: Meridian Books, 1957), 392–425.

[3] This way of stating the central thesis can be seen in Wellhausen's description of his conversion to the Grafian Hypothesis: "In the summer of 1867, I learned through Ritschl that Karl Heinrich Graf placed the Law later than the Prophets, and, almost without knowing his reasons for the hypothesis, I was prepared to accept it." Wellhausen, *Prolegomena*, 3.

understanding, which follows the biblical presentation, the prophets are the successors of Moses and call the nation back to obedience to the Law promulgated by Moses. They apply the Mosaic Law to their current situations, drawing attention to violations of the law and reminding kings and their subjects of the consequences of disobedience threatened in the law. In the new understanding, the prophets cannot remind people of the Law, because in their time the Law does not exist, at least not in the written form now found in the Pentateuch. Instead, the prophets are religious innovators, and the Law is derived from them, a codification of their original spiritual insights. The theology of Deuteronomy is dependent on the great prophets of the eighth century (Isaiah, Hosea, and Amos), and the Priestly literature (throughout Genesis-Numbers) is dependent on seventh- and sixth-century prophets (like Jeremiah and Ezekiel) for the democratization of religion, the concern with guilt, and the triumph over idolatry.

With the new understanding of Israel's religious history offered by the Documentary Hypothesis, the prophets are not only given a new position in relation to the Law and a new function as the source of revealed religion, but they are also given a new status or value: the prophets are the high point of Israel's religious history. The progression from prophetic religion during the monarchy to priestly religion during the exile is viewed as a tragic decline, and the driving force of this decline is taken to be the introduction of written Law. On the Deuteronomistic reforms of Josiah, Wellhausen writes, "With the appearance of the law came an end to the old freedom. ... There was now in existence an authority as objective as could be; and this was the death of prophecy."[4] His view of the Priestly literature, which he believed to have been introduced by Ezra, is that it made the cultus the principal element of religion, which "appears to amount to a systematic decline into the heathenism which the prophets incessantly combated."[5] The decline of religion from the prophets to the teachers of the law is Wellhausen's account of the origin of Judaism.

Duhm's Contribution to Grafianism: Reimagining the Prophets

Wellhausen's basic understanding of the historical relationship between the prophets and the law was embraced by Duhm, and his theory of Jeremiah's composition is in full conformity. Duhm believed that the legal material in the Pentateuch postdates the work of the prophets and is clearly inferior. In his last major work, Duhm writes, "The lawgiver is the antithesis of the prophet. Judaism, which no longer understood the prophets, nor the earlier period as a whole, chose for itself the lawgiver. ... The people of Yahweh became the people of the Torah."[6] The opposition between the prophet and lawgiver or scribe (and the late dating of the latter) has been observed to be central to

[4] Wellhausen, *Prolegomena*, 402.
[5] Wellhausen, *Prolegomena*, 423.
[6] Bernhard Duhm, *Israels Propheten* (Tübingen: J. C. B. Mohr, 1916), 319. Cited in Walther Zimmerli, *The Law and the Prophets: A Study of the Meaning of the Old Testament*, James Sprunt lectures 1963 (Oxford: Blackwell, 1965), 28.

Duhm's source division of Jeremiah. Duhm could identify a passage as non-prophetic, and thus inauthentic, if it seemed to urge obedience to the law, threatened retribution for disobedience, or was overly concerned with idolatry. It might seem surprising that Duhm would deny that Jeremiah's authentic speeches could show any priestly or deuteronomistic influence since Jeremiah was the son of a priest and his early ministry coincided with the Deuteronomistic reforms of Josiah. However, in keeping with the Grafian perspective, Duhm maintains an absolute distinction between the spirit of the prophets and the spirit of the priests and scribes. As was seen in the previous chapter, he is able to keep Jeremiah untouched by priestly and scribal corruption by creating a biography in which the young prophet criticizes the cult in Anathoth as crude folk religion and opposes reforms according to deuteronomistic law as superficial. In this way, both Duhm's theory of the composition of the book of Jeremiah and his reconstruction of the life of the prophet embody the struggle between prophecy and the law central to the Grafian reconstruction of Israel's religious history as presented by Wellhausen.

As was observed, this dichotomy between prophet and scribe was not only the basis for Duhm's source-critical analysis of Jeremiah, but it also provided the significance of his results: the discovery of a true core of prophetic literature and the reconstruction of a true prophetic biography which serve as standards to judge the religious degeneracy and historical inaccuracy of the later views of prophecy added to the book by scribes and teachers of the law. This observation can now be restated: the perspective of the Documentary Hypothesis supplies the central presuppositions of Duhm's work on Jeremiah and the results are intended to confirm the same perspective.

It might be thought that Duhm's work on Jeremiah was simply an application of Wellhausen's perspective on the Pentateuch to a prophetic book. However, this could only be the case if Duhm had come to his position on the basis of Wellhausen's work. In fact, his early acceptance and advocacy of the Documentary Hypothesis wins him "the honour of being the first German apologist for Grafianism."[7] This distinction is based on the publication of his book *The Theology of the Prophets as a Basis for the Inner History of the Development of Israel's Religion*, in 1875,[8] one year before Wellhausen

---

[7]   R. J. Thompson, *Moses and the Law in a Century of Criticism since Graf*, VTSup 19 (Leiden: Brill, 1970), 56. John Rogerson credits August Kayser (*Das vorexilishce Buch der Urgeschichte Israels und seine Erweiterungen*, Strasbourg, 1874) as the first scholar in Germany to champion the idea that the *Grundschrift* was a unity and postexilic (Rogerson, *Criticism in the Nineteenth Century*, 259). Thompson and Kuenen (whom both Thompson and Rogerson cite) both recognize August Kayser as an earlier proponent of the theory than Duhm, but they both insist that Duhm was the first to champion the theory in Germany. (Thompson, *Moses and the Law*, 56; Abraham Kuenen, *An Historico-Critical Inquiry into the Origin and Composition of the Hexateuch: Pentateuch and Book of Joshua* [London: Macmillan, 1886], xxiii–xxxv.) Perhaps this is because they count Kayser as Alsatian (both Kayser and Graf studied in the Alsatian city of Strasbourg with Èdouard Reuss, who had argued in his teaching since 1833 that the law is later than the prophets) even though Kayser wrote in German and Alsace was annexed by Germany in 1871. Between his comments on Kayser and Duhm, Kuenen writes, "We have reached the point at which our allies in Holland, England, and Alsatia were awaiting, so to speak, the adhesion of their German friends" (Kuenen, *Origin of the Hexateuch*, xxxv).

[8]   Bernhard Duhm, *Die Theologie der Propheten als Grundlage für die innere Entwicklungsgeschichte der israelitischen Religion* (Bonn: Marcus, 1875).

began to argue publicly for the Grafian position in his articles on the composition of the Hexateuch.[9]

The primary achievement of Duhm's book, as is apparent from the title, is a rethinking of the prophetic literature that would pave the way for the acceptance of the new presentation of Israel's religious history. Kuenen summarizes Duhm's approach:

> Provisionally accepting the results obtained, on this point [whether the Torah preceded the prophets], by Vatke, myself, Kayser, and others, Duhm proceeds to investigate the historical conditions and the internal development of prophecy, to see whether the whole history, external and internal, can be consistently traced out on the assumption of the non-existence of the priestly legislation. The result is that, in the whole course of his masterly investigation, he is never once driven back upon the Mosaic Law for explanations or illustrations of the growth of prophecy.[10]

To write a history of the prophets without reference to the Pentateuchal Law, Duhm could not rely on the traditional story of the development of Israel's religion that followed the presentation of Israel's history in the historical narratives. In the new telling, as R. J. Thompson observes, "the prophets assumed gigantic proportions as the real founders of Israelite faith while the Mosaic Law was reduced to a less significant position in the post-exilic period."[11] In Duhm's reconstruction, the Law is not merely assigned a less significant place to make room for the prophetic literature; it is actually set in opposition to the prophetic literature as its destroyer: Thompson concludes his summary of Duhm's reconstruction, "The Levitical system which gave the death-blow to prophecy in the post-exilic age could never have been its nursing mother in earlier times."[12] From this overview of Duhm's work on the prophets beginning over twenty-five years before his work on Jeremiah, it can be seen that Duhm was no passive recipient of the new thinking on the history of Israel's religion. Instead, especially in the area of estimating the role and worth of the prophetic literature, Duhm was not only an enthusiastic advocate but also a major contributor to the rise of the Grafian hypothesis and its new view of Israel's history.

Duhm's primary contributions to the Grafian reconstruction of history were to isolate a body of prophetic literature free from the taint of priestly or scribal thinking and to create a biography of a true prophet that could be used as standards for judging the religious degeneracy and historical inaccuracy of the later literature (including the additions in Jeremiah). Once again the suspicion arises whether that Duhm simply picked the passages that conform to his preferences (for prophetic literature over legal literature) or, more precisely, has fit the evidence from the book into a historical scheme that cannot be substantiated from the book itself. Again, Duhm and his supporters can respond that their division of the evidence is not based simply on modern preferences or categories, but on objective features of the text: primarily the division between

---

[9] Julius Wellhausen, "Die Composition des Hexateuchs," *Jahrbücher für Deutsche Theologie*, 21 (1876), 392–450, 531–602; 21 (1877), 407–79.
[10] Kuenen, *Origin of the Hexateuch*, xxxvi.
[11] Thompson, *Moses and the Law*, 57.
[12] Thompson, *Moses and the Law*, 57.

poetry and prose, but also including the "deuteronomistic" vocabulary and form of the inauthentic work. The fact that when the materials of the book are divided on formal and stylistic grounds the resulting categories correspond to the concerns of two different periods in the Grafian reconstruction of Israel's history lends some credibility to the idea that the differences are due to different sources. However, there is another explanation of this alignment. To see it one must first consider how the Grafian reconstruction of Israel's history (particularly its opposition of prophecy and law), like Duhm's reconstruction of the prophet's biography and his Romantic aesthetics, is deeply rooted in the use made of the poetry in prophetic books by Robert Lowth.

Herder's Lowthian Influence on German Biblical Scholarship

The previous chapter described how the influence of Lowth on German biblical scholarship came in a variety of ways. First was the direct influence of Lowth's Lectures on Hebrew Poetry which were widely known among German scholars through the edition published in Germany by Michaelis in 1758. Second was the pervasive influence of Romanticism in German culture. The dominant conceptions of literature, art, history, and national identity in nineteenth-century Europe were colored by Romanticism, and German Romanticism gave a special place to the model of the Biblical prophets as understood by Lowth. Third was the work of individual Bible scholars who both laid the foundations of nineteenth-century German biblical scholarship and were clearly building on the work of Lowth. The most prominent of these were Michaelis, Eichhorn, and Herder. Of these three, the one who both drew most heavily on Lowth and played the largest part in preparing the way for the Documentary Hypothesis was Herder.[13]

Herder's Contributions to the Study of Biblical Prophetic Literature

The foundational contribution of Lowth that Herder and others passed on to nineteenth-century German biblical scholarship was the consideration of the biblical authors and their works in terms of human achievement or contribution to human history. Lowth had urged that Hebrew poetry, especially the poetry in the prophetic books, could be understood as great literature and the Hebrew prophets could be ranked among the great authors of literary history. The prophetic books, and particularly the poetry in

---

[13] Eichhorn is often credited as the father of German Higher Criticism and the initiator of the historical development that led to the Documentary Hypothesis. The reason for giving Herder a more prominent place is that Eichhorn was deeply influenced by Herder, in particular the Lowthian aspects of his approach, and it is being argued here that the Documentary Hypothesis flows out of Lowth's approach to the prophets. Cheyne wrote, "Eichhorn is never weary of confessing that he lives upon Herder's ideas." Thomas Kelly Cheyne, *Founders of Old Testament Criticism: Biographical, Descriptive, and Critical Studies* (London: Methuen, 1893), 17. In broad strokes, it can be said that Eichhorn's primary contributions were his approach to the text as potential historical evidence and his willingness to question the veracity of its accounts. Herder's primary contributions were to approach the text as literature and his provision of the basic historical framework and assumptions that undergird the Documentary Hypothesis.

them, took on a new status with the Hebrew bible as the greatest literature. At the same time, the understanding of the prophets was transformed. Lowth's approach introduced a new extrinsic standard for recognizing and evaluating prophecy. Prophecy could no longer be assumed to be prophecy simply because it was spoken by a prophet, nor could it be assumed to be inspired simply because it was in the Bible. With Lowth's understanding of prophecy as poetry, one could judge that a text was more prophetic or less prophetic, more inspired or less, based on how impassioned, sublime, and poetic it was.

Herder's work on Hebrew poetry not only made Lowth's new view of the Bible as literature foundational for German biblical scholarship but expanded it from the sphere of literature to other realms of human achievement, particularly the development of national culture, which in turn became part of the education of the human race. Herder extended Lowth's identification of prophetic inspiration with poetic inspiration to include the inspiration of all agents of national and or general human progress. Those individuals whose lives and teaching serve to lift up their nation or the human race are recognized as geniuses inspired by the divine spirit that guides human history. As in Lowth, it is primarily the inspired prophets in the Bible who serve as the models of the "enlightening influences," the "genius[es] of humanity" and the "guardians of our race."[14] Thus the prophets take on the role of the true founders of the nation of Israel and their work becomes the nation's greatest contribution to the progress of humanity.

Herder's reconception of the prophets as inspired agents of national and human progress had an important corollary that also became foundational for nineteenth-century biblical scholarship. If historical progress comes through inspired prophetic geniuses who bring new enlightenment to humanity, then it is only natural to think that the primary obstacles to progress would be retrograde elements whose lack of inspiration causes them to oppose the geniuses and cling to what is known and familiar, to established traditions and institutions. If the work of agents of enlightenment is characterized by its creativity, originality, and freedom, the work of these reactionaries who stand in the way of progress will be imitative, derivative, and bound by convention. This is because they lack inspiration or have no contact with the animating Spirit of human history. In the previous chapter, it was shown how Herder gives an intimation of the identity who it was in Israel's history who filled the role of the uninspired foil to the inspired prophets: the legal rigorists who turned the living system of Moses into a lifeless mass and idolized his commandments[15] and the priests who stood in relation to the prophet as body to soul.[16] Once again, Herder's conservative view of the texts prevented him from drawing out the full implications of his theory. After all, he believed that both the laws and the priesthood were instituted by Israel's greatest prophet, Moses. However, his understanding of the opposition between prophets on the one hand and legal enforcers and priests on the other proved to be foundational for the nineteenth-century reconfiguration of Israel's religious writings and history.

---

[14] Johann Gottfried von Herder, *The Spirit of Hebrew Poetry*, trans. James Marsh (Burlington: Edward Smith, 1833), 2:57.
[15] Herder, *Hebrew Poetry*, 1:272.
[16] Herder, *Hebrew Poetry*, 1:279.

Herder's understanding of the dichotomy between the prophets and the priests and legal enforcers is closely related to a third feature of his system that was foundational for nineteenth-century German biblical scholarship: a historical scheme in which the age of the prophets is the high point of Israel's religious and literary history. The idea of a decline from the age of the prophets to the age of priests and scribes can be inferred from the passages in which Herder discusses the priests and legalists.

> How few priests … ever opposed themselves to the progress of corruption? Under the judges and kings did not corruption indeed always begin with them?[17]

> What would have been the conduct of [Moses] had he appeared in those times … when his system of laws, once living in all its members, had become a lifeless mass, when the least of his precepts had been converted into a golden calf.[18]

The idea of corruption in Herder's presentation of the priests implies a historical decline from a better time to a worse time. The contrast between the former better time and the latter worse time is more clear in his comment on the laws; the age of Moses with its living system has declined into an age of legalism with its lifeless mass. The hints of a historical scheme of decline arise from Herder's basic contrast between prophets and priest and scribes. This scheme plays out in the scholarship of the ensuing century. The basic scheme is that the prophets (for Herder, including Moses), who as original geniuses are agents of religious and political progress, bring Israel's religion to its high point; then the legalists and priests, who lack the creative genius to envision further progress or even to understand the spirit of the original geniuses, bring Israel's religion into decline by clinging to the outward forms left by the original geniuses.

New Framework for Israel's Religious History

Herder's presentation of the opposition between the prophet Moses and those who perverted his law is especially remarkable for the way it lays the foundation for the most distinctive element of later historical criticism: the historical schema of decline from original prophetic religion to derivative legalistic religion. Herder provides the basic historical framework scholars leading up to the time of Duhm and Wellhausen used to reshape the Old Testament and the history of Israel's religion. The general note of decline into legalism makes Thompson conclude that the Grafian Hypothesis owes less to evolutionary theory and Hegelianism (with their schemes of progressive upward development) than to the Romanticism of writers like Herder. Thompson cites a description of Wellhausen's general perspective on Israel's religious history to show the affinity between Wellhausen and Romantic writers like Herder: "What evolution there was, was really devolution, for it was a backward movement from the life of the green tree to the dead wood of legalism."[19]

---

[17] Herder, *Hebrew Poetry*, 1:279.
[18] Herder, *Hebrew Poetry*, 1:272.
[19] Thompson, *Moses and the Law*, 36. Thompson quotes William Lang Baxter and refers to his work, *Sanctuary and Sacrifice* (1895), 102; however, the sentence is a paraphrase rather than a direct quotation.

A closer examination of Herder's understanding of Israel's religious history shows that it anticipates the Grafian scheme (of Wellhausen and Duhm) in more than the general idea of decline. In his presentation of Israel's history, Herder makes use of an idea that emerged in the eighteenth century: that human history follows a course similar to the growth of an individual from infancy to adulthood. A classic statement of this idea is found in Gotthold Ephraim Lessing's *Education of the Human Race* (1777–80). For Lessing, like other Enlightenment thinkers, history's long and gradual education of the human race would finally lead to an age of perfection that corresponds to mature adulthood.[20] In contrast, Jean-Jacques Rousseau, anticipating later Romantics, envisioned a decline from the golden age of the childhood of the human race. Rousseau begins *Emile* (1762), his classic work on education, stating, "Everything is good as it leaves the hands of the Author of things; everything degenerates in the hands of man."[21] Although Herder incorporates Rousseau's more pessimistic scheme, he occupies a mediating position, which sees cycles of progress followed by decline: "The human race, each nation … moves from bad to good and better, from better to bad and worse."[22]

The pattern of rise from childhood and decline into old age marks Herder's presentation of Israel's religious history in *The Spirit of Hebrew Poetry*. The prophetic achievement of Moses in providing the structure of Israel's social, religious, and literary systems is not the beginning of Israel's history but rather the early high point it reached after the long period of the patriarchs. The first volume of his *Spirit of Hebrew Poetry* is mainly concerned with the pre-Mosaic traditions (primarily the early narratives of Genesis), which Herder considers the raw material of Israel's literature. The Genesis narratives are poetic in their simplicity, sincerity, and sublimity: characteristics they will pass on to Hebrew poetry that draws from them. One who rightly understands these earliest Hebrew traditions will understand that Hebrew poetry is "the poetry of herdsmen; a poetry breathing the spirit of their covenant relation, that is, of the family bond, by which they were united, and the relation of friendship by which the patriarch of the race stood to God."[23] The first volume concludes with a portrait of the prophet Moses, who reforms the institutions of Egyptian civilization on the basis of these early pastoral Hebrew traditions in order to create the purified religious, political, and literary culture of Israel. The value of the simple pastoral age lay mainly in its preparation for the prophetic achievement of Moses. In itself, it lacked the order and complexity necessary for national greatness. Its literature stands as the entryway (*Zugang*) to the actual building (*Gebäude*) of Hebrew poetry.[24] In short, the first age of Israel's history has the character of the childhood stage. It is succeeded by the youthful manhood of Moses's age in which what is best in it is embodied in laws, institutions,

[20] Gotthold Ephraim Lessing, *The Education of the Human Race*, trans. F. W. Robertson, 3rd ed. (London: Henry S. King [1777–80], 1872).

[21] Jean-Jacques Rousseau, *Emile: Or on Education*, trans. Allan Bloom (New York: Basic Books, 1979), 37.

[22] Johann Gottfried von Herder, "Ueber die neue Deutsche Literatur: Erste Sammlung von Fragmenten," in *Sämtliche Werke*, vol. 1, ed. Bernhard Suphan (Hildesheim: Georg Olms, 1967), 151–2.

[23] Herder, *Hebrew Poetry*, 1:237.

[24] Johann Gottfried von Herder, *Vom Geist der ebräischen Poesie*, 3rd ed. (Leipzig: Johann Ambrosius Barth, 1825), 1:310.

and sacred literature. Eventually this age gives way to the old age of decline and corruption into priestly religion and legalism.

Those familiar with Wellhausen's work can appreciate the similarities of Herder's three-stage presentation of Israel's history to his own three-stage history: the simple natural religion of J and E; the ethical monotheism of D; and the complex, priestly, and legalistic religion of P. The obvious difference is that whereas Herder follows the traditional idea that Deuteronomy is the work of Moses, Wellhausen assigns it to the age of Josiah.[25] However, even though in Wellhausen's presentation, the date of the central period has been shifted forward over five hundred years, its character as the period of prophetic genius remains remarkably similar. Just as in Herder's presentation, the laws of Moses are a codification and institutionalization of his prophetic reform of the early natural religion, in Wellhausen's presentation, Deuteronomy is the product of the eighth- and seventh-century prophetic reform of earlier natural religion.[26] "Deuteronomy is the progeny of the prophetic spirit," argues Wellhausen, because it embodies the prophetic vision: monotheism and the belief that God "asks nothing for Himself, but asks it as a religious duty that man should render to man what is right."[27] As in Herder's presentation, the central period sees not only the prophetic reform but also the reduction of Hebrew religion to a written law, so in Wellhausen's presentation, the time of Josiah's "discovery" of Deuteronomy is the first time that the Torah becomes a written authority.[28] In Wellhausen as in Herder, the codification and institutionalization of the prophetic spirit in the Mosaic law, intended to purify and establish the state, has the unintended effect of strengthening the priests and the later legal enforcers who corrupt and undermine the state.[29] In each of these aspects, Herder's understanding of Israel's religious history anticipates the Grafian model in which the prophetic genius stands at the acme of the history. Herder provides the outline of a persuasive historical framework that becomes the dominant model when later scholars are able to fill it out with biblical texts that fit the various stages. The source-critical work of his contemporary, Eichhorn, helps to free the texts from their traditional places in the canon so that they can be reassigned to the new historical framework, which owes much to Herder.[30] In Duhm's commentary, this relocation of texts reaches the book of Jeremiah.

---

[25] The other major difference is that whereas Herder does not question the Mosaicity of the P material, Wellhausen assigns it to the third stage, the stage of dead legalism. Herder seems reticent to find anything but *potential* corruption in the actual texts of the Bible, especially those which spring from the prophetic genius of Moses.

[26] For Wellhausen, the early period of natural religion is primarily the time of the judges and the early monarchy. For Herder it is the time of the patriarchs.

[27] "Israel" in Wellhausen, *Prolegomena*, 487–8.

[28] Wellhausen, *Prolegomena*, 402.

[29] Wellhausen, *Prolegomena*, 488. For Wellhausen, the introduction of the written law was "the death of prophecy." Wellhausen, *Prolegomena*, 402.

[30] Herder appears to have been unable to conceive of how his reorientation of Old Testament studies would be augmented and advanced by source criticism. In the last question in the dialogue of vol. 1 of *The Spirit of Hebrew Poetry*, Alciphron asks about "those hypotheses, which explain the diversity of [the patriarchal] traditions in the use of the words Jehovah and Elohim." Euthyphron responds that little can be added to the work of "a recent author" (i.e., Eichhorn, the first volume of whose *Einleitung in das alte Testament* [1780] had appeared three years before Herder published his first volume on Hebrew poetry). He suggests that the divisions are over-precise in a matter that admits

Literary Criteria Used to Determine Religious Value and Historical Provenance

It has now been shown how Herder's work prepares the way for Duhm in two important areas that go beyond Lowth: (1) his presentation of prophets as individual geniuses of human progress whose work is threatened by the representatives of institutional religion (priests and legal enforcers) who cling to outward forms and (2) his presentation of Israel's religious history as reaching its zenith in the prophets and then sinking into dead legalism. Although these are both momentous contributions to the general outlook shared by Duhm and the other creators and defenders of the Grafian model, their formative significance for Duhm's work on Jeremiah is only clearly understood in association with Herder's most direct anticipation of Duhm, the linking of poetry and prophecy. As has been observed, this link is inherited from Lowth. However, Herder combines it with his broader philosophical and historical theory so that poetic form is associated with prophetic genius as opposed to priestly tradition and with the early and better stage of Israel's history.

The first association Herder makes with poetry, the association with prophetic—as opposed to priestly—religion, is a result of his extension of the idea of prophetic inspiration from poetic inspiration (as in Lowth) to the inspiration of agents of human progress. Those individuals whose lives and teaching serve to lift up the human race are recognized as geniuses inspired by the divine spirit that guides human history. It is only natural that these exalted spirits would express themselves in "inspired" and exalted language. Herder asks, "Who, in speaking in the name of God, would speak in a manner unworthy of his majesty and dignity? Who that is inspired speaks coldly and without elevation?"[31] Writing that is "cold" and "without elevation" must be the work of uninspired writers, those who do not have direct contact with the spirit animating history. These writers do not have direct contact with the spirit animating history, and thus their writing is not original but derivative. On the other hand, the uninspired representatives of institutional or traditional religion (priests and legal enforcers) depend on the genius and inspiration of others. Herder's acceptance of the traditional ascriptions of the authors of the biblical books (particularly Moses's role in writing the Torah) prevents him from fully working out the implications of his understanding. However, the connection he draws between literary inspiration and creative genius makes it possible to judge the spiritual and historical value, and the authors of texts (inspired prophets or uninspired priests and scribes) by literary criteria. If a text is not inspiring it is likely to be uninspired. Material (such as laws, sermons, and genealogies) that lacks the signs of inspiration (such as imagination, originality, expression, passion, and creativity) cannot be attributed to an inspired prophet (such as Moses or Jeremiah) and are more likely to be the work of an uninspired priest or scribe. This methodological approach is what Thompson refers to when he writes, "Herder's aestheticism was in the air when criticism began."[32] The use of aesthetic criteria to distinguish sources

---

little certainty, and he concludes that it makes little difference since everyone will recognize that the traditions have a single source, "the family of Shem." Herder, *Hebrew Poetry*, 1:265-266.

[31] Herder, *Hebrew Poetry*, 2:50-51.

[32] Thompson, *Moses and the Law*, 45.

and judge historical and religious value provides the basis both of the Documentary Hypothesis of the Pentateuch (which isolates the uninspired, non-prophetic prose of the Deuternomistic and Priestly sources) and Duhm's theory of the composition of Jeremiah (which also isolates the uninspired, non-prophetic prose).

The second and more distinctive association that Herder draws is between poetry and antiquity. For Herder poetry is older than prose. If this idea can be found in Lowth, it is not conspicuous. However, Lowth's celebration of the ancient poetry of the Hebrews as natural, spontaneous, and simple rather than polished, labored, and precise helps to lay the groundwork. The historical application of Lowth's reorientation of poetic values can be seen in the work of the English critic Hugh Blair, whose lectures provide a direct link between Lowth and Wordsworth and were popular in Germany as well as in England. Commenting on the superiority of biblical poetry over modern poetry, Blair writes that modern poetry's "superfluities and excrescencies of Style, were the result of imitation in after times; when composition passed into inferior hands and flowed from art and study more than from native genius."[33] This passage shows how the contrast between native genius and imitation can be understood historically as a contrast between early literature and later literature.

Herder's conviction that poetry precedes prose is not a simple working out of the implications of Lowth's position. Herder presents a full history of the development of Israel's literature according to the scheme of childhood, adulthood, and old age. In fact, it appears that it was primarily his understanding of literary or philological development that shaped his understanding of religious and social development rather than vice versa. Certainly in *The Spirit of Hebrew Poetry*, literary and linguistic development is primary. Eugene Reed summarizes the stages in Herder's scheme of linguistic development:

> In the childhood of mankind, the primitive nation is conditioned by fright, fear, and then wonder. When the child becomes a youth "his primitive wildness gives way to a politic calm; his mode of life, the character of his thought divest themselves of their fire, the melody of his speech flows sweetly from his tongue, like that of Homer's Nestor, and rings musically in the ear" ([Herder, "Fragments," in *Sämtliche Werke*,] I, 153). This is the poetic age. When the youth becomes a man, he ceases altogether to be a poet. Political organization makes inevitable the formulation of abstract concepts, and as a result, the age of prose is born.[34]

This three-stage scheme has obvious similarities to Herder's presentation of Israel's religious history outlined above. It is of great significance that as the religious history reaches its high point in the prophetic work of Moses, the literary or linguistic history reaches its high point in the poetic age. In this way, Herder draws on Lowth's identification of prophecy and poetry and reinforces it by giving it historical and

---

[33] *Lectures on Rhetoric and Belles Lettres* (1783), quoted in David B. Morris, *The Religious Sublime: Christian Poetry and Critical Tradition in 18th-Century England* (Lexington: University Press of Kentucky, 1972), 164. Blair's passionate defense of the poetry of "Ossian" helped to fuel the enthusiasm for his Celtic poetry in Germany.

[34] Eugene E. Reed, "Herder, Primitivism and the Age of Poetry," *MLR* 60 (1965): 555.

evaluative significance. Prophetic poetry becomes the great achievement of the nation in the prime of its social and religious history.

Herder's evaluation of prophetic poetry's worth and place in history provides the impetus for scholars who came after him to distinguish prophetic poetry from what is early and preparatory and what is late and derivative. It also makes literary quality a key criterion for determining the historical setting for texts. In this regard, it is highly significant that in Herder's history of Israel's literature, poetry does not arise from abstract prose but from primitive myths and traditions. It is prose (e.g., laws and sermons) that draws on poetry; prose results from the codification and abstraction of the poetic achievement. The implication is that the poetry of the prophets could not be drawn from the prose of the law; the law is abstracted from the earlier poetry (in Herder, the poetic myths of the patriarchal narratives). Here is the literary foundation for the defining thesis of the Grafian movement: the law follows the prophets. Herder himself is kept from following out the implications of his reversal of poetry and prose by his conventional understanding of authorship of the Old Testament books. At most, he can note that prophets do not always speak the exalted poetry that one would expect of them. For example, he observes the contrast between the "sublime and oracular declarations" of Balaam and "the far feebler language of many of the later prophets, which almost sinks to the level of prose."[35] It remains for Duhm to suggest that cold and pedestrian prose could not possibly come from the true prophets from the age of Israel's literary prime but must have been added by priests and scribes in Israel's old age who tried to pass off their prose additions as the work of inspired prophets.

Summary of Herder's Contribution

It was noted in the introduction to this discussion of Herder that his work lies at the roots of both German Romanticism and German biblical studies in the nineteenth century. His contributions to both can now be summarized. For German Romanticism, Herder lays a foundation in large part by his development of Lowth's association of prophet and poet. Herder adds to Lowth's work the idea of the prophet/poet as a creative genius through whose individuality the spirit of history raises up nations and reveals truth to humanity. For nineteenth-century German biblical studies, Herder provides a new historical framework that interprets the conflict between prophet and priest as the historical decline from the time of creative geniuses to the time of small-minded adherents to the letter of the prophets' words. Herder's literary and religious history tells the story of the preparation of Israel for the emergence of prophetic religion and then its decline as their creative work hardened into lifeless traditions and institutions. That it was Herder (drawing on Lowth) who laid out this history helps to explain why it came to be assumed that authentic literature from the prophetic period could be recognized by its literary quality, or more precisely, its approximation to Romantic poetry.

These features of Herder's contribution to Old Testament studies are the very ones that were remarked as the distinctive features of Duhm's treatment of Jeremiah: the

---

[35] Herder, *Hebrew Poetry*, 2:52.

opposition of prophet and institutional religion, the history of decline from the prophetic period, and literary quality as the criterion of religious value and historical reliability. The explanation of how Duhm's work came to be so dominated by Herder's ideas can be considered both in general and specific terms. In general, it can be remarked that Duhm began his studies of the Old Testament in a time heavily influenced by Romanticism in the German universities and especially in biblical studies. More specifically, direct lines of scholarly influence can be traced from Herder to Duhm. One line of scholarly tradition runs from Herder through the scholars who contributed to the Grafian revolution in Pentateuchal studies that was eagerly embraced and promoted by Duhm. Another runs through Duhm's teacher Heinrich Ewald.[36]

From Herder to Duhm I: The Pre-Grafians

It has already been noted how Duhm presents his first major work on the prophets as a contribution to theories of Graf, Kayser, and Kuenen, which he held to be proved beyond reasonable doubt. The influence of Herder on this line of scholarship can be seen in the way each of the scholars who played a major role in the new thought on the Pentateuch refer back to pioneering work of Herder's student, Wilhelm Martin Leberecht de Wette (1780–1849).[37] De Wette was the first to suggest a late date for Deuteronomy and deny the accuracy of the picture of cultic religion in Chronicles.[38] De Wette was Herder's pupil in the Weimar gymnasium and sat under his preaching.[39] Smend suggests that it was Herder's influence that caused de Wette to become a student of theology.[40] Throughout his life, de Wette referred to Herder with gratitude for his great influence on his general and theological education. He writes, "[Herder] appeared to me on the dry steppe of theological criticism and rationalism like an inspired seer, pointing me up to those eternally green pastures soaked by the water of the life. I have always regarded him as the forerunner of a rejuvenated theology, which is both inspired and inspiring."[41] De Wette's work on Chronicles was augmented by

---

[36] These two lines of scholarly tradition from Herder to Duhm were suggested by R. J. Thompson's similar suggestion for Wellhausen: "The critical succession from Wellhausen back to Herder can be established along these two lines of parentage. In the one line are Wellhausen, Ewald, Eichhorn and Herder. In the other, Wellhausen, Vatke, de Wette and Herder." Thompson also notes that each of four modern investigators of the tradition leading up to Wellhausen—Kraus, Hahn, Perlitt, and Smend—have pointed back to the same source: Herder. Thompson, *Moses and the Law*, 46.

[37] Wellhausen refers to Wilhelm Vatke, Èdouard Reuss, and Leopold George as "disciples of Martin Lebrecht de Wette, the epoch-making pioneer of historical criticism in this field. He indeed did not himself succeed in reaching a sure position, but he was the first clearly to perceive and point out how disconnected are the alleged starting-point of Israel's history and that history itself." Wellhausen, *Prolegomena*, 7.

[38] W. M. L. de Wette, *Beiträge zur Einleitung in das Alte Testament* (Halle: Schimmelpfennig, 1806–7).

[39] Karl Barth, *Protestant Theology in the Nineteenth Century* (Grand Rapids, MI: Eerdmans, 2002), 468.

[40] Rudolph Smend, *Deutsche Alttestamentler in drei Jahrhunderten* (Göttingen: Vandenhoeck & Ruprecht, 1989), 40.

[41] De Wette expressed his gratitude to Herder as the man, "der auf meine allgemeine und theologische Bildung durch seine Schriften so viel Einfluß gehabt, der mir auf der dürren Steppe des theologischen Kriticismus und Rationalismus als ein begeisterter Seher erschien und mich auf die ewiggrüne, vom Wasser des Lebens getränkte Weide hinwies, den ich immer als den Vorläufer einer

the philological work of his supporter Wilhelm Gesenius (1786–1842), well known for his Hebrew grammar and lexicon. Rogerson sums up his evaluation of the relation between Gesenius and de Wette: "For over thirty years, Gesenius taught many of the results that are to be found in de Wette's early critical writings."[42] Gesenius in turn taught both Wilhelm Vatke (1806–82) and Èdouard Reuss (1804–1891), urging Vatke to read and thoroughly digest the work of de Wette.[43] Vatke, who was the first to work out a unified history of Israel in which the Priestly literature was a product of the final postexilic stage, was strongly influenced by both de Wette and Herder.[44] In an early letter, he wrote, "Herder ist ebenfalls mein Mann."[45] Reuss, who was the first to teach the idea that the prophets came before the law,[46] also shows the influence of Herder and de Wette. It was Reuss's students at Strasbourg, August Kayser (1821–1885) and Karl Heinrich Graf (1815–1869), who worked out the Pentateuchal theory in the form that Duhm knew it (Duhm calls the theory the "Grafian Hypothesis"[47]). In this way, it can be seen that the scholarly investigation of the Pentateuch that came to fruition in the works of Duhm and Wellhausen had its roots in the work of Herder.

W. M. L. de Wette: Hebrew Religion versus Judaism

The most obvious element of continuity between Herder and these pioneers of the source criticism of the Pentateuch is their adoption of the historical schema in which the achievements of the prophetic poets are later compromised by rigid adherents to the cult and written law. This outline of Israel's religious history suggested by Herder becomes the central organizing principle for understanding Israel's religious history in de Wette's work.[48] In his *Biblische Dogmatik* (1813), he divides Israel's religious history into two sharply distinguished periods: the preexilic period of Hebrew religion (*Hebraismus*) and postexilic period of Judaism (*Judenthum*).[49] Hebrew religion is characterized by freedom and universalism; Judaism is characterized by legalism,

---

verjüngten begeisterten und begeisternden Theologie betrachtet habe." Quoted by Smend, *Deutsche Alttestamentler*, 10.

[42] Rogerson, *Criticism in the Nineteenth Century*, 57.

[43] "[Gesenius] earnestly advised young Wilhelm Vatke to read, mark, and inwardly digest [de Wette]." Cheyne, *Founders of OT Criticism*, 62. Cheyne draws this anecdote from Heinrich Benecke's study of Vatke, where it appears that Gesenius was advising Vatke to read de Wette in order to balance out the conservative influence of his new Hebrew and Arabic teacher, Ewald. Heinrich Benecke, *Wilhelm Vatke in sienem Leben und seinen Schriften* (Bonn: Emil Strauss, 1883), 27.

[44] de Wette, *Biblische Theologie des Alten Testaments* (1848).

[45] Benecke, *Wilhelm Vatke*, 34.

[46] Reuss had told his students Graf and Kayser his views as early as 1833 but did not publish them until after his students had published them in their own works. Thompson, *Moses and the Law*, 33.

[47] "Die Graf'sche Hypothese," Duhm, *Theologie der Propheten*, 17.

[48] De Wette presents himself as an advocate of the philosophy of his friend Jakob Friedrich Fries (1773–1843). Rogerson, *Criticism in the Nineteenth Century*, 36–43. However, de Wette's adherence to Friesian philosophy does not negate the influence of Herder because the two thinkers have much in common: in particular, their search for an alternative source of truth in literature and intuitive understanding.

[49] The Old Testament section of de Wette's *Biblische Dogmatik* is titled "Religion des Alten Testaments oder Hebraismus und Judenthum." Wilhelm Martin Lebrecht de Wette, *Biblische Dogmatik: Alten und neuen Testaments: oder kritische Darstellung der Religionslehre des Hebraismus, des Judenthums und des Urchristenthums*, 3rd ed. (Berlin: G. Reimer, 1831), 62.

ritualism, and particularism: "Whereas Hebrew religion was a matter of life and inspiration, Judaism is a matter of the concept and literalism."[50] In the period of Judaism, slavery to the letter of the law led to the decline of prophecy.[51] The law for de Wette is Deuteronomy, which was written in the time of Josiah and gained dominance in Israel's religion during the exile. Chronicles, which shows Israel following the law before the exile, is an anachronistic projection of Judaism onto the time of Hebrew religion. This basic understanding of Israel's history, in which the law stands between Hebraism and Judaism, is the one that came to dominate Old Testament studies in the time of Wellhausen and Duhm. It is particularly clear in the final section of Wellhausen's *Prolegomena*, in which he makes a sharp distinction between preexilic Israel and postexilic Judaism.[52] De Wette's early presentation of this central feature of the Grafian Hypothesis explains Wellhausen's comment that de Wette was a "clever chap" who anticipated everything he had done in the Old Testament.[53] De Wette's historical scheme in turn can be found in seed form in Herder's work on prophetic poetry.

Wilhelm Vatke: Hegelian Philosophy of History

Wilhelm Vatke built on the work of de Wette by developing a three-part scheme of Israel's history with similarities to Herder's scheme. In Vatke's scheme, there is a long struggle between an original religion of nature (prominent in the early myths and legends) and a later religion of spiritual individualism (prominent in the prophetic literature). The conflict was resolved in the Persian period, and the results are codified in the late legal, wisdom, and poetic material.[54] Comparison of Vatke's understanding of Israel's history to Herder's shows that while Vatke's positive evaluation of the final period is a departure from Herder's understanding, his characterization of the first two stages is a natural development of Herder. Vatke's innovative positive view of the final period can be explained as a result of his thoroughgoing Hegelianism. His three stages are intended as an illustration of Hegel's well-known thesis, antithesis, and synthesis so that the literature of the final period is seen to resolve and transcend the conflict of the earlier periods. The continuity between Vatke's historical scheme and Herder's and de Wette's is most obvious in his description of the first two stages: the progress of religion from the primitive to the prophetic. His characterization of the literature of the early period as "mythical" develops the idea that myth is the expression of the genius of a youthful people, a key element of Romanticism that both Herder and de Wette helped to establish in biblical scholarship. Similarly, his

---

[50] "Während der Hebraismus Sache des Lebens und der Begeisterung war, ist das Judenthum Sache des Begriffs und des Buchstabenwesens." de Wette, *Biblische Dogmatik*, 114.

[51] de Wette, *Biblische Dogmatik*, 54.

[52] "Israel and Judaism" in Wellhausen, *Prolegomena*, 315–66.

[53] Rudolph Otto writes, "Wellhausen sagte mir gelegentlich in Bezug auf de Wette: 'Ein gescheiter Kerl! Was ich im alten Testmente gemacht habe, steht ja schon alles bei ihm.'" Rudolph Otto, *Kantisch-fries'sche Religionsphilosophie und ihre Anwendung auf die Theologie: Zur Einleitung in die Glaubenslehre für Studenten der Theologie* (Tübingen: J. C. B. Mohr [Paul Siebeck], 1909), 130.

[54] Rainer Albertz, *A History of Israelite Religion in the Old Testament Period*, vol. 1, OTL (Louisville, KY: Westminster John Knox, 2005), 4–5.

characterization of the prophetic contribution as spiritual individualism accords well with Herder's Romantic idea of the prophets as inspired representatives of individual religion.

One area in which Vatke developed Herder's ideas is particularly important as a precursor to Duhm's approach. Vatke's work is celebrated as marking the turn to a fully historical investigation of Israel's religion, and this includes the determination of which texts provide reliable historical evidence. In Vatke's historical work, Herder's description of the Genesis narratives as mythical and de Wette's description of Chronicles and Deuteronomy as projections of later periods onto the earlier history allow him to discard large portions of the Old Testament as evidence of the historical periods to which they refer. At the same, time he elevates the importance of the prophetic literature as historical evidence. Building on Herder's idea of the prophetic literature as spontaneous effusions of great men at important junctures in Israel's history, Vatke treats the prophetic literature as primary historical evidence of Israel's religion at the time each prophet spoke.[55] He then uses the historical reconstruction of Israel's religious development based on this evidence to evaluate the historicity of the historical books and to determine the date of the legal material.[56] In this way, the poetic "authenticity" of prophetic writings established by Lowth and Herder (i.e., the aesthetic evidence that they are the work of an inspired poet) is used by Vatke and other historical critics to guarantee the historical authenticity of the prophetic writings (their reliability as evidence of their time of origin). This reliance on aesthetic criteria to judge historical reliability is a central feature of Wellhausen's source-critical reconstruction of the Pentateuch and Duhm's reconfiguration of the book of Jeremiah.

Ultimately, the failure of Vatke's overall historical scheme to win adherents is an indication of the pervasive influence of Herder's Romanticism. The "triumph of Grafianism" by the end of the nineteenth century can be seen as the triumph of de Wette's and Herder's vision of the rise and fall of Israel's religion over Vatke's vision of its continuous progress. The historical theory of Graf, Kuenen, and Kayser that Wellhausen and Duhm took and championed is in its basic outline the one enunciated by de Wette's over half a century earlier: Israel's decline from Hebrew religion and its inspired prophets to legalistic Judaism and its priests and scribes. The distinguishing tenet of the Documentary Hypothesis, the postexilic date of the Priestly source, in essence takes Vatke's method of reassigning texts to their true historical period and uses it to defend de Wette's theory of decline over Vatke's theory of progress.

---

[55] William Irwin writes, "Vatke's outstanding contribution to Pentateuchal criticism was his demonstration that the prophets are a primary, and major, source of evidence for religious conditions and practices against which to test the antiquity of the priestly legal system. And when we see that this is precisely the core of Wellhausen's argument in the *Prolegomena*, it becomes apparent what it was that he had learned 'most and best' [from Vatke]." William A. Irwin, "The Significance of Julius Wellhausen," *JBR* 12 (1944): 165. Irwin is refuting W. F. Albright's charge that Wellhausen must have been a Hegelian since Vatke was overtly a Hegelian and Wellhausen had written, "[From Vatke] I gratefully acknowledge myself to have learned best and most." Wellhausen, *Prolegomena*, 15.

[56] Vatke's use of the prophetic literature as authentic literary evidence is similar to the use that F. C. Baur and other nineteenth-century New Testament critics made of the "authentic" epistles of Paul.

Romantic Historicism over Hegelianism

Wellhausen and Duhm, though they draw heavily on Vatke, are eager to distance themselves from his position. To them, he is an example of a scholar who let his philosophical system predetermine his historical work, and they understand their own work as objectively historical, unbiased by any philosophical system.[57] Wellhausen's evaluation of Vatke appears in a review of Strauss's *Leben Jesu*, which appeared in 1835—the same year as Vatke's *Biblische Theologie*. Wellhausen writes,

> Philosophy does not precede, but follows [biblical criticism], in that it seeks to evaluate and to systematize that which it has not itself produced. The authors—who were friends—of the two great theological works of 1835 were certainly Hegelian. But, that which is of scholarly significance in them does not come from Hegel. As Vatke is the disciple of, and the one who brings to completion the work of, de Wette, so Strauss completes the work of the old rationalists.[58]

This passage is remarkable because it not only expresses Wellhausen's view of the relation of biblical criticism and philosophy, but it also shows his understanding of Vatke and de Wette. What is valuable in Vatke comes from de Wette (i.e., scientific criticism); what is dispensable in Vatke comes from Hegel (i.e., philosophy). Wellhausen seems oblivious to de Wette's philosophical presuppositions—most likely because they are his own. From the vantage point provided by the distance of an intervening century, it now appears that Wellhausen and the Grafians did not simply choose history over philosophy, but instead chose one philosophical version of history over another. In broad strokes, they chose Herder's Romanticism, in which history's high points come in the form of inspired individuals, over Hegel's Idealism, in which history is moving upward toward a final resolution through the conflict of varying forms of consciousness.

To be more precise, the Grafians chose the historicism of Leopold von Ranke and Johan Gustav Droysen, which critiqued Hegelian and Enlightenment views of history from the perspective of Herder's Romantic individualism and Romantic nationalism. Both the Hegelian and the historicist schools of historiography formed in the wake of the loss of confidence in an earlier understanding of history of in which the time of classical Greece and Rome was held up as the golden age and therefore the standard for judging other cultures and historical periods.[59] Enlightenment thinkers including Hegel believed that historical progress had elevated the present

---

[57] Duhm draws a contrast between Vatke's approach to the question of the development of Israel's religion with his "theories of the philosophy of religion" and Graf and Orth's objective approach to the "archeological materials in the pre-exilic texts" and Kuenen and Kayser's "literary historical research." Duhm, *Theologie der Propheten*, 18.

[58] Craig Bartholomew's translation of a quotation from Lothar Perlitt, *Vatke und Wellhausen* (Berlin: A Töpelmann, 1965), 204. Craig G. Bartholomew, "Uncharted Waters: Philosophy, Theology and the Crisis in Biblical Interpretation," in *Renewing Biblical Interpretation*, ed. Craig Bartholomew, Colin Greene, and Karl Möller, Scripture & Hermeneutics 1 (Grand Rapids, MI: Zondervan, 2001), 17.

[59] Isaiah Berlin, *Three Critics of the Enlightenment: Vico, Hamann, Herder* (Princeton, NJ: Princeton University Press, 2000), 15.

age above earlier historical periods, including the classical period, and that that progress would continue toward a better age. In essence, they transferred the golden age to the future. Historical events and ages could be evaluated the standard of that future age and were significant insofar as they contributed to or blocked progress toward it.

Historians like Droysen and von Ranke rejected this "teleological" view of history and, following the path marked out by thinkers like Lowth and Herder, argued that the accomplishments of each people and age should be understood on their own terms. However, this threated a kind of historical and cultural relativism and created a pressing question for historians: What would count as historically noteworthy? Herder's Romantic theory of creative geniuses (rooted as it has been seen, in the Lowthian presentation of inspired prophets) who founded lasting institutions provided two criteria for answering this question. Herder believed that the genius of an individual could be directly appreciated by modern readers (or historians) because they shared some measure of the common human Spirit. This belief is the basis of Herder's hermeneutic of *Einfühlung*, or empathy.[60] Added to this subjective criterion was the objective criterion of lasting historical effect.[61] Those works which stood the test of time could be judged to be the works of a genius, an individual who helped to express the one human spirit guiding history. Gadamer's description of the historical school of in relation to Hegel and Herder would be just as apt as a description of the Grafians' view of history:

> We remember how the historical school distinguished itself from Hegel. Its birth certificate, as it were, is its rejection of the aprioristic construction of world history. Its new claim is that not speculative philosophy but only historical research can lead to a universal view of history. It was Herder's critique of the Enlightenment's schema of the philosophy of history that made this development possible. … Against the Enlightenment's teleological view of history, … [Herder argued] that to think historically … means to acknowledge that each period has its own right to exist, its own perfection.[62]

---

[60] The word *Einfühlung*, whether or not it was coined by Herder, first appeared in late eighteenth-century Germany and gained currency through his work. The English word "empathy" came into the language in the early twentieth century as an attempt to translate *Einfühlung*. Richard Burnett observes that Barth traces the roots of both historicism and psychologism back to Herder and especially to his hermeneutics of empathy. Richard E. Burnett, *Karl Barth's Theological Exegesis*, WUNT 2/145 (Tübingen: Mohr Siebeck, 2001), 142. Schleiermacher's principle of divination clearly owes something to Herder's principle of empathy (Burnett, *Barth's Exegesis*, 153). Gadamer observes that "in hermeneutics, what corresponds to the production of genius is divination, the immediate solution, which ultimately presupposes a kind of con-geniality." Gadamer, *Truth and Method*, trans. Joel Weinsheimer and Donald Marshal, 2nd ed. (New York: Continuum, 2000), 189. This observation reveals the link between Herder's concept of genius and his concept of empathy: what genius creates, empathy understands by re-creating. Gadamer refers to the approach of Herder and Schleiermacher as Romantic hermeneutics. Gadamer, *Truth and Method*, 174–218.

[61] Gadamer notes the importance of this "criterion of success" in both Herder and Ranke. Gadamer, *Truth and Method*, 203.

[62] Gadamer, *Truth and Method*, 200–1.

190 Jeremiahunder the Shadow of Duhm

The Grafians rejected Vatke's Hegelianism and in its place chose de Wette's Romantic historicism, which is grounded in Herder. The central idea of the de Wette's Romantic history of Israel is that the nation reached its perfection in the age of the prophets. It was in this age through the prophets that the spirit of the nation came to full expression and made its distinctive contribution to human history. Thus both the Grafian view of Israel's history and the historicists view of human history are grounded in the new view of the prophets of Israel that Herder founded on Lowth reading of the poetic sections in the prophetic books.

A more obvious example of the Grafians debt to Herder's Romanticism can be seen in Lothar Perlitt's description of Wellhausen's critical tastes: he had "almost constitutional aversion to everything artificial, schematic, constructed, secondary, derived" and a corresponding attraction "to the original, the organic, the natural, the simple."[63] These two sets of qualities could easily be applied to Duhm's division of authentic and inauthentic speech in Jeremiah, and they are also, of course, the defining characteristics of good and bad literature for the Romantics and Herder, and behind them for Lowth.

From Herder to Duhm II: Heinrich Ewald

The other line of scholarly tradition connecting Herder and Duhm runs through Heinrich Ewald (1803–1875), who taught both Duhm and Wellhausen at Göttingen. Ewald had been trained by Eichhorn, Herder's close associate, and Cheyne notes that portraits of Eichhorn and Herder hung on the walls of Ewald's study, "as if to remind him of the aim and spirit of their common enterprise."[64] In regard to Duhm and Wellhausen, Ewald occupies an unusual position because, although he is acknowledged by both as a major source of their thought, he was a fierce opponent of the Grafian Hypothesis, which it was their life work to promote. The tension can be seen in Wellhausen who dedicated his *Prolegomena* "to my unforgotten teacher Ewald" and yet wrote elsewhere that Ewald was "the principal hindrance" (*der grosse Aufhalter*) to progress on the road laid out by de Wette and Vatke.[65] Due largely to Ewald's influence, the idea that an Elohistic source (Ewald's "Book of Origins") was the unifying foundational document (*Grundschrift*) of the Pentateuch (supplemented by the other sources) was the dominant theory throughout the middle decades of the nineteenth century.[66] It was primarily this "supplementary hypothesis" that the Grafians sought to overturn by arguing for a late date of the Priestly material. However, although the Grafians disagreed with Ewald's theory of the composition of on the Pentateuch, they highly valued his work on the

---

[63] Craig Bartholomew's translation from Perlitt, *Vatke und Wellhausen*, 211. Bartholomew, "Uncharted Waters," 19.

[64] Cheyne, *Founders of OT Criticism*, 71.

[65] Rogerson, *Criticism in the Nineteenth Century*, 91.

[66] Cheyne estimates that Ewald's work "held back progress" (i.e., blocked the rise of the Grafian hypothesis) in biblical studies for thirty years: due to Ewald, the ideas of Vatke's *Biblische Theologie des Alten Testaments* (1848) did not come into wide influence until the publication of Wellhausen's *Geschichte Israels*, I (1878). Cheyne, *Founders of OT Criticism*, 107.

prophets. Wellhausen wrote of Ewald's two-volume work on the prophets, "This is Ewald's exegetical masterpiece. The prophets were congenial to him, and he penetrated more deeply into their nature than any of his predecessors."[67] Considering Ewald's work on the prophets provides a firsthand perspective on the tradition of interpretation of the prophets as it passed from Herder to Duhm through Ewald.

Ewald's Gifts to the Grafians

Ewald's work on the prophets may be said to have prepared for Duhm's work in two ways: his specific contributions to the study of prophecy, which Duhm took up in his own works on the prophets, and his contributions to the Grafian theory. In view of their opposition to Ewald's source-critical theory, it is surprising to see how many elements in his work the Grafians found congenial to their reconstruction of Israel's history. First and foremost was Ewald's historical method. Ewald's study of the prophets in terms of the unique contributions of unique personalities to their unique historical situations (an approach he inherited from Lowth and Herder) provided an alternative to the historical schemes of Vatke and Strauss, which were discredited by their dependence on Hegelian philosophy. Ewald's romantically conceived prophets allowed future biblical historians a way to maintain their historical idealism (their belief that the divine or ideal realm was expressing itself in human history) without reference to a teleological standard to measure the degree of enlightenment that each stage reached. The revelatory divinity of the prophets' messages did not need a standard external to history, but could be validated by each prophet's own originality, intensity, and integrity, and the eventual acceptance of his message. In the minds of his contemporaries, Ewald gave the study of Israel's religion a solid objective, scientific, and historical basis to replace the aprioristic philosophical approaches.[68] This is surely what they intended by referring to him as "the Ranke of Hebrew history."[69] Looking back on the period, scholars today can see a deeper significance in the title, as they discern the similarity of Ewald's approach to Ranke's historicism with its replacement of the Hegelian philosophy of history with Romantic hermeneutics.[70]

The second element of Ewald's scholarship that contributed to the Grafian hypothesis was his individual treatment of the classical prophets. Ewald's work on the prophets included a detailed account of each of the major writing prophets arranged in historical order. This was of great help to the Grafians because of a curious feature of their work: although they propounded a theory of Israel's development that held the prophetic literature to be the consummation of the history, their work primarily

---

[67] Julius Wellhausen, *Festschrift zur Feier des hundertfünfzigjährigen Bestehens der Königlichen Gesellschaft der Wissenschaften zu Göttingen, Bëitrage zur Gelehrtengeschichte Göttingens* (Berlin, 1901), 71. Quoted in Zimmerli, *Law and Prophets*, 19.

[68] "The first scientific historical work [on biblical history] was by H. Ewald." Israel Abrahams, "Jews," in *Encyclopedia Britannica: A Dictionary of Arts, Sciences, Literary and General Information* (New York: Encyclopedia Britannica, 1911), 15:373.

[69] Cheyne, *Founders of OT Criticism*, 105.

[70] Gadamer, *Truth and Method*, 197–203.

focused on the Pentateuchal sources that either pre- or postdated the prophetic period Ewald's work on the prophets filled this gap, and Duhm's own work on the prophets can be seen as an attempt to fully integrate Ewald's work with the new theory of Israel's religious history. Duhm's intent to both build on and surpass Ewald's work is evident in the full title of his first major work: *The Theology of the Prophets as Foundation* [Grundlage] *for the History of the Inner Development* [*or Evolution,* Entwicklung] *of Israelite Religion.* Like Ewald's work, Duhm's believed his was not founded on a philosophical theory, but on individual consideration of each prophet in his historical situation. However, unlike Ewald's work, Duhm's would not be content to provide fragmentary pictures of the historical backgrounds of the various individual prophets but would work toward a comprehensive picture of the historical development of Israel's religion. It would return to the achievement of de Wette and Vatke, but this time on the basis of solid historical evidence.

A third element of Ewald's work that benefited the Grafians is his theory of prophecy as the way that divine truth first breaks into the world. Herder's conception of the prophets as original and creative geniuses who stand at the origins of national institutions and traditions helped de Wette and Vatke incorporate the prophets into their schemes of religious history. Ewald radicalizes Herder's conception by incorporating it into his theory of how divine truths (i.e., all moral and religious truths) must necessarily come into the world. Ewald develops portraits of the prophets as individuals who had such firm conviction of the truth they had received that they were compelled to proclaim the truth to the people to whom it applied and to maintain it in the face of all opposition. Ewald located "the genuine prophetic element" in the compulsion that will "leave a man no rest until he proclaims [his divine conception]," the "extreme force with which [it] springs forth."[71] This is why, Ewald explains, a prophet was called a *nābî'*: the term "denotes originally a loud, clear speaker … who declares the mind and words of another."[72] The nature of the prophet as one compelled to speak the truth he has received determines prophecy's universal and necessary form: the "violence and the immediateness" of its activity.[73] From this characterization of the form of prophecy, Ewald draws a striking conclusion:

> Historically, therefore, this form must have originated in an unavoidable necessity.
>   We have now arrived at the main principle, that the prophetic form is the earliest in which higher and divine truths and conceptions can start into life, that on that account prophecy belongs peculiarly to early antiquity and the youth of the human race.[74]

The logic of Ewald's conclusion is that the only situation that would make it necessary for divine truth to be delivered in such a violent and immediate manner is one in which the divine truths were not already known: "We must imagine a time," he writes,

---

[71] Heinrich Ewald, *Commentary on the Prophets of the Old Testament,* trans. J. Frederick Smith, TTFL 9 (London: Williams & Norgate, 1875), 1:7-8.
[72] Ewald, *Prophets of the Old Testament,* 1:8 (emphasis original).
[73] Ewald, *Prophets of the Old Testament,* 1:10.
[74] Ewald, *Prophets of the Old Testament,* 1:11.

"when the higher truths themselves had no existence amongst men."[75] To imagine this time, modern readers would have to take themselves out of the present day in which the divine truths have become universally known and familiar. The present day differs from the time of the prophets in that "what first glowed as a hidden, but mightily outbreaking fire quite within the inmost heart of holy men, has now become a visible light set up in the world without [i.e., external to] men."[76] Ewald's argument can be summed up by saying that since the prophets experienced their preaching as the outbreaking of the fire of truth, they must necessarily have lived in the period of darkness before the enlightenment of divine truth.

The Grafians could hardly fail to see how Ewald's argument supported their own reconstruction of the history of Israel in which the prophets precede the law. Ewald does not merely argue that the law seems unnecessary for the prophets in light of their creative genius, or that it seemed fitting that their youthful freedom and spontaneity would come before the order and discipline of the law. He argues that his historical investigation of the individual prophets had uncovered the universal form of prophecy, and that the character of this form makes it a logical necessity that divine truth cannot have entered the world before the prophets. To the Grafians, this must have appeared a striking independent confirmation of their conception of the prophets as the original geniuses of Israelite religion. Their investigation of the books of history and law had carved out a unique role for prophets, and Ewald's investigation of the prophetic books uncovered prophets who perfectly fit that role. The hand fit the glove. The Grafians believed that this was because their reconstruction of the composition of the Pentateuch and the history of Israel and Ewald's reconception of the prophets had both discovered aspects of the same historical reality behind the biblical texts.

This study has suggested an alternative explanation for the fit: both the glove and the hand belong to Herder. Ewald's model of prophecy, in which prophets are compelled to speak the divine truths newly entering the world, is deeply rooted in the tradition that begins with Lowth's derivation of prophetic poetry from sublime experiences and that takes on significance for history with Herder's theory that the providential spirit of history achieves human enlightenment through the agency of inspired geniuses. The Grafians' framework of history, in which the age of the prophets with its youthful freedom is succeeded by the age in which their insights have hardened into law and ritual, is rooted in the tradition that begins in Lowth's discovery in the prophetic literature of a poetry of youthful originality, simplicity, and vigor and that includes Herder's historical scheme in which the national history reaches its youthful prime in the time of the prophets. In light of their common roots in Herder's Romanticism, it is no great surprise (and is no confirmation of either's work) that Ewald's prophets fit the role of the prophets in the Grafian history of Israel's religion.

Ewald's Direct Anticipation of Duhm

In Duhm's work on the prophets, particularly in his commentary on Jeremiah, Ewald's Romantic reconceptions of the Hebrew prophets and the Grafians' Romantic

---

[75] Ewald, *Prophets of the Old Testament*, 1:11.
[76] Ewald, *Prophets of the Old Testament*, 1:13.

reconstruction of Israel's history were fully integrated and achieved a kind of consummation. It was as if two branches of the same family tree had come together in marriage. Ewald not only prepared for their marriage in the work of Duhm work by grooming the Hebrew prophets to be compatible with the Grafian history; he also provided Duhm with the methodological approach by which he was able to reconfigure the texts of the prophetic books to make them serve as evidence for the reconceived prophets and the reconstructed history. However in this his most direct contribution to Duhm's work, Ewald was not drawing as much from the biblical scholarship of Herder and his followers as he drew from the very foundations of Romanticism as laid down in Lowth's work on the poetry in the prophetic books.

The first direct contribution of Ewald's work to Duhm's work on the prophets was his reconception of the aim of interpreting the prophetic books. Whereas in most interpretation of these books before Lowth the aim of interpretation was assumed to be the clarification of the message or purpose of the books, for Ewald (like Lowth) the aim of interpretation was to recover the original experiences of the prophet. As has been seen, for Ewald the "directness and immediateness" of the prophetic experience and prophetic action were the essential characteristics of prophecy. The violence that accompanied the coming into history of the novel divine conceptions was what gave the prophets assurance of the validity of their ideas. The implication of this view for interpreting the prophetic literature is that to fully understand a prophetic text, the interpreter must not only grasp the meaning of its statements but also "vividly realize again the period of its nativity."[77] This is not simply a matter of locating the prophets in their original historical settings, but also of re-creating the original prophetic experiences in the experience of the reader. The aim of a direct appreciation of the experience of the prophets is the reason Ewald gives for limiting his study to what the prophets themselves wrote. The stories about the prophets, whether in the historical or prophetic books, come to the reader mediated by the thoughts of the later writers, but "in their own writings [the prophets] have most distinctly and trustworthily laid bare their spirit" with the result that, through their writings, readers can "know in their inmost hearts these heroes of divine truth and admire their genuine greatness."[78]

Ewald's understanding of the value of prophetic literature as a medium through which the heart of the reader can draw near to the heart of the prophet is the full flowering of Herder's Romantic hermeneutics of *Einfühlung*, which in turn is rooted in Lowth's estimation that the value of the prophetic books lies in the poetry, understood as expressions of the sublime experiences of the prophets. Ewald's interest in prophetic experience clearly influenced his student. Duhm singles out his teacher as the scholar who "probably deserves the most praise" for his appreciation of "the psychological factor in its significance for the formation of religious thoughts and concepts."[79] Ewald

---

[77] Ewald, *Prophets of the Old Testament*, 1:103.

[78] Ewald, *Prophets of the Old Testament*, 1:2.

[79] Duhm, *Theologie der Propheten*, 34 (quoted in Rudolph Smend, *From Astruc to Zimmerli: Old Testament in Scholarship in Three Centuries*, trans. Margaret Kohl [Tübingen: Mohr Siebeck, 2007], 109). Smend adds that, in terms of psychological interpretation, Duhm went "far beyond Ewald and any restriction to psychology." Smend, *Astruc to Zimmerli*, 109. The intense interest in prophetic psychology, found in Ewald and Duhm, was to characterize studies of the prophets in the early twentieth century. It is especially evident in the work Hermann Gunkel (1862–1932) and Gustav Hölscher (1877–1955), and, as will be seen, in Sigmund Mowinckel's work on Jeremiah (1914).

is the most obvious source of Duhm's conviction that authentic prophecy must be original to the prophet (not derived from tradition) and must take the form of passionate (poetic) outbursts that lay bare the heart of the prophet. This foundational assumption of Duhm's is rooted in the same Romantic tradition as his judgment that the most valuable part of the book of Jeremiah is the authentic poetry of the prophet, and that what makes it valuable is "the voice" it gives "to the individual self" and "the masterful expression" it gives to "the feelings, and the emotional state of the prophet."[80]

This leads to a second aspect of Ewald's work in which he develops the tradition of Lowth and Herder in a way that prepares for Duhm's work. Ewald helps to lay the groundwork for Duhm's signal contribution to Jeremiah studies, the methodological priority of the task of distinguishing the "authentic words" of the prophet from the work of later authors. The necessity of this critical task arises out of Ewald's understanding of the prophets as the first conduits through which divine truths came into the world. A logical consequence of Ewald's theory is that once truth has become widely known, the need for prophecy diminishes. It is an irony of religious history as interpreted by Ewald that the greatest prophets did the most to bring the age of prophecy to an end by making the eternal truths widely known. Unfortunately, according to Ewald, people kept speaking and writing as prophets long after the "the few simple universal truths" had been announced by the true prophets. The result was that along with the original truths there "have been further added a large mass of derived mixed truths, mere ideas and usages, which have become sacred and legal"; thus, "it is not strange that it should become very difficult to rise to the living source of pure truth."[81] This then becomes the first task of the interpreter: to sort out the original pure truth from the mass of mixed truth that was added later.

Ewald adds a further element to the rationale for this critical sorting. Prophecy did not merely disappear; it degenerated. Even in the time of the prophets, prophets began to go astray from their true purposes. They might slip from the true "ecstasy" of authentic prophetic experience into mere "madness," or transfer their conviction of inspiration to their own ideas, or begin to use their respected positions for personal gain or political influence.[82] They might also attract followers who wished to be prophets but lacked the inspiration of the authentic prophet: "As in all human things, tradition and imitation very early succeeded to primitive originality."[83] It was these imitators and traditionists whose work Duhm believed had accumulated on top of the original work of the inspired prophet Jeremiah. It was his work to strip away these layers of accretion in order to uncover the authentic writings of the inspired prophet.

Unlike Ewald and scholars of the nineteenth century, these scholars were less inclined to see the prophets' experiences as revelatory (as the irruption into history of the divine, or transcendent, or sublime); rather, they sought to explain the Hebrew prophets' experiences as typical of prophetic experience in other religions (especially those of the Ancient Near East) and as able to explained psychologically without recourse to spiritual or supernatural causes.

[80] Duhm, *Das Buch Jeremia*, KHC 11 (Tübingen: J. C. B. Mohr, 1901), xiii.
[81] Ewald, *Prophets of the Old Testament*, 1:14.
[82] Ewald, *Prophets of the Old Testament*, 1:15-22.
[83] Ewald, *Prophets of the Old Testament*, 1:19.

Ewald not only provided Duhm with the aim, and the methodological priority of his approach to the prophets, but he also provided him with his key methodological tool: using the form of the speech (poetry or prose) to determine whether it is authentic prophetic speech or a later non-prophetic addition. Ewald wrote that "violence and immediateness" is the "distinctive and unique" character of prophecy, the "form ... essential to all prophecy."[84] "Prophecy," he says, "is not possible without this natural and spontaneous form."[85] The later non-prophetic additions Ewald characterized as "tradition and imitation" with content that was "sacred and legal."[86] Although he does not explicitly identify the division between authentic prophetic material and later non-prophetic with the division between poetry and prose, the entrenched dichotomies in Ewald's work between spontaneous and imitated, original and traditional, immediate and detached and the way they line up with the dichotomy between prophetic and legal or priestly are clearly rooted in the Romantic dichotomy between poetic and nonpoetic, which is in turn rooted in the way Lowth distinguished the poetic sections from the nonpoetic in Jeremiah and the other books of Hebrew prophecy. In this way, Ewald not only reinforces the way nineteenth-century scholars understood the difference between prophetic and legal literature (as early and inspired or later and derivative), but he also regrounds it in the Romantic understanding of the difference between poetic and nonpoetic composition. This provided Duhm with the tool he needed to bring the book of Jeremiah into conformity with the Grafian view of history, in which the prophets precede the law: treating poetic form as the prime indication that a passage is prophetic and authentic.

Evaluation: Whether Common Conclusions Strengthen Credibility

Having reviewed the relationship between Duhm's work on the prophets and the development of the Grafian reconstruction of Israel's religious history, the discussion can return to the central question of the chapter: does the conformity of Duhm's historical conclusions founded on his theory of the composition of Jeremiah to the widely accepted historical model of Israel's religious history add to the plausibility of compositional theory? The analogy would be to two scientists who reach the same conclusions working with different methods or different sets of evidence, or two mathematicians who reach the same conclusion with a different sequence of proofs. The concurrence would not only add to the credibility of their common conclusion but also to the methods they used to reach the conclusions. The strength added to Duhm's model would seem to be would be even greater than in these examples because it is not merely one other scholar's conclusion with which his conclusions align but the conclusions of many of the foremost biblical scholars of his day.

---

[84] Ewald, *Prophets of the Old Testament*, 1:10-11.
[85] Ewald, *Prophets of the Old Testament*, 1:11.
[86] Ewald, *Prophets of the Old Testament*, 1:19, 14.

How a Hypothetical Interpreter Might Have Reach Duhm's Conclusions

To assess the degree of credibility this concurrence provides to Duhm's model, the way he and the other scholars arrived at their common conclusions came to can be compared with a scenario that would provide a high degree of credibility for his model of Jeremiah's composition. The scenario begins with an interpreter who comes to the book of Jeremiah and is puzzled to find that the book presents two types of material as the speech of the prophet: poetic speeches and prose speeches. As she examines these two types of material, she sees that the differences between them in style and wording as well as in religious outlook are so pronounced that she is driven to the conclusion that they cannot both have been spoken (or written) by the same person. Having come to doubt the veracity of the book's presentation, she is faced with the question of which (if either) of the two types of material was actually spoken by the prophet. She finds that although the poetic material fits well with what is known from other sources about the prophet Jeremiah and his time period, there are anachronistic elements in the prose material that make it impossible that it was written during the prophet's lifetime. Working on the basis of the likely authenticity of the poetic speeches, the interpreter sees that they provide evidence about the historical prophet and his message that is quite different from the book's portrayal, in particular its portrayal of the prophet's relationship to the written law. Turning to the inauthentic prose speeches, the knowledge that they were written after the fall of Jerusalem helps her to see their value as evidence of an exilic community trying to come to terms with the catastrophe by explaining it as the consequence of disobedience to a written law.

At this point, the interpreter comes across the work of scholars who have been working on the interpretation of the Pentateuch and the historical books. As was the case with the interpreter's work on Jeremiah, their literary and historical investigations had caused them to doubt the veracity of the historical presentations in the books and to see them as being composed of incompatible sources from various historical periods. When the sources were read in their correct historical contexts, a picture of the history of Israel's religion emerged that differed sharply from the history presented by the books. The most notable difference was that the system of laws that the books present as being written in the time of Moses was actually written much later, primarily in the exilic and postexilic periods. A notable implication of this discovery is that it discredits the idea that the preexilic prophets could have called for obedience to the ancient written law. The interpreter could hardly fail to see that what she had discovered through her investigation of the book of Jeremiah fits perfectly with the discovery of these other scholars. They concur that the seventh-century prophet Jeremiah could not have been an advocate of the written law, but that this feature of the book's portrayal was due to later advocates of the law attributing their perspective to Jeremiah as they also attributed their laws to Moses. The interpreter of Jeremiah would surely be justified in regarding the close alignment of her historical results with the results other scholars had obtained by investigation of the Pentateuch as a significant confirmation of the validity of her conclusions about the book of Jeremiah as well as of their significance as confirmation of the historical discoveries of the Pentateuch scholars.

If this had been the way that Duhm and the scholars responsible for the Documentary Hypothesis had come to common conclusions about the historical relationship between the prophets and the written law, it would certainly bolster the credibility of Duhm's historical conclusions as well as his compositional model. Of course, this is not the way it actually happened. Before suggesting how Duhm's conclusions about Jeremiah turned out to conform to the conclusions of the Grafian scholars, it can be pointed out how improbable it would be that the scenario just described could have ever happened without Duhm's assumptions and aims. In the scenario, it is the features of the book of Jeremiah itself that drive the interpreter to her conclusions. It seems unlikely this would ever happen. The interpreter's first step depends on her finding the difference between the poetic and prose speeches of Jeremiah so irreconcilable that she is driven to discredit the book's presentation and deny that the speeches could have the same author. A case for multiple authorship on the basis of differences style, diction, or form is very difficult to make because there are so many other plausible explanations. It is hard to deny that an author might have chosen one style for one purpose or occasion and another style for another purpose or occasion. Differences in outlook in the speeches might provide stronger reason for abandoning the book's presentation of Jeremiah's speech. But again, there are many other possible explanations, especially given Jeremiah's decades-long career during which his views could have changed.[87] There even more plausible explanations for these differences when it is recognized that the book (both the poetry and the prose) presents not only Jeremiah's perspective but also the sometimes conflicting perspective of Yahweh. These considerations make it implausible that an interpreter would be driven to the theory that the differences between poetic speeches of Jeremiah and the prose speeches of Jeremiah could only be explained by positing two different authors with incompatible perspectives.

The second step of the hypothetical interpreter, that she would determine that the prose speeches of Jeremiah must be inauthentic and written after the destruction of Jerusalem, is also implausible. In the scenario, it was supposed that the interpreter was driven to this conclusion by anachronisms in the prose speeches and the greater fit of the poetic speeches with what was known about the time period. In fact, there are no notable instances of anachronisms in the prose speeches or anything that makes it unlikely that they were spoken during the ministry of Jeremiah and before the destruction of Jerusalem and Judah that many of them predict.[88] From the other sources of information about this period in Judah (the fullest are in 2 Kings 22–25 and 2 Chronicles 34–36), the most notable events other than the destruction and exile at the hands of the Babylonians are the discovery of the Book of the Law and the promulgation by priest and prophet of the warning based on it that disobedience of the law (and breaking the covenant) would bring foreign invasion, destruction, and exile. Thus the Deuteronomistic style, diction, or concerns that characteristic of many of

[87] His career stretches over at least forty years: from the time of his call (*c.* 627 BC) well into the first decades in the next century and including years before the discovery of the Book of the Law (*c.* 621 BC) and years after the destruction of Jerusalem (586 BC).

[88] The warnings or announcements of the destruction of Jerusalem and exile before the events in the prose speeches do not strain credulity any more than the similar warnings or announcements in the poetic speeches.

Jeremiah's speeches in prose can hardly be called anachronistic. If it were assumed that the poetic speeches and the prose speeches could not both be spoken by the prophet and it was asked which are more likely to represent his public speeches, there would be several reasons for choosing the prose. Unlike the poetic speeches, the prose speeches are regularly explicitly tied to specific events in the life of Jeremiah and are often explicitly introduced as messages to be delivered by Jeremiah to various historical audiences. The prose speeches also align more closely with Jeremiah's speeches in the only narratives about him (those in the book of Jeremiah). In these narratives, he speaks exclusively in prose.[89] These considerations do not prove the authenticity of the prose speeches; they merely show that there is no conflict with them and what is known about Jeremiah's time that would make it necessary to deny that Jeremiah spoke them. Thus it would be improbable that an interpreter working only with the book of Jeremiah and what was known from other sources about him and his time would ever come to the conclusion that the prose speeches could not have the same author as the poetic speeches or that they must have been written after the time of Jeremiah. It would thus also be improbable that the interpreter would come to doubt that Jeremiah delivered messages that urged adherence to the ancient laws.[90]

How Duhm Reached His Conclusions

The reasons that it was likely that Duhm would reach these conclusions that another interpreter would be unlikely to reach should be apparent from the previous chapters on his work. Duhm was predisposed by the cultural situation and scholarly tradition he was in to read the poetic sections of a prophetic book as if they had been written by a poet similar to a Romantic poet and to understand the poetic features as the inevitable expressions of the passionate temperament, creative powers, and tender sensibility of such a poet. For this reason, Duhm believed that passages of "low quality" and "clumsy form"—and this includes all of the prose speeches attributed to Jeremiah—"cannot be objectively brought into line with the undoubtedly genuine creations of Jeremiah."[91] The corresponding association of the literary inspiration that made the poetry great and prophetic inspiration explains why there could be no question for Duhm whether it was poetry or the prose that was most likely to be authentic. The conclusions Duhm reached based on his beliefs about the necessary form, style, and literary quality of true prophecy were reinforced by his belief about the message of true prophets. Duhm was predisposed to read the speeches of Jeremiah as the speech of a figure who resembled a creative artist, a visionary genius, a religious reformer, a liberal theologian, or an enlightened biblical scholar. At the same time, he was predisposed to read speeches that call for adherence to a written law as the work of figures like a tradition-bound literary critics, reactionaries, dogmatic and legalistic religious figures (whether Jews,

---

[89] The one exception is the saying of the palace women that Jeremiah tells Zedekiah he heard in a vision (Jer. 38:22b).

[90] It has been pointed out before that it is not only the prose speeches but also the poetic speeches that urge adherence to the ancient law (Jer. 6:19) and consider it to have been given in the time of Moses (Jer. 2:6-8).

[91] Duhm, *Jeremia*, vii (emphasis added).

Catholics, or conservative Protestants), and those who understand the scriptures to be the Word of God. When the two sets of speeches are read as expressing the perspectives of these two opposed groups, they can hardly be thought of as the speeches of one author.

The dichotomy between these two groups in Duhm's thinking characteristic of a view of human history that was shared by many of his contemporaries—including to different degrees the scholars who propounded the Documentary Hypothesis. At the core of this view is the belief in a dialectic antagonism between two groups: the progressives who move humanity forward and the reactionaries who hold them back. This has been the basic struggle in all ages—particularly in humanity's religious, or spiritual, development—and perceiving it provides the framework for understanding what is good and bad in history and religion throughout the ages including the present age. It is the struggle between "leading spirits" of every age and the "laity." The latter are "Bible believers," who have turned the work of the leading spirits and prophets of the past into "laboriously constructed systems," which they must guard against the new prophets of their day. They are supported by the work of "classicists," "systematists," and "theologians." But the "historian[s] of religion" expose their scriptures as the work of uninspired scribes and show them to be aligned with the enemies of the prophets they claim to follow.[92]

It would provide a sufficient explanation of how Duhm and the proponents of the Documentary Hypothesis came to similar conclusions to demonstrate that they began with similar assumptions about religion, history, prophets, scribes, written laws, inspiration, good literature, and so on and that they employed similar methods (judging historical authenticity and religious worth by literary style, etc.). However, this is not the most significant factor in what actually happened. That is that Duhm himself already convinced of the truth of the Grafian reconstruction of the history of Israel's religion—and, as has been observed, one of it first and foremost proponents— long before his work on Jeremiah. His work on the prophetic books throughout his career can be understood as an attempt to bring them into alignment with the historical model he accepted as true. The book of Jeremiah presents a formidable problem for this attempt. In Duhm's own words, he experienced reading the book as the work of the prophet as an oppressive nightmare. As has been seen, at the core of the Grafian reconstruction was the idea that the prophetic literature and the prophets behind it represented the high point in Israel's literature from which it declined in to the lesser literature of the legal material and the high point in Israel's religion from which it declined into the and legalistic scribal religion of Judaism. This theory runs aground in the book of Jeremiah in which the largest part of the speech of one the greatest prophets does not conform to the Grafian expectations for inspired literature. Moreover the prophet's message in many of these speeches, that failure to obey the Law will lead to the consequences threatened by the Law, is at odds with the Grafian understanding of the relationship between prophets and the Law. It is particularly problematic that alignment of this message as well as of language and style in which it presented appear to suggest Jeremiah's sympathy for and perhaps active participation

---

[92] Duhm, *Jeremia*, 189–90.

in the covenant renewal program of Josiah based on the Book of the Law discovered in the Temple. This program which urged obedience to a written law is the turning point in the Grafian history, the birth of scribal religion which brought an end to prophetic religion, the birth of Judaism that brought an end to the religion of Israel. It is a scandal that the prophet Jeremiah does not oppose the program of outward conformity to a written law that is the antithesis of the prophetic religion of inner sensitivity of spirit.

Duhm's commentary provides a solution to these problems. He solves the literary problem by denying the authenticity and veracity of whatever does not fit the model. This maneuver accomplishes two things for the Grafian reconstruction: it delivers a prophet and a prophetic literature that conforms to their literary and theological expectations, and it simultaneously makes available a large body of material (over half the book) that can be used as evidence for filling in the picture of a group that is crucial to their historical scheme but can only be known through literature attributed to them: the exilic, deuteronomistic scribes. Duhm solves the historical problem by reemploying the material he identifies as authentic to create an alternative biography of the prophet and alternative history of his time that are characterized by opposition between the prophet and scribal advocates for the Book of the Law. Duhm's achievement of his aims, freeing himself from the nightmare, is the primary reason Duhm's conclusions fits so well with the conclusions of Grafian scholars. Duhm was Grafian scholar. This explanation of how Duhm's work and the work of the other Grafians reached common conclusions does not mean that their conclusions cannot be true, but it does mean that the fact that they reached common conclusions cannot strengthen the credibility of their conclusions and methods as much as it would have if they had reached their conclusions independently as in the hypothetical scenario.

Conclusion to Part One

At this point, the reader of the book of Jeremiah is better equipped to evaluate whether the compositional model and biography of the prophet offered by scholars for interpreting the book are likely to be necessary or helpful. The investigation of the origins of the two interpretive aids in the Duhm's commentary raised the question of whether their primary use was to bring the book into conformity with Duhm's personal aesthetic and theological preferences. However, there were three features of his work that seemed to support his claim that his compositional and biographical models brought the book into conformity with the actual historical reality behind the book. The first feature that lent credibility to his work was that it was based on objective feature of the text: the division between poetry and prose. The second feature was that investigating the prophet's life using only the poetic speeches as evidence produced a compelling biography. The third feature is that the opposing views Duhm found in the two main stages of the book's composition (and in the conflict he described between Jeremiah and his historical opponents) closely parallel the views of two stages in the presentation of the history of Israel's religion agreed upon by many of the most prominent biblical scholars of the modern period. The last three chapters have considered the support provided for Duhm's model for each of features in turn.

It has been shown that Duhm's views of prophetic poetry, of prophets, and of their place in the history of Israel's literature and religion are much more than his own personal preferences but were widely shared by many of the most influential biblical scholars of the nineteenth and twentieth centuries. However, the objectivity of these views was brought into question by the demonstration of how the work of these scholars was driven and shaped various currents of contemporary thought. The fact that many of these views and the currents of thought have as a source a particular explanation of the poetry in the prophetic books undermined the argument that Duhm's models were given a greater claim to objectivity by the fact that they were based on the objective difference between poetic and prose speeches in the book. They are actually based on a particular understanding of the differences between the poetry and prose, the same understanding that provides the foundation for the theories of the true nature of character of prophets and their relationship to priests and scribes that made Duhm's biographical and compositional reconstructions so compelling to himself and his contemporaries.

These considerations raised the question of whether the interpretive aids introduced by Duhm are grounded in historical truth. If his accounts are not true, then the reader of Jeremiah would not only be justified in leaving them aside as unnecessary and unhelpful; she should be advised to avoid them as misleading guides likely to produce a false or distorted readings of the book. The scholars recommending these interpretive models could respond that although Duhm was a man of his time and his work was influenced by his environment, he could still be credited with discovering the basic truth about the historical prophet and the composition of the book, and that although this the presentation of the standard model in Duhm's work had its excesses and inaccuracies, subsequent scholarship has dealt with these rough spots, confirmed Duhm's basic perceptions, and put them on stronger foundations. The next two chapters examine the more widely accepted forms of Duhm's biographical and compositional models in the works of John Skinner and Sigmund Mowinckel. The reader of Jeremiah is thus advised to reserve final judgment on whether to rely on the elements of the standard model until she has considered them in their new, improved forms.

Part Two

The Fruits of Duhm: The Standard Form of Duhm's Model in the Twentieth Century

5

Skinner's Biography of the Prophet

Introduction to Part Two: Skinner and Mowinckel and the Standard Approach to Jeremiah

The first part of this book examined Bernard Duhm's novel approach to the book of Jeremiah and its roots in the eighteenth- and nineteenth-century thought. The reason for this examination was to help readers of Jeremiah evaluate elements of Duhm's theory which scholars since the time of his commentary have offered as necessary introductory background: in particular, a model of the book's composition that distinguishes between authentic and inauthentic material primarily on the basis of literary form and a reconstruction of the biography of the prophet based solely on the material deemed authentic. It was argued that Duhm's compositional and biographical theories, which he presented as the objective results of a historical investigation, had more the character of creative transformations of the book designed to bring the prophet and his literary work into conformity with certain contemporary understandings of the nature of prophecy. These transformations, in turn, were required to facilitate their use as exemplars for contemporary models of artistic creation, historical progress, and religious meaning. If this account of Duhm's work is correct, it could give readers of Jeremiah reason to doubt whether these elements Duhm's approach were necessary or even helpful for reading the book and even whether they were likely to be true.

At this point, a reader who might admit that viewing Duhm's theory in light of its roots raises questions about its validity could still object that Jeremiah scholarship today is much less influenced by Duhm's theory than scholarship in the twentieth century and that even when Duhm's compositional model and reconstructed biography provided the foundation for the dominant paradigm for understanding the book, they had been modified in ways that might give them a better claim to truth. It is part of aim the third and final part of this book to address the first objection and show how Duhm's compositional model continues to have a significant (inhibitive) effect on present Jeremiah scholarship. This second part of book is intended to address the second objection: that it was only in modified form that Duhm's theory dominated Jeremiah scholarship in much of the twentieth century. This will be accomplished by evaluating two influential works that extended and modified Duhm's work on Jeremiah and which have a better claim to represent the paradigm that dominated

Jeremiah scholarship in the last century. John Skinner's *Prophecy and Religion: Studies in the Life of Jeremiah* (1922) gave the biography of the prophet made possible by Duhm's method what is probably its fullest and perhaps most engaging form. Sigmund Mowinckel's *Zur Komposition des Buches Jeremia* (1914) gave the compositional model pioneered by Duhm its most recognizable and influential form. The present chapter will examine Skinner's biography of the prophet to see if it offers readers an account of the prophet that is more helpful for reading the book, less open to the suspicion of being ideologically driven, and more likely to be historically accurate. In a similar manner, the following chapter will examine Mowinckel's compositional model to see if it is more likely to be helpful, objective, and accurate than the compositional model of Duhm.

Skinner's Achievement of Duhm's Biographical Aim

The first feature of John Skinner's biography of Jeremiah in *Prophecy and Religion* that strikes the reader acquainted with Duhm's commentary is that it is a much fuller and more developed account than Duhm's biography. Although Duhm saw as a chief end of his work the recovery of the true historical biography of the prophet, in his 1901 commentary, the presentation of the biography was limited to a few pages in the introduction and the scattered commentary on specific passages that Duhm believed gave evidence of Jeremiah's life. John Skinner's 1922 monograph may be said to bring Duhm's biographical aim to full fruition as a book-length retelling of the prophet's life. Skinner's biography begins with Jeremiah's birth in Anathoth and ends—over three hundred pages later—with Jeremiah's death-bed charge to his friend Baruch.[1] Although Skinner's biography certainly goes into considerably more depth than Duhm's, it is clearly a development not only of Duhm's biography but also of the biographical approach he pioneered.

The primary element of continuity is that, like Duhm, Skinner reconstructs most of his biography on the basis of the historical contexts he believes he can determine for isolated pieces of the poetry (primarily in chs 1–25) that, like Duhm, he considers to be authentic records of the prophet's speech. It is a remarkable aspect of Skinner's work that only the last third of his book relies heavily on the prose narratives concerning Jeremiah that are the most obvious biographical material in the book.[2] As in Duhm's biography of Jeremiah, Skinner's primary interest is the period before the events narrated in these accounts, the period from his call (*c.* 626) to his first recorded public appearance (*c.* 604). This period, to which none of the book's accounts of the prophets life are explicitly linked, Skinner believes to be the determinative years of the prophet's life, and he believes he can reconstruct a full account. Although he follows Duhm in this, it is a remarkable feat that Skinner is able to write a detailed account of this

---

[1] John Skinner, *Prophecy and Religion: Studies in the Life of Jeremiah* (Cambridge: Cambridge University Press, 1922), 18, 346–9.

[2] Like Duhm, Skinner believes the prose narratives are the work of Baruch (which Skinner describes as the scribe's "memorabilia"). *Prophecy and Religion*, 231.

period that stretches to almost two hundred pages based almost solely on the poetry of the book. What makes his feat even more remarkable is that although the text of Jeremiah regularly offers clear designations of the setting for the prose of the book, it does not designate the historical setting for any of this poetry,[3] and there is no explicit indication that any of it was written in the period Skinner uses it to reconstruct.

Skinner's Work Founded on Duhm's Theories

This amazing project of breaking the first twenty-five chapters into very small units, discarding those thought to be inauthentic, and then constructing a full, coherent biography of the prophet by piecing together the units would have been unthinkable without the previous work of Duhm. The foundational contribution of Duhm that makes Skinner's project possible is that idea that the poetic units are individual effusions of the prophet on various occasions. Following Duhm (and biblical scholars stretching back to Lowth), Skinner understands Jeremiah's poetry as "a lyrical outpouring of private emotion"[4] in which his "state of mind [is] revealed."[5] This view of Jeremiah's poetry has been shown to be the inheritance of Romantic literary theory, which is grounded in a particular understanding of the poetry of the prophetic literature in the Hebrew Bible. The emphasis on spontaneity is the crucial element for using the poetry as biographical evidence because if to the degree that it is recognized that the poetry shows signs of intentional artistry calculated to produce a rhetorical effect or conjure up a dramatic situation, its value as psychological and biographical evidence is compromised.

At one point, Skinner raises a doubt about the Romantic theory of poetry on which his biographical reconstruction depends. Considering the theory that Jeremiah's poetry arises from visionary ecstasy (a poetic theory closely aligned to the Romantic conception of inspiration) Skinner distinguishes between the "the voluntary working of the imagination, which is the essence of poetry, and the automatic working of it."[6] The idea that poetry is essentially a voluntary production is at odds with the idea his approach depends on, the view of prophetic poetry as an automatic product of a vision, a disturbing event, or a strong emotion. However, before he concludes the sentence that acknowledges a truth about poetry that threatens to undermine his whole project, he dismisses the idea of Jeremiah's poetry as anything but automatic: "The difference between the voluntary ... and the automatic ... is perhaps only a difference of degree. ... In literature, it must always be a very delicate task if not impossible to discriminate between them."[7] Skinner will not attempt to judge whether any of Jeremiah's poems might be something other than automatic products; if they were, it would undermine their reliability as biographical evidence.

---

[3] The only explicit indications of historical setting in Jeremiah 1–25 are attached to passages in prose: two in Josiah's reign (1:2, 3:6) and two in Zedekiah's reign (after the writing of the scroll in Jehoiakim's reign; 21:1, 24:1).

[4] Skinner, *Prophecy and Religion*, 55.

[5] Skinner, *Prophecy and Religion*, 127.

[6] Skinner, *Prophecy and Religion*, 49.

[7] Skinner, *Prophecy and Religion*, 49.

Along with this fundamental belief about the nature of poetry, Skinner also builds on a number of specific historical theories found in Duhm that allow him to treat the poetry (and some of the prose) in chs 1–25 as a collection of evidence for reconstructing the early ministry of the prophet. The first is the belief that material found in the first part of the book must date from the first part of the prophet's life.[8] This unfounded assumption sits awkwardly with Skinner's and Duhm's more fundamental belief that the book is a jumble of historical evidence that depends on modern interpreters to put it into correct chronological order.

A second historical theory of Duhm's necessary for Skinner's reconstruction is the idea that the descriptions, or prophecies, of invasions of Judah by a foe from the north (mostly in chs 4–10) were inspired by a Scythian invasion of Palestine (c. 626, only mentioned in Herodotus, c. 430).[9] Without this theory, the depictions—which include portrayals of Jerusalem under siege (6:1-8) and then destroyed and of her inhabitants exiled (9:19, 10:20)—would naturally be read as referring to the Babylonian invasions. Since the Babylonian invasions were limited to the reigns of Jehoiakim and Zedekiah, acknowledging that they referred to Babylon would invalidate Duhm's and Skinner's use of these passages to recreate Jeremiah's early ministry, which was primarily in the reign of Josiah.[10]

A third historical—or perhaps compositional—theory of Duhm's that makes Skinner's reconstruction possible is the idea that the poetry (and some of the prose) or Jeremiah 1–25 makes up the basic contents of the scroll that Jeremiah dictated to Baruch in the fourth year of Jehoiakim (the so-called *Urrolle* of 604, Jer. 36:1-4, cf. 36:32).[11] His argument is that this scroll is the same scroll mentioned in 25:13, and that 25:1-13, which begins with a reference to the twenty-three year ministry of Jeremiah, from his call to fourth year of Jehoiakim (25:1-3), the period Skinner reconstructs, is the concluding summary of the scroll.[12] The identification of the scrolls in 25:13 and 36:2 seems probable particularly since the same year is given for both accounts. However, the identification of the contents of the scroll with the contents of chs 1–25, particularly with the poetry of these chapters, is more problematic. One weakness of this theory is that 25:13 refers to the scroll as "this scroll, which Jeremiah prophesied against all the nations" and 36:2 describes the contents of the scroll as "all the words I have spoken to you against Israel and Judah and all the nations," but Jeremiah 1–25 contains very little that concerns the judgment of the nations.[13] Jeremiah's prophecies

---

[8] Skinner, *Prophecy and Religion*, 54.
[9] Skinner notes that it was Eichhorn who introduced this theory. Skinner, *Prophecy and Religion*, 39.
[10] The invasions from the north could not have been during the reign of Josiah if it is assumed (as Duhm and Skinner do) that prophecies cannot refer to future events which are not already at least on the horizon. Skinner gets around the natural reading of these texts as referring to Babylon with his theory that although they were originally composed in response to the Scythian threat, they were later reapplied to Babylon. Skinner, *Prophecy and Religion*, 38–40, 236–7.
[11] "Everything goes to show that [the contents of the roll are] all comprised within the first 25 chapters of the present book." Skinner, *Prophecy and Religion*, 239, n. 2. Duhm also believed that the basic contents of the scroll, he calls it the *Buchrolle*, were to be found in chs 1–25. Duhm, *Das Buch Jeremia*, KHC 11 (Tübingen: J. C. B. Mohr, 1901), xxi.
[12] Skinner, *Prophecy and Religion*, 240.
[13] Of the few passages in these chapters that refer to the future of the nations (3:17; 4:2, 14; 9:26; 10:25; 12:17; 16:19; 18:7-9) only 4:2, 14, 10:25, and 16:19 are in poetic form.

against the nations (MT 46:1–51:64) follow directly after 25:13 in the LXX. Skinner deals with this weakness in his theory in a manner reminiscent of Duhm's methods. He solves the problem by "omitting the superfluous clauses" in 25:1-13, so that, in his emended text, 25:13 simply refers to "this scroll" even though both the MT and the LXX have "this scroll which Jeremiah prophesied against all the nations."[14]

Skinner's Work Follows Duhm's Method

Duhm's understanding of the nature of the poetic material and his historical theories provide Skinner with the raw material for his biography of the prophet—one that resembles Duhm's creation but is richer and more elaborate. Like Duhm, Skinner uses the isolated and then selected bits of Jeremiah 1–25 to weave together a biographical tapestry whose pattern is determined by an elaborate combination of certain fixed historical dates with a narrative of the development of Jeremiah's literary skill, theological insight, and personal piety. The dates may be said to provide the warp of the biographical tapestry, and the scheme of personal development, the woof. The primary dates are: the invasion of the Scythians (626); the discovery of the Book of the Law (621); the battle of Megiddo, in which Josiah was killed (608); and the battle of Carchemish, in which the Babylonians established supremacy in Palestine (605). The invasion of the Scythians and the battle of Carchemish correspond with, respectively, Jeremiah's call (*c.* 626) and his first dated pronouncements twenty-three years later (604, the fourth year of Jehoiakim), and thus mark the beginning and end of the period of his early ministry (Jer. 25:3).

The pivotal date in Skinner's scheme is the discovery of the Book of the Law in discovery of the Book of the Law in the eighteenth year of Josiah (621). On the basis of a series of historical hypotheses, Skinner is able to place almost every fragment of poetry he isolates from chs 1–25 into either the pre- or post-reform period.[15] If a poetic unit threatens invasion, it must come before the reform since the Scythian invasion was five years earlier. If a unit denounces the popular religion of idolatry, it must come before or during the reform since the reform weakened the popular religious practices. If, on the other hand, it denounces social immorality or religious indifference, it must be from after the reform. This is on the supposition that Jeremiah's participation in the reform led to persecution in his home town (a plausible reading of Jeremiah 11) and caused him to relocate to Jerusalem (a speculative theory that is at least possible). When he came to the city, he was shocked by the decay of society and of the national religion centered on the temple. If a poetic unit calls for repentance, it comes from before or during the reform, but if it expresses a sense of irrevocable doom, it must come from after Jeremiah had grown disillusioned with the reform.

---

[14] Skinner, *Prophecy and Religion*, 240–1.
[15] This use of the "Deuteronomistic" reform of Josiah as the pivotal date echoes the foundational procedure of the Grafian position. Graf started with de Wette's dating of Deuteronomy to the time of Josiah and used it as a pivot to argue that the combination of J and E must be dated earlier than Josiah's time because D (including Deuteronomy) presupposes it, and P must be dated later because it presupposes D.

Into this basic redistribution of poetic units based on their supposed relation to key historical dates, Skinner weaves in a complementary way of ordering the units based on their place in a narrative of Jeremiah's gradual growth in religious insight. The basic pattern of Skinner's developmental scheme portrays the prophet as growing increasingly disillusioned with all forms of external and national religion as he faces increasing opposition and alienation. Rather than driving him to despair, these drive Jeremiah to cry out to God in personal prayer and in so doing enable him to reach a level of individual and interior religion unparalleled in the time before Christ.[16] The prophet's first and central disappointment is with the reform of Josiah.[17] He sees that outward conformity to a legal code does not necessarily produce interior change. Even worse, he sees that the idea in Deuteronomy that God has made a covenant with Israel produces complacency and false security. Later, especially after the death of Josiah, Jeremiah watches in dismay as the people trade their superstitious reliance on the law and covenant for a superstitious reliance on the Temple and the sacrificial system.[18] He comes to realize that the sacrificial system not only gave false security to Israel but that a physical temple and animal sacrifices are no part of true religion. Having found himself in opposition to both priest and scribe, he realizes that the prophets cannot be trusted either since they prop up the false religions of the priests and scribes with their prophecies of good fortune. Finally, cut off from all forms of exterior religion, Jeremiah pours out his heart to God in his lyrical confessions. This is the high point of both his poetic achievement and his growth in religious insight and personal piety; it is also the high point of Israelite religion.[19] Contrary to previous scholars, Skinner believed that the confessions did not date from the time of Jeremiah's opposition to kings described in the prose narratives. In his account, they are not the result of the outward persecution and opposition that he faced from the king's court, but rather the climax of his earlier spiritual crisis that led to his discovery of interior religion, which in turn allowed him to stand against the external powers of his day without wavering. The confessions are Jeremiah's Gethsemane before he goes to his trial and suffering before the rulers of Jerusalem.[20]

Skinner Makes Jeremiah Compelling to His Contemporaries

With this biography of Jeremiah, Skinner brings to fruition the efforts of Duhm and other historical-critical scholars looking for the true prophet behind the book. His portrait of Jeremiah has features that made Duhm's Jeremiah compelling to himself and his contemporaries: the reconstructed prophet is both believable and admirable. Skinner provides an account of the prophet that his contemporaries accept as "true"

---

[16] Skinner, *Prophecy and Religion*, 201–3.
[17] Skinner, *Prophecy and Religion*, 150–3. Breaking from Duhm, Skinner believes that Jeremiah actually participated in the reforms of Josiah. Skinner, *Prophecy and Religion*, 106–7. Duhm, *Jeremia*, xi.
[18] Skinner, *Prophecy and Religion*, 168–70.
[19] Skinner, *Prophecy and Religion*, 222–8.
[20] Skinner, *Prophecy and Religion*, 209–10.

in two senses: it conforms to their understandings of history and the real world, and makes him a proponent of what they consider authentic religion. How Skinner's biography achieved these two aims can be considered in turn beginning with how his account was able to make not only the prophet Jeremiah but the whole phenomenon of Israelite prophecy credible as history.

Conformity to Expectations about History

An obvious way that Skinner's account makes Jeremiah believable to his contemporaries is his explanations of the prophetic speeches about the future. Skinner explains each passage that the book presents as Yahweh's declarations of future judgment as the result of Jeremiah's "premonition of judgment" or "presentiment of coming doom" based on his keen observations of current events.[21] These explanations have two features to commend them to Skinner's readers, the idea that Jeremiah's speeches come from his own intuitions provides an alternative to the idea that they are actual messages from God, and the idea that they represent his informed presentiments provides an alternative to the idea that Jeremiah was given knowledge of the future before it happened. Duhm provides similar explanations, but Skinner asserts that these explanations are always necessary due to the nature of prophecy. This is a "principle" of prophecy that he takes from his teacher, A. B. Davidson: "Prophecies are usually suggested by some great movement among the nations, in which Yahweh's presence is already felt."[22] This principle explains why the poems about the foe from the north cannot have been written about the Babylonians (the northern foe repeatedly named in the book) but must have originally been written about the Scythians (who are never named in the book). If these poems are to be attributed to the early part of Jeremiah's ministry, they could not possibly refer to the threat of Babylonian invasion since the Babylonians are not even a dominant power yet. To suggest otherwise would be to go against Davidson's principle; it would be a suggestion "contrary to the analogy of prophecy."[23] In his biographical reconstruction, Skinner has isolated every prophecy from its literary context and reassigned it to historical context that can explain it consistent to the "analogy of prophecy."

It is not only Jeremiah's life and words that Skinner is attempting to make consistent with contemporary understandings of historical truth. Like Duhm, Skinner wants to present a historically believable account of Hebrew prophecy and Hebrew religion. Skinner praises Duhm for his "historical view of religion," which, he says, "has had no more brilliant exponent than Duhm."[24] The central feature of this historical view is that growth in religious insight or practical piety can come about only through a long and gradual rise from lower forms of religion to higher forms. "The historical evolution of religion," says Skinner, has in it a ladder of innumerable steps.[25] New

---

[21] Skinner, *Prophecy and Religion*, 53.
[22] Skinner, *Prophecy and Religion*, 38. Quoted from A. B. Davidson, *Nahum, Habakkuk and Zephaniah* (in *Cambridge Bible for Schools*), 14.
[23] Skinner, *Prophecy and Religion*, 42.
[24] Skinner, *Prophecy and Religion*, 331.
[25] Skinner, *Prophecy and Religion*, 228.

achievements in religion must arise naturally from the previous stages. This insistence on historical continuity explains why Skinner charges Duhm with departing from the "historical view of religion" when Duhm asks why God did not give Jeremiah a full view of the new heart as understood by Christians.[26] The historical view demands that God only work with what is available in the present circumstances and not skip ahead to what will be possible in a later age. Skinner's view of religious history conforms to a defining characteristic of the historiography of the late nineteenth and early twentieth century: that for something complex and structured to be accepted as believable it had to be explained as the result of a long gradual rise from simple natural things.

In *Prophecy and Religion*, the "historical view of religion" is expressed in Skinner's insistence that classical prophecy is a natural development from the primitive ecstatic and mantic prophecy. Approaches that sharply distinguish between the classical and the primitive Hebrew prophets or the prophets among Israel's neighbors, Skinner judges to be "unhistorical" because a "sudden advance in religious enlightenment involves an absolute breach of continuity."[27] Instead, Skinner believes the development of classical prophecy from early *nabi'ism* should be thought of as "closely analogous to the development of self-conscious reason in man from the rudimentary intelligence of the lower animals."[28]

Skinner's adherence to the "historical view of religion" provides the framework not only for his presentation of the evolution of Hebrew prophecy but also for his presentation of the evolutionary growth of Jeremiah's as a poet and a prophet. He explains every development in Jeremiah's growth in piety and religious insight in terms of a response of the present state of Jeremiah's mind to a new historical environment. The combination of this evolutionary account of Jeremiah's development and the psychological account of his speeches (they result from an experience akin to poetic inspiration or religious ecstasy) this way allowed Skinner to offer his readers a biblical prophet they could accept as historically believable.

Conformity to Protestant Liberalism

Skinner's efforts to provide historically believable accounts of prophecy and religion are not only in conformity with the historiography of the late nineteenth and early twentieth centuries, but also with the liberal Protestant theology that had its greatest influence around the same time. Theologians like Albrecht Ritschl and Adolf von Harnack offered accounts of Christian theology characterized by "maximum acknowledgement of the claims of modern thought" particularly scientific and historical thought.[29] They sought to present the essence of Christianity in a way that would make it less open to the criticisms that modern thinkers had made of traditional Christianity. This included presenting Israel's religion as Skinner does as a gradual evolution from lower forms to higher with minimum reference to the implausible supernatural elements.

---

[26] Skinner, *Prophecy and Religion*, 331.
[27] Skinner, *Prophecy and Religion*, 4, n. 1.
[28] Skinner, *Prophecy and Religion*, 4, n. 1.
[29] Claude Welch, *Protestant Thought in the Nineteenth Century, Volume 1, 1799–1870* (New Haven, CT: Yale University Press, 1972), 142.

Conformity to classic Protestant Liberalism by historical criticism of the Bible is certainly not confined to Skinner's historical-critical approach to Jeremiah. The liberal theological beliefs and aims that shape Skinner's and Duhm's work on Jeremiah were widely shared by biblical scholars of their time, especially those associated with (German) "higher," or "historical," criticism. The influence ran both ways. Not only was biblical criticism shaped by the beliefs of Liberalism; these theological beliefs were often founded on or formed in response to the conclusions of biblical criticism. Liberal theologians were deeply influenced by the kind of historical criticism of the Bible and often took the conclusions of their studies as foundational—particularly the Grafian model of Israel's religious history. Like Duhm, Skinner was a strong advocate for the Grafian model (or the Documentary Hypothesis in which it is embedded). He studied at Edinburgh under A. B. Davidson, whose students, including Robertson Smith, were in the vanguard of scholars who brought the revolution in Old Testament studies from Germany to England.[30] The work of Smith and Skinner provided many English speakers with their primary introductions to the work of Wellhausen and Duhm. These historical critics of the Bible and liberal theologians accepted that traditional evaluations of the Bible's truth and authority had been undermined by historical scholarship, and they sought to reestablish the value of the Bible on the more reliable scientific and historical basis offered by historical critics.

It has been argued in the preceding chapters on the roots of Duhm's approach that the historical-critical method and Grafian model that formed the context of his work were intended to provide an account of the history of Israel's religion that would not only be accepted as a contribution to factual history but also be believed as a contribution to true religion. In the wake of the ascendency of scientific naturalism and enlightenment rationalism, many people were looking for an account of the world and of human history that would allow for transcendence, significance, and purpose. If this desire was a shaping influence in nineteenth-century biblical criticism, it was an even more obvious influence in nineteenth-century theological liberalism. The prominent theologians sought an alternative to traditional Christianity that they not only perceived to be unscientific and credulous in its belief in the supernatural but also childish and naive in its view of God, exclusive and culturally bound in its ecclesiology, fear- and guilt-driven in its soteriology, superstitious in its rituals, repressive and manipulative in its ethics. They not only found these undesirable elements in dogmatic Christianity but in the Bible itself. At the same time they recognized much that was valuable in Christianity and sought to preserve what best in the Bible—as well as be able to claim that their alternative religious view was grounded in the Bible. The understood their new religious system not as an innovation but as a recovery of true religion which had been obscured by tradition both in the history of Christianity and in the composition of the Bible.

Liberal theologians worked together biblical critics in the project of recovering the true history behind the Bible that would allow them to distinguish between the true religion hidden in the text and the detritus of tradition which obscured the truth. This

---

[30] George Adam Smith, "The Late Professor A. B. Davidson, DD. LL.D.," in *The Biblical World*, ed. William R. Harper, New Series, vol. 20 (Chicago, IL: University of Chicago Press, 1902), 167.

model derives in part from the Romantic idea of the poetic or innovative geniuses whose works were only poorly understood by their followers or contemporaries and must be recovered by modern scholars. For the liberal theologians, the perfect religion of Jesus had already appeared in Israel in certain prophets and psalmists, poetic geniuses whose achievements were not appreciated by the rest of their nation. Harnack describes the situation before Christ: "The spring of holiness had long been opened; but it was choked with sand and dirt … the rubbish which priests and theologians had heaped up so as to smother the true element of religion."[31] The rubbish was the religious nationalism, crude supernaturalism, dead legalism, and superficial ritualism that led to Judaism and the Catholic Church. According to both Harnack and Wellhausen, the true religion that Jesus recovered was the combination of "ethical ideas and the religious individualism of the prophets."[32] In both biblical criticism and theological liberalism, true religion was associated with prophets and false religion was associated with scribes.

Examination of Duhm's work on Jeremiah has shown the attempt to free prophetic religion from scribal religion as central to his agenda, and the same could be said of Skinner's work. Skinner is even more forthright about his agenda to recover true religion by which he believes was first achieved by the Hebrew prophets. This is the significance of the title of his book: *Prophecy and Religion: Studies in the Life of Jeremiah*. The book is intended to demonstrate how, in the life of Jeremiah, the individual consciousness of Israelite prophecy and social morality of Israelite religion came together to form true personal religion.

> This close and permanent association between religion and prophecy is the distinctive feature of the Old Testament dispensation. … The ethical genius of religion direct[ed] the vision of the prophet to the eternal principles of the divine government, while the insight of the prophet drew forth from the national faith the essential truth about God which at last gave the world a perfect religion.[33]

The course of Jeremiah's life and the growth of his prophetic consciousness allowed him to transform the national religion by turning it "from the formalism of an external worship, and the legalism of a national covenant" and by drawing out the essential truth that "God [is found] in the heart of the individual."[34] Just as theological

---

[31] Adolf von Harnack, *What Is Christianity?*, trans. Thomas Bailey Saunders (New York: G. P. Putnam's, 1901), 52.

[32] Walter Homolka, *Jewish Identity in Modern Times: Leo Baeck and German Protestantism* (Providence, RI: Berghahn Books, 1995), 23. Some Jewish scholars such as Leo Baeck embraced the idea of Protestant Liberalism that Israel's greatest contribution to religion was the ethical monotheism taught by Jeremiah and the other prophets. Baeck built on Harnack's *Essence of Christianity* (1902) with his own *Essence of Judaism* (1905). However, other Jewish thinkers saw in this idea of liberal Protestantism latent anti-Semitism or even an existential threat to Judaism or the Jewish people. Eugene Borowitz identifies the threat in a question: If Israel, as Baeck asserts, "exists for the sake of its idea, ethical monotheism" and if this idea "can be known by any person of religious consciousness, why does one need Judaism? … On what basis can one argue that the idea cannot survive without the Jewish people?" Eugene B. Borowitz, *Choices in Modern Judaism*, 2nd ed. (Springfield, NJ: Behrman House, 1996), 70–1.

[33] Skinner, *Prophecy and Religion*, 5–6.

[34] Skinner, *Prophecy and Religion*, 227.

liberals believed that they could liberate ethical, interior, individual religion from its entanglement with conventional Christian doctrine and practice, Skinner believed that Jeremiah brought to culmination the prophetic mission "to liberate the eternal truths of religion from their temporary national embodiment and disclose their true foundation in the immutable character of God and the essential nature of man."[35] Jeremiah was able to set these eternal truths free from Israel just as the nation was in its death throes.[36] Not only was Judah about to be taken into exile, but more significantly, Josiah's promulgation of the Deuteronomic law was the beginning of the end for Israelite religion.[37] Deuteronomy unleashed the scribal and priestly religion of reliance on the covenant, external obedience to the law, and sumptuous ritual and ceremony.[38] This was the rubbish that Harnack believed had smothered the true element in Israel's religion, and that Duhm and Skinner believed had covered the authentic prophetic writings of Jeremiah.

Conformity to Historicism

Like nineteenth-century higher criticism, nineteenth-century theological liberalism can be seen to be closely associated with Romanticism. Theological liberalism and Romanticism are both grounded in a particular understanding of prophecy that they used to challenge what they perceived as dead traditionalism, and both came to be seen as answering a felt spiritual need created by scientific and rationalistic materialism. Another connection between theological liberalism and historical criticism is a view religious history shaped by nineteenth-century historicism. Central to the historicist approach is the ideas that each nation has its own unique contribution to make to the general education of humanity and that this contribution comes through great individuals whose lives give expression to the characteristic spirits of their nations. This idea has its roots in Herder's presentation of the achievement of the biblical prophets as Israel's greatest contribution to the history of religion. Herder's idea was developed by higher critics and liberal theologians into a presentation of Israel's religious history culminates in the lives of the prophets. This is the essence of the Grafian reconstruction, which provides the foundation for Skinner's work on Jeremiah.

Skinner's work is located in this historicist project of showing Israel's contribution to the human progress as can be seen in his presentation of his work as a study of the unparalleled "alliance of prophecy and religion in Israel" that became "one of the most influential factors in … the Education of the Human Race."[39] That Skinner's contribution to this project is a biography of a prophet is particularly significant because of the centrality of the biography of genius in historicist accounts of human progress. These individuals give expression to the spirit of their nation and contribute to the education of humanity. As an introduction to his biography, Skinner traces in Ewald and Wellhausen the growing appreciation of Jeremiah as the figure in whom prophecy

---

[35] Skinner, *Prophecy and Religion*, 14–15.
[36] Skinner, *Prophecy and Religion*, 351.
[37] Skinner, *Prophecy and Religion*, 96.
[38] Skinner, *Prophecy and Religion*, 106–7.
[39] Skinner, *Prophecy and Religion*, 1.

in Israel achieved not only its greatest insight into the "universal essence of religion"[40] but also its greatest expression, or embodiment. Skinner quotes with approval A. B. Davidson's estimation of the achievement of Jeremiah: "The book of Jeremiah does not so much teach religious truths as present a religious personality. Prophecy had already taught its truths, its last effort was to reveal itself in a life."[41]

Skinner's biography of Jeremiah serves to crown the accomplishments of nineteenth-century biblical criticism and theology by showing what they had isolated as the true element in Israelite religion coming to expression in the life of individual. It was shown in Chapter 3, how Duhm's biography of Jeremiah brought the prophet's life into conformity with the lives of Romantic poets and artists. Skinner also traces a development of the prophet as poet with a biography that has many parallels to lives of Romantic poets. An example would his references to "the wild and desolate scenery on which his native Anathoth looks down" and "the harvest which Jeremiah's quiet eye must have gleaned in youth, not merely from permanent features of the landscape but from the familiar pictures of rural life and the ordinary interests and occupations of men."[42] This could easily be a description of the effect on Wordsworth of growing up in the Lake District with its wild and desolate scenery and colorful rural inhabitants.

Conformity to Accounts of Crises of Faith

Although the Skinner's biography of Jeremiah, like Duhm's, has many similarities to nineteenth-century biographies of artists, geniuses, and reformers, a closer analogy would be with the accounts of crises of faith that were a widespread phenomenon of the nineteenth century in novels and biographies. The progress of the natural science and biblical criticism was experienced by many in the nineteenth century as devastating challenges to traditional Christian belief. The crises of faith these challenges brought about in pious young intellectuals are recorded in thousands of accounts in novels, biographies, and autobiographies.[43] The accounts have many standard elements: pious youth in the shelter of traditional faith; early religious enthusiasm (often evangelical or Tractarian); disillusionment; erosion of traditional beliefs through exposure to modern scientific, historical, and critical studies; painful break from family and church; discovery of deeper personal and moral religion; and steadfast endurance of opposition from church and traditional institutions.

In many of these accounts, the crisis of faith comes when the individual becomes acquainted with the works of liberal theology or biblical criticism. However, the life pattern can be observed in the lives of the theologians and historical critics themselves.

---

[40] Skinner, *Prophecy and Religion*, 15–16.
[41] Skinner, *Prophecy and Religion*, 16–17. Quoted from A. B. Davidson, "Jeremiah" in Hasting's *Dictionary of the Bible*, II, 576.
[42] Skinner, *Prophecy and Religion*, 22.
[43] "Beyond the canonical writers of the period [1840–1895], there are hundreds of writers publishing thousands of novels about the crisis of faith." Elizabeth Deeds Ermarth, *The English Novel in History: 1840–1895* (New York: Routledge, 1997), 41. Prime examples of the novel of crisis of faith, or the novel of doubt, are *The Nemesis of Faith* (J. A. Froude, 1849); *The Autobiography of Mark Rutherford* (William Hale White, 1881); *Robert Elsmere* (Mrs. Humphry Ward, 1888); and *The Way of All Flesh* (Samuel Butler, 1903).

Protestant theologians whose lives fit the basic pattern include Ritschl, Harnack, and especially Schleiermacher (whose life might be said to have created the pattern).[44] The elements of these accounts can also be seen in the lives of prominent biblical scholars whose embrace of the findings of historical criticism led to crises in their personal faith, alienation from family and church, and opposition from academic and ecclesiastical authorities. For the story of how biblical scholarship led to a personal crisis of faith, De Wette's life is probably best known. For the story of rejection and alienation, one thinks of the life of Bishop Colenso of South Africa.[45] For the story of steadfast devotion to one's personal scholarly vision, the life of Ewald has already been suggested, and the life of Robertson Smith also readily comes to mind.[46]

It can now be seen how the biography of Jeremiah that resulted from the historical-critical method has a strong resemblance to the lives of the nineteenth-century theologians and biblical scholars who broke with traditional Christianity. Skinner's Jeremiah is an individual, who in light of the crisis of his age, sought "a deeper foundation of his prophetic relationship with God than the things that were shaken and ready to pass away."[47] This came through a personal crisis of faith that offered Jeremiah the choice either to "despair of religion" or to "find in himself ... the germ and pledge of a new religious relationship."[48] What makes Skinner's story of Jeremiah's triumph over his crisis of faith strikingly similar to the stories of nineteenth-century liberal theologians and biblical critics is that the parts of Israel's religion that Jeremiah comes to realize are "shaken and ready to pass away" are practically identical to the parts of orthodox Christianity that liberal theologians and biblical critics came to doubt.

The two central crises faith in Skinner's biography are Jeremiah's loss of faith in the Deuteronomic reform and his loss of faith in the sacrificial system. In regard to the Deuteronomic reform, Jeremiah does not merely come to see that superficial conformity to God's commands is insufficient. He comes to see that the underlying problem is trust in a written word of God; he takes his stand against "the illusion of infallibility and finality attaching to the written word, as if it were superior to the living voice of prophecy or the dictates of the religious sense."[49] In regard to Israel's sacrificial system, Jeremiah does not merely come to see that sacrifice cannot substitute for true devotion and moral reform. He comes to see that sacrifice is "non-essential" for fellowship with God, and further, that it could never have been commanded by God in the first place:[50] "The whole system, and all laws prescribing or regulating it,

[44] Wilhelm Dilthey's monumental *Life of Schleiermacher* (1870) is significant not only for the pattern of life it presents but also for making biography central to appreciating the contribution of the theologian. He argued that Schleiermacher's significance could not be understood without reference to his life. Richard Crouter, *Friedrich Schleiermacher: Between Enlightenment and Romanticism* (New York: Cambridge University Press, 2005), 21.
[45] Thomas Kelly Cheyne, *Founders of Old Testament Criticism: Biographical, Descriptive, and Critical Studies* (London: Methuen, 1893), 196–204.
[46] See, e.g., James Bryce's biography of Robertson Smith, which recounts his "courage ... in confronting his antagonists in the ecclesiastical court," his triumph over "the party of repression." James Bryce, "Robertson Smith," in *Studies in Contemporary Biography* (New York: Macmillan, 1905), 316, 325.
[47] Skinner, *Prophecy and Religion*, 218.
[48] Skinner, *Prophecy and Religion*, 219.
[49] Skinner, *Prophecy and Religion*, 121.
[50] The error Jeremiah rebuked was "the notion that Yahwe had ever instituted sacrifice at all." Skinner, *Prophecy and Religion*, 182–3.

... lie outside the revelation on which the national religion of Israel was based."[51] Since Deuteronomy contains laws regulating sacrifice, Skinner concludes that Jeremiah must have rejected the book's claim "to be a divine law imposed on Israel" and tradition's ascription of "the origins of the most ancient ritual codes to the authority of Moses" and that he must have come to believe instead that "such laws ... were unauthorized additions to the covenant made with the fathers."[52]

In short, the great crisis of Jeremiah's life is his conversion to the Grafian view of the Mosaic Law. Building on his doubt that there could be an infallible written word of God, Jeremiah is able to satisfy "the dictates of the religious sense" when he is able to see through the popular illusion that God had ever given Israel any laws concerning priests, sacrifices, or a temple. He realizes that the Priestly legal materials were not part of the original revelation but were added by later editors and constituted "a perversion of the historic religion of Israel from its native ethical genius."[53] He thus uncovers not only the truth about the compositional history of the laws falsely attributed to Moses but also the true history of Israel's religion. Here Jeremiah built on the work of earlier historical critics: Amos, who discovered that "sacrifice was unknown in the wilderness," and Hosea, who held the view that "the desert sojourn was the ideal period in Israel's history."[54] These historical-critical insights allowed him to come close to the pure ethical religion of Ritschl and Harnack, built on the recognition that "a perfect religious relationship is possible without sacrifice at all."[55]

These observations about the biography of Jeremiah, which result from following a historical-critical approach to the book similar to Duhm's, explain Perdue's observation that Skinner's Jeremiah appears as "something of an Adolf von Harnack."[56] This characterization applies not only to Skinner's Jeremiah but also to Duhm's and those of others who follow his method. The anachronistic nature of this result raises questions about the objectivity of the method. The reader would have reason to be suspicious of a scholar who pretended not to know how his study of Jeremiah produced the image of a nineteenth-century liberal theologian: "I took whatsoever gold was found in Jeremiah, then I cast it into the fire, and this liberal theologian came out." In light of the foregoing discussion of the method, a more truthful account would admit that the result was in some measure due to the scholar's original perception of the book. In the terms of

---

[51] Skinner, *Prophecy and Religion*, 182–3.

[52] Skinner, *Prophecy and Religion*, 183.

[53] Skinner, *Prophecy and Religion*, 184.

[54] Skinner, *Prophecy and Religion*, 181.

[55] Skinner, *Prophecy and Religion*, 181. James Orr explains why, in Ritschl's theology, sacrifice for sin was unnecessary for reconciliation with God: "Ritschl rejects absolutely the ordinary satisfaction theory of the death of Christ ... [because in his system] There is no Principle in the character of God demanding the punishment of sin for its own sake; no wrath of God against sin ... from which ... the sinner needs deliverance. The sole obstacle to his reconciliation with God lies in his own guilt-consciousness, and in the distrust of God which this engenders. For the removal of this there is needed no such atonement for sins as the ordinary theory supposes, but only the full Revelation of the Fatherly love and forgiving grace of God." James Orr, *The Ritschlian Theology and the Evangelical Faith* (London: Hodder and Stoughton, 1897), 149–50.

[56] Leo G. Perdue, "The Book of Jeremiah in Old Testament Theology," in *Troubling Jeremiah*, ed. A. R. Pete Diamond, Kathleen M. O'Connor, and Louis Stulman, JSOT Sup 260 (Sheffield: Sheffield Academic Press, 1999), 321.

the apocryphal story of how Michelangelo came to carve an angel out of the marble from Carrara, one can imagine the scholar saying, "In the massive stone of the book of Jeremiah, I saw the figure of a liberal theologian waiting to be freed. Then my task was easy; I simply chipped away whatever didn't look like Harnack."

Evaluation of Skinner's Work

The Objectivity of Skinner's Work

In light of the outcome of his work, the question can be asked whether Skinner's work is any more likely to be objective than Duhm's. Both of them come up with an account of Jeremiah's life and belief system that is suspiciously similar to the lives and beliefs of certain modern theologians and biblical scholars (similar, in fact, to their own lives and beliefs). However, the way Skinner achieves this outcome differs somewhat from the way Duhm achieved his. Skinner is less reliant on Duhm's primary contrivance: dismissing as inauthentic whatever does not fit his model. Although Skinner accepts Duhm's theory that the book has been freely redacted by members of a Deuteronomistic school, he seldom follows Duhm's regular practice of dismissing passages as inauthentic because they have Deuteronomistic elements.[57] This difference from Duhm is in keeping with the most significant way Skinner's biography differs from Duhm's: unlike Duhm who denied that Jeremiah participated in the (Deuteronomistic) reforms of Josiah,[58] Skinner believed that Jeremiah initially participated in the reform but later grew skeptical of it when it failed to produce ethical change.[59]

Part of the appeal of Skinner's book to his contemporaries was the way he is able to incorporate more of the book's presentation of Jeremiah while maintaining Duhm's achievement of making it usable by liberal theologians and Grafian biblical scholars, who understood the rise of scribal and priestly religion to correspond to the demise of the true prophetic religion of Israel. This understanding is expressed in the dictum of Skinner's teacher Davidson, which he quotes with approval: "Pharisaism and Deuteronomy came into the world the same day."[60] Skinner's work attempts to reconcile this religious perspective which pits prophets against priests and scribes with the book's presentation of Jeremiah as participating in the reform, which was led by priests and scribes and which was based on the book that they looked to for authority. Part of his attempt rests on three ways in which his work departs from Duhm's. First, Skinner draws a stronger distinction between the Deuteronomic law itself and the scribal religion that was based on it. Even Davidson's dictum, which does not simply

---

[57] "There is no doubt that the collected prophecies of Jeremiah passed through the hands of the Deuteronomic school, and were freely edited by them. His discourses have been interpolated, amplified, in some instances rewritten. But the deliberate invention of an incident which had no point of contact in the authentic record of his life is a procedure to which no assured parallel is found in the book." Skinner, *Prophecy and Religion*, 102.

[58] Duhm, *Jeremia*, xi.

[59] Skinner, *Prophecy and Religion*, 106–7.

[60] Skinner, *Prophecy and Religion*, 96.

equate the perspective of Deuteronomy with Pharisaism, leaves open this possibility. Skinner notes that Deuteronomy is not solely concerned with external religion, but like Jeremiah calls for a circumcision of the heart.[61] In his account, it is not primarily Deuteronomy, but mainly the book's misguided advocates who preached a message that encouraged false trust in legal obedience, temple rituals, and the national covenant.[62] Second, Skinner presents a more nuanced picture of Jeremiah's religious development in which his early enthusiasm for the reform faded as he saw the superficiality of its results. In his biographical reconstruction, he assigns to an early stage of Jeremiah's career passages marked by Deuteronomism, and he assigns to a later period passages that suggest opposition to scribal or priestly religion.

The difference between Duhm's and Skinner's way of bringing the book into conformity with liberal Protestantism and the Grafian model of Israel's history is on clear display in their treatment of Jer. 31:31-34, the passage that proclaims the new covenant Yahweh will make with Israel in the future. Duhm argues that text is clearly not the work of a Jeremiah rather an "outburst from the scribes."[63] Its inauthenticity is clear not only from its clumsy prose form but also from its perspective. It envisions a new covenant, but not a new Torah, which shows that unlike Jeremiah its authors do not recognize that the problem is the Torah itself not failure of the people to observe the Torah. The hope of its scribal authors is "that every member of the Jewish people would know the law by heart and understand that all Jews are scribes."[64] By exposing the inauthenticity, Duhm is able to free Jeremiah from the taint of scribal Judaism.

In Skinner's discussion of the authenticity of the passage, he engages directly with Duhm's denial. He posits that Duhm's interpretation of the passage depends on reading it as the work of a postexilic legalist and then asserts that it could be given a different interpretation if it is read as the work of Jeremiah, "whose constant effort was (in the words of Dr. Davidson) to draw men's minds away from all that was external— sacrifices, Temple, ark and law-book—to that which was inward and real.'"[65] Read as the words of Jeremiah, the passage can be seen as an affirmation of "the inwardness or true religion—the spiritual illumination of the individual mind and conscience, and the doing of God's will from a spontaneous impulse of the renewed heart."[66] Skinner summarizes the two possible interpretations: "We may read into the words a view of religion so profoundly spiritual and personal that it is hardly conceivable that anyone else than Jeremiah could have written them. On the other hand they may be interpreted in a trivial and formal sense which would stamp them unmistakably as the composition of a late Jewish legalist."[67] It is on this basis, rather than on the question

---

[61] Skinner, *Prophecy and Religion*, 107.

[62] Skinner, *Prophecy and Religion*, 106–7.

[63] Duhm, *Jeremia*, 255.

[64] Duhm, *Jeremia*, 255.

[65] Skinner, *Prophecy and Religion*, 325.

[66] Skinner, *Prophecy and Religion*, 229–330. There is an interesting parallel between Skinner's concept of true religion and the Romantic concept of true poetry which is not marked by external conformity to poetic rules and forms but by its expression of the spontaneous impulse of an individual heart under the influence of inspiration.

[67] Skinner, *Prophecy and Religion*, 320.

of poetic or prose form, that Skinner judges the authenticity of the passage.[68] If it has a profound grasp of internal, individualistic religion must be judged to be authentic. If it is concerned with trivial and formal religion (i.e., obedience to a written law or reliance on a national covenant) it must be inauthentic. However, judging whether the religious view of the passage is true or merely trivial will depend on whether it was written by a profound prophet or a Jew. It can now be seen that Skinner and Duhm are asking the same question of the passage, and although Skinner comes to a different answer authenticity, they have the same ultimate result: Jeremiah's character as a profound prophet (one who understands the nature of true religion as grasped by Protestant Liberalism) is reinforced by freeing it from suspicion of admixture with Jewish legalism. If Duhm achieves his result by chipping away the parts of the book that do not fit his preexisting vision, it can be asked if Skinner was able to achieve his similar result by pouring the parts into a preexisting mold.

The Plausibility of Skinner's Work

If Skinner's account of Jeremiah's life and beliefs may not have a substantially better claim to objectivity than Duhm's, his account of the composition of the book can claim greater plausibility. By granting the prophet a greater sympathy for Deuteronomic law and allowing the Deuteronomic editors a greater sympathy with Jeremiah's message, Skinner removes one of the greatest implausibilities of Duhm's compositional model: the need to explain why a theological party that bitterly opposed the prophet during his life (calling for his death) preserved the authentic records of his ministry (including evidence of the opposition) and chose to present their own messages as his words.[69] Whether readers also find Skinner's biography of the prophet more plausible because of the explanations he offers for the parts of Jeremiah's story that differ from their experience (messages from God, prophecies of future events, catastrophes and invasions initiated by God, etc.) will depend on the extent to which they share the worldview of Skinner and likeminded modern interpreters. However, in considering whether explanations like Skinner's are necessary for modern readers to make sense of the book, there is another factor that should be taken into account. It cannot be assumed that modern interpreters will share Skinner's view of the Bible. For Skinner and his presumed audience, the Bible was still a source of authority, and he and his

---

[68] Unlike Duhm, Skinner does not simply assume that all poetry must have been written by the prophet; instead, he believes that he can judge the authenticity of a passage by whether it displays the literary quality worthy of a great poet. Thus, for example, Jeremiah cannot have written Lamentations because the "poetic genius" of its writer is "inferior," and the poet "adopts the artificial form of the acrostic" (Skinner, *Prophecy and Religion*, 279. Skinner repeats Lowth's denial that prophets could write acrostics. *Poetry of the Hebrews*, 244). On the other hand, four passages from Jeremiah 31, whose authenticity has been debated (31:2-6, 25, 26, 18-20, 21, 22), cannot be denied to Jeremiah because of their unsurpassed "originality of conception, vividness of imagination, and depth of feeling." Skinner, *Prophecy and Religion*, 302. Skinner's criterion for authenticity is not poetic form but conformity to Romantic literary values. This gives his judgments less claim to objectivity than Duhm's.

[69] Skinner exposes this weakness in Duhm's compositional account when he writes, "The mere fact that the prophecies of Jeremiah were edited by the Deuteronomic school shows that there was no antagonism between them." Skinner, *Prophecy and Religion*, 107.

audience assumed that it was a primary source of knowledge about true religion, as well as about authentic humanity. Without these assumptions about the Hebrew Scriptures, it is difficult to understand why scholars like Skinner went to such lengths to bring its literature and its account of Israel's into conformity with modern sensibilities and convictions.

The fortunes of Skinner's biographical reconstruction in the twentieth century appear to have depended to some degree on the fortunes of Protestant Liberalism, with its unique combination of views about religion, history, morality, and human potential. *Prophecy and Religion* was probably the most popular work on Jeremiah for much of the century (it went through ten editions between 1922 and 1963). Its popularity was probably primarily among Christian believers who were sympathetic to Skinner's theological perspective. Pastors and laypeople could enjoy its uplifting vision and engaging style. Among biblical scholars, Skinner's biographical reconstruction has proven to be more short-lived. An important marker of its waning influence was the sustained attack on the "Skinnerian" approach in Robert Carroll's 1981 book, *From Chaos to Covenant.*[70] It would be hard to find a scholar from the last part of the twentieth century who supported Skinner's identification of the foe from the north or his judgments about the contents of the *Urrolle.* This was not so much because his historical theories had been shown to be false or less credible than other theories as because the outcomes his theories allow were less likely to be found necessary or useful. There was less need for a biblical justification for leaving traditional religion behind for a higher religion of interiority or for boldly questioning the authority of written revelation. More and more, Biblical scholarship in the latter twentieth century was no more expected to provide justification for theological perspectives than it was for theories of poetry.

Although Skinner's biographical results became less useful—and thus less persuasive—to scholars, the same is not true of the assumptions on which his results were grounded—assumptions he inherited from Duhm. Skinner's work, which was willing to question Duhm's assumption that the prose speeches were inauthentic, was founded on Duhm's assumption that the poetic speeches were authentic. It was necessary for his historical approach and his historical results that the poetic speeches be understood as authentic: that is that they represent reports of speeches that Jeremiah at various points in his career, and that understanding them depends on recovering those historical (or social) contexts. This assumption was very useful, perhaps necessary, for the work most Jeremiah scholars for most of the twentieth century. This belief justified their historical approaches to the book (their attempts to discover the history, and the history of composition, behind the book), and it undergirded their historical conclusions. If biblical scholars were no longer expected to provide historical justifications for certain theological perspectives, they were still expected to provide historical justifications for their reconstructions of Israel's literature and religion. Jeremiah scholars were expected to provide explanations of the phenomenon of Israelite prophecy and the development of the prophetic literature in

[70] Robert P. Carroll, *From Chaos to Covenant: Prophecy in the Book of Jeremiah* (New York: Crossroad, 1981), 7.

terms of the history and religions of their ancient near eastern context. Much of this work was founded on assumed authenticity of the poetry. This assumption was not only useful for justifying the results of twentieth-century biblical scholarship but for justifying biblical scholarship itself. It proved more to be much more enduring than the biographical reconstructions Duhm and Skinner had used it to produce. As their theories about Jeremiah's life lost their hold on Biblical scholarship, their theory about the poetry in the book became even more deeply entrenched.

Three Unhelpful Results of Skinner's Assumption about Poetry in Jeremiah

In the last decades of the twentieth century, it began to become clear that the historical approaches to Jeremiah which had proven useful for generating theories about the history and compositional process that lay behind the book were less useful for understanding the book in its present form. This led to calls for scholarship to move beyond these historical approaches. However, it did not lead to a reexamination of the primary assumption that validated the historical approaches. It seems that the assumption about the nature of the poetry was too deeply entrenched; scholars were too confident in its truth to question it. This examination of the biographical reconstruction Skinner built on Duhm's assumption about the poetry can close by considering three unhelpful results of the assumption that appear in Skinner's work on Jeremiah—and continue to appear in work on Jeremiah from Duhm's time to the present.

The first unhelpful result is the one that scholars dissatisfied with Duhm's and Skinner's historical approach have most readily recognized. The assumption that the poetry in Jeremiah is comprised of authentic utterances from various occasions has prevented scholars from investigating the present literary contexts of the poetic sections and the present sequence of the text and from considering whether the poetic sections are parts of extended literary creations. Skinner's work is a clear example of this unhelpful result. Although his work mainly deals with poetic sections in Jeremiah 1–25, he never considers them as they appear in the book but only isolated from their literary contexts, given biographical contexts by his elaborate sorting system, and then presented in a new chronological order of his own making. More recent scholars have recognized this weakness in approaches like Skinner's and have sought to correct this it by offering compositional theories in which the original (authentic) poetic speeches have been placed in a meaningful order by an editor (whether a later Deuteronomic editor or Jeremiah editing his own early works). Chapters 7 and 8 of this study will show how that although these theories have enabled the recent scholars to see much more of the cohesiveness of sections with poetry in them, their retention of Duhm's and Skinner's assumption about the authenticity of the poetry has prevented them from considering whether any of the cohesiveness of these sections could be due to the author(s) of the poetic passages wrote them as parts of extended compositions.

A second unhelpful result of considering poetry as authentic evidence has gained much less attention. Treating the poetic speeches in Jeremiah as evidence of the prophet's speeches on various occasions prevents readers from seeing how these poetic speeches by various characters contribute to the text's presentation of these characters. In Duhm's work, the obvious obstacle to perceiving the book's presentation of its characters is the denial of the authenticity of the prose speeches. Treating the prose speeches as representing the agendas of postexilic scribes keeps the reader from considering what they contribute to the characterization of Jeremiah and Yahweh when they are read as they appear in the book's presentation: primarily as Yahweh's messages to the people spoken through Jeremiah before the fall of Jerusalem. Skinner's work is comparatively free from this unhelpful result of Duhm's assumption about the prose speeches because he is willing to accept them as (at least based on) actual speeches of Jeremiah before the fall of Jerusalem. Although Skinner still obscures the text's characterization of Yahweh by reading his warnings and pronouncements of judgments as the premonitions and predictions of Jeremiah, he at least allows them to be read in the context of Jeremiah's prophetic ministry.

In Skinner's work, it is primarily Duhm's assumption of the authenticity of the poetry that results in him skewing the book's characterization. The main distortion is of the character of Yahweh, the main speaker in the book. Skinner regularly reads the poetic speeches of Yahweh as speeches of Jeremiah even though the book seldom offers any reason for identifying Jeremiah as the speaker—even in the role of messenger conveying Yahweh's speeches. A typical example is Skinner's comment on Jer. 11:15-16, a speech in which Yahweh castigates the people for coming into his house and offering sacrifices even though their deeds are vile. Skinner writes, "Here we have an utterance of Jeremiah's private reflexions on the new attitude of the people to the Temple and its worship."[71] In this passage as in many other passages in Skinner's work, Yahweh's judgment becomes Jeremiah's religious insight.

Skinner's consistent explanations of Yahweh's speeches as expressions of Jeremiah's feelings, insights, or premonitions are out of keeping with one of the striking characteristics of the book: Jeremiah often speaks in opposition to Yahweh's word. However, even when explaining passages in which Jeremiah and Yahweh argue with each other, Skinner does not break from his understanding of the speeches in the book of Jeremiah. He explains that "Jeremiah was the first to introduce into prophecy this opposition between conscience and feeling, or between the voice of God and the impulse of the heart."[72] According to Skinner's explanation, the conflict between Yahweh and Jeremiah is simply another name for the conflict between the prophet's conscience and his feelings.

A possible analogy to Skinner's interpretation would be an interpretation of the *Bacchae* in which the conflict between Pentheus, the authoritarian king of Thebes, and Dionysus, the free-spirited god of wine, is read as an internal conflict between Pentheus' sense of duty and his need for leisure.[73] This interpretation would involve

---

[71] Skinner, *Prophecy and Religion*, 168.
[72] Skinner, *Prophecy and Religion*, 48.
[73] This analogy might seem to beg the questions of the nature and author(s) of the speeches in Jeremiah, since it is well known that the *Bacchae* is a drama and that it was written by Euripides (not Pentheus). However, it is not being assumed here that poetic speeches in Jeremiah are part of a dramatic portrayal. It is simply being pointed out that Skinner's assumption, which requires him to read the speeches as isolated historical records, prevents him from considering the possibility of dramatic presentation even when the text displays a key feature of dramatic presentation, speeches which work together as dialogues.

a serious misunderstanding of the characterization of both Pentheus and Dionysius. Disbelief in the actual existence of Dionysius would not be sufficient to drive a reader to this interpretation. The reader would have to be persuaded that Pentheus is the speaker of not only his own speeches but also the speeches of Dionysius. An interpreter might be able to persuade a reader of this interpretation, if she were able to convince the reader that the presence of iambic trimeter showed that they must be records of actual speeches (or that this meter is characteristic of the speech of kings of Greek city-states). The assumption that poetic form is an indicator that a speech in the book of Jeremiah must be a record of what the prophet said on a particular historical occasion plays this role in Skinner's interpretation—and in most interpretations of Jeremiah up to the present.

These two unhelpful results of the assumption of that poetic form is an indication of authenticity are the corollaries of a more fundamental unhelpful result of the assumption: it prevents interpreters from considering other more natural possibilities for the significance of poetic form. The assumption that the poetry in the book of Jeremiah must be his spontaneous effusions called forth by historical events or psychological states, keeps interpreters from considering that the poetry may have been intentionally crafted to portray situations or characters. This is how interpreters explain the poetry of Homer, Euripides, Vergil, Dante, Shakespeare, or Milton. Most interpreters of Jeremiah appear not even to consider this possibility. Skinner, as was seen, brings it up only to dismiss its implications, which would undermine his use of the poetry as biographical evidence, the foundational justification of his approach. He, like other interpreters of Jeremiah, is locked into explaining prophetic poetry according to a Romantic theory of the source of poetry that was common in the nineteenth century. It is an irony of twentieth-century study of the Israel's prophetic literature that in a time when general literary criticism was leaving behind Romantic theories of poetry for ones that emphasized intentional artistry, these same Romantic theories were becoming further entrenched in biblical criticism.[74] Of course, the biblical scholars did not consider Duhm's assumption about the poetry of Jeremiah a Romantic theory or a helpful supposition to facilitate their historical approach; they saw it as the one of the "assured results of modern scholarship." The part the best-known presentation of Duhm's compositional theory of Jeremiah played in helping his assumption achieve this status is the subject of the next chapter.

---

[74] In the early part of the twentieth century, Romantic literary theory was called into question by neo-classical, or formalist, critiques. In his 1919 essay, "Tradition and the Individual Talent," T.S. Eliot argues that good poetry is not primarily the product of an extraordinary personality or sublime experiences but rather of intentional literary craftsmanship. What counts, according to Eliot, "is not the 'greatness,' the intensity, of the emotions, the components, but the intensity of the artistic process." The poet may express personality, experience, or emotions, but there is no reason these must be personal to the poet. Eliot writes: "Impressions and experiences which are important for the man may take no place in the poetry, and those which become important in the poetry may play quite a negligible part in the man, the personality." (T. S. Eliot, "Tradition and the Individual Talent," in *Criticism: the Major Texts*, ed. Walter Jackson Bate [Chicago: Harcourt Brace Jovanovich, 1970], 528.) This impersonal theory of poetry turned attention away from the character and situation of the poet, and redirected the attention to the poem itself—and the characters and situations evoked by the arrangement of the poem's components.

6

Mowinckel's Theory of the Composition of the Book

Mowinckel's Contribution to the Standard Compositional Approach

As Skinner's biography of Jeremiah can be seen as the standard form of the biographical approach employed by Duhm, Duhm's compositional approach to the book of Jeremiah received its standard form in the work of Sigmund Mowinckel. In his 1914 *Zur Komposition des Buches Jeremia*, Mowinckel introduced the designations A, B, and C for the three main types of material identified by Duhm (poetic oracles, biographical prose, and prose sayings). Mowinckel's designations and his allocation of passages to the three categories continue to provide the starting point for discussions of the composition of Jeremiah.[1] The basic character of this standard compositional theory can now be examined by comparing Mowinckel's presentation to Duhm's on four major points of the theory:

1. The book of Jeremiah is not a book in the modern sense but a collection of materials relating to the prophet; therefore, the first task of criticism is to distinguish the component parts based on their relationships to the historical prophet.
2. Besides the narratives, which offer biographical evidence about the life of the prophet (Type B), there are two other main types of material in Jeremiah: authentic sayings of the prophet (Type A) and inauthentic additions (Type C), which have been put into the mouth of the prophet. Since the additions offer a tendentious presentation of the message and activity of the prophet, they must be carefully distinguished from his authentic speeches, which provide reliable evidence.

---

[1] T. R. Hobbs writes that "with relatively few modifications, [Mowinckel's modification of Duhm's] position has been subsequently adopted by Volz [1928], Rudolph [*HAT* 12, 1947], and Hyatt [*IB* 5, 1956]." T. R. Hobbs, "Some Remarks on the Composition of and Structure of the Book of Jeremiah," in *A Prophet to the Nations: Essays in Jeremiah Studies*, ed. Leo Perdue (Winona Lake, IN: Eisenbrauns, 1984), 176. One could now add Bright (*AB* 21, 1965) and Thompson (*NICOT*, 1980) and many others.

3. The primary criterion for distinguishing the authentic speeches (Type A) from the inauthentic additions (Type C) is their literary genre: authentic speeches can be recognized by their stirring poetry, and the additions can be recognized by their dull, pedestrian prose.

4. The authentic speeches (Type A) are short lyrical sayings delivered in response to events in the life of the prophet. They were collected and incorporated into the book with little attempt at coherent organization or presentation. Thus interpreting them will involve isolating them from their present literary context and determining their place in the biography of the prophet.

On each of these points, it will be demonstrated that although Mowinckel is in basic agreement with Duhm's position, he has also sought to improve upon it by modifying its perceived weaknesses, systematizing its central observations, and supporting it with new argumentation. What Mowinckel has to contribute to each point is primarily derived from form criticism and tradition criticism,[2] approaches that came to prominence after Duhm made his primary contribution to Jeremiah studies. In brief, it can be said that Mowinckel sought to update Duhm's compositional theory of Jeremiah by supplementing it with the form-critical work of Hermann Gunkel (1862–1932). This is in fact how Mowinckel presents his own work,[3] and it is this combination of Duhm's source analysis with Mowinckel's form-critical presentation that provides the basic shape of the standard approach to the composition of Jeremiah. The standard approach will now be examined by first laying out Mowinckel's contributions to each of the four central points, then examining the influences that shaped the approach (and that shaped the form-critical method Mowinckel incorporates into the approach), and finally considering the effects of the approach on reading and interpreting the book of Jeremiah.

Point One: Compositional Analysis Is the First Priority

On the first point, Mowinckel's belief that Jeremiah is a composite book and thus that compositional analysis is the first priority of interpretation is the obvious significance of his primary contribution to Jeremiah scholarship: the systemization of Duhm's division of the book into three types of material. The title and subject matter of his work on Jeremiah, *Zur Komposition des Buches Jeremia*, also indicate that compositional analysis is his central concern. In the introduction to this work, he presents it as

---

[2] Mowinckel described his approach as traditio-historical. In his view, Gunkel's work was traditio-historical as well, even though he called it form criticism. Sigmund Mowinckel, *The Spirit and the Word: Prophecy and Tradition in Ancient Israel*, FCBS (Minneapolis, MN: Fortress, 2002), 20.

[3] Sigmund Mowinckel, *Zur Komposition des Buches Jeremia* (Oslo: Jacob Dybwad, 1914), 17. In the conclusion of his book, Mowinckel notes that his work has very few citations because he wrote it during a forced *Otium* (leisure) at a sanatorium where he was without his books. However, he singles out two sources he feels obliged to acknowledge: Duhm, the pioneer of the historical approach to the composition of Jeremiah; and Gunkel, who personally taught him to identify oracles and different styles in prophetic books. (Mowinckel studied with Gunkel at Giessen between 1911 and 1913, Mowinckel, *Zur Komposition*, xii.) Without the benefit of Gunkel's teaching, he says, he could never have written his book. Mowinckel, *Zur Komposition*, 66–7.

an effort to extend the compositional analysis of the Pentateuch to the prophetic books. He suggests that previous attempts to discern the compositional history of the prophets have failed because they relied on assumptions carried over from their work with the prose of the Pentateuch.[4] The authors of these attempts imagined the prophets to be writers and saw their task as uncovering the authentic literary work as originally composed by the prophet. This led them to look for long compositions and logical order that had been obscured by the editors. Mowinckel offers as a corrective the form-critical view that prophets were orators who delivered short oracles that were later written down, collected, and included in the book without logical arrangement. Thus Mowinckel affirms the source-critical aim of compositional analysis even though he questions the assumptions and methods. In fact, his own assumptions and methods can be seen as a radicalization of the source-critical approach: he is more doubtful about the possibility of finding coherence in the present form of the book, and he finds a much more complex compositional history and many more and much smaller compositional units. Mowinckel believes that the previous critics, even though they discerned multiple sources, have failed to grasp adequately the main principle (*Hauptregel*) of interpreting prophetic books: that they are composite works (*Sammlerwerke*).[5]

On this point, it is not immediately clear to what degree Mowinckel believes his criticism of the earlier source critics applies to Duhm. Mowinckel's praise of Duhm as a pioneer in compositional study[6] is probably on the grounds that he was more radical than any of his predecessors in limiting the speeches ascribed to Jeremiah and in drawing a strong distinction between Jeremiah's speeches and the inauthentic additions. His criticism of Duhm's overemphasis on authenticity[7] may indicate that Mowinckel thinks Duhm is still too willing to think of the prophet as a writer whose speeches have a logical coherence. In any case, Mowinckel's adoption of Duhm's basic compositional categories shows that he affirmed Duhm's overall picture of a fragmented book but wanted to amend it and give it methodological clarity through form-critical analysis.

Point Two: Authentic Speeches Must Be Distinguished from Inauthentic Speeches

On the second point, the sharp distinction between authentic and inauthentic sources, Mowinckel strongly endorses this fundamental contribution of Duhm. This is the primary significance of his division of the book into the three types, A, B, and C. The distinction between the first-person speeches (A and C) and the third-person narratives (B) is quite obvious and had been recognized before Duhm by many scholars (who often credited the speeches to Jeremiah and the narratives to Baruch). What

---

[4] Mowinckel, *Zur Komposition*, 3.
[5] Mowinckel, *Zur Komposition*, 3.
[6] Mowinckel, *Zur Komposition*, 66–7.
[7] Mowinckel, *Zur Komposition*, 17.

Duhm added and Mowinckel codified was the separation of A and C as authentic and inauthentic material.

Initially, it might appear to someone reading *Zur Komposition des Buches Jeremia* that Mowinckel is not interested in isolating the authentic words of the prophets. In his first paragraph, he charges earlier studies of the composition of the prophetic books with making a "fundamental error": namely, "making it [their] aim to distinguish between the 'genuine' and 'false' (*echt und unecht*) and thus consciously or unconsciously making their judgment of authenticity the defining standard of the question of composition."[8] In a later passage, he blasts Duhm's attempts to determine authenticity as responsible for a critical "act of violence" (*Gewalttätigkeit*).[9] However, throughout his study, Mowinckel clearly argues for the authenticity of the A material. He writes,

> The Collection A gives the impression of an authentic, lightly edited tradition; it almost always has the genuinely (*echt*) prophetic, metrical form; most of its oracles can be recognized by form and content as works of one and the same man; this man appears as a distinctly stamped individual, clearly different from most other prophets. Thus we have in A, if anywhere, the *ipsissima verba* of Jeremiah.[10]

In light of Mowinckel's interest in identifying what is authentic in Jeremiah, his criticism of earlier compositional studies must have a narrow focus. It appears that his primary criticism is that by "authentic," source critics often mean *written* by the prophet. Mowinckel, in keeping with his form- or tradition-critical perspective, wants to stress that the prophet only spoke the words. His theory that someone else collected the prophet's sayings and wrote them down takes away the expectation found in earlier studies that the authentic material might take the form of an extended logically arranged document composed by the prophet. Mowinckel believes that form criticism has shown that brevity and lack of arrangement are characteristics of authentic prophetic speech.[11]

In *Zur Komposition des Propheten Buches*, Mowinckel presents the three main types of material as the work of three different authors whose various views of prophecy caused them to present Jeremiah in different ways:

A comes from a faithful collector and preserver of the prophetic tradition;
B from an historical author and an admirer of the person and life of the prophet;
C … from an author who transformed the tradition according to a theory and a
     pattern.[12]

---

[8] Mowinckel, *Zur Komposition*, 3.
[9] Mowinckel, *Zur Komposition*, 17.
[10] Mowinckel, *Zur Komposition*, 21.
[11] Mowinckel, *Zur Komposition*, 3.
[12] Mowinckel, *Zur Komposition*, 39. Mowinckel finds at least two other sources in Jeremiah: the D source in chs 30 and 31, and the "oracles against foreign peoples" in 46–51. He considers both of these to be late, inauthentic additions. Mowinckel, *Zur Komposition*, 14–17, 45–8.

This presentation of the three sources shows Mowinckel's basic agreement with Duhm's assessment that the prophetic oracles and biographical narratives (A and B) have a high degree of historical value whereas the speeches are highly tendentious and thus have little historical value. Mowinckel sharpens Duhm's assessment of the third source by making it the work of a single person and identifying its theological perspective. Whereas for Duhm the additions were the work of various postexilic scribes, legal experts, and priests, Mowinckel sees them as Deuteronomistic work. The Deuteronomistic perspective that C promotes is that the fall of Jerusalem was God's punishment for the nation's idolatry and other sins against God that were forbidden in the written law of Moses. This message, put in the mouth of Jeremiah by the C author, is sharply distinguished from the perspective of the authentic oracles of Jeremiah (source A). The authentic oracles were primarily concerned with personal social morality, and though Jeremiah might have thought of this morality as a divine law, "there is not a trace anywhere [in his authentic oracles] that this law was understood as firmly described in writing."[13]

Mowinckel also attributes to the Deuteronomistic influence the nonhistorical view of prophecy that Duhm found in the additions. He believes that the understanding of prophecy that the C speeches assumes is an inconsistent amalgam of features drawn from various periods in the actual historical development of prophecy: at different times, Jeremiah appears as a foreteller, a miracle worker, and most of all as a lawgiver, a writer of canonical books, a preacher, and a minister.[14] As in Duhm's presentation, Mowinckel disparages the C-source for both its literary style and its religious content, and like Duhm, he reserves his strongest denunciations for its failure to represent adequately the historical prophet. From the magnificent oracles of Jeremiah, the Deuteronomistic C-source can only extract sermons about sin and punishment, "from the diversity … monotony, from the wealth of the ideas and thoughts, genres and moods … poverty of language and content, and from the many personal outbursts and feelings, from the whole specific individuality of the great man … a shadowy figure, a dogmatic theory."[15] This extremely negative view of the late source explains why Mowinckel, like Duhm, believed that it was important to distinguish and isolate the inauthentic material as the first step of interpretation.

In a later work, *Prophecy and Tradition* (1946), Mowinckel offered a modification of his own earlier understanding of the nature of the C material.[16] Instead of describing C as a written source, the work of a single author, Mowinckel now proposed that C was the work of a "circle of tradition" in which the certain words of Jeremiah were "transmitted and transformed" under the influence of the Deuteronomistic theology of the traditionists.[17] With the understanding that C was a product of an oral tradition

---

[13] Mowinckel, *Zur Komposition*, 35.

[14] Mowinckel, *Zur Komposition*, 37.

[15] Mowinckel, *Zur Komposition*, 39.

[16] Full title: *Prophecy and Tradition: The Prophetic Books in Light of the Study of the Growth and History of the Tradition.* This early work can now be found in a lightly edited form in the first nine chapters of Mowinckel, *Spirit and Word*, 1–80.

[17] Mowinckel, *Zur Komposition*, 56. Mowinckel attributes his earlier view that C was a "source" to "an unnecessary and unfounded partial concession to Duhm's view." Mowinckel, *Spirit and Word*, 136, n. 12. However Duhm never portrayed this material as a single written source but as an accumulation of individual additions to the original sources written by Baruch.

that stretched back to Jeremiah, it was possible to identify ideas in C that might have originated from Jeremiah. This solved a problem for scholars like Duhm and Mowinckel who were puzzled that what they viewed as one of the highest religious achievements recorded in the book of Jeremiah, the denunciation of the material sacrificial cult, came in the middle of a passage of Deuteronomic prose, the Temple Sermon of ch. 7. Mowinckel's new theory allowed the enlightened content to be ascribed to the inspired prophet and the prosaic form to the (presumably less-inspired) traditionists.

It might be thought that Mowinckel's new tradition-critical emphasis on the long period or oral transmission separating the historical speeches from their written form would undermine his faith in the ability of criticism to discover the *ipsissima verba* of the prophet or that it would soften the sharp distinction he drew between authentic and inauthentic material. In fact, the opposite is true. *Prophecy and Religion* is a sustained argument for the compatibility of tradition criticism with source-critical methods and aims. Mowinckel's book appears to have been occasioned by the direction tradition criticism was being taken by practitioners like Ivan Engnell, who saw the discipline as superseding literary criticism and abandoning its quest to recover authentic sources.[18] In response, Mowinckel argues that both tradition criticism and literary criticism are needed: in Jeremiah, literary criticism's task is to discover the contents of Baruch's roll (the *Urrolle*), and tradition criticism's task is to discover the "original Jeremian nucleus" of the Deuteronomistic traditions.[19] Their common aim is to recover the authentic life and message of Jeremiah. Studies like Engnell's that limit themselves to the synthesis in which the text now exists might "contribute to the picture of religious shape of Judaism,"[20] but Mowinckel seeks "a deeper understanding"[21] that comes from going behind the tradition where "the powerful figures of the prophets [loom]."[22] He ends his work with a section titled "*Ipsissima Verba*," which could be described as a rallying cry for the traditional aims of historical criticism:

> Research … cannot submit to a "Do Not Enter" sign [that forbids the search for the *ipsissima verba* of the prophets]. … We will attempt to ascertain their words, get hold of the original sayings … as they once sounded in the streets and the marketplaces of Jerusalem and by the gates of the temple. We will attempt to find them by all means within our power—through form criticism, tradition history, and literary criticism.[23]

---

[18] See, e.g., Ivan Engnell, "The Traditio-Historical Method in Old Testament Research," in *A Rigid Scrutiny*, ed. John T. Willis (Nashville, TN: Vanderbilt University Press, 1969), 3–11. However this essay by Engnell was first published in 1959 and responds to Mowinckel's 1946 *Prophecy and Tradition*.

[19] Mowinckel, *Spirit and Word*, 18.

[20] Mowinckel, *Spirit and Word*, 47.

[21] Mowinckel, *Spirit and Word*, 37.

[22] Mowinckel, *Spirit and Word*, 80.

[23] Mowinckel, *Spirit and Word*. Although additional chapters follow in *Spirit and Word*, these are the final words of Mowinckel's original *Prophecy and Religion*. One might compare the rhetorical cadence of Mowinckel's peroration to Churchill's speech after the British retreat from France, "We shall defend our island, whatever the cost may be, we shall fight on the beaches, we shall fight on the landing grounds, we shall fight on the fields and the streets, we shall fight in the hills; we shall never surrender."

Duhm's quest to recover the authentic words of Jeremiah from under the layers of additions found a formidable champion in Mowinckel.

Point Three: Poetic Form Is the Primary Criterion for Distinguishing Authentic Speech

The third point of the standard model of Jeremiah's composition is that the primary distinction between Jeremiah's authentic words and the later additions is the poetic form of the authentic words. On this point, Mowinckel has adopted Duhm's approach but made a major modification. Duhm was the pioneer of the approach to Jeremiah that equated authenticity with metrical form. However, as has been noted, he limited the authentic speeches to those in the five-beat *qînâ* lament form. This limitation, which has found few followers, was emphatically rejected by Mowinckel: "It must be called an unparalleled critical act of violence when Duhm implements his declaration that Jeremiah may only employ the five-beat meter with numerous false explanations and the most outrageous excisions, frequently excising precisely the most characteristic words."[24] Though rejecting Duhm's strict metrical limitation, throughout his work Mowinckel relies on Duhm's basic assumption that authentic prophetic speech is metrical. Speaking of the A source, he writes, "By far the greatest part of these oracles and songs are metrical, as the prophetic style demands from the outset."[25] The loosening of the metrical requirement allows Mowinckel to expand the material considered to be authentic: from about 280 verses in Duhm[26] to about 400 verses in his own list of passages in Source A.[27] Although Mowinckel (like Duhm) distinguishes the A texts from the C on several other grounds (their style, their diction, their view of religion, their view of prophecy, their use of headings), the fundamental distinction remains their poetic form.

As on other points, on the identification of authenticity with metrical form, Mowinckel takes his cue from Duhm, but he looks to form criticism to provide validation of Duhm's view. As evidence for his claim that prophetic style demands poetic form, Mowinckel draws on two lines of argument made by form critics. The primary argument comes from narratives about the prophets in the historical books, particularly those that show the prophets as ecstatics and speakers of prophetic oracles (predictions about the future). By connecting these passages with the poetry of the written books of prophets, the poetry can be explained as the result of ecstatic experiences. This is the approach taken by Hermann Gunkel. He gives this explanation of meter: "The prophets, who received their ideas in times of exalted inspiration and uttered them under the influence of over-flowing emotions, could only speak in poetic rhythm."[28] He gives a similar explanation of the prophet's use of poetic imagery, allusions, and other

---

[24] Mowinckel, *Zur Komposition*, 20.

[25] Mowinckel, *Zur Komposition*, 20.

[26] Duhm's own estimation. Bernhard Duhm, *Das Buch Jeremia*, KHC 11 (Tübingen: J. C. B. Mohr, 1901), xvi.

[27] Mowinckel, *Zur Komposition*, 20–1.

[28] Hermann Gunkel, "The Israelite Prophecy from the Time of Amos," in *Twentieth Century Theology in the Making*, ed. Jaroslav Pelikan (New York: Collins, 1969), 66.

oblique approaches: "In mysterious times of ecstasy, [revelations] appeared obscure and shadowy before the soul of the prophet."[29] The other argument that prophetic speech must be metrical comes from comparative religion. Mowinckel argues that the theory that "the real form [of the prophetic saying] is poetic and metric" is "endorsed ... by the epic traditions and the parallel analogies from the ancient Arabic visionaries."[30] His source for the Arabic parallel is Gustav Hölscher,[31] who argues that the Hebrew prophets were similar to the Arabian *Kâhin*, shamanistic soothsayers who spoke prophecies when possessed by a *Jinnī*. Their words, observes Hölscher, "are always rhythmically formed, indeed in the oldest meter of Arabic poetry."[32] Once again, Mowinckel uses form-critical arguments (or more precisely here, the kind of comparative-religion arguments often employed by the form critics) to bolster an idea that derives from Duhm and became a central feature of the standard compositional approach to Jeremiah.

Point Four: Authentic Sayings Must Be Isolated from Their Literary Context

The fourth and final point of the standard approach is that the authentic sayings are short lyrical pieces that appear in collections with little intentional order, and thus that each authentic saying must be isolated from its present literary context and placed in a historical context before its meaning can be understood. On this point, Mowinckel's influence is the most pronounced because although Duhm's work suggests that he was operating with these assumptions, Mowinckel states them as guiding methodological principles. Although Duhm does not draw attention to the brevity of the authentic oracles, the oracles he isolates are quite short. On average, they are about four verses long with some only one or two verses long.[33] As for the possibility of meaningful order, Duhm indicates that some of the units are parts of cycles consisting of four or five poems and that they originally had a "more or less chronological" order, which has now been obscured by the editors who broke them apart and moved them from their original places because they did not understand their significance.[34]

Brevity and Self-Sufficiency of Units Demanded by Form Criticism

The understanding of the brief extent and negligible order of the oracles that is implicit in Duhm's commentary becomes the explicit methodological starting point in Mowinckel's Jeremiah studies. He begins his work on the composition of Jeremiah by pointing out a "fundamental error" in previous compositional studies of the prophets: assuming that the prophetic books are "logically arranged" according

---

[29] Gunkel, "Israelite Prophecy," 69.
[30] Mowinckel, *Spirit and Word*, 43.
[31] Mowinckel, *Spirit and Word*, 132, n. 14.
[32] Gustav Hölscher, *Die Profeten: Untersuchungen zur Religionsgeschichte Israels* (Leipzig: J. C. Hinrichs, 1914), 92–3.
[33] Duhm estimates that the authentic poetry (which is around 280 verses) comprises approximately sixty poems. Duhm, *Jeremia*, xiii, xvi. He groups them by the periods of Jeremiah's life in which they originated. Duhm, *Jeremia*, xiii–xiv.
[34] Duhm, *Jeremia*, xiii, xiv, xxi.

to a "uniform plan" and are made up of extensive "speeches." Mowinckel presents his work as a corrective based on facts about prophetic literature that have become firmly established: that the prophetic books are composite works and that their basic component, the prophetic oracle "has no arrangement … is usually very brief … [is] a completely self-contained unit, and has nothing to do with anything that stands next to it."[35] Thirty years later, in his work on prophecy and tradition, he writes concerning the length of prophetic speeches: "The separate, self-contained prophetic message … is generally very brief."[36] Concerning the possibility of meaningful connection between individual speeches, he writes, "The apparent connections that exist, on closer examination, prove to be secondary."[37]

The grounds for Mowinckel's foundational assumptions lie primarily in form criticism. Mowinckel acknowledges this when he writes that although Duhm had begun to realize the brevity and abruptness of the oracles, it was only "through the suggestions of Gunkel in his excellent sketch of Israelite literature that clarity was achieved."[38] In his writing on prophecy, Gunkel extended the work of scholars like Ewald and Duhm who turned the focus onto the "secret experiences of the prophet," the overwhelming internal compulsion that convinced the prophets that they possessed divine truths that needed to be spoken. Gunkel augmented this view of prophecy with the newly developing disciplines of abnormal psychology and comparative religion. The strange experiences of individuals suffering from mental illnesses or shamanistic soothsayers provided analogies for the experiences of the prophets. The relevance of these analogies to the prophetic literature was urged in part based on the perceived continuity in the development Israelite prophecy from the early *nĕbî'îm* in the time of the judges to the prophets of the exile and beyond. If prophecy originally arose out of these ecstatic psychological experiences, it could hardly be expected to take the form of extensive and coherent argument (at least not until prophets became writers, something which only began with Ezekiel). Instead, since "prophetic apprehension … consists of a sudden illumination like lightning," the oracles that resulted would naturally be characterized by a marked "movement from one subject to another. Isolated individual elements, uprooted from their context, are abruptly placed together. One stone is heaped upon another, mere fragments."[39]

Mowinckel's belief that modern scholarship had shown that Jeremiah's oracles must be brief was supported by Gunkel's scheme of the development of prophetic speech forms by gradual evolution from short and simple to long and complex: the earliest prophecies were only one or two words, and it was not until the time of Ezekiel, who was the first prophet to write his own book, that long complex compositions became possible.[40] In Gunkel's estimation, Jeremiah came at the stage in which "prophets had learned to express themselves with great clarity in brief statements, made up of two,

[35] Mowinckel, *Zur Komposition*, 3.
[36] Mowinckel, *Spirit and Word*, 41.
[37] Mowinckel, *Spirit and Word*, 45.
[38] Mowinckel, *Zur Komposition*, 17. Gunkel's "sketch of Israelite literature" that Mowinckel refers to is apparently "Die Israelitiche Literatur," in *Die orientalichen Literaturen*, ed. Paul Hinnenberg, Die Kultur der Gegenwart 1/7 (Leipzig: B. G. Teubner, 1906), 51–102.
[39] Gunkel, "Israelite Prophecy," 71. Originally published as "Propheten II. Seit Amos" (1913).
[40] Gunkel, "Israelite Prophecy," 64–6. See also Hermann Gunkel, "The Prophets: Oral and Written," in *Water for a Thirsty Land: Israelite Literature and Religion*, ed. K. C. Hanson, Fortress Classics in

three, or a few more long lines."[41] Mowinckel carries Gunkel's observation over into his work on the composition of Jeremiah; he is not a page into his work before he distinguishes his approach from previous approaches with the corrective statement that oracles are "mostly very brief, 2 to 5 verses, less frequently 10–12, rarely more than 15–20."[42]

Mowinckel's fixed belief in the brevity of the oracles and their lack of relationship with adjacent oracles in the text determines the methodological priorities for interpreting Jeremiah. These truths about oracles, recently discovered by form criticism, dictate that "the correct division (*Einteilung*) of the units (*Abschnitte*) is ... the first and most difficult work of exegesis, which has almost never been satisfactorily achieved."[43] Here again, he directly echoes Gunkel.[44] For the exegete who attempts this work, Mowinckel lays down rules for judging the extent of a unit: (1) Prophetic formulas indicate the beginning or end of a saying. (2 & 3) When a saying has delivered the basic formal elements of its type, or fulfilled the purpose of its type (e.g., it has said something about the future or what should be done), it has reached its conclusion. (4) A saying can have only one dominant image.[45] Each of these rules is designed to prevent exegetes from overestimating the extent of individual units. Mowinckel also aims to prevent exegetes from finding unwarranted connections between the units. The only kind of connections he recognizes are those between the parts of a "prophetic liturgy" (a composite form described by Gunkel). However, before one can claim to have identified a prophetic liturgy, Mowinckel insists that a number of demands must be met: (1) the liturgy must conform to a recognizable pattern, (2) it must have a uniform "imaginative picture," (3) the connection between units must be necessary (i.e., the units must be unclear and defective when isolated), (4) the units must have common or symmetrical stylistic features.[46] The third demand is the heart of Mowinckel's defense against the perception of unity in the poetic sections of the prophets: it is not enough to show that a connection is possible, or probable; it must be necessary. The text is assumed to be fragmentary; the burden of proof lies with those who attempt to find unity in the text.[47]

Biblical Studies (Minneapolis, MN: Fortress, 2001), 88–93. Originally published as "Die Propheten als Schriftsteller und Dichter" (1923).

[41] Gunkel, "Prophets: Oral and Written," 92. Gunkel cites as examples: Jer. 2:1-3, 4-9, 10-13, and 14-19.

[42] Mowinckel, *Zur Komposition*, 4.

[43] Mowinckel, *Zur Komposition*, 17.

[44] "The study of the style of the prophets must begin with the units in which their utterances were made. ... [I]n general they are not indicated in the tradition of the text we possess, and many scholars, who have not yet realized the necessity of this task ... still think in terms of units which are much too large." Gunkel, "Israelite Prophecy," 64.

[45] Mowinckel, *Spirit and Word*, 49.

[46] Mowinckel, *Spirit and Word*, 50-1. Mowinckel's argument in his early work that Jer. 14:1–15:4 is not "a liturgy as Gunkel defined this literary term" is, in part, that it fails to meet these demands. Mowinckel, *Zur Komposition*, 22-3.

[47] Here as throughout *Spirit and Word*, Mowinckel's primary target is Ivan Engnell. Engnell had argued that the servant passages in Isaiah 40–55 should be read in light of the other passages in these chapters. Mowinckel responds that "it is necessary [for Engnell] to provide actual evidence that these different passages really refer to and need each other, and that they require the greater connection to provide a clear sense with an unmistakable point." Mowinckel, *Spirit and Word*, 47.

The Necessity of Recovering Historical Context for
Interpreting Spoken Messages

Mowinckel's program for interpreting the authentic prophetic sayings is not limited to distinguishing them from adjacent units in the text. He believes that the true significance and value of the units can only be grasped when they are isolated from their present context and placed in a new context. In response to scholars like Engnell who emphasized the importance of the present literary context, he writes, "Stressing the general exegetical principle that the interpretation should be determined 'according to the context' is obviously correct. No exegete has denied it. But again we have to ask: which context?"[48] In the argument that follows, Mowinckel is only concerned to deny the importance for exegesis of the literary context, to show that the present placement of oracles is of little concern because it is "secondary." However, Mowinckel's repeated disparagement of the present context as "secondary" raises the question of what the context is that he believes to be primary. The answer appears in his descriptions of the units he wishes to isolate: "It is … the individual saying—determined by the situation … which is the original unit."[49] For Mowinckel, it is the historical situation in which each isolated saying was first spoken that determines the meaning of the text—or perhaps more accurately, the multitude of individual meanings. Conversely, the value of the text comes from what it is able to reveal about the original situations of the isolated sayings. He writes that although investigating the sayings in their collected form may provide knowledge about Judaism's view of prophecy, "deeper understanding" will come from "insight into the concrete situation of the detached saying."[50] For Mowinckel, like Duhm and Skinner, the context that provides the isolated saying with both its meaning and value is the original historical situation.

Mowinckel's exegetical principle that the historical rather than the literary context is determinative for meaning is grounded in two form-critical beliefs about prophetic speech. Both are apparent in Mowinckel's description of the prophets: "The prophets were men of the spoken word, who appeared with brief sayings ('messages'), determined by the situation and the moment."[51] The reason that meanings of the isolated units are determined by their original historical contexts is that they are thought of as the written records of spoken words and as messages. Spoken words have their primary, or original, meaning in the situation in which they were spoken. What they signify depends on their historical context: who spoke these words, in what role, for what reason, to whom, in response to what situation, and so on. Dependence on historical context is much less common in written works since the writer, knowing that the context in which the text will be read will be different from the one in which it is written, crafts the text so that it is independent of the original context. The description of the prophetic books as collections of words spoken on various occasions suggests

---

[48] Mowinckel, *Spirit and Word*, 47.
[49] Mowinckel, *Spirit and Word*, 43.
[50] Mowinckel, *Spirit and Word*, 47, 37.
[51] Mowinckel, *Spirit and Word*, 43–4.

that understanding the significance of the books will depend on knowing about the occasions.

A similar implication arises from Mowinckel's description of the prophetic writings as being composed of messages. The genre of message is characterized by a high degree of dependence on situational context for determining meaning. This is less true of other genres such as narratives, laws, or proverbs. Understanding a message usually depends on determining who said it and why, what audience and situation it is intended to address, and so on. This is why, for example, interpreting the letters of Paul often depends on determining the situation in the church to which the message of the letter is addressed, whereas it is comparatively less important to determine the audience of the stories about Paul in Acts. The assumption that prophetic sayings were originally spoken words and messages makes it necessary to recover their original historical contexts to determine their meaning.

As with the other points of the modern compositional model of Jeremiah, the necessity of reading the "authentic prophetic sayings" in their original historical contexts was advocated by Duhm, but it was given methodological clarity and justification by Mowinckel by means of the new perspectives offered by form criticism. It is from form criticism that Mowinckel draws the belief that the authentic prophetic sayings in Jeremiah are records of spoken words that took the form of messages. That orally delivered speeches stand behind the prophetic literature might be called the first principle of the form- and tradition-critical approaches to the prophetic books. Gunkel states emphatically, "The prophets were not originally writers but speakers."[52] Before Ezekiel or Deutero-Isaiah, all prophecies were originally delivered orally by the prophet before an audience.[53] The story of Jeremiah having Baruch write down the words Yahweh spoke to him in previous years is taken as evidence that the present book contains collections of sayings that were originally publicly spoken.

The characterization of prophetic speeches as "messenger speech" could be called the culmination of the form-critical study of the prophets. The classic statement of the "messenger speech" theory is *Grundformen prophetischer Rede* (1960) by Claus Westermann. Although Westermann's work was published well after Mowinckel's primary contributions to Jeremiah studies (1914, 1946), the historical introduction of his work traces the growth of the messenger speech theory back to Ludwig Köhler's designation of the phrase "thus says the Lord" as the "messenger formula" in his form-critical work on Deutero-Isaiah (1923).[54] Mowinckel does not refer to prophetic speech as messenger speech in his early work on the composition of Jeremiah (1914), but he makes substantial use of the idea in his later work on prophecy and tradition (1946), citing Köhler's observation of the "messenger formula"[55] as an indication that the prophets presented their words as messages.[56] Mowinckel appropriated an idea

---

[52] Gunkel, "Prophets: Oral and Written," 87.

[53] "Wherever it is impossible to conceive of a prophet himself delivering a prophetic word to an audience, such a word certainly belongs to a later time of prophecy." Gunkel, "Prophets: Oral and Written," 87.

[54] Claus Westermann, *Basic Forms of Prophetic Speech* (Philadelphia, PA: Westminster, 1967), 36–40.

[55] Mowinckel, *Spirit and Word*, 130, n. 6.

[56] Mowinckel, *Spirit and Word*, 36. The emphasis on messenger speech found in *Prophecy and Tradition* (1946) does not appear in the earlier *Komposition des Buches Jeremia* (1914). It appears

from form criticism that validated his belief that prophetic sayings were short, orally delivered, and dependent on their historical context for meaning.

The following statement by Mowinckel can serve as a summary of his fundamental belief about the material he isolated as authentic sayings of the prophet (Type A poetry):

> It is an assured result both of the historical-psychological and form-critical investigation … that the prophets did not act as orators with long speeches and a connected development of ideas according to modern logic. … They were Yahweh's messengers who stepped forward with concise, spontaneous, topical, brief messages from Yahweh in a concrete situation.[57]

Mowinckel grounds Duhm's way of treating the (poetic) passages he considered authentic prophetic speech in what he presents as truth about prophetic speech akin to a scientific law: prophetic speech must be short and historically bound (i.e., arising from and addressed to a specific historical/social situation). The law of prophetic speech dictates rules about how it must be interpreted: interpreters must not look for long compositions or logical coherence and they must not look for its significance in the present literary context but only in the (reconstructed) original historical context. These assumptions and the corresponding interpretive approach are not new contributions of Mowinckel but can be seen to be guiding the work of Duhm. What Mowinckel believes he has added is methodological justification—from two main sources: the historical-psychological conclusions of older scholars like Ewald and Duhm and the form-critical conclusions of more recent scholars like Gunkel and Köhler. In Mowinckel's work, Duhm's assumptions are augmented with form-critical investigation and have become the assured results of modern scholarship. With this justification, Mowinckel believes he has transformed Duhm's view of the nature of authentic prophetic speech into an "assured result" of modern scholarship.

Evaluation of Mowinckel's Work

Whether Mowinckel Strengthened the Case for Duhm's Model

Now it can be asked whether Mowinckel was actually able to strengthen Duhm's compositional model with support from form criticism. In support of the foundational element of the model, the belief that the authentic words of the prophet are limited to the poetic passages, the strongest argument the form critics can offer is the one that Duhm and other source critics relied on: that Hebrew prophecy must take the form of poetry because it is the result of ecstatic experiences and thus allegedly prophetic material that does not have poetic form must be inauthentic. The claim that a prophet was unable to speak (or speak as a prophet) except in poetic form seems hard to defend.

---

that Mowinckel appropriated an idea that came to prominence between the works through the work of Koehler and others.

[57] Mowinckel, *Spirit and Word*, 36.

Even if the poetic sections of the prophetic books are best explained as the result of the prophet's ecstatic experiences, there is little reason to deny that the prophet could have given speeches that were not grounded in an ecstatic experience, or perhaps chose to represent the results of an ecstatic experience in a nonpoetic form. That prophetic speech cannot be authentic if it lacks poetic form is a belief that Duhm seems to be among the first to have expected to be taken seriously. It was noted in the overview of Duhm's work that although his whole compositional theory is clearly founded on this belief he never explicitly states it, and it was suggested that this might have due his recognition of its indefensibility. It was reserved for form critics to state it as principle of interpreting prophetic speech that its "real form is poetic and metric"[58] or that the prophets "could only speak in poetic rhythm."[59]

Explaining the poetic form of some of sections of the prophetic books in terms of ecstatic experiences faces its own challenges. As has been pointed out, this explanation must deal with the observation that the usual reason for poetic form is that an author decided to write poetry (or to intentionally craft his or her speech in a way that distinguishes it from naturally occurring speech). Mowinckel and the other form critics attempt to blunt the force of this observation by drawing a close connection between prophets behind the prophetic books and ecstatic prophets in the historical books. This is same expedient Lowth employed almost two centuries earlier in his attempt to explain the poetry in the prophetic books as the result of ecstatic inspiration. However, the justification for this explanation provided by the portrayals of the ecstatics is weak. The fact that certain ecstatics (mostly centuries before Jeremiah) were called "prophets" and played music hardly proves that the poetic form of speeches found in the book of Jeremiah were the result of ecstatic experiences. The new examples of "prophetic speech" the form critics adduced from other ancient Near Eastern religions have the same weakness as justification for claims about the poetry in the prophetic literature. They may suggest that roots in ecstatic experiences are one possible explanation of poetic form in the Hebrew prophetic literature, but to demonstrate that this is the best explanation of any particular poetic passage in the prophetic books would require an argument for why it is more likely explanation than other possible explanations, including that the prophet (or other writer) chose to write in poetic form. The mere fact that some Hebrew ecstatics or Arabic shamans sang or spoke in metric from when they were "prophesying" provides little justification for the claim that material displaying metric form in the prophetic literature must be an authentic record of the speech of a prophet, and even less justification for the claim that material without metric form could not have been based on the speech of a prophet.

It is interesting to observe that Mowinckel appears unwilling to embrace the direct claim that the poetic form in prophetic speech is always the result of ecstatic experience. A comparison of his earlier and later work on the prophets appears to show him growing more willing over time to give the intentional choices of the prophet a greater role in explaining the form of prophetic speech. In his first work on Jeremiah (1914), the prophet is presented as sometimes speaking in the "characteristic style

---

[58] Mowinckel, *Spirit and Word*, 43.
[59] Gunkel, "Israelite Prophecy," 66.

of a *Nabi*, which clearly betrays its origin in ecstasy and enthusiasm" (e.g., 4:5-8, 13; 5:10) but more often clothing his messages in a variety of different forms borrowed from other contexts.[60] This presentation closely follows Gunkel.[61] In a later article (1934), he distinguished between the early prophets who spoke under the impulse of violent frenzies regarded as possession by the Spirit, and the later "reforming prophets" (including Amos, Hosea, Isaiah, and Jeremiah) who spoke out of the more tranquil conviction that they had received Yahweh's word.[62] However, at this point he is still not willing to discount the principle that prophecy is the result of ecstasy. Even though the later prophets display less of the "extreme ecstatic manifestations," he writes, the "ecstatic substratum" is retained and continues to function as a criterion for recognizing that their words come from Yahweh.[63] Most importantly for his work on Jeremiah, Mowinckel confirms his belief that in all of the prophets, poetic form is the spontaneous product of ecstasy (even if it is no longer associated with outward frenzy or music): "the word suddenly comes to them … in a flash, the idea and image are there and involuntarily become rhythmic words."[64] However, in a lecture a few years later (1938), he gives a very different account of prophetic inspiration and its relation to the poetic or metrical form of prophecies:

> The normal occurrence of inspiration within the prophets … is … an attitude of submissive and expectant inward concentration and listening, in which ideas from God arise in their mind and images form in their imagination, their inward eye, and become words to which they themselves then more or less give the clearest and most impressive form, most frequently a rhythmic-poetic one.[65]

In this passage, Mowinckel has broken away not only from the characterization of inspiration as ecstatic frenzy but also from the explanation of poetic form, particularly of metrical speech, as the spontaneous result of this kind of experience.

This late view of Mowinckel's, that the poetic form of prophetic speeches is the result of the prophet's intentional choice for effective communication, has the merit of offering a more plausible account than the explanation of poetic form as the result of ecstatic experience. It provides a more likely account of features of the poetic passages such as artistry, rational arguments, and variety of mood and effect. What Mowinckel appears not to realize is that this account of poetic form cuts at the root of his model of Jeremiah's composition. The model is founded on the identity of prophecy with poetry, and this depends on Lowth's fusion of prophetic inspiration and poetic inspiration as two ways of describing an identical experience—an ecstatic experience that spontaneously overflows as prophetic poetry. The fundamental reason for denying

---

[60] Mowinckel, *Zur Komposition*, 18–19. The idea that the prophets appropriate forms from other settings is a key idea in Gunkel's presentation of the prophets. Gunkel, "Israelite Prophecy," 73–4.

[61] "Prophecy adopted foreign genres in the course of its development … a sign of the zeal with which they contended for their people's hearts." Gunkel, "Prophets: Oral and Written," 99–100.

[62] Mowinckel, "'The Spirit' and the 'Word' in the Pre-Exilic Reforming Prophets," *JBL* 53 (1934): 207.

[63] Mowinckel, "Spirit and Word," 207, 215.

[64] Mowinckel, "Spirit and Word," 215.

[65] Mowinckel, *The Old Testament as the Word of God*, trans. Reidear B. Bjornard (New York: Abingdon Press, 1959), 25.

the authenticity of the prose in Jeremiah is that it lacks the poetic features that would show its origin in an authentic prophetic experience. If the poetic form of Jeremiah's speech was simply chosen for clear and impressive communication, then there is no good reason why he could not have chosen a prose form instead. The logic of denying that Jeremiah could have written in prose form depends on the belief that the poetic form of his authentic speech is not a choice: it is the natural, spontaneous—and thus necessary—form that prophetic (i.e., "inspired") speech must take. Mowinckel had already begun to undermine this belief when he acknowledged the later prophets borrowed the forms from non-prophetic sources to present their messages. It opens up the possibility the prophets could have borrowed nonpoetic forms. Jeremiah, for example, could have chosen to present some of his messages in the form and style of Deuteronomy or of the reformers of his day, perhaps believing that it would add authority or clarity to what he had to say. This admission would obviously remove the foundation from a theory founded explaining the difference between speeches in poetic form and speeches in prose form in terms of authenticity and inauthenticity.

Mowinckel's gradual abandonment of the theory that poetic form (and other characteristics of poetry) in the poetic books are the effects of ecstatic experiences also undermines a second assumption of Duhm's that Mowinckel attempted to establish as assured result of scholarship: that the records of authentic speeches of prophets must be short and unconnected to each other. If as he writes, the prophetic speech of the "reforming prophet" can be characterized as "clear, reasoned, moral and religious exposition,"[66] the claim that it must be concise and without complex development becomes harder to defend.

Mowinckel's other arguments for the brevity and unrelatedness of the units he regards as authentic are not very convincing. He offers an argument from the form of the poetic units in the prophetic books calling attention to "the traditional introductions and conclusions that generally frame the individual saying and identify it as a separate saying (in the book of Amos for example)."[67] Although Mowinckel's work can be praised for bringing methodological order to observations about introductory and conclusive formulas and techniques, his work cannot show that whether the units that he has isolated by observing their introductions and conclusions are were originally short speeches or simply elements in a longer compositions—in an extended poetic section of a prophetic book, they could be called stanzas. The example of Amos that Mowinckel offers is actually a case in point against his argument since the book begins with what is commonly recognized as a lengthy composition (1:2–2:16) made up of poetic stanzas delimited by their use of introductory and conclusive formulas.

Mowinckel's primary argument that these formulas introduce and conclude individual sayings is largely based on the assumption that these "traditional introductions and conclusions" are used in the "traditional" way: that is, the way they are used in speeches in the narratives about prophets outside the prophet books. His arguments come from a section titled "Starting Points: Outside the Prophetic Books," which seeks to determine the form (including length) units in the prophetic books

---

[66] Mowinckel, "Spirit and Word," 208.
[67] Mowinckel, *Spirit and Word*, 43.

must take based on a survey of the "prophetic legends" in historical books and the practices of the Arabic visionaries.[68] The weakness of this argument, that should be evident to a form critic, is that the speeches in these sources have a different context than the speeches in a book like Jeremiah. In their assumed historical contexts when they were first spoken, the prophetic speeches could be short because both speaker and audience were well aware of the context. In the historical books, the speeches can be short because the reader also knows the context from the surrounding narrative. An important feature of the poetic sections in Jeremiah (and in other prophetic books) is that the reader is not provided with a clear historical context from a prose narrative (or a superscription: e.g., "in the fourth year of Jehoiakim"), and thus the poetry must stand on its own. In this situation, the significance (or the context that would provide significance) must be conveyed by the poetry itself (or its literary context) and this requires a quite different form—one that is often longer and more complex in which "traditional" elements must play different roles than they would in historically occurring speech.

Arguments from the form of prophetic speeches in the historical books are also the primary support Mowinckel offers for the third assumption of Duhm's that he attempts to strengthen with form criticism: that is, the necessity of identifying the original historical or social context of the individual sayings. These arguments have the same weaknesses. Mowinckel argues that the authentic poetic speeches must be located in historical setting based on their forms. However, rather than attend to the form of the poetic units themselves, Mowinckel and other form critics attempt to identify the "basic form of prophetic speech" from prophetic speeches in the narrative histories or from the prophetic literature of other ancient Near Eastern religions and then read the short units isolated from the prophetic books as if they took this form. The "basic form" that form critics often insist defines the nature of prophetic speech is the "message form." The idea that prophetic speeches must be messages provides a rationale for why determining their significance depends on recovering the original situation in which they were spoken. That is the nature of a message: it addresses a specific situation.

The problem with these attempts to characterize the poetic material in Jeremiah as messages is that although the speeches of the prophets in the historical narratives usually take the form of messages from Yahweh to specific historical audiences and function as messages in the historical situations their narratives portray, this is rarely the case with the poetic material in the Jeremiah. They are not given a historical setting, they are not presented as messages, and their form does not conform to the conventions of messages (e.g., addressing the intended audience with second person pronouns). It is ironic that the prose speeches in Jeremiah which Mowinckel denies are authentic prophetic speech clearly have all these features. One example of many would be in Jeremiah 7, in which Jeremiah is given a prose message to declare to the people worshipping in the temple: "The word that came to Jeremiah from Yahweh: 'Stand in the gate of Yahweh's house and proclaim there this word, and say, "Hear the word of Yahweh all you men of Judah who enter these gates to worship Yahweh …. Amend your (m.pl.)

---

[68] Mowinckel, *Spirit and Word*, 40–3.

ways and your doings, and I will let you dwell in this place" ' " (7:1-3). This speech and most of the other prose speeches in Jeremiah are clearly presented as messages but form critics perversely insist on characterizing them as sermons all the while insisting that the poetic material, which seldom has any of these characteristics, must be understood as messages.[69] A further irony of the form critics' insistence that the poetic speeches in Jeremiah must be considered to have the same basic nature as the speeches in historical books and their denial that the prose speeches cannot have the same nature is that the prophetic speeches in the historical books are almost all in prose.

The difficulty of accounting for the form critics' insistence on reading the poetic speeches as messages in terms of the messages themselves, reader might wonder if there are other explanations for how they came to this "assured result." One explanation is that this designation supports the historical-critical conviction that to discern the significance of units of text they must be isolated from their literary contexts and relocated in historical contexts—contexts that readers could not guess without the help of historical critics. This conviction could also explain the form critical insistence that the poetic speeches must be read as "prophecies" (i.e., predictions) or "judgments" (i.e., predictions of punishment with a rationale). These descriptions, which are quite apt for many (perhaps most) of the prophetic speeches in the narratives about the prophets in the historical books and in Jeremiah or for the prose speeches in Jeremiah, do not fit for much of the poetic material in Jeremiah.[70] Many poetic depictions of disaster or destruction that appear to be evocations of present situations rather than predictions of future ones (e.g., Jer. 4:29-31, 6:22-26, 8:16, 9:17-19, 14:2-6). However, the belief that authentic prophetic speech must be predictions of the future (because the basic form of prophetic speech is judgment) and that prophetic predictions must be premonitions called forth by historical developments dictates that understanding these passages will depend on identifying the particular historical situation that called them forth, and this will require historical reconstruction.

The form critics recognize that much of the material in the prophetic books does not actually fit these forms. This is the logic of the term "basic form." The basic form expresses the true nature of the prophetic speech even though the prophets significantly modified the forms to adapt them to new circumstances or they creatively appropriated other forms from other social settings to effectively convey their messages or predictions. While this might be possible, overall it seems like a dubious way of dealing with the evidence in the book: first assuming its basic form and nature based on evidence from outside of the book and then providing explanations for why the evidence in the book doesn't usually conform to the assumed form or nature. The "basic form of prophetic speech" risks becoming a Procrustean bed into which all authentic

---

[69] One feature that the poetic speeches do often share with the clear prophetic messages in the prose narratives of the historical books and in the prose narratives and speeches in the book of Jeremiah is the phrase "Thus says Yahweh" Form critics following Köhler call this phrase "the messenger formula." I argue in Chapter 7 that this is a misleading title and that the phrase cannot be relied on to identify the speech in which it occurs as a message.

[70] A quick count of passages in Jeremiah that include the most common characteristic of the judgment speech—"therefore" (*lākēn* or *'al-kēn*) between a reason for judgment and a threat of future judgment—shows that there are almost forty in prose speeches and less than twenty in poetry.

prophecy must be made to fit. In an earlier work, I observed that the form critic Claus Westermann was forced to describe almost every example of what he identified as a basic form of prophetic speech (the "judgment against the nation") in the poetry of the prophetic books in terms of expansions, adaptations, omissions, inversions, and finally the dissolution of the form altogether:[71] I commented, "The difficulty of describing all the animals at the zoo as cows with various expansions, additions, omissions, and inversions might suggest that a 'paradigm shift' is in order."[72]

The Dominance of Mowinckel's Model

Mowinckel's insistence that it is the "assured result" of scholarship that the authentic material in Jeremiah is restricted to units of poetry and that these must be "concise, spontaneous, topical, brief messages from Yahweh in a concrete situation"[73] appears difficult to maintain based on the investigation of the book alone. It was not Mowinckel alone who believed that this was the truth about the composition of Jeremiah, the truth that Duhm had discovered and that biblical scholarship had confirmed. These results—enshrined in his system of Type A (authentic prophetic poetry), Type B (prose narratives), and Type C (inauthentic prose sermons)—provided the basic model for Jeremiah studies for most of the twentieth century. This raises the question of why this theory gained and maintained such prominence.

A basic explanation that helped illuminate Duhm's approach to the book was that it allowed interpreters to privilege the parts of the book that could be made to fit with their aesthetic tastes and theological perspectives. Denying the authenticity of the Type C prose speeches frees the prophet Jeremiah from aspects of the book that do not measure up to Romantic standard of great literature or liberal Protestantism's idea of true religion. This seems to be at least part of what Duhm's compositional theory provides for Mowinckel and other twentieth-century scholars. It was noted, for example, how Mowinckel looks to the Authentic A material for "deeper understanding" as opposed to the understanding of Judaism that can be had been investigating the C material or present form of the book.[74] The case can also be made that form criticism in general represents a revival of Romanticism. Gunkel, for example, referred to himself as a "neo-Romantic"[75] and worked throughout his scholarly career to call biblical criticism back to Herder's Romantic projects and perspective.[76] However, Duhm and

---

[71] Claus Westermann, *Basic Forms of Prophetic Speech* (Philadelphia, PA: Westminster, 1967), 36–40, 176–88, 205–10.

[72] Joseph M. Henderson, "The Structure of Jeremiah 4:5–6:30" (Master's Thesis, Asbury Theological Seminary, 1998), 20.

[73] Mowinckel, *Spirit and Word*, 36.

[74] Mowinckel, *Spirit and Word*, 18, 47.

[75] John Hayes writes that Gunkel pointed to four contemporary movements that provided the background for form criticism: "neo-Romanticism, comparative religion, history of religion, and psychology." John H. Hayes, *An Introduction to Old Testament Study* (Nashville, TN: Abingdon, 1979), 123–4.

[76] Gunkel wrote concerning historical criticism's failure to follow the literary-historical program suggested by Herder: "When will the testament of the great Herder finally be executed?" Hermann Gunkel, "Forward to the Third Edition (1910)," in *Genesis*, trans. and ed. Mark Biddle (Macon, GA: Mercer University Press, 1997). In a way parallel to the work of Hamann and Herder, Gunkel presents his work as intended to combat "the modernizing of exegetes who, without historical

Mowinckel's model continued to dominate Jeremiah studies long after the high point of the influence of liberal theology and Romantic aesthetics on biblical studies around the turn of the twentieth century.

Another explanation of the widespread reliance on Duhm and Mowinckel's model of the composition of Jeremiah is that the assumptions it embodies about relationships between prophecy and the Law, or between literary types and religious outlooks were necessary to maintain what were considered the great achievements of biblical criticism: primarily the Grafian alternative to the Bible's presentation of Israel's history and the Documentary Hypothesis but also many other scholarly discoveries such as Duhm's source critical theory of the book of Isaiah. While the efforts to achieve and maintain these theories may have originally be fueled by theological or literary agendas, as the influence of these systems waned, scholars still desired to defend the achievements in their field. Since belief in the self-presentations of the Biblical books continued among Jewish and Christian believers who believed in the basic truth of their scriptures, the scholarly alternative would continue to need defense especially from scholars from these believing communities.

Mowinckel himself was a Christian who believed that the Bible was the Word of God with "significance for a living Christian faith."[77] In a series of lectures for a nontheological audience, he sought to help Christians come to a correct understanding what it means refer to the Old Testament as inspired, or as revelation. The two options in his presentation are the belief of "the fundamentalist with his dogma of verbal plenary inspiration" and the belief of "the realist with a historical view of the Bible."[78] He begins to explain his theory of inspiration in a chapter titled "The Principle Solution Is a Historical View of the Bible," with the explanation, "All [the prophets] stand with both feet in the midst of a *concrete historical situation*, speaking to their contemporaries out of it."[79] In light of this, Mowinckel says later, interpreting the Bible "includes the duty to obtain the clearest possible picture of 'when, where, who, to whom, how, under what circumstances,' that is, all the concretizing and visualizing of the situation that can be obtained only through historical study."[80] For Mowinckel, it is the essence of a realistic, historical view of the Bible to believe that its words must be interpreted as conditioned by the historical contexts in which they arose. This is the only way that readers can "see the Old Testament as it really is and not to view it … through dogmatic glasses."[81]

In Mowinckel's insistence that the authentic prophetic material in Jeremiah must be poetic, must be short, must be unconnected to the other short prophetic sayings, and must be read in the context in which it was originally spoken, there is a strange new kind of dogmatism. No one must question the "assured result" of scholarship that the book

---

reflection and influenced by rationalism, know nothing of the 'effects' of the *pneuma* and render 'Spirit' a pure abstraction." Quoted in Robert A. Oden, *The Bible without Theology: The Theological Tradition and Alternatives to It*, NVBS (San Francisco, CA: Harper & Row, 1987), 31. From Gunkel's *The Influence of the Holy Spirit* (1888).

[77] On the cover of his book written for popular audiences, the title *The Old Testament as the Word of God* is followed by the words "Its significance for a living Christian faith." Mowinckel, *Word of God*.

[78] Mowinckel, *Word of God*, 125

[79] Mowinckel, *Word of God*, 27 (emphasis original).

[80] Mowinckel, *Word of God*, 47.

[81] Mowinckel, *Word of God*, 5.

of Jeremiah is incoherent. It cannot be read as a book but requires the aid of scholars to explain what the brief, isolated parts of the book meant in their original historical situations. Again and again, Mowinckel must caution against being tempted by signs of meaningful connections or extended compositions; these, he warn, will all turn out to be illusory. His warning is well-expressed by a later scholar: "The exploration of supposed, larger, cumulative, literary entities will not repay the labour."[82] The reader of Jeremiah coming to the book may be surprised to find this figure standing in front of it warning readers against any attempt to find coherence. Her situation can be compared to that of the traveler who on arriving at the famed Emerald City is met at the entrance by the Guardian of the Gate, who insists that before entering the city each traveler must be equipped with a pair of green spectacles which cannot be removed and to which the Guardian alone holds the key. The traveler might be forgiven for wondering what she might see if she entered the city without the glasses. Although she accepts the Guardian's warning that without the spectacles she would be dazzled, she can't help wondering to herself if he might be something of a humbug.

---

[82] William McKane, *A Critical and Exegetical Commentary on Jeremiah*, ICC (Edinburgh: T&T Clark, 1986 and 1996), vol. 1, lxxiv.

Part Three

Moving beyond Duhm: Discerning the Coherence in Jeremiah 2–20

Rhetorical Critics and Jeremiah 2–10

Scholars Look for Literary Coherence and Find Dramatic Portrayal

Failure to Reject Duhm's Approach Results in Failure to Perceive Jeremiah's Unity

Parts One and Two presented the origins and standard form of an approach to the book of Jeremiah that dominated the twentieth century. This approach was argued to be dependent on Romantic conceptions of poetry from the eighteenth century and heavily influenced by currents in late nineteenth-century German thought: particularly theological liberalism, philosophical idealism, and historicism. The aims and methods of this approach promoted the assumptions that the text of the book is fragmentary and unorganized, a jumble of historical documents primarily valued as evidence of the history that lies behind the book. Because this approach achieves its historical reconstruction by breaking the book into parts, removing the parts from their literary contexts, and relocating them in supposed historical contexts, it works against understanding the unity and significance of the book as a whole.

At this point, those who know something of the history of Jeremiah scholarship might find themselves agreeing with at least parts of the foregoing characterization and criticism. However, they would be quick to point out that much has changed since the middle of the twentieth century. Especially in the last quarter of the twentieth century, Jeremiah scholars became dissatisfied with the results of Duhm's approach, often for the reasons given here: the failure to illuminate the present form and significance of the book as a whole. As a result, many have sought to move beyond Duhm's aims of reconstructing the biography of the prophet and the composition of the book to the aims of explaining its present form. Likewise, they have sought to move beyond Duhm's methods to new methods intended to describe the unifying elements of the book. Given these developments summed up by Brueggemann's observation that scholars now aspire "to move beyond the historical-critical categories of Sigmund

Mowinckel and Bernhard Duhm,"[1] one could well ask why the criticism of Duhm's approach has any more than historical interest. If scholarship has indeed moved beyond the approach of Duhm, why not simply draw the veil of charity over the failures and excesses of previous generations and get on with the constructive work of reading the book of Jeremiah?

The reason is that scholarship has in fact not moved beyond Duhm. The argument of Part Three will be that although Jeremiah scholarship has made many advances in the last half century, it has failed to break free from some of the erroneous assumptions and misguided methods that are the heritage of Duhm's approach. In particular, the renewal of interest in the whole book in its present form—a laudable characteristic of scholarship beginning in the late twentieth century—has been held back by the failure to relinquish elements of a method that insisted on treating the book as a conglomeration of incompatible sources. Thus it will be urged here that if scholars truly wish to "move beyond" Duhm, they must be willing question his foundational assumptions, which have guided over a century of Jeremiah scholarship.

The remaining chapters will examine the work of scholars who have attempted to move Jeremiah scholarship forward by offering attempts to describe the unity of the book. The present chapter will describe attempts that can be classified as rhetorical criticism, and the following chapter will describe the attempts of redactional criticism. It will be argued that each attempt falls short because of its failure to break free from parts of Duhm's model. In broad strokes, the rhetorical critics failed to break free from Duhm's project of reconstructing the historical Jeremiah (represented by Skinner's biography), and the redaction critics failed to break free from Duhm's source-critical assumption (embedded in Mowinckel's compositional model) that poetry must predate prose. At the same time, both redactional and rhetorical approaches have uncovered a feature of the text which both undermines the assumptions of Duhm and points the way forward to a better understanding of the unity of the book: dramatic presentation. These two chapters will illustrate the successes and failures of the rhetorical and redactional approaches by evaluating their investigations of Jeremiah 2–10 and 11–20: portions of Jeremiah which Duhm, Mowinckel, and Skinner assumed to be disorganized collections of authentic poetic materials from the prophet's early ministry mixed together with prose added by later editors. The final chapter will argue that the unity of Jeremiah 2–10 and 11–20 can only be seen by laying aside Duhm's biographical aims and source-critical assumptions.

The Dominance and Decline of Historical-Critical Aims

Before turning directly to the scholarly approaches that attempted to give accounts of the unity of the book, a brief historical survey will illustrate how these new approaches are characteristic of a shift in Jeremiah studies, and in biblical studies as a whole, which characterized the last decades of the twentieth century. The shift can be illustrated

---

[1]   Walter Brueggemann, "Preface," in *Reading the Book of Jeremiah: A Search for Coherence*, ed. Martin Kessler (Winona Lake, IN: Eisenbrauns, 2004), ix.

by considering the difference between two books on Jeremiah published by the same author, Leo Purdue, the first in 1984 and the second in 1994.

The Dominant Historical-Critical Approach in the Twentieth Century

In 1984 Perdue and Kovacs published, *A Prophet to the Nations*, a collection of representative essays on Jeremiah from the previous decades. Of the twenty-two essays, all but two were first published after 1950 and most (thirteen) come from the 1960s and 1970s.[2] These essays demonstrate the dominance of the historical-critical approach to Jeremiah pioneered by Duhm for most of the twentieth century. The titles of the section groupings reveal that the contributors are working within the framework of the biographical and compositional models laid out by Skinner and Mowinckel. The first eight essays are in sections titled "The Date of Jeremiah's Call," "Jeremiah, Deuteronomy, and the Reform of Josiah," and "The Foe from the North." These issues arise from the attempt to reconstruct the early years of Jeremiah's ministry using the poetry of Jeremiah 2–20 as evidence—in essence, Skinner's (and Duhm's) biographical project. The next six essays are in a section titled "The Composition of Jeremiah." These essays discuss the relationships between the three types of material identified by Mowinckel as A, B, and C.[3] A section of six essays follows titled "The Quest for the Historical Jeremiah: Call and Confessions"—a return to the biographical approach. The final two essays are in a section titled "New Directions in Jeremiah Research," and certainly several of the book's authors attempt to break away from the standard approach and pursue new directions, and each of them does have something new to offer. Still, by and large, the essays share the biographical and compositional aims of the standard historical-critical approach and to a large degree its methodological approaches and foundational assumptions as well. Thus the collection is a testament to the dominance of Duhm's approach to Jeremiah throughout the majority of the twentieth century.[4]

The interests and aims of the essays in Perdue and Kovac's anthology help to explain the attraction of the standard approach throughout the twentieth century. Given their aims, the assumption inherent in the standard approach that the book of Jeremiah is fragmentary, poorly organized, and primarily valuable for reconstructing ancient history did not seem a serious detraction from the value of the book. Scholars who followed the standard approach might be puzzled with the objection that their approach treated the book as primarily useful for historical evidence, if it was implied that they minimized the book's literary or theological value. They could respond that they were helping to recover the great poetry of Jeremiah and that good theology is

---

[2] Leo G. Perdue and Brian W. Kovacs, *A Prophet to the Nations: Essays in Jeremiah Studies* (Winona Lake, IN: Eisenbrauns, 1984).

[3] Four of them begin with paragraphs on Duhm and Mowinckel.

[4] The introductory essay by Perdue, "Jeremiah in Modern Research: Approaches and Issues," deals with the same biographical and compositional issues. Perdue and Kovacs, *Prophet to the Nations*, 1–32. As has been noted, it was a standard practice in the twentieth century to begin commentaries on Jeremiah with introductions containing sections on the biography of the prophet and the composition of the book.

based on the facts of history. This view of theology's dependence on reconstructed history characterized the classic Liberalism of the early twentieth century (as was shown in previous chapters), and it could be demonstrated that a similar view was also characteristic of the neoorthodox theology offered as an alternative to liberalism. Thus for much of the century, neither the dominant theological perspectives nor the dominant exegetical perspectives gave much reason for dissatisfaction with the results of the standard historical-critical approach to Jeremiah. Instead the historical reconstructions of the life of the prophet and of the growth of the tradition were considered valuable (perhaps essential) contributions to theological reflection and historical scholarship, and the theologians and exegetes who grounded their work in these historical reconstructions had a strong belief in (and a strong interest in maintaining) the validity of the approach that enabled them.

The "Collapse of History" in the Last Decades of the Twentieth Century

Although the standard historical-critical approach to Jeremiah has continued to exert its influence throughout the twentieth century and into the twenty-first, there is no doubt that in the last decades of the twentieth century the dominant approach to Jeremiah faced a significant challenge as did the historical-critical approach to the Bible in general. The nature of this new situation in Jeremiah studies and biblical studies is suggested in the title of a book Leo Perdue published in 1994—a decade after the anthology he edited. *The Collapse of History* is a study of what was the current state of Old Testament theology using Jeremiah scholarship for its primary examples.[5] Perdue estimates that "for at least a generation ... active revolt against the domination of history and historical method has been underway."[6] "Revolt" is perhaps too strong of a word, but his estimation that a shift had begun to occur about a generation earlier (i.e., in the 1960s and 1970s) is sound. What actually occurred is better described by the word "collapse" in his title. There was a growing sense that the historical-critical method had collapsed under its own weight, or simply run out of steam, leaving biblical scholarship to cast about for viable alternatives. The collapse of the dominant method explains the resulting state of methodological "fragmentation" or "pluralism" Perdue describes.[7] There had been no unified attack on the historical method, nor had a distinct alternative arisen that appeared likely to replace the standard approach. The central results of the historical-critical approach were not convincingly refuted but continued to serve as the foundational assumptions for prominent scholarship. There was, however, a sense that the standard approaches were yielding diminishing returns and that maintaining the increasingly complex and convoluted system necessary to justify the increasingly hypothetical and trivial results was no longer worth the effort. In Jeremiah studies, the fragmentation of the text and the preponderance of historical concerns had become sources of dissatisfaction. This led to calls to move beyond the

---

[5] Leo G. Perdue, *The Collapse of History: Reconstructing Old Testament Theology* (Minneapolis, MN: Fortress, 1994).

[6] Perdue, *Collapse of History*, 4.

[7] Perdue, *Collapse of History*, 5–6.

standard historical-critical approaches to approaches that would illumine the structure and agenda of the present form of the text.

Two of the most promising new approaches that appeared in the last decades of the twentieth century were rhetorical criticism and redaction criticism. The remainder of this chapter will offer a critique of rhetorical criticism by evaluating the results of rhetorical analyses of Jeremiah 2–10. The following chapter will offer a critique of redaction criticism by evaluating the results of redaction analyses of Jeremiah 11–20.

The Rhetorical Approach to Jeremiah: An Alternative to the Standard Approach

The advent of rhetorical criticism in Old Testament studies is often associated with James Muilenburg's 1968 SBL presidential address "Form Criticism and Beyond."[8] Muilenburg urged attention to the literary features of texts that he believed were the result of intentional artistry. This represented a significant challenge to form criticism's attempt to explain these features as formal conventions that gave evidence of the original settings of the speech forms. He also advocated going beyond form criticism's interest in small units isolated by their formal patterns and introductory and conclusive formulas. Instead, he encouraged interpreters to think of the units isolated by literary analysis as component parts of larger literary compositions—not individual literary fragments. The introductory and conclusive formulas, he understood to be rhetorical devices that not only mark the boundaries of compositional units but also link them with other units to form literary compositions. Muilenburg's work thus reopened the possibility of extended literary compositions and meaningful coherence in Jeremiah that form-critical approaches like Mowinckel's had denied. More fundamentally, he presented an alternative to the Romantic theory that poetry is the automatic product of poetic natures or poetic experiences. In his understanding, poetry is primarily the result of intentional artistry.

Muilenburg's rhetorical approach had a wide influence on Jeremiah studies. His special interest in the book is evidenced by the number of examples in his presidential address drawn from Jeremiah, as well as by several articles he wrote on the book. His commentary on Isaiah 40–66 provides a model for rhetorical criticism of prophetic poetry with many features easily applicable to interpretation of Jeremiah.[9] Although he never finished his commentary on Jeremiah,[10] two of his students, Jack Lundbom and William Holladay, have each contributed a major work on the rhetorical analysis of

---

[8] Delivered at the SBL national convention on December 18, 1968, at the University of California, Berkeley; published as James Muilenburg, "Form Criticism and Beyond," *JBL* 88 (1969): 1–18. Muilenburg's address and Childs' *Biblical Theology in Crisis* (1970) are the most obvious historical markers of the beginning of the shift of emphasis toward the final form of the text that marked biblical studies in the last decades of the twentieth century.

[9] James Muilenburg, "Isaiah 40–66," in *IB*, ed. George A. Buttrick (New York: Abingdon, 1956).

[10] His student Jack Lundbom writes, "Muilenburg hoped in his retirement years to write a Jeremiah commentary, but managed only a very rough draft of chapters 1–20, before giving up the work." Jack Lundbom, *Jeremiah 1–20: A New Translation with Introduction and Commentary*, AB 21A (New York: Doubleday, 1999), xv.

Jeremiah and a commentary on Jeremiah employing a rhetorical approach. However, although they have uncovered significant evidence of unity and intentional artistry, their concern to maximize the amount of authentic material has kept them from a decisive break with the biographical approach to the book.

Lundbom's 1975 work, *Jeremiah: A Study in Ancient Hebrew Rhetoric*,[11] follows Muilenburg's method of first isolating and then relating literary units on the basis of rhetorical devices. His study confines itself to two primary devices, chiasmus and inclusion, which he finds in a great variety of passages both large and small. In his view, the whole of chs 1–20 is held together by an intricate set of verbal recurrences. Holladay's 1976 work, *The Architecture of Jeremiah 1–20*,[12] likewise finds an elaborate artistic unity in the material that previous scholarship often regarded as chaotic. In contrast to Lundbom's limited focus, Holladay finds a great variety of linking devices such as catchwords, assonance, alliteration, and many of his own invention such as "adjunction by pre-existing association."[13] Along with his rhetorical analysis, Holladay also offers complex redactional theories in which Jeremiah himself is the primary redactor of several editions of his work.

The argument in both Lundbom's and Holladay's work that Jeremiah is largely responsible not only for the poetry but also for much of the prose of the book is intended as challenge to the compositional theories like those of Duhm, Mowinckel, and Skinner which deny the authenticity of most of the prose. The primary argument they employ against these earlier theories is that the verbal subtleties and compositional complexity they observe in the text are indications of a rhetorical skill best attributed to Jeremiah (or Baruch). Prose passages that display this artistry and take part the complex designs with poetic passages should thus be attributed to Jeremiah. Their arguments against the conclusions of scholars like Skinner and Duhm have an unintended irony. The rhetorical critics attempt to counter the standard compositional theory ends up putting rhetorical criticism at the service of primary aim of that theory: to recover the biography of the prophet behind the book. The central concern remains establishing the authenticity passages—that is, their value for biographical reconstruction. In this way, the work of these rhetorical critics can be seen not as a reversal of the biographical approach but rather as a continuation.

Holladay's work in particular is marked by his concentration on the historical prophet's life and his confidence that this can be reconstructed. His first work on Jeremiah was in fact a biography of the prophet,[14] and he begins his monumental commentary declaring his conviction that "the data for reconstruction of the chronology of Jeremiah's career, and for the establishment of fairly secure settings for his words and actions, are attainable."[15] Holladay's readiness to name the year, and often the very

---

[11] Jack Lundbom, *Jeremiah: A Study in Ancient Hebrew Rhetoric*, 2nd ed. (Winona Lake, IN: Eisenbrauns, 1997).

[12] William Lee Holladay, *The Architecture of Jeremiah 1–20* (Cranbury, NJ: Associated University Presses, 1976).

[13] Holladay, *Architecture of Jeremiah*, 170.

[14] William Lee Holladay, *Jeremiah: Spokesman Out of Time* (Philadelphia, PA: United Church Press, 1974).

[15] William Lee Holladay, *Jeremiah 1: A Commentary on the Book of the Prophet Jeremiah, Chapters 1–25*, Hermeneia (Philadelphia, PA: Fortress, 1986), 1.

month, in which verses (or even parts of verses!) were first spoken or recorded goes beyond the audacity of Skinner's speculations and may be without parallel in Jeremiah scholarship. Like Skinner, Holladay constructs a complex historical framework for linking pieces of the text to externally established historical dates. Central elements in Holladay's framework include his theories that Jeremiah often delivered his speeches at septennial readings of Deuteronomy and that the two versions of the scroll dictated to Baruch (the *Urrolle* of ch. 36) can be distinguished in the text.[16] Although Holladay's biographical reconstruction is novel and is set in opposition to earlier biographies at several points,[17] it is evident that he is in basic agreement with aims and methods that characterized earlier biographical approaches like those of Duhm and Skinner. Even in his attempts to overturn the assumption that the prose speeches are inauthentic, Holladay relies on the assumptions and methods of the standard approach he seeks to oppose: he uses the assumed authenticity of the poetry as the measure of the authenticity of the prose.[18] The irony of Holladay's approach is not only that he ends up reinforcing the approach of those whose conclusions he opposes, but that he has done so using the tools of an approach (rhetorical criticism) that offered him an alternative to the standard approach. By its very nature, rhetorical analysis should direct attention to the artistry of the text and to the effect it has on its audience rather than to the life of the artist who crafted it.

Dramatic Presentation in Jeremiah 2–10

Shifts in Speaker and Audience as Evidence of Dramatic Presentation

Although Holladay's commitment to the biographical approach prevented him from making the break from the standard compositional approach that rhetorical criticism promised, the intense scrutiny to which he subjected the book brought attention to many of its overlooked features, and his rhetorical perspective made possible new estimates of the significance of these features. Holladay's sustained observation of one of these features has radical implications for understanding the nature of the book of Jeremiah. This feature is the frequent shifts between speakers and audiences. Throughout much of the book, particularly in the passages identified as poetic (such as the majority of Jeremiah 2–10), Holladay demonstrates that the text can be divided into speeches by observing who is speaking to whom. The identity of the speakers and audiences is sometimes indicated by a superscription, sometimes by the content (which would only be appropriate to one speaker), and often by the use of personal

---

[16] Holladay, *Jeremiah 1*, 1–5.

[17] Most notably, Holladay, like Philip Hyatt before him, argues for a "low chronology" for Jeremiah's biography in which 627 ("the thirteenth year of Josiah," Jer. 1:2) is the date of Jeremiah's birth, not the beginning of his ministry. His ministry, and first recorded words, would then commence late in Josiah's reign, well after the reform of 622. Holladay, *Spokesman out of Time*, 17–22.

[18] William Lee Holladay, "Prototypes and Copies: A New Approach to the Poetry-Prose Problem in the Book of Jeremiah," *JBL* 79 (1960): 351–67; William Lee Holladay, "A Fresh Look at 'Source B' and 'Source C' in Jeremiah," *VT* 25 (1975): 394–412.

pronouns.[19] In source- and form-critical studies, these shifts had often been relied on as indicators of seams between disparate sources or original prophetic speeches. Holladay's rhetorical approach showed that these shifts could be intentional features and not necessarily indications of separate sources. In his 1986 commentary, he observed about Jeremiah 4–10, "Analysis suggests that the interchange of speakers plays a role in the poetic structure of the units."[20] He built on his observation by offering carefully argued distinctions between speakers and presenting his identifications of speakers beside the speeches in the text in the manner of a dramatic script. For example, Jer. 8:20-22a appears as:

> PEOPLE: The harvest is past, the summer is gone …
> JEREMIAH: By the shattering of my fair people I am shattered …
> YAHWEH: Is there no Balm in Gilead? . . .[21]

Although the shifts in speaker and the possibility of intentional dramatic presentation had not totally escaped consideration in previous scholarship, Holladay is correct to note that the interchange of speakers had "not been dealt with systematically by the commentators heretofore."[22] Holladay's suggestion that the shifts in speaker and audience, a feature of the text more obvious than the shifts between poetry and prose, are the result of intentional dramatic portrayal opens up new possibilities for understanding the basic nature of the text. At the same time, it calls into question central assumptions about the nature of the text that are the heritage of the standard historical approach. Unfortunately, Holladay remained so committed to these older assumptions and to the biographical approach they facilitate that he was unable to follow out the implications of his discovery.

The evidence of dramatic portrayal challenges the standard historical approach. This challenge can be illustrated by observing the incompatibility of the standard biographical approach to Jeremiah 2–10 and an approach that recognizes the extent of dramatic portrayal in these chapters. The conflict is striking in Holladay's interpretation of Jeremiah 2–10. On the one hand, Holladay finds evidence of extensive dramatic portrayal. On the other, Holladay uses isolated speeches as bit of historical evidence for reconstructing Jeremiah's early life. Holladay comes to Jeremiah 2–10 in the role of the historical critic like a detective looking for any clues that might betray when each speech was spoken by Jeremiah, as well as where, and to whom. In Jer. 4:4-31, for example, he relies on theories concerning the battle of Carchemish, the "great drought," and the burning of the first scroll in order to date 4:5-8, 13-18, and 29-31 in the early summer of 605; 4:9-12 in December 601;

---

[19] The gender and number of the personal pronouns, whether independent, attached to prepositions, or indicated by verbal forms, are often used to identify the audience (e.g., whether f.s. or m.pl.). Unfortunately, this feature is difficult to convey in English translations since standard English does not distinguish gender and number in the second person.

[20] Holladay, *Jeremiah 1*, 137.

[21] Jer. 8:20-22a. Holladay, *Jeremiah 1*, 288. Holladay follows the practice used to indicate speakers in some versions of the Song of Solomon.

[22] Holladay, *Jeremiah 1*, 137. In his opinion, Jeremiah's introduction of dramatic dialogue into his prophetic oracles was an advance comparable to the advances made in Greek drama by Sophocles.

and 4:19-28 in the early weeks of 600.[23] Holladay the historical biographer labors to provide similarly precise dates for the rest of 4–10. Yet for these same chapters, Holladay the rhetorical critic argues that the integrated structure of the whole takes the form of an extended chiasm[24] and that this poetry is characterized by dramatic presentation.[25]

The Nature of Dramatic Portrayal

To assert that passages of Jeremiah are characterized by intentional dramatic portrayal means that the shifts in speaker can be understood as representing the interchange of speeches in a dialogue. Although dialogue is a good indicator of dramatic portrayal, it is not its essential characteristic (there may also be dramatic monologue). What makes a work dramatic is that it has been artfully contrived to portray persons or situations by means of creating speeches that represent what those persons might have said in those situations. The speeches are written in a way that the competent reader can infer the situation and the speaker from the text alone. A familiar example of dramatic portrayal is Browning's poem "My Last Duchess." The first line, "That's my last Duchess painted on the wall," is carefully crafted to reveal a speaker (a duke), a situation (showing a painting), and an audience (someone who does not recognize the subject of the painting). Similarly, the first line of Song of Solomon, "Let him kiss me with the kisses of his mouth, for your love is better than wine," dramatically presents a woman addressing her (presumably absent) lover. These dramatic speeches have the appearance of reports of actual speech because they are created to represent actual speech. But unlike reports of actual speech, the dramatic speakers and situations that provide the interpretive contexts of these speeches are not the historical speakers and their situations but the persons and situations that the speeches were created (or employed) to portray.

Examples of Dramatic Speech in Jeremiah 2–10

A clear example of dramatic portrayal occurs in Jeremiah 6:4-6, which pictures generals launching their plans to destroy Jerusalem:[26]

> "Prepare for war against her;
> > Up, and let us attack at noon!"
> "[Too bad], the day is declining,
> > The shadows of evening lengthen."

---

[23] Holladay, *Jeremiah 1*, 152.

[24] He argues that the major units of 4:5–6:30 follow the pattern A, B, C, D, A′, C′, B′, apparently a kind of chiasm with a twist. Holladay, *Jeremiah 1*, 136.

[25] Holladay, *Jeremiah 1*, 137–8.

[26] Several of the examples in this section are based on analysis I did for my master's thesis. Henderson, "The Structure of Jeremiah 4:5–6:30." An earlier form of the central section of this chapter was published as Joseph M. Henderson, "Jeremiah 2–10 as a Unified Literary Composition: Evidence of Dramatic Portrayal and Narrative Progression," in *Uprooting and Planting: Essays on Jeremiah for Leslie Allen*, ed. John Goldingay, LHB/OTS 459 (New York: T&T Clark, 2007), 116–52.

"Up and let us attack at night,
    And destroy her palaces."[27]

These speeches transport the reader to the enemy camp at the decisive moment just before the city is stormed. They portray ruthless invaders who are so eager to destroy the city that they will even break military convention to attack at night. Treating these speeches as historical reports of the authentic speech of Babylonian generals would be absurd. The most obvious clue is the poetic form (the commands of generals do not usually emerge as poetry),[28] but it is also worth noting the stylized way that these speeches represent the events of a whole day in one compressed dialogue (i.e., the first speech represents the situation before noon and the other two, after dusk). These speeches are clearly not a report of a spy from Jerusalem who has sneaked into the enemy council. They are the creation of a poet who has carefully crafted them to conjure up the scene and the feeling of doom in the imagination of the readers. Holladay, like most scholars, treats this dramatic presentation as a creative way that Jeremiah chose to warn the people of Jerusalem of what might come in the future.[29] Although this interpretation is possible, it should be noted that there is nothing in the passage that would identify Jeremiah as the speaker or would indicate that it refers to a future event. (Holladay's interpretation comes not from the passage but from the extrinsic idea that prophetic speeches take the form of God's messages about the future delivered by the prophet.) The primary effect of the passage does not depend on identifying who originally spoke or wrote the lines and when, but on identifying the dramatic speakers and situation: the enemy generals during a siege.

In another example, the dramatic effect depends on the reader or hearer identifying the dramatic speaker and situation. Jer. 4:19-21 presents an anguished cry in the midst of an enemy invasion:

[My womb, my womb! I writhe as in birth pangs.][30]
    Oh, the walls of my heart!
    My heart is beating wildly;
I cannot keep silent,
for I hear the sound of the trumpet,
    the alarm of war.
Disaster overtakes disaster,
    the whole land is laid waste.
Suddenly my tents are destroyed,
    my curtains in a moment.

---

[27] All citations from Jeremiah are based on the NRSV. "The LORD" has been regularly emended to "Yahweh" without note. All other emendations are noted by square brackets.

[28] It appears that the whole exchange may have a chiastic form A-B-C-C′-B′-A′ with the parallelism of the B line ("Up and let us attack at _____") especially obvious. If this is the case, it would provide further evidence that the dialogue is not naturally occurring but artistically crafted.

[29] Holladay, *Jeremiah 1*, 205.

[30] My translation. For *mēʿeh* translated "womb," see Gen. 25:23, Ruth 1:11, Ps. 71:6, and Isa. 49:1. For *ḥûl* translated as "writhing in childbirth," see Isa. 26:17, 45:10, 51:2.

How long must I see the standard,
>   and hear the sound of the trumpet?

In previous scholarship, the speaker of this cry has routinely been assumed to be Jeremiah. In fact, the passage has served as a central example of several different theories of prophetic speech. In the Romantic view, it is taken as an example of the sensitive poet's sublime experiences. Lowth quotes it as an example of the sublime expression of terror, one remarkable for its "wonderful force and enthusiasm."[31] In the comparative-religions or psychological view, the passage is taken as evidence of the ecstatic nature of prophecy. Gunkel calls this passage "a moving description of how the fearful vision pursued [Jeremiah], and how the human instrument, too weak to bear the enormous weight of the divine message, had to succumb to it."[32]

However, it is not at all clear that Jeremiah is the speaker or that it is a vision of the future. The text does not name him as the speaker, and there are several strong indications that the speaker is actually Daughter Jerusalem (i.e., the city pictured as a woman).[33] Jerusalem is explicitly named as the addressee of the preceding speech ("announce to Jerusalem," 4:16), which concludes by directly addressing her: "This is your (f.s.) doom, and it is bitter; it has reached your (f.s.) very heart" (4:18). Her answering cry picks up the word "heart" ("Oh the walls of my heart," 4:19) and combines it with the feminine imagery of womb and birth pangs. The cues alerting the reader that a woman speaks continue with the domestic vocabulary of "curtains" and "tents" (4:20), evoking the conventional sphere of women. These words recur in a closely parallel speech later in the book (10:19-20).[34] In this later speech, which also follows an address to a woman (10:17), the speaker refers to "my children," who could easily be the inhabitants of Jerusalem pictured as her children, but are unlikely to be the children of the childless prophet.[35] The only reason to identify Jeremiah as the speaker of the cry in 4:19-21 is the presupposition that he speaks all of the poetry (or all of the poetry not clearly spoken by Yahweh). Likewise, the only reason to identify the terror and anguish of the cry as the result of a visionary experience is the presumption that prophetic speech must be about the future. Without this presumption, the terror and anguish could naturally be read as provoked by a present military invasion. The

[31] Robert Lowth, *Lectures on the Sacred Poetry of the Hebrews*, trans. G. Gregory (Boston, MA: Joseph T. Buckingham, 1815), 386–7.

[32] He adds, "When the ecstasy left him, he felt as though he had been beaten by clubs … [the] condition of *stupefaction*." Hermann Gunkel, "The Israelite Prophecy from the Time of Amos," in *Twentieth Century Theology in the Making*, ed. Jaroslav Pelikan (New York: Collins, 1969), 52.

[33] Henderson, "The Structure of Jeremiah 4:5–6:30," 37–8. Three other studies identifying Lady Jerusalem as the speaker of these two speeches are Kenro Kumaki, "A New Look at Jer. 4:19–22 and Jer. 10:19–20," *AJBI* 8 (1982): 113–22; Barbara Bakke Kaiser, "Poet as 'Female Impersonator': The Image of Daughter Zion as Speaker in Biblical Poems of Suffering," *JR* 67 (1987): 164–82. Mark E. Biddle, *Polyphony and Symphony in Prophetic Literature: Rereading Jeremiah 7–20* (Macon, GA: Mercer University Press, 1996), 20–1.

[34] Cf. the speech to the desolate woman Zion in Isaiah 54 with its references to her children [54:1], tents, and curtains [54:2].

[35] In Yahweh's rebuke (4:22), which follows Jerusalem's cry (4:19-21), he refers to the people as "stupid children." It is likely that this is an oblique reproach of their mother, Jerusalem, who raised them in such a way that "they are skilled at doing evil, but do not know how to do good" (4:22). Cf. 5:7aβ: "Your (f.s.) children have forsaken me."

passage dramatically portrays the invasion of Jerusalem by creating a speech for the city that sounds like a woman crying out over the destruction of her home.

Mark Biddle, who identifies Jerusalem as the speaker of both passages, notes that although Timothy Polk recognizes the evidence that Jerusalem speaks, he persists in identifying Jeremiah as the speaker. Biddle conjectures, "Polk's thesis seems to be that, since the tradition identifies the prophet Jeremiah as the immediate human agent of all the speech contained in the book, every first person language specimen involves, to some degree or on some level, the prophetic persona." To Polk's approach, he poses an incisive question: "Can the integrity of distinct voices survive such a program?"[36] Biddle's question applies with greater force to scholars who follow the standard historical approach to Jeremiah, which mandates that poetry must be authentic prophetic speech and that prophetic speech must take the form of messages spoken by the prophet. The problem is especially pronounced for Holladay. His perception of dramatic presentation in Jeremiah can be credited with his usual care to preserve the "integrity of distinct voices," but his commitment to the biographical approach and its assumptions about prophetic speech can be blamed for his failure to recognize Jerusalem as the speaker of this passage.

Yahweh's Speech as Dramatic Speech

At this point, those committed to the standard approach, which understands the poetry of Jeremiah 2–10 as a collection of prophetic oracles, might be willing to concede that the voices of enemy generals or Lady Jerusalem can be heard in the passages just discussed. However, they would be quick to point out that these two passages are rare exceptions in a section dominated by speeches in which the first person speaker is clearly Yahweh. Given the preponderance of speeches that follow the expected form of prophetic speeches—Yahweh's warnings, spoken through his prophet—they would suggest that in these two passages, the prophet employs an unusual poetic technique for warning the people of the coming destruction of Jerusalem. They could point to these two passages as examples of how prophets adopted a great variety of borrowed forms to fulfill the purpose of the basic form of prophetic speech.

This line of argument, which can be named the "basic forms of prophetic speech" approach,[37] might be convincing if Yahweh's speeches in Jeremiah 2–10 fulfilled the expectations this approach raises. In fact, they do not. This can be illustrated by examining the expectations raised by the designation of the basic forms of prophetic speech as "messenger speech."[38] As was shown above, this designation, which received its classic statement in Claus Westermann's form-critical work, was adopted by

---

[36] Biddle, *Polyphony and Symphony*, 21, n. 11.

[37] Westermann notes that it was Gunkel who pioneered this approach, one which distinguishes between the basic form and borrowed (or foreign) forms. Claus Westermann, *Basic Forms of Prophetic Speech* (Philadelphia, PA: Westminster, 1967), 26.

[38] Westermann identifies several basic forms of prophetic speech (including the judgment speech to an individual, the judgment speech to the nation, the judgment speech to a foreign nation, and the salvation speech to the nation); however, all of these have the characteristics of being messenger speech and of being an announcement about the future. Westermann, *Basic Forms of Prophetic Speech*, 94–5.

Mowinckel to describe the poetry of Jeremiah. It added support to his ideas that the units of prophetic speech are short and that they receive their significance when they are read in light of their original historical context (the situation which provoked the message or which it addresses). These assumptions, in turn, facilitated the biographical approach to the poetry of Jeremiah. They allowed scholars from Duhm to Skinner to Holladay to use isolated units of Jeremiah's poetry as historical evidence for reconstructing his biography. Westermann's theory that the message form was the distinguishing characteristic of prophetic speech provided ready-made answers to the questions of speaker, audience, and situation: Yahweh's speeches were orally delivered to the people or leaders of Judah by Jeremiah in his role as Yahweh's messenger. For Yahweh's speeches in Jeremiah 2–10, however, three features of the text resist the expectations about speaker and audience raised by the "messenger speech" theory. First, Yahweh's speeches are seldom addressed directly to the people or leaders. Second, many of Yahweh's speeches either answer or are answered by the speeches of other speakers to form stylized dialogues. Third, Yahweh's speeches can be distinguished from Jeremiah's speeches, which often express a divergent perspective. Observation of these three features will suggest that in Yahweh's speeches he is portrayed as speaking without the mediation of Jeremiah as a messenger.

Yahweh's Speech: Unexpected Addressees

The first feature of Yahweh's poetic speeches that does not fit the messenger speech model is that few of them are addressed to Jeremiah's contemporaries in Judah. This is in contrast to the prose speeches which actually are mostly presented as messages from Yahweh addressed to the leaders or people of Judah.[39] In the prose messenger speeches, the audience is clear from the second masculine plural verb forms and pronominal suffixes. For example: "Amend your (m.pl.) ways and your (m.pl.) doings and let me live with you (m.pl.) in this place" (7:3) and "I will cast you (m.pl.) out of my sight as I cast out all your (m.pl.) kinsfolk, all the offspring of Ephraim" (7:15). It would be evident from these verses themselves that Yahweh addresses the men of Judah even if this were not also specified in the introduction (7:1-2), in which Yahweh explicitly commands Jeremiah to deliver this message to the men of Judah in the temple gate. Unlike these prose speeches, the poetic speeches of Jeremiah 2–10 for the most part lack this kind of introduction, and there are only a few second masculine plural forms that might refer to the people of Judah.[40] In spite of this, interpreters regularly assume that the poetry speeches must represent messages to the people of Judah like the prose speeches.[41]

---

[39] However, many are addressed to Jeremiah and have the form of words *about* the people.

[40] Passages which might be addressed directly to the people of Judah include: Jer. 2:28 (m.s.); 4:3-4; 5:18 (possibly prose), 31b; 8:8, 17; 9:3 (ET 9:4). Some passages which could be addressed to Judah are embedded in speeches addressed to other audiences: 4:5b-6 and 5:21-22, 26 are in speeches addressed to messengers; 6:16-17 is in a speech addressed to the nations or the earth (6:18-19).

[41] Of course, these same interpreters regularly assume that many of the messages in prose cannot be actual messages delivered by Jeremiah.

One group of poetic speeches whose addressees indicate that they are better understood as dramatic representations than as messenger speech are those with feminine singular addressees.[42] In chs 4–6 the addressee is identified as Jerusalem (4:16, 5:1, 6:8) or Daughter Zion (4:31, 6:23),[43] but in chs 2 and 3 the woman addressed seems to be Israel (2:3, 14, 26, 31; 3:6-10, 20).[44] In the past, these female characters have been treated as mere metaphors for the city or country they represent, and the addressing them has been considered merely an oblique way of addressing the people of Judah. The inadequacy of this approach becomes apparent when it is observed that in the text these women have distinct characters with personal opinions (2:25), emotions (4:19), wishes (4:14), and responsibilities (2:35). They have clothes (2:34, 4:30), homes (4:20, 10:20), belongings (10:17), lovers (2:25, 4:25), and children (10:20).[45] Most important in terms of dramatic presentation, they have speaking parts. Israel, Yahweh's wayward bride, engages in an extended dispute with him (2:17-25, 33-37),[46] and Jerusalem, the adulteress whose lovers have turned on her, cries out first in panic (4:19-21, 31b) and then afterward in pain and grief (10:19-20). Yahweh's speeches addressed to these women bring to life climactic moments in his relationships with them. It is not impossible that Jeremiah performed these dramatic speeches for the people of Judah, impersonating the outraged husband and his unrepentant wife. However, in the text, the operative setting of these speeches is not a historical situation in the life of Jeremiah but a dramatic situation in the life of Yahweh and his bride.

Another set of speeches whose addressees do not fit the messenger model are the principal speeches of chs 4–6, each of which begins with a cluster of imperatives. These speeches are often considered prime examples of prophetic speech because they concern the onslaught of the northern foe that the historical Jeremiah prophesied would come. At first glance, the masculine plural form of the introductory imperatives might be thought to indicate that they are messages addressed to the men of Judah.

> 4:5: Declare in Judah, and proclaim in Jerusalem ...
> 4:16: [Warn this nation]. ... Proclaim against Jerusalem ...
> 5:1: Run ... through the streets of Jerusalem ... search [her] squares ...
>   to see if you can find one person ... who does justice ...
> 5:10: Go up through her vine-rows and destroy ...
> 5:20: Declare in the house of Jacob, proclaim it in Judah ...
> 6:1: Flee for safety. ... Blow the trumpet. ... Raise the signal
> 6:9: [Glean, glean][47] as a vine the remnant of Israel ...
> 6:16: Stand at the crossroads and look, and ask for the ancient paths...

---

[42] Jer. 2:2, 17-25, 33-37; 3:1-5, 13, 19; 4:7, 18, 30; 5:7; 6:8, 23, 25-26; 7:29; 7:19.

[43] The sole exception is 6:25-26, which addresses "my daughter people."

[44] These verses naming Israel are all in close proximity to the verses with a feminine singular addressee; however, they all use masculine forms to refer to Israel except 3:6-10. The arguments for understanding the woman addressed to be Israel as distinct from Judah will be laid out in the section on narrative progression.

[45] The children of Jerusalem (10:20) are presumably the inhabitants of the city. Thus the speeches addressed to her are not spoken directly to the people but to their "mother."

[46] Israel's speeches are subordinated to Yahweh's speeches with the phrase "you (f.s.) said" (2:20, 23, 25, 35). Thus the dispute is not technically a dramatic dialogue but rather a monologue in which Yahweh rehearses an earlier dispute with Israel.

[47] Following the Septuagint.

A more careful consideration of these passages reveals that, apart from 6:1 and 6:16,[48] they are not addressed to the people but instead to those who will destroy the people, examine the people, and warn the people. Perhaps to salvage the messenger speech interpretation, the commands to warn or to search have been read as addressed to the messenger Jeremiah. This is often assumed to be the case for 4:5, 4:16, 5:1, and 5:20.[49] However, although it might appear that Jeremiah is addressed if one only reads the English translations, the plural imperatives in the Hebrew text rule out the prophet as the addressee.

These erroneous identifications of the addressees were avoided by Holladay because of his attentiveness to the questions of dramatic speaker and audience. His rhetorical approach with its emphasis on introductory techniques and meaningful repetitions allowed him to offer an intriguing alternative. The similarity of these commands that introduce the major sections of 4–6 led him to consider them as a group. If the question of audience is asked of the whole set of introductions, a profile quickly emerges. The addressees as a group (m.pl.) are asked to bring destruction on the nation (5:10, 6:9), to affirm Yahweh's judgments or examine the evidence for them (5:1), and to relay his messages (4:5, 4:16, 5:20). These roles do not fit any single human audience, but Holladay realized that they fit well with roles played by beings in the spiritual realm he referred to as the "heavenly court."[50] The idea that the great god(s) was surrounded by a host of lesser spiritual beings was common in the ancient Near East,[51] and although these beings played a much smaller role in Israelite religion,[52] they are represented in several Old Testament texts and provide the best explanation for numerous passages

---

[48] There is good reason to take even these two speeches, which at first glance seem to address their audience directly, as dramatic speech. 6:1-8 dramatizes the imminent destruction of Jerusalem, and it seems unlikely that this is all for the sake of the Benjamites, who are addressed in the opening imperatives. Instead, by "overhearing" the warnings to the Benjamites to flee the city, the intended audience is shown the grave danger Jerusalem faces. In 6:16 the advice to the people to seek the ancient paths is followed by a report of their response: "But they said, 'We will not walk in it.'" Yahweh is not directly addressing the people but relating an earlier exchange between himself and the people. His addressees, to whom he is relating this exchange, appear to be the "nations," the "congregation," and the "earth" (4:18-19), who serve as witnesses of his people's rebellion.

[49] J. Philip Hyatt, "Jeremiah," in *IB*, ed. George A. Buttrick (New York: Abingdon, 1956), 844. Peter Craigie, Page Kelly, and Joel Drinkard Jr., *Jeremiah 1–24*, WBC 26 (Dallas, TX: Word Books, 1991), 87. William McKane, *A Critical and Exegetical Commentary on Jeremiah*, ICC (Edinburgh: T&T Clark, 1986 and 1996), vol. 1, 90.

[50] This solution is suggested by Holladay, *Jeremiah 1*, 149. A similar identification of the audience of m.pl. commands has been made for Isa. 40:1, "Comfort (m.pl.), comfort my people, says your God." James Muilenburg writes, "Already in the opening lines we hear Yahweh addressing the members of his council." Muilenburg, "Isaiah 40–66," 422–3. Earlier proponents of this of this reading of Isaiah 40 are Frank Moore Cross ("The Council of Yahweh in Second Isaiah," *JNES* 12 [1953]: 274-7) and H. W. Robinson ("The Council of Yahweh," *JTS* 45 [1944]: 155). An expanded defense of the divine council as the audience of these commands can be found in Henderson, "The Structure of Jeremiah 4:5–6:30," 45–52.

[51] H. W. Robinson, "The Council of Yahweh," *JTS* 45 (1944): 151-7. E. Theodore Mullen Jr., *The Assembly of the Gods in Canaanite and Early Hebrew Literature*, HSM 24 (Chico, CA: Scholars Press, 1980).

[52] In biblical literature, the deity of these figures is radically undercut by the absolute supremacy of Yahweh, and they remain for the most part shadowy background figures which hover between existence and metaphor.

like these in which the second-person audience of Yahweh's speech is plural.[53] Although they are often unnamed, it is likely that members of Yahweh's cosmic audience are addressed by name in Jer. 6:18-19 as the "nations," the "congregation," and the "earth" (cf. also the "heavens" called as witnesses in 2:12). However, it is not the names but the familiar roles they play that allow careful readers like Holladay to recognize the members of the divine council as the audience of the introductory imperatives: the calls to destroy the nation suggests their role as Yahweh's military hosts, the challenge to search the city for counterevidence of Yahweh's judgments suggests their role as his council, and the calls to relay his messages suggests their role as intermediaries.

If these speeches are spoken to Yahweh's spiritual hosts, then the relevant setting is not the temple gate or the royal palace, but the heavenly council of Yahweh. They dramatically portray critical moments in that council just as the speeches of the enemy generals portrayed a decisive moment in their council. Even if the divine council cannot be identified as the audience of all of these speeches, the plural imperatives rule out Jeremiah as the audience, and the speeches stand in marked contrast to the prose accounts of the prophet delivering messages to the people. In those accounts, Jeremiah is the speaker of a message to the king or a group of people who are addressed by Yahweh. Yahweh does not appear as a character in the account, but only as the source of the message. In these poetic speeches of Yahweh, however, the mediation of Jeremiah is not mentioned, and Yahweh speaks directly to his council as he speaks elsewhere in the poetry to Daughter Jerusalem, to his bride Israel, and to Jeremiah.

Yahweh's Speech: Part of Dramatic Dialogues

If the addressees of Yahweh's speeches are one indication that they are better understood as dramatic portrayal of direct speech than as historical reports of messenger speeches, another indication is that his speeches both answer and are answered by the speeches of other speakers. An example of Yahweh responding to another speech is his stinging rebuke immediately following Daughter Jerusalem's cry in 4:19-21:

> [Surely] my people are foolish,
> > They do not know me;
> They are stupid children,
> > They have no understanding.

The effect of the whole scenario depends on the striking contrast between Daughter Jerusalem agonizing over the destruction of her land (and by implication her children, the people of the land [cf. 10:20]), and Yahweh who, unimpressed with the suffering of

---

[53] Many other passages in the prophets featuring imperatives addressed to unnamed m.pl. audiences fit well with the divine council. The addressees could be divided up by what they are commanded to do: Destroyers: Isa. 13:2, 18:2, Jer. 12:9, 48:26, 50:14, 50:26-29, 51:3, 51:11-12, 51:27, Joel 2:1, 3:9, Amos 3:9, 3:13; Helpers (comforters): Isa. 35:3-4, 40:1, 40:3, 48:20aß, 57:14aß, 62:10-11; Messengers: 18:2, 48:20, Jer. 46:14, 50:2, Joel 3:9; Praisers: Isa. 12:4, Jer. 31:7; Lamenters: Isa. 13:6, 22:4, Jer. 9:10, 9:17, 22:10, Ezek. 19:1. Though the members of the divine council may not be the best choice for the addressees of all these commands, they are certainly plausible for most of them.

the city, is instead impressed with her children's stupidity which caused the suffering. The poet has made the speech of Yahweh answer the speech of Jerusalem (and her speech answer to Yahweh's prior speech to her 4:16-18) in a stylized dramatic dialogue. The rebuke is not the record of what Yahweh said to Judah through Jeremiah; it is a dramatic portrayal of how Yahweh answered Jerusalem's cries of distress. His words are no more a record of his actual speech than the cry of the personified city is a record of the people's speech. Other speeches of Yahweh that function as responses include the parallel rebuke of Daughter Jerusalem after her complaint over her destruction (10:21), the call for true repentance after Israel's apparent repentance (4:1-2), and the encouragement to Jeremiah to pour out wrath after his complaint that he is tired of holding it in (6:11b-12).

Not only does Yahweh respond to other speakers; they respond to him. These responses include the confession of guilt by Israel's sons (3:22b-23) following Yahweh's invitation for them to return (3:22a), and the hymn to Yahweh, the true living God (10:6-10) following his warning against serving the false impotent idols of the nations (10:1-5).[54] Although there were no doubt people in Jeremiah's day who shared the sentiments expressed in these poetic responses, the speeches are clearly not records of feedback that the prophet received after delivering his messages. They are components of dramatic interchanges between Yahweh and Israel constructed to portray the situation between them at critical points in their relationship.

Perhaps the most impressive examples of dramatic interchanges in these chapters are those between Yahweh and Jeremiah. Twice Jeremiah responds to commands addressed to the divine council (5:1, 6:9). That the prophet responds suggests that he is pictured as privy to the declarations in the council (cf. 23:22). Like Isaiah who volunteers to fulfill the mission he (over)hears in Yahweh announce in his council (Isa. 6:8), Jeremiah also acts on what he hears in the council. In 5:1-9 Yahweh commands searchers to look for righteous individuals in Jerusalem (5:1-2), and after an initial negative report (5:3, perhaps spoken by a member of the council), Jeremiah determines to conduct his own search to see if he can find someone overlooked by the first search. When even the sympathetic Jeremiah finds both great and small to be rebellious (5:4-5), Yahweh declares there is nothing left for the city but judgment (5:7-9). In 6:9-15 Yahweh commands his agents to glean through the remnant of his vineyard Israel. Having heard this, Jeremiah tries to warn the people, but finding no one who will listen, he complains that he is no longer able to hold in the divine wrath. At this point, Yahweh tells him to pour it out on the people. In both of these interchanges, the extent of the people's rebellion and the justice of Yahweh's judgment are portrayed by representing the failure of the sympathetic prophet to find an alternative to destruction. Yahweh's speeches and Jeremiah's speeches answer each other in a stylized dialogue that can hardly be report of an actual conversation but instead has the marks of dramatic portrayal.[55]

---

[54] Because this hymn is absent from the Septuagint, it is probably not original to the context. However, it appears to have been added by an intelligent poet who has enhanced the drama of the chapter by crafting a fitting hymn that the people sing in response to Yahweh's command.

[55] One indicator of dramatic portrayal is the compression of time. Both of these interchanges represent in a single conversation a series of events that would take some time to occur. In one

Yahweh's Speech: Distinct from Jeremiah's Speech

These dialogues between Yahweh and Jeremiah are examples of a third feature of the poetic speeches that identifies them as dramatic portrayals rather than messenger speech. Not only the speeches, but the characters of Yahweh and Jeremiah can be clearly distinguished. Jeremiah is not merely a mouthpiece through which Yahweh addresses the people; he is an independent speaker, a character in the drama. The most striking example of the interplay between the character of Yahweh and the character of Jeremiah is their emotional exchange in 8:18–9:3 (ET 9:4). Here Jeremiah's speeches expressing his agony over his poor people's demise (8:18-19a, 20-23 [ET 9:1]) are rebuffed by Yahweh's speeches expressing his anger at his people's wickedness and idolatry (8:19b, 9:1 [ET 9:2]).[56] In Jeremiah's final speech, he conveys his grief with an implausible wish:

> O that (*mî-yittēn*) my head were a spring of water,
>   and my eyes a fountain of tears,
>   that I might weep day and night
>   for the slain of my poor [lit., "daughter"] people!
>
> (8:23 [ET 9:1])

Yahweh counters with an implausible wish of his own:[57]

> O that I (*mî-yittnēnî*) had in the desert
>   a traveler's lodging place,
>   that I might leave my people
>   and go away from them!
>
> (9:1 [ET 9:2])

In response to the devastating punishment of his daughter people, Jeremiah is so heartbroken that he cries out for a way to express his sympathetic grief more fully. In stark contrast, Yahweh is so angry and disgusted with his people's continuing rebellion that all he wants to do is get as far away from them as possible. Possibly because of the influence of the messenger-speech theory, previous interpreters have failed to perceive the marked distinction between sympathy and anger in this dialogue. Even Walter

---

of Jeremiah's speeches, an entire sequence of action is presented: being disappointed by the poor, going to the great, and being disappointed by them as well. Similarly, in 6:10-11b, a single speech presents: trying to find someone to warn, concluding no one will listen, and being filled with wrath. This is the same technique employed in the dramatic speeches of the enemy generals: a speech spoken before noon (6:4a) and two speeches from the end of the day (6:4b and 6:5) are joined in a single conversation.

[56] For an analysis of the dramatic interchange of speakers in this passage, see Joseph M. Henderson, "Who Weeps in Jeremiah VIII 23 (IX 1)?: Identifying Dramatic Speakers in the Poetry of Jeremiah," *VT* 52 (2002): 191–206. This article argues that an important criterion for distinguishing the speech of Jeremiah is the term "my daughter people" (*bat-'ammî*).

[57] The poetic form and the artful parallels between the two speeches are evidence of the literary craft employed in creating this dramatic dialogue.

Brueggemann, who is more attuned than most to the possibility of drama, can write that in Jer. 8:23 (ET 9:1) "Yahweh/Jeremiah dissolves in tears of love and anger."[58] This is to miss a central element in the dramatic portrayal not only in this passage but throughout Jeremiah 2–20: Jeremiah's sympathy for the people and his advocacy on their behalf is pitted against Yahweh's wrath toward his people and his fixed intent to punish them.[59] Blurring the distinctions between their perspectives and allowing their characters to merge results in a severe diminution of the dramatic effect.

Arguments for Messenger Speech Answered

The analysis of speakers and audiences has shown that few of the poetic speeches in Jeremiah 2–10 have the speakers and audiences that the messenger speech model would lead readers to expect. Instead of Yahweh speaking through Jeremiah to the people, Yahweh and Jeremiah are portrayed as independent speakers. This finding is in opposition to Westermann's categorical claim that "in The Book of Jeremiah ... a literary separation of the word of Yahweh and the word of the prophet is *not* possible."[60] However, up to this point the analysis has not addressed what Westermann believes to be the primary evidence of messenger speech: the so-called "messenger formula" (*Botenformel*), "thus says Yahweh."[61] Each occurrence of this phrase (fifteen times in connection with the poetry of Jeremiah 2–10) is thought by some interpreters to indicate that the speech in which it occurs must be a message, that it must be spoken by Jeremiah as Yahweh's messenger.

Two observations undermine the interpretation of this phrase as a messenger formula. First, although the phrase does often occur in the prose accounts of prophets delivering speeches as messengers, the differences between those speeches and the poetic speeches raise the possibility that similar elements may have different functions in the two kinds of speeches.[62] Second, in several instances the phrase cannot indicate that Jeremiah is speaking as a messenger. In 6:6 and 6:9 the phrase introduces commands to the besiegers of Jerusalem, and in 5:4 it introduces a speech to Jeremiah (also in 15:19, 26:2, 30:2, 33:25, 34:2, 35:13, and 37.7). It is implausible

---

[58] Walter Brueggemann, *Theology of the Old Testament: Testimony, Dispute, Advocacy* (Minneapolis, MN: Fortress, 1997), 253.

[59] Dramatic interchanges which display this distinction between Jeremiah (J) and Yahweh (Y) include: 4:6 (Y), 4:8 (J); 4:9 (Y), 4:10 (J); 5:4-5 (J); 5:7-9 (Y); 5:12-13 (J), 5:14-17 (Y); 5:30-31a (J), 5:31b (Y); 6:10-11a (J), 6:11b-12 (Y); 9:9 (ET 9:10) (J), 9:10 (ET 9:11) (Y); 14:11-12 (Y), 14:13 (J), 14:14-16 (Y), 14:17-22 (J); 15:1-4 (Y); 15:10-11 (J), 15:12-13 (Y). In most of these passages, the speakers are quite clear, but in some of the less clear passages, speakers have been suggested based on the distinction between sympathy and wrath. An additional distinction that arises from these passages is Jeremiah's tendency to blame the priests and prophets for misleading the people (4:9; 5:5, 12, 30-31a; 14:13) and Yahweh's response that the people are also guilty and deserve punishment (5:7-9, 14-17, 31b; 14:16). Besides these dramatic dialogues, another indicator of the distinction between Yahweh's position and Jeremiah's is Yahweh's repeated injunction that Jeremiah not pray for the people (7:16, 11:14, 14:11, 15:1).

[60] Westermann, *Basic Forms of Prophetic Speech*, 95.

[61] Westermann, *Basic Forms of Prophetic Speech*, 93, 102.

[62] At the end of the previous chapter, other problems were observed to result from Westermann's attempt to derive the basic forms of prophetic speech from the speeches in the prophetic accounts.

that Jeremiah would deliver messages to himself or to Jerusalem's destroyers telling them to attack.[63]

The occurrence of the phrase in speeches which are clearly not messages and in speeches which, as shown above, are spoken independently by Yahweh discredits the messenger theory and bolsters two alternative explanations of the phrase. One is that the phrase could be part of Yahweh's speech, a way for him to emphasize the authority of what he is saying.[64] Another possibility is that the phrase is an editorial indicator that stands outside the dramatic dialogue. This second possibility is strengthened by the fact that around twenty-five occurrences of this phrase and the related phrase *něʾum yhwh* in the Masoretic Text of Jeremiah are not found in the Septuagint text. This is probably evidence of an editorial tendency to add indicators of the divine origin and authority of Yahweh's speech.[65] It is quite likely that this tendency observed in the differences between Masoretic and Septuagint Text goes back beyond the Septuagint tradition and thus provides an explanation for some of the occurrences found in both texts. In any case, whether spoken by Yahweh or a narrator (or added by an editor), these phrases can be understood as "authority formulas" rather than as messenger formulas, which must be relayed by Jeremiah. This allows Yahweh's speeches to be interpreted as independent dramatic speeches.

Arguments from the Book's Presentation Answered

Some interpreters may object that even if the poetic speeches do not take the form of messages, and even if the phrase "thus says Yahweh" cannot be relied upon to indicate messages, the speeches should still be read as messages from Yahweh spoken by Jeremiah because this is how the book presents its material. In Jeremiah 1, the book is introduced as "The words of Jeremiah ... to whom the word of Yahweh came" (1:1-2), and the following account relates how Yahweh put his words in the prophet's mouth (1:9) and sent him to speak to the people (1:17). The rest of the book includes several accounts of Jeremiah publicly delivering Yahweh's messages and even an account of how he had them recorded on a scroll (ch. 36). The record of these public messages is often identified with the poetry of the first twenty (or twenty-five) chapters.

[63] Westermann's conclusions about messenger speech in Jeremiah rely on the earlier work of Wildberger's. In his work, Wildberger counted 107 messenger speeches in which the messenger formula is used correctly, and 23 in which it is used incorrectly ("Unrecht gebraucht"). In other words, by his estimation in one out five times in Jeremiah the phrase is used in speeches that are not messages from Yahweh. Hans Wildberger, *Jahwewort und prophetische Rede bei Jeremia* (Zurich: Zwingli, 1942), 73. The high incidence of "incorrect usages" raises the question whether Wildberger and Westermann's designation of the phrase is valid.

[64] The formula *něʾum yhwh*, "says Yahweh," can be understood to function in a similar way. Paul Noble writes, "The n'm formulas function as 'attention markers' ... It can give a saying special emphasis; in such cases the n'm formula is essentially equivalent to 'And mark my words!'" "The Function of N'm Yhwh in Amos," *ZAW* 108 (1996): 623. H. Van Dyke Parunak comes to a similar conclusion. H. Van Dyke Parunak, "Some Discourse Functions of Prophetic Quotation Formulas in Jeremiah," in *Biblical and Hebrew Discourse Linguistics*, ed. Robert Bergen (Dallas, TX: Summer Institute of Linguistics, 1994), 511.

[65] These two possibilities are explored by Samuel Meier, who also provides a thorough critique of Westermann and an in-depth consideration of ancient Near Eastern parallels in Samuel Meier, *Speaking of Speaking: Marking Direct Discourse in the Hebrew Bible* (New York: Brill, 1992), 273–98.

However, although the book clearly presents Jeremiah as receiving Yahweh's words and delivering them as messages to the people, it is far from clear that the poetry of the first twenty chapters is the record of those words and messages. To determine whether the introductory presentation of Jeremiah applies to especially to the poetry (the common assumption), the arguments presented above can be examined in order. First, although Jeremiah 1 begins "The words of Jeremiah … to whom the word of Yahweh came" this obviously cannot apply literally to the whole book, which includes words *to* Jeremiah, and narratives *about* Jeremiah. If it is asked which words in the book are presented as words from Yahweh to Jeremiah, an initial answer can be provided by observing the more than forty sections throughout the book that begin the same way as Jeremiah 1, with the phrase, "The word of Yahweh came to Jeremiah/me." Almost all of the speeches introduced by this phrase are in prose: all but six in the Masoretic Text and all but two in the Septuagint.[66] Thus the book clearly introduces numerous prose speeches as words of Yahweh to Jeremiah, but only a few poetic speeches.

The second reason given for reading the poetry of Jeremiah 2–10 as messages is that Jeremiah 1 presents Jeremiah as commissioned to deliver Yahweh's words to the people. Again, although the book contains numerous speeches that take the form of messages to the people or leaders of Judah delivered by Jeremiah, almost all of them are in prose. For example, if one examines the prose speeches introduced as words of Yahweh given to Jeremiah, about half can be clearly identified as messages the prophet is to speak to the people of Judah or their leaders. This is evident from their direct naming of their audiences or their second masculine plural pronouns. (The other half of these speeches are presented as private communications to Jeremiah.) To these prose messages explicitly introduced as Yahweh's words to Jeremiah can be added numerous other prose speeches (either standing alone or occurring in narratives) that are clearly presented as given by Yahweh to be delivered by Jeremiah. In fact, in all of the narrative accounts of Jeremiah speaking as a messenger, the prophet routinely speaks his messages in prose.[67] In stark contrast, the analysis above of the poetry of 2–10 has shown that only a handful of the poetic speeches of Yahweh might directly address the people of Judah or their leaders (2:2; 4:3-4; 5:31b; 8:8, 17; 9:3 [ET 9:4]),

---

[66] Introductions to poetic passages using the phrase "the word of Yahweh came to Jeremiah [or "me"]" in the MT alone are: 2:1, 46:1, 47:1, 49:34. The introductions in both the Masoretic Text and the Septuagint are: 1:4 and 14:1, but neither of these introduces a message to the people. 1:4 introduces a personal word to Jeremiah, part of his call. 14:1, "The word of Yahweh that came to Jeremiah concerning the drought," is immediately followed by a poetic description of a drought that does not seem to be spoken by Yahweh (14:2-6). Yahweh's word to Jeremiah comes in 14:10-12 and 13-17a. If—as seems likely to me—the phrase "you shall say to them this word" in 17a applies to the preceding word about "sword and famine" in 14:13-16, then this passage (13-16) could be the "word of Yahweh about the drought" referred to in 14:1, and it would be a message to the people. However, like almost every other message Jeremiah is to deliver to the people it is in prose.

[67] Although the book primarily presents Jeremiah as delivering message in prose, there are some places where the words that he receives from Yahweh or delivers to his contemporaries are represented in poetry. At least some of the poetry in the passages about the nations (chs 46–51) and about the future hope of Israel (chs 30–31) is presented as given to Jeremiah by Yahweh. It is not clear, however, whether they were actually intended to be spoken as messages (see 25:13, 30:1-4, 46:1). There are also some isolated passages in which Yahweh commands Jeremiah to speak a message that is presented in poetic form (e.g., 3:11-13, 21:11-12, 25:30-31).

and none of these has any indication that they were spoken through the mediation of Jeremiah as a messenger.[68]

One possible exception to this absence of messenger-speech indicators in the poetry of Jeremiah 2–10 is of particular importance since it is the first verse of the section. In the Masoretic Text, 2:1-2bα reads, "The word of Yahweh came to me, saying, 'Go and proclaim in the hearing of Jerusalem.'" This introduction is one of the over forty which use the formula "The word of Yahweh came to Jeremiah," and the instructions to Jeremiah to speak what follows in Jerusalem is clearly the introduction of a message. However, this introduction is also one of the four that occur only in the Masoretic Text. The Septuagint has only "and he said," and the discrepancy between the two texts suggests that longer introduction in the Masoretic Text is an editorial addition, perhaps an attempt to supply a fitting introduction where an earlier introduction dropped out. The impression that the longer introduction is secondary is strengthened by its rough fit with the poetic speeches that follow. Whereas the introduction names Jerusalem as the addressee, the following speech is addressed to a bride who followed Yahweh in the wilderness (i.e., a feminine personification of all Israel at the time of the exodus, 2:2b). The following chapters (chs 2–3) are moreover addressed broadly to Israel (and as will be argued below, largely to northern Israel). Thus nothing in these speeches is directly relevant to Jerusalem until 4:3.[69] If this evidence is taken to indicate that the longer introduction is secondary, its value for determining the genre of the following poetry (i.e., providing evidence that they were originally messages) is clearly diminished.

However, one might still object that even if the introduction is secondary, the final form of the book (i.e., the Masoretic Text) presents what follows 2:1-2 as a message from Yahweh to Jerusalem delivered by Jeremiah. In response to this objection, it could be argued that affirming the Masoretic Text's presentation of 2–10[70] as a prophetic message to Jerusalem does not necessarily entail identifying the individual units of 2–10 as records of divine messages Jeremiah delivered in Jerusalem. The introductory formula could be read as a canonical or book-level indicator. Its function would be to indicate that what follows has the authority of the prophet Jeremiah and should be read as Yahweh's word to Jerusalem. This function would be similar to the function of the introduction to the whole book in the first chapter if that chapter is intended to introduce all that follows as "the words of Jeremiah" (1:1) or as the words of Yahweh

---

[68] The case is similar in Jeremiah 11–20, in which the passages which might be spoken by Yahweh and might directly address the people or leaders of Judah are limited to 13:18-19, 13:24 (an anomalous m.pl address in the middle of a speech with a f.s. addressee), and 15:11 in the Masoretic Text. (In the Septuagint, followed by many interpreters, the speaker appears to be Jeremiah not Yahweh.) 13:18-19 appears to be a message from Yahweh to the royal family delivered by Jeremiah. If the introduction, "Say (m.s.) to the king and queen [mother]," is addressed to Jeremiah by Yahweh, 13:18-10 would be the one poetic passage in Jeremiah 2–20 that is clearly a message from Yahweh to the people of Judah to be delivered by Jeremiah.

[69] That is, apart from the aside to Judah in a speech to northern Israel (2:28), and perhaps also the vision of the future given to northern Israel, which presents the sons of Israel joining the sons of Judah and worshipping in Jerusalem (3:14-18).

[70] Perhaps the superscription only applies to 2:3–4:2, or 2:3–6:30 (since the phrase "the word of Yahweh came to Jeremiah/me" is in 7:1), or 2:3–52:34. It is not clear the extent of the passage that 2:1-2 is intended to introduce.

spoken through the prophet's mouth (1:9). Those responsible for the introductory chapter could hardly have intended that every word of the book should be read as originally spoken by Jeremiah or spoken by Yahweh through Jeremiah. The intended effect (or affirmation) is more akin to referring to the Torah as the books of Moses, or the Psalter as the psalms of David, or the whole Scriptures as the Word of God. These general canonical or theological designations cannot be the sole determinants of the genres, speakers, situations, historical origins, and authorship of the contents of individual passages. These aspects of individual passages must be ascertained by internal indications as well. Even a synchronic reading of the book of Jeremiah will acknowledge that a third-person account *about* Jeremiah and a first-person speech *by* Jeremiah are not "the words of Jeremiah" (1:1) in the same sense. Competent reading of the book will involve attention to the genres of the individual components. Since, as this chapter has demonstrated, there is little internal evidence that the poetic speeches of Jeremiah 2–10 were delivered as prophetic messages and ample evidence that they are dramatic portrayals, competent readers will not read 2:1-2 in the Masoretic Text as an indication that all of the following speeches through ch. 10 are prophetic messages delivered by Jeremiah.[71]

The third reason many argue that, in the book's presentation, the poetry of 2–10 must be read as messages are several references in to a book, or scroll, that contains the words that Yahweh gave to Jeremiah throughout his ministry up until the fourth year of Jehoiakim (25:1-3, 13; 36:1-2). The idea that the contents of this scroll, understood as an early edition of Jeremiah, consisted primarily of the poetry of 2–20 is an assumption that was foundational to the standard approach to the book articulated by Duhm, Mowinckel, and Skinner and one that is still common today. However, it is an assumption that has little support from the text. There is no indication that the contents of the scroll were in poetry (though, in the Septuagint, 25:13 introduces the oracles against the nations, MT 46–51, which are in poetic form). There is also no indication that the scroll includes material already presented in the book of Jeremiah (i.e., in the chapters before ch. 25), and the book gives little indication whether the material in 2–24 originates from before or after the fourth year of Jehoiakim. The explicit references to time periods are limited to: "In the days of King Josiah" (3:6, in prose) and "When Zedekiah sent Passhur ..." (21:1, after Jehoiakim's reign). Furthermore, the contents of 2–24 do not fit well with the descriptions of the contents of the scroll: "All the words I have uttered against [that land] ... [what] Jeremiah prophesied against all the nations" (25:13) and "all the words I have spoken to you against Israel and Judah and all the nations" (36:2). The obvious discrepancy is that both descriptions include prophesies against "all the nations," but there are very few words about the nations in 2–24 (2:17, 9:25-26, 12:14-15, 18:7-10, all in prose). Also

---

[71] It is not impossible that the speeches are both messages and dramatic portrayals. In fact, this is the necessary conclusion of those convinced that the speeches are messages, but who are also aware that they contain dramatic portrayal. Holladay is a prime example. His assumption about messenger speech and his observation of dramatic presentation drive him to the conclusion that Jeremiah must have delivered his speeches in several voices, performing his productions like a ventriloquist. Although this is possible, it is an unnecessary supposition if one recognizes how slender the evidence is for considering these speeches public pronouncements (i.e., as prophetic messages).

the stated purpose of the scroll ("that the house of Judah will hear all the evil which I intend to do to them, so that everyone may turn from his evil way") does not fit well with the poetry of 2–24. It may however fit with the prose, which sometimes holds out the possibility of repentance (e.g., 3:14, 7:3-7, 11:2-7, 17:19-27, 18:1-11; cf. 26:1-6, 35:15).[72]

Considered together, the book offers more reasons to dissuade readers from looking for the contents of the scroll in 2–25 than to encourage them. As has been argued in previous chapters, a likely motivation for this identification of the poetry with the contents of the scroll is that it makes the poetry of 2–20 available for reconstructing the early ministry of the prophet. However, the book does not appear to be interested in that project and does not present its materials in manner that facilitates it. For example, it only offers explicit designations of time periods for two events before the reign of Jehoiakim: 1:2 (cf. 25:3) and 3:6. In any case, the fact that the book presents Jeremiah having Baruch record messages Yahweh sent him to speak to the people cannot be used evidence that the poetic speeches of 2–10 or 2–20 are messages. This chapter has demonstrated that very few poetic passages take the form of prophetic messages to the people in contrast to numerous prose passages which are clearly presented as messages.

This section has shown that the common assumption that the poetry of 2–10 consists mostly of prophetic messages in not necessitated by the presentation of the book. At the same time, it has shown that prose speeches throughout the book are regularly identified as messages: they take the form of messages (in their speakers and addressees), and they have the expected subjects and purposes of messages. This finding is the reverse of what the assumptions of the standard approach would lead one to expect. Of course, scholars committed to that approach could argue that the evidence offered here relies on a naive synchronic reading, one uninformed by established source and form-critical conclusions. The introductory phrases indicating that prose speeches are messages of Yahweh for Jeremiah to deliver to the people are to be considered secondary additions. The prose speeches were given the form of messages from Yahweh by the Deuteronomists who composed them. The narratives about Jeremiah in which he delivers prose messages are also late and unreliable, if not entirely fictitious. To address the validity of each of these historical-critical claims would be out of place in this section on whether the book presents the poetry as messages. The primary conclusion is that the judgment that the poetic speeches offer dramatic portrayals and do not need to be considered messages is easily compatible with the presentation of the book. However, a secondary conclusion has also become apparent: namely, that the judgment of the standard approach that the prose speeches do not derive from Jeremiah is in direct opposition to the presentation of the book. It is the book's repeated assertion that the prose speeches were put into Jeremiah's mouth by Yahweh. This is plainly contradictory to the assertion of the standard approach that they were put into his mouth by the Deuteronomists. The source-critical question

---

[72] Admittedly, there are some poetic passages in 2–25 that call for repentance, and several of the prose passages that call for repentance are followed by descriptions of the people's failure to repent, thus closing the possibility of repentance.

of who is correct about the origin of these words, the book or the twentieth-century scholars, can only be decided by proving or disproving the source-critical claims mentioned above. However, it is clear that the book and the scholars of the twentieth century cannot both be correct.

Advantages of the Recognition of Drama

If it is accepted that the poetic speeches of Yahweh are not records of messages delivered by the prophet but rather dramatic representations of divine speech in which Yahweh speaks independently, then the poetic speeches of all the speakers in Jeremiah 2–10 can be understood as elements of dramatic portrayals. With this understanding, the portraits of the various characters come into focus, and there emerge as well a rich variety of striking scenes and moving situations: Yahweh arguing his case before the divine council, the human enemies planning an attack in their council, Yahweh dispatching his agents and messengers, the prophet desperately searching for someone to warn, and Yahweh rebuffing the wailing of Daughter Jerusalem and the weeping of Jeremiah. In previous scholarship, these dramatic scenes have been only dimly perceived by interpreters whose focus was set on the historical situations they believed they could discover behind the text. Their attempt to trace the development of Jeremiah's thought caused them to interpret Yahweh's angry rebukes of the faithlessness of his bride (his view of Israel's idolatry) as evidence of Jeremiah's participation in the reforms of Josiah (or of the Deuteronomists' attempts to enlist the authority of Jeremiah in their struggle against the religions of Babylon). Their investigation of prophetic psychology led them to interpret the cries of Daughter Jerusalem at the onslaught of the invading armies as a specimen of the secret experiences of the prophets. Their attempt to connect Jeremiah's ministry to datable events caused them to treat Yahweh's speeches summoning destroyers as speeches of Jeremiah giving expression to his troubled premonitions occasioned by the Scythian invasions or by the defeat of the Assyrians at Carchemish.

That these dramatic scenes have remained obscure is only one of the negative effects of the standard historical-critical approach. A more significant loss was the blurring of the portraits of the principal characters. Some characters such as Daughter Jerusalem and the members of the divine council were silenced all together, but the chief damage to the dramatic characterization was the confusion of the speeches of Jeremiah and the speeches of Yahweh. As has been seen, the most common procedure was to interpret the speeches Yahweh speaks to various audiences as messages and thus to make them speeches Jeremiah speaks to the people of Judah and Jerusalem. Given the dramatic nature of the text, this procedure is tantamount to reassigning the lines of the lead character to a secondary character. It has the result of elevating this secondary character into the lead role and fundamentally altering the distinctive characterization of both characters. It might be thought that interpreting Yahweh's speeches as messages would still allow them to function as revealing his character since he is understood as the sender of the messages. While this might be true of scholars who think that God can actually send messages, it does not seem to be the case with many twentieth-century scholars. "Messenger speech" was not understood in a way that implied that the contents of the message are what the prophet actually heard Yahweh say. That Yahweh is not regarded as the original speaker of the messages is obvious when "messenger speech" is taken as evidence of the messenger's psychology, the development of his thought, or events in his life that inspired the messages. The prophet's choice to speak in the person of God—the essence of the messenger form—is taken to be a product of his strong conviction of the truth of his message or of its relevance to the current situation.[73] The effect of the common assumption that "a literary separation of the word of Yahweh and the word of the prophet is *not* possible"[74] is not to silence the voice of the prophet but to silence the voice of Yahweh.

It might be thought that reading Yahweh's speeches as dramatic representations rather than messages simply takes his speeches out of the mouth of the prophet and puts them into the mouth of a shadowy dramatist. Yahweh goes from being a function of prophetic consciousness to being a fictional character. However, recognizing Yahweh's speeches as dramatic does not force the judgment that he is fictional. One subgenre of drama is historical drama, and dramatic representation is often meant to represent something real. The Jeremiah portrayed in these chapters is surely meant to represent the real historical prophet, and there is every reason to believe that the authors as well as the original readers believed in a real, speaking God. The designation of these speeches as dramatic is not a judgment about the historicity or reality of its subjects; it is a judgment about their relationship to history or reality as it is known outside the text.

The significance of recognizing the text as dramatic can be illustrated by imagining a person who believed that Shakespeare's *Henry V* was a collection of speeches from court records and war reports. When she realized that it was actually a drama, much of what she had learned from it about English history and Henry's life, she would still rightly hold to be true: she would still believe, for example, that Henry defeated the French at Agincourt. However, she would have a different conception of how the text related to the history, and this would have significant implications for her interpretation. She would no longer need an explanation of how the chronicler had access to the French war councils, and she would no longer need a theory to explain why fifteenth-century royalty spoke in iambic pentameter.

It is true that recognizing the poetic speeches of Jeremiah 2–10 as dramatic portrayals will mean that some questions about its origin will have to remain unanswered. If the poetry of the book is understood to be related to the historical prophet as an intentional portrayal of his life rather than as a natural product of his life, the historical-critical use of the poetry as evidence for reconstructing his psychology, the development of his thought, or his biography will be deemed inappropriate. The dramatic understanding of the speeches may thus cut off one line of access to the life and mind of the historical prophet as reconstructed by the scholars of the last century. On the other hand, it

---

[73] Brevard Childs parodies this understanding as leading to such conclusions as: "The formula 'Hear the word of God' is only an idiom for saying, 'This is what I as a sensitive religious person think.'" Brevard S. Childs, *Biblical Theology in Crisis* (Philadelphia, PA: Westminster, 1970), 101.

[74] Westermann, *Basic Forms of Prophetic Speech*, 95.

also opens to view the life and mind of Jeremiah, Israel, Jerusalem, and Yahweh as portrayed by the biblical text.

Failure to Perceive the Implications of Dramatic Portrayal

The preceding observations on the potential gains of recognizing the presence of dramatic presentation in Jeremiah 2–10 raise the question of why so few interpreters have realized these gains. The explanation offered here is that these interpreters have failed to break free from the standard historical-critical approach and the assumptions of Duhm which facilitate it. This failure is particularly obvious in the work of Holladay for two reasons. First, although Holladay made great progress in describing the dramatic presentation in the poetry of Jeremiah, he failed to appreciate the implications of his work for historical criticism. Many of the standard historical-critical assumptions about the poetry and prose of Jeremiah and about the use of the poetry for the standard aims are called into question by the evidence of dramatic presentation in Jeremiah 2–10. However, Holladay's recognition of the dramatic nature of the text did not lead him to reconsider those dubious assumptions, and he vigorously pursued the discredited aims, in particular the attempts to reconstruct Jeremiah's early ministry and recover the contents of his scroll. Second, although Holladay was an advocate of the rhetorical approach, which sought to turn attention to the artistry and unity of the text and to describe the effect of the whole on readers, he failed to realize the promise of his discoveries for achieving these rhetorical-critical aims because of his continued adherence to the standard assumptions and aims. The dramatic portrayal to which Holladay drew attention is evidence of literary handiwork that could put the search for intentional artistic ordering on firmer ground than the old Romantic notions of inspired effusions. More significantly, the recognition of dramatic portrayal opens up possibilities for comprehending the artistic structure and unity of sections like 2–10, but Holladay was unable to see this unity because he was locked in to outmoded views of the text. The way the structural unity of Jeremiah 2–10 comes to light when the poetry is understood as dramatic presentation and the way the standard assumptions prevented scholars like Holladay from perceiving the unity will be demonstrated in the final chapter of this study. The remainder of the present chapter will show why the recognition of drama should have given scholars adequate reason to abandon the standard uses of the poetry of Jeremiah 2–10 that they inherited from Duhm.

The basic reason the recognition of dramatic presentation undermines the standard approach is that it compels a new assessment of the genre of the material, and its genre has characteristics that make it ill-suited for use as evidence in the standard historical-critical pursuits. To say that dramatic presentation is an indicator of the genre of the poetry of Jeremiah 2–10 depends on the conclusion that dramatic presentation is not merely a technique these chapters occasionally employ for rhetorical effect; it is their regular mode of presentation. The mode of presentation, or genre, of the poetry throughout this section can be described as dramatic portrayal. This conclusion is supported by the demonstration above, which accounted for a large number of the poetic passages in Jeremiah 2–10. The dramatic nature of many more passages in this section will be demonstrated in the final chapter. The comprehensive use of dramatic presentation is also well documented in Holladay. Furthermore, an increasing number of scholars in the decades since Holladay's work have not only recognized numerous instances of dramatic presentation but have gone on to describe the text as a whole in terms that suggest the genre of dramatic portrayal.[75] Ronald Clements writes that "the most suitable classification" of what the book offers is "a '*presentation*' of Jeremiah … a *reflection* of the life of the prophet." It is significant that Clements offers his assessment as an alternative to the assessments of genre offered by proponents of the standard form: "[The book] is neither a shapeless anthology nor yet a biography. Nor is it simply a collection of important addresses given on prominent public occasions."[76] Walter Brueggemann provides a similar assessment of the genre and draws a similar contrast when he writes that the book's presentation of the prophet is "more like a portrait … than an objective report." On the basis of his recognition that the book provides a "portrait" rather than a "report," Brueggemann calls for a new interpretive approach that "pays attention to the power of language to propose an imaginative world."[77]

Dramatic Portrayal Invalidates the Biographical Approach

Brueggemann's recognition that the new assessment of genre calls for a new approach is particularly significant. The argument of the present study is that the new assessment of genre calls for the abandonment of some old approaches. The first obsolete approach is one that is central to Holladay's work: the reconstruction of the biography of Jeremiah. The invalidity of the biographical approach to Jeremiah 2–10 in light of the recognition of its dramatic genre is highlighted by several considerations. The basic procedure of the standard biographical approach, as represented by Skinner or Holladay, is to use the poetry as evidence of the historical or biographical situation in which it was produced. However, the basic character of dramatic portrayal is that its speeches have been crafted to evoke a situation *different* from the situation of the author. If the poetic speeches of Jeremiah 2–10 are dramatic portrayals, then the details historical critics relied on to determine their original settings are likely to be cues that the poet included to help realize the dramatic setting of the speeches. As has been seen, Holladay, like Skinner and a host of other scholars, has scoured the poetry for historical hints that would help him link passages to events in the life of Jeremiah. For example, he takes

---

[75] Partial recognition of the dramatic genre can be seen in earlier works. Baumgartner draws attention to Jeremiah's "skill of creating a kind of dialogue between human being and God by combining the prophetic lament with the oracle." Walter Baumgartner, *Jeremiah's Poems of Lament*, trans. David E. Orton (Sheffield: Almond, 1988), 100. Gerhard von Rad observes that "Jeremiah's speech has a strong tendency to become diffuse, and it has epic and even dramatic qualities." Gerhard von Rad, "Jeremiah," in *Old Testament Theology*, trans. D. M. G. Stalker (New York: HarperCollins, 1965), 195.

[76] Ronald E. Clements, "Jeremiah's Message of Hope: Public Faith and Private Anguish," in *Reading the Book of Jeremiah: A Search for Coherence*, ed. Martin Kessler (Winona Lake, IN: Eisenbrauns, 2004), 139 (emphasis added).

[77] Walter Brueggemann, *A Commentary on Jeremiah: Exile and Homecoming* (Grand Rapids, MI: Eerdmans, 1998), 11, 15.

the reference to a drought in 3:3 as evidence that the verse must have come from the time of the "great drought" and thus must be dated later the rest of the verses in ch. 3. If the speech in which this reference occurs (3:1-4), a speech Yahweh addresses to his estranged wife Israel, is recognized as dramatic portrayal, then the reference to the drought will be interpreted as part of the dramatic situation. It may well refer to a historical drought. If so, the poet probably included it to help establish the time of the dramatic situation when Yahweh addressed the speech to his wife. However, the speech offers no evidence of whether the poet was writing during the situation portrayed or weeks, years, or decades later. If the speech is dramatic portrayal of a moment in the relationship of Yahweh and his bride, then using the reference to drought to pluck out one sentence and assign it to an event in the life of the prophet is highly dubious. Holladay, like many before him, is unwilling to relinquish his biographical and source-critical projects and the dubious procedures and assumptions that facilitated them (e.g., the belief that the poetry flowed out of the prophet in response to external and internal crises).

That the recognition of dramatic presentation invalidates the use of the poetry as biographical evidence is supported by another consideration. If dramatic speeches are by definition speeches that have been artfully designed to convey a situation, it is unlikely that they will make contain solid historical evidence of the situation in which they were written. Evidence known to be artfully contrived would be inadmissible in a court, and it will likewise prove to be unreliable for a biographer or a historian. It would be ridiculous to use Browning's line "That's my last Duchess painted on the wall" as biographical evidence that the poet must have been a duke. However, the dramatic speeches of Yahweh or Lady Jerusalem have repeatedly been used as evidence of circumstances in Jeremiah's life. This practice is also inappropriate for speeches that have Jeremiah as their dramatic speaker—even if it is assumed that Jeremiah is the dramatist who wrote them. It is unlikely that someone could use the lines "Whose woods are these? I think I know. His house is in the village though" to convict Robert Frost of trespassing. However, a very similar method has been a staple of Jeremiah scholarship for over a century. The argument is not that dramatic poetry can have no historical value. It might accurately portray a historical situation or might even provide clues about the poet (e.g., that he was grieved about the plight of Jerusalem or was familiar with the poetry of Hosea). The argument is that as artistic representations or portrayals of speech, the speeches cannot be used as direct evidence of the situation in which they originated in the same way that records of historical speech can be used. The barrier that the dramatic nature and poetic form of the speeches in Jeremiah 2–10 provide to biographical reconstruction is clearly perceived by Timothy Polk. "In my opinion," he writes, "it violates the integrity of the text, *qua* poetry, to replace the given literary context with the conjectured historical occasion of the writing process and so to construe the text as referring to the authorial circumstances rather than the literary subject as it is literarily defined."[78]

---

[78] Timothy Polk, *The Prophetic Persona: Jeremiah and the Language of the Self*, JSOT Sup 32 (Sheffield: University of Sheffield Press, 1984), 165.

Dramatic Portrayal Invalidates the Use of Jeremiah 2–10 as Authentic Prophetic Speech

The recognition of the poetry of Jeremiah 2–10 as dramatic poetry casts doubt not only on using it as evidence of Jeremiah's biography but also on using it as evidence of authentic prophetic speech. Since the time of Duhm, who identified the poetry of these chapters as the authentic literary productions of the prophet-poet, scholars have relied on this material as evidence of how Jeremiah must have actually spoken. This evidence was highly prized for two historical-critical pursuits. For source critics like Duhm, the authentic speech of Jeremiah served as a touchstone for evaluating the authenticity—or, more often, inauthenticity—of other portions of the book. For form critics or tradition critics, the authentic speeches were primary evidence for identifying the "basic forms" of prophetic speech, for discerning their *Sitze im Leben*, and reconstructing the historical development of Israelite literature.

Recognizing the speeches of these chapters as dramatic poetry creates several problems for the uses to which they have been put in the historical-critical approaches. First, as has been shown above, the recognition that they are dramatic portrayals undermines the judgment that they are historical reports. This does not necessarily mean that they were not delivered publically or that they were not presented by Jeremiah. It means that they are not records of the prophet's natural speeches addressing historical situations but speeches created (or employed) to represent the prophet (and other speakers) in dramatically conceived situations. The characteristics of the dramatic speeches (their diction, their phraseology, their forms) should be thought of as part of the attempt to represent the speech of Yahweh, Daughter Jerusalem, the inhabitants of northern Israel, some enemy generals, or the prophet. Thus they can have little value for determining the characteristics or forms of Jeremiah's naturally occurring speech. Unlike these other characteristics, the poetic form, which is common to all these speakers, is not a characteristic of their speech per se but of the dramatic mode in which they are presented. It is the characteristic speech of the work of a poet or dramatist. Although Jeremiah might well be the dramatist responsible for these speeches, there is no reason to think that only prophets are capable of poetic composition or dramatic portrayal. Even if he were the dramatist, the speeches he created would be evidence of dramatic speech not prophetic speech.

Conclusion

These considerations show why the dramatic nature of the speeches in Jeremiah 2–10 (which Holladay's willingness to credit the text with for intentionality, artistry, and coherence helped him to uncover) undermine his attempt to use isolated passages as evidence to reconstruct the biography of Jeremiah. Holladay appears to have intended his biography to be a superior alternative to biographies like Duhm's and Skinner's—a life of the prophet that was not at odds the life presented in the book; however, he ended up reinforcing Duhm's and Skinner's misguided method. Had he more fully grasped the implication of his discovery of the nature of the text, he might have had the satisfaction of seeing that it undermined the validity of reconstructed biographies like Duhm's. It also significantly weakens the rationale for denying that the prose speeches and poetic speeches the book presents as Jeremiah's could have been spoken by the same person: whether the dramatic character of the prophet portrayed by the book or the dramatist—who could be the prophet himself.

The possibilities of understanding both types of speeches as speeches of the character Jeremiah and the differences between various speeches in these chapters as primarily due to the variety of dramatic speakers and dramatic settings are a significant steps toward achieving another of Holladay's purposes: the rhetorical-critical aim of appreciating the artistry and coherence of the present form of the book. Recognition of dramatic presentation in the text also opens up a new possibility for the nature of the coherence in chs 2–10: temporal progression. The dramatic presentations could be arranged chronologically: not in the order in which they were written but in the order of the events they were designed to portray—like scenes in a drama. In short, they could tell a story. This possibility for chs 2–10 (as well as chs 11–20) will be explored in the final chapter. The next chapter shows redactional studies looking for coherence chs 11–20 were stymied in their attempts by their failure to relinquish Duhm's assumptions about the poetry and the prose but that, like Holladay, they were able to uncover evidence of the dramatic nature of the text.

8

Redaction Critics and Jeremiah 11–20

Scholars Look for Theological Coherence and Find Dramatic Portrayal

The introduction to Part Three presented Jeremiah scholarship of the last few decades as dissatisfied with the standard historical-critical approaches inherited from Duhm because they failed to illuminate the present form of the book. New approaches sought to "move beyond" Duhm by offering accounts of the theological or ideological perspective of the book and its literary structure. However, the argument of these final three chapters (7, 8, and 9) is that these new approaches have not in fact moved beyond Duhm insofar as they have failed to break free from the assumptions and critical methods designed to facilitate his historical and biographical aims. The argument of the entire study is that these assumptions and methods, which dominated Jeremiah scholarship in the twentieth century, are not only unhelpful for reading the book but are also wrong. Duhm's erroneous assumptions and invalid methods are based on a faulty understanding of the nature, or genre, of the book. What Duhm took to be fragments of authentic prophetic poetry mixed together with the work of later hands are actually elements of extended literary presentations. This alternative assessment of the nature of the book provides the necessary justification for attempts to find meaningful order and purpose in the present form of the book. Although scholars attempting to understand the book in its present form have not fully rejected Duhm's assessment, they have uncovered new evidence that it is wrong: particularly their observations of literary coherence and dramatic presentation. To the extent that scholars have not seen that this evidence undermines the validity of the standard assumptions and methods and have continued to found their work on these invalid assumptions and methods, they have failed to achieve their own aim of illuminating the present form of the book.

The previous chapter argued that rhetorical criticism of Jeremiah, despite its many gains, failed to adequately describe the present form of the book because it was unable to break free from the standard historical-critical assumptions and aims. The present chapter will argue the same about a second major approach that has sought to account for the present form of the book: redaction criticism. Redaction criticism has a closer relationship to the older historical-critical methods than rhetorical criticism. Whereas rhetorical criticism (at least in theory) is not dependent on historical-critical reconstructions, redaction criticism depends on the source-critical identification of texts that stand behind the present form. Its perpetuation of the historical-critical project of tracing the history of the text's composition sets it apart from other approaches of the period in which Perdue perceived "the collapse of history." However, it is adapted to this new environment by its aim of accounting for the structure and purpose of the present form (what it calls "the final form") of the book.

The close connection between redaction criticism and source criticism has meant that the redaction-critical approach to Jeremiah is more deeply enmeshed in the assumptions and methods of Duhm than the rhetorical-critical approach. Rhetorical criticism of Jeremiah need not have depended on Duhm's assumption of the authenticity of the poetry, and the methodological priorities of rhetorical criticism (identifying literary units and describing their relationships) are clearly distinct from Duhm's priorities (distinguishing authentic prophetic evidence from later additions). The perpetuation of Duhm's and Skinner's biographical project in the rhetorical criticism of Lundbom and Holladay is largely a historical accident. Although Duhm's methods and assumptions are only incidental features of rhetorical criticism of Jeremiah, they are inherent features of much of the redaction criticism. Redaction criticism's methodological priority (distinguishing the early material from the late material) is the same as Duhm's. Furthermore, much of the redaction criticism of Jeremiah takes as foundational Duhm's basic assumption that the division between poetry and prose should be interpreted as a division between early and late material.

The present chapter will argue that the perpetuation of Duhm's methods and assumptions has prevented redaction critics from adequately describing the book of Jeremiah. It will make this argument by demonstrating the weakness of redactional accounts of Jeremiah 11–20. This section of Jeremiah has attracted the attention of redaction critics because of its mixture of what was assumed to be authentic prophetic poetry and later Deuteronomistic prose. This chapter will show how slight the evidence is for this assumption and how unsatisfying the results based on it are as accounts of the nature and purpose of Jeremiah 11–20. The chapter will then use the evidence of dramatic presentation in Jeremiah 11–20 uncovered by redaction critics to suggest that the dramatic nature of the text points to an alternative understanding of the relationship between its poetry and prose. Finally, the chapter will argue that the dramatic nature of the material in these chapters demands new methodological priorities, and it will demonstrate the superiority of interpretation based on these priorities to interpretation based on the priorities of redaction criticism by contrasting the results of applying each method to Jeremiah 11–20.

The History of the Redactional Approach to Jeremiah

Before turning to the analysis of redaction critical accounts of Jeremiah 11–20, a brief overview of the historical development of the redactional approach is necessary to set the stage. Any history of the redactional approach to Jeremiah will have to provide an explanation for the survival and flourishing of this historical-critical method in the period supposed to be characterized by the "collapse of history." A partial explanation, mentioned above, is that while redaction criticism employs historical-critical methods, its purpose is to provide an account of the structure and message of the final form of the text. However, the oddity remains in Jeremiah scholarship that many redaction-critical theories build on the standard compositional theory derived from Duhm, who denied the coherence of the present form of the text and castigated the last contributors to the book as scribes and Torah teachers with no inspiration and with no understanding of God or prophets. Duhm's approach, which viewed the late material as Jewish rubbish that had to be cleared away before the authentic prophetic literature could be appreciated, makes an unusual basis for the redactional approach, which attributes the structure and message of the book to the authors of this late material. The short explanation of redaction criticism's dependence on Duhm is that while it often retained his basic assumption that the poetry represented the earliest material and the prose speeches the latest, its understanding of the character and value of the late sources was dramatically different from Duhm's understanding. The story of the gradual reversal of Duhm's evaluation of the prose material is the basic story of the development of the redaction-critical approach to Jeremiah.[1]

An initial step toward the reevaluation of the prose was taken by Mowinckel. Although the general effect of Mowinckel's work was to solidify the work of Duhm in a form that became the standard historical-critical theory of the book's composition, he also initiated some new directions in understanding the character of the different materials, particularly the prose speeches. Already in his 1914 work, Mowinckel brought together many of the prose passages that Duhm had simply discarded as inauthentic additions and presented them as a third major source, the "Deuteronomistic C Source," in which he observed distinctive formal characteristics. In his later work (1946), Mowinckel refined his theory by re-characterizing the prose speeches as "traditionary material" (rather than as a written source) and offering a description of how a school of prophets had passed on Jeremiah's messages in oral form and freely adapted them to meet the needs of their communities in the exile.[2] The idea that the sermons were an oral tradition gave them a more positive value: they might contain a core of authentic Jeremianic material and at the same time have a theological relevance for later times.[3] Mowinckel's perspective was developed and popularized in Germany by Wilhelm Rudolph's influential commentary, which described the C material as a presentation of Jeremiah's message for the exilic synagogue.[4]

By attributing a theological agenda to the prose speeches, Mowinckel paved the way for a redactional theory of the book which credited the Deuteronomists not only

---

[1] Both Louis Stulman and Hetty Lalleman-de Winkel provide helpful overviews of this history. Louis Stulman, *The Prose Sermons of the Book of Jeremiah: A Redescription of the Correspondences with Deuteronomistic Literature in the Light of Recent Text-critical Research*, SBLDS 83 (Atlanta, GA: Scholars Press, 1986), 17–31; Hetty Lalleman-de Winkel, *Jeremiah in Prophetic Tradition: An Examination of the Book of Jeremiah in the Light of Israel's Prophetic Traditions*, CBET 26 (Leuven: Peeters, 2000), 9–48.

[2] Sigmund Mowinckel, *The Spirit and the Word: Prophecy and Tradition in Ancient Israel*, FCBS (Minneapolis, MN: Fortress, 2002), 136, n. 11. *The Spirit and the Word* (2002) includes *Prophecy and Tradition* (1946).

[3] This softening of Duhm's harsh judgment of the prose can also be seen in Skinner's work. Skinner sometimes finds in the prose sermons an authentic core, which he believes yields true autobiographical evidence (most notably in Jeremiah 11, which he takes as evidence of Jeremiah's participation in Josiah's reforms). John Skinner, *Prophecy and Religion: Studies in the Life of Jeremiah* (Cambridge: Cambridge University Press, 1922), 97–103.

[4] Wilhelm Rudolph, *Jeremia*, 2nd ed., HAT 12 (Tübingen: J. C. B. Mohr, 1958).

with contributing the prose speeches but also with editing the earlier materials to give the book its final form. The first full-blown redactional account of the book that followed this mode was J. Philip Hyatt's 1951 article, "The Deuteronomistic Edition of Jeremiah."[5] In Hyatt's system, the Deuteronomistic redactors were represented by the letter D, because they were not only responsible for the prose sermons (Mowinckel's C source) but also for the selection and arrangement of the earlier materials. In one sense, Hyatt's theory of a comprehensive Deuteronomistic redaction is a reversal of Duhm and Mowinckel's compositional agenda since it finds the significance of the book in the agenda of the latest source rather than the historical evidence of the earliest source. In another sense, Hyatt's theory is a radical extension of Duhm and Mowinckel's perspective since it greatly increases the importance of the Deuteronomistic authors and editors they had discovered in the book.

Subsequent scholarship built on Hyatt's theory that a comprehensive Deuteronomistic redaction was the dominant factor in the present shape of the book. This account of the composition of Jeremiah was bolstered by the popularity of Martin Noth's redactional account of the composition of the "Deuteronomistic history" (in Deuteronomy, Joshua, Judges, Samuel, and Kings).[6] Noth argued that the Deuteronomistic school did not simply add a final layer of tradition but instead reworked existing materials to give the present text its literary shape and theological purpose. According to Noth, the theological perspective of the Deuteronomistic historians could most easily be observed in the speeches they composed and placed in the mouths of central characters at decisive moments of the history. These speeches provide the framework, both structural and ideological, for the whole work. Noth's theory was readily applicable to the book of Jeremiah: the Deuteronomistic speeches in Jeremiah, which are presented as spoken by the prophet, are actually the free compositions of the Deuteronomists, and they provide the structural and ideological framework of the book of Jeremiah.

Hyatt's theory that the present form of Jeremiah was largely a product of exilic Deuteronomists was given its fullest presentation in works by Ernest Nicholson and Winfried Thiel in the early 1970s. Nicholson's book, *Preaching to the Exiles*, argued that the Deuteronomists were exilic preachers who were the heirs of an oral Jeremiah tradition that they freely adapted to their own didactic and kerygmatic purposes: to explain the catastrophe of 587 BC and to urge repentance by offering hope.[7] As in Mowinckel's work, Nicholson's supposition of an oral tradition made it possible to argue that the prose sermons could be rooted in the historical message of Jeremiah as well as shaped by exilic concerns. A distinctive element of Nicholson's theory was his proposal that the Deuteronomistic preachers were not only responsible for the prose sermons but also for the narratives (both Mowinckel's C and B material). Thus, for Nicholson, the Deuteronomistic preachers are responsible for most of the prose of the book, and it is their homiletic concerns which dominate the outlook of the

---

[5]   J. Philip Hyatt, "The Deuteronomistic Edition of Jeremiah," *VSH* 1 (1951): 71–95.
[6]   Martin Noth, *Überlieferungsgeschichtliche Studien* (Halle: Max Niemeyer, 1943).
[7]   Ernest W. Nicholson, *Preaching to the Exiles: A Study of the Prose Tradition in the Book of Jeremiah* (New York: Schocken Books, 1971).

book. Nicholson presents his work, which emphasizes oral tradition, as a challenge to "literary" approaches like Duhm and Hyatt's, which understand the composition of the book in terms of written sources. However, like Hyatt's theory, Nicholson's theory has the effect of greatly extending the role of Duhm's Deuteronomistic editors. In his work, Mowinckel's Deuteronomistic C Source has swallowed up the source B narratives that Duhm and Mowinckel considered biographical or historical accounts.

A more direct heir to Hyatt's redactional approach is found in Winfried Thiel's two volumes on the Deuteronomistic redaction of the book of Jeremiah.[8] Thiel identifies traces of Deuteronomistic editing in all parts of the book. Of particular importance for the study of Jeremiah 11–20 is his theory that in the first half of Jeremiah, the editor's hand can be seen in complexes of material designed to present stylized scenes of the prophet's ministry.[9] The editor could join source materials into complexes by grouping common themes, by employing catchwords (*Stichworte*), or by imposing formal patterns. Significantly, these complexes could include both poetry and prose. The original poetry has been incorporated into the literary designs and theological agenda of the Deuteronomistic editors. Like Nicholson, Thiel identifies the agenda of the Deuteronomists to consist primarily of explaining the 587 BC catastrophe to the survivors and encouraging them to obedience with a message of eventual salvation. This is the agenda Duhm and Mowinckel found in the Deuteronomistic additions. Thiel finds that this agenda of Mowinckel's Type C governs the Type A poetry as well. Thus, like Nicholson's extension of the Type C prose to include the Type B narratives, Thiel's redactional theory extends the influence of Duhm's redactors over a greater part of the book.

The theory of a comprehensive Deuteronomistic redaction provides the basis and justification for many of the current redactional attempts to describe the structure and perspective of Jeremiah. First, by providing an explanation of the present form of the book as the result of a coherent theological agenda rather than as a haphazard attempt to preserve historical records, it justifies the attempt to identify a unified purpose. Second, by crediting those responsible for editing and adding to the Jeremiah tradition with intelligence and purpose, it opens up the possibility of artistry and intentionality in the arrangement of materials. At the same time, it leaves intact the basic assumptions of the standard historical approach (particularly, its use of poetic form to distinguish supposed authentic oracles from supposed Deuteronomistic sermons). In its updated redactional form, the standard compositional model has not only survived the "collapse of history" but has also become the dominant means for answering questions about the theological perspective and literary structure of the final form of Jeremiah.

The advantages for reading the book offered by theories of a comprehensive Deuteronomistic redaction come with a potential weakness: dependence on the validity of the standard compositional model. The redactional theory stands or falls with Duhm's assumption that Jeremiah's speeches in prose are the work of Deuteronomistic redactors who used the figure of the prophet for their own theological purposes. If

---

[8] Winfried Thiel, *Die deuteronomistische Redaktion von Jeremia 1–25*, WMANT 41 (Neukirchen-Vluyn: Neukirchener, 1973); Winfried Thiel, *Die deuteronomistische Redaktion von Jeremia 26–45*, WMANT 52 (Neukirchen-Vluyn: Neukirchener, 1981).

[9] Thiel, *Jeremia 1–25*, 161–2.

there are reasons to doubt that assumption (as this study has suggested), then the redactional theories founded on it are threatened with the fate of houses built on sand.

Three Redactional Studies of Jeremiah 11–20

The validity and results of the redactional approach to Jeremiah can be evaluated by examining redactional studies of Jeremiah 11–20. This unit has attracted redactional studies because it contains both the "confessions" of Jeremiah (11:18-20, 12:1-6, 15:15-18, 17:14-18, 18:19-23, 20:7-13), considered quintessential samples of the authentic poetry of Jeremiah, and several of the major "prose sermons" (Mowinckel's Type C: 11:1-14, 16:1-15, 17:19-27, 19:1-13), considered to be examples of the work of the Deuteronomists responsible for the final form of the book. The model for redactional analysis of these chapters was provided in the 1973 work of Thiel. Other German scholars built on his redactional approach to these chapters throughout the next two decades.[10] Then, in the space of three years beginning in 1987, three book-length redactional studies of Jeremiah 11–20 were published in English, drawing on the earlier German studies.[11] The first two were based on dissertations by Kathleen O'Connor (1988)[12] and Pete Diamond (1987) working independent of each other.[13] The third, based on lectures given by Mark Smith (1990), draws heavily on the work of O'Connor and Diamond.[14] The titles of the three monographs reveal a common approach:

The Confessions of Jeremiah: Their Interpretation and Role in Chapters 1–25 (O'Connor)
The Confessions of Jeremiah in Context: Scenes of Prophetic Drama (Diamond)
The Laments of Jeremiah and Their Contexts: A Literary and Redactional Study of Jeremiah 11–20 (Smith)

The focus on the "confessions," or "laments," of Jeremiah in each of the three titles is in keeping with the standard historical-critical approach, which singles out these

---

[10] Thiel, *Jeremia 1–25*; Ulrike Eichler, "Der klagende Jeremia" (1978); Franz Hubmann, *Untersuchungen zu den Konfessionen* (1978); Norbert Ittmann, *Die Konfessionen Jeremias* (1981); Ferdinand Ahuis, *Der klagende Gerichtsprophet* (1982). Diamond provides a helpful chart, which gives an overview of Ittmann, Ahuis and Hubmann's redactional analyses of the laments in Jeremiah 11–20. A. R. Pete Diamond, *The Confessions of Jeremiah in Context: Scenes of Prophetic Drama*, JSOT Sup. 45 (Sheffield: JSOT Press, 1987), 197, n. 32.

[11] As will shortly be pointed out, these books are first about the confessions and then only secondarily about their contexts in Jeremiah 11–20. Furthermore, both Kathleen O'Connor and Mark Smith make a point of going beyond the immediate context in chs 11–20 to consider the larger context of 1–25. However, as the bulk of the discussion in all three of these books focuses on Jeremiah 11–20, I will refer to them as studies of Jeremiah 11–20.

[12] Kathleen M. O'Connor, *The Confessions of Jeremiah: Their Interpretation and Their Role in Chapters 1–25* (Atlanta, GA: Scholars Press, 1987), 125–63.

[13] Diamond, *Confessions in Context*.

[14] Mark S. Smith, *The Laments of Jeremiah and Their Contexts: Preliminary Observations about Their Literary Interplay in Jeremiah 11–20*, SBLMS 42 (Atlanta, GA: Scholars Press, 1990).

sections as the authentic poetry of the prophet. At the same time, each of the three also signal its intent to read the confessions in their present literary context. This is keeping with the newer interest in the literary structure and theological agenda of the present form of the text. As will appear, each of the three studies is able to combine the standard compositional model with the concern for the present form by means of the redactional theory of Hyatt and Thiel. The shortcomings of this theory will appear in the weaknesses of the three studies: their inability to confirm the standard historical-critical assumptions, the dependence of their redactional analyses on these assumptions, and the inadequacy of their resulting accounts of the present form of the text.

The Assumed Authenticity of the Laments

The studies of O'Connor, Diamond, and Smith each begin with an extended consideration of the laments in isolation from their literary contexts.[15] They rightly perceive that their redactional theories depend on establishing the prior existence of the laments. Since the laments are mostly in poetic form, the supposition of their priority is supported by the standard assumption that poetic form in Jeremiah indicates authenticity. However, O'Connor, Diamond, and Smith also recognize that in the case of the poetic laments, form-critical observation does not necessarily support the assumption of authenticity. Each of the studies takes as its point of departure the challenge to the authenticity of the laments based on the theory advanced by Reventlow, Gerstenberger, and Gunneweg that the formulaic lament language indicates their original use as part of cultic or national lament.[16] An additional challenge to the authenticity of the laments (as Smith notes[17]) comes from Carroll and Pohlmann on the basis of a radical extension of the dominant redactional theory: if the prose sermons were composed to address the needs of a later audience and then put in the mouth of Jeremiah, then perhaps the poetic laments were as well.[18]

Excursus: The Laments in Modern Historical Criticism

By choosing the laments as their subject matter and beginning their studies with the debate over their authenticity, O'Connor, Diamond, and Smith appear to recapitulate the history of twentieth-century scholarship on Jeremiah 11–20. In the latter half of the nineteenth century and the first half of the twentieth century, the laments were not only the main attraction of Jeremiah 11–20 but also arguably the main attraction

---

[15] O'Connor, *Confessions of Jeremiah*, 7–80; Diamond, *Confessions in Context*, 21–125; Smith, *Laments and Their Contexts*, 1–29.

[16] Erhard Gerstenberger, "Jeremiah's Complaints: Observations on Jer. 15 10–21," *JBL* 82 (1963); A. H. J. Gunneweg, "Konfession oder Interpretation im Jeremiabuch," *ZThK* 67 (1970); Henning Graf Reventlow, *Liturgie und prophetisches Ich bei Jeremia* (Gütersloh: Gerd Mohn, 1963).

[17] Smith, *Laments and Their Contexts*, xvii.

[18] Robert P. Carroll, *Jeremiah: A Commentary*, OTL (Philadelphia, PA: Westminster, 1986); Karl-Friedrich Pohlmann, *Die Ferne Gottes – Studien zum Jeremiabuch: Beiträge zu den "Konfessionen" im Jeremiabuch und ein Versuch zur Frage nach den Anfängen der Jeremiatradition*, BZAW 179 (Berlin: de Gruyter, 1989).

of the whole book. Read as Romantic lyrics, the poetic laments were thought to offer windows into the great soul of the prophet. In Ewald's understanding, the laments of the prophet arise from the combination of his melancholy nature and the perversity of the Jewish people. Although he allowed the intrusion of personal feeling into Jeremiah's prophecy to be "forgivably human," he considered it a sign of the decline of prophecy from its heights in the "strong and manful" Isaiah.[19] It was Wellhausen who reversed Ewald's negative judgment of the laments and placed them instead at the highpoint of prophetic religion, the point at which prophecy broke through into individual religion (*die individuelle Religiosität*).[20]

Following Wellhausen's view that they represented the unique achievement of the historical prophet, the laments came to occupy a central place in several twentieth-century schemes for understanding Israel's history and religion. For form critics, they showed how intense individual experience could mold traditional forms into new forms.[21] For the early sociological and comparative-religions approach, they were evidence of a unique kind of prophetic experience. For attempts to recast the religious history of Israel on the Grafian model followed by Duhm and Skinner, they provided the first expressions of a new personal religion forged by a great soul whose disillusionment with priestly and legal religion led him into an intimate relationship with God in which he participated in unmediated discourse.[22] In the closely related thought of Protestant Liberalism, Jeremiah's achievement in the laments foreshadowed Christianity's liberation of religion from Judaism, the Reformation's liberation of religion from Catholicism, and the Enlightenment's liberation of religion from dogmatism. These models of religion and history help to explain the intense interest in the laments in the twentieth century and the necessity that they be authentic.

Duhm's source-critical division of the book facilitated these assumptions and approaches to the laments since he deemed their poetic form to be an indicator of authenticity. Along with other aspects of Duhm's theory, later scholars like Mowinckel sought to give the authenticity of the laments support from form criticism. However, form criticism initially posed a threat to their authenticity since they did not conform to what was considered the standard form of prophetic speech. Instead, it was recognized early on that in their formal structure as well as in their subject matter, the laments had many similarities to the individual laments found

---

[19] Heinrich Ewald, *Commentary on the Prophets of the Old Testament*, trans. J. Frederick Smith, TTFL 9 (London: Williams & Norgate, 1875), vol. 3, 69.

[20] Julius Wellhausen, *Israelitische und jüdische Geschichte*, 6th ed. (Berlin: Georg Reimer, 1907), 147. Skinner writes, "In a few incisive paragraphs [Wellhausen] has emphasized the positive value of [Jeremiah's] experience in a way that has profoundly influenced all subsequent exposition. Accepting his view we find that Jeremiah's specific greatness lies in the sphere of personal religion. The strongly marked emotionalism of his temperament is ... perhaps a necessary condition of ... heart to heart converse with God." Skinner, *Prophecy and Religion*, 15.

[21] Baumgartner writes, "Out of the deep sorrow of this rich life, what is basically a completely new song type has been born." Walter Baumgartner, *Jeremiah's Poems of Lament*, trans. David E. Orton (Sheffield: Almond, 1988), 98.

[22] John Skinner writes about the Jeremiah revealed by the confessions: "It was a great step in the history of religion to turn from the formalism of an external worship, and the legalism of a national covenant, and to find God in the heart of an individual. ... Jeremiah took that step, and opened up a way of access to God." Skinner, *Prophecy and Religion*, 227.

primarily in the Psalms. These formal affinities led some scholars to question the authenticity of the laments: if the laments were dependent on the individual laments in the Psalms, and if the Psalms did not receive their form until after the exile, then the "laments of Jeremiah" could not be those of the preexilic prophet.[23] Gunkel[24] and later Baumgartner[25] sought to counter these doubts by arguing that the laments were not dependent on particular psalms but only on the general form of the individual lament, which both Jeremiah and (later) the psalmists employed. This lament form clearly predated Jeremiah since examples could be found as early as the time of the monarchy in Israel and even earlier in Egypt and Mesopotamia. Furthermore, in the view of Gunkel and Baumgartner, which became the dominant view in the twentieth century, the laments of Jeremiah did not strictly follow the form but showed signs of having been adapted to express distinct individual complaints. With these arguments, the authenticity of the laments remained largely unchallenged and the laments were kept available as evidence for the standard critical projects of biographical and historical reconstruction. However, this form-critical debate had shown that although it was not implausible that Jeremiah had spoken the laments, when they are isolated from their literary contexts, there is little in their form or content that would identify them as specifically Jeremianic.

These form-critical findings are not acknowledged by all three of the studies. O'Connor continues the old attempt to reconstruct the origins and literary history of the laments prior to their inclusion in the present text. She claims that the laments were each publicly presented by Jeremiah to prove his authenticity as a prophet and then later collected for the same reason.[26] Furthermore, she asserts that the original collection, from which the later editors drew, included the laments in their present order, a sequence that represents Jeremiah's growth in confidence and hope.[27] O'Connor's historical and compositional claims are speculative, and her reading of the laments as increasing in hopefulness and confidence is at odds with the common understanding that they grow more despairing. Her proposal that the purpose of the early collection of laments was to authenticate Jeremiah as a prophet is shown to be doubtful by Diamond. In a review of her work, he points out that, far from authenticating Jeremiah's prophetic ministry, the laments in isolation would actually undermine it: particularly those which present Jeremiah's prophecies and requests as unfulfilled (11:18-19, 17:14-18, 18:19-23), or those which present Jeremiah as challenging Yahweh's integrity or his own vocation (12:1-4, 15:15-18), especially when these latter are answered by a challenge or rebuke from Yahweh (12:5, 15:19-20).[28]

---

[23] Baumgartner cites Bernhard Stade (1887), Gustav Hölscher (1914), and Nathaniel Schmidt (1901). Baumgartner, *Jeremiah's Poems of Lament*, 15–6.

[24] Hermann Gunkel, *Die israelitische Literatur* (Darmstadt: Wissenschaftliche Buchgesellschaft, 1963), 38.

[25] "In asserting Jeremiah's dependence on the Psalms today … it is no longer a matter of the prophet's dependence on individual psalms but on the psalms' style." Baumgartner, *Jeremiah's Poems of Lament*, 101. Originally published as *Die Klagegedichte des Jeremia*, BZAW (Giessen: Alfred Töpelmann, 1917), vol. 32.

[26] O'Connor, *Confessions of Jeremiah*, 85.

[27] O'Connor, *Confessions of Jeremiah*, 93–4.

[28] A. R. Pete Diamond, "Review of *The Confessions of Jeremiah: Their Interpretation and Their Role in Chapters 1–25*, by Kathleen O'Connor," *JBL* 108 (1989): 696.

Diamond and Smith, who follows him,[29] are more cautious about asserting authenticity or defending an original composition. Diamond's careful form-critical analysis of the individual laments allows him to reject Reventlow's claim that the laments could not be authentic because their language is "radically ambiguous." Like Baumgartner before him, Diamond is able to demonstrate that although some of the laments adopt the language of cultic lament, several are given their distinctive character by reference to prophetic concerns.[30] Although this makes it plausible that they were spoken by Jeremiah, it hardly constitutes proof of their authenticity. A further conclusion of Diamond's form-critical analysis is that "the confessions do not comprise a uniform formal group."[31] Unlike O'Connor, Diamond is willing to admit that there is little evidence that they were part of an earlier source. He notes that it is difficult to defend a proposed sequence or to find a plausible motivation for an earlier collection of laments.[32] He astutely observes that both the impetus to read the laments as spoken by Jeremiah and the impetus to discern "significant sequentiality" arise not from the content of the individual laments but rather from their placement in the book: "The more the passages are isolated from their present literary setting, the more opaque and indeterminate become attempts to maintain a reading of them in relationship to the prophetic mission, especially the Jeremianic mission."[33] Only in their present context can the laments be identified as the speech of Jeremiah.

The failure to justify the assumption that the laments were part of a previous source or had an original historical context distinct from their present literary context is a major weakness in the redactional accounts of Jeremiah 11–20 offered by O'Connor, Diamond, and Smith. The nature of this weakness is apparent in an odd lapse in Smith's work. At one point, he states confidently that "the laments' original purpose conspicuously contrasts, and therefore highlights, their additional function in their redactional context."[34] However, the only original purpose he suggests is "to defend Jeremiah's ministry," a purpose he seems to have drawn from O'Connor's argument, which he later calls "problematic on a number of grounds."[35] Without the supposition of an original purpose or setting for the laments, the need for a redactional explanation of how they achieved their new purpose and setting is obviated. The three redactional

---

[29] Smith, *Laments and Their Contexts*, 28–9.

[30] Diamond, *Confessions in Context*, 123.

[31] Diamond, *Confessions in Context*, 122. Diamond's assessment is shared by Louis Stulman: "The confessions in my opinion are far too diverse and complex to be subsumed under a single rubric or literary function." Louis Stulman, "Review of *The Confessions of Jeremiah in Context: Scenes of Prophetic Drama* by A.R. Diamond," *CBQ* 51 (1987): 317.

[32] Diamond, *Confessions in Context*, 145, 189–90.

[33] Diamond, *Confessions in Context*, 189, cf. 123–4, 145.

[34] Smith, *Laments and Their Contexts*, xviii.

[35] "The present order of the laments and the ending of 20:13 may function as a defense of the prophetic ministry, but such a view is problematic on a number of grounds." Smith, *Laments and Their Contexts*, 28. It is possible that Smith does not find the idea that the laments function as a defense of the prophet's ministry problematic but only the view that the present order and ending of Jeremiah 11–20 support the defense. However, this sentence summarizes O'Connor's argument for her thesis that the laments serve as a defense, and since Smith does not provide his own argument for O'Connor's thesis and he relies elsewhere on her argument, he appears to undermine the grounds for his claim that the laments originally functioned as a defense.

studies do not provide sufficient rationale for supposing that the laments ever had a purpose or setting other than their present purpose and setting in the book, and yet their redactional analyses are founded on the prior existence of the poetry.

They provide even less justification for considering the prose speeches to be secondary additions. No doubt, they expect their readers will simply accept the inauthenticity of the prose as one of the assured results of modern scholarship. However, even if they were able to establish that the prose could not be authentic and must have been written or added years after the ministry of Jeremiah, this would still not constitute proof that it was later (far less that it provides the editorial frame). These conclusions would require them to demonstrate that the poetry was earlier: that it could not have been written by the same author(s) who contributed the prose or added by still later author(s). The unproven assumption that the poetry must be authentic or at least predate the prose is the inheritance from the standard approach to Jeremiah. Previous chapters have shown the basis of this assumption to be weak, and the present discussion shows that these redaction critics have done little to strengthen it.

The Redactional Analyses of Individual Passages

Reliance on the unsupported assumption of the secondary nature of the prose characterizes the redactional analyses of each of the three interpreters of Jeremiah 11–20. O'Connor starts with the assertion that Jer. 11:21-23 and 12:6 are "clearly redactional prose comments."[36] She attempts to support her assertion about 11:21-23 by showing that the unit has its own structural integrity and its own concerns that distinguish it from the adjacent poetic units (11:18-20 and 12:1-3).[37] However, these features of 11:21-23 are easily explained by the obvious fact that the unit is a speech with a different speaker (Yahweh) than the speaker of the two adjacent speeches (Jeremiah). This explanation of the differences in terms of different speakers obviates the need for the redactional explanation in terms of different authors. O'Connor's designation of Yahweh's speech as a "comment" or "midrash" on the preceding speech of Jeremiah[38] gives it a purpose that is only plausible on the assumption that, as prose, it must derive from a later editor who added it to the original poetic source. Without this prior source-critical assumption, it would seem obvious that the primary purpose of the speech is to present Yahweh's response to Jeremiah's complaint. A secondary purpose is to convey relevant details about the context of Jeremiah and Yahweh's speeches (e.g., that the opponents Jeremiah complains about are the "men of Anathoth," 11:21). For O'Connor, this purpose—in her words, "to explain what has been left vague"—about the context, provides the grounds for designating the prose speech a "comment" or "midrash."[39] However, she gives no reason why a poetic speech and a prose speech that clarifies its context must come from different sources. In fact, as has been shown above, the difficulty of discerning the context of the poetic speeches when they are isolated

36 O'Connor, *Confessions of Jeremiah*, 15.
37 O'Connor, *Confessions of Jeremiah*, 16.
38 O'Connor, *Confessions of Jeremiah*, 15, 18.
39 O'Connor, *Confessions of Jeremiah*, 18.

from adjacent prose speeches is one reason for questioning her claim that they were part of an earlier collection of prophetic laments with no prose. O'Connor's similar explanations of other prose speeches (18:18, 16:1-13, 20:1-6)[40] as midrashic additions to adjacent poetic passages have the same weakness: although they are plausible on the assumption that the poetic laments must predate the prose, this assumption is one for which O'Connor is unable to provide an adequate defense.

Like O'Connor's redactional analyses, Diamond's also rely on the assumed priority of the poetry. Diamond identifies 11:21-23, 15:13-14, and 18:18 as plausible redactional expansions of adjacent poetry.[41] In each case, Diamond argues that the "dissonances" between the prose units and poetic units and differences in form, vocabulary, and imagery show that their present connection is secondary.[42] Like O'Connor, Diamond does not consider whether the differences and dissonance between speeches could be explained by the difference of speakers or the dissonances between their speech aims or their perspectives (his "redactional additions" are spoken by Yahweh or Jeremiah's enemies and the adjacent "preexisting material" is spoken by Jeremiah). However, even if one grants Diamond's claim that the present proximity of the poetic and prose passages is secondary, it is not necessary to grant his larger claim that this proximity is the work of the editor(s) who added the prose. This claim, that it is the prose which is secondary, is crucial to Diamond's overall theory: that the literary structure and theological perspective of Jeremiah 11–20 were given it by an editor (or editors) whose agenda is best discerned in the addition of prose units.

In part, the validity of Diamond's redactional analyses depends on the plausibility of the literary and theological intentions he suggests motivated the editorial expansions. Whether his suggestions provide a compelling account of the structure and purpose of Jeremiah 11–20 will be considered below. Here, it is important to note that his redactional analyses depend on the premise that the prose is later than the poetry. But Diamond does not attempt to prove this premise; in fact, as was shown above, his own work undermines the case for the prior existence of the poetry. His reliance on the assumed secondary nature of the prose appears throughout his analyses of the individual passages in which he treats indicators that speeches are written in prose as evidence that they must be editorial additions. He expends considerable effort to demonstrate the prose form of each "redactional addition" and its affinity with other "Deuteronomistic" prose (Type C) passages. Likewise, he takes pains to demonstrate the poetic form of adjacent laments and their affinity with the "Jeremianic material" (Type A poetry).[43] Diamond appears to believe that by simply demonstrating that the prose belongs to Mowinckel's Type C and the poetry to Mowinckel's Type A, he has given evidence that the prose passages are later additions. However, this only constitutes

---

[40] O'Connor, *Confessions of Jeremiah*, 56-7, 107, 111.

[41] Diamond, *Confessions in Context*, 123. This is a more conservative estimate than either O'Connor's or those of the previous redactional works with which Diamond interacts. Smith's discussion of the redaction of the individual laments follows Diamond's work. Smith views 11:21-23 and 18:18 as editorial expansions but does not follow O'Connor's suggestion that 16:1-13 and 20:1-6 are midrashic expansions as well. Smith, *Laments and Their Contexts*, 5-6, 18.

[42] Diamond, *Confessions in Context*, 28.

[43] Diamond, *Confessions in Context*, 26-8, 91-4.

evidence if one takes for granted the validity of Mowinckel's judgment that Type A is authentic, or at least earlier, than Type C.[44] Diamond either expects his readers to share this common assumption or he relies on the validity of the earlier theories of Nicholson and Thiel, who themselves share the assumption handed down from Duhm and Mowinckel.[45] Although Diamond presents his work as an independent confirmation of Thiel's and Nicholson's theories, his analyses of the individual passages on which he founds his conclusions rely are largely dependent on the unproven assumptions of these theories inherited from Mowinckel and Duhm.

The Resulting Account of the Present Form of the Text

Thus far it has been argued that, judged solely on historical-critical grounds, these redactional studies are unconvincing because their analyses depend on claims they are unable to defend yet unwilling to discard. It remains to consider how successful these studies are in achieving their redaction-critical aim: to illumine the role the laments play in the final form of the text. In terms of the broader discussion of Jeremiah scholarship, it can be asked whether they have been able to move beyond the perceived weaknesses of the older historical-critical methods by providing a better account of the canonical text's structure and purpose.

Literary Structure

In their analysis of the literary structure of Jeremiah 11–20, the three redactional studies have made significant progress beyond the older source- and form-critical studies. Their detailed analyses of how the individual laments were incorporated into their present contexts bring to light the multiplicity of literary connections between the laments and their contexts, in particular between the laments and adjacent prose units. Their demonstration of the interdependence of the laments and their contexts helps to ensure that Jeremiah scholarship will never return to the time when an investigation of the laments could be considered adequate without consideration of their literary contexts.

To acknowledge the many connections these redactional studies identify in Jeremiah 11–20, it is not necessary to accept their explanation of the connections: that they are the work of redactors who added the prose. In fact, their success in demonstrating

---

[44] In light of the history of scholarship, the argument is circular. Diamond's arguments that the prose passages have been added to the poetic laments in 11–20 rely on Mowinckel and Duhm's assumption of the priority of poetic form, and this assumption relies, in part, on the picture of Jeremiah as a lamenting poet based on the assumed authenticity of the laments in 11–20.

[45] E.g., to demonstrate that 11:21-23 must be the work of "a later editor," Diamonds points to its parallels with the "prose traditions" and then notes that Nicholson and Thiel identify the prose as the work of Deuteronomistic editors (Diamond, *Confessions in Context*, 28, 203, n. 37). At several points, it appears that Diamond simply assumes the basic validity of the earlier redactional approaches of Thiel and Nicholson. For example, he faults Holladay's attempt to identify the rhetorical structure of Jeremiah 11–20 because it fails to take account of the "recent redactional studies ... of Thiel and E. Nicholson, who see Dtr. editorial activity as constitutive for the present form of the book [and] suggest that the confessional materials play a subordinate function within the larger Dtr. complexes" (Diamond, *Confessions in Context*, 134).

the vital part the laments plays in the text's present structure actually weakens their redactional arguments. The more clearly it is perceived how integral the laments are to the structure of the present text, the less credible it will appear that they were ever part of an earlier text with a different structure.[46] Most of the coherence these redactional studies find in the present text could have been identified by the rhetorical studies that attribute the literary structure to Jeremiah or Baruch. As in the case of the rhetorical critics, what allowed the redaction critics to move beyond the older view of a fragmentary text was a compositional theory that credited those responsible for the present form of the text with some degree of intelligence and literary skill.

Not only are the redactional studies able to demonstrate the literary unity of the laments and their immediate contexts, but all three of them also discern meaningful structure in the larger section that includes the laments. Despite disagreements on many details, they all agree that Jeremiah 11–20 coheres as a literary unit and that the whole sequence of its component units builds up to a final climax (chs 18–20).[47] The success of their individual conclusions about literary structure will be considered in the next chapter. It can be said here, however, that the evidence these studies provide of extensive literary structure effectively counters the widespread opinion that there is little coherence to be found in the book of Jeremiah. In his commentary on Jeremiah, published only a year before the first of these studies (1986), William McKane stated categorically, "The exploration of supposed, larger, cumulative, literary entities will not repay the labour."[48] These three studies discredit McKane's counsel of despair.

Theological Purpose

Along with their effort to describe the literary structure of the final form of the text, the three studies also attempt to discern its purpose. The conclusions they draw concerning the text's purpose are much more dependent on their redactional theories than their conclusions about its structure. In broad strokes, they identify the purpose of the text with the purpose of the prose writers whom they credit with the final determinative redaction of the text. The inadequacy of their designation of the purpose of Jeremiah 11–20 provides a further reason for questioning the assumptions about poetry and prose on which their redactional accounts rely.

All three studies conclude that the primary purpose of Jeremiah 11–20 is theodicy: to justify God's action in bringing about the destruction of Jerusalem and the exile of her people.[49] O'Connor and Diamond attempt to present this conclusion as the result of their redactional analyses of the individual laments. They observe that

---

[46] John Barton notes this as a general problem for redaction criticism, a problem he calls "The Disappearing Redactor." John Barton, *Reading the Old Testament: Method in Biblical Study* (Philadelphia, PA: Westminster, 1984), 56–7.

[47] O'Connor, *Confessions of Jeremiah*, 158; Diamond, *Confessions in Context*, 180–1; Smith, *Laments and Their Contexts*, 59–60.

[48] William McKane, *A Critical and Exegetical Commentary on Jeremiah*, ICC (Edinburgh: T&T Clark, 1986 and 1996), vol. 1, lxxiv.

[49] O'Connor, *Confessions of Jeremiah*, 156; Diamond, *Confessions in Context*, 182; Smith, *Laments and Their Contexts*, 61–4.

a primary effect achieved by the addition of prose units to the laments is to situate the laments in concrete situations in the life of the prophet. Since these situations all involve opposition to Jeremiah from various groups in Judah and Jerusalem, they conclude that the redactors incorporated the laments as evidence of the nation's opposition to God's word and his prophet—evidence intended to exonerate God by showing the people's guilt. However, this judgment of redactional intent cannot be derived from the mere fact that the laments occur in the context of scenes of opposition. The redactors could have had other reasons for portraying opposition to Jeremiah: for example, to portray the hardships of Jeremiah's ministry or to present his reactions as exemplary. O'Connor and Diamond characterize alternative reasons like these as "biographical," and they believe their redactional analyses disprove them.[50] However, their demonstration that, in their present context, the laments present scenes from Jeremiah's life would seem to strengthen rather than weaken the impression that the purpose for their inclusion is to some degree biographical.

A second argument for identifying the purpose of Jeremiah 11–20 as theodicy appears more credible. All three studies claim that the effect of the redactional additions to the laments is to connect them with nearby prose sermons, which have theodicy as their principal intent. O'Connor notes that the prose sermons all evidence a concern with the people's failure to hear the word of Yahweh, and she concludes that the laments are employed "to illustrate the people's rejection of God's word in the person of the prophet and hence to justify the fall of the nation."[51] Diamond similarly judges that the laments provide a "concrete illustration of the nation's opposition to Yahweh … through refusal to heed his prophetic messenger."[52] Smith concurs: "The laments now placed with the introductory prose sections illustrate how the condition of the prophet reflects divine judgment against the people."[53] All three studies conclude that redactors have employed the laments as illustrations of the theodicy argument that is the purpose not only of the prose sermons but also of the whole of Jeremiah 11–20.

The argument for this conclusion about purpose is on firm ground in its observation of the interconnectedness of the prose speeches and poetic laments; however, its designation of these two elements "prose sermons" and "illustrations" introduces unsupported assumptions that undermine the validity of the argument. Using the term "sermons" for the prose speeches presupposes that they are the work of preachers and thus that their subject must be theological and their purpose homiletic. In Jeremiah scholarship, the term "prose sermons" also carries with it Mowinckel's theory, taken up by Nicholson, that the preachers of the sermons were exilic Deuteronomists. In regard to the prose speeches of Jeremiah 11–20, the interpretation that they are the sermons of exilic preachers is hardly self-evident since they are all presented as spoken by Yahweh to Jeremiah (or through him to the people and leaders of Judah) in the years before the exile. The decision to discount the text's presentation depends on a host of historical-critical assumptions about the nature of prophetic speech, the evolution of Israel's

---

[50] O'Connor, *Confessions of Jeremiah*, 158; Diamond, *Confessions in Context*, 182–3.
[51] O'Connor, *Confessions of Jeremiah*, 158.
[52] Diamond, *Confessions in Context*, 153.
[53] Smith, *Laments and Their Contexts*, 39, citing Diamond, *Confessions in Context*, 153.

religion, the composition of the Pentateuch, and so on: in short, the assumptions of the dominant compositional theory of Jeremiah originating in Duhm and passed down in Mowinckel's terms such "prose sermons."

The term "illustrations" as a designation of the laments arises as corollary of the "prose sermon" theory when it is viewed from the redactional perspective. As has been noted, an inductive study of the laments themselves yields little reason to think of them as illustrations. The argument that dictates that the laments must be considered illustrations is deductive. The logic runs as follows: If it is assumed that the prose passages are "sermons" of the exilic preachers, and it is further assumed that these preachers are the redactors who gave Jeremiah 11–20 its final form, then the homiletic purpose discerned in the sermons must also be the purpose of the whole passage. Thus, materials in the passage that do not obviously share the purpose or generic characteristics of their sermons must be preexisting sources, which have been incorporated into the preachers' work as illustrations.

That this is the logic of Diamond's study is apparent on the last full page of his work. Revisiting the question of the authenticity of the laments, he notes that although the intrinsic evidence for their authenticity is slight, it is preferable to consider them authentic because this conforms to the explanation that the fit between the laments and later prose is "a product of exploiting authentic material which was readily serviceable for incorporation into the double-axis pattern [i.e., the literary structure of Jeremiah 11–20 given to it by the Deuteronomists] and the buttressing of apologetic interests [i.e., the theodicy argument]."[54] In other words, the authenticity of the laments should be assumed because of the compatibility of the assumption with the idea that the laments were preexisting material available to be incorporated as illustrations. The assumption that the laments are illustrations drawn from earlier material allows a redaction critic to disregard whatever purposes the laments themselves might have as subordinate to the theodicy agenda of the final form of the text. Diamond concludes,

> The authenticity question makes little difference in the attempt to establish a valid reading of these difficult passages. For this, we are dependent on the Dtr. context-building which has effected a dramatic portrayal of the prophetic mission in the development of its theodicy argument.[55]

Determining whether the laments are authentic is unimportant to Diamond because his redactional analysis leads him to believe that their original purpose has been replaced by the theodicy argument of the final form of the text. What he fails to recognize is that his redactional analysis actually depends on the assumed authenticity of the laments. His theories that the prose provided contexts for preexisting poetry and that the "prose sermons" were illustrated with preexisting laments are dependent on the assumptions of Mowinckel's compositional theory, which takes as its first principle the authenticity of the poetry, particularly the laments.

---

[54] Diamond, *Confessions in Context*, 190.
[55] Diamond, *Confessions in Context*, 191.

Both Diamond and O'Connor attempt to cast their identification of theodicy as the purpose of Jeremiah 11–20 as a result of their fresh rhetorical analyses. In the final sections of their studies, they both observe that their discovery that the laments now support the theodicy agenda parallels Nicholson's discovery of theodicy as the agenda of the narrative prose.[56] Apparently, they intend their readers to regard this surprising consensus as a confirmation of their common conclusion: that the book was given its structure and purpose by exilic Deuteronomists. However, in light of the preceding discussion, the similarity of their conclusions can be seen as the predicable outcome of their common assumptions. If scholars refuse to question Mowinckel's theory that the Type C prose consists of the sermons of exilic Deuteronomists, then they must interpret the growing evidence of the coherence of the book in terms of a more comprehensive Deuteronomistic influence. Consequently, they will identify the purpose of more and more of the book with the theodicy agenda of the Deuteronomists.

Since the time of Duhm, the idea that the prose was a late addition was closely connected with the idea that its purpose was to "explain the cause of the exile" according to the simple legalistic "theory of retribution" in which "all the people's misfortune is the result of sinning against Yahweh's word."[57] The novelty of Nicholson's theory is its ability to reduce the prose narratives to elements of the theodicy agenda Duhm found in the prose speeches. Diamond and O'Connor (following previous redaction critics like Thiel and Hubmann) perform the same service for the poetic laments.

The Inadequate Account of the Text

Up to this point, the primary criticism of the three redactional studies has been that they rely on unsupported compositional theories. In response, it could be argued that in the absence of earlier forms of the text, all compositional theories will necessarily be hypothetical but that one hypothesis can be judged stronger than another by its ability to offer a superior explanation of the present form of the text. Thus, if these redactional studies provide a compelling reading of the text, they strengthen the case for the standard compositional model on which they rely. In actuality, they weaken the case for the compositional model they assume by providing accounts of the present form of the text that are less compelling than those they intend to replace.

The inadequacy of the redactional explanation of Jeremiah 11–20 appears in their central conclusion: that the purpose of the whole passage is theodicy. Their judgment that the intent is to argue for God's justice does not square well with a passage remarkable for some of the strongest accusations of divine injustice in the Hebrew Bible:

Why does the way of the wicked prosper? ... You plant them, and they take root. (12:1b-2)
You have been to me like a deceitful brook, like waters that fail. (15:18)
Should good be repaid with evil? (18:20)
Yahweh, you have enticed me and I was enticed;

[56] O'Connor, *Confessions of Jeremiah*, 156; Diamond, *Confessions in Context*, 188.
[57] Bernhard Duhm, *Das Buch Jeremia*, KHC 11 (Tübingen: J. C. B. Mohr, 1901), xvii, xix.

you are stronger than me and you have prevailed. (20:7)

The whole unit concludes with Jeremiah's bitter wish that he had been killed in the womb (20:14-18), an implicit protest against Yahweh, who appointed him a prophet while he was in the womb (1:5). This protest is met with silence, and not one of Jeremiah's charges is answered with a defense of divine justice.[58] These make strange illustrations for a text attempting a theodicy.

Of course, it was not in these poetic laments but in the prose speeches that the redaction critics claim to have discovered the theodicy agenda. However, theodicy is a poor description even of the prose speeches. Although these speeches spoken by Yahweh certainly lay the blame for the coming destruction on the sinful people, what they threaten is not the disinterested application of legal consequences but rather the outbreak of divine fury. Passage after passage depicts a divine rage that staggers human comprehension: Yahweh will set fire to his people and consume them (11:16), lift Jerusalem's skirts over her face to expose her shame (13:26), repay the people's sin double (16:18), turn his back on them in their day of trouble (18:17), and make them eat the flesh of their sons and daughters (19:9), because in his anger "a fire is kindled that will burn forever" (15:14, 17:4). Alternating with Yahweh's fiery wrath is his bitter grief: "I have given the beloved of my heart into the hands of her enemies.... She has lifted up her voice against me—therefore I hate her" (12:7-8, cf. 13:11, 15:5-9, 18:13-17). Although it is clear from Yahweh's speeches that his hatred and wrath were incited by the people's rebellion, it is hard to believe that the primary intent of presenting Yahweh's caustic denunciations and angry threats is to persuade exiles that the devastation wrought by his anger is just or reasonable. To identify theodicy as the primary agenda of Yahweh's speeches, it is necessary to isolate them from their present literary contexts, relocate them in hypothetically constructed historical contexts (an exilic or postexilic setting), and interpret them as if they were the compositions of simpleminded preachers or scribes who were motivated solely by narrowly conceived theological interests. In short, it is necessary to take the view of the prose speeches developed by Duhm and Mowinckel.

The curious outcome of these redactional studies is that although they move beyond the old source-critical approaches by attempting to read the laments in their present literary context, the account they offer of the present form of Jeremiah 11–20 is actually less compelling than the older source- and form-critical approaches, which considered the laments in isolation. The redaction critics warn against biographical and psychological approaches,[59] which offer accounts readers might judge to be more like their own understanding of the text. Those studies—Skinner's or von Rad's, for example—at least offer an explanation of what gives the figure of

---

[58] In 12:5-6, Yahweh's response suggests that Jeremiah should be prepared for even greater unjust suffering. In 15:19, Yahweh responds to Jeremiah's complaint of abandonment by saying that he will take him back on the condition that he turn from the worthless [complaints] and start saying something worthwhile again.

[59] Diamond (*Confessions in Context*, 182) warns against the psychological and biographical approaches of many authors including Skinner and von Rad. Skinner, *Prophecy and Religion*; von Rad, "Jeremiah." Diamond's argument that the identification of the theological (theodicy) agenda undermines the identification of biographical or psychological interest appears in O'Connor and

Jeremiah and his laments their affective power: the laments are the outpouring of a great soul in anguish or are intended to portray a suffering servant of Yahweh. The only explanation available to the redaction critics is that the Deuteronomistic preachers imprudently chose illustrations that overpowered their message. They end up with an implausible explanation as a result of trying to pour the new wine of present-form interpretation into the old wineskins of the standard compositional model. When the source criticism of Duhm was ascendant, the judgment that the Deuteronomistic prose was secondary led scholars to discard it as irrelevant to the interpretation of the authentic laments. In the redaction criticism of these authors seeking to move beyond source criticism, the judgment that the prose is secondary leads them to appoint it the sole arbiter of the meaning of the laments. The irony of this conclusion is that what they consider the most distinctive and vivid passages of Jeremiah 11–20, the passages that initially drew the interest of the three interpreters, must be viewed as mere supporting evidence for the didactic or apologetic purposes of the prose writers. The poetic laments, which O'Connor describes as "vivid, original and extremely concrete," must be subordinated to the prose sermons, which she describes as "rigidly formulaic."[60] Likewise, Diamond must caution that readings of the text which focus on the pathos or exemplary nature of Jeremiah's suffering "fail to interpret these texts in a manner which adequately considers the regulatory role of their contextual utilization."[61] In the final pages of their studies, the three writers seem to strain against the straitjacket of their redaction-critical conclusions, perhaps sensing that they have disallowed the interpretations of the text that readers (including themselves) find most compelling.

Two Promising Developments in Redaction Criticism

The failure of these three redactional studies to provide an adequate account of the purpose and structure of Jeremiah 11–20 might suggest that the redactional approach to Jeremiah will not be able to overcome the perceived shortcomings of the older form of historical criticism. However, at the time of these studies, new developments in redactional studies of Jeremiah held out the promise of better results. First, there was a growing willingness to question the foundational assumptions of the older compositional models, particularly Duhm's assumption that poetic form indicates authenticity. Second, there was a growing recognition of dramatic presentation as a feature of the final form of the text. Taken together, these developments pointed the way to a new approach to the text that could yield a more compelling account of its structure and purpose.

Smith as well, but it is less pronounced. O'Connor, *Confessions of Jeremiah*, 158. Smith, *Laments and Their Contexts*, 67.

[60] O'Connor, *Confessions of Jeremiah*, 151.

[61] Diamond, *Confessions in Context*, 158.

Redaction Critics Willing to Challenge Duhm's Assumptions

The new willingness to challenge Duhm's assumptions appears in three other redaction-critical studies of Jeremiah that appeared around the time of O'Connor, Diamond, and Smith. First is the commentary of William McKane (1986), which combines the redaction-critical method with a text-critical analysis of the extant manuscripts that is unrivaled in its detail. The result is a kind of *reductio ad absurdum* of the source and redactional methods. Instead of suggesting a discrete number of sources or redactional layers with identifiable settings or agendas, McKane finds several independent sources and redactional additions in almost every passage, often in each verse or phrase. Unlike Hyatt, Thiel, and the three studies discussed above, McKane finds no evidence of a comprehensive redactional agenda; each addition was simply triggered by something in the existing text so that the text gradually accumulated like graffiti on a bathroom wall. Eventually the evolving text, or "rolling corpus," snowballed into the texts we have today.[62] This account of the text's growth leaves many unanswered questions about why the text was ever passed on or accepted as scripture, and few are likely to embrace McKane's radical skepticism about the possibility of finding significant order or purposeful presentation in the book. However, in its excesses, McKane's work provides an unintentional critique of the redaction-critical method. Few of his individual redactional suggestions are any less probable than the suggestions of more conservative redaction critics like O'Connor and Diamond, who see the redactional additions as primarily limited to the prose. This raises questions about why redaction critics stop where they do. In particular, McKane's ability to offer redactional proposals for poetic additions that are as plausible as previous redactional suggestions for the prose additions shows how artificial and tenuous Duhm's old source-critical division really is.

A second redactional study that is willing to disregard the barrier between the poetry and the prose is Mark Biddle's analysis of Jer. 2:1–4:2 (1990).[63] Since these chapters are almost entirely in poetic form, the redactional analysis cannot rely on the standard poetry/prose division for identifying sources. Instead, Biddle identifies redactional layers within the poetry on the basis of shifts in theme, structure, and addressee. Whether or not Biddle's compositional theory finds any acceptance, his attempt to extend redactional analysis to the poetry is a significant breakthrough. On the one hand, it further undermines the old historical-critical use of the "authentic" poetry as evidence to reconstruct the biography of the prophet and thus frees the interpreter to consider what purpose the poetry serves in the book. On the other hand, it undermines the redactional use of the "authentic" poetry as preexisting material that the prose writers could employ for their purposes. If redactors could write poetry, poetic form loses its value as an indicator of an authentic, and thus early, source.[64]

---

[62] McKane, *Commentary*, xlix–li.

[63] Mark E. Biddle, *A Redaction History of Jeremiah 2:1–4:2*, AThANT 77 (Zürich: TVZ, 1990).

[64] Biddle's idea that redactors could add poetry was anticipated by Thiel, who allowed that redactors could add poetry in the style of the existing material. Thiel, *Jeremia 1–25*, 41. Thiel does not show an awareness of how this admission erodes the validity of his division between early poetry and late Deuteronomistic prose.

A third redactional study that undermines the old assumption of the poetry's authenticity is Robert Carroll's commentary, which appeared in the same year as McKane's (1986). Whereas McKane and Biddle radicalize the redactional approach to Jeremiah by extending detailed redactional analysis to the poetry, Carroll radicalizes it in another direction. Building on redactional studies like those of Nicholson and Thiel, he finds the prose of the book to reflect the agenda of exilic writers. The portrait it offers of Jeremiah is largely a fiction created to further their ideological agendas. However, Carroll goes further than Nicholson and Thiel by questioning what makes the poetry any more likely than the prose to provide reliable historical data about the ministry and message of the prophet. If the prose narratives and redactional framework are ideological constructions, then why should the expectations they raise (e.g., of a written scroll or an early ministry) have any weight in the question of the authenticity of the poetry?[65] Like the prose, the poetry should also be examined for evidence that it is part of a late depiction of Jeremiah created to serve ideological agendas. Carroll's radical skepticism about the historical value of the book is hardly more likely to win adherents than McKane's radical skepticism about structural coherence. However, as with McKane, his disregard of the common source-critical assumptions has shown how vulnerable they are. In particular, he has shown that the assumption of the poetry's authenticity is a shaky foundation.

Carroll's work is remarkable in that it not only recognizes the weakness of Duhm's assumption but also acknowledges that this weak assumption is the foundation of its own redactional approach. In a bold challenge to the foundational assumption of the majority of twentieth-century Jeremiah scholarship, Carroll calls the authenticity of the poetry a "dogma [that] cannot be established by argument, [but] can only be believed."[66] However, he also admits that his redactional reconstruction depends on "taking the core of the poetic oracles as the work of the poet/prophet Jeremiah (probably the only a priori judgment used in this book)."[67] Thus, Carroll recognizes that his foundational assumption is an a priori judgment that cannot be supported by argument. This is tantamount to a confession that his whole redactional analysis is a castle built in the air.

Carroll's redactional study of Jeremiah, along with those of McKane and Biddle, are indications that belief in Duhm's assumption that poetic form represents authenticity is crumbling. Carroll characterizes it as indefensible. McKane and Biddle, when they postulate poetic additions in their redactional analyses, treat it as dispensable.[68] However, few redaction critics have recognized the degree to which their own analyses are compromised by the weakness of this foundation. Questioning whether poetic form guarantees authenticity not only undermines the old source- and form-critical attempts

---

[65] Carroll, *Jeremiah*, 47–8.

[66] Carroll, *Jeremiah*, 47.

[67] Robert P. Carroll, *From Chaos to Covenant: Prophecy in the Book of Jeremiah* (New York: Crossroad, 1981), 9.

[68] It is worth noting that William Holladay (in his commentary published in the same year as McKane's and Carroll's) also offered a complex account of the composition that disregarded Duhm's assumption that the division of poetry and prose is a division between authentic and inauthentic material. Holladay, *Jeremiah 1*.

to reconstruct the biography of Jeremiah from the poetry but also the redaction-critical attempt to reconstruct the exilic situation of the prose. Hyatt and Thiel's theory of a comprehensive Deuteronomistic redaction relies heavily on Duhm and Mowinckel's assumption that the division between poetry and prose should be interpreted as a division between authentic and inauthentic, early and late. In order to read the prose speeches in the context of the theological concerns of exilic Deuteronomists, they must first be disassociated from their context in the preexilic ministry of Jeremiah (their context in the book's presentation). The primary justification for proposing a later context for the prose speeches is their alleged inauthenticity based on their dissimilarity from the presumably authentic poetic speeches. If, however, the poetry cannot provide reliable evidence of the historical prophet's style, diction, and concerns, then the argument that the Deuteronomistic style, diction, or concerns of the prose speeches prove their inauthenticity collapses.

Those redaction critics who argue for a comprehensive Deuteronomistic redaction by the authors of the prose speeches might counter that their judgment that the prose speeches are inauthentic is based not only on the dissimilarity between the prose speeches and the poetry but also on the similarity between the prose speeches and the prose speeches in Deuteronomy and the Deuteronomistic history. This argument from similarity is weaker, however, because there are several plausible alternative historical explanations of the similarities.[69] Since almost all would agree that Deuteronomy predates Jeremiah and that the prophet's early life coincides with the Deuteronomistic reform of Josiah, it would seem hard to deny that Jeremiah could have shared some of the concerns of the Deuteronomists or employed some of their characteristic diction or speech forms. Many scholars, including Skinner, have argued that Jeremiah was an active supporter of the reforms, at least initially. Others have argued that he must have been acquainted with Deuteronomy even before the reforms.[70] Even if Jeremiah was unfamiliar with Deuteronomy or in opposition to the reforms, it is still quite likely that he could have used contemporary language or speech forms that were also used by the Deuteronomists.[71] A strong argument in favor of these alternative

---

[69] Moreover, there are also significant differences between the perspective of the book of Jeremiah and that of the Deuteronomistic history: in particular, as Gordon McConville persuasively argues, there is little parallel in the historical books (Joshua–Kings) to Jeremiah's message of future hope for the nation. J. Gordon McConville, *Judgement and Promise: An Interpretation of the Book of Jeremiah* (Winona Lake, IN: Eisenbrauns, 1993).

[70] Yehezkel Kaufmann writes that Deuteronomy "must have been an element in Jeremiah's education; he studied it in his youth in the priestly school of Anathoth and absorbed its language and its spirit." Yehezkel Kaufmann, *The Religion of Israel: From Its Beginning to the Babylonian Exile*, trans. Moshe Greenberg (Chicago, IL: University of Chicago Press, 1960), 417. Kaufmann argues convincingly against the radical opposition of Jeremiah and Deuteronomy (417–19), and states the main contention of the first chapters of this study (414): "Wholesale excisions and condemnation of passages on literary and aesthetic grounds are certainly unjustified. Scholars have freely cut and altered the text of Jeremiah to make it conform with their preconceived notion of what a true prophet and poet would have written." The historical case for Jeremiah's use of Deuteronomistic thought and language has recently been argued by Mark Leuchter. Mark Leuchter, *Josiah's Reform and Jeremiah's Scroll: Historical Calamity and Prophetic Response*, Hebrew Bible Monographs 6 (Sheffield: Sheffield Phoenix, 2006).

[71] The classic statement of this argument was given is John Bright's claim that the prose speeches were written in "the characteristic prose style of the seventh/eighth centuries." Bright, *Jeremiah*, lxxi. Others who have supported this argument include Holladay and Helga Weippert. William Lee

explanations of the Deuteronomistic character of the prose speeches is that in all of the accounts of Jeremiah speaking (and in his letter to the exiles), he regularly speaks in (Deuteronomistic) prose. The claim (made by Nicholson and others) that these prose accounts are also creations of later Deuteronomists assumes the inauthenticity of the prose speeches and is open to the same criticisms: it rests on dissimilarity of the prose and the poetry and the similarity of the prose to the Deuteronomic literature, and both of these features can easily be explained in terms of the influence of Deuteronomy on Jeremiah and his preexilic contemporaries. Previous chapters have argued that the denial that Jeremiah could have been responsible for the prose did not derive from a recognition that it was historically implausible but from the need for Jeremiah to conform to preconceived ideas of what was worthy of true prophets or poets, or the need to fit Jeremiah into a preconceived scheme of the history of Israel's religion.

Once it is admitted that Jeremiah could be responsible for prose passages and that later redactors could be responsible for poetic passages, the hierarchical structure of the text supported by Duhm's reading of the poetry/prose distinction collapses. Both poetic units and prose units could be either preexisting material (perhaps written by Jeremiah) or material composed later to give the text its present form and purpose. This recognition casts doubt on redactional approaches that identify the form and purpose with the supposed intentions of authors responsible for only one element of the present text. It also clears the way for a new attempt to discern the form and purpose of the present text unhindered by the old historical-critical assumptions of Duhm.

Redaction Critics Who Recognize the Dramatic Nature of the Text

At the same time that redactional studies were beginning to reveal the inadequacy of approaches based on the dominant historical-critical assumptions, some redaction critics were beginning to appreciate a feature of the text that suggested a new and more promising approach. The previous chapter related how William Holladay's attempt to describe the structure of the early chapters of Jeremiah in terms of rhetorical artistry turned up evidence of dramatic presentation. A similar account can now be given of redaction critics whose close analysis of the text led them to the same discovery.

A prominent example appears in the work of Mark Biddle. It was noted above that in his first major work on Jeremiah, he offered a redactional analysis of Jer. 2:1–4:2 that, like the work of Thiel, McKane, and Carroll, extended the search for sources and redactional layers to the poetic material.[72] In his redactional analysis, Biddle observed that shifts in speaker and audience (largely between f.s. and m.pl. addressees) are an important feature of the text, and he interpreted them as indicators of various redactional layers (as McKane often does). However, in a second work on Jeremiah, which considers chs 2–20, Biddle offers a new explanation of this feature of the

---

Holladay, "A Fresh Look at 'Source B' and 'Source C' in Jeremiah," *VT* 25 (1975): 394–412; Helga Weippert, *Die Prosareden des Jeremiabuches*, BZAW 132 (Berlin: de Gruyter, 1973). The argument (employed by some of these scholars) for the basic authenticity of the prose speeches based on their similarities with the presumably authentic poetry is less compelling since it is founded on the same weak assumption their more skeptical opponents rely on (i.e., the authenticity of the poetry).
[72] Biddle, *Redaction History*.

text: "By analyzing the interplay of the various voices in the book … it may be possible to discover the contours of an extended dialogue."[73] Biddle's analysis of these voices involves him in the identification of the speaker and audience of each speech in the text. On this basis, his work could be called the most significant dramatic analysis of Jeremiah since Holladay. Although Holladay understands the dramatic presentation to be a product of rhetorical artistry the prophet himself and Biddle understands it to be the achievement of a later editor, their agreement on the effect helps to confirm the dramatic nature of the text.

A second example of a redaction critic whose close analysis of the text led to the discovery of its dramatic nature is Pete Diamond in his work *The Confessions of Jeremiah in Context*, which has been discussed above. The subtitle of his study, "Scenes from a Prophetic Drama," and the titles of the two main sections: "Part I: Dramatic Dialogue between Prophet and God," and "Part II: Dramatic Dialogue—Prophet and God versus Israel," indicate Diamond's recognition of the dramatic character of Jeremiah 11–20. Although Diamond's discovery of drama in the text can be attributed to his own independent analysis, he also indicates the support of earlier works that also find dramatic presentation in these chapters. Thiel, whose detailed presentation of a theory of a comprehensive Deuteronomistic redaction set the pattern for works like Diamond's, argued that Jeremiah 10–20 was composed of a series of stylized dramatic scenes of prophetic suffering.[74] Diamond also cites with approval a study that goes further in realizing the significance of the text's dramatic nature.[75] Based on a detailed formal and rhetorical analysis of Jer. 14–15.9, W. A. M. Beuken and H. W. M. van Grol conclude that "the supposed liturgic character of the text … and also the [Deuteronomistic] sermonlike character … can be made relative and the dramatic character of the text appears to dominate."[76] This conclusion goes further than Diamond is willing to follow since, as has been shown, it is the Deuteronomistic agenda that he finds dominant. In actual fact, the treatment of the text as dramatic dialogue that Diamond's section titles seem to promise is not borne out in the sections themselves.[77] Furthermore, most of Diamond's comments on the dramatic nature of the text only come in the last ten pages of his book.[78] This would seem to suggest that although

---

[73] Mark E. Biddle, *Polyphony and Symphony in Prophetic Literature: Rereading Jeremiah 7–20* (Macon, GA: Mercer University Press, 1996), 11.

[74] Thiel, *Jeremia 1–25*, 161–2.

[75] Diamond, *Confessions in Context*, 280, n. 5.

[76] W. A. M. Beuken and H. W. M. van Grol, "Jeremiah 14,1–15,9: A Situation of Distress and Its Hermeneutic, Unity and Diversity of Form–Dramatic Development," in *Le Livre de Jérémie: Le prophète et son milieu, les oracles et leur transmission*, ed. Pierre Bogaert (Leuven: Leuven University Press, 1981), 341.

[77] Oddly, although the two section titles do not fit as descriptions of the chapters they include, they fit quite well with the two cycles into which Diamond divides Jeremiah 11–20: "Cessation of the prophet–God dialogical pattern in Cycle One [11:18–15:21] may relate, in part, to the shift of attention to the conflict between prophet and nation over the message. If there is any sense in which the label 'dialogue' is proper for Cycle Two [18:12–20:18], it would have to be in relation to the implicit dialogue between the prophet and his opponents." Diamond, *Confessions in Context*, 144.

[78] Diamond, *Confessions in Context*, 181–91. However, there are several earlier instances in the book in which Diamond perceives how speeches respond to each other in a dialogical manner. E.g., in his analysis of 18:1–23 he rejects Thiel's "pattern analysis" of the chapter "because it would obscure the dialogical framework … which lends the stylized scene its peculiar dynamic." Diamond, *Confessions in Context*, 172.

Diamond recognizes the dramatic character of these chapters, he has not realized the significance of this recognition for the methods he employs. In this way, Diamond's study reflects the general situation of redaction criticism of Jeremiah: although it has hit upon evidence of the weakness of Duhm's assumptions about poetry and prose and evidence of dramatic presentation that incorporates both poetry and prose, it has not yet been able to break free of the old historical-critical model that this evidence throws into doubt.

The Dramatic Nature of Jeremiah 11–20 Demands New Methodological Priorities

In the introduction to his study of Jeremiah 11–20, Diamond offers wise advice on the question of method:

> There is the need to confront repeatedly current research interests, aims, and methods with a close analysis of the nature of the texts themselves, open to the possibility that the inherent characteristics of the text will offer guidelines and place constraints upon our own attempt at interpretation—metaphorically speaking, that the inherent conventions of the confessions will say "read me this way" and establish by this a hierarchy of priorities in the attempt to achieve a valid reading of them.[79]

The history of Jeremiah scholarship since the last decades of the twentieth century has shown how close analysis by several interpreters including Holladay, Biddle, and Diamond himself opened their eyes to the dramatic characteristics of the text. The recognition of these characteristics calls for a new assessment of the nature of the text. If the text is judged to be dramatic in nature, this will necessitate a new interpretive approach that offers an alternative to current research aims and assumptions. In Diamond's terms, there will have to be a new hierarchy of interpretive priorities suited to the dramatic nature of the text. This new set of priorities can now be presented and then illustrated by application to Jeremiah 11–20.[80] Finally, the new interpretive priorities and the resulting analysis of Jeremiah 11–20 can be compared to the priorities that guided the studies of O'Connor, Diamond, and Smith and their analyses. The superiority of the new approach based on recognition of the dramatic nature of the text will serve as additional reason for abandoning the approach based on the faulty assumptions of Duhm.

---

[79] Diamond, *Confessions in Context*, 17.

[80] The three "priorities of dramatic interpretation" presented here are almost identical to Mark Biddle's questions for three "levels of analysis" of "the symphony of voices in the book of Jeremiah": Identity, Characterization, and Dialogue. Biddle, *Polyphony and Symphony*, 8–11. I believe that I developed these three priorities independently as will appear in my analysis of the dramatic speeches in Jer. 4:5–6:30 in my master's thesis. Henderson, "The Structure of Jeremiah 4:5–6:30," 56–73, 101–4. However, I note that I had read Biddle's work by the time I finished my thesis in 1998, and I am happy to acknowledge Biddle's pathbreaking work.

Priorities of Dramatic Interpretation

First: Identify Speakers

The first priority of an approach that recognizes dramatic presentation in a text must be identifying the dramatic speakers. Speeches are the building blocks of drama, and for them to have the intended effects of developing characters, representing dialogue, or evoking dramatic situations, it is imperative that the reader know for each speech who is speaking. For the majority of the speeches in Jeremiah, the identity of the speaker is not hard to discern. However, interpreters have often failed to identify some obvious speakers because of the agenda or assumptions they bring to the text: for example, they assume that because Jeremiah is Yahweh's messenger, the individual speeches of Jeremiah and Yahweh cannot be distinguished. In some passages, the speaker is admittedly quite difficult to identify, particularly in poetic dialogues where the changes in speaker may be indicated only by subtle differences in tone or content. The general process of identifying the speakers should therefore begin with speeches whose speakers are obvious and use these to build up profiles of the characters (particularly their characteristic concerns and diction). These profiles can then be used to help identify the speakers in the more difficult cases.

In Jeremiah 11–20, it is not hard to identify Jeremiah or Yahweh as the speaker of most of the speeches. To begin with Jeremiah, it can be observed that his part is not limited to the speeches that are usually classified as his laments (11:18-20, 12:1-6, 15:15-18, 17:14-18, 18:19-23, 20:7-13). To these must be added his cries of woe in light of the difficulty of his whole life since birth (15:10, 20:14-18). Two additional passages that are spoken by Jeremiah come from the scene in ch. 14, in which Yahweh rejects the prayers of the people. The first is clearly marked as Jeremiah's speech ("then I said," 14:13), but the other is harder to identify as spoken by Jeremiah, especially since it seems to be introduced as a message from Yahweh ("You shall say to them this word," 14:17-18). A number of factors nevertheless indicate that it is Jeremiah and not Yahweh whose thought and concerns are represented: the distinctive diction (particularly the terms *bat-ʿammî*, "my Daughter People," and *šeber*, "wound"),[81] the sympathy for the people in a context in which Yahweh is expressing his unyielding anger toward them, and the placing of blame on the prophets and priests. All of these are characteristics of Jeremiah's speech not only in Jeremiah 11–20 but in chs 2–10 as well.[82] In light of these features, it is best to understand the initial phrase in 14:17 as referring to the preceding speech of Yahweh (14:15-16).[83] A final speech that can be attributed to Jeremiah with some confidence is Jer. 13:15-17, in which the prophet begs the leaders of Judah to listen to the word of Yahweh. Although the speaker is not

---

[81] In the article "Who Weeps in Jeremiah VIII 23?" I argue that these terms are not used by Yahweh but rather in laments directed to Yahweh throughout both Jeremiah and Lamentations. Joseph M. Henderson, "Who Weeps in Jeremiah VIII 23 (IX 1)?: Identifying Dramatic Speakers in the Poetry of Jeremiah," *VT* 52 (2002).

[82] Joseph M. Henderson, "Jeremiah 2–10 as a Unified Literary Composition: Evidence of Dramatic Portrayal and Narrative Progression," in *Uprooting and Planting: Essays on Jeremiah for Leslie Allen*, ed. John Goldingay, LHB/OTS 459 (New York: T&T Clark, 2007), 131–3.

[83] Henderson, "Who Weeps in Jeremiah VIII 23?" 202–3.

explicitly identified, the multiple references to Yahweh in the third person suggest that Yahweh is not the speaker, and the prophet is the only other character in the drama whose speech is characterized by these concerns.

Speeches by Yahweh dominate Jeremiah 11–20 and thus cannot be discussed exhaustively here.[84] However, some of the most important features of his speech can be noted. In the discussion of the laments, it was noted that three of them are answered by speeches from Yahweh (11:21-23, 12:5-6, 15:19-21). When viewed in the context of the rest of Yahweh's speeches, there is no need to suggest that these three answers of Yahweh are oracular words given to Jeremiah in response to his cultic laments. Instead, in the drama, it is simply assumed that Yahweh and Jeremiah can speak directly to each other and even carry on a conversation. Yahweh speaks to Jeremiah, telling him twice not to pray for the people (11:14, 14:11-12), and two of his other speeches to Jeremiah (14:14-17, 15:1-4) form part of an extended dialogue centering on the futility of the people's prayer. These speeches of Yahweh to Jeremiah show that Yahweh can speak independently from Jeremiah. This means that unless it is clear that Yahweh is addressing Jeremiah's contemporaries by means of the prophet, Yahweh's speech should not be classified as messenger speech. Some speeches to consider in this regard are the four bitter laments of Yahweh concerning the sin and judgment of his "beloved" (i.e., Jerusalem or Judah, portrayed as the woman Yahweh loves, 12:7). In two of these speeches, he directly addresses her (13:20-27, 15:5-9), and in two, he talks about her (12:7-11, 18:13-17). None of these speeches indicate that they are to be relayed to the people by Jeremiah.[85] The people are not directly addressed.[86] The characters in the dramatic situation these speeches evoke are not Jeremiah and the people, but Yahweh and his beloved.

Other speeches of Yahweh in Jeremiah 11–20 *can* be correctly described as messenger speeches. One clear example is in 11:1-5, which begins, "The word that came to Jeremiah from Yahweh: 'Hear the words of this covenant, and speak to the men of Judah and the inhabitants of Jerusalem. You shall say to them.'" What follows (11:2b-5a) is clearly messenger speech. This conclusion is supported not only by the introduction of the speech but also by its direct address to the people (2 m.pl.) to whom Jeremiah was to take the message. Other comparably clear messenger speeches include: 11:6b-8, 13:12-14, 15:2b, 16:11b-13, 17:19-27, 18:6-11, 19:3b-9, 19:11b-13, 19:15, and 20:4b-6. Although Jeremiah is portrayed as actually speaking these messages to the people, they are properly considered Yahweh's speech because he is the first-person speaker. The aims of the speech, the perspective, and the concerns are Yahweh's. Jeremiah is simply the mouthpiece.

A third speaker has fewer lines but is important nonetheless. This is the voice of the people, or their representatives, who hold out hope that Yahweh will relent from his wrath and that peace can be reestablished without further judgment. The voice of

---

[84] Yahweh is the speaker of roughly two-thirds of Jeremiah 11–20.

[85] The phrases "Thus says Yahweh" in 18:13 and "says Yahweh" (*nĕ'um yhwh*) in 15:9 do not mark the speeches in which they occur as messenger speech since, as was argued in the previous chapter, these phrases should not be understood as messenger formulas.

[86] Except perhaps in the anomalous 13:23, which has a m.pl. addressee in the middle of a speech with a f.s. addressee (Jerusalem) in all the other verses (13:20-27).

these speakers can be heard in the two prayers (14:7-9, 19-22) pleading for Yahweh not to forsake them in the midst of the drought. Although these might be thought to be the prayers of Jeremiah,[87] they are distinguished from his speech by the use of the first common plural and particularly by the parallels between their perspective and temple theology: their reliance on Yahweh's name (14:7, 9, 21), their assumption that Yahweh is in their midst (14:9), and their references to Zion (14:19) and Yahweh's throne (14:21).[88] Although these prayers seem orthodox, contrite, and pious, they are both rejected by Yahweh. Another speech that can be assigned to these people who place their hope in the temple is 17:12-13. Like the two prayers in ch. 14, this speech is a seemingly pious prayer in the first common plural, referring to Yahweh's throne and the sanctuary, and using the title "the hope of Israel" to refer to Yahweh.[89] This brief survey completes the identification of speakers for most of the speeches in Jeremiah 11–20.

Second: Characterize Speakers

The second priority in an approach based on recognizing drama in the text is to describe the characters in the passage as they are revealed in the totality of their speeches (as well by what is said about them and how they interact in the dramatic situations). This priority overlaps somewhat with the first priority. It was already noted that the usual way to identify an initially ambiguous speech is to see if it fits the developing profile of one of the characters. Thus, the circular movement between identifying the speaker of individual speeches and grasping the character of the speaker will be a feature both of an interpretive analysis of a dramatic passage as well as of a competent reading of the passage.

The dominant impression that one receives from surveying the speeches of the prophet is of extreme tensions in his character. Jeremiah is twice commanded not to intercede for the people (11:14, 14:11), but he reports that he has (18:20). He cries out for vengeance (18:23) and also says that he will weep for those who will not repent (13:17). He expresses extreme disappointment with Yahweh (15:18) as well as confessing trust in him (16:19). It may be tempting to resolve these tensions source-critically, but the situation of the prophet in the drama provides an alternative reading that is more compelling. The drama portrays an unthinkable time in the history of Yahweh and his people: Yahweh has come to hate his beloved (12:8); he is calling destroyers to demolish his own inheritance (12:9). Like a child in the midst of a messy divorce, Jeremiah will necessarily have conflicting emotions. Jeremiah is called to be a prophet in a time when the traditional prophetic roles of urging the people to repentance and interceding on their behalf are futile (13:23, 15:1). The message of judgment that Jeremiah must deliver is one that he strives against mightily but unsuccessfully (20:9).

---

[87] In an earlier article, I myself assigned these prayers to Jeremiah. Henderson, "Who Weeps in Jeremiah VIII 23?," 192. Others who assign these prayers to Jeremiah include Diamond and Thiel. Thiel, *Jeremia 1–25*, 182; Diamond, *Confessions in Context*, 161.

[88] Beuken and van Grol assign these prayers to the people and note the temple theology. Beuken and van Grol, "Jeremiah 14,1–15,9," 327.

[89] This title, which occurs in both 14:8 and 17:13, is not used elsewhere in the Hebrew Bible.

The character of Yahweh is also notable for tensions that can be seen in the three different types of Yahweh speeches noted above: messages to the people to be spoken by Jeremiah, personal words to Jeremiah, and private words spoken to or about his beloved. In the source-critical and redactional analyses, the tension between these speeches was resolved by considering the first to be late Deuteronomistic prose sermons, the second to be oracular elements of Jeremiah's laments, and the third to be part of the authentic poetry of Jeremiah. A dramatic reading takes all three of these types of speeches as elements in the entire body of Yahweh's speeches, which reveals his character in the drama. A possibility for how these diverse speeches could contribute to a unified dramatic portrayal of Yahweh is suggested by the differences in audience. Only the first group of speeches, the messenger speeches, is represented as being intended for public hearing. The second are spoken to Jeremiah, and in the third, even Jeremiah is not clearly present. In light of these different audiences, it can be seen that in his public words to the people, Yahweh sternly warns (11:3), urges repentance (17:24-27, 18:11), and declares the consequences of disobedience (11:8, 15:4, 16:3, 19:4-9). In his private speech, he expresses his bitter grief over his beloved people (12:7), his hopeless dream that she will repent (13:27), his desperation at the failure of his severe punishment (15:6), and his outrage at being rejected for other lovers (18:13-15). The dramatic situation being portrayed in these two types of speech is analogous to the situation of a parent with a rebellious child. When confronting the son or daughter, the talk must center on impersonal warnings and consequences, but in private, the parent can pour out anger and grief. This dramatic situation provides an explanation of why Yahweh's public speeches are in rhetorical prose that employs the language of the agreement between him and the people (i.e., the Deuteronomistic covenant), while the private speeches are in poetry with vivid personal imagery.

Third: Identify Dialogues

The third priority for interpreting a dramatic text is to determine the scope of the dramatic dialogues and scenes.[90] The first reason this interpretive task is important is that the individual speeches receive their significance from the dialogues and scenes of which they are components. Knowing the limits of those dialogues helps to clarify this significance. The second reason this task is important is that it reveals the major units that make up the whole drama (in this case, Jeremiah 11–20).

The clearest example of a dramatic dialogue comes in 14:1–15:4, in which the people's prayers and Jeremiah's argument are all rebuked by Yahweh. Other clear examples of dialogue are two interchanges between Jeremiah and Yahweh previously identified as laments: Jeremiah (11:18-20), Yahweh (11:21-23), Jeremiah (12:1-4), Yahweh (12:5-6); and Jeremiah (15:10), Yahweh (15:11-14), Jeremiah (15–18), Yahweh (19–21). One of the features of these three dramatic dialogues is that several of the responding speeches do not directly address the concerns of the previous speeches. For

---

[90] This interpretive task cannot be completely divided from the previous tasks. E.g., the identity of the speakers of the prayers in 14:7-9 and 19-22 was determined by the role the prayers play in the dialogue from 14:7 to 15:4.

example, Jeremiah's complaint in 12:1-4 about Yahweh's failure to punish the wicked is answered by Yahweh's surprising retort that things are only going to get worse (12:5-6). O'Connor comments, "Despite this evasion, or more precisely, because of it, the verse fits the pattern of Yahweh's responses to indictments against his justice elsewhere in the OT."[91] This technique of presenting dramatic dialogue in which the speakers seem to talk past each other heightens the dramatic effect: each character has such a strong agenda that, instead of responding in the previous speaker's frame of reference, he or she attempts to reframe the dialogue. This kind dialogue presents an extra challenge for readers because they are not only asked to understand what each speaker is saying but also to discern the rhetorical strategies and aims of the speakers.

The dialogue that poses the greatest challenge to the dramatic approach is 17:5-18. Several of its speeches are wisdom sayings whose speakers are initially ambiguous. However, since the voices of the speakers who are overconfident in the temple (17:12-13) and the voice of Jeremiah (17:14-18) have already been identified, it becomes possible to make plausible identifications of the remaining speakers in the dialogue. The wisdom speech describing the fates of the wicked and the godly (17:5-8) can be assigned to Jeremiah's enemies.[92] They may be suggesting that their prosperity indicates their piety and that Jeremiah's misery indicates that he trusts in himself. Jeremiah replies that it is not so easy to know what is in people's hearts (17:9). Yahweh then enters the conversation declaring that he can discern what is in people's hearts as well as give them what they deserve. He also warns that prosperity can disappear quickly (17:10-11). The confident speakers once again assert their confidence based on the temple and distinguish themselves from those who forsake Yahweh and are doomed (meaning Jeremiah). Jeremiah then prays that in the coming day of evil these enemies will be shamed, not he (17:14-18). This way of reading the passage as a coherent drama offers a clear alternative to previous interpretations, which see the passage as merely a jumble of various sources, or the prophet's "miscellaneous file."[93]

This discussion of the major dialogues in Jeremiah 11–20 completes the initial stages of a new analysis of the passage based on the recognition of its dramatic character. The implications of this new analysis for understanding the structure and purpose of this passage will be presented in the next chapter. However, the initial results of approaching the passage with the three methodological priorities suited to dramatic presentation can now be compared to the results achieved by O'Connor, Diamond, and Smith. Their redactional approach is characterized by three priorities of historical criticism, a methodological agenda introduced to Jeremiah studies by the historical-critical studies of Duhm and Mowinckel. A critique of these priorities as applied to Jeremiah 11–20 by O'Connor, Diamond, and Smith will demonstrate how unsuited

---

[91] She cites as additional examples Yahweh's evasive replies to Job in Job 38–41, to Habakkuk in Hab. 1:5, and to Jeremiah in Jer. 15:10-21. O'Connor, *Confessions of Jeremiah*, 21.

[92] The introductory phrase "Thus says Yahweh" does not occur in the Septuagint and thus may be secondary. One indication that Yahweh is not speaking is that the speech refers to him as "Yahweh," rather than "I," three times. If the Masoretic Text introduction is retained, it is still possible to identify Jeremiah's enemies as the speakers: they are presenting their wisdom saying as the word of Yahweh as Hananiah presents his false prophecy in Jer. 28:2.

[93] Bright, *Jeremiah*, 119.

they are to the dramatic presentation and how they prevent these scholars from recognizing the dramatic speakers and situations.

Priorities of Historical Criticism

First: Determine Sources

The first priority of the historical-critical approach is to determine the sources of the material. This is why O'Connor, Diamond, and Smith all begin their studies with the question of the authenticity of the laments. However, if the laments are recognized to be components of a drama, this question becomes much less urgent. If the text were a letter or a decree, it might be necessary for interpretation to settle the question of authorship first, but dramas are usually written in such a way that they can be understood and appreciated without knowing the identity of the author. Examining the individual speeches of a drama for evidence of their source or author raises the dangerous possibility that the question of authorship will be confused with the question of who is speaking. In fact, this is just what O'Connor, Diamond, and Smith (and many before them) do in their treatment of the laments. They use the elements of the speeches that indicate that Jeremiah is their speaker (such as the prophetic diction and concerns) as evidence for settling the question of whether Jeremiah is their author. Their inability to prove that the laments were original compositions of Jeremiah, as well as their ease in showing that in the present text they are clearly spoken by Jeremiah, are just what one would expect if the speeches are part of a drama in which Jeremiah is first and foremost a dramatic character. The questions of whether the dramatist could have employed authentic material in his presentation or whether Jeremiah himself could be the dramatist are not unimportant for interpreting the drama, but they can hardly be the first interpretive priority.

The distortion of the text's dramatic presentation that arises from prioritizing the question of source is not that great for Jeremiah's speeches since reading the speeches as reports of Jeremiah's actual speech is not radically different from reading them as dramatic representations of his speech. However, a much greater distortion arises in the case of the speeches of Yahweh, which dominate the passage. For these speeches, the practice of beginning the analysis with the assumption that poetry indicates the authentic words of the prophet and prose indicates later additions results in misidentifying the speakers. Yahweh's poetic speeches are taken to be the speeches of Jeremiah to the people of Judah in the role of a messenger[94] even though there is no evidence in the text that these speeches are messages or that they were ever spoken by Jeremiah. Yahweh's prose speeches are taken to be writings or sermons of exilic Deuteronomists.[95] Identifying Yahweh's speeches as "prose sermons" makes it

---

[94] E.g., Yahweh's angry denunciation of his people in 18:13-17 is described by Diamond as a "prophetic proclamation" and by O'Connor as a "poetic oracle of judgment." Diamond, *Confessions in Context*, 172; O'Connor, *Confessions of Jeremiah*, 109.

[95] The central part of all of the passages in Jeremiah 11–20 that Stulman identifies as "passages commonly ascribed to the C corpus" (i.e., "prose sermons") were identified in the dramatic analysis given above as messages from Yahweh: 11:1-14, 16:1-15, 17:19-27, 18:1-12, 19:2b-9, 19:11b-13. Stulman, *Prose Sermons of Jeremiah*, vi.

almost impossible to appreciate the text's dramatic presentation. First, it obscures the dramatic setting presented by the text in which Yahweh speaks to Jeremiah or to the people (through his prophetic messenger) in the years before the exile. The placement of these prose speeches at beginnings of the major scenes indicates their crucial role in establishing the settings throughout the whole passage. Second, it divorces the prose speeches from their speaker, Yahweh, and reassigns them to speakers unknown to the dramatic presentation. In the presentation of the text, these speeches are spoken by Yahweh; their concerns, diction, and style are his. It is Yahweh who is responsible for the "theodicy agenda," the polemical view of idolatry, the concern for covenant loyalty, as well as for the "Deuteronomistic" perspective and language, including both the distinctive diction and the "rigidly formulaic,"[96] "pedestrian,"[97] "verbose and repetitious"[98] style. Although it is possible that some of these features can be explained in terms of the authors and editors and their exilic or postexilic situations, this kind of explanation cuts against the text's intention to present Yahweh's speaking to Jeremiah and the people in the period leading up to the exile.

Second: Describe Form

The second priority of the historical-critical approach is to describe the forms of the texts isolated by the analysis of sources. This explains why the first major sections in the works of O'Connor, Diamond, and Smith are form-critical evaluations of the individual laments.[99] For the analysis of a dramatic text, it may be helpful to notice how the use of conventional language and speech patterns provides the reader with clues to understanding the nature and implied dramatic setting of various speeches or dialogues. However, as practiced in traditional form criticism as well as by the three interpreters of Jeremiah 11–20, the result of the formal analysis is to isolate further the individual elements of the text in the search for their original social contexts. Thus, Diamond introduces his form-critical analysis with the question of whether the laments are part of a cultic genre, a legal genre, or a special prophetic genre.[100] Just as the attempt to identify the author of the laments obscures their role as speeches in a larger dialogue, so the attempt to identify the formal and social settings of the laments often obscures their roles in larger compositions that are designed to evoke dramatic situations.

  If the text is recognized to be a dramatic composition, then the primary reason these first two historical-critical priorities are inappropriate is that they divide the elements of the text into categories alien to the dramatic presentation. Once one has recognized the dramatic nature of Jeremiah 11–20, it will be apparent that O'Connor's, Diamond's, and Smith's choice to begin with the analysis of the isolated laments will necessarily skew their interpretation of the dramatic presentation. This is not simply

---

[96] O'Connor, *Confessions of Jeremiah*, 151.
[97] Bright, *Jeremiah*, lxxi.
[98] Nicholson, *Preaching to the Exiles*, 7.
[99] O'Connor, *Confessions of Jeremiah*, 7–80; Diamond, *Confessions in Context*, 21–125; Smith, *Laments and Their Contexts*, 1–29.
[100] Diamond, *Confessions in Context*, 22.

because, as was shown above, there is little source-critical or form-critical rationale for considering the laments as a group. It is because the speeches of Jeremiah in the laments are elements of a dramatic portrayal, and their meaning cannot be grasped in isolation from their dramatic contexts. They must be understood not only in light of their dramatic situations, which are portrayed through the dialogues they are components of, but also in light of the character of Jeremiah, which is developed primarily by his speeches throughout Jeremiah 11–20, speeches of which the laments are only one part.

Failure to consider some of Jeremiah's speeches because they do not conform to formal patterns will result in a distortion of the dramatic portrayal. A noteworthy example is O'Connor's exclusion of Jeremiah's final speech in Jeremiah 11–20, his dramatic curse of the messenger who announces his birth (20:14-18). Because this speech is a curse rather than a lament, O'Connor disregards it (and the similar curse in 15:10) as part of the portrayal of Jeremiah in 11–20.[101] By excluding this passage and 15:10, O'Connor is able to argue that Jeremiah 11–20 presents Jeremiah as "the prophet of Yahweh's praises"[102] and that the movement of Jeremiah 11–20 is growing crescendo "of burgeoning confidence and hope" culminating in the triumphant praise of 20:13.[103] O'Connor's interpretation of the dramatic presentation is only possible if one walks out before the final scene. Her peculiar reading is only an extreme example of how the dramatic presentation of Jeremiah 11–20 is commonly misread when the elements of its dramatic portrayal are improperly isolated to achieve source- and form-critical aims.

Third: Determine History of Composition

The third priority of the historical-critical approach is to understand the history of composition by which the elements isolated by source- and form-critical analyses came to occupy their present positions in the text. This agenda appears in the redactional theories of all three studies of Jeremiah 11–20. Although the focus on the present form of the text is welcome to the dramatic approach, the assumption in the redactional theories (carried over from source and form theories) that the unity of the passage is an editorial achievement creates hindrances to a full dramatic reading. First, the redactional analyses, although they attempt to explain the unity of the text, are committed to the idea that the original sources are discernible despite the redactional work. One result is an emphasis on the "seams" between adjacent units: that is, the irreconcilable differences between their perspectives, forms, and diction that must be explained as evidence that the units originated from different sources. This emphasis often runs counter to appreciating the dramatic presentation either because it overemphasizes the disunity in a composition, or it offers an alternative reading to elements that are intended to indicate the presence of multiple speakers. Another result is that the kind of unity suggested is often based on superficial devices such as catchwords, chiastic ordering, or formal patterning.[104] Thus, these studies often pass

---

[101] O'Connor, *Confessions of Jeremiah*, 79–80.
[102] O'Connor, *Confessions of Jeremiah*, 3.
[103] O'Connor, *Confessions of Jeremiah*, 94.
[104] O'Connor, *Confessions of Jeremiah*, 111–12.

over the dramatic unity in which diverse speeches are elements of coherent dialogues or work to together to create stylized dramatic scenes.

The second hindrance the redactional analysis creates for a dramatic reading is that it introduces a hierarchy between speeches that is alien to dramatic presentation. When O'Connor, Diamond, and Smith identify the prose speeches in Jeremiah 11–20 as redactional additions, they make the laments of Jeremiah subordinate to the additions. The role that the "original speeches" play in the text must be explained in terms of the intentions of the editor(s) who added the "later speeches." The distortion this causes to the dramatic presentation can be illustrated by considering the effect of identifying the perspective of (some of) the speeches of one character in a drama with the perspective of the dramatist. If someone believed that the text called "Hamlet" contained the authentic poetry of the historical prince of Denmark, he might also believe that those who added the later inauthentic material (notably the prose speeches) were motivated by an agenda that can be discerned in some of these speeches, perhaps those of King Claudius. If the Claudius party (who wished to exonerate the king and blame Prince Hamlet for the collapse of the monarchy) is also judged to be responsible for the final form of the text, then it would be obvious that the records of Hamlet's private musings were included as evidence documenting the paranoia and dementia that led to his delusional accusations and treachery. To the redaction critics who identify the perspective of Jeremiah 11–20 with the perspective of Yahweh's prose speeches (read as exilic sermons), it is obvious that Jeremiah's laments were included as evidence of the people's sin that led to the exile. The conclusion that this "theodicy agenda" is the primary purpose of Jeremiah 11–20 illustrates a third hindrance to appreciating the dramatic presentation in the passage. Redaction-critical approaches regularly reduce the significance of passages to such narrowly conceived ideological or theological agendas.[105] The reader can judge what a disservice this represents for dramatic literature remarkable for its heartrending portrayals of Yahweh decreeing the destruction of his beloved and Jeremiah fighting in vain to hold back his prophetic fire.

This chapter has not only demonstrated how the failure to break free from the assumptions and methods of the dominant historical-critical approach to Jeremiah has kept redaction critics from realizing their goal of illuminating the literary structure and theological significance of the final form of the text; it has also shown how some of these critics began to realize the frailty of the old assumptions and to discover features of the text that challenged these assumptions and held out the promise of a better understanding of the present text. The previous chapter traced similar

---

[105] In redactional analyses that seek to identify the *ideological* agendas of the editors, the basic agenda usually turns out to be the attempt to exonerate themselves and discredit rival political groups by blaming them for the exile. Carroll, *Jeremiah*; Carolyn J. Sharp, *Prophecy and Ideology in Jeremiah: Struggles for Authority in Deutero-Jeremianic Prose* (New York: T&T Clark, 2003). Redactional analyses that find a *theological* agenda in the final form of the book (like O'Connor, Diamond, and Smith) are closely related to canonical approaches to the book such as those of Brevard Childs. Childs, "Jeremiah," 338–54. The theological agenda they find in the canonical form of the book is primarily to exonerate God by blaming Judah for the exile. The similarity between these two judgments of the book's agenda lends credence to Walter Brueggemann's suggestion that "ideological" and "canonical" approaches are "two sides of the same coin." Walter Brueggemann, *Exile and Homecoming: A Commentary on Jeremiah* (Grand Rapids, MI: Eerdmans, 1998), xi.

developments in rhetorical criticism of Jeremiah. The final chapter will show how the discovery of dramatic presentation in Jeremiah 2–10 and 11–20 has opened the way to understanding their literary structure and how the rhetorical and redaction critics were unable to see this because of their continued adherence to the aims or methods and the assumptions of Duhm.

9

Dramatic Portrayal and Narrative Coherence in Jeremiah 2–10 and 11–20

The two previous chapters gave examples of both rhetorical studies of Jeremiah 2–10 and redactional studies of Jeremiah 11–20 that came to recognize a central feature of the text: dramatic presentation. Scholars following these approaches found evidence that the speeches in these chapters were designed to depict dramatic characters and evoke dramatic situations. However, the previous chapters also showed that these same scholars could only offer skewed accounts of the dramatic characters and situations because they continued to cling to elements of Duhm's assumptions, agendas, and methods, which dominated twentieth-century Jeremiah scholarship. Adherence to Duhm's assumption that poetic form is an indicator of authenticity caused them to assign Yahweh's poetic speeches to Jeremiah and his prose speeches to exilic Deuteronomists. Adherence to Duhm's biographical agenda caused rhetorical critics to misread cues intended to evoke dramatic situations as clues that inadvertently reveal situations in the life of Jeremiah. Adherence to Duhm's methodological approach caused redaction critics to assign dramatic speeches to early and late editions of the text and subordinate the early speeches to the supposed agenda of the late ones. Both rhetorical and redaction critics failed to realize that the dramatic character of the text they discovered poses a challenge to Duhm's system. Recognizing this feature of the text undermines Duhm's basic assumption that poetic form indicates authenticity by providing an alternative explanation of the poetry and prose division, and it casts doubt on the validity of his biographical agenda and compositional approach by suggesting that the text is a unified artistic creation rather than a collection of authentic and inauthentic records.

The refusal of rhetorical and redaction critics to abandon Duhm's system in spite of evidence that undermines its validity has not only clouded their perception of the dramatic characters and situations; it has also prevented them from achieving their aim of illuminating the structure and purpose of the present form of the text. This failure is noteworthy since, as has been described, these new approaches came to prominence because of their promise to overcome the failure of older historical-critical approaches to provide a satisfying account of the present form of the text. If the accounts of the present book of Jeremiah offered by rhetorical and redaction criticism are no more compelling than those offered by form and source criticism (or less compelling, as in the case of the redactional accounts of Jeremiah 11–20), the new approaches will have failed to demonstrate their worth.

That the rhetorical and redactional approaches of the last decades have made significant progress in discerning the unifying structure of Jeremiah was demonstrated in the descriptions of Lundbom's and Holladay's observations of Jeremiah 2–10 and O'Connor's, Diamond's, and Smith's observations of Jeremiah 11–20. All of these scholars turned up an impressive amount of new evidence of intentional literary structure that help put to rest the older views that these chapters of Jeremiah are a "hopeless hodgepodge" of loosely related materials. However, although they showed the possibility of literary structure and found many specific signs of this structure, these scholars remained committed to Duhm and Mowinckel's assumption that the text was fundamentally a collection of disparate materials. This assumption limited the kind and degree of structure they could expect to find in the text.

The last two chapters argued that the discovery of dramatic presentation in the text calls for a reassessment of the nature of the text, including the nature of its structural unity. New possibilities for structure were turned up when the text of Jeremiah 2–10 and 11–20 were analyzed with methods appropriate for texts employing dramatic presentation. In particular, it was shown that units of text thought to derive from different sources are actually individual speeches in extended dramatic dialogues and that the speeches of the primary speakers (Yahweh and Jeremiah) contributed to dramatic characterizations that were developed across a number of scenes. Many of these dramatic dialogues and scenes have been observed by the rhetorical and redaction critics. However, these critics have not, for the most part, been able to perceive a more comprehensive type of unity that holds together the dramatic dialogues and scenes of Jeremiah 2–10 and 11–20. The principal relationship of the scenes in these two sections is temporal progression; their unity comes from their participation in two extended dramatic narratives.

This final chapter defends the judgment that Jeremiah 2–10 and 11–20 are unified by temporal progression as a more compelling account of the text than the rhetorical accounts of Jeremiah 2–10 as unified by a complex pattern of structuring devices (e.g., chiasms and *inclusios*) and the redactional accounts of Jeremiah 11–20 as unified by a pattern of sermons and illustrations. The failure of these studies to perceive the narrative unity and their explanation of the unity in terms of a pattern imposed by an editor (whether Jeremiah or Deuteronomists) is attributed to their commitment to Duhm and Mowinckel's assumption that the text is fundamentally a collection of historical records. The evidence of dramatic presentation in the text given in previous chapters serves as an initial challenge to this assumption. The evidence of narrative progression in the text is presented in this final chapter as a further challenge Duhm's assumption: it indicates that the components of these chapters (both poetry and prose) are elements of unified literary compositions not a collection of (authentic and inauthentic) historical records.

The Narrative Coherence of Jeremiah 2–10

The analyses of Jeremiah 2–10 in the work of Lundbom and Holladay has been singled out for investigation because the rhetorical approach they employ holds out the promise of appreciating the artistic structure of the present form of the text. A primary aim for both scholars is to overturn the judgment of the standard compositional approach that the poetry of Jeremiah has no meaningful structure. This challenge is obvious in the title of Holladay's 1976 *The Architecture of Jeremiah 1–20*. Both Lundbom and Holladay find the poetry elaborately structured by an intricate system of *inclusios*, chiasms, and a variety of other rhetorical techniques.[1] Observation of these techniques, primarily by looking for patterns of repeated words and parallel structures, allows Lundbom and Holladay to delimit the compositional units in the text and describe the relationships between them. The attention they pay to the structural unity and rhetorical artistry of the present form of the text yields many novel observations and intriguing suggestions.

Despite their advances in understanding the artistry and unity of the materials in Jeremiah, the proposals for structure suggested by these rhetorical studies suffer from three weaknesses. First, the subtlety of many of the rhetorical techniques they purport to find in the text raises doubts about whether readers or hearers could have been expected to perceive or appreciate them. Second, the overreliance on patterns of repeated words as the primary techniques of literary unity means that their observations of structure do not go much beyond defining individual units and noting parallels between units. It may be a solid observation that Unit A in ch. 4:5-31 has verbal and formal similarities with Unit A′ in ch. 6:1-8,[2] but it is not clear how this observation adds to the reader's understanding or experience of either of these passages. Third, the notion of structure or architecture suggested by Lundbom and Holladay often seems to be overly spatial and static. Parallel columns and balanced symmetries are appropriate to an edifice or a picture but seem less appropriate for a literary work that is experienced by readers (or hearers) as a linear succession. With the "architectural" structures found by Lundbom and Holladay, one often wonders to what degree the structures were suggested by considering blocks of text on the written page.

These weaknesses can be considered symptomatic of a more fundamental flaw in the rhetorical approach of Lundbom and Holladay. Their search for structure primarily takes the form of an attempt to discover a hidden pattern imposed on disparate units rather than a description of how the components of the composition were designed to work together to achieve a unified effect. Their understanding of structure can be attributed to their failure to break free from the standard assumptions about the nature of the poetry in Jeremiah. The primary assumption is that each poetic unit originated in

---

[1] Each of these scholars has contributed an important monograph on Jeremiah (William Holladay, *The Architecture of Jeremiah 1–20* [Lewisburg, PA: Bucknell University, 1976]; Jack Lundbom, *Jeremiah: A Study in Ancient Hebrew Rhetoric*, SBL Dissertation Series 18 [Missoula, MT: Scholars, 1975]) as well as a major commentary (Holladay, *Jeremiah 1: A Commentary on the Book of the Prophet Jeremiah*, Chapters 1–25, Hermeneia [Philadelphia, PA: Fortress, 1986]; Lundbom, *Jeremiah 1–20*, Anchor Bible [New York: Doubleday, 1999]).

[2] Holladay, *Jeremiah 1*, 136.

a historical context that provides its basic meaning. As has been shown, this assumption has become entrenched in the form-critical descriptions of the poetry in the prophetic books as collections of short speeches that take the basic form of oracles or messages (forms that depend on their historical contexts for meaning). The rhetorical criticism of Lundbom and Holladay does not move beyond these declarations of form criticism about what prophetic speeches must be.

Lundbom and Holladay could not challenge the form-critical system that makes poetic units available as authentic evidence because of their own commitment to the biographical approach. The result is that in their work, the present context of the poetic units must be considered secondary. Whatever coherence these originally independent units have must be an editorial achievement (even if the editor is Jeremiah), and the coherence cannot be more than superficial because recognition of meaningful coherence in the present literary context threatens to degrade the value of the independent parts as evidence of the situations in which they were composed. Thus, the most the editor is allowed to do is group the materials by content, arrange it into patterns, or add a few linking words and framing devices. The resulting "structure" is at best a curiosity, and its value for understanding the meaning and significance of the poetry can be estimated by the pains that Lundbom and Holladay take to dismantle the structure in order to use the isolated units to determine the original contents of the *Urrolle*, the identity of the northern foe, the date of Jeremiah's call, and so on.

Lundbom and Holladay's perpetuation of the standard approach's agenda of recovering the history behind the present text keeps them from fully perceiving the story of Yahweh and Israel that Jeremiah 2–10 creates for its audience. To perceive the effect a text is designed to have on its audience would seem to provide a better description of the aims of rhetorical criticism than to discover the devices used to "structure" a text. Similarly, a text's structure may be better described as the way its components work together to create its effect than as the pattern into which its components are arranged. Of course, an appropriate estimation of a text's effect or structure will depend on the nature of the text. In the case of Jeremiah 2–10, it will be argued here that the text is intended to provide its audience with a narrative portrayal of Yahweh's relationship to Israel and that its structure is a narrative to which each of the dramatic scenes contribute.

Defining the Unit (Jeremiah 2–10): Three Views of Its Unity

Understanding the elements of Jeremiah 2–10 as scenes in a narrative progression provides a more organic and observable unity for the text. The difference between narrative unity and previous understandings of the text's unity can be shown by comparing three ways of distinguishing Jeremiah 2–10 as a compositional unit.

In most studies following the standard compositional approach, there is little concern for structure and little expectation of unity. The individual records of Jeremiah's speeches (or fragments of his speeches) are thought to be merely gathered into a collection. In this collection, some find evidence of editorial groupings and others see traces of earlier collections, or cycles. Still others view the collection as a "hopeless hodgepodge thrown together without any discernible principle at all."[3] This

---

[3]   John Bright, *Jeremiah*, 2nd ed., AB 21 (Garden City, NY: Doubleday, 1965), lvi.

lack of unity is only to be expected in a collection of historical documents, and it provides little hindrance to interpretation if the individual speeches are only related by common authorship. Commentaries following the standard approach often treat Jeremiah 2–10 as a unit. However, this is not because of any perceived compositional unity but only because the documents it contains are mostly in poetic form and stand between the prose call of Jeremiah in ch. 1 and the beginning of the laments in ch. 11. The documents in these chapters can be considered together because they are mostly the same kind of material (authentic oracles) and may mostly originate from the same early period in Jeremiah's ministry. These perceived similarities give the contents of Jeremiah 2–10 about the same degree and kind of unity as marbles collected in a bag because most of them are the same color.

A second way of distinguishing Jeremiah 2–10 as a unit is based on observing a rhetorical technique—one such as Lundbom and Holladay might observe. At the beginning and end of these chapters, repeated diction suggests the presence of an *inclusio*, or framing device, which marks the boundaries of the compositional unit. In the first verse of poetry in ch. 2, Yahweh recalls how the young bride Israel followed him (literally, "walked after me," *lektēk ʾaḥăray*) in the wilderness. The verbal root *hlk* is repeated in the last verses of poetry in ch. 10, with the confession "mortals as they walk (*hōlēk*) cannot direct their steps" (10:23). A more striking repetition occurs in the adjacent verses. In the second verse of poetry, the nation is portrayed as the first fruits of Yahweh's harvest, sacred to him, with the result that "all who ate of it (*kol-ʾōklāyw*) became guilty; disaster came upon them" (2:3). The image of devouring (*ʾkl*) the nation recurs in the final verse of ch. 10, which calls on Yahweh to pour out his wrath on the nations because they have "devoured (*ʾaklû*) Jacob" (10:25).

Relying on this *inclusio* to define the unit has some apparent weaknesses. For the audience to perceive the repetitions at the end of ch. 10 as indications of the end of the unit, they would have to have kept these two words in mind throughout the reading of nine chapters. The likelihood of this depends largely on how prominent the words were in their first occurrence as well as how rare the words are in general usage and in Jeremiah 2–10. On these counts, *hlk*, a very common word, would barely register with the audience, but *ʾkl*, a less common word, might possibly stand out. Even if this *inclusio* were recognized as framing 2–10, it is difficult to see what it would add to understanding the significance of the whole beyond marking it as a unit.[4]

If the verbal repetitions alone are observed, it is difficult to argue that the connections between 2:2-3 and 10:23-25 are intentional or significant. However, the argument is much stronger if the reader pays attention to the temporal settings of these passages. The two images at the beginning of ch. 2 (the bride and the firstfruits) are pictures of Israel at the time of the exodus ("in the wilderness," 2:2). The two speeches at the end of ch. 10 are spoken by a person in the time of the exile ("the nations have laid waste [Jacob's] habitation," 10:25). Thus, they depict two contrasting moments in Israel's history. In the first, the people faithfully walk after Yahweh, like a new bride with her

---

[4] Although neither Holladay nor Lundbom make much of this *inclusio*, the criticisms of it apply with more or less the same force to many similar rhetorical techniques they identify as structural elements in the text of Jeremiah.

husband (2:2), and in the second, their independent wandering leads to the confession that "it is not in man who walks to direct his steps" (10:23). In the first picture, they are Yahweh's prized firstfruits, zealously protected from the nations that would devour them (2:3); in the second, having lost Yahweh's protection, they have been devoured by the nations (10:25). Along with the contrast, there is also an implicit comparison: in the time of the exile as in the time of the exodus, Israel finds itself without land, king, or temple, wholly dependent on Yahweh for protection and guidance.

Although this contrast and comparison add to the interpretive significance of the two passages, the argument that these passages—nine chapters apart—provide a frame for the chapters remains somewhat weak without further support. This support comes when it is observed that the whole nine chapters are unified by a temporal progression—the third way of describing the unity of Jeremiah 2–10. With this view, these parallel verses can be seen as the opening and closing scenes of a story. They not only imply the boundaries of a compositional unit; they also indicate the timeframe of the story: from the time of the exodus to the time of the exile. The parallelism of the beginning and end indicate that in the exile, Israel's story has come full circle. The chapters in between tell how the nation moved from the initial situation to the final situation: the story of Israel from exodus to exile.

All that was necessary to understand the relationship between 2:2-3 and 10:23-25 was to attend to the situations the two units were intended to portray and then note the difference in when they occurred. This same attention is all that is necessary to perceive the narrative progression in Jeremiah 2–10. Unfortunately, the dominant historical agenda of relating each unit to a situation in Jeremiah's life has made it almost impossible to attend to the situations portrayed in the text. The following overview of Jeremiah 2–10 will describe the occasions that the various units portray and note how they are related by temporal progression: how they tell a story. At each point, it will also be shown how critics following the dominant approach were blinded to this aspect of the text by their commitment to the agenda and assumptions of the standard compositional theory developed by Duhm and Mowinckel.

This story can be considered in three parts: (1) Israel's history of infidelity from the entry of the whole nation into the land through the exile of northern Israel (chs 2–3), (2) Judah's continued refusal to repent in the face of northern invasions culminating in the fall of Jerusalem (chs 4–9), (3) Israel's reliance on Yahweh in the aftermath of the exile (ch. 10).

Israel's Story from Exodus to Exile

United Israel and Northern Israel (Chapters 2–3)

The opening scene of a dramatic presentation is crucial for establishing the situation and time period. As has been observed, 2:1-3 fulfills this narrative requirement with its clear presentation of Yahweh and Israel's relationship during the time of the wilderness wandering. The next scene (2:4-8) continues the story of the nation by presenting the entry into the land. Yahweh is pictured as recounting the story for "the house of Jacob, and all the tribes of Israel" (2:4). He recalls how their "fathers" forgot what he had done for them in delivering Israel from Egypt and leading them in the wilderness (2:6). Then he speaks directly to all the tribes of Israel: "I brought you into a plentiful land ... but when you entered you defiled my land" (2:7). After recounting how the leaders of those first Israelites in the land rejected Yahweh, the speech concludes: "Therefore once more I accuse you, says Yahweh, and I accuse your children's children" (2:9). For at least the first few verses of this speech, it is hard to deny that the early history of Israel is being presented.

However, by the end of the speech, many interpreters have jumped directly from this setting in the early period of Israel's history to a setting in the life of Jeremiah. Craigie writes, "Jeremiah is the messenger through whom the divine declaration of the legal suit is declared."[5] That Jeremiah speaks here must be assumed, perhaps on the basis of the "messenger formula" in 2:5. However, the passage identifies Yahweh as the speaker while Jeremiah and his mediatory role are not mentioned until 3:6.[6] As for the audience of this passage, Thompson identifies them as "members of Judah, the southern kingdom" perhaps "at some covenant festival."[7] But the passage contains at least three specific indications of the audience of this passage: it is identified as "all the tribes of Israel" (2:4), specifically all those whose fathers were delivered from Egypt (2:5), and all those who entered the land (2:7). Concerning the occasion, for Bright and others, the reference to false worship "seems clearly to reflect pre-reformation conditions."[8] In the passage, however, the false worship is assigned to the period of the first Israelites in Canaan (and only by extension to their descendants, 2:9).

The differences between what the passage portrays and what the interpreters find in it can be explained by the persistence of the biographical approach to the text. The interpreters are less interested in the situation portrayed by the passage than in the situation that can be reconstructed if it is assumed that the passage is a record of a speech Jeremiah delivered. The reason this interest in what lies behind the text is especially pronounced in interpretation of the poetry of the book's first chapters has been explained in Chapter 5. In the biographical approach exemplified by Skinner, the poetic speeches of these chapters, regarded as authentic documentary evidence, are used to reconstruct the first two decades of Jeremiah's ministry, from his call (*c.* 627 BC, the thirteenth year of Josiah's reign, 1:2) to the first events recorded in the prose accounts (*c.* 609 BC, the beginning of Jehoiakim's reign, 26:1). Since there is little clear indication in the poetry that it originated in Jeremiah's early years (or in Jeremiah's time at all), inferences must be made on the flimsiest of evidence as seen in the interpretation of Jer. 2:2-9 above. A reference to early Israel's idolatry (2:7) must originate early in Josiah's reign because after his reforms there could have been little idolatry in Judah. A reference to the leaders of early Israel mishandling the law (2:8)

[5] Peter Craigie, Page Kelly, and Joel Drinkard Jr., *Jeremiah 1–24*, WBC 26 (Dallas, TX: Word Books, 1991), 29.
[6] Jeremiah's role as a messenger appears in the heading in 2:1-2a "The word of the Yahweh came to me saying, 'Go and proclaim in the hearing of Jerusalem.'" However, it has already been pointed out that this heading only occurs in the Masoretic Text and sits loosely with the following passage, which is not addressed to Jerusalem but Israel.
[7] J. A. Thompson, *The Book of Jeremiah*, NICOT (Grand Rapids, MI: Eerdmans, 1980), 167.
[8] Bright, *Jeremiah*, 17.

must have been part of a speech Jeremiah delivered at a covenant festival in Judah (perhaps on the assumption no one referred to the law except at covenant festivals).

The next long section (2:14-37) continues the story of Israel primarily through Yahweh's address to her as a woman who rebels against him to go after other lovers. Perceiving the time period being portrayed depends on correctly identifying the woman. The preceding section suggests that all Israel is being addressed. However, the reference in the opening verses of the section (14-16) to a masculine Israel ("Israel a slave? Is he a homeborn servant") may picture Israel as Jacob, who often represents the northern nation. This is confirmed when the woman addressed is warned against putting her trust in Egypt and Assyria (initially in 2:18 and finally in 2:39). The situation these warnings evoke is the last years of independent northern Israel when a succession on kings vacillated between dependence on Egypt and Assyria (cf. 2 Kgs 15–17, Hos. 4:13, 7:11, 8:9, 12:1). The final warning, "From [Egypt] too you will come away with your hands upon your head" (2:37), vividly represents the results of King Hoshea's policy of secretly paying tribute to Egypt (2 Kgs 17:4). When Assyria discovered it, Israel was attacked and the alliance with Egypt proved useless in preventing the occupation of the land and the deportation of thousands of its citizens. In Jer. 2:18-37, this exile of Israel's people is presented as the result of Yahweh's anger at his sinful wife for her adultery with her lovers, Egypt and Assyria.

In opposition to this understanding of the passage, most interpreters of the last hundred years have insisted that the woman must be Judah during the time of Jeremiah. The difficulty is that there is no evidence that Judah ever put its trust in Assyria during Jeremiah's time. Josiah's reign, when Jeremiah began his ministry, was marked by independence from Assyria, which was in its final decline. One standard response to this historical difficulty is to push the date of the warnings back to some early time in Jeremiah's life when Assyria still had some semblance of power.[9] Another response, recognizing the first response to be historically dubious, is to say that Assyria represents Babylon.[10] Thus, a warning to Israel against depending on Egypt and Assyria (2:14-19) should be read as a warning to Judah against depending on Egypt and Babylon. This forced reading is the result of the fixed assumption that the poetry of these chapters can have no background other than the ministry of Jeremiah.

The following passage (3:1–4:2) begins with the question, "If a man divorces [or sends away] his wife and she goes from him and becomes another man's wife will he return to her?" (3:1). Apparently northern Israel failed to heed Yahweh's warning and he has now divorced her by abandoning her to conquest and her people to exile. This divorce is the result of her adulteries described in the previous section. However, in opposition to this interpretation, modern interpreters insist that Judah of Jeremiah's day is the divorced woman, though they usually fail to suggest in what sense Yahweh has sent her away.

Up to this point, it might be possible to doubt that 2:14-3:5 has northern Israel in view, but in 3:6-10 the text makes this identification explicit. Yahweh says to Jeremiah, "Have you seen what she did, that faithless one, Israel, how she went up on every high

---

[9] E.g., Bright, *Jeremiah*, 14.
[10] Holladay, *Jeremiah 1*, 3.

hill and under every green tree and played the whore? ... and her false sister Judah saw it" (3:6b, 7b). Israel is (unusually) portrayed as a woman, her harlotry is described in the exact words used to accuse the sinful woman in 2:20, and she is distinguished from her sister Judah, making it clear that the northern nation alone is in view. Yahweh continues, "For all the adulteries of that faithless one, Israel, I had sent her away with a decree of divorce" (3:8b). Here, the divorce of 3:1 is clearly presented as Yahweh's divorce of northern Israel. The presentation of the text at this point is so clear that it is almost impossible to maintain that it presents Judah as the sinful woman Yahweh divorced. The only expedient left for this view is to deny the presentation of the text. Thus, in order to maintain the assumption of the biographical approach that the background of Jeremiah 2–3 must be the Judah of Jeremiah's day, commentators regularly discredit 3:6-10 as late prose that misinterprets Jeremiah's authentic poetry.

In the text's presentation, the question of 3:1—whether northern Israel can return to Yahweh and her people return from exile—dominates 3:1–4:2. Initially, it seems impossible that Yahweh would have her back after adultery, divorce, and flagrant prostitution (3:1-5). However, during the time of Josiah, there is an unexpected turn of events. Because Judah has refused to learn from the example of her older sister Israel and stubbornly followed the pattern of adultery and refusal to repent, she has become even guiltier than Israel. On the basis of this new situation and the faithful love of Yahweh, Jeremiah is commissioned to go and offer a chance for northern Israel to return to her God and for her people to return to their land.

> Yahweh said to me: Faithless Israel has shown herself less guilty than false Judah.
> Go, and proclaim these words to the North and say:
> Return O Israel, says Yahweh.
>> I will not look on you in anger,
> for I am merciful, says Yahweh;
>> I will not be angry forever.
>
> (3:11-12)

It is amazing to observe that many scholars are so convinced that "Israel" cannot mean northern Israel that they deny that this message to the "North" addresses northern Israel. They insist that the Israel here called to return is all Israel or Judah; the prose introduction, which distinguishes Israel from Judah and indicates that it is northern, they dismiss as a late misinterpretation. The argument offered for this denial of the text's presentation is that the repentance call is in poetic form; poetic form is a mark of authentic messages of Jeremiah; and the authentic messages of Jeremiah were addressed to Judah, not northern Israel.[11]

It is sometimes added that comparison between northern Israel and Judah does not appear in the authentic poetry of Jeremiah and does appear in Ezekiel. This

---

[11] William McKane, *A Critical and Exegetical Commentary on Jeremiah*, ICC (Edinburgh: T&T Clark, 1986 and 1996), vol. 1, 71–2; John Skinner, *Prophecy and Religion: Studies in the Life of Jeremiah* (Cambridge: Cambridge University Press, 1922), 46; Mark Biddle, *A Redaction History of Jeremiah 2:1–4:2*, AThANT 77 (Zürich: TVZ, 1990), 96; Philip Hyatt, "Jeremiah," in *IB*, ed. George A. Buttrick (New York: Abingdon, 1956), 826.

argument is Cambridge circular since most of these interpreters have already ruled out the poetry of Jeremiah having any concern with northern Israel. However, if the poetry of Jeremiah 2–3 does concern northern Israel, then it would seem that it invites comparison with the following chapters, which concern Judah. In fact, the appeal for true repentance that brings northern Israel's story to a close (4:1-2) leads into a parallel appeal to Judah and Jerusalem to change their ways or face judgment (4:3-4).

The Judgment of Judah and Jerusalem (Chapters 4–9)

In the large central section of Jeremiah 2–10, chs 4–9, the focus turns from northern Israel to Judah and Jerusalem as indicated by the opening warning to the "men of Judah and Jerusalem" (4:2).[12] The setting presented in this section is primarily the time period of the successive invasions of Judah by the Babylonians up to and including the destruction of Jerusalem in 586.[13] This is the time of Jeremiah's ministry, and the prophet is portrayed both as an agent of Yahweh and a member of the sinful nation: sometimes he brings Yahweh's words of warning or judgment, and sometimes he seeks to avert Yahweh's judgment or simply weeps over the fate of the people. However, as the dramatic analysis in ch. 6 argued, Yahweh and Jeremiah are for the most part independent speakers, and Yahweh's speeches should not be attributed to Jeremiah (as messenger speeches) unless the text makes clear that Jeremiah is speaking Yahweh's words clearly indicated in the text (e.g., 3:12).

A dominant aspect of the dramatic portrayal in this section is the vivid evocation of war and disaster that accompanies the invasions of Judah. A prominent example is the panicked cry of Jerusalem as the invaders threaten her home, her children, and her life (4:20, 22, 31). Unfortunately, as was observed in the dramatic analysis, interpreters often fail to perceive the dramatic situation because they read Jerusalem's speech (4:19-21) as the speech of Jeremiah in order to use it as evidence of prophetic experience. Treating this speech as a prophetic oracle of Jeremiah not only obscures the dramatic speaker but also obscures the time of this scene in the narrative progression. The speech presents Lady Jerusalem crying at the time of the invasion: "I hear the sound of the trumpet. ... Suddenly my tents are destroyed. ... How long must I see the standard?" There is no indication in the text that these things are being heard or seen ahead of time as a prophetic oracle or vision.

The impetus to read Jerusalem's speech as a prophecy comes not from the text but from the assumption that poetry must be authentic prophetic speech. This assumption became entrenched in studies of the prophets through the form-critical judgment that the distinguishing character of prophetic speech is the announcement

---

[12] Although Jer. 4:1-4 can be considered a hinge passage, the best place to draw the line between the first two major sections of Jer. 2-10 is probably between 4:3 and 4:4. Thus, "Jeremiah 4–9" should be read in this discussion as shorthand for "Jer. 4:2–9:25".

[13] Since the northern foe is never named, it is not out of the question that some of the passages could refer to another northern invader as in the old Scythian theory. However, since the passage includes the destruction of Jerusalem at the hands of the Babylonians and the time period of the whole passage is during the ministry of Jeremiah, the Babylonians must be the primary invader being portrayed.

of future events.[14] When this form-critical judgment is combined with the form-critical judgment that prophetic speech is messenger speech and the source-critical judgment that poetic form indicates authentic prophetic speech, the result is that the poetic portrayals of the horror of invasion in Jeremiah 4–9 are regularly treated as Jeremiah's prophecies of coming judgment even though many of them give no indication that Jeremiah is speaking or that the situation evoked is in the future.[15] The text's presentation does include passages that present Jeremiah or Yahweh warning of future catastrophe, but these are relatively few and often in prose.[16] Without the form-critical assumption, the portrayals of war can be appreciated as dramatic scenes from the last days of Judah: the ominous approach of the enemy (4:7, 13; 6:22-33), the frantic preparations of the people (4:5; 6:1; 8:14), the terrifying onslaught (4:29, 5:17, 6:25, 8:16), the inescapable siege (6:3-6), and the desolate aftermath (9:10, 19, 21-22 [ET 9:11, 20, 22-23]). The immediacy of these depictions gives the reader a sense of being present as the invasions occur.

Both the prophetic predictions and the portrayals of invasion are woven together in the narrative progression that can be observed throughout chs 4–9. The progression is not a clear linear story. Instead, it is presented in a series of dramatic vignettes that portray critical moments in the story. Even among these, it is not always clear that time has progressed when the text moves from one scene to the next. Instead, many scenes seem to repeat earlier scenes. For example, the invaders are shown setting out from their country at least three different times (4:7, 16; 6:22-33), and several times they gather around Jerusalem (4:17, 31; 6:3-7, 25). These could represent successive invasions (e.g., 604, 598, and 588 BC); however, there are few clear details that would allow readers to connect the various pictures of invasion with the various historical invasions. The general impression left on the reader is similar to that of watching a sandcastle threatened by successive waves crashing onto a beach. However, although the image of waves may express the back-and-forth movement in the chapters, this is not the whole picture. Two additional features of the situation must be added to complete the image: first, each of the incoming waves reaches further up the beach because the tide is coming in; and second, the castle finally falls.

---

[14] E.g., Gene Tucker concludes his search for the basic form of prophetic speech, saying, "The most common and distinctive form of prophetic speech is the prophecy. … The genre is defined by two factors which appear with regularity: the prophet (1) presents a communication from God (2) announcing future events." Gene M. Tucker, "Prophetic Speech," in *Interpreting the Prophets*, ed. James Luther Mays and Paul J. Achtemeier (Philadelphia, PA: Fortress, 1987), 38–9. See also Westermann's observation of "what is by far the most predominant function of the prophetic speech: An announcement is almost always made in it. … The announcement can proclaim judgment or salvation." Claus Westermann, *Basic Forms of Prophetic Speech* (Philadelphia, PA: Westminster, 1967), 94.

[15] It is interesting to note that, as in the case of the form-critical judgment that characteristic prophetic speech is messenger speech, the form-critical judgment that prophetic speech is an announcement of the future fits quite well with most of allegedly inauthentic prose speeches in Jeremiah but not very well with the allegedly authentic poetic speeches.

[16] Poetic references to the future: 4:23-26; 5:6, 15-17; 6:12, 15, 19, 21; 8:10, 12; 9:10 (ET 11), 24 (ET 25). Prose references to the future: 4:9, 11-12, 27; 5:18-19; 7:1-15, 32-34; 8:1-3; 9:14-15 (ET 15-16). Furthermore, these predictions are often followed by a portrayal of the actual occurrence of the disaster they predict: Jer. 4:13, 29; 6:22-24; 8:14-16; 9:16-18 (ET 17-19). In this way, the warnings are fitted into the story.

The way in which the text achieves this dramatic portrayal of increasingly devastating invasions that finally result in the fall of Jerusalem is through an ingenious alternation of recurring scenes. That these recurring scenes are the key to the structure of this section of Jeremiah was recognized by William Holladay. In his commentary, he carefully notes the recurrences in vocabulary, form, and dominant motif.[17] On the basis of these observations, he proposes that the structure of Jer. 4:5–6:30 is determined by arrangement of recurring scenes into a (somewhat) chiastic pattern: A (4:5-31), B (5:1-9), C (5:10-17), D (5:20-9), A′ (6:1-8), C′ (6:9-15), B′ (6:16-30).[18] By drawing attention to these recurrences, Holladay has made a significant advance in perceiving the structure of the passage. However, he failed to notice a crucial feature of the recurrences he observed: within each set of recurrences, the scenes that occur later in the text depict situations that occur later in the narrative.

Of course, Holladay was kept from observing this feature because in keeping with form-critical dictates, he regards the scenes of the invasions to be a record of Jeremiah's oracles. In keeping with the biographical and compositional agenda, Holladay is not as interested in the situations these "oracles" portray as he is in discerning when the prophet spoke them: that is, what historical events prompted his sense of impending disaster.[19] The biographical agenda and form-critical assumptions determine his conventional judgment of the nature and structure of the passage. His designation of 4:5–6:30 as the "foe cycle"[20] represents the assessment that these chapters contain a thematic collection of (mostly) authentic oracles. His description of the structure as a chiastic pattern (A, B, C, D, A′, C′, B′) represents the limits of structure an editor could impose on a collection of records.

The narrative structure of Jeremiah 4–9 can now be observed by examining five sets of recurrences and noting how in each set the later recurrences represent further developments in the situation or later episodes in the story. The first set of recurrences in 4–9 is made up of three clusters of urgent commands to seek safety in light of the looming invasion. These commands, which dramatically introduce major scenes of invasion, are similar in form, purpose, and vocabulary. At the same time, comparing them shows a clear temporal progression. The first cluster of commands (4:5-6) urges people to flee for safety to the fortified cities and to Jerusalem. In the second cluster (6:1), Jerusalem is no longer safe and the Benjaminites are called to go out from the midst of Jerusalem and find refuge further south. In the third cluster (a question and two commands), there is a note of resignation: "Why do we sit still? Gather together, let us go to the fortified cities and perish there" (8:14). At this point, neither Jerusalem nor any of the cities can offer safety; the end has come. The story moves from an initial scene that holds out the hope of survival to a scene where all that remains is despair.

A second set of recurrences are a series of references to Yahweh's wrath as fire. These represent the implementation of Yahweh's warning that his wrath would "go

---

[17] Holladay, *Jeremiah 1*, 132–3.
[18] Holladay, *Jeremiah 1*, 136.
[19] E.g., he observes, "At least initially the material describing the foe from the north was stimulated by Carchemish." *Jeremiah 1*, 134.
[20] Holladay, *The Architecture of Jeremiah 1–20* (Cranbury, NJ: Associated University Presses, 1976), 31.

forth like fire and burn with none to quench it" (4:4).[21] This image is picked up in 5:14 when Yahweh tells Jeremiah, "I am now making my words in your mouth a fire and this people wood." The narrative thread is continued in 6:11 when Jeremiah complains that he is full of the wrath of Yahweh and weary of holding it in. In response, Yahweh tells him to pour it out.[22] Thus, the story moves from a scene of potential judgment to a scene of actualized judgment.

The third set of recurrences, images of refining, is closely related to the second set, images of fiery wrath, and carries it into ch. 9. In 6:27, Jeremiah is portrayed as refiner or tester of the people pictured as metal. This is probably in view of the fire he pours out on them, thus "the lead is consumed by the fire" (6:29). Jeremiah's refining is to no avail (6:29-30); so in the end, Yahweh takes over: "Now, I will refine them and test them" (9:7 [ET 9:8]). If this is to be read together with the previous passages in which fiery wrath recurs, the following story arc appears: Yahweh threatens that his wrath is coming if the people do not repent; they do not, and so he puts his wrath in Jeremiah; Jeremiah tries to hold it in but cannot. The fiery wrath poured out by Jeremiah is ineffective to refine the people; so Yahweh determines to refine them himself with the wrath he threatened.

A fourth set of recurrences is the pictures of the people as a fruitless vineyard (perhaps drawing on the earlier picture of Israel as a choice vine gone bad [2:21]). These three vineyard images are plagued with thorny textual and interpretive issues. Nevertheless, it is not difficult to see that they are related both thematically and sequentially.

> 5:10 Go up through her vineyard and destroy,
>> But do not make a full end;
>> Strip away her branches, for they are not Yahweh's
> 6:9 [Glean, glean] as a vine the remnant of Israel;
>> Like a grape gatherer pass your hand again over its branches
> 8:13 When I wanted to gather them, says Yahweh,
>> There are no grapes on the vine, no figs on the fig tree,
>> Even the leaves are withered.

Whether the gleaning (6:9) and gathering (8:13) are understood as intended to destroy the vines or to find fruit that would avert their destruction, the progressive nature of the passages can be seen. The first verse represents a first pass through the vineyard: "do not make a full end." The second verse represents a second pass: "pass your hand again" (*hāšēb*) to gather what was left the first time, the "remnant." Holladay refers to this second pass as a "mopping up process,"[23] and the Rabbinic commentator

---

[21] The vocabulary is repeated in the prose of 7:14: "My wrath will be poured out on this place. . . . It will burn with none to quench it." The prose prophecies are generally inserted in the narrative at the time when they are fulfilled rather than the time when they were spoken.

[22] Although 5:14 only uses the term "fire" and 6:11 only uses the term "wrath," the connection between them is clear in 4:4. Cf. 20:9 where it is fire that Jeremiah is weary of holding in.

[23] Holladay, *Jeremiah 1*, 213.

Rashi remarks that the image is of gleaning the higher branches for what was missed in the first picking.[24] The third verse laments the futility of making a third pass.

A fifth set of recurrences is the thrice-repeated refrain: "'Shall I not punish them for these things?' says Yahweh, 'and shall I not avenge myself on a nation such as this?'" (5:9, 29; 9:8 [ET 9:9]). Obviously, there can be no observable development in verbatim repetition. However, since each refrain follows another round of Yahweh's punishment and the people's refusal to repent, the refrain becomes more pointed and the answer more obvious each time: with each new exposure of the people's stubborn wickedness, there is greater reason for them to be punished.

In each set of recurrences, the final scene occurs in the poetry of 8:13–9:8 (ET 9:9). This passage draws together the narrative threads introduced in chs 4–6 and brings each one to a critical moment. The defense measures have failed, the people are resigned to perish, Jeremiah's warning and Yahweh's chastisement have had no effect, there is nothing in the vineyard of Israel left worth saving, and repeated efforts to refine them have yielded only dross. The section (4:5–9:8 [ET 9]) appropriately ends with the final repetition of the refrain, "Shall I not punish them? … Shall I not avenge myself?" All of the narrative threads have come together; there is nothing left for Jeremiah to do but weep (8:23 [ET 9:1]) and nothing left for Yahweh to do but take his vengeance and punish the nation. The narrative is approaching its conclusion; the next section will depict the fall of Jerusalem.

The culmination of the text's portrayal of the invasion in chs 8 and 9 is regularly overlooked by scholars limited to the standard compositional approach. Their assessment of the nature of these chapters is summed up well in the name Holladay gives them: the "secondary foe cycle."[25] To these scholars, Jeremiah 8–9 is simply a collection of additional oracles separated from the other oracles about the foe (Jeremiah 4–6) by the prose sermon in ch. 7. Chapter 7 does indeed come in 6:9–8:13, a passage that seems to have more of a topical rather than a narrative structure. The beginning and end of the passage are marked by the second and third recurrences of the gleaning imagery. In between them, the narrative pauses while the various "fruits" that might make Israel worth saving are considered. The corrupted fruit passages may be arranged in the kind of chiasm that Lundbom and Holladay often find in the text.[26]

Gleaning (6:9-12)
    Prophets (6:13-15)
        Law (6:16-19)
            Sacrificial System (8:20-21)
                Temple (7:1-15)
            Sacrificial System (7:21-26)
        Law (8:4-9)
    Prophets (8:10-12)
Gleaning (8:13)

---

[24] Cited by McKane, *Jeremiah*, 145.

[25] Holladay, *The Architecture of Jeremiah 1–20*, 31.

[26] If this is the case, and if the Masoretic Text extra in 8:10b-12 (a "doublet" of 6:13-15) is secondary, it would be an instance of an editor heightening the structure found in the existing text by adding poetry.

The prose speeches about the temple (7:1-7, 8-15) fit into the structure as one group of examples (the central example, if the chiastic structure is accepted) of things that gave the people of Israel false hope.[27] When the gleaning reveals that there is no fruit in the remnant worth saving (8:13), the narrative resumes with the scenes in which there is no hope of avoiding judgment.

The narrative now comes to the climax: the punishment of the nation, the fall of Jerusalem. Jerusalem's fall is portrayed in the second half of ch. 9 (9:9-21 [ET 10-22]) by Yahweh's announcement that he will destroy the city (9:10 [ET 11]) followed by a prophecy of the exile (9:11-15 [ET 12-16]) and a series of laments raised by the women of the fallen city (9:16-20 [ET 17-21]). Although many interpreters have recognized the climactic nature of these laments, they have been prevented from understanding their place in the narrative of 2–10 by the assumption that the laments are authentic prophetic speech (and thus must be spoken by the prophet) and the form-critical judgment that prophetic speech must be about the future. They commonly take these laments to be a novel type of prophecy in which Jeremiah predicts the downfall of the city by imagining the kind of laments he expects the people will sing when that future event occurs. Although this is not impossible, it has the effect of obscuring the dramatic situation vividly evoked by the laments (the time of mourning at the destruction of Jerusalem) and foregrounding a setting that the text does not suggest (the previous time in Jeremiah's ministry when he received or delivered a prophetic word about the destruction). In the narrative of the text, these laments portray the fall of Jerusalem, the culmination and climax of the story of Judah and Jerusalem's punishment for their wickedness and stubborn refusal to repent.

The Exiles' Praise and Jerusalem's Complaint (Chapter 10)

The final section of Jeremiah 2–10 presents scenes from the aftermath of Jerusalem's fall. The first scene portrays the exiles in their new situation confronted with the idol worship of the foreign culture. Yahweh's warning against following the idolatry of the nations is followed by two hymns (10:6-10, 12-16) in which the exiles exalt Yahweh over the idols of the nations. These hymns recall the beginning of the story in which Israel was devoted to Yahweh in the wilderness outside of the land and had not yet been corrupted by idolatry. The story returns to the choice between the true God and the worthless gods (in both chs 2 and 10, the gods are *hebel* [2:5; 10:15]). In the exilic

---

[27] It is interesting to note that the passage employs the dramatic technique of telescoping time like several of the poetic units (e.g., 5:1-4, 6:3-5). 7:1-7 presents Yahweh promising the people (through Jeremiah) that if they will amend their ways and not trust in "deceptive words" about the temple, they will remain in the land. 7:8-15 presents a speech on a later occasion when Yahweh says that because the people have trusted in "deceptive words" and have not amended their ways, the temple will be destroyed and the people will be cast out of the land. Thus, the passage presents a story by presenting two scenes back-to-back. Treating the two scenes as one authentic historical speech ("The Temple Sermon," which is the same as 26:16, e.g., J. A. Thompson, *The Book of Jeremiah*, NICOT [Grand Rapids, MI: Eerdmans, 1980; reprint, 1989], 272–4) or treating the first scene with its conditional promise as an editorial expansion (e.g., John Skinner, *Prophecy and Religion: Studies in the Life of Jeremiah* [Cambridge: Cambridge University Press, 1922], 170–1) obscures the dramatic presentation.

context of ch. 10, the false alternative is "the way of the nations" (10:2): the worship of the astral deities (10:3) and extravagant idols (10:9) of the wealthy empires who are ridiculed in the international language of Aramaic (10:11). The hymns praising Yahweh and denouncing idols represent Israel's turn toward the true God, a reversal of the turn away from him at the beginning of Israel's history in ch. 2.[28]

This portrayal of the exile is often misinterpreted by scholars whose first concern is to distinguish authentic and inauthentic material in the text. With this methodological priority, the cues in the text designed to suggest the exilic situation are taken to be indicators of the text's exilic origin and, thus, its inauthenticity. Further evidence of inauthenticity is the possibility of textual expansion: MT 10:6-8 and 10 are absent from the LXX (and 10:9 is in a different order),[29] and 10:12-16 is a doublet with 51:15-19. However, although this text may have been expanded during the exilic time period, what is remarkable is the unified portrait the resulting text gives of the exilic scene. The exilic editor[30] appears to have added a tightly unified three-part hymn (10:6-10) closely modeled on a preexisting three-part hymn (10:12-16/51:15-19).[31] If this is the case, it offers a striking example of the editor's ability to enhance the existing narrative and dramatic presentation and to compose poetry.

The hopeful tone struck by the joyful praise of the Israelites in exile is extinguished when the scene shifts to the bitter laments of Jerusalem in ruins. As is often the case in a tragedy, a ray of hope before the final catastrophe serves to deepen the gloom of the conclusion. As with the recurrences in 4–9, this final section furthers the narrative by presenting a scene that deliberately recalls the form and imagery of an earlier passage in order to present a subsequent situation. The cries of the ruined Jerusalem (10:18-20) reprise the anguished cries of Lady Jerusalem in 4:19-21. There her cries were those of a woman in the midst of invasion: "Suddenly my tents are destroyed, my curtains in a moment. How long must I see the standard and hear the sound of the trumpet?" (4:20b-21). Here, the picture has changed to the aftermath of her destruction: "My tent is destroyed, and all my cords are broken; my children have gone from me, and they are no more; there is no one to spread my tent again and set up my curtains" (10:20). As in the earlier scene, Jerusalem's cries are met with a blistering rebuke from Yahweh (10:21), showing that even Jerusalem's destruction has not exhausted his wrath.

At this point, as the narrative draws to a close, there comes a surprising recurrence of a report that destruction is coming from the north (10:22). At first, this might seem to mar the narrative progression: the story seems to have gone back to the beginning when the northern foe first set out. Although the text certainly means to recall these earlier passages, the succession of earlier reports did not present an identical event but several similar events, waves of invasion each eliciting a different

---

[28] That the "house of Israel" is addressed in 10:1 (cf. "portion of Jacob," 10:16) may represent a return to the use of "Israel" to mean the whole nation, the north and south joined in exile.

[29] Evidence from Qumran suggests that the LXX is based on a Hebrew *vorlage*. Frank Moore Cross writes, "The Qumran Jeremiah [4QJerb] omits the four verses [10:6-8 and 10] and shifts the order of [10:9] in identical fashion." Frank Moore Cross, *The Ancient Library at Qumran*, rev. ed. (Garden City, NY: Doubleday, 1961), 187, n. 38.

[30] It is worth remembering that Jeremiah's ministry stretched into the exile.

[31] An original hymn and an added hymn closely modeled after it:

response: first fleeing to Jerusalem, then away from Jerusalem, then to the cities resigned to perish. The response to this final threat of northern invasion, coming after the destruction of Jerusalem, is a new development (perhaps representing the renewed threat of invasion that caused the remaining inhabitants to flee to Egypt, cf. Jer. 41:17-18). Instead of commands to the people to prepare for the invasion, there are petitions addressed to Yahweh to mitigate or divert the invasion. The speaker accepts the necessity of correction but pleads that Yahweh will correct him (or "her" if the speaker is Jerusalem) "in just measure," recognizing that another invasion could "bring [him or her] to nothing" (10:24). Finally, the speaker prays that Yahweh will divert his anger (and probably the invasion) away from Israel onto the foreign nations who have devoured Israel (10:25). This final prayer thus appeals to the status of Israel at the beginning of the story: a people sacred to Yahweh who would bring evil on all who ate it (2:3).

Israel's Tragedy Obscured by the Biographical Approach

Before leaving these chapters behind, their literary and theological character can be briefly suggested. First, although the focus of these chapters is clearly Yahweh and Israel, the character of Jeremiah has not disappeared from the story. Instead, the outline of his character is sharpened. His primary role in these chapters is a reluctant agent of Yahweh's judgment. In most of the scenes in which he appears, he challenges Yahweh's verdict that there is nothing in the people worth saving, or he seeks to prevent the execution of Yahweh's sentence of destruction. His failure in each case serves to dramatically validate Yahweh's judgment.

At the same time, Jeremiah's advocacy for the sinful people serves another function in the drama. It provides a perspective that understands the people's situation as tragic and pitiable. Although the dominant voice is the angry Yahweh, the minority perspective of the sympathetic Jeremiah is not silenced. An even more striking feature is that the sinful Jerusalem is given a speaking part. Her cries can hardly fail to arouse the sympathy of the reader. In the standard biographical approach, which treats the poetry as messenger speech, the only voices allowed are those of Yahweh and Jeremiah. From the divine perspective, Jerusalem can only be seen as an unfaithful wife and a defiant prostitute. When the text is understood as drama, it can be seen that although Yahweh's perspective is dominant, the drama also includes Jerusalem's own perspective in which she is a pitiable character, bereaved of her home and children by Yahweh's wrath.

The overall effect of Jeremiah 2–10 is tragic. It evokes the terror and pity that Aristotle singled out as the intended effects of tragedy. However, unlike classical Greek tragedy, there is no tragic hero whose bold assertion of will in the face of his or her inescapable fate compels a degree of admiration. Israel's history of infidelity and waywardness in

Original Hymn (10:12-16/51:15-19)	New Hymn (10:6-10)
A: Yahweh, Creator (12-13)	A: Yahweh, King of the Nations (6-7)
B: Stupidity of created idols (14-15)	B: Stupidity of the nations' idols (8-9)
A': Yahweh, Creator (16)	A': Yahweh, King of the Nations (10)

spite of multiple chances to turn back to Yahweh is only foolish and shameful. Their perversity and the severity of Yahweh's punishments make the whole drama extremely bleak. The few bright spots only serve to heighten the gloom. Yahweh's plan to reunite Judah and Israel and bring them back to Jerusalem with rejoicing (3:14-19) brings out the appalling wickedness of the people's infidelity, which dashes his plan. Even the exile's apparently sincere praise of Yahweh's sovereignty is coupled with the cries of the bereaved Jerusalem under his indignation and wrath.

In its theological perspective, the drama can certainly be said to give ample justification for Yahweh's decision to punish his people with exile. However, the overall effect cannot be described as theodicy, as it is sometimes described by redaction critics emphasizing the editorial role of Deuteronomists, whose alleged agenda is to explain the exile as the result of Israel's breach of the covenant. Neither is the effect to vindicate Jeremiah's astute reading of the moral state of his people and its inevitable result—as Duhm and some proponents of the biographical approach would have it. The pathos evoked by the people's plight and the horror evoked by the extent of Yahweh's wrath cannot be explained by these readings that emphasize the justice of the punishment. Rather than exalting Yahweh's justice, the repeated pictures of Israel's wickedness increase the sense of despair, the sense that Israel is incapable of pleasing Yahweh. Although the destruction Yahweh inflicts on his people is acknowledged to be just, the emphasis is on its severity and the inability of the people to bear it. The despair over the hopeless wickedness of the people and the unbearable wrath of Yahweh is expressed in the final verses of the composition:

> I know, O Yahweh, that the way of man is not in himself
> That it is not in man who walks to direct his steps
> Correct me, Yahweh, but in just measure
> Not in thy anger, lest thou bring me to nothing.
>
> (Jer. 10:23-24)

Israel's only hope is that Yahweh would relent of his wrath or turn it on their enemies (10:25, on the basis of his promise to bring evil on any who would "devour" Israel, 2:3).

That the composition ends in prayers to Yahweh for mercy suggests an underlying function for the entire drama. Like the prayers, the drama gives expression to the people's experience of the invasions and destruction of their country. As in the book of Lamentations or in many of the laments in the Psalms, the severity of Yahweh's wrath and the devastating effects of his punishment are portrayed with the hope that he will be moved to relent. The depiction of Yahweh's condemnation of the faithlessness and perversity of his people confesses their guilt. This assessment of the underlying purpose of Jeremiah 2–10—that it allows a sinful and devastated people to address their God—reverses the common assessment that it is intended to address the people as a message from God.

That this tragic story of Yahweh and Israel has seldom been clearly perceived can be partly attributed to the dominance of the standard compositional and biographical approaches to Jeremiah. This is not only because they directed the focus of scholarly attention from what lies on the surface of the text to what lies behind the text.

Recognizing Jeremiah 2–10 as a unified literary composition would involve questioning the merits of the approaches and their hard-won gains. Accepting the evidence of intentional artistry, dramatic portrayal, and narrative unity would challenge the biographical theory that these chapters are composed of evidence for reconstructing the early ministry of Jeremiah. Many of the clues that interpreters used to deduce the historical origins of the individual speeches would be seen as intentionally crafted elements of the dramatic portrayal. Once it was perceived how a speech fits into a dialogue, or how the situation the dialogue portrays fits into the overall story, it would be harder to justify the attempt to find a place for it in the biography of Jeremiah. For the biographical approach, this would close up a major source of historical evidence used to bring to light the historical Jeremiah and his times. The recovery of the great work of dramatic poetry in Jeremiah 2–10 (the tragic story of Yahweh and Israel from exodus to exile) might come at the cost of abandoning the biography of prophet that generations of twentieth-century scholars labored so long to create.

The Narrative Coherence of Jeremiah 11–20

The previous chapter argued that just as adherence to the biographical agenda of Duhm kept rhetorical critics from fully appreciating the dramatic presentation in Jeremiah 2–10, adherence to the compositional model of Duhm and Mowinckel kept redaction critics from fully appreciating the dramatic presentation in Jeremiah 11–20. The second half of this chapter will argue that the assumptions embedded in Duhm and Mowinckel's compositional model also kept redaction critics from perceiving the narrative unity of Jeremiah 11–20. The primary assumption they retained from Duhm is that the prose speeches are inauthentic compositions added to authentic poetry. In their redactional analyses, this assumption provides the foundation of their theory that the structure of the final form of the text is the work of editors whose Deuteronomistic theological agenda finds expression in the prose sermons. Previous chapters exposed the dubious grounds for this assumption; this section will demonstrate how it obscures the structure of the text.

Although the theory of a comprehensive Deuteronomistic redaction is unable to provide a satisfying account of the text's structure, its advantages over the older source-critical theories should be acknowledged. The previous chapter noted that by crediting the editors of Jeremiah with intelligence, artistic skill, and a coherent theological agenda, the redactional theories of Hyatt, Nicholson, and Thiel provide a rationale for looking for intentional arrangement in the text. Working from this perspective, O'Connor, Diamond, and Smith are able to perceive the fundamental aspects of the structure of Jeremiah 11–20. All of them move beyond the old source-critical view of these chapters as simply a collection of materials that happen to contain the majority of Jeremiah's poetic confessions, to the observation that Jeremiah 11–20 is a coherent literary unit. O'Connor and Smith go further by identifying a defining characteristic of the major structural subunits. O'Connor observes that "all five [confessions] appear closely connected with prose sermons,"[32] and Smith observes that each of the four

---

[32] Kathleen M. O'Connor, *The Confessions of Jeremiah: Their Interpretation and Their Role in Chapters 1–25* (Atlanta, GA: Scholars Press, 1987), 112.

major sections he finds in Jeremiah 11–20 has two parts, "an introductory prose narrative plus prophetic lament."[33] On this basis, they come up with similar divisions of the section into subunits. O'Connor divides the unit into five subunits: Jeremiah 11–12, 13, 14–16, 17, 18–19;[34] Smith into four: Jeremiah 11–12, 13–15, 16–17, 18–19.[35]

The theory of a comprehensive Deuteronomistic redaction, which allowed Smith and O'Connor to perceive the structural units in Jeremiah 11–20, kept them from appreciating the nature of the structural relations within the units because it was founded on Duhm and Mowinckel's erroneous assumption that the prose is the work of later theologians and preachers. Guided by this assumption, the three redactional studies all concluded that the overarching purpose of Jeremiah 11–20 is didactic or homiletic, and that its prose sections and poetic sections contribute to this purpose as sermons and illustrations. The prose "sermons" are the plain statement of the Deuteronomistic theodicy argument that Yahweh had to judge Judah because of its disobedience, and the laments provide examples of one kind of disobedience: rejecting Yahweh's prophet. The previous chapter demonstrated that theodicy could hardly be the purpose of unit as a whole or even the prose speeches. Furthermore, it observed that describing the prose speeches as "sermons" seriously distorts the dramatic presentation of the text. It interprets speeches that the text clearly presents as words Yahweh spoke to Jeremiah (or through him to the people) before the exile as sermons that Deuteronomistic theologians or preachers addressed to exilic audiences.

When Yahweh's prose speeches are read in the context presented in the text (rather than the context of their origin as theorized by Duhm and Mowinckel), their relationship with Jeremiah's poetic laments becomes clear. Like Jeremiah's laments, Yahweh's speeches to Jeremiah are set in situations before the exile. More precisely, they are set in situations before the invasions (described in Jeremiah 4–9), which they regularly refer to as future events. Once it is seen that Yahweh's speeches and Jeremiah's laments are presented as occurring in the same time period, there is no obstacle to the possibility that they portray successive events. This possibility becomes a probability when the dramatic nature of the text is perceived, since dramatic episodes are usually related to each other by temporal progression. Because the redactional theories disallow this kind of organic unity, redaction critics are forced to describe the relationships between speeches in terms of static patterns (e.g., each unit contains both a speech and a lament) or superficial links (e.g., repeated images and catchwords[36]) and divisions (e.g., superscriptions). In this way, the redactional accounts of structure are quite similar to the rhetorical approaches of Lundbom and Holladay. Like the

---

[33] Mark S. Smith, *The Laments of Jeremiah and Their Contexts: Preliminary Observations about Their Literary Interplay in Jeremiah 11–20*, SBLMS (Atlanta, GA: Scholars Press, 1990), 40.

[34] O'Connor, *Confessions of Jeremiah*, 130–1.

[35] Smith, *Laments and Their Contexts*, 40. The differences between Smith and O'Connor's divisions arise from O'Connor's judgment (correct in my view) that 14:1-9 begins a new section even though it is not in prose and her judgment (incorrect in my view) that the prose of 16:1-18 is connected with the preceding lament in 15:15-18 rather than the subsequent lament in 17:14-18. O'Connor, *Confessions of Jeremiah*, 112. Diamond's division of the unit into three subunits (Jeremiah 11–13, 14–17, 18–19) relies on the more superficial feature of similar superscriptions in 11:1, 14:1, and 18:1. A. R. Pete Diamond, *The Confessions of Jeremiah in Context: Scenes of Prophetic Drama*, JSOT Sup (Sheffield: JSOT Press, 1987), 149, 182.

[36] O'Connor, *Confessions of Jeremiah*, 111.

rhetorical critics, the redaction critics are committed to the theory that any significant structure is the result of an editorial arrangement imposed on originally independent materials.[37] It would endanger their redactional or biographical theories by obscuring the evidence they rely on if these critics were to recognize the narrative progression and dramatic portrayal of the text.

Six Dramatic Episodes

Although temporal progression, or narrative development, is a basic feature of dramatic presentation, a more characteristic structural feature of extended dramatic presentations is the succession of dramatic episodes. A dramatic episode is not simply a section of drama that represents an action occurring in a single locale. An episode is the basic building block of dramatic presentation and must fulfill certain expectations and requirements: for example, furthering the narrative or developing the characterization of the main characters. Aristotle observed that a drama must be a whole with a beginning, a middle, and an end,[38] and the same is true of a dramatic episode. Each part of an episode has a function in its dramatic presentation. The beginning of an episode must establish the dramatic situation; it must provide the relevant context for making sense of the following action or dialogue. This is particularly important in a dramatic presentation that cannot rely on lights or a curtain to distinguish an episode from the previous episode, or a change of scenery to suggest a new situation. It calls for particular dramatic skill when the dramatist does not rely on a narrator to introduce the episode but uses the speeches of the first speakers in the episode to reveal the situation while simultaneously initiating the dialogue. In the poetic episodes of Jeremiah 2–10, this is often accomplished by the commands or questions of the first speaker that reveal his or her identity as well as the identity of the audience. The middle, or body, of an episode shows the reactions of the characters to the new situation, or their interaction with each other. This usually calls for dramatic dialogue. The conclusion of an episode often accentuates the personal significance, or emotional effect, of the main action or dialogue on the characters. In a Greek drama or a modern musical, this could be achieved by a poetic chorus or song. In a Shakespearian drama, it could be achieved by a soliloquy in which a character pours out his or her emotional response after the other characters have left the stage.

Once interpreters have recognized the presence of dramatic dialogues, dramatic representation of speech, and dramatic characterization of speakers in Jeremiah 11–20, they might reasonably expect the passage to be composed of dramatic episodes. This expectation proves true. In fact, each of six major structural subunits takes the form of a dramatic episode. This can be demonstrated by observing how the beginning,

---

[37] Like Mowinckel, who lays down the general rule that "the apparent connections that exist, on closer examination, prove to be secondary," those seeking to discern the original historical contexts of the isolated units of Jeremiah must be wary of the discovery of meaningful structure. It might endanger their historical-critical projects by suggesting that the present literary context of the units provides sufficient guidance to their meaning. Sigmund Mowinckel, *The Spirit and the Word: Prophecy and Tradition in Ancient Israel*, FCBS (Minneapolis, MN: Fortress, 2002), 45.

[38] *Poetics* 1450.b.25–30.

Table 9.1 Dramatic Episodes in Jeremiah 11–20

Episode	Introductory situation	Controversy/Dialogue	Emotional response
1	11:1-17	11:18–12:6	12:7-13
2	13:1-14	13:15-19	13:20-27
3	14:1-6	14:7–15:4	15:5-20
4	16:1-18	16:19–17:13	17:14-18
5	17:19–18:12	18:13-17	18:18-23
6	19:1-15	20:1-6	20:7-18

middle, and end of each subunit fulfill the corresponding functions of the three parts of a dramatic episode. Each unit begins by establishing the dramatic situation, usually with a public message of judgment (usually in prose). This is followed by a controversy about the judgment (often in dialogue form). The unit concludes with an emotional response to the judgment and dialogue (usually in poetry) either by Yahweh or Jeremiah. Table 9.1 indicates the beginning, middle, and end of each of the six episodes. Summary overviews of the six episodes will illustrate how each one has a beginning, a middle, and an end that fulfill their individual functions as parts of a coherent episode.

The first episode (11:1–12:14) is introduced with a dramatic representation of Yahweh sending Jeremiah first to announce the conditions of his covenant and then to announce the judgment because the people had broken his covenant. The dramatic technique of telling the story by presenting speeches from two different times was observed to be a common technique in Jeremiah 2–10.[39] The "Deuteronomistic" language and concerns of these messages can be attributed to the attempt to depict Jeremiah's participation in the reforms of Josiah. Jeremiah's announcement of judgment brought opposition from his townsmen, and in the body of the episode, his speeches ask Yahweh first to judge his enemies and then to deal with the other wicked people in the land. These responses suggest that Jeremiah thinks the problem is limited to a group of wicked people and that judgment could be averted if these individuals were dealt with. Yahweh counters this false hope, warning that the wickedness is much more pervasive reaching even to Jeremiah's family. Yahweh will protect his prophet, but he is going to lay waste to the land. The episode is concluded with Yahweh's lament over his beloved, whose rebellion has enraged him. The invading armies that will come and conquer the people are not merely the legal consequence for breaking the covenant law; they are the devouring sword of a scorned lover.

In the second episode (13:1-27), the sign of the loincloth sets up the situation by portraying Yahweh's intention to spoil the pride of his people. Since there is no indication that this sign was intended for anyone other than Jeremiah, it appears Yahweh wants to convey to his prophet the anguish he feels in ruining a people closer to him than his garments. In the central section, Jeremiah's pleading with the leaders of the people suggests that he thinks they may still repent and avoid judgment. This thought is shattered by the speech of an infuriated Yahweh that concludes the

---

[39] E.g., 5:1-4, 6:3-5, 7:1-15.

episode: he vows to expose the shame of Lady Jerusalem because it is impossible that her people would repent.

The third episode (14:1–15:20) is the only one introduced with poetry: the portrayal of a terrible drought. However, the ensuing prayers of the people indicate that they interpret the drought as Yahweh's judgment for sin and, thus, give the introduction a function similar to Yahweh's messages of judgment in prose. In the dialogue about the drought, Yahweh rejects the prayers of the people (or temple party) as well as Jeremiah's attempt to shift the blame to the prophets. The dialogue is followed by Yahweh's exasperated speech, in which he recounts the harsh but fruitless treatment he has used with Jerusalem. The episode ends with a second emotional outpouring, Jeremiah's complaint to Yahweh that his ministry of announcing judgment has only brought him persecution and misery. Yahweh responds with an offer of continued personal protection if Jeremiah will continue to speak his words about the people's destruction.

In the fourth episode (16:1–17:18), the situation is introduced by Yahweh's commands to Jeremiah that he not marry or attend funerals, and Yahweh's instruction that Jeremiah explain to the people that this signifies the coming exile. This message sparks a series of speeches in which an overconfident temple party tries to assure themselves that they are the righteous people under Yahweh's blessing. The subtext of their message—that Jeremiah, with his message of judgment, is among the wicked who are under Yahweh's curse—calls forth Jeremiah's emotional call for vindication that concludes the episode.

The situation that begins the fifth episode (17:19–18:23) is portrayed in two challenges from Yahweh for the people of Judah to change their ways: the call to keep the Sabbath and the message of the potter's house. His prose messages indicate that he is still willing to spare them if they will repent. The people's blunt refusal to repent calls forth Yahweh's outraged resolve to demolish them. Their plots to silence Jeremiah call forth the prophet's impassioned cry for vengeance.

In the sixth episode (19:1–20:18), the situation is presented by the message that accompanies Jeremiah's breaking of the pot, a public declaration of the coming destruction of Jerusalem. The depiction of the ensuing controversy is achieved by a narrative rather than the usual dialogue: Pashhur beats and imprisons Jeremiah, and Yahweh declares that Pashhur and all Judah will go into exile in Babylon. In Jeremiah's final emotional response, he expresses his confidence that Yahweh will give him vengeance on his persecutors (such as Pashhur), but then in a shocking reversal, he curses the man who brought the news of his birth.

The division between the six dramatic episodes outlined in Table 9.2 approximates the unit divisions proposed by Diamond, Smith, and O'Connor.

The similarity between Smith's and O'Connor's unit divisions and the division achieved by dramatic analysis results from their observation that each major unit includes a "prose sermon" and a lament. Examination of the dramatic episodes reveals that each does indeed include at least one prose speech and one poetic speech of the prophet.[40] Although

---

[40] The discrepancy between Smith's four units, O'Connor's five, and the six dramatic episodes seems to result from Smith and O'Connor's inconsistent application of their principle. Both Smith and O'Connor include ch. 18 with ch. 19 even though ch. 18 has its own prose speech (18:5-11) and

Table 9.2 Comparison of Unit Divisions for Jeremiah 11–20

O'Connor	(11 — 12) (13) (14 — 15 — 16) (17) (18 — 19 — 20)
Diamond	(11 — 12 — 13) (14 — 15 — 16 — 17) (18 — 19 — 20)
Smith	(11 — 12) (13 — 14 — 15) (16 — 17) (18 — 19 — 20)
Henderson[a]	(11 — 12) (13) (14 — 15) (16 — 17) (18) (19 — 20)

[a] For the sake of simplicity, the chart does not show that I have found that 17:19-27 fits better as part of the introduction of 18 than as the conclusion of 16–17. If this passage is judged to be secondary to the main structure of Jeremiah 11–20, it would bring my unit divisions into closer conformity with the other three.

Smith and O'Connor correctly identified this feature, the theory of the Deuteronomistic redaction kept them from seeing its significance. All of the episodes but one begin with one of Yahweh's prose speeches because these speeches provide an effective way to introduce the dramatic situation. Their warnings of impending judgment (usually publicly proclaimed) establish the situations and set in motion the controversies and dialogues in the bodies of the episodes. All the episodes include poetic laments because they provide effective conclusions to the dramatic situations.[41] Their emotional responses to the actions of Yahweh or human opponents portray the personal import of the dramatic action of the episodes for their characters.

The obstacles that the theory of Deuteronomistic redaction presents for appreciating the text's presentation can now be more clearly described. First, reading Yahweh's speeches as exilic sermons makes it almost impossible to perceive the dramatic situation portrayed in each episode. A primary dramatic function of these speeches, which stand at the beginnings of five of the six episodes, is to establish the dramatic situations: a controversy or action that resulted from something Yahweh said to Jeremiah (or through him to the people) in the time before the Babylonian incursions. Second, identifying the nature of these units as homiletic or didactic makes it almost impossible to perceive the relationship between the prose speeches and the laments. When the text is read as homiletic material, the prose speeches are understood as the plain statement of the argument, the primary focus of the text, and the laments and other materials are viewed as supporting evidence. This represents a reversal of the text's dramatic presentation in which the prose speeches serve to prepare the audience for the portrayal of the characters whose interactions and experiences constitute the primary focus.

Jeremiah's Story: From Prophet of Reform to Prophet of Doom

A major concern of the three redactional analyses of Jeremiah 11–20 is identifying the theological agenda. This is a natural concern given their view of the text as the homiletic work of preachers or theologians. However, once it becomes clear that the text has the character of a dramatic portrayal, questions about the theological agenda cannot have

prophetic lament (18:19-23). Smith includes ch. 13 with chs 14–15 even though it has its own prose speech (13:8-14) and poetic prophetic speech (13:15-17).

[41] As has been noted, the first two episodes conclude with the emotional poetic responses of Yahweh rather than Jeremiah. The prophet's laments in these episodes belong to the body sections rather than the conclusions.

the same priority. A more natural question to ask of a drama is whether it is tragic or comic. To begin to answer this question, the obvious place to look is at the end of the drama. It was noted above that, unlike a unit in a theological discourse, which states its point or perspective at the beginning and then illustrates it, a dramatic episode usually gives its clearest indication of its significance or perspective in its conclusion. What is true of the individual episodes is truer still of the complete dramatic composition. Its nature is made clear by its ending.

The final episode of Jeremiah 11–20 ends with Jeremiah cursing the day of his birth (20:14-18). This alone is enough to identify the dramatic perspective of the composition as tragic. When this final lament is considered along with Jeremiah's laments in each of the other five episodes of Jeremiah 11–20, it can also be said that Jeremiah is the central tragic figure of this composition (unlike Jeremiah 2–10, which tells the tragic story of Israel). The song of confident praise (20:11-13) that immediately precedes Jeremiah's final lament might raise doubts about this judgment of the tragic nature of the text. However, as has already been observed in relation to the praise of exiles (10:6-16) near the end of Jeremiah 2–10, tragedies regularly introduce a moment of bright hope or personal triumph just before the final catastrophe, with the effect of deepening the darkness of the final episode. Still, the reader of Jeremiah 11–20 is left to wonder what caused the drastic change in perspective between the two final speeches of Jeremiah.

One possible explanation is that the final speech presents Jeremiah at a later time after a reversal of fortune. However, since Jeremiah's praise comes from his confidence that Yahweh will vindicate him by taking vengeance on his enemies, the reversal would have to be the triumph of his personal enemies; this does not fit with what is known of Jeremiah's life and it seems to provide an unlikely occasion for his final lament. Furthermore, if Jeremiah is lamenting the triumph of his enemies, who want to kill him and silence his message, his wish that he had been killed (and thus silenced) before his birth would make little sense. The alternative explanation to which the drama drives the reader is that it is Jeremiah's vindication and deliverance themselves that call forth his final lament. Yahweh's deliverance of Jeremiah from opponents like Pashhur signifies the vindication of his prophetic message, but his message is Judah's destruction. Yahweh's vengeance on Pashhur, who tried to silence Jeremiah's message, signifies that the prophesied destruction cannot be averted. Jeremiah's unusual tragedy does not lie in his death or in the failure of his vocation but rather in his life and the success of his vocation—to bring about the destruction of his people. This explains his wish that he had been killed before he was born, before he was able to fulfill the vocation given to him before he was formed in the womb (1:5).[42]

With this understanding of the tragic nature of Jeremiah 11–20, the broad outline of the whole composition can be suggested. Initially, Jeremiah is eager to be Yahweh's spokesman. He endorses the declaration of Yahweh's covenant stipulations ("So be it,

---

[42] As has often been noted, his final lament seems to look back to Jeremiah 1 (cf. 15:10) so that it concludes not only 11–20 but also 1–20. An intriguing possibility is that the call narrative in Jeremiah 1 was originally the introduction to 11–20 (or some form of it), and 2–10 was inserted later. This might explain the ill-fitting introduction to 2–10 in the Masoretic Text of Jer. 2:1-2a: it may have originally introduced Jeremiah 11, which it fits better.

Yahweh," 11:5) believing that he will be an agent of the reform of his nation (probably as part of the reforms of Josiah's time). However, as the story progresses, he comes to realize that the outcome of his prophetic ministry will not be the reform of his nation but rather its destruction. He had underestimated the stubborn wickedness of Judah and the unrelenting wrath of Yahweh. When this realization comes, it is too late to back out of his ministry. Yahweh's promise of personal protection depends on Jeremiah's continuing to speak his words of destruction (15:19-21). Finally, Jeremiah must speak his message of "violence and destruction"—not only because of Yahweh's external coercion, but also because of internal compulsion (18:7-9).

The calls for vengeance in Jeremiah's laments show this progression as well. His first calls for vengeance and judgment on the wicked are compatible with his hopes for the salvation of his nation: he asks Yahweh to protect the life of his reforming prophet from enemies in his hometown (11:18-20) and to rid the land of the wicked people who prevent its flourishing (12:1-6). As the story progresses, Jeremiah's wrath toward his opponents expands until it closely parallels the wrath of Yahweh toward the sinful nation, the wrath that will bring the destruction of the entire nation (17:18, 18:21-23). The final declarations of the coming destruction of Jerusalem are portrayed as Yahweh's answer to the prophet's cries for vengeance and his vindication of his prophet against his enemies (20:4-6). In this way, Jeremiah becomes complicit in the national destruction he had originally thought he could help prevent.

Jeremiah's Tragedy Obscured by Duhm's Assumptions

This brief overview of the tragic story of Jeremiah portrayed by Jeremiah 11–20 allows a critique of the redaction-critical assessment that the theological agenda of Jeremiah 11–20 is to justify the exile according to Deuteronomistic theology. First, in agreement with this assessment, it can be affirmed that Yahweh's prose speeches take the Deuteronomistic perspective as foundational and establish this as the controlling perspective of the whole composition. The opening episode lays out the theology of the conditional covenant: obeying Yahweh's law will result in the enjoyment of the blessings of the land but disobeying his law will bring the covenant curses (11:1-13). Each of the five succeeding episodes begins with a speech or scene that assumes and enunciates this Deuteronomistic perspective: the nation's disobedience of Yahweh's covenant stipulations brings the consequences laid out in the covenant—including exile.

The redaction critics fail to see that the Deuteronomistic perspective is also foundational for the controversies, actions, dialogues, and laments that follow the prose speeches. This can be illustrated with Jeremiah's laments. Jeremiah attributes the trouble of Judah to the wicked people who think they can avoid the consequences of disobeying Yahweh (12:4). Unless he thought that judgment for disobedience could be averted by repentance and obedience, he would not have initially found Yahweh's words a delight (11:5, 15:16). Unless he thought that the judgment of the nation was sealed by their rejection of Yahweh's prophet (Deut. 18:17, 2 Kgs 17:13), he would not have lamented his own prophetic vocation (15:10; 20:7-9, 14-20). Without the Deuteronomistic perspective enunciated in Yahweh's speeches, Jeremiah's story would not make sense. This is one reason why Duhm's attempt to purge the Deuteronomistic elements from the text was misguided and detrimental for understanding the book. It is also why the redactional theory that the poetry originally existed without the prose is untenable. The poetic speeches depend on the prose speeches not only to provide their dramatic contexts and narrative motivations but also to present their theological foundation. Without this foundation, the dramatic portrayal would collapse.

Once it has been acknowledged that the Deuteronomistic perspective is foundational to Jeremiah 11–20 and the prose speeches are essential, it must be observed that these prose speeches and their theological perspective are merely the starting points for the dramatic interactions and of the tragic story that are the focus of the drama. Yahweh's speeches provide the occasions for the arguments, pleas, conflicts, and rebukes that make up the bodies of the episodes and for the heartbreaking expressions of anguish, exasperation, rage, and despair that bring the episodes to their culminations. The fact that, according to the Deuteronomistic covenant, Judah's disobedience must be punished is not presented as the logical conclusion of an argument but as a presupposition that helps define the situation of the dramatic struggle. The covenant presents a tragic predicament for Yahweh—and eventually Jeremiah—because it demands that he punish his beloved people. However, as the drama unfolds, the emerging portraits of Yahweh and Jeremiah transcend the covenantal framework: the destruction of Judah will come not merely as consequence of covenant violation but also as the pouring out of the irrepressible wrath of Jeremiah, the rejected reformer, and Yahweh, the spurned lover.

On the basis of Duhm's source-critical theory that the prose is later than the poetry, the redactional accounts of Jeremiah 11–20 all understand the poetic laments to be subordinate to the prose speeches (historical evidence appended to the sermons as illustrations). This understanding is the reverse of the relationship of the two kinds of speeches in the text. Yahweh's prose speeches are subordinate to the poetic laments of Jeremiah and Yahweh—not because the poetic laments come from a later source but because they come later in the dramatic episodes—at their conclusions. The introductory prose speeches are not only subordinate in the sense that they support the climactic poetic speeches but also in the sense that the poetic speeches condition the effect of the prose speeches on readers. Yahweh's messages, characterized by the Deuteronomistic language of rules, agreements, violations, and consequences, have a different effect for the readers who read them as part of Jeremiah 11–20 than they would have had for those hearing them publicly delivered by Jeremiah. In their dramatic context in Jeremiah 11–20, they are the speeches of the grieved and angry Yahweh and Jeremiah. The formal language of the prose messages masks the deep anguish and bitter anger of the speakers as revealed in the private laments. Their effect in the dramatic presentation can be approximated by imagining the restrained speech of a wife reading the legal stipulations of a divorce to her unfaithful husband—all the while filled with unspoken anger, love, grief, and despair. These dramatic effects of the text's presentation cannot be appreciated by scholars who read the prose speeches as the sermons of exilic theologians who imposed their agenda on preexisting poetry. Not only the speakers and situations of the individual speeches but also the literary structure and theological perspective of the whole composition are obscured by continued adherence to the source-critical theory of Duhm.

Conclusion

The last three chapters have demonstrated the continuing influence of Duhm's assumptions on Jeremiah scholarship of the last decades of the twentieth century. Scholars sought to move beyond the older historical-critical approaches, such as the biographical approach of Skinner or the tradition-critical approach of Mowinckel, whose focus on the history or the history of composition behind the text was thought to give insufficient attention to the present form of the text. New approaches such as rhetorical and redaction criticism allowed scholars to make many significant advances in perceiving the literary artistry, formal structure, and theological agenda of the present text. However, as has been demonstrated, their efforts were limited by their inability to move beyond the basic assumptions of Duhm—the same assumptions that informed the work of previous works like those of Skinner and Mowinckel. Duhm's assumption that the poetry is primarily valuable as authentic evidence of Jeremiah's historical ministry and message kept rhetorical critics from fully perceiving the story of Israel presented in Jeremiah 2–10. The assumption that the prose speeches must be late additions of Deuteronomistic theologians kept redaction critics from fully perceiving the story of Jeremiah's early ministry presented in Jeremiah 11–20. In this way, Duhm's assumptions prevented scholars of the last decades of the twentieth century from achieving their aim of illuminating the present form of the book.

This study will conclude by considering whether in the twenty-first century, scholars studying the book of Jeremiah are finally ready to abandon the unfounded and unhelpful assumptions of Duhm. A starting point for this assessment comes from *Reading the Book of Jeremiah: A Search for Coherence* (2004), a collection of essays published one hundred years after Duhm's *Jeremia*. In the preface, Walter Brueggemann offers his assessment of the current state of Jeremiah studies:

> The current discussion seeks to move beyond the historical-critical categories of Sigmund Mowinckel and Bernhard Duhm and the classic formulation of three sources, A, B, and C. In Jeremiah as in other parts of biblical scholarship, the new questions concern the inadequacy of historical readings of a positivistic kind and the prospect of synchronic readings, either through ideological analysis that seeks to show that ideology shapes the book, or through canonical readings that find a large theological intentionality to the whole book.[43]

Initially, this assessment seems to suggest a clear rejection of Duhm's source-critical analyses of Jeremiah. However, further reflection raises the question of whether scholars are actually ready to reject Duhm's assumptions or whether they are merely interested in shifting the focus from Duhm's diachronic study of the history behind the text to synchronic study of the theology or ideology of the present form of the text. In the latter case, there would be little to differentiate this shift of focus from the shift of focus characteristic of the

---

[43] Walter Brueggemann, "Preface," in *Reading the Book of Jeremiah: A Search for Coherence*, ed. Martin Kessler (Winona Lake, IN: Eisenbrauns, 2004), ix.

last decades of the twentieth century. As the last three chapters have shown, scholars who sought to move beyond Duhm's agenda by attending to the literary shape and theological intention of the present form of the text produced inadequate accounts of the present form because they failed to move beyond Duhm's basic assumptions. Whether this will also be true of scholars in the twenty-first century remains to be seen.

Fresh Jeremiah scholarship that follows the synchronic, ideological, or canonical approaches mentioned by Brueggemann holds out the promise of investigation of the text unfettered by Duhm's assumptions but often shows a disappointing reluctance to leave these assumptions behind. The case of Louis Stulman is representative. In a 1999 essay by Stulman (which Brueggemann offers as an example of the new "synchronic contributions"),[44] he offers an analysis of Jeremiah 1–25 that he claims will focus "not on the literary growth and development of [the text, but on] its own focal concerns, dominant attitudes and functions in the present *Sitz im Buch*."[45] However, in a footnote to this description, Stulman makes a crucial admission:

> Although the present study attempts to focus on the present form of the text of Jeremiah, it is nonetheless impossible (or for that matter desirable) to divorce entirely diachronic from synchronic concerns. As such, this chapter accepts as well established, for example, the following "historical-critical" claims: … [Including the claim that] the prose sermons represent a later development of the text, most probably a development of the earlier poetry.[46]

Here, Stulman acknowledges that his analysis depends on the fundamental assumption of Duhm, that poetry is earlier than prose, and his description of Yahweh's prose speeches as "sermons" betrays his acceptance of Mowinckel and Nicholson's theory that they are the work of Deuteronomistic preachers. Guided by these historical-critical assumptions, Stulman predictably arrives at the same basic understanding of the final form of the text as the redactional studies surveyed in the last two chapters. In his attempt to describe the theological or ideological "*Tendenz*" of the final form of the text he writes, "[The] univocal prose [of] 'C' tames and 'codifies' the wild and multiphonic voices of the poetry," and "'C's' ideology … places the whole … within the context of reciprocal justice, thereby domesticating the turbulent and unrestrained poetry."[47] As with the redactional studies, Stulman perpetuates Duhm's practice of setting the wild and passionate poetry against the dull and domesticated prose, as original material and later additions. The only significant difference from Duhm is that the focus on the final form of the text leads Stulman and the redaction critics to give the last word to dull and domesticated prose Duhm sought to discredit.

---

[44] Walter Brueggemann, "Next Steps in Jeremiah Studies," in *Troubling Jeremiah*, ed. A. R. Pete Diamond, Kathleen O'Connor, and Louis Stulman, JSOT Sup 260 (Sheffield: Sheffield Academic Press, 1999), 407.

[45] Louis Stulman, "The Prose Sermons as Hermeneutical Guide," in *Troubling Jeremiah*, ed. A. R. Pete Diamond, Kathleen O'Connor, and Louis Stulman, JSOT Sup 260 (Sheffield: Sheffield Academic Press, 1999), 36.

[46] Stulman, "Prose Sermons," 36–7, n. 12.

[47] Stulman, "Prose Sermons," 61, 62.

Contrary to Stulman's assertion, it does seem at least possible that new "synchronic" approaches could proceed without reference to diachronic theories of the history of the text's composition. However, the actual ideological and canonical approaches that Brueggemann presents as recent alternatives to Duhm's approach continue to depend on Duhm's source-critical assumptions. They routinely identify the ideology or theology of the present canonical form of the book with the agenda of prose writers because these are considered to be the latest additions to the book in the dominant diachronic scheme. This is apparent in Brueggemann's observation that "in ideological criticism and canonical reading, there is a great push beyond the 'person' (persona?) of the prophet to the claims of the 'book.'"[48] These critics are not only attempting to leave behind the attempt to recover the historical "person" of the prophet (that Duhm and Skinner attempted to recover) but also the attempt to discern the "persona" of the prophet as portrayed by the book, because for them the "claims of the book" are equivalent to the claims of Mowinckel's C source read as Deuteronomistic sermons. The C source, and thus the book, cannot be interested in the person of the prophet because that is the interest of the A source. Once again, these critics, with their focus on the agenda of the final form, maintain Duhm's fundamental opposition of the poetic and prosaic, and break from him only by privileging the prosaic.

This approach to the book based on Duhm and Mowinckel's formulation of the three sources A, B, and C is the one that Brueggemann judges is still "apparent at the present time," a century after Duhm's work. In his assessment of the current state of Jeremiah studies, he writes,

> The distinction between poetry and prose is an important one, and the linkage between them is more or less unsettled. It does seem apparent at the present time that the prose material with a Deuteronomic accent is a powerful shaping force for the final form of the text. This recognition means that the chapters that might seem ponderous or heavy-handed are to be taken with greater seriousness for our reading of the whole of the book.[49]

Brueggemann's counsel that scholars should make their peace with the ponderous and heavy-handed Deuteronomic prose because it shaped the final form is based on Duhm's judgment that the prose must be inauthentic because poetic form is the mark of authentic prophetic speech. Thus, although Brueggemann's counsel appears to turn Duhm's perspective on its head by giving more weight to the prose than the poetry, even upside down, Duhm's system continues to determine the outcomes of Jeremiah scholarship. More than a century after the appearance of Duhm's commentary, Jeremiah scholarship remains under the shadow of Duhm.

---

[48] Brueggemann, "Preface."
[49] Brueggemann, "Preface," ix.

Epilogue: Pete Diamond and the Voice of Yahweh

In a commentary on Jeremiah published in 2003, Pete Diamond wrote, "Everywhere Yahweh is the central fictive speaker in the rhetoric of Jeremiah."[1] Diamond's comment may seem to state the obvious: any competent reader could see that Yahweh is the first-person speaker of most of the passages in Jeremiah. However, those acquainted with the history of Jeremiah scholarship in the last century could appreciate Diamond's observation as a hard-won insight that required him to overcome sizable obstacles presented by common assumptions about the book. These assumptions woven into the dominant historical-critical paradigm of the book's composition had the effect of obscuring the centrality of Yahweh's speech; they directed attention away from the speeches of Yahweh to the historical authors who stand behind the text. Yahweh's speeches were primarily understood as the speech, or writing, of either Jeremiah or exilic Deuteronomists. Diamond's lifetime of contributions to Jeremiah studies challenged these assumptions and broke new ground in understanding the nature of the book. In these ways, he laid the basis for better understanding Yahweh's speeches and portrait of Yahweh they provide.

Diamond's first major work, *The Confessions of Jeremiah in Context* (1987), stood at the turning point in the history of critical scholarship on Jeremiah. His aim of reading the confessions in context is representative of a major shift away from the older historical criticism, which isolated material like the confessions and attempted to read them in a reconstructed historical context. The shift of focus to the literary contexts in the final form of the text opened new possibilities for understanding the coherence and purpose of the text. At the same time, Diamond's decision to begin with the isolated confessions showed his dependence on the earlier scholarship, particularly its assumption that poetic material is more likely to be early or authentic. This dual relationship with older source criticism (accepting its basic assumptions but questioning their significance) locates Diamond's work in group of redaction-critical approaches to Jeremiah that include a number of German works (notably Thiel) from the decades before Diamond's work and was soon to include several major English works (including O'Connor, Smith, Biddle, Seitz, and Stulman). Diamond's work relied

---

[1] A. R. Diamond, "Jeremiah," in *Eerdman's Commentary on the Bible*, ed. John Rogerson and James Dunn (Grand Rapids, MI: Eerdmans, 2003), 615.

on common assumptions, employed similar methods, and predictably came to similar conclusions.

However, Diamond's willingness to question some of the "assured results" of the standard paradigm on the basis of fresh analyses of the text enabled him to uncover significant weaknesses in some of its fundamental assumptions. Unlike other redaction critics, Diamond openly acknowledged that his study found little support for the assumption that the poetry predates the prose. After a detailed form-critical assessment of each of the poetic confessions, he concluded, "The confessions do not comprise a uniform formal group."[2] Furthermore, Diamond failed to find evidence that they were part of an earlier source. He observed that without the framework provided by their present context, it is difficult to defend a proposed sequence[3] or to find a plausible motivation[4] for an earlier collection of laments. In a discussion of whether the laments are distinctly prophetic or merely cultic, he wrote, "The more the passages are isolated from their present literary setting, the more opaque and indeterminate become attempts to maintain a reading of them in relationship to the prophetic mission, especially the Jeremianic mission."[5]

Diamond's failure to find any support for assuming the authenticity—or even priority—of the poetic material lent support to Robert Carroll's judgment that the standard assumption of the poetry's authenticity is a "dogma [that] cannot be established by argument, [but] can only be believed."[6] Like Carroll, he used this observation to undermine the legitimacy of the older attempt to reconstruct the life of Jeremiah. Unfortunately, also like Carroll, Diamond continued to rely on the standard assumption even after he had demonstrated its weakness. Carroll admitted to needing the assumption of the priority of the poetry (an assumption he called "the only a priori judgment"[7] he would use in his work) to demonstrate the secondary nature of the prose, the foundation of his redactional account. Similarly, throughout his redactional analysis of individual passages, Diamond relied on the assumption that poetry is prior to prose without offering any justification. He offered demonstrations that passages are in prose or that they include Deuteronomistic language as sufficient evidence for the conclusion that they are editorial additions. Thus, his clearer insight into the weakness of the standard historical-critical foundation of other redaction critics did not prevent Diamond from following their approaches and replicating their results.

Of course, the positive results of redactional approaches like Diamond's for understanding Jeremiah 11–20 are considerable. A signal achievement of these works was to demonstrate that the confessions, or laments, had significant links with the

---

[2] A. R. Pete Diamond, *The Confessions of Jeremiah in Context: Scenes of Prophetic Drama*, J SOT Sup 45 (Sheffield: JSOT Press, 1987), 122. Diamond's assessment is shared by Louis Stulman: "The confessions in my opinion are far too diverse and complex to be subsumed under a single rubric or literary function." Louis Stulman, "Review of A. R. Diamond, *The Confessions of Jeremiah in Context: Scenes of Prophetic Drama*," *CBQ* 51 (1987): 317.
[3] Diamond, *Confessions in Context*, 145.
[4] Diamond, *Confessions in Context*, 189–90.
[5] Diamond, *Confessions in Context*, 189, cf. 123–4, 145.
[6] Robert P. Carroll, *Jeremiah: A Commentary*, OTL (Philadelphia, PA: Westminster, 1986), 47.
[7] Robert P. Carroll, *From Chaos to Covenant: Prophecy in the Book of Jeremiah* (New York: Crossroad, 1981), 9.

materials in their immediate literary contexts (whether poetry or prose) and further that the whole section in which they occur, Jeremiah 11–20, has some degree of structural unity. For example, Diamond and several of the other redactional studies agree that chs 11–20 build toward a climax in the final chs 18–20. This new perception of the unity of the text was made possible by their theory that the Deuteronomistic authors or editors gave shape to the present form of the text. Crediting the authors or editors of Jeremiah with intelligence and purpose gave these redaction critics the grounds for looking for signs of artistry and intentionality in the arrangement of materials.

Unfortunately, these gains came at considerable cost. The theory of Deuteronomistic redaction Diamond followed skews the readers' ability to judge the genre, purpose, and theological perspective of the text. On the assumption that the Deuteronomists are responsible not only for Yahweh's prose speeches but also for the structure (which integrates the preexisting material), the genre and agenda of the whole composition is identified with the genre and agenda discovered in the prose speeches. Because the prose speeches are considered to be Deuteronomistic sermons, the genre of the whole is described as homiletical, or paraenetic. Because the agenda of the Deuteronomistic preachers is determined to be exonerating the deity for Judah's exile, the agenda of the whole composition is assumed to be theodicy. Jeremiah's confessions and the rest of the supposedly preexisting non-Deuteronomistic material are said to have been incorporated into the sermons of the Deuteronomists as sermon illustrations, or documentary evidence of the wickedness of people. The purpose of Jeremiah's confessions is identified as providing historical proof that the people of Judah rejected God's prophet and thus that he cannot be blamed for their demise. The application of the theory of the Deuteronomistic redaction and its theodicy agenda to the poetic sections of Jeremiah 11–20 was the end result of a long process in modern Jeremiah criticism. Beginning with Mowinckel's identification of the Deuteronomistic preachers as authors of this type C prose, Deuteronomistic editing was found by Nicholson and others to be behind the type B narratives as well. With the redaction-critical studies of 11–20, it has subsumed the Type A poetry as well. To borrow the words of Gordon McConville, the "dead hand of the Deuteronomist" has been drawn over the entire book.[8]

The weakness of the theory of Deuteronomistic redaction as it applies to Jeremiah 11–12 is apparent from its poor fit with the actual material of these chapters. It would take quite a bit of explaining to convince a reader unacquainted with Duhm and Mowinckel's compositional theory that Jeremiah 11–20 had a theodicy agenda. These chapters are justly best known for Jeremiah's anguished prayers, which include some of the strongest accusations of Yahweh for injustice in the Hebrew Scriptures. Furthermore, the portrait of Yahweh the text paints can hardly be said to emphasize his justice. Diamond's descriptions of the characterization are especially helpful here. Commenting on Yahweh's declaration that he will ignore his people's cries for help in

---

[8] Gordon McConville, "Review of Jeremiah 37-52: A New Translation with Introduction and Commentary (Anchor Bible, 21C) by Jack R Lundbom," *JSOT*, New Series, 58, no. 2 (October 2007): 600.

ch. 11, Diamond wrote, "The hate and rage of a betrayed husband issue in Israel's doom (11:7-13)."[9] Commenting on Yahweh's promise to publically expose his adulterous wife in ch. 13, he wrote, "The demise of the nation represents God's personal pitiless violence."[10] Although the text certainly emphasizes the wickedness and recalcitrance of the God's people, it does not portray Yahweh's response as the measured application of just consequences but as the violent outburst of an unbridled fury. The description of this portrayal as theodicy is not encouraged by attention to text's presentation but rather forced by adherence to a compositional theory.

Although Diamond concurred both in his early and later work with ascription of a theodicy agenda to Jeremiah 11–20, in one of his last articles he offered a telling critique of the approach that produced it. He wrote,

> Redaction criticism settles for a linear, monological reading that obliterates the complexity of polyphonic poetics, settling eventually on a single privileged voice somewhere along the stages of linear, historical compositional genesis. The question is whether the critic prefers the voices of earlier compositional layers or of some later stage in the ideological poetics at work in the production of the scroll.[11]

This trenchant criticism does strike one false note. The voice that redaction critics, including Diamond himself, privilege does not seem to be one they prefer. When one redaction critic argued for identifying the meaning of the text with what she calls the "rigidly formulaic" prose of the Deuteronomists in place of what she calls the "vivid, original and extremely concrete" poetry,[12] it seems unlikely that she was guided by her personal preference. Rather, her reading was constrained by the straitjacket of her methodological approach, a combination of Duhm's source-critical assumptions with redaction criticism's insistence that the final form is the arbiter of meaning. Diamond's concurrence with the judgment that the genre of 11–20 is paraenetic and its purpose is theodicy shows that the extent to which he was able to break free from entrenched assumptions was only partial.

Even in this early work, however, Diamond observed features in the text that pushed him toward a new understanding of the genre and purpose. The new judgment can be seen in his subtitle of his first major work: *Scenes of Prophetic Drama*. He explained in the concluding chapter of this work: "As a play, which apart from minor scenic comments relies primarily on dialogue to create a sense of narrative development ... the literary complex 11–20 narrates or portrays the course of Jeremiah's prophetic mission as a dialogue in which prophet, Yahweh, and nation are the participants."[13] Diamond's close reading of the text enabled him to grasp the primary nature and coherence of the

---

[9] Diamond, "Jeremiah," 568.

[10] Diamond, "Jeremiah," 569.

[11] A. R. Pete Diamond, "Interlocutions: The Poetics of Voice in the Figuration of YHWH and His Oracular Agent, Jeremiah," *Interpretation* 62, no. 1 (January 2008): 53.

[12] Kathleen M. O'Connor, *The Confessions of Jeremiah: Their Interpretation and Their Role in Chapters 1–25* (Atlanta, GA: Scholars Press, 1987), 151.

[13] Diamond, *Confessions in Context*, 181–2.

literary composition. First, its reliance on speeches to depict situations in the mission of the prophet indicates the dramatic nature or genre of the passage. Second, the best explanation of the text's shifts in style, vocabulary, concerns, and perspectives between adjacent passages is often the alternation of dramatic speakers whose speeches answer each other and thus form what Diamond recognizes as dramatic dialogues. Third, the dialogues are components of what he refers to as "stylized scenes," which are the basic units of the literary structure. Fourth, the primary relationship of the scenes to each other (as well as the relationship of the speeches that make up the scenes) is narrative development: they work together to tell a story.

The recognition of the dramatic and narrative character provides an alternative to the account of the text offered by the standard compositional model. The basic difference is that the speeches are understood to be "fictive" representations of speech (to use Diamond's term) rather than historical records of speech. By definition, fictive speech is speech employed to portray characters or situations. This means that elements of the speeches in Jeremiah 11–20 that in previous accounts were treated as clues that might betray the identity of the author or of the historical situation in which the speech was originally spoken or written are actually intentional elements included, or even created, by the author(s) to develop a dramatic character or evoke a dramatic situation. Thus the vocabulary, style, concerns, perspective, and agenda of the speeches are only secondarily those of the author(s); they are primarily those of the dramatic characters. This is not to deny that characters portrayed in Jeremiah 11–20 (including Yahweh) would have been understood by their authors and audiences as real persons. Indentifying a speech as "fictive" does not necessarily mean that its speakers are fictional, as Diamond sometimes seemed to argue. There is a genre called "historical" drama. The nature and the degree of correspondence between these portrayals and historical reality cannot be determined simply by noting that they are portrayals.

Recognition of the dramatic character of the text also provides an alternative account of the coherence of the text. The obvious difference is that what were formerly viewed as disruptive compositional seams can be understood as shifts in dramatic speakers. Recognizing the presence of dramatic dialogue does not mean denying that the text is composite or that its history of composition may be complex. A drama could be revised many times and could employ previously existing material (including records of historical speeches). However, it does mean that shifts in style or perspective alone cannot be taken as evidence of multiple hands. A more fundamental difference in the way that reading a text as dramatic accounts for its coherence is that the coherence is understood to be primarily functional or organic. The various speeches, dialogues, and scenes are primarily unified as elements that work together (like parts of a machine or organs in living thing) to achieve the intended portrait. To use the analogy of a painting, perceiving the unity of a painted portrait does not come primarily from positing that parts of the painting came from the same paint tube or were added with the same type of brush stroke. Neither does perceiving the unity depend on identifying which parts were painted last. The unity comes from the portrayal of the subject that the work was created to provide.

Recognition of dramatic portrayal also provides a different account of the structure of the text. This is evident by comparing the two accounts of Jeremiah 11–20: one that sees the text as a collection of prose sermons with poetic documentary material that supports the agenda of the sermons, the other that sees the text as dramatic presentation composed of scenes that tell different parts of a story. Most of these scenes begin with one of Yahweh's speeches in prose that serve the crucial function of establishing the dramatic situations. The text makes it clear that these introductory speeches are messages from Yahweh to be delivered to the people of Judah or Jerusalem by Jeremiah. The content of the messages—calls for repentance or announcements of coming judgment—signal to the audience that these situations took place before the threatened catastrophe. Yahweh's introductory speech in the initial scene (11:1-5) has the most important role in this regard since it introduces the opening situation of the whole dramatic composition (Jeremiah 11–20). Its call to heed Yahweh's covenant and choose the covenant blessings over the covenant curses deliberately evokes the time of Josiah's covenant renewal and reforms based on the newly discovered Book of the Covenant. Jeremiah's enthusiastic response initiates the opening question of the story, whether his ministry can bring repentance and avert the covenant curses. When the Deuteronomistic language of this message and Yahweh's other messages is interpreted as a function of the theological perspective or agenda of exilic preachers or editors, the preexilic situation of the dramatic situation is obscured—as is the agenda or motivation of one of the central characters in drama, Yahweh. Diamond's works stand uneasily astride these two understandings of the text. On the one hand, his adherence to the standard compositional model appears even in his commentary when he begins his unit on Jeremiah 11–12 with extended discussion of the confessions isolated from their literary context, thus severing them from Yahweh's prose speeches, which establish the time frame of the story. On the other hand, even in his early work he had already recognized that Jeremiah 11–20 tells the story of "the course of Jeremiah's prophetic mission."[14]

Diamond's critical gains—both in questioning the standard assumptions and recognizing the dramatic nature of Jeremiah 11–20—bore fruit in the form of new insights about the text's portrayal. This is particularly true of his advances in understanding the text's portrayal of Yahweh. His recognition of the dramatic nature of the text (or the fictive nature of the speeches) allowed him to consider both Yahweh's poetic speeches and his prose speeches as elements in the text's portrayal of his character. It has already been observed how Diamond brought attention to Yahweh's fiery anger over his people's betrayal. This aspect of his portrayal emerges primarily from what can be called Yahweh's poetic laments in chs 12, 15, and 18 but also from the brief narrative and prose speeches in ch. 13 about the ruined loincloth. Yahweh's prose speeches in ch. 13 are a significant exception because unlike most of Yahweh's prose speeches (and like his poetic speeches), there is no indication that these speeches were to be communicated to the people as messages. This highlights a key feature of the whole group of Yahweh's speeches: they fall into two clearly discernible categories: public and private. The private speeches are important elements in developing what Diamond referred to as "divine interiority."[15] As he demonstrated, Jeremiah 11–20 (which justly

[14] Diamond, *Confessions in Context*, 181–2.
[15] Diamond, "Interlocutions," 59.

celebrated its portrait of inner life of the prophet) also provides a rich evocation of the inner life of Yahweh as he approaches the point in his story when he will pour out his wrath on his beloved people.

What makes Diamond's elucidation of the text's portrayal of Yahweh particularly insightful is his recognition that the portrayal of the inner life painted by the private speeches colors the audience's perception of Yahweh's public messages. The private speeches all occur in scenes that also include public messages. The effect created is that the audience understands Yahweh's relatively staid public statements as spoken by a character whose inner life is in turmoil. When Yahweh is exhorting the nation to repentance, enumerating the consequences of breaking the covenant, denouncing the folly of idolatry, or declaring the immanence of judgment in measured rhetorical prose, he is all the time seething with fury at his people's betrayal and broken with grief over what they have become. As Diamond writes, "Whatever deuteronomic 'rationality' fronts the surface of God's rhetoric, it acts as a façade, a mask for divine interiority."[16] Yahweh's messages to his rebellious people, which explain their situation in terms of the impersonal consequences of their law breaking, are sent by a character wracked with interior pain revealed in the private speeches in which he pours out his anger and grief.

Another of the observations that Diamond's understating of the dramatic nature of the text allowed gets to the heart of the portrayal of Yahweh in Jeremiah 11–20. Diamond notices that the dialogue between Yahweh in the opening scene (chs 11–12) "create[s] a parallelism between Jeremiah and Yahweh." The parallelism is twofold. First, the conspiracy of the men of Anathoth against Jeremiah mirrors the rejection of the covenant by the people of Judah, a rejection Yahweh calls a conspiracy against him. Second, after revealing to Jeremiah that his own household will act treacherously against him, Yahweh bursts out with a cry of agony that his own house, the beloved of his soul, has rebelled against him. The opening scene thus sets the audience up to understand the experiences of Jeremiah as reflecting the experiences of Yahweh. As Jeremiah's message falls on deaf ears, as he experiences not only rejection but violent opposition, as he becomes unable to hold back his anger toward his persecutors, and as he is torn between his desire to see disaster averted and his desire to have his word vindicated, the audience realizes that what is true of Jeremiah is even more true of Yahweh.

Diamond observes that in the second half of the composition (chs 16–20) Jeremiah's private speeches are no longer answered by Yahweh's private responses to him.[17] In these last scenes, Yahweh's interior life is evoked not through his speeches but through Jeremiah's. The concluding speeches of Jeremiah (in ch. 20) bring to completion not only the composition's portrait of Jeremiah but also its portrait of Yahweh. Jeremiah rejoices that Yahweh will vindicate his message and bring vengeance on his enemies. But then, reflecting that his triumph and the triumph of his message will mean the destruction of his people, he curses the day of his birth. As Jeremiah gives voice to his experience, the audience receives a hint of what it must mean for Yahweh that he

[16] Diamond, "Interlocutions," 59.
[17] Diamond, *Confessions in Context*, 144.

is about to pour out the wrath that has burned in his bones for centuries and what it must mean for him to know that the covenant he established with his beloved people will bring about their destruction at his own hands.

Finally, the fruit of Diamond's work can be understood by the fresh understanding of the purpose of Jeremiah 11–20. The purpose of a dramatic portrayal can't be summed up in one main point or central argument like homiletical work. As drama its primary purpose is to offer a truthful and compelling portrait, in this instance a terrifying and heartbreaking portrait of Yahweh and his prophet. Although the drama has no narrow theological or ideological agenda, it is not difficult to discern some of the intended effects on its audience, the exiled people of Judah. The drama does not allow them to understand their plight merely as punishment: that the exile is the consequence of breaking the law, so they must now repent and obey the law if they want to be restored to the land. Instead, they are confronted with the deep personal anguish their betrayal has caused Jeremiah and Yahweh. They are not allowed to understand their loss and suffering as the result of impersonal consequences or misfortune. Instead, they must face the terrible reality that their God is enraged with them. They are made to recognize their inveterate wickedness in such a way that they are stripped of any hope that they could depend on their own obedience for restoration. Instead, they are forced to admit that their only hope is that Yahweh might relent from his wrath: that his love for them, which both caused his wrath and held it back for so long, still remains; that in wrath Yahweh will remember mercy.

Bibliography

Abrahams, Israel. "Jews." In *Encyclopedia Britannica: A Dictionary of Arts, Sciences, Literary and General Information*, 371–410. Vol. 15. New York: Encyclopedia Britannica, 1911.

Abrams, M. H. *The Mirror and the Lamp: Romantic Theory and the Critical Tradition.* New York: W. W. Norton, 1958.

Abrams, M. H. *Natural Supernaturalism: Tradition and Revolution in Romantic Literature.* New York: W. W. Norton, 1971.

Albertz, Rainer. *A History of Israelite Religion in the Old Testament Period.* Vol. 1. OTL. Louisville, KY: Westminster John Knox, 2005.

Balfour, Ian. *The Rhetoric of Romantic Prophecy.* Stanford, CA: Stanford University Press, 2002.

Barth, Karl. *Protestant Theology in the Nineteenth Century.* Grand Rapids, MI: Eerdmans, 2002.

Bartholomew, Craig G. "Uncharted Waters: Philosophy, Theology and the Crisis in Biblical Interpretation." In *Renewing Biblical Interpretation.* Edited by Craig Bartholomew, Colin Greene, and Karl Möller, 1–39. Scripture & Hermeneutics 1. Grand Rapids, MI: Zondervan, 2001.

Barton, John. *Reading the Old Testament: Method in Biblical Study.* Philadelphia, PA: Westminster, 1984.

Barzun, Jacques. *From Dawn to Decadence: 500 Years of Western Cultural Life: 1500 to the Present.* New York: HarperCollins, 2000.

Baumgartner, Walter. *Jeremiah's Poems of Lament.* Translated by David E. Orton. Sheffield: Almond, 1988.

Benecke, Heinrich. *Wilhelm Vatke in sienem Leben und seinen Schriften.* Bonn. Emil Strauss, 1883.

Berlin, Isaiah. *The Roots of Romanticism.* 2nd ed. Princeton, NJ: Princeton University Press, 2013.

Berlin, Isaiah. *Three Critics of the Enlightenment: Vico, Hamann, Herder.* Princeton, NJ: Princeton University Press, 2000.

Beuken, W. A. M., and H. W. M. van Grol. "Jeremiah 14,1–15,9: A Situation of Distress and Its Hermeneutic, Unity and Diversity of Form–Dramatic Development." In *Le Livre de Jérémie: Le prophète et son milieu, les oracles et leur transmission.* Edited by Pierre Bogaert, 168–73. Leuven: Leuven University Press, 1981.

Biddle, Mark E. *Polyphony and Symphony in Prophetic Literature: Rereading Jeremiah 7–20.* Macon, GA: Mercer University Press, 1996.

Biddle, Mark E. *A Redaction History of Jeremiah 2:1–4:2.* AThANT 77. Zürich: TVZ, 1990.

Blackwell, Thomas. *An Inquiry into the Life and Writings of Homer.* London: For E. Dilly, at the Rose and Crown in the Poultry, near the Mansion-House, 1735.

Blair, Hugh. *A Critical Dissertation on the Poems of Ossian.* London: T. Becket and P. A. De Hondt, at Tully's Head in the Strand, 1763.

Blake, William. *Blake's Poetry and Designs.* 2nd ed. NCE. New York: W. W. Norton, 2008.

Blayney, Benjamin. *Jeremiah and Lamentations: A New Translation with Notes Critical, Philological, and Explanatory.* 2nd ed. Edinburgh: Oliphant & Balfour, 1810.

Borowitz, Eugene B. *Choices in Modern Judaism.* 2nd ed. Springfield, NJ: Behrman House, 1996.

Boyle, Nicholas. *Goethe: The Poet and the Age.* New York: Oxford University Press, 1992.

Bright, John. *Jeremiah.* 2nd ed. AB 21. Garden City, NY: Doubleday, 1965.

Brueggemann, Walter. *A Commentary on Jeremiah: Exile and Homecoming.* Grand Rapids, MI: Eerdmans, 1998.

Brueggemann, Walter. "Next Steps in Jeremiah Studies." In *Troubling Jeremiah.* Edited by A. R. Pete Diamond, Kathleen O'Connor, and Louis Stulman, 404–22. JSOT Sup 260. Sheffield: Sheffield Academic Press, 1999.

Brueggemann, Walter. "Preface." In *Reading the Book of Jeremiah: A Search for Coherence.* Edited by Martin Kessler, ix–x. Winona Lake, IN: Eisenbrauns, 2004.

Brueggemann, Walter. "Questions Addressed in the Study of the Pentateuch." In *The Vitality of Old Testament Traditions.* Edited by Walter Brueggemann and Hans Walter Wolff. Atlanta, GA: Westminster John Knox, 1982.

Brueggemann, Walter. *Theology of the Old Testament: Testimony, Dispute, Advocacy.* Minneapolis, MN: Fortress, 1997.

Bryce, James. "Robertson Smith." In *Studies in Contemporary Biography,* 311–26. New York: Macmillan, 1905.

Burnett, Richard E. *Karl Barth's Theological Exegesis.* WUNT 2/145. Tübingen: Mohr Siebeck, 2001.

Carroll, Robert P. *From Chaos to Covenant: Prophecy in the Book of Jeremiah.* New York: Crossroad, 1981.

Carroll, Robert P. *Jeremiah: A Commentary.* OTL. Philadelphia, PA: Westminster, 1986.

Cheyne, Thomas Kelly. *Founders of Old Testament Criticism: Biographical, Descriptive, and Critical Studies.* London: Methuen, 1893.

Childs, Brevard S. *Biblical Theology in Crisis.* Philadelphia, PA: Westminster, 1970.

Childs, Brevard S. "Jeremiah." In *Introduction to the Old Testament as Scripture,* 338–54. Philadelphia, PA: Fortress, 1979.

Clements, Ronald E. "Jeremiah's Message of Hope: Public Faith and Private Anguish." In *Reading the Book of Jeremiah: A Search for Coherence.* Edited by Martin Kessler, 135–47. Winona Lake, IN: Eisenbrauns, 2004.

Clements, Ronald E. *One Hundred Years of Old Testament Interpretation.* Philadelphia, PA: Westminster, 1976.

Craigie, Peter, Page Kelly, and Joel Drinkard Jr. *Jeremiah 1–24.* WBC 26. Dallas, TX: Word Books, 1991.

Cross, Frank Moore. *The Ancient Library at Qumran.* Rev. ed. Garden City, NY: Doubleday, 1961.

Cross, Frank Moore. "The Council of Yahweh in Second Isaiah." *JNES* 12 (1953): 274–7.

Crouter, Richard. *Friedrich Schleiermacher: Between Enlightenment and Romanticism.* New York: Cambridge University Press, 2005.

Cullhed, Anna. "Original Poetry: Robert Lowth and Eighteenth Century Poetics." In *Sacred Conjectures: The Context and Legacy of Robert Lowth and Jean Astruc.* Edited by John Jarick, 25–47. LHB/OTS 457. New York: T&T Clark, 2007.

Diamond, A. R. Pete. *The Confessions of Jeremiah in Context: Scenes of Prophetic Drama.* JSOT Sup 45. Sheffield: JSOT Press, 1987.

Diamond, A. R. Pete. "Interlocutions: The Poetics of Voice in the Figuration of YHWH and His Oracular Agent, Jeremiah." *Interpretation* 62, no.1 (January 2008): 48–65.

Diamond, A. R. Pete. "Jeremiah." In *Eerdman's Commentary on the Bible*. Edited by John Rogerson and James Dunn, 543–616. Grand Rapids, MI: Eerdmans, 2003.

Diamond, A. R. Pete. "Review of *The Confessions of Jeremiah: Their Interpretation and Their Role in Chapters 1–25*, by Kathleen O'Connor." *JBL* 108 (1989): 694–6.

Dickson, Gwen Griffith. *Johann Georg Hamann's Relational Metacriticism*. Berlin: de Gruyter, 1995.

Duhm, Bernhard. *Das Buch Jeremia*. KHC 11. Tübingen: J. C. B. Mohr, 1901.

Duhm, Bernhard. *Die Theologie der Propheten als Grundlage für die innere Entwicklungsgeschichte der israelitischen Religion*. Bonn: Marcus, 1875.

Eliot, T. S. "Tradition and the Individual Talent." In *Criticism: The Major Texts*. Edited by Walter Jackson Bate, 525–9. Chicago, IL: Harcourt Brace Jovanovich, 1970.

Engnell, Ivan. "The Traditio-Historical Method in Old Testament Research." In *A Rigid Scrutiny*. Edited by John T. Willis, 3–11. Nashville, TN: Vanderbilt University Press, 1969.

Ermarth, Elizabeth Deeds. *The English Novel in History: 1840–1895*. New York: Routledge, 1997.

Ewald, Heinrich. *Commentary on the Prophets of the Old Testament*. Translated by J. Frederick Smith. 5 vols. TTFL 9. London: Williams & Norgate, 1875.

Frei, Hans. *The Eclipse of Biblical Narrative: A Study in Eighteenth and Nineteenth Century Hermeneutics*. New Haven, CT: Yale University Press, 1974.

Gadamer, Hans Georg. *Truth and Method*. Translated by Joel Weinsheimer and Donald Marshal. 2nd ed. New York: Continuum, 2000.

Gerstenberger, Erhard. "Jeremiah's Complaints: Observations on Jer. 15 10–21." *JBL* 82 (1963): 393–408.

Gunkel, Hermann. *Die israelitische Literatur*. Darmstadt: Wissenschaftliche Buchgesellschaft, 1963.

Gunkel, Hermann. "Foreword to the Third Edition (1910)." In *Genesis*. Translated by Mark Biddle. Edited by Mark Biddle. Macon, GA: Mercer University Press, 1997.

Gunkel, Hermann. "Fundamental Problems of Hebrew Literary History." In *What Remains of the Old Testament and Other Essays*. Translated by A. K. Dallas. Edited by A. K. Dallas, 57–68. New York: Macmillan, 1928.

Gunkel, Hermann. "The Israelite Prophecy from the Time of Amos." In *Twentieth Century Theology in the Making*. Edited by Jaroslav Pelikan, 48–75. Vol. 1. New York: Collins, 1969.

Gunkel, Hermann. "The Prophets: Oral and Written." In *Water for a Thirsty Land: Israelite Literature and Religion*. Edited by K. C. Hanson, 85–132. Fortress Classics in Biblical Studies. Minneapolis, MN: Fortress, 2001.

Gunkel, Hermann. "What Is Left of the Old Testament?" In *What Remains of the Old Testament and Other Essays*. Translated by A. K. Dallas. Edited by A. K. Dallas, 13–56. New York: Macmillan, 1928.

Gunneweg, A. H. J. "Konfession oder Interpretation im Jeremiabuch." *ZThK* 67 (1970): 395–416.

Hamann, J. G. "Aesthetica in Nuce: A Rhapsody in Cabbalistic Prose (1762)." In *Classic and Romantic German Aesthetics*. Edited by J. M. Bernstein, 1–23. New York: Cambridge University Press, 2003.

Harnack, Adolf von. *What Is Christianity?* Translated by Thomas Bailey Saunders. New York: G. P. Putnam's Sons, 1901.

The HarperCollins Study Bible: New Revised Standard Version, Including the Apocryphal/ deuterocanonical Books. San Francisco, CA: HarperSanFrancisco, 2006.

Hayes, John H. *An Introduction to Old Testament Study*. Nashville, TN: Abingdon, 1979.

Henderson, Joseph M. "Duhm and Skinner's Invention of Jeremiah." In *Jeremiah Invented: Constructions and Deconstructions of Jeremiah*. Edited by Else K. Holt and Carolyn J. Sharp, 1–15. LHB/OTS 595. New York: T&T Clark, 2015.

Henderson, Joseph M. "Jeremiah 2–10 as a Unified Literary Composition: Evidence of Dramatic Portrayal and Narrative Progression." In *Uprooting and Planting: Essays on Jeremiah for Leslie Allen*. Edited by John Goldingay, 116–52. LHB/OTS 459. New York: T&T Clark, 2007.

Henderson, Joseph M. "The Structure of Jeremiah 4:5–6:30." Master's Thesis, Asbury Theological Seminary, 1998.

Henderson, Joseph M. "Who Weeps in Jeremiah VIII 23 (IX 1)?: Identifying Dramatic Speakers in the Poetry of Jeremiah." *VT* 52 (2002): 191–206.

Hepworth, Brian. *Robert Lowth*. Twayne's English Authors 224. Boston, MA: G. K. Hall, 1978.

Herder, Johann Gottfried von. *Sämtliche Werke*. Vol. 1. Edited by Bernhard Suphan. Hildesheim: Georg Olms, 1967.

Herder, Johann Gottfried von. *The Spirit of Hebrew Poetry*. Translated by James Marsh. 2 vols. Burlington: Edward Smith, 1833.

Herder, Johann Gottfried von. *Vom Geist der ebräischen Poesie*. 3rd ed. 2 vols. Leipzig: Johann Ambrosius Barth, 1825.

Heschel, Abraham J. *The Prophets: An Introduction*. New York: Harper & Row, 1962.

Hobbs, T. R. "Some Remarks on the Composition of and Structure of the Book of Jeremiah." In *A Prophet to the Nations: Essays in Jeremiah Studies*. Edited by Leo Perdue, 175–91. Winona Lake, IN: Eisenbrauns, 1984.

Holladay, William Lee. *The Architecture of Jeremiah 1–20*. Cranbury, NJ: Associated University Presses, 1976.

Holladay, William Lee. "A Fresh Look at 'Source B' and 'Source C' in Jeremiah." *VT* 25 (1975): 394–412.

Holladay, William Lee. *Jeremiah 1: A Commentary on the Book of the Prophet Jeremiah, Chapters 1–25*. Hermeneia. Philadelphia, PA: Fortress, 1986.

Holladay, William Lee. *Jeremiah 2: A Commentary on the Book of the Prophet Jeremiah, Chapters 26–52*. Hermeneia. Minneapolis, MN: Fortress, 1989.

Holladay, William Lee. *Jeremiah: Spokesman Out of Time*. Philadelphia, PA: United Church Press, 1974.

Holladay, William Lee. "Prototypes and Copies: A New Approach to the Poetry–Prose Problem in the Book of Jeremiah." *JBL* 79 (1960): 351–67.

Hölscher, Gustav. *Die Profeten: Untersuchungen zur Religionsgeschichte Israels*. Leipzig: J. C. Hinrichs, 1914.

Holt, Else K., and Carolyn J. Sharp, eds. *Jeremiah Invented: Constructions and Deconstructions of Jeremiah*. New York: Bloomsbury T&T Clark, 2015.

Homolka, Walter. *Jewish Identity in Modern Times: Leo Baeck and German Protestantism*. Providence, RI: Berghahn Books, 1995.

Hyatt, J. Philip. "The Deuteronomistic Edition of Jeremiah." *VSH* 1 (1951): 71–95.

Hyatt, J. Philip. "Jeremiah." In *The Interpreter's Bible*. Edited by George A. Buttrick. Vol. 5. New York: Abingdon, 1956.

Irwin, William A. "The Significance of Julius Wellhausen." *JBR* 12 (1944): 160–73.

Johnson, Paul. *The Birth of the Modern: World Society 1815–1830*. New York: HarperCollins, 1991.

Kaiser, Barbara Bakke. "Poet as 'Female Impersonator': The Image of Daughter Zion as Speaker in Biblical Poems of Suffering." *JR* 67 (1987): 164–82.

Kaufmann, Yehezkel. *The Religion of Israel: From Its Beginning to the Babylonian Exile.* Translated by Moshe Greenberg. Chicago, IL: University of Chicago Press, 1960.

Klatt, Werner. *Hermann Gunkel: Zu seiner Theologie der Religionsgeschichte und zur Entstehung der formgeschichtlichen Methode.* FRLANT 100. Heft der ganzen Reihe. Göttingen: Vandenhoeck & Ruprecht, 1969.

Kuenen, Abraham. *An Historico-Critical Inquiry into the Origin and Composition of the Hexateuch: Pentateuch and Book of Joshua.* London: Macmillan, 1886.

Kugel, James L. *The Idea of Biblical Poetry: Parallelism and Its History.* New Haven, CT: Yale University Press, 1981.

Kugel, James L. *Poetry and Prophecy: The Beginnings of a Literary Tradition.* Ithaca, NY: Cornell University Press, 1990.

Kumaki, Kenro. "A New Look at Jer. 4:19–22 and Jer. 10:19–20." *AJBI* 8 (1982): 113–22.

Lalleman-de Winkel, Hetty. *Jeremiah in Prophetic Tradition: An Examination of the Book of Jeremiah in the Light of Israel's Prophetic Traditions.* CBET 26. Leuven: Peeters, 2000.

Legaspi, Michael. *The Death of Scripture and the Rise of Biblical Studies.* New York: Oxford University Press, 2010.

Lewis, C. S. "Donne and Love Poetry in the Seventeenth Century." In *John Donne's Poetry,* NCE. Edited by A. L. Clements, 144–60. New York: W. W. Norton, 1966.

Lewis, C. S. *Studies in Words.* 2nd ed. New York: Cambridge University Press, 1967.

Lessing, Gotthold Ephraim. *The Education of the Human Race.* Translated by F. W. Robertson. 3rd ed. London: Henry S. King [1777–80] 1872.

Leuchter, Mark. *Josiah's Reform and Jeremiah's Scroll: Historical Calamity and Prophetic Response.* Hebrew Bible Monographs 6. Sheffield: Sheffield Phoenix, 2006.

Lowth, Robert. *Isaiah: A New Translation with a Preliminary Dissertation and Notes, Critical, Philological and Explanatory.* 2 vols. London: J. Dodsley, T. Cadell, 1778.

Lowth, Robert. *Lectures on the Sacred Poetry of the Hebrews.* Translated by G. Gregory. Boston, MA: Joseph T. Buckingham, 1815.

Lundbom, Jack. *Jeremiah 1–20: A New Translation with Introduction and Commentary.* AB 21A. New York: Doubleday, 1999.

Lundbom, Jack. *Jeremiah: A Study in Ancient Hebrew Rhetoric.* 2nd ed. Winona Lake, IN: Eisenbrauns, 1997.

McConville, J. Gordon. *Judgement and Promise: An Interpretation of the Book of Jeremiah.* Winona Lake, IN: Eisenbrauns, 1993.

McConville, J. Gordon. "Review of Jeremiah 37–52: A New Translation with Introduction and Commentary AB 21C by Jack R Lundbom." *JSOT,* New Series, 58, no. 2 (2007): 599–601.

McKane, William. *A Critical and Exegetical Commentary on Jeremiah.* 2 vols. ICC. Edinburgh: T&T Clark, 1986 and 1996.

Meier, Samuel. *Speaking of Speaking: Marking Direct Discourse in the Hebrew Bible.* New York: Brill, 1992.

Milton, John. "Paradise Lost." In *Complete Poems and Major Prose.* Edited by Merritt Y. Hughes, 211–469. New Jersey: Prentice Hall, 1957.

Morris, David B. *The Religious Sublime: Christian Poetry and Critical Tradition in 18th-Century England.* Lexington: University Press of Kentucky, 1972.

Mowinckel, Sigmund. *The Old Testament as the Word of God.* Translated by Reidar B. Bjornard. New York: Abingdon Press, 1959.

Mowinckel, Sigmund. " 'The Spirit' and the 'Word' in the Pre-Exilic Reforming Prophets."
   JBL 53 (1934): 199–227.
Mowinckel, Sigmund. *The Spirit and the Word: Prophecy and Tradition in Ancient Israel.*
   FCBS. Minneapolis, MN: Fortress, 2002.
Mowinckel, Sigmund. *Zur Komposition des Buches Jeremia.* Oslo: Jacob Dybwad, 1914.
Muilenburg, James. "Form Criticism and Beyond." *JBL* 88 (1969): 1–18.
Muilenburg, James. "Isaiah 40–66." In *The Interpreter's Bible.* Edited by George A. Buttrick,
   381–773. Vol. 5. New York: Abingdon, 1956.
Mullen, E. Theodore, Jr. *The Assembly of the Gods in Canaanite and Early Hebrew
   Literature.* HSM 24. Chico, CA: Scholars Press, 1980.
Nicholson, Ernest W. *Preaching to the Exiles: A Study of the Prose Tradition in the Book of
   Jeremiah.* New York: Schocken Books, 1971.
Norton, David. *History of the English Bible as Literature.* Cambridge: Cambridge
   University Press, 2000.
Noth, Martin. *Überlieferungsgeschichtliche Studien.* Halle: Max Niemeyer, 1943.
O'Connor, Kathleen M. *The Confessions of Jeremiah: Their Interpretation and Their Role in
   Chapters 1–25.* Atlanta, GA: Scholars Press, 1987.
Oden, Robert A. *The Bible without Theology: The Theological Tradition and Alternatives to
   It.* NVBS. San Francisco, CA: Harper & Row, 1987.
Orr, James. *The Ritschlian Theology and the Evangelical Faith.* London: Hodder and
   Stoughton, 1897.
Otto, Rudolph. *Kantisch-fries'sche Religionsphilosophie und ihre Anwendung auf die
   Theologie: Zur Einleitung in die Glaubenslehre für Studenten der Theologie.* Tübingen: J.
   C. B. Mohr (Paul Siebeck), 1909.
Parunak, H. Van Dyke. "Some Discourse Functions of Prophetic Quotation Formulas
   in Jeremiah." In *Biblical and Hebrew Discourse Linguistics.* Edited by Robert Bergen,
   489–519. Dallas, TX: Summer Institute of Linguistics, 1994.
Perdue, Leo G. "The Book of Jeremiah in Old Testament Theology." In *Troubling Jeremiah.*
   Edited by A. R. Pete Diamond, Kathleen M. O'Connor, and Louis Stulman, 320–38.
   JSOT Sup 260. Sheffield: Sheffield Academic Press, 1999.
Perdue, Leo G. *The Collapse of History: Reconstructing Old Testament Theology.*
   Minneapolis, MN: Fortress, 1994.
Perdue, Leo G. "Jeremiah in Modern Research: Approaches and Issues." In *A Prophet
   to the Nations: Essays in Jeremiah Studies.* Edited by Leo G. Perdue. Winona Lake,
   IN: Eisenbrauns, 1984.
Perdue, Leo G., and Brian W. Kovacs, eds. *A Prophet to the Nations: Essays in Jeremiah
   Studies.* Winona Lake, IN: Eisenbrauns, 1984.
Plato. "Euthyphro." In *Plato: Complete Works.* Edited by John M. Cooper, 1–16.
   Indianapolis, IN: Hackett, 1997.
Pohlmann, Karl-Friedrich. *Die Ferne Gottes – Studien zum Jeremiabuch: Beiträge zu
   den "Konfessionen" im Jeremiabuch und ein Versuch zur Frage nach den Anfängen der
   Jeremiatradition.* BZAW 179. Berlin: de Gruyter, 1989.
Polk, Timothy. *The Prophetic Persona: Jeremiah and the Language of the Self.* JSOT Sup 32.
   Sheffield: University of Sheffield Press, 1984.
Prickett, Stephen. *Words and the Word: Language, Poetics and Biblical Interpretation.*
   New York: Cambridge University Press, 1986.
von Rad, Gerhard. "Jeremiah." In *Old Testament Theology.* Translated by D. M. G. Stalker,
   191–219. Vol. 2. New York: HarperCollins, 1965.
Reed, Eugene E. "Herder, Primitivism and the Age of Poetry." *MLR* 60 (1965): 553–67.

Reventlow, Henning Graf. *Liturgie und prophetisches Ich bei Jeremia*. Gütersloh: Gerd Mohn, 1963.

Robinson, H. W. "The Council of Yahweh." *JTS* 45 (1944): 151–7.

Rogerson, J. W. *Old Testament Criticism in the Nineteenth Century: England and Germany*. 1st Fortress Press ed. Philadelphia, PA: Fortress, 1985.

Roston, Murray. *Prophet and Poet: The Bible and the Growth of Romanticism*. Evanston, IL: Northwestern University Press, 1965.

Rousseau, Jean-Jacques. *Discourse on the Sciences and Arts*. Translated by Judith R. Bush. Edited by Roger D. Masters and Christopher Kelley. Vol. 2 of *The Collected Writings of Rousseau*. Hanover, NH: University Press of New England, 1992.

Rousseau, Jean-Jacques. *Emile: Or on Education*. Translated by Allan Bloom. New York: Basic Books, 1979.

Rudolph, Wilhelm. *Jeremia*. 2nd ed. HAT 12. Tübingen: J. C. B. Mohr, 1958.

Schlegel, Friedrich. *Philosophical Fragments*. Translated by Peter Firchow. Minneapolis: University of Minnesota, 1881.

Sharp, Carolyn J. *Prophecy and Ideology in Jeremiah: Struggles for Authority in Deutero-Jeremianic Prose*. New York: T&T Clark, 2003.

Sherwood, Yvonne. *Biblical Blaspheming: Trials of the Sacred for a Secular Age*. New York: Cambridge University Press, 2012.

Skinner, John. *Prophecy and Religion: Studies in the Life of Jeremiah*. Cambridge: Cambridge University Press, 1922.

Smart, Christopher. *Christopher Smart: Selected Poems*. Edited by Karina Williamson and Marcus Walsh, Penguin Classics. New York: Penguin Books, 1990.

Smend, Rudolph. *Deutsche Alttestamentler in drei Jahrhunderten*. Göttingen: Vandenhoeck & Ruprecht, 1989.

Smith, George Adam. "The Late Professor A. B. Davidson, DD. LL.D." In *The Biblical World*. Edited by William R. Harper, 167–77, New Series, Vol. 20. Chicago, IL: University of Chicago Press, 1902.

Smith, Mark S. *The Laments of Jeremiah and Their Contexts: Preliminary Observations about Their Literary Interplay in Jeremiah 11–20*. SBLMS 42. Atlanta, GA: Scholars Press, 1990.

Stow, Calvin E. "Review of *Lectures on the Sacred Poetry of the Hebrews*, by Robert Lowth." Translated by G. Gregory (1839). *NAmerR* 31 (1830): 337–79.

Stulman, Louis. "The Prose Sermons as Hermeneutical Guide." In *Troubling Jeremiah*. Edited by A. R. Pete Diamond, Kathleen O'Connor, and Louis Stulman. *JSOT* Sup 260. Sheffield: Sheffield Academic Press, 1999.

Stulman, Louis. *The Prose Sermons of the Book of Jeremiah: A Redescription of the Correspondences with Deuteronomistic Literature in the Light of Recent Text-critical Research*. SBLDS 83. Atlanta, GA: Scholars Press, 1986.

Stulman, Louis. "Review of *The Confessions of Jeremiah in Context: Scenes of Prophetic Drama*, by A.R. Diamond." *CBQ* 51 (1987): 316–18.

Taylor, Charles. *The Ethics of Authenticity*. Cambridge, MA: Harvard University Press, 1991.

Thiel, Winfried. *Die deuteronomistische Redaktion von Jeremia 1–25*. WMANT 41. Neukirchen-Vluyn: Neukirchener, 1973.

Thiel, Winfried. *Die deuteronomistische Redaktion von Jeremia 26–45*. WMANT 52. Neukirchen-Vluyn: Neukirchener, 1981.

Thiselton, Anthony. *New Horizons in Hermeneutics*. Grand Rapids, MI: Zondervan, 1992.

Thompson, J. A. *The Book of Jeremiah*. NICOT. Grand Rapids, MI: Eerdmans [1980] 1989.

Thompson, R. J. *Moses and the Law in a Century of Criticism since Graf.* VTSup 19. Leiden: Brill, 1970.

Traina, Robert. *Methodical Bible Study.* New York: Biblical Seminary in New York, 1952.

Voltaire. *Candide, or Optimism.* Translated by Henry Morley. New York: Barnes & Noble Books, 2003.

Warton, Joseph. *An Essay on the Genius and Writings of Pope.* London: M. Cooper at the Globe in Paternoster Row, 1756.

Weippert, Helga. *Die Prosareden des Jeremiabuches.* BZAW 132. Berlin: de Gruyter, 1973.

Welch, Claude. *Protestant Thought in the Nineteenth Century, Volume 1, 1799–1870.* New Haven, CT: Yale University Press, 1972.

Wellhausen, Julius. *Israelitische und jüdische Geschichte.* 6th ed. Berlin: Georg Reimer, 1907.

Wellhausen, Julius. *Prolegomena to the History of Ancient Israel: With a Reprint of the Article "Israel" from the Encyclopedia Britannica.* New York: Meridian Books, 1957.

Westermann, Claus. *Basic Forms of Prophetic Speech.* Philadelphia, PA: Westminster, 1967.

de Wette, Wilhelm Martin Lebrecht. *Biblische Dogmatik: Alten und neuen Testaments: oder kritische Darstellung der Religionslehre des Hebraismus, des Judenthums und des Urchristenthums.* 3rd ed. Berlin: G. Reimer, 1831.

Wildberger, Hans. *Jahwewort und prophetische Rede bei Jeremia.* Zurich: Zwingli, 1942.

Wilson, Edmund. *To the Finland Station: A Study in the Writing and Acting of History.* New York: New York Review of Books, 2003.

Wimsatt, William K., Jr., and Cleanth Brooks. *Literary Criticism: A Short History.* New York: Random House, 1957.

Wood, Robert. *Essay on the Original Genius and Writings of Homer.* London: T Payne at the Mews Gate and P. Elmsly in the Strand, 1775.

Wordsworth, William. *William Wordsworth: The Major Works*, Oxford World's Classics. Edited by Stephen Gill. New York: Oxford University Press, 2000.

Young, Edward. *Conjectures on Original Composition.* London: For A. Millar in the Strand; and R. and J. Dodsley in Pall-Mall, 1759.

Zimmerli, Walther. *The Law and the Prophets: A Study of the Meaning of the Old Testament.* James Sprunt Lectures 1963. Oxford: Blackwell, 1965.

Subject and Author Index

Abrahams, I. 191
Abrams, M. H.
  "natural supernaturalism" 85, 122,
    141, 164
  poetics of lamp v. mirror 73, 85
aesthetic quality used as evidence of
    authorship 47, 98, 104
  by Duhm 8, 13, 39–41, 52–3
  by Lowth 99
  by Michaelis 99
  by Skinner 221
Albertz, R. 186
artistic inspiration
  as antidote to Enlightenment
    disenchantment 84–5
  "natural Supernaturalism" 85–6, 122, 164
"authentic," meaning "useful as evidence" 7,
    17–19, 35, 51, 187, 280, 291, 302
authorship of Jeremiah 19–23
  book's presentation 100–1
  four fifths denied to Jeremiah by Duhm
    37, 100–1
  how important for interpretation 18
  traditional ascription 101, 111

Balfour, I. 71, 137–8
Barth, K. 184, 189
Bartholomew, C. 188, 190
Barton, J. 296
Baruch
  as artistic redactor 256–7, 296
  as the author of the prose narratives 33,
    35, 40, 43, 44–5, 118, 149, 206
  as a scribe 44, 147–8
  character drawn by Duhm 44, 152
  character in the book 44, 147–8, 152
Barzun, J. 127–8
Baumgartner, W. 278, 290–2
Benecke, H. 185
Berlin, I.
  on Hamann and Herder 130

on Romantic historicism 188
  Romanticism as "expressionism" 72–3
Beuken, W. A. M. 306, 310
Bible as literature 19, 62–3, 88–9
  alternative to classical models 131
  Authorized (King James) Version 62–3
  Luther's German translation 63
  model for German literature 133
Biddle, M. 26, 245, 327
  pioneer of dramatic analysis 3,
    262, 305–7
  radical redactional theory 302–3, 349
biography of Jeremiah, historical
    reconstruction 7, 31–2
  a Künstlerroman 123, 216
  by Duhm 14, 33–4
  by Holladay 256–9, 278–80
  by Skinner 15
  crisis of faith model 216–18
  focused on early ministry 114, 206
  isolated poetic passages the primary
    evidence 14, 206
  necessary to create an "admirable"
    prophet 46, 48, 116–17, 119
  necessary to remove supernatural
    elements 118–19, 210–12
  not required by the book, 113–15
  parallel to lives of historical critics and
    liberal theologians 216–19
  parallel to Wordsworth's
    autobiography 124
Blackwell, T. 128–9, 133
Blair, H. 73, 129, 182
Blake, W.
  Bible as literary model 61
  prophetic poet 120–1, 143
  prophetic poetry answers Enlightenment
    disenchantment 62, 84–5, 89
Blayney, B. 57–9, 110
Borowitz, E. B. 214
Bright, J. 2, 304, 312, 314, 322, 325–6

Brueggemann, W. 26, 316
    affirms Deuteronomistic redaction
        12, 238
    conflates speech of Jeremiah and
        Yahweh 269
    observes attempt to "move beyond"
        Duhm 12, 251–2, 346–8
    recognizes dramatic portrayal 269, 278
Bryce, J. 217
Burnett, R. 189

Carroll, R. 26
    authenticity of poetry, a "dogma [that]
        cannot be established" 303, 350
    criticism of "Skinnerian" biographical
        approach 222
    ideological approach 316
    radical redactional theory 289, 303, 305
Cheyne, T. T. 129, 136, 142–43, 176, 185,
        190–91, 217
Childs, B. S. 255, 276, 316
Clements, R. E. 278
coherence of the text 2–3
    as evidence of authorship 20
    as imposed by late editors 5, 337–9
    by architectural arrangement
        (patterning) 321–2, 330, 332, 338
    by rhetorical devices 321, 338
    mere collection 230, 234–6, 322–3
    narrative progression 3, 6, 97, 281, 320,
        322–4, 328–33, 338
    search for 346
Craigie, P. 265, 325
Cross, F. M. 265, 334
Crouter, R. 217
Cullhed, A. 73

Davidson, A. B.
    brought Grafian revolution to United
        Kingdom 213
    Deuteronomy Pharasaic 219–20
    prophecies triggered by current
        events 211
    prophetic truth revealed in Jeremiah's
        life 216
    taught Skinner 213, 219
de Wette
    adumbrates Grafian history 184,
        187, 192

crisis of faith 217
dates Deuteronomy to Josiah's time
    186, 209
opposes Hebrew religion to
    Judaism 185–6
Romantic historicism 190
studied under Herder 184
Vatke's and Wellhausen's inspiration
    184–8, 190
Deuteronomistic diction and concerns
    as indicator of inauthenticity 49,
        304, 350
    depicts Jeremiah's part in Josiah's
        reforms 340
    disparaged 231, 314
    in Jeremiah's speech 21, 148–52
    in prose narratives 304–5
    in Yahweh's (public) messages 21,
        314, 345
    not surprising in time of Josiah
        198–9, 304
Deuteronomists (exilic)
    as authors of prose narratives 286–7
    as authors of the Deuteronomistic
        history (Deut.-2 Kgs) 286
    as authors of the prose speeches 5
        12, 285
    as having theodicy agenda 4–5, 287,
        296–301, 314, 336, 351–2
    as redactors gave text structure 4–5,
        12, 286–7
    disparaged by Duhm 44
    only known through supposed writings
        201, 314
Deuteronomy
    as a product of Josiah's time 172, 180,
        184, 186–7, 209
    as an attempt to silence the prophet
        word 157
    as causing the decline of Israelite
        religion 215
    as source of false security 210, 220
    as the origin of "Pharisaism" 219–20
    attributed to Moses 138, 199
    attributed to scribes 147, 154
    concern with interior religion 156, 163
    does not hold Jerusalem or the temple to
        be inviolable 159
    Jeremiah appeals to its covenant 148, 150

Jeremiah appeals to its warning of exile
148, 151–2
Jeremiah cites 150
part of Jeremiah's education 304
public reading the occasion of Jeremiah's
sermons 257
the "Book of the Law" found in Josiah's
time 147
Diamond, A. R.
on pre-existence of poetic
laments 349–50
breaks with redaction criticism 352
recognized dramatic nature of
text 352–3
speeches as fictive 349, 353
"divine interiority" 354–5
Dickson, G. G. 130–31
divine communication, verbal
presumed by the book 119, 276
problematic for modern interpreters
118–19, 211, 275–6
Documentary Hypothesis, *see* History of
Israel (or Israel's religion), (Grafian)
reconstruction of
dramatic characters 3, 275
divine council 264–6
identification of 257–62, 308–13
obscured by "messenger speech" theory
275–6, 309
peace and prosperity (temple) party
309–10, 312, 341
dramatic dialogue 3, 5, 266–8, 311–13
develops a dramatic episode 339
misread as multiple sources 313, 315
presented by Holladay 257–8
dramatic presentation 3
defined 259
examples in Jeremiah 258–69
non-biblical examples 259, 276, 279, 316
recognized
by Beuken and van Grol 306
by Biddle 305–6
by Brueggemann 278
by Clements 278
by Diamond 306–7
by Holladay 257–8
by Polk 262, 79
by Thiel 287, 306
telescoping of time 260, 267–8, 333, 340

undermines Romantic poetics 277
undermines use of text as historical
evidence 276–81
dramatic settings/situations
established at the beginning of a
dramatic episode 339
for all of Jer. 11–20: prexilic 21
for Jer. 1–2: before Jeremiah's time 324–7
for Jer. 9:9-21: destruction of
Jerusalem 333
for Jer. 10: early exile 333–5
for Jer. 11: Josiah's reform 340
obscured by search for historical context
258–9, 275, 278–9, 314, 324–5,
334, 342
Duhm, B.
alters text to fit agenda 105
antagonism toward the book of Jeremiah
36–9, 112, 158, 164, 200
believes Jeremiah was martyred by
scribes 119, 125, 157, 166
believes the Torah is false 152, 154
creating a religious alternative to
orthodox Christianity 102–3, 167
disinterest in the structure of Jeremiah
36, 112
low view of Jews and Judaism 38, 40–1,
87, 95–6, 116, 173, 220, 285
opposition to "Bible believers" 166–7, 200
pioneer of the dominant paradigm of
Jeremiah scholarship 32–4, 43, 52,
174–5, 200
pronouncements without justification
(evidence) 7, 107–8, 152–5, 161–2
proponent of the Grafian model
15, 174–6
Romantic poetics 96–7, 104, 106
selective use of evidence 150, 152, 156,
161, 219
self-confidence 107–9
self-presentation as a historian 34–6,
103, 113
self-understanding as prophet 108–9, 144
theological opinions as criteria for
authenticity 40–1
threat of subjectivity 46–7, 52–3
translation of Jeremiah (1903) 110
understanding of historical progress
199–200

Eichhorn J. G.
 "father of higher criticism" 136
 influenced by Herder 136
 trained Ewald 190
Eliot, T. S. 2, 225
Engnell, I. 232, 236–7
Ermarth, E. D. 216
Ewald, H.
 biographies of prophets 191–6
 contributions to Grafian project 191–3
 held back acceptance of Documentary
  Hypothesis 190
 interest in prophetic psychology 192–4
 low view of Jews 290
 man of opposition 143
 prophecy as self-expression 195
 Romantic historicism and hermeneutics
  191, 193–4
 studied under Eichhorn 142
 taught Duhm and Wellhausen 142

"Foe from the North," the 24, 32, 253
 Babylonian 21, 24, 211, 328, 340
 identified as Scythian 34, 114, 117–19,
  208, 275
form critical assumptions about
  prophetic speech
 "basic form" approach misreads
  evidence 262
 "judgement speech" obscures setting
  260–1, 328–9
 "messenger speech" obscures speakers
  and audiences form 262
 "messenger speech" not indicated by
  "messenger formula" 269–70, 325
Frei, H. 131, 133, 139

Gadamer, H. G. 139, 189, 191
genius
 agent of human progress 140, 215
 agent of the Spirit of History 189
 biblical prophet as model 120, 138–41
 biographical development
  (*Bildungsroman*) 141, 162
 creator of religion 214
 expresses national spirit 10, 141, 162
 fidelity to personal vision 141, 143
 Jesus as 165, 214
 model for Duhm's Jeremiah 162–6

opposition from traditional and
 institutional figures 141, 144,
 163, 200
recognized by elevated literary style
 181, 182
Romantic poet as model 14, 119
roots in Kant 149
understood through empathy 189
Gerstenberger, E. 289
Grafian reconstruction of the history of
 Israel 7
 decline from religion of Israel to Judaism
  173, 185, 195
 embodied in the Documentary
  Hypothesis 14–15, 18, 171–3
 fits Duhm's model of Jeremiah 14
 historicist 188–90
 must evolve gradually 211–12
 prophets precede the law 172–3,
  183, 193
 Wellhausen's work the classic
  presentation 172
Gunkel, H.
 evolution of prophetic speech 235–6,
  241
 interest in prophetic psychology 194,
  235, 261
 introduces "messenger speech"
  theory 238
 meter the result of passion 233–4, 240
 "neo-Romantic" 245
 on laments 291
 pioneer of form criticism 228, 236
 pioneered "basic form" of prophetic
  speech approach 241, 262
 taught Mowinckel 228
Gunneweg, A. H. J. 289

Hamann, J. G.
 criticism of Michaelis and Bacon as
  rationalists 130, 131
 influence on Herder, his student, and
  German Romantics 73, 130
 inspired by Lowth 73, 130, 133
Harnack, A. 212, 214, 215, 217–19
Hayes, J. 245
Henderson, J.
 masters thesis on Jer. 4:5–6:30 3, 245,
  259, 261, 265, 307

"Who Weeps in Jeremiah VIII 23?" 3,
268, 308, 310
Hepworth, B. 99, 129
Herder, J. G.
accepts basic historicity and traditional
authorship of biblical books 177, 18
architect of Romantic nationalism
135, 137
contrasts priests and scribes with
prophets 177
draws on Lowth 130–5
influence on German historical criticism
135–7, 141–2, 144–6
leading figure in German
Romanticism 130–5
makes prophecy a human
achievement 177
On the Spirit of Hebrew Poetry 130
promoter of German literature 132–5
Heschel, A. 1
historical criticism, history of
"collapse of history" 19, 254
common roots with Romanticism
11, 135
development of Documentary
Hypothesis 171–3, 184–94,
187–93
dominance in Duhm's time 42
rise of historical consciousness 115
turn from in the late twentieth
century 3, 6
historicism, *see* Romantic historiography
Hobbs, T. R. 227
Holladay, W.
argues for authenticity of prose
speeches 256
biographical agenda 256–7, 262,
277–9, 322
finds evidence of drama 257–8
Jeremiah structured by rhetorical
devices 256, 321
studied under Muilenburg 256
Hölscher, G. 194, 234, 291
Homolka, W. 214
Hosea, as an influence on Jeremiah 119,
124, 165, 218
Hyatt, J. P. 227, 257, 265, 286–9, 302, 304,
327, 337
builds on Mowinckel 227

pioneers theory of comprehensive
Deuteronomistic redaction 286–9,
304, 337

incoherence of the book of Jeremiah
posited
by Bright 2, 322
by Duhm 37
by McKane 2, 247, 296, 302
by Mowinckel 229
inspiration
as ecstatic experience (or enthusiasm)
16, 22, 79–81
as expression of the national spirit
(*Volksgeist*) 10, 133–4, 140–1,
163, 215
as the common source of poetry and
prophecy 9, 78–81, 89
by Nature 122
by the Holy Spirit 78–9, 89–90
by the Muse 78
in Duhm 81, 96
measured by literary qualities 89, 98, 181
transformed by Lowth 77–80
Irwin, W. A. 187

Jeremiah (book)
as literature 101–2
fragmentation in historical critical works
11, 111, 235–6, 254–5
historical/biographical presentation 276
interest in the present form 255, 347
truth (historicity) of its portrayal 23–5,
102, 111, 297, 353
Jeremiah (character in the book) 3, 5
advocate for the Law and the covenant
150, 154–6, 200
comes to share Yahweh's anger and grief
344, 355
described as false portrayal by Duhm
40, 201
extreme tensions in character 310
(false) prophets his primary
opponents 158–60
first-person narrator 20
"push beyond" (interest in) person/
persona 300, 301, 348
reluctant prophet of doom 335, 343, 355
a scandal to Duhm and Grafians 200–1

sympathy (for Daughter People) 268–9,
    308, 335
  understood as a portrayal/persona 278
Jeremiah (historical prophet)
  after 586 B. C. 21
  extent of involvement with Josiah's
      reforms 32, 114, 174, 200–1, 210, 304
  message to Northern Israel 327–8
  priestly family 160, 304
  prophetic call 114, 257
  temple sermon 114
Jeremiah (modern portrayal)
  genius of humanity 162, 165–6
  Grafian historical critic 218
    doubts authority of Deuteronomy
        217–18, 154
    realizes priestly legal materials a
        perversion 218
  literary giant 119
  lyric poet 41, 64, 123, 210
  martyr 119, 125
  national bard 109, 121
  pioneer of interior religion 210, 214–15,
      217, 220
  poète maudit 125–6
  psychologist 163
Jeremiah 2–10
  the story of Israel and Yahweh 3,
      24–5, 322–37
  as lament 336
  authorship 20–3
  frame 323–4
  tragic 335–6
  unsuitable for biographical
      reconstruction 336–7
Jeremiah 11–20
  the story of Jeremiah's early prophetic
      career 3, 24–5, 337–46, 354
  authorship 20–3
  presupposes Deuteronomistic
      perspective 345
  summary 340–1
  tragic 343
Jeremiah scholarship, history of modern
  attempts to "move beyond Duhm" since
      the late twentieth century 11–12,
      16, 19, 32, 42–3, 111–12, 233,
      251–2, 254–5, 267, 283, 295–6,
      300–1, 346–8

Duhm as pioneer 7, 3, 32–4
  twentieth-century characterized by
      priority of historical concerns 3, 18,
      228, 253
Jeremiah, dominant paradigm for
      interpretation in the twentieth
      century
  A-B-C designation of Mowinckel 7, 12,
      33, 227–33, 245–6, 346–8
  established by Duhm 6, 11, 13, 15, 42–3,
      51, 253–4
  modifications to Duhm's model 42
  Validity/Truth 12–13, 43, 167, 196–202,
      284, 287–8
Jerusalem (Daughter) as a dramatic
      character/speaker 260–2, 264, 266–
      7, 275, 279, 309, 328, 334–5, 341
Johnson, P. 127
Johnson, S. 93–4, 123
Josiah's reforms
  pivotal date in the Grafian history
      172, 201
  pivotal date in Skinner's biography 209
  the "death of prophesy" 173
  see also Jeremiah (historical
      prophet): extent of involvement
      with Josiah's reforms

Kaiser, B. B. 261
Kant, I. 85, 139
Kaufmann, Y. 304
Kuenen, A. 174–5, 184, 187–8
Kugel, J. 55–6, 71, 89
Kumaki, K. 261
Künstlerromane, lives of (Romantic) poets
      and artists 9, 123–4
  dependent on Lowth's reconception of
      prophets 14
  as framework for Jeremiah's biography
      123–4, 164, 216

Lalleman, H. 285
Laments ("Confessions") of Jeremiah
  as achievement in individual religion
      210, 290
  as elements in the portrayal of
      Jeremiah 315
  as evidence, "illustrations," in theodicy
      argument 297–8, 342

as pre-existing source 289, 291–3
as Romantic lyrics 290
assume Deuteronomistic perspective 344
authenticity challenged and defended
   289, 291
emotional conclusions of dramatic
   episodes 339–40, 342
tragic conclusions, include Jeremiah's
   curse of his birth 315, 355
Legaspi, M. 129
Lessing, G. E. 139, 179
Leuchter, M. 304
Lewis, C. S. 59, 93–4
Liberalism, classic (German) Protestant
   as the theology of Jeremiah 15, 216–21
   conforms to contemporary scientific
      beliefs 212
   extracts true religion from
      tradition 213–14
   individual and interior religion 214
   prefers prophets to scribes and
      priests 219
   relation to historical criticism 213–14
   sacrifice unnecessary 218
Lowth, R. 54–144
   at the root of (German) historical
      criticism 135–7, 176–7
   at the root of German
      Romanticism 126–31
   challenges neoclassicism with prophetic
      poetry 58–60, 65, 68
   discovers poetry in the prophetic books
      54–7, 90–1
   effects for reading prophetic
      poetry 87–94
   forges Romantic poetics 64–5, 68, 70–5
   his *Isaiah* a model for Romantic poetry
      60–3, 67
   influence on Herder 130–5
   makes biblical prophets models for
      Romantic poets 120–2
   makes prophetic inspiration the measure
      of good poetry 77–81
   popularity in Germany 129, 135
   promotes biblical poetry as great
      literature 89
   uses literary style as evidence of
      inspiration 99
Lundbom, J. 2–3

biographical approach 322
finds chiastic structure 256, 321
studied under Muilenburg 255

McConville, J. G. 20, 304, 351
McKane, W. 327
   discourages search for coherence 12,
      247, 296
   radical redactional theory 302–5
   text a "rolling corpus" 302
Meier, S. 270
meter
   as natural product of inspiration 79–80,
      94, 233–4, 225, 240, 276
   considered essential for prophecy
      233, 240
   considered essential to poetry 56, 59–62,
      66, 70, 93
   Duhm achieves through emendation
      105, 233
   not obvious in Hebrew poetry 55–7, 9
   parallelism as evidence of 56
   qinah lament meter as criterion of
      authenticity 47–8, 53, 233
   the result of intentional art 61, 70,
      93, 241
methodological priorities
   determined by the text 17–18,
      20, 307–12
   of Duhm 42, 168, 284
   of Ewald 195
   of historical criticism 42, 312–15
   of modern Jeremiah studies 4, 6,
      18, 31–2
   of Mowinckel 227–9, 236
   of redactional critics 312–15
   of rhetorical critics 284
Michaelis, J. D.
   considered a rationalist by Hamann 130
   publishes Lowth's *Lectures* in Germany
      129–30, 135
   taught Eichhorn 136
   uses literary style as evidence of
      inspiration 99
Milton, J
   a "Hebrew in soul" 75, 121
   as model for Romantic poets 124, 141
   as national bard of England 75, 121
   non-rhyming poetry 61

presents Biblical poetry as English
      poetry 62
Morris, D. 182
Moses
  as prophetic prophet 138
  as "genius of humanity" 138
  opposed to legalism 146
  source of Israel's Law 151, 173, 177,
      179–80, 199, 273
Mowinckel, S.
  A-B-C compositional model, *see*
      Jeremiah, dominant paradigm
      for interpretation: A-B-C
      designation of
  attempts to validate Duhm' assumption
      about poetry 229–31, 233, 239–40
  builds on Duhm's compositional
      model 228
  changes view on ecstatic origin of
      prophecy 240–2
  declares "messenger speech" theory
      "assured result" 15, 239, 242, 245–7
  defends necessity of historical-critical
      approach 228–9, 232, 237–9,
      243, 246
  denies written law before Jeremiah 231
  disparages prose speeches 231
  employs "messenger speech" theory
      237–9, 243–5
  insists on fragmentary text 230, 234–6,
      239, 247, 339
  low view of Judaism 232, 237, 245
  prose speeches a Deuteronomistic
      source 285–6, 299, 351
  search for *ipsissima verba* 230, 232
  studied under Gunkel 228
  views prophets as speakers not
      writers 229–30
Muilenburg, S. 2, 255–6, 265
Mullen, T. 265

narrative, *see* coherence of the
      text: narrative progression
Nicholson, E. W.
  built on by later redaction critics 295,
      299, 303, 347
  extends theory of Deuteronomistic
      redaction to prose narratives 286–7,
      297, 305, 337, 351
  posits theodicy agenda 299

subordinates "vivid" poetry to
      "formulaic" prose 301, 352
Norton, D. 62
Noth, M. 286

O'Connor, K. 26, 312
  finds coherence in final form 320,
      337–8, 341–2
  finds hopeful trajectory in Jer. 11–20 by
      excluding conclusion 315
  posits "confessions" comprised a
      preexisting source 291–2, 312–14
  posits theodicy agenda 297, 299
  prose speeches as midrash 293–4
  redactional study of "confessions" in
      context 288–90, 349
Oden, R. 246
Orientalism 65, 133
Orr, J. 218
"Ossian" 62–3, 133, 182
  influenced by Lowth 62, 133
  model for German literature 133–4
Otto, R. 186

Paine, T.
  Bible: poetry mixed with "trash" 99–100
  prophecy stripped of religious meaning
      83–4, 86–7, 89–90
  view of prophets drawn from
      Lowth 83, 90
Parunak, H. V. 270
pathos, divine 1, 4
Perdue, L.
  1984 anthology illustrates historical-
      critical approach to Jeremiah 32
  critique of Skinner's biography
      218, 253–4
  uses Jeremiah scholarship to illustrate
      "collapse of history" 254, 284
Plato 63, 131, 139
poetic diction and imagery
  classical tropes 70–1
  Hebrew *Mashal* 71
  neoclassical expectations 65–8
  Romantic explanation 71
  Romantic taste 68
poetic form as a criterion of authentic
      prophetic speech 18–19, 47–8,
      290, 348
  Duhm claims he discovered 52

Duhm presents as the "end result" of
work 52–3
embedded in Mowinckel's A-B-C
classification system 51
foundational assumption of modern
Jeremiah studies 5
necessary for historical-critical projects
8, 222–3
necessary for Skinner's biographical
reconstruction 223
obscures the identity of dramatic
speakers and situations 223–5,
261–2, 329
"poets could only speak in poetic form"
seems untenable 53, 240
prevents recognition of book's
characterization 223–4
primary obstacle to perceiving the
coherence of the book 6, 223, 225
provides an appearance of objectivity for
Duhm's judgments 47–8, 202
questioned
by Biddle 302
by Carroll 303
by McKane 302
rooted in the Romantic understanding
of inspiration 18, 196, 202
used without providing
justification 7, 293
used to both deny and defend the
authenticity of the prose 15, 18, 257
poetic speeches (modern assumptions)
authentic ("oracles") 5, 12, 31, 51,
230, 233
brief 97, 230, 234–7, 239, 242–3
depend on biographical context 96, 114,
223, 237–9, 243
messages 15, 207, 243–4, 263–74, 313
spontaneous 97, 141, 196, 207, 225,
239, 241–2
unrelated to literary context 230, 234–6
useful as evidence 2, 23, 51, 197, 201,
207, 223
poetic speeches
assume Law to be ancient 155–6, 160–1
crafted to portray speakers and
situations 22, 275
difficult to determine author and
historical context 19, 199,
243–4, 294

elements of dramatic portrayals 281
make effective conclusions 345
often evocations of present situations
(not prophecies about the future)
244, 329
often portray private emotion 311,
345, 354–55
portray natural speech 92, 276
preexisting source doubtful 22, 292,
345, 350
public delivery doubtful 22, 271,
273, 313
seldom presented as messages 22, 243–4,
263–4, 271, 273–4, 313
urge obedience to the Law 155–6, 160–1
variety of speakers and audiences 23,
223, 263, 277
Yahweh the primary speaker (w/o a
messenger) 87, 119, 224, 266,
268–9, 275
poetry in Jeremiah
an objective feature of the text 48, 53
as Romantic poetry 69
could be secondary 305
difficult to determine extent 104–5
discovered by Lowth 58
presented typographically by
Blayney 57–8
presented typographically by Duhm 58
poetry in the Hebrew Bible
characterized by parallelism 54–7
lacking obvious meter 55–7, 59
poetry in the prophetic books
as a model for Romantic poetry 10, 60–3
as great literature 89–90, 94–5
as Romantic poetry 90–1, 93–4
denied by Jerome 56
discovered by Lowth 54–6
lacks poetic accent marks in MT 55–6
parallelism as evidence 54–7
presented typographically 57–9, 67
poetry
inherently "fictive," or dramatic 22,
92–3, 260
intentional production 22, 71, 92–4,
97, 207
mimetic 70, 73–4, 78, 85, 92
Pohlmann, K. F. 289
Polk, T. 262, 279
Prickett, S. 61, 73, 81, 133

priests (in historical criticism)
  opponents of prophetic geniuses 144–55,
    177–8, 181
  representatives of external religion 145
  their law the "death of prophecy" 173
  their temple and sacrifice inessential to
    religion 210
prophesy as foretelling
  assumed by prose and poetic
    passages 119
  denied as essential by Herder 137
  explained as premonitions 40, 211, 224,
    244, 275
  maintained by Lowth 84, 137
  questioned by Duhm 118–19
  questioned by Paine 83
prophetic experience/psychology, interest
    in 6, 123, 194, 261, 275–6
prophetic religion (of preexilic Israel)
    opposed to scribal/priestly religion
      (of postexilic Judaism) 7
  assumed by Duhm 49, 154, 200
  Duhm's reconstruction of Jeremiah
    designed to support 157, 200–1
  grounded in Herder's Romantic scheme
    of history 145, 178–83
  in liberal Protestantism 214, 219
  Jeremiah's "confessions" brought into the
    scheme 290
  not supported by account of Josiah's
    reform in Kings 157
  not supported by the book of Jeremiah's
    account of prophets and
    scribes 200–1
  primary feature of the Grafian history of
    Israel's religion 173–4
  Skinner's reconstruction of
    Jeremiah designed to support
    214–15, 219–21
prophets (Hebrew)
  as agents of human progress 121, 138–
    42, 146, 181
  as creators of national literature 138–40
  as founders of Israelite religion 175
  as great historical figures 89
  as national leaders 10, 137–8
  as pioneers of interior religion 124
  as (Romantic) poets 10, 63, 83, 121–2
  as visionary geniuses 10, 138–9,
    177–8, 192–3

prose narratives, authorship 43, 118, 286–7,
    299, 303, 351
prose speeches (modern assumptions)
  as redactional expansions
    ("midrash") 293–5
  inauthentic 7, 52, 227, 8
  "sermons" 5–6, 313–14, 338, 342,
    345, 351
  the work of exilic Deuteronomists 285–
    6, 345, 349, 351
prose speeches
  "Deuteronomistic" diction and concerns
    107, 197–8, 304, 314
  as incorporating authentic tradition
    233, 285–6
  as records of actual prophetic speeches
    22–3, 198–9, 224
  function in the text 23, 314, 327,
    341–2, 354
  future-oriented 6, 338
  primarily messages from Yahweh 5, 263,
    266, 274–5, 324

redaction criticism 3–7
  dependent on source criticism 283–5,
    287–8, 304
  justifies and illumines coherence of text
    295–6, 337, 350
  interest in final form of Jer. 11–20
    284–5, 288–9
  makes latest source the arbiter of
    significance 301, 316, 348, 351–2
  radical redactional theories 302–3
  reduces significance to narrow
    ideological/theological agendas
    316, 348, 352, 356
Reed, E. 182
Reventlow, H. G. 34, 289, 292
rhetorical criticism 2
  allows extended literary
    compositions 255
  challenges form criticism 255
  launched by Muilenburg 255
  (over) focused on rhetorical devices 2–3,
    256, 322
  posits intentional artistry 255, 257
  should focus on rhetorical effect
    257, 321–2
rhetorical devices 2, 256
  catchwords 256, 287, 315, 322, 338

chiasm 16, 256, 259, 320–1, 332
inclusion 256, 320–1, 323
Robinson, H. W. 265
Rogerson, J. W. 8, 135, 172, 174, 185, 190
Romantic aesthetic values 68, 131
    Duhm's chief criteria of
        authenticity 8, 69
    match German character 128, 134
    specific values
        colloquialness 66, 68
        naturalness 66, 68–9, 76, 93
        originality 81, 144, 193, 195, 22
        simplicity 66, 104, 132
    Wellhausen's taste 190
Romantic hermeneutics (of Einfühlung, or
        empathy) 11, 91, 115
    and expressivism 189, 194
    and historicism 189, 191
Romantic historiography,
        historicism 188–90
    follows the growth of an individual
        179–80, 182
    in Skinner's biography of
        Jeremiah 215–16
    rooted in Herder's Romanticism 189–90
Romantic poetics
    alternative to (neo)classical poetics 8–9,
        65, 68, 71
    dominant in nineteenth century 98
    expressionism 9–10, 14, 71–4, 132, 166,
        195, 230
    "poetics of the lamp" 73, 85
    poetry a product of passion 71–3, 80
    poetry precedes prose 182–3
    poetry spontaneous or natural 71–2,
        132, 187, 207
    rooted in Lowth's presentation of
        Hebrew prophets 9
Romanticism, German
    and German Nationalism 127–9
    leading figures 126
    opposition to French classicism and
        rationalism 10, 127–8, 133–5
    roots in English Romanticism 128
    roots in Lowth's lectures 129–31
    Sturm und Drang movement 81–2,
        128, 130
Roston, M.
    on Longinus 75
    on Lowth's Isaiah 57

on neoclassical poetic paraphrases of
        biblical poetry 66–7
    on Ossian 62
    on pre-Romantic poets 120
Rousseau, J. J. 68, 128, 179
Rudolph, W. 285

Schlegel, F. 81, 126
scribes (in Jeremiah)
    Baruch records Jeremiah's propecies 147
    Shaphan's family saves Jeremiah's life 152
scribes, Deuteronomistic (in Duhm or
        other historical critics)
    agents Josiah's reform 157
    creators of the book of Jeremiah
        38–9, 147
    enemies of the prophet Jeremiah
        38–9, 147
    opponents of Jesus 167
    opponents of prophetic geniuses 145–6,
        177–8, 181
    oppose written "Law of Yahweh" to
        prophetic "word of Yahweh" 157–60
    precursors of modern "Bible believers"
        166–7, 200
    responsible for Deuteronomy 154
    responsible for Jeremiah's
        martyrdom 157
    wrote the Law to undermine
        prophets 157
Sharp, C. J. 11, 27, 316, 360
Sherwood, Y. 126
Skinner, J.
    biographical method 209–10
    compositional model more plausible
        than Duhm's 221–2
    develops Duhm's biography of Jeremiah
        206, 208
    founded on Romantic poetics 207
    historicism 215–16
    low view of Judaism 220–1
    makes Jeremiah a historical
        critic 217–18
    makes Jeremiah a liberal theologian
        212–14, 217–19
    manipulates evidence 209, 220–1
    popularity 222
    question of subjectivity 218–21
    unfounded assumptions 208
Smart, C. 60–1, 64, 120, 125

Smend, R. 52, 108, 184–5, 194
Smith, M.
  describes structure of Jer. 11–20 296,
    320, 337–8, 341–2
  draws on O'Connor and Diamond
    288, 294
  finds theodicy agenda 297
  redactional study of laments in context
    288–9, 292, 313–16, 349
Smith, R. 213, 217
Stow, C. E. 136
Stulman, L.
  attempts synchronic interpretation 347
  privileges "Deuteronomistic
    prose" 347–8
  retains Duhm's assumption 347–8
sublime, the
  biblical literature as example 75, 77, 83,
    86, 99, 104, 121, 133, 179, 183, 261
  in Duhm 112, 135
  in Longinus, 74–5, 104
  in Romanticism 75
  result of inspiration 78, 120, 193
  result of passionate experience 74–5,
    140, 163
  transformed by Lowth 73–5, 86
synchronic as opposed to diachronic focus
  12, 19, 273–4, 346–8

Taylor, C. 85
Thiel, W.
  extends theory of Deuteronomistic
    redaction to poetry 286–9, 295,
    299, 302–6, 310, 337, 349
  recognizes dramatic presentation
    287, 306
Thiselton, A. 115
Thompson, J. A. 136, 174–5, 178, 181, 184,
  185, 227, 325, 333
Traina, R. 2

unity of the text, *see* coherence of the text
"*Urrolle*" 232, 257
  held to contain the poetry of Jer. 1–25,
    208, 270, 273–4
  more likely to contain Jer. 46–51,
    208–9, 273
  more likely to contain prose
    speeches 274

scroll in Jer. 25 208
scroll in Jer. 36 208, 303

Vatke, W.
  draws on Herder and de Wette 186–7
  Hegelian historical scheme 186, 188
  influence on Duhm 176
  influence on Wellhausen 187
  prophetic literature as historical
    evidence 187, 192
  rejected as too philosophical
    187–8, 190–1
Voltaire 127
Von Rad, G. 278, 300–1

Warton, J. 128
Weippert, H. 304, 305
Welch, C. 212
Wellhausen, J.
  authenticity of prophetic writings 187
  classic form of the Documentary
    Hypothesis 18
  contributor to the Grafian theory 172–5,
    178, 180, 186, 190
  builds on de Wette 186
  builds on Vatke 187–8
  Jeremiah's "confessions" the highpoint of
    prophetic religion 290
  links to Herder 184–5
  low view of Judaism 173, 178
  "the prophets preceded the law" 172
  religion of Israel v. Judaism 186
  Romantic aesthetic values 190
  Romantic historicism 189–90
  self-understanding as historian 34, 188
  studied under Ewald 142–3, 190–1
Westermann, C.
  classic presentation of "messenger
    speech" theory 238, 262–3, 269–70
  prophetic and divine speech
    indistinguishable 269, 276
  prophetic speech, "announcement of
    judgment/promise" 329
  reduces prophetic speech to "basic form"
    245, 262, 269
Wildberger, H. 270
Wilson, E. 112
Wimsatt, W. K. 74
Wood, R. 128, 129

Wordsworth, W.
  autobiographical *Prelude* paralleled
    by reconstructed biography of
    Jeremiah 123–5, 140–1, 164, 216
  biblical (prophetic) poetry a model
    64–5, 68, 75
  poetry, "the spontaneous overflow of
    powerful emotions" 9, 73, 76
  "Preface" to *Lyrical Ballads*, manifesto of
    Romanticism 64–5
  Romantic literary theory drawn from
    Lowth 64–5, 71
  takes up the mantle of prophetic
    bard 121–3

Yahweh (character in Jeremiah)
  betrayed lover 4, 24, 340, 356
  bringing foreign invasions 24, 310, 340
  mercy 327, 356
  primary speaker 2, 359
  public vs. private speech 311, 345, 354–5
  source of messages 25
  wrathful 4, 24–5, 299–300, 310, 340–1,
    352, 356

Yahweh's speeches
  as Deuteronomistic sermons 313–14,
    338, 342
  as impossible to distinguish from
    prophet speech 262, 269, 276, 328
  as prophetic self-expression 87, 195,
    224, 276
  as scribal "midrash" 293
  distinct from Jeremiah's speech
    268, 308
  dramatic addressees 263–6
  fictive 349
  in dialogues 266–9
  includes messages 309
  includes poetic laments 354
  notable tensions 311
  often unmediated (not through a
    messenger) 309
  public prose and private poetry 311, 345
  to his council 263–6
Young, E. 66, 128

Zimmerli, W. 108, 143, 163, 173,
  191, 194

Scripture Index

Gen. 1	172	1 Sam. 1:24	151
1:1	75	10:5-10	79
1:3	104	19:24	79
16:12	143	19:20-24	79
25:23	260		
		2 Chron. 34-36	198
Exod. 15	138	35:35	23
Deut. 10:16	148	Ps. 51:11	89
15:12	150	71:6	260
18:17	344	90	138
18:18-22	118	137	99
18:22	158		
28-30	148	Isa. 1:1	114
28:15	152	1:2	67
28:25	150	1:3	57
28:26	150	12:4	266
28:37	152	13:2	266
28:64-68	148	13:6	266
29	150	18:2	266
30:6	148	26:17	260
30:10	148	35:3-4	266
32	138	40-55	235
		40:1	265–6
Josh. 18:1	151	40:3	266
		45:10	260
Judg. 5:12	64	48:20	266
5:27	64	49:1	260
5:28	64	51:2	260
		54:1	261
Ruth 1:11	260	54:2	261
		57:14	266
2 Kgs 3:15	79	59:21	79
15-17	326	61:1	79
17:4	326	62:10-11	89, 266
17:13	344		
22-22	198	Jer. 1	271
22-23	147, 157	1-20	44, 343
22-25	114, 198	1-20	44
23	148	1-25	207–9

1:1	160, 272–3	2:20	25, 105, 264, 327
1:1-2	270	2:23	264
1:1-3	114	2:24	124
1:2	114, 207, 257, 274, 325	2:25	264
		2:26	148–9
1:2-10	274	2:28	263, 272
1:2-20	274	2:33-37	264
1:2–2:16	242	2:35	105, 264
1:4	271	2:36	24
1:5	300, 343	2:37	326
1:9	118–19, 270, 273	2:39	326
1:12	118	3:1	25, 326–7
1:17	270	3:1-4	278
1:19	125	3:1–4:2	326–7
2	323	3:1-5	264, 327
2-3	264, 272, 324–8	3:3	279
2-10	3, 20–5, 257–69, 272–81, 320–37	3:6	20, 207, 273–4, 325
2:1	20, 271	3:6-7	327
2:1-2	272, 273, 325, 343	3:6-10	114, 264, 326–7
		3:8	24, 327
2:1-3	236, 324	3:10	148
2:1–4:2	302, 305	3:11	20
2:2	264, 271–2, 323–4	3:11-12	327
		3:11-13	271
2:2-3	323–5	3:12	328
2:3	105, 264, 323–4, 335–6	3:13	264
		3:14	274
2:4	324–5	3:14-18	272
2:4-8	324	3:14-19	336
2:4-9	236	3:17	208
2:5	325	3:18	24
2:6	25, 325	3:19	264
2:6-7	24	3:20	264
2:6-8	199	3:22-23	267
2:7	25, 325	4-6	264
2:8	24, 155, 159, 325	4-9	328–33
2:9	325	4-10	208, 258
2:10-13	236	4:1	105
2:11	24	4:1-2	267, 328
2:12	266	4:1-4	328
2:14-16	326	4:2	109, 328
2:14-19	302, 305	4:2–9:25	328
2:14-37	326	4:3	272, 328
2:14–3:5	326	4:3-4	263, 271, 328
2:17	105, 273	4:4	148, 328, 331
2:17-25	264	4:4-31	258
2:18	24, 326	4:5	265, 329
2:18-37	326	4:5-6	263, 330

4:5-8	241, 258	5:14-17	269
4:5-31	321, 330	5:17	329
4:5–9:8	332	5:18	263
4:5–6:30	3, 259, 330	5:18-19	329
4:6	269	5:20	264–5, 330, 340
4:7	264, 329	5:21-22	263
4:8	269	5:26	263
4:9	159, 163,	5:29	163, 332
	269, 329	5:30-31	269
4:9-12	258	5:31	159, 263,
4:10	20, 269		269, 271
4:13	241, 329	6:1	264–5
4:13-18	258	6:1-8	208, 265, 330
4:14	105, 264	6:3	105
4:16	261, 264–5	6:3-5	333, 340
4:16-18	267	6:3-6	329
4:17	329	6:3-7	329
4:18	261	6:4	105, 268
4:18-19	265	6:4-6	259
4:19	261, 264	6:5	268
4:19-21	260, 261, 264,	6:5-6	163
	266, 328	6:6	269
4:19-21	334	6:8	264, 267
4:19-28	259	6:9	264–5, 267,
4:20	261, 264, 328		269, 331
4:20-21	334	6:9-12	332
4:22	261	6:9-15	267, 330
4:23-26	329	6:9–8:13	332
4:25	264	6:10-11	268–9
4:29	329	6:11	331
4:29-31	244, 258	6:11-12	267, 269
4:30	264	6:12	329
4:31	264	6:13	148
5:1	264–5, 267	6:13-15	332
5:1-2	267	6:15	329
5:1-4	333, 340	6:16	159, 264–5
5:1-9	267, 330	6:16-17	263
5:3	267	6:16-19	160–1, 332
5:4	20, 269	6:16-30	330
5:4-5	156, 267, 269	6:18	161
5:5	269	6:18-19	263, 266
5:6	329	6:19	160–1, 199, 329
5:7	261, 264	6:19-21	148
5:7-9	267, 269	6:21	329
5:9	332	6:22-23	329
5:10	241, 264–5, 331	6:22-24	329
5:10-17	330	6:22-26	244
5:12-13	269	6:23	264
5:14	331	6:25	329

6:25-26	264	8:13–9:8	332
6:27	331	8:14	329–30
6:29	331	8:14-16	329
6:29-30	331	8:16	244, 329
6:30	245, 259, 261,	8:17	263
	265, 272,	8:18-19	268
	307, 330	8:18–9:3	3, 268
7	101, 232,	8:19	268
	243, 332	8:20-21	332
7:1	20, 272	8:20-22	258
7:1-2	263	8:23	268–9, 332
7:1-3	243	9:1	268, 332
7:1-7	333	9:1-15	24
7:1-15	45, 329, 332, 340	9:2	105, 268
7:2	22	9:3	263, 271
7:3	44, 263	9:4	263, 268, 271
7:3-7	274	9:7	331
7:4	24	9:8	331–2
7:8-15	333	9:9	269, 332
7:9	156	9:9-21	333
7:11	326	9:10	266, 269,
7:14	331		329, 333
7:14-15	24	9:11	269, 329
7:15	263	9:11-15	333
7:16	269	9:12-16	148
7:19	264	9:13	149, 160
7:21-26	332	9:14-15	329
7:25	25	9:16-18	329
7:27	22	9:16-20	333
7:28	105	9:17	266
7:29	264	9:17-19	244
8-9	332	9:19	21, 208, 329
8:1	159	9:20	329
8:1-3	329	9:21-22	329
8:2	148, 163	9:22-23	329
8:4	105	9:24	156
8:4-9	332	9:25-26	273
8:5	156	9:26	148, 208
8:7	156, 161	10	333–5
8:8	39, 44, 147,	10:1	334
	152–3, 155–8,	10:1-5	267
	161, 263, 271	10:2	334
8:8-9	147, 153–6,	10:3	334
	159–61, 167	10:6-8	334
8:9	156–7, 161, 326	10:6-10	267, 333–5
8:10	159–61, 329	10:6-16	343
8:10-11	160–1, 332	10:7	25
8:11	160	10:9	334
8:13	105, 331–3	10:10	25, 334

10:11	334	11:18-23	125
10:12	25, 163	11:18–12:6	340
10:12-16	333–5	11:18–15:21	306
10:15	333	11:21	24, 293
10:16	25, 163, 334	11:21-23	293–5, 309, 311
10:17	261, 264	12:1	326
10:18	156	12:1-2	299
10:18-20	334	12:1-3	293
10:19-20	261, 264	12:1-4	292, 311–12
10:20	21, 208, 264,	12:1-6	288, 308, 344
	266, 334	12:4	344
10:21	267, 334	12:5	292
10:22	21, 334	12:5-6	300, 309, 311–12
10:23	323–4	12:6	293
10:23-24	336	12:7	309, 311
10:23-25	323–4	12:7-8	300
10:24	335	12:7-11	309
10:25	208, 323–4, 336	12:7-13	24, 340
11	209, 285	12:8	310
11-20	3–6, 20–4,	12:9	105, 266, 310
	287–301,	12:14	21
	306–17, 337–46	12:14-15	273
11:1	20, 338	12:16	44
11:1-5	24, 309, 354	12:17	208
11:1-10	148	13	118, 352, 354
11:1-13	149, 344	13:1	20
11:1-14	288, 313	13:1-14	340
11:1-17	340	13:1-27	340
11:1–12:14	340	13:3	163
11:2-5	309	13:8	20
11:2-7	274	13:8-10	272
11:3	22, 311	13:8-14	342
11:3-4	25	13:11	300
11:4	44	13:12	22
11:5	20, 24, 79, 344	13:12-14	309
11:6	20	13:13	159
11:6-11	25	13:15-17	308, 342
11:6-8	309	13:15-19	340
11:7-13	352	13:17	21–2, 310
11:8	311	13:18-19	272
11:9	20	13:19	21
11:13	163	13:20-27	309, 340
11:14	24, 269, 309–10	13:22-27	25
11:15-16	224	13:23	309–10
11:16	300	13:24	272
11:18	163	13:26	300
11:18-19	291	13:27	311
11:18-20	288, 293, 308,	14	308, 310
	311, 344	14:1	20, 271, 338

Reference	Pages
14:1-6	340
14:1-9	338
14:1–15:4	236, 311
14:1–15:20	341
14:2-6	244, 271
14:7	310
14:7-9	310–11
14:7–15:4	311, 340
14:8	310
14:9	310
14:10-12	271
14:11	20, 24, 269, 310
14:11-12	269, 309
14:13	20, 269, 308
14:13-16	271
14:14	20
14:14-16	269
14:14-17	309
14:15-16	308
14:16	269
14:17	308
14:17-18	308
14:17-22	269
14:18	159
14:19	310
14:19-22	311
14:21	310
15:1	20, 25, 269, 310
15:1-4	269, 309
15:2	309
15:4	236, 311
15:5-9	300, 309
15:5-20	340
15:6	311
15:7	163
15:9	309
15:10	24, 146, 163, 308, 311, 315, 343–4
15:10-11	269
15:10-21	312
15:11	272
15:11-14	311
15:12-13	269
15:13-14	294
15:14	300
15:15-18	288, 292, 308, 338
15:16	1, 344
15:18	299, 310
15:19	269, 300
15:19-20	292
15:19-21	309, 344
15:21	306
16-20	355
16:1-13	294
16:1-15	288, 313
16:1-18	338, 340
16:1–17:18	341
16:3	311
16:10	22
16:10-11	148
16:11	149
16:11-13	309
16:18	300
16:19	208, 310
16:19–17:13	340
17:4	300
17:5-8	312
17:5-18	312
17:9	166, 312
17:10-11	312
17:12-13	310, 312
17:13	310
17:14-18	288, 291, 308, 312, 338, 340 341, 344
17:18	20
17:19	148, 274, 288, 309, 313, 342
17:19-27	340
17:19–18:12	341
17:19–18:23	149
17:22	44
17:24	311
17:24-27	296, 351
18-20	20, 338
18:1	274
18:1-11	313
18:1-12	306
18:1-23	20, 23
18:3	20
18:5	342
18:5-11	309
18:6-11	208, 344
18:7-9	273
18:7-10	44
18:11	300
18:12–20:18	309
18:13	

18:13-15	311	22:8-9	148–9
18:13-17	300, 309,	22:8-14	152
	313, 340	22:10	266
18:17	25, 300	22:13	105
18:18	24, 155–6,	22:15-16	147
	158, 294	22:16	157
18:18-23	125, 340	22:21	105
18:19-23	288, 291,	22:22	105
	308, 342	23:4-5	157
18:20	38, 299, 310	23:9	105
18:21-23	344	23:10	148
18:23	24, 310	23:11	159
18:26	125	23:14	148
18:28	125	23:20	157
18:32	125	23:22	100, 118, 267
18:36-38	125	23:29	90
18:43-44	125	23:32	166
19:1-13	288	24:1	114, 207
19:1-15	340	24:7	148
19:1–20:18	341	25:1	114
19:2-9	313	25:1-13	208–9
19:3-9	309	25:1-3	208, 273
19:4-9	311	25:3	209, 274
19:9	300	25:11	21
19:11-13	309, 313	25:12	118
19:13	22	25:13	148, 208–9,
19:14	20–1		271, 273
19:15	309	25:30-31	271
19:19	24	26	150, 158
20	4, 355	26:1	114, 325
20:1-3	20	26:1-3	152
20:1-6	24, 294, 340	26:1-6	274
20:3	22	26:2	269
20:4	21	26:3	152
20:4-5	25	26:4	151–2
20:4-6	309, 344	26:4-5	152, 161
20:7	20, 299–300	26:4-6	148, 151, 161
20:7-9	344	26:6	152
20:7-13	288, 308	26:7	158
20:7-18	340	26:8	158
20:9	310, 331	26:9	151
20:11-13	343	26:11	22, 151, 158
20:13	292, 315	26:13	44, 151
20:14-18	300, 308,	26:16	158, 163, 333
	315, 343	26:24	152
21:1	21, 114, 207, 273	27:1	114
21:2	22	27:16	159
21:11-12	271	28	158
22:4	266	28:1	114

28:1-14	118	34:17	150
28:2	312	34:20	150
28:3	159	35:1	114
28:9	118, 158	35:13	269
28:15-17	118	35:15	274
28:16-17	118	36	44, 270
28:47	163	36:1	114
29	101	36:1-2	273
29:1	114	36:1-4	208
29:1-14	118	36:2	148, 208, 273
29:1-2	114	36:4	44
29:10	118	36:6	21, 44
29:13	148	36:9	35
29:14	148	36:10	44, 147
29:19	163	36:12	147
29:20-13	158	36:15	44
29:24-28	159	36:17-18	44
29:24-32	158	36:18	44
30-31	271	36:20	147
30:1-4	271	36:21	147
30:2	148, 163, 269	36:26	147
30:6	163	36:32	viii, 44, 147, 208
30:10	163	36:33	44
30:20	105	37-38	150
31	52, 101, 221	37:7	269
31:2-6	221	37:15	147
31:7	105, 266	37:20	147
31:8	105	38:22	114
31:11	105	38:22	199
31:18-20	221	40:1	114
31:21	221	40:7	21
31:22	221	41:17-18	335
31:25	221	41:18	21–2
31:26	221	43	44
31:31-34	38, 45, 148–9, 220	43:3	21–2, 44
31:33-34	156	44:1	114
32	44	44:10	149
32:1	114	44:10-11	148
32:23	148–9	44:23	149
32:32	159	45:1	44, 148
33:25	269	45:4	44
33:32	90	46-52	44
34	150, 152	46-51	271
34:1	114	46:1	271
34:8-22	150	46:1–51:64	209
34:13	150	46:14	266
34:13-14	148	47:1	271
34:14	150	48:20	266
		48:26	266

49:34	271	3:9	266
50:2	266		
50:14	266	Amos 1:1	114
50:24	105	3:9	266
50:26-29	266	3:13	266
51:3	266		
51:11-12	266	Mic. 1:1	114
51:15-19	334–5		
51:27	266	Hag. 1:1	114
51:60	148		
52:25	147	Zeph. 1:1	114
Ezek. 1:1-2	114	Zech. 1:1	114
3:23	79	12:1	79
19:1	266		
		John 3:8-10	130
Hos. 1:1	114		
4:13	326	2 Pet. 1:21	90
Joel 2:1	266	2 Tim. 3:16	79, 90
2:28	79		

CPSIA information can be obtained
at www.ICGtesting.com
Printed in the USA
LVHW080257020821
694299LV00009B/253